THE RECEPTION OF CICERO IN THE EARLY ROMAN EMPIRE

Cicero was one of the most important political, intellectual, and literary figures of the late Roman Republic, rising to the consulship as a "new man" and leading a complex and contradictory life. After his murder in 43 BC, he was indeed remembered for his life and his works – but not for all of them. This book explores Cicero's reception in the early Roman Empire, showing what was remembered and why. It argues that early imperial politics and Cicero's schoolroom canonization had pervasive effects on his reception, with declamation and the schoolroom mediating and even creating his memory in subsequent generations. The way he was deployed in the schools was foundational to the version of Cicero found in literature and the educated imagination in the early Roman Empire, yielding a man stripped of the complex contradictions of his own lifetime and polarized into a literary and political symbol.

THOMAS J. KEELINE is Assistant Professor of Classics at Washington University in St. Louis. His research and teaching interests extend to all aspects of the ancient world and its reception, with a particular focus on Latin literature and the history of education and scholarship. He has published articles and reviews in the fields of Latin literature, lexicography, metrics, the history of classical scholarship and the classical tradition, and textual criticism.

THE RECEPTION OF CICERO IN THE EARLY ROMAN EMPIRE

The Rhetorical Schoolroom and the Creation of a Cultural Legend

THOMAS J. KEELINE

Washington University in St. Louis

CAMBRIDGE
UNIVERSITY PRESS

CAMBRIDGE
UNIVERSITY PRESS

University Printing House, Cambridge CB2 8BS, United Kingdom

One Liberty Plaza, 20th Floor, New York, NY 10006, USA

477 Williamstown Road, Port Melbourne, VIC 3207, Australia

314–321, 3rd Floor, Plot 3, Splendor Forum, Jasola District Centre, New Delhi – 110025, India

79 Anson Road, #06–04/06, Singapore 079906

Cambridge University Press is part of the University of Cambridge.

It furthers the University's mission by disseminating knowledge in the pursuit of education, learning, and research at the highest international levels of excellence.

www.cambridge.org
Information on this title: www.cambridge.org/9781108426237
DOI: 10.1017/9781108590594

© Thomas J. Keeline 2018

First published 2018

Printed and bound in Great Britain by Clays Ltd, Elcograf S.p.A.

A catalogue record for this publication is available from the British Library.

Library of Congress Cataloging-in-Publication Data
NAMES: Keeline, Thomas J., author.
TITLE: The reception of Cicero in the early Roman empire : the rhetorical schoolroom and the creation of a cultural legend / Thomas J. Keeline.
DESCRIPTION: Cambridge : Cambridge University Press, 2018. | Includes bibliographical references and index.
IDENTIFIERS: LCCN 2018022102 | ISBN 9781108426237 (alk. paper)
SUBJECTS: LCSH: Cicero, Marcus Tullius – Appreciation. | Rhetoric, Ancient.
CLASSIFICATION: LCC PA6346 .K445 2018 | DDC 875/.01–dc23
LC record available at https://lccn.loc.gov/2018022102

ISBN 978-1-108-42623-7 Hardback

For Monica

Contents

Preface

Feeling certain that I would write a dissertation on Latin poetry, in my third year of graduate studies at Harvard I thought I should choose a Latin prose author for my Special Examinations. To give myself a bit of breadth, I reasoned, before settling down in my narrow corner to dissertate. Thus began a fateful year of fortnightly meetings in Kathy Coleman's study in the Widener Library, reading and discussing Cicero. After my special exams were over, as I was casting (read: flailing) about for a suitable dissertation topic, Kathy suggested that I might consider the reception of Cicero in Tacitus and Pliny. I remember the moment quite distinctly: I was walking out of the back of the library, somewhat frustrated after an afternoon spent with Varro, and Kathy was walking in – unsurprisingly, she was getting ready to get back to work as I was getting ready to flop on the couch. I turned the idea over in my head as I headed home; I had taken her Pliny seminar the year before, and it all seemed to make good sense. Well, one thing led to another, and the scope of the dissertation soon broadened into a more general study of Cicero's reception in the early Empire. This book is a revised version of that dissertation. I should say that I still really like poetry.

The debts that I've accumulated along the way are larger than I'll ever be able to repay, but I can at least put some of them on public record. Emma Dench and Richard Tarrant were the other members of my dissertation committee and exemplary readers; both have also read parts of the present book. I have benefited greatly from discussions with and help in various forms from William Altman, Christopher Burden-Strevens, Sean Dolan, Alain Gowing, Brandon Jones, Tim Moore, Victoria Pagán, Carl Springer, Morris Tichenor, Chris van den Berg, Matthijs Wibier, and Andrew Wright. The Department of Classics at Washington University in St. Louis has provided the ideal environment for me to work in and the ideal colleagues for me to work with, and the members of the Ancient Mediterranean Studies Writing Group here also read and discussed the book's fifth chapter. The two anonymous readers for the Press deserve particular thanks for improving every page of the book with their detailed and constructive comments. Michael Sharp has throughout been the ideal editor, nurturing this project from an unfinished dissertation into its final form. Iveta Adams is a copy-editor nonpareil: she has removed more authorial idiosyncrasies, inconsistencies, infelicities, and outright errors than I'd care to admit. Finally, Chris Whitton, in a feat of extraordinary generosity and chalcenteric endurance, read through the whole of my manuscript in less than 48 hours and offered countless insightful comments – all this without ever having met me in person. I am profoundly grateful to all of the above, and it goes without saying that after so much good help, whatever nonsense remains is entirely my fault.

It would take a Cicero to try to put into words what I owe to Kathy Coleman, and I don't think even he could manage. From the day she encouraged me to enroll in her Pliny seminar, she has taken me under her wing. She read every word of the original dissertation more times than I can count, and improved it immeasurably in style and substance. As if that were not enough, she did the same thing again with the present book, prompting me at a critical moment to get to work and reading and commenting on each chapter as I completed it. But this is typical: Kathy reads and comments on everything I send her, and so I end up sending her everything. I shudder to think of what she has not done over the past few years because she's been too busy licking my ill-formed ideas into shape, but I cannot imagine a better mentor.

My first son was born as I was finishing the dissertation; my second son as I was starting the book; and my daughter entered the world as the book went into production. Somehow my wife has found the time for all of us and for a more than full-time job besides. This book is dedicated to her.

Note on Texts and Abbreviations

Unless otherwise noted, translations are my own, although I have borrowed the occasional felicitous phrase from Loeb versions. Abbreviations for Latin authors follow the *TLL* but eschew the consonantal *v* (except schol. Bob. = scholia Bobiensia); Greek authors LSJ (except Cass. Dio = Cassius Dio); modern periodicals *L'Année philologique*. All other abbreviations are explained at the beginning of the bibliography. Asconius is cited by page number from Clark (1907) and the scholia Bobiensia by page and line number from Stangl (1964).

Introduction

In the predawn light of October, AD 75, a 13-year-old trudges bleary-eyed through the streets of Rome. Cocks are not yet crowing, but occasional sounds can be heard as the city slowly stirs from slumber. Our youth is excited and nervous: he is on his way to his first day of school under the *rhetor's* tutelage, the place where he will spend the rest of his teenage years learning the art of oratory.[1] He is about to make the acquaintance of a man long dead, a man whom neither his parents nor his grandparents knew personally, but who will be of fundamental importance for the next few years of his life: Marcus Tullius Cicero. In the rhetorical classroom he will spend countless hours reading Cicero's speeches and writing declamations about him or in imitation of him. He will be exposed to a very particular version of this famous figure, with some aspects played up and others played down – sometimes to make him a more exemplary classroom icon, sometimes as a legacy of political decisions made a century ago – and he will have this version thrashed into his head for years.[2] But of course he will not stay a schoolboy forever; he will eventually leave the *rhetor's* school and embark on the *cursus honorum*, or a legal career, or a military campaign, or any of the other professional paths open to an upper-class youth of education and ambition. And yet even as an adult, those first impressions and that schoolroom image of Cicero will stick with him. When Roman literary authors talk about Cicero, we see in their texts the same themes and points of emphasis that originally developed in the rhetorical classroom. Education wields an enormous influence on the shaping of history and memory, and even more so in an age before printed books, television, and the internet. I will show the extent and nature of that influence on the

[1] For the basic details of the schoolday and schoolroom, see Bonner (1977) 126–145, Cribiore (2001) 127–159, Bloomer (2011) 12–17, and Cribiore (2015). The guess of October as a plausible date is based on Mart. 10.62; Martial is also a witness to the early start to the schoolday (14.223).
[2] Literally: as a snippet of Pompeian schoolroom graffiti reminds us (*CIL* iv.4208), "If you don't like Cicero, you will be beaten," *si ti[bi] Cicero do[let], uap[u]labis*. See p. 30 below.

I

afterlife of Cicero, one of Rome's most famous sons. This book is the story of what, how, and why our young 13-year-old will learn about Cicero, and what he might do with what he learned. It is the story of Cicero's reception in the early Roman Empire.

It is a truism that Cicero is a "school author," a cornerstone of the ancient curriculum. He is synonymous with rhetorical education in authors as diverse as Martial and Messius.[3] The truism is true: Cicero really was central to the rhetorical schoolroom. My purpose in this book is to explore what that schoolroom centrality means, and what its consequences are. What are the effects of having a particular image of Cicero hammered into you for years? What are the consequences of focusing on this author as *the* paragon of oratorical excellence? In this investigation we will have to try to set aside our own preconceptions arising from two millennia of reception; the way things turned out is not necessarily the way that they had to be. The Cicero I describe will be simultaneously strange and familiar. From a modern perspective, it is an undeniably partial and indeed flattened image. Cicero was remembered, as Tadeusz Zielinski wrote, for his life and his works[4] – but not for all of them. So much that the ancient world could have engaged with it simply does not; their Cicero is in some ways but a shadow of the original man, and yet it is a towering shadow that later generations struggled mightily to escape from. This partial Cicero, stripped of the complex contradictions of his own lifetime and refashioned into a literary and political symbol, *is* the Cicero of the early Empire, and he is largely created in the imperial schoolroom.

The seeds of this reception were sown by Cicero himself and by political forces in the immediate aftermath of his death. In his own lifetime he was very conscious that he was shaping his reputation for posterity; in the *Pro Archia*, for example, he writes, "Everything that I did, already then when I was doing it I realized that I was scattering and planting the seed of myself in the world's everlasting memory" (*ego uero omnia quae gerebam iam tum in gerendo spargere me ac disseminare arbitrabar in orbis terrae memoriam sempiternam, Arch.* 30).[5] Cicero was also well aware of how important the schoolroom would be as the mediator of his reception. Not only does he publish his work – already a deliberate act of image management – but he

---

[3] E.g. Mart. 5.56.3–5; a member of the so-called *quadriga Messii*, Cass. *inst.* 1.17.7; cf. *GL* VII.449–514.
[4] Zielinski (1929) 9.
[5] Instances of this self-conscious self-presentation are legion; think, for example, of the way that Cicero remodels the image of his exile *post reditum* (see p. 164 below and May [1988] 88–127). On Ciceronian self-fashioning, see recently Dugan (2005), Steel (2005), Kurczyk (2006), van der Blom (2010), Pieper (2014), Scheidegger Lämmle (2017).

publishes speeches specifically for the edification of young students (*Att.* 2.1.3; cf. 4.2.2); he talks constantly of the use of his writings in the school-room (e.g. *Brut.* 123, where his texts displace orators of the older genera-tion); he even goes so far as to augur that schoolboys will learn some of his speeches off by heart (*ad Q. fr.* 3.1.11).[6] Cicero knew full well how impor-tant the schoolroom would be in preserving the monument that he had labored to build for himself.

The political forces at work in the decades following Cicero's death also helped shape what was presented in the schoolroom. While for any number of reasons his ghost might seem an unlikely bedfellow for the living Octavian, in fact Cicero's outspoken opposition to Mark Antony made him a perfect ally of the new regime after Actium.[7] As the years rolled on, of course, the political context changed dramatically: the issues that were so lively and important in the 20s BC were a dead letter a century later.[8] And yet the schoolroom curriculum was very conservative and consistent. The fundamental terms of Cicero's reception were set early on, frozen and fossilized in the tumultuous years following his death, and they remained remarkably constant. Sensitive and sophisticated writers like Seneca the Younger, Tacitus, and Pliny can put those terms to different uses, but the issues surrounding Cicero that were debated in Augustan declamations continued to be replayed in the classroom of Quintilian a century later and beyond.

Is the Cicero of the schoolroom the only "Cicero" that survived into the early Empire? Perhaps not, and I cannot claim that I have exhausted all interpretive possibilities. Nothing absolutely compelled ancient audiences to engage only with a partial Cicero. Whatever we know of Cicero today, antiquity, at least in theory, could have known too. But we should remember that essentially every literary author we read – to say nothing of the politicians and advocates and countless other voices that have perished without echo today – was schooled in the rhetorical tradition that I discuss in this book; the influences that I describe were foundational for everyone. I see the schoolroom as the predominant factor conditioning Cicero's early reception, and I want to bring out the interest in the very

[6] Stroh (1975) 21, 52–53 perhaps goes too far in believing that Cicero's overriding concern in publishing his speeches was to provide examples for the rhetorical classroom, and recent work like that of Steel (2005) has shown just how sophisticated Cicero is in using publication to shape his public persona. Nevertheless, Stroh is right to emphasize that Cicero was eager for canonization as a school author. Cf. the humor of Horace on his own schoolroom fate (*epist.* 1.20.17–18).
[7] This theme will be developed particularly in chapter 3.
[8] On the evolution in the ways Romans in the early Empire looked back at their Republican past, see esp. Gowing (2005).

particular – and flattened and simplified – Cicero that the ancient school-room so influentially presents. Ancient authors are not limited to what they learned in the schoolroom, and we will see some go far beyond it, but even this we can only properly appreciate when we understand its schoolroom foundation.

The seeds of Cicero's afterlife were sown by Cicero himself and by post-mortem political propaganda, but they were tended by the rhetorical teachers and nourished to maturity in their classrooms. Cicero's reception in the early Empire is decisively influenced by the Roman rhetorical schoolroom.

An Orientation

It is a topos to say that the object of one's proposed study has been ("unfairly" or "surprisingly") neglected by scholarship. I cannot claim that the reception of Cicero has been entirely neglected, but it has been the subject of only a handful of significant studies, especially as concerns its earliest period.[9] The most important and extensive of these is Tadeusz Zielinski's *Cicero im Wandel der Jahrhunderte* (fourth edition 1929), which for all its many virtues treats the first century only briefly, being concerned with the reception of Cicero from antiquity through the French Revolution. Zielinski's work is really an attempt at large-scale cultural history viewed through the figure of Cicero, focusing on three *Eruptionsperioden*, first the expansion of Christianity, then the Renaissance, and finally the Enlightenment.[10] His treatment of the period that I examine is thus super-ficial by design, and he occasionally makes odd statements, claiming for example that Cicero was first acknowledged as the head of Roman literature in the time of Quintilian.[11] Nevertheless, among many acute observations Zielinski does briefly advert to the importance of the schoolroom.[12]

There is also the eminently readable and intensely personal *2000 Jahre Cicero* of Bruno Weil (1962), which is likewise sweeping in scope – encompassing, as the title promises, the two millennia from Cicero's

---

[9] For brief comments on some of the twentieth-century scholarship not mentioned here, see Kennedy (2002) 481–483. Kennedy's essay itself is a whirlwind tour of Cicero's reception from antiquity to the nineteenth century.

[10] Zielinski (1929) 2–3.

[11] Zielinski (1929) 36: "So kam es, daß erst jetzt, zur Zeit seines zweiten säkularen Gedenktages, Cicero das anerkannte Haupt der römischen Literatur war." We will see by contrast that Cicero was accorded this status almost from the moment of his death.

[12] E.g. Zielinski (1929) 10, 15. His foundational discussion of *Cicerokarikatur*, i.e. a negative tradition critical of Cicero, also acknowledges the importance of declamation (280–288).

death to Weil's present – and prone to dubious or misguided inferences.[13] Weil is not concerned with the schoolrooom and passes through the period that I discuss in about thirty pages. Besides the monographs of Zielinski and Weil, three collections of essays devoted to Cicero's afterlife have recently been published, William Altman's *Brill's Companion to the Reception of Cicero* (2015a), Nancy van Deusen's *Cicero Refused to Die: Ciceronian Influence through the Centuries* (2013), and Gesine Manuwald's *The Afterlife of Cicero* (2016). The first of these focuses almost exclusively, the second and third exclusively, on Cicero's later reception. Finally, Catherine Steel's *Cambridge Companion to Cicero* (2013) concludes with six essays on Cicero's reception, one treating the imperial period.

The other book-length treatments of Cicero's reception are unpublished dissertations, Gambet (1963), Lavery (1965), Wright (1997), and Sillett (2015), the last of which I have not seen.[14] Both Gambet and Lavery proceed chronologically – Gambet up to AD 79, Lavery through the reign of Hadrian – in an attempt to assemble and appraise all the surviving evidence. Lavery's dissertation takes the form of passages and commentary, capped by a brief conclusion in which he identifies three strands of reception: one negative, one positive, and one eulogistic of Ciceronian oratory without touching on his life. It is to be certain a good collection of material, and from the notes to individual passages some insights may be gleaned, but otherwise Lavery's work remains atomistic commentary that is not unified in the pursuit of broader claims.[15] Gambet, on the other hand, is both more sensitive and much more thorough, having written a hundred more pages than Lavery on a less expansive time period. He also, like Zielinski, correctly observed the importance of rhetorical education.[16] Nevertheless, his treatment of the schoolroom remains superficial, and his methodical examination of each author in chronological order, always followed by a judgment about whether the writer in question liked Cicero or not, prevents him from seeing the unifying themes that originate in the declamatory classroom and pervade the thoughts of writers in the first century and beyond. What he is really concerned with is establishing

---

[13] For example, Weil believes that there was a ban on Cicero's writings under Augustus (pp. 38, 41, 46–55). Weil himself was a lawyer, not a professional classicist, and fled the Nazis. He identified with Cicero both as an advocate and as an exile, and hoped desperately for a "return to Cicero" in post-war Germany. See Altman (2015b) 215–219.

[14] Also Petzold (1911), whose third chapter briefly considers Cicero's *laudatores* and *obtrectatores* after his death; the schoolroom is touched on cursorily pp. 55–58. I know Sillett (2015) only from its abstract, from which it appears complementary to but not co-extensive with my project.

[15] The schoolroom finds occasional brief mention; see Lavery (1965) 45–46, 164, and 181.

[16] So most clearly stated in his conclusion, e.g. Gambet (1963) 231, 237–238.

a "positive" and a "negative" tradition – his focus is on Cicero's posthumous "reputation" – and he is obsessed with determining the sincerity of the various witnesses to these traditions.[17] He also thinks that he detects a fall and then a rise in Cicero's fortunes, but this proves illusory on closer examination.[18] Furthermore, he stops his investigation at the death of the Elder Pliny, thus omitting three of the most important witnesses to Cicero's early *Fortleben*: Quintilian, Tacitus, and Pliny the Younger (to say nothing of Plutarch and the Greek historians and the pseudepigrapha I discuss).

Wright (1997) disregards the influence of the schoolroom and declamation, but rightly emphasizes the ideological dimension of Cicero's early reception.[19] His study ranges from the triumviral period through the early Julio-Claudian era, and he observes that you do not find the complex array of reactions to Cicero that you might have expected.[20] While we differ on numerous points of detail and I cannot agree with all of his conclusions, his focus on ideology productively moves beyond the reductionistic "positive" and "negative" traditions that had characterized earlier work. I should note that even though Wright downplays the declamatory influence on Cicero's reception, he is a particularly sensitive reader of declamation, as shown in his article from 2001 (an appendix to the thesis).

There have also been book chapters and articles treating various aspects of Cicero's first-century reception, among which the two most significant for my purposes are Michael Winterbottom's "Cicero and the Silver Age" (1982) and Robert Kaster's "Becoming 'CICERO'" (1998). Winterbottom makes many trenchant observations, particularly regarding Quintilian. He does not, however, deal as much with the declamatory tradition, and he lacks the space to go into detail except as concerns Quintilian. Kaster focuses on how Cicero's writing and style became identified with his life in the declamatory tradition. His essay is useful, but deliberately limited in scope; he modestly disclaims a full treatment of Cicero's early reception, concentrating on the declaimers preserved in Seneca the Elder. Other

---

[17] Sincerity or lack thereof is a persistent concern, e.g. Gambet (1963) 57–60, 91, 246–247.

[18] E.g. Gambet (1963) 33, 85, 92, 118, 147, 190, 218, 230–231, 233, 239, 249. Some of this speculation is built on a misreading of the evidence (see his p. 118 on the phrase *nemo ausus est*), some on simply ignoring the clear fact that, as demonstrated throughout my book, Cicero was read as a foundational part of the school curriculum through the entirety of this period. This notion is not confined to Gambet; see e.g. Bishop (2015) 289–290, 293–294; van der Blom (2016b) 88. Wright (1997) 214–236 refutes the notion of a "Ciceronian dark age" in detail.

[19] Wright's thesis did not become available to me until my own work was substantially complete, but it has not led me to alter any of my arguments.

[20] Wright (1997) 4.

recent contributions include the chapter by Alain Gowing (2013), a sensitive look at two concrete examples of Ciceronian reception in Seneca the Younger and Quintilian. Bishop (2015) considers the Cicero of Asconius and the Cicero of Macrobius, implicitly and rightly marking the contrast between the oratorical Cicero of the early Empire and the philosophical Cicero of later centuries. More general overviews include Pierini (2003) and Richter (1968), both concerned above all to place on record and summarize the first-century evidence, and van der Blom (2016b), a brief treatment with emphasis on Cicero's self-fashioning as found in his preserved speeches.

Thus while workers have toiled in these fields before, there remains a considerable crop to harvest. By choosing a broad but restricted chronological basis and looking at the evidence through the lens of rhetorical education (see "Scope and Structure" below), I hope to show just how important the schoolroom was in mediating Cicero's memory. Such an investigation does not merely help us understand Cicero's imperial reception. A deep dive into the waters of a single – indeed *the* single – Roman rhetorical model sheds a different kind of light on ancient educational practices from that provided by broader surveys.[21] Moreover, such a study addresses questions of Roman identity and ideology. Scholars have recently emphasized how important declamation and rhetorical education were in forging "Roman-ness" in elite Roman men, and these same educational forces also preserved and transmitted imperial ideology. I explore how and why the particular case of Cicero was, as Emma Dench puts it, "so good to think with as a Roman exemplar in the early imperial period."[22] Indeed, the investigation of the early Empire's relationship with one of its most significant late Republican predecessors is part of a broader conversation about the construction of memories of the Roman Republic in the early Empire, a conversation in which the schoolroom is generally ignored.[23] I show that it is of vital importance in transmitting and indeed creating the

---

[21] Indispensable surveys include Marrou (1964), Bonner (1977), Morgan (1998), Cribiore (2001), and more interpretively Bloomer (2011). See also the essays in Bloomer (2015a).

[22] Dench (2013) 122. On the importance of declamatory education in shaping ancient *mentalité*, see e.g. Beard (1993), Bloomer (1997a), Bloomer (1997b) 110–153, Gunderson (2003), Migliario (2007) 17–22, Bloomer (2011) 170–191. From a somewhat different perspective, Connolly (2007) explores the implications of rhetoric and rhetorical education in constructing the "state of speech," i.e. the entirety of the Roman *res publica*. See her pp. 237–261 on declamation and Quintilian.

[23] The periodization of "late Republic" and "early Empire" is not necessarily self-evident, especially to ancient authors, for whose understanding see Sion-Jenkis (2000) 53–64. (In the *Dialogus* Tacitus in fact implicitly dates the beginning of the Empire to Cicero's death: see p. 272 below.) Further on these issues Gowing (2005) 3–6, whose definition of "Republic" I here follow: "a chronological as well as cultural marker, to denote the period between the end of the Roman monarchy in 509 BC and

memories which imperial authors preserve. Furthermore, the whole history of Latin prose literature after Cicero is in part a set of responses to his overwhelming influence, as mediated by the rhetorical schools. Whether we want to understand nuances of imperial Latinity, or Seneca's style, or Tacitus' intertextuality, or Pliny's anxieties, we must first understand not just Cicero, but how Cicero was understood by later authors. I hope finally that by coming to grips with later authors' reception of Cicero, we might gain better insight into our reception too: we are none of us free from the biases and filters that shape our understanding, but by seeing those of others we might be able to be more conscious of our own.

Scope and Structure

My study of Cicero's reception begins where his own control over his legacy ended: the moment of his death. The living Cicero's self-fashioning has been extensively studied in recent scholarship,[24] and while I have derived considerable profit from such discussions, I will not rehash them here. Although I constantly make reference to Cicero's life and works in what follows, my goal is not so much to talk about the "real" Cicero – if indeed any Cicero is not simply someone's (re)construction – as the imperial reception of the man. As a result I start with authors writing after Cicero's death and follow their lead backwards and forwards. The endpoint for my investigation is, roughly speaking, the age of Pliny, Tacitus, and Plutarch, and I have at least some discussion of most authors who wrote between 43 BC and AD 117.[25] I have also constantly found it useful to bring in later testimony as important witnesses to an earlier tradition, and so texts as diverse as Cassius Dio's *Roman History* and undatable pseudo-Ciceronian writings find their place alongside works written squarely in the first century. The reasons for this are made clear when the texts are discussed, as are questions of dating, when relevant.

The book consists of seven chapters followed by a brief epilogue. It is broadly divided into two parts joined by a central linking chapter. The first four chapters, arranged thematically rather than chronologically, focus on

the beginning of the Augustan principate in 31 BC" (6). On memories of the Republic in the Empire, see Gowing (2005) and Gallia (2012).

[24] Cf. n. 5 above.

[25] The notable exception is Sallust (*ca.* 86–35 BC), who represents a special case. Even if he was writing a year or two after Cicero's death, his *Bellum Catilinae* is the report of events he lived through, and his portrait of Cicero was not subject to the influence of the Ciceronian school curriculum but rather his personal knowledge of and interactions with the man himself. Wright (1997) 10–29 discusses Cicero in Sallust.

the rhetorical schoolroom and its pervasive influence; the final two chapters are case studies of the reception of Cicero in Tacitus and Pliny, which have Quintilian as their educational fulcrum. The bridge is the fifth chapter, a study of Cicero in Seneca the Younger, which spans the gap both chronologically and thematically between the evidence of Seneca the Elder, Seneca the Younger's father, and Quintilian, Seneca the Younger's reactionary conservative successor. The studies of Seneca, Tacitus, and Pliny, while grounded in the classroom, also move beyond it – just as these three authors were grounded in the tradition of rhetorical education but rose above it. In the first half of the book we see Cicero "flattened" as he is textualized and transformed from a living man into words on a page, but this very textualization also allows for a sort of reinflation by more sophisticated authors as they put to various uses the icon that Cicero has become. In particular we see in the later chapters a debate not just over Cicero the educational figure, but also over Cicero the educational theorist.

In the first chapter I establish how a Ciceronian speech was taught in the early Empire, focusing on Cicero's *Pro Milone*. By triangulating among three ancient sources (Asconius, Quintilian, and the scholia Bobiensia), I try to reconstruct how the speech would have been taught in the ancient rhetorical classroom. Careful scrutiny of the preoccupations and interests of these teachers reveals what students in the early Empire would have learned about Cicero from their closest surviving link to the man: his speeches. The emphasis in the rhetorical classroom is always on Cicero's supreme skill as a speaker and his status as exemplary orator; appreciation and imitation of his rhetorical artistry is all-important.

Having discussed how Cicero was read in the ancient classroom, I turn next to the other major activity of the rhetorical school, the practice of writing declamations and rhetorical exercises. In my second, third, and fourth chapters I examine ancient schoolroom declamations about Cicero and declamations written in his persona, including "spurious" pseudo-Ciceronian texts. Certain dominant themes and emphases immediately appear, and they continue to reappear in literary treatments of the man. Chapter 2 further develops the idea of Cicero as the model for eloquence, the factor which ensured his centrality to a school curriculum dedicated to teaching that very quality. I argue that this reputation was not inevitable, but once established proved unshakable and undergirded his entire reception. Cicero becomes identified as the "*uox publica*," and I consider various ways in which his eloquence was discussed in the schoolroom, including comparisons with Demosthenes and the notion of an oratorical decline since Cicero's day, and show that these discussions have ramifications far outside the classroom walls.

The rhetorical schools contended that Cicero's eloquence led to his death, and that death is the subject of my third chapter. Cicero's death was simply the historical event most significant for his reception, and its details were replayed again and again in declamation. These declamations were themselves first subject to the influence of imperial ideology, then acted as propagators of it, and I show how declamation played a central role in shaping history and memory. What young men learned about Cicero's death at school reappears in their literary writings as adults, whether they are historians like Velleius Paterculus or poets like Juvenal. Indeed, the declamatory version of events even influences Greek writers like Plutarch, Appian, and Cassius Dio.

While Cicero's death was the most salient historical component of his reception, it was not the only one, and in my fourth chapter I discuss the other elements that recur with some frequency in later discussions of the man: his consulship as a *nouus homo*, his exile, and his activities in the aftermath of Caesar's assassination. I view all of these through the prism of pseudepigraphic texts, that is, texts that are ascribed to Cicero or his contemporaries but that are in fact products of the rhetorical schools. Declamation was naturally dialectic, and these themes give scope for both praising and blaming Cicero. There was, however, no simple dichotomy between a positive and a negative tradition, but rather a wealth of material that could be accommodated by enterprising speakers to the demands of the case at hand. Here too I show how the themes and points of emphasis that developed in the rhetorical classroom are echoed in history and literature. The chapter closes with a brief coda on an underappreciated part of pseudepigraphic technique, the use of intertextual allusions.

In chapter 5 I move away from detailed scrutiny of the ancient rhetorical classroom to broader case studies of how sophisticated literary authors make use of their rhetorical training and rise above it. Seneca the Younger is the son of Seneca the Elder and must have been steeped in the rhetorical tradition that his father preserves, and we do indeed see that version of Cicero in his writings. And yet Seneca engages – and chooses *not* to engage – with Cicero in wholly new ways. He ignores Cicero's philosophy; he forges his own stylistic path; he knows Cicero's letters but goes his own way in epistolography too, embracing a radical generic experiment; he rejects Cicero's broad educational vision. In his wholesale spurning of Cicero, he sets the stage for the neo-Ciceronian reaction of Quintilian, who was in a sense his successor as an imperial tutor.

Quintilian's classroom is the pivot for chapters 6 and 7, which comprise case studies of Cicero in Pliny the Younger and Tacitus. Pliny was Quintilian's pupil, and Tacitus quite possibly was as well; Pliny and Tacitus were moreover friends and correspondents. I show first that Quintilian puts forth a simplified program of neo-Ciceronianism: Cicero, he says, was Rome's best orator, and since his day oratory has gone into a decline. Cicero also provided a guide to eloquence in his rhetorical treatises and courtroom speeches. Thus, Quintilian argues, if contemporary students wish to attain Cicero's greatness, they must do what the great man prescribes and follow in his educational footsteps.

In chapter 6 I demonstrate that Tacitus repudiates these ideals in his *Dialogus de oratoribus*. He mounts a sophisticated theoretical rebuttal of Quintilian's neo-Ciceronianism, but he does so in a remarkable fashion, cloaking his rejection in Ciceronian style and language. He thus rejects Cicero by subverting Cicero's own words. With cleverly destructive intertextuality, Tacitus actually explodes the entire genre within which he is working; while playing by its rules and conventions, he claims that the game can no longer be played and won. In a masterpiece of Ciceronian eloquence he argues that Ciceronian eloquence is no longer possible; the change in political circumstances from the late Republic to the early Empire has closed that route forever.

In the seventh and final chapter I show how Pliny, by contrast, tries to put Quintilian's Ciceronian classroom principles into practice in the rough and tumble world of Roman life and letters. He is nevertheless acutely conscious that neither his native talent nor the changed political circumstances allow him to do so successfully. His *Epistulae* thus show a persistently uneasy anxiety of influence, as he both desires to be compared with his great model and avows that he is not worthy of such an honor. I investigate both Pliny's explicit mentions of Cicero in the *Epistulae* and some more subtle Ciceronian echoes and motifs in those letters. I demonstrate that his relationship with Cicero remains an unresolved and unresolvable tension throughout his work.

In an epilogue I draw all these threads together and provide an aperçu on the late antique and early medieval reception of Cicero, which is very different. Throughout the early Empire, Cicero had been little valued as a philosopher, not least because those who wanted to read philosophy could read his Greek sources. With the advent of Christianity and the progressive erosion of Greek in the West, however, his stock as a philosopher began to rise. It became less and less necessary to look to him as a model of a Latinity whose character had fundamentally shifted, and less and less possible to understand or relate to the political situation of a completely alien time, but more and more desirable to find improving moral elements in his *philosophica*. Augustine, a Greekless Christian, encapsulates this trend, and I briefly explore the decisive role of Cicero's philosophical works in his formation.

CHAPTER I

Pro Milone: *Reading Cicero in the Schoolroom*

Practice the *sortes Seruianae* and open your copy of Servius' commentary on Vergil to a random page. Fate led me to page 72 of the Harvard edition's second volume, which comments on *Aen.* 1.105–108. Here we find notes on nine lemmata, eight of which are concerned simply to gloss basic linguistic information: e.g. 105 DAT LATVS *inclinatur*, PRAERVPTVS *in altum leuatus*, 106 DEHISCENS *ualde hiscens*, 108 TRIS *Latinum est. genetiuus enim pluralis quotiens in "ium" exit, accusatiuum pluralem in "is" mittit.* These elementary notes are intended for schoolboys just beginning to make their formal acquaintance with the Latin language and its literature. It was a curious feature of the Roman educational system that the most sophisticated Latin poetry, the likes of Vergil and Horace, was rendered into little more than a treasure trove of grammatical curiosities for the plunder of schoolmasters.[1]

This educational oddity arose because the Romans assigned the reading of poetry to the *grammatici*, the teachers of the ancient grammar school. It would be an unfair caricature to paint all their comments as exclusively concerned with instruction in proper Latinity, but it is certainly safe to say that they tailored their commentary to suit the level of their audience. Sophisticated literary criticism was not the order of the day; straightforward explanation and exegesis predominated.[2] Prose reading, by contrast, fell almost entirely to the more advanced *rhetor*, under whose tutelage entire speeches would be read.[3] The "boys" were young men by the time

---

[1] Bonner (1977) 189–249 provides the most convenient overview of Roman grammatical education; earlier Marrou (1964) 274–281. On Servius in particular, see Kaster (1988) 169–197.

[2] And this is one of the reasons that we tend to form an unfavorably low opinion of the abilities of the scholiasts. Such a verdict is often unfair, as they do sometimes show themselves to be sensitive critics, but it is in any event analogous to judging modern criticism by an edition of Shakespeare aimed at middle-schoolers.

[3] I see no reason to doubt, as Reinhardt and Winterbottom (2006) xxix do, that speeches were studied from beginning to end in the schoolroom. As we shall see, Quintilian provides extensive commentary on the *Pro Milone* from its *exordium* through to its *peroratio*, as do the scholia Bobiensia and

they arrived at the rhetorical school,[4] and they were at this point concerned to fit themselves for an appropriate public career. Poetry was out. They were rather in want of training in the art of oratory, and reading the best orators – Cicero above all – conduced to this end. Such students no longer had any need of being told the rules for forming third-declension genitives plural. They needed instead to learn how best to persuade an audience: the proper arrangement of a speech, sophisticated techniques of argumentation, how to keep one's listeners attentive and agreeably disposed, and so forth. When we turn then to the commentary tradition of prose authors, which reflects the teaching practices of the rhetorical schools, we find an entirely different world from that of Servius *et al.* Gone – or at any rate almost gone – are basic explanations of vocabulary and syntax, that staple of the grammarian's diet. Instead, more sophisticated analysis of the form and function of different aspects of the speeches becomes the main fare.

In this chapter I will focus on reconstructing that world, concentrating on how one read the *Pro Milone* of Cicero. Although somewhat neglected in today's classrooms, the *Pro Milone* is a brilliant speech and was highly esteemed in antiquity,[5] and we are singularly fortunate to have three separate sources of early imperial commentary on it: Asconius, the scholia Bobiensia, and Quintilian. This triptych of sources, taken together, presents a remarkable (and unique) picture of how a speech was read in the ancient world. Moreover, although the speech was exceptionally well regarded in antiquity, it was probably not exceptional in terms of its teaching: what we reconstruct for this speech probably holds good, *mutatis mutandis*, for other popular Ciceronian speeches.[6] This investigation will

---

Asconius. Furthermore, at *inst.* 2.5.7–12 Quintilian clearly gives instructions for how to read and interpret a speech from beginning to end (see p. 22 below); cf. Theon ch. 13 on the similar reading of whole speeches (preserved in Armenian, but accessible in Patillon [1998] 102–105; see too pp. xcviii–c of his introduction). Winterbottom (1982) 247–248 agrees in this straightforward interpretation. It would not have taken native speakers of Latin an intolerably long time to go through a Ciceronian speech in such detail, nor would it be necessary for every pupil to have a copy of the speech: oral recitation and exposition would have been standard.

[4] Quintilian is vague on the appropriate age for pupils to enter the rhetorical school, saying that the student should leave the grammarian's tutelage *cum poterit* (*inst.* 2.1.7). Bonner (1977) estimates that "boys would normally have joined the school of rhetoric by the age of fifteen ... as the course proceeded, they would become *adulescentuli* or *iuuenes*, and stay until around eighteen" (137); Reinhardt and Winterbottom (2006) "hazard the guess that pupils normally learnt rhetoric from 13 or 14 to 18" (xxv).

[5] Quintilian, for example, calls it a *nobilissima oratio* (*inst.* 11.3.47) and a *pulcherrima oratio* (*inst.* 4.2.25); Asconius says that Cicero *scripsit ... hanc quam legimus ita perfecte ut iure prima haberi possit* (42C).

[6] In antiquity Cicero's most popular speeches included, as we shall see, the *Verrines, Catilinarians, Pro Milone,* and *Philippics,* but even less expected gems like the *Pro Cluentio* were evidently taught in the schoolroom.

thus shed light both on the practical business of Roman education and, more importantly for my purposes, on how pupils were first exposed to Cicero in the early imperial classroom, where he was stripped of his complexities and presented above all as a model for oratory.

"*The* early imperial classroom" – can we even speak of such a thing? In some ways presenting imperial education as a unified entity continues in the tradition of Henri-Irénée Marrou and Stanley Bonner, who, tending to take literary sources as statements of historical fact, saw ancient education as a whole as relatively static. This simplified narrative has been challenged, and it is clear that we must make some allowances for individual variation across time and place.[7] Nevertheless, Raffaella Cribiore's investigation of Egyptian education has confirmed the fundamental correctness of the picture that Marrou and Bonner present; as she writes, "the evidence of the papyri remarkably agrees with the information transmitted by writers such as Plutarch, . . . Libanius, . . . and Quintilian."[8] The variation that she observes is mostly in the details, and her work shows the continuity of educational practice across temporal and geographic boundaries. Thus she does not hesitate to claim that "an educated man who lived in Alexandria, Oxyrhynchos, or Panoplis was not basically different from one who resided in Antioch or Rome."[9] I think therefore that we can fairly use the shorthand of "imperial education" to denote the common educational practices of the Roman Mediterranean world in the first few centuries AD, so long as we bear in mind that this is to some degree always an idealized model that cannot capture every detail of the reality of ancient education in the actual classroom.[10] The introduction to Cicero that I will describe was thus, broadly speaking, a shared student experience throughout the Romanized world, spanning differences in time, space, and even social class.[11]

---

[7] A sophisticated probing of Marrou's historiography of education is Too (2001), including a fascinating look into Marrou's own intellectual background.

[8] Cribiore (2001) 6.

[9] Cribiore (2001) 240. Morgan (1998) comes to the same conclusions, e.g. pp. 3–4: "What [schoolmasters] taught, at any given level, recurs again and again in the surviving evidence in remarkably similar forms across vast geographical distances, a wide social spectrum and a timespan of nearly a thousand years . . . Surviving descriptions and examples of the exercises used to teach literacy and numeracy and their associated disciplines suggest that much the same exercises in the same order were taught, from the third century BCE onwards, everywhere from the palaces of kings and emperors to the village street." Similarly her pp. 24–25 and esp. 44–47 in more detail.

[10] The basic details of the ancient schoolroom are well summarized and discussed by Bonner (1977) 126–145, Cribiore (2001) 127–159, Bloomer (2011) 12–17, and Cribiore (2015).

[11] Social class admittedly to a lesser degree, since a rhetorical education was the province of a select few. Nevertheless, it might just as well be enjoyed by an Egyptian tax collector as by a Roman orator (see e.g. Morgan [1998] 197). I will concentrate primarily on the literary elite, simply because they produced most of the texts that we can draw on today; they were also the ones to grow up and

The *Miloniana* Commentary Tradition: Sources

Our three sources of commentary on the *Pro Milone* are not entirely unproblematic, and we cannot just press them into service willy-nilly and hope to produce a coherent picture of the first-century classroom. Quintilian is in many ways the most straightforward, but of course he does not simply give us a line-by-line commentary. He makes several general statements about the *Pro Milone*, has a few examples of insightful and detailed explication, and offers a host of minor comments on the speech. These will be woven together from scattered parts of the *Institutio oratoria* in my exposition, which will thus reflect how he might have taught the speech to an actual class; he was, after all, a real teacher, and it seems likely that he drew his examples in the *Institutio* from the abundant store he had built up over years in the classroom. I will also occasionally mention examples of his comments on other speeches, particularly those that are consciously programmatic or unconsciously revealing of methodology.[12]

Asconius, by contrast, does provide a line-by-line commentary preceded by an extensive introduction. We can very clearly reconstruct just what he would have taught, but we are nowhere explicitly told that his teaching would have taken place in a classroom. We know little about Asconius' life: he was possibly a senator, probably Paduan, and certainly lived in the first century AD. Some have taken literally the idea that he writes for the benefit of his sons, but this flies in the face of all Roman conventions.[13] While he

become Rome's leaders. While methods of education remained broadly constant, the interests of the political and literary elite doubtless differed from those of the less privileged. (The son of a village scribe, for example, was much less likely to be fitting himself for a senatorial career at Rome.) And so while students' introduction to Cicero was a shared experience, what they went on to do with that acquaintance may have varied.

[12] Stroh (1975) 271 n. 106 contends that Quintilian knew only the *Pro Milone, Pro Ligario*, and possibly the *Pro Cluentio* really well: "das dürften die Musterstücke gewesen sein, die er mit seinen Schülern im Zusammenhang interpretiert hat." (Cf. too Stroh [1975] 301.) While Quintilian must have known those speeches well and taught them to his own students, the indices to Russell's (2001) Loeb volumes show clearly that Quintilian quoted from a wide range of Cicero's orations. His "real" knowledge is not limited to just this handful.

[13] Marshall (1985), for example, firmly believes that "the address to his sons is no mere literary device" (38; see 32–38 *passim*). Winterbottom (1982) 246, on the other hand, shows a more reasoned caution: "It is not clear to me if Asconius' own commentary reflects his teaching in a school," with n. 2, "He addresses his sons; but that may be a show, as with the Elder Seneca." Lewis (2006) tries to have it both ways, saying that "it is surely right to see [Asconius'] aim in writing to be the instruction of his sons ... this aim does not preclude his envisaging a wider audience for his work" (xv–xvi). It seems to me that this "wider audience" is Asconius' true target, while his sons just may happen to fit the requisite mold as well. Writing for the instruction of one's sons is entirely conventional (Roos [1984] 199–200 gives a list of ancient works dedicated to sons); just consider Quintilian's pose of writing for his son and the son of his dedicatee. Cf. Coleman (1988) ad Stat. *silu.* 4.7.54–56 with discussion of

does take some pains to maintain this pose throughout the work,[14] surely his addressees were merely conventional. He plainly put far too much effort into the work for it to be intended for an audience of two,[15] and the fact that it at some point entered circulation is further reason for suspecting that such was the intent all along. Nor can we believe that he was writing for learned audiences like a Verrius Flaccus, for much of his commentary is simply too basic to be intended for a true "scholarly public": it seems unlikely that a Roman scholar would have needed instruction in basic senatorial procedure, whereas a young man training for the *cursus honorum* very well might.[16] Asconius does not deal exclusively in the basics, but he does deal a fair bit in them, and he seems concerned to pitch these explanations to the youth on the cusp of a political career. A schoolroom audience is the simplest and most plausible hypothesis that accounts for all the facts.

The scholia Bobiensia are the most problematic of the sources, chiefly because of their dating, but they also prove exceptionally fruitful. The scholia themselves are preserved on a fifth-century palimpsest, but they without question reproduce much that is older.[17] Nevertheless, this is clearly not a "pure" first-century source. Some considerable care will thus need to be applied when using its comments as representatives of an earlier tradition, but there was a real conservatism and continuity in the Roman educational tradition, and in the absence of evidence to the contrary, I will take the Bobbio scholia as representing the teaching methods and concerns of the early Empire, even if in some cases we may actually be dealing with slightly later material.[18] While these notes are dramatically different in

---

simplified history written for the benefit of the studious youth; one thinks of Cato writing out his Roman history μεγάλοις γράμμασι for his son (Plut. *Cat. ma.* 20.5).

[14] The sons are addressed at Ascon. 43C (*quid sit diuidere sententiam ut enarrandum sit uestra aetas, filii, facit*; see p. 54 below), and the second-person plural is pervasive (e.g. 27C *demonstrasse uos memini me hanc domum in ea parte Palatii esse*, of Scaurus' house).

[15] Note that he commented on more speeches than what we have today, and possibly on the whole Ciceronian corpus (so Madvig [1828] 21). See Marshall's (1985) extensive and persuasive discussions (1–25); he concludes that "it can be said that Asconius probably wrote on a very large number of Cicero's speeches" (19).

[16] See e.g. p. 54 below for the note on *diuisio*; Marshall (1985) 32–33 argues in similar fashion that the commentaries' "simple style" might suit an audience in their late teens. See too Lewis (2006) xiv on the word *enarratio*, which "implies an expository narrative, designed for guidance and education, perhaps sometimes on a fairly basic level."

[17] See *CLA* 1.28 for palaeographical and codicological details. The only serious *Quellenforschung* into the Bobiensia is Hildebrandt (1894) 33–62, now ripe for updating. His conclusion is that the scholia we have today were excerpted from a fourth-century commentary, itself derived from a rhetorical and historical commentary from the second century, which in turn derived its historical notes from the late first century (p. 63). Similarly Zetzel (1974) 116.

[18] Cf. Winterbottom (1982) 246: "And [the scholia Bobiensia] do, or may, reproduce the sort of thing a practising *rhetor* would have told his pupils as they read through a speech of Cicero in class."

external form from Quintilian, in discussing the *Pro Milone* they exhibit tremendous thematic similarities with him, which is not surprising if each source is reflective of classroom teaching.

The Bobiensia suffer from subsidiary textual problems as well; the text is missing whole sections (most regrettably twenty pages commenting on sections 49–101 of the speech), but more than enough is preserved for our purposes here. The scholarly consensus, such as it is, seems to be that the scholia borrow some material – if only indirectly – from Asconius.[19] This means that we must exercise caution when dealing with close similarities between Asconius and the Bobiensia, since they may not necessarily represent independent sources converging on the same ideas. Nevertheless, if the scholia's concerns are the same as those of Asconius, they are witness to a continuity of common interest. Furthermore, the scholia are by no means slavish imitators; all the rhetorical and some of the historical notes are clearly independent of Asconius' influence.[20]

Pro Milone: Background to the Speech and Outline

Like the second *Philippic* and the *actio secunda* of the *Verrines*, the *Pro Milone* ranks as one of Cicero's most famous speeches even though he never actually delivered it. Unlike those two cases, however, Cicero did in fact give a speech on 8 April[21] 52 BC on behalf of Milo, but it is not the masterpiece that has been transmitted to us. Instead, the sources tell us, Cicero lost his nerve in the face of a *corona* composed of Pompey's soldiers and stammered through an inadequate and unavailing oration. He nevertheless prepared a thoroughly revised version for publication, which was a resounding success: as the story goes, he sent a copy to Milo in exile at Massilia, who supposedly replied that he was fortunate that Cicero had not delivered the revised speech as his actual defense – otherwise he would have been denied the opportunity to enjoy the excellent mullet of Marseilles.[22]

---

[19] Some have, however, denied any connection. Even if the Bobiensia do draw on Asconius, it is not clear whether they are working through an intermediate source (or sources); Hildebrandt (1894) 53–55 summarizes the question and plumps for an intermediary. The testimonial apparatus in Stangl (1964) is very helpful for spotting possible Asconian parallels, but almost none appear to be *ad uerbum*, and some are so general as only to indicate that the two are commenting on the same speech.

[20] For historical differences, see e.g. p. 56 below on *diuisio*, along with nn. 55 and 86.

[21] Possibly 7 April. See succinctly Lewis (2006) and Marshall (1985) ad Ascon. 30C with more details; most fully Ruebel (1979) 239–249.

[22] As retailed by Cassius Dio (40.54.3), whose account of the trial itself is rather overdone: he claims that Cicero was so terrified that he could only manage to utter a few words of his speech before

The political background to the case is complex, but the basic issue at hand is simple enough. Milo stands accused of the murder of his arch-rival (and Cicero's arch-enemy) Clodius, who was killed in a skirmish between Clodian and Milonian gangs along the Via Appia near Clodius' estate. After Clodius' death there was great political upheaval, with the infamous Sextus Cloelius using Senate House furniture as a funeral pyre for his dead friend – and burning down the Curia itself in the process. Because of the highly charged nature of the case and the general chaos surrounding it, Pompey, recently appointed sole consul, created a special panel of judges and instituted a special procedure for trying the case. The details of the laws are not of great importance for our purposes, but they are conveniently summarized by A. C. Clark:

> The special objects of these laws were to secure brevity in the proceedings, to make corruption impossible, and to curb the eloquence of the orators. The hearing of evidence was to be the chief part of the trial. Two hours only were allowed for the speech of the prosecuting counsel, and three for the reply. The jurors who were to vote were only chosen out of a larger body on the morning of the last day; an ingenious provision which put bribery out of the question.[23]

The reality appears to be that Milo and Clodius happened upon each other by chance and that the fight broke out spontaneously, as all three of our commentators affirm.[24] Clodius was wounded in the fray, and Milo apparently ordered his partisans to follow him into an inn and finish him off. Cicero, by contrast, bases his whole defense on a sort of false dilemma: one of these men ambushed the other, he claims repeatedly. It cannot have been Milo. Since it cannot have been Milo, it must have been Clodius. Milo thus acted in self-defense, in accordance with the laws of both nature and mankind. Cicero also gives something of a nod to the line of defense adopted by Brutus in a published pamphlet, namely that Milo's killing of Clodius was done for the benefit of the state and should be praised, not

---

sitting down again. That this cannot be true is clear from the fact that Quintilian is able to cite from both the speech Cicero actually delivered (as taken down by stenographers) and from the version revised for publication: see *inst.* 4.3.17 and 9.2.54; cf. Ascon. 42C and schol. Bob. 112.10–13 St. On the two versions, see e.g. Stone (1980), Dyck (2002), Steel (2005) 118–121; Melchior (2008) reassesses the reasons that Cicero would publish a losing speech.

[23] Clark (1895) xxv.

[24] See e.g. Quint *inst.* 6.5.10, Ascon. 41C, schol. Bob. 111.24–28 St. According to Asconius, the jurors thought the same thing (*uidebantur non ignorasse iudices inscio Milone initio uulneratum esse Clodium, sed compererant, postquam uulneratus esset, iussu Milonis occisum*, Ascon. 53C). Fotheringham (2013b) 8–10 provocatively but unconvincingly wonders whether Cicero's version of events is necessarily a lie.

punished.[25] The ancient commentary tradition thus focuses primarily on Cicero's rhetorical brilliance in painting a persuasive picture of his version of the events in order to convince the jury. Lying is perfectly acceptable; Quintilian even explicitly theorizes about when an orator is allowed to defend the guilty and to bend or break the truth (*inst.* 12.1.34–45), and he gives practical advice for how best to do so (*inst.* 4.2.88–94).[26] All is fair in love and war and persuading the judges. That Cicero lost the actual case is for the most part immaterial. Although the commentators do make brief apologias for Cicero's failure (see pp. 36 and 41 below), there is in general little concern for reality in rhetorical teaching – consider only the themes of the declamations. For the classroom, the entire universe consists in the hermetically sealed and hermeneutically closed world of the speech itself.

I append here a brief outline of the speech for those readers not yet catechized on its every detail by a Quintilian or an Asconius. My discussion of the commentary tradition will in the main assume this structure as well.[27]

I.   *Prooemium* (*Mil.* 1–6)
   a.   Begins from the unusual circumstances of the trial, viz. that it is being conducted under armed guard.
   b.   Tries to secure the jurors' good will by various expedients.
   c.   Briefly states the defense's primary contention: that Clodius set an ambush for Milo.

II. *Praeiudicia* (*Mil.* 7–22)
   a.   Cicero must dispel three possible *praeiudicia* before proceeding to the *narratio* of the case. This is unusual.
   b.   *Praeiudicium* 1: Any confessed killer stands already condemned (*Mil.* 7–11).
   c.   *Praeiudicium* 2: The Senate has already decreed the killing *contra rem publicam* (*Mil.* 12–14).

---

[25] On Brutus' pamphlet, see Quint. *inst.* 3.6.93, 10.5.20, Ascon. 41C, schol. Bob. 112.15–16 St. See also p. 31 below. Brutus was not alone in this belief; Cato too may have voted for acquittal in the trial on these very grounds (Ascon. 53–54C): *fuerunt qui crederent M. Catonis sententia eum* [i.e. *Milonem*] *esse absolutum; nam et bene cum re publica actum esse morte P. Clodi non dissimulauerat et studebat in petitione consulatus Miloni et reo adfuerat.*

[26] Cf. Ascon. 70C *non praeterire autem uos uolo esse oratoriae calliditatis ius ut, cum opus est, eisdem rebus ab utraque parte uel a contrariis utantur*; 13C *hoc Cicero oratorio more, non historico, uidetur posuisse.*

[27] This outline is based on that of Clark (1895) l–lvii and Fotheringham (2013b) 22–23; cf. the detailed discussion of Wisse (2007). For a historical overview of the whole course of Cicero's and Milo's relationship, focusing on the murder of Clodius, its antecedents, and its consequences, see Lintott (1974). Craig (2002) 596 lists further bibliography on the speech. Berry (2000), a translation with introduction and notes, is also particularly useful.

d. *Praeiudicium* 3: Pompey himself has already declared Milo guilty (*Mil.* 15–22).

III. *Narratio* (*Mil.* 23–31)

a. Briefly tells the story of the "ambush" from Milo's perspective.

b. The dilemma, according to Cicero: who set an ambush for whom? The ambusher is guilty; the ambushed merely acted in self-defense.

IV. *Argumentatio* (*Mil.* 32–71)

a. Various arguments are adduced to prove that Clodius set the ambush for Milo.

  i. Clodius would have wanted Milo's death (*Mil.* 32–34); Milo would not have wanted Clodius' (*Mil.* 35).

  ii. Clodius was violent by his very nature (*Mil.* 36–41); not so Milo (*Mil.* 41–43).

  iii. The time and day of the ambush would have been impossible for Milo to plan in advance; not so for Clodius (*Mil.* 45–51).

  iv. The place: the ambush took place virtually on Clodius' property (*Mil.* 53–54).

  v. Clodius was traveling light and ready for action; Milo was encumbered by his wife and others (*Mil.* 55–56).

b. More general arguments

  i. Milo was justified in manumitting his slaves (*Mil.* 57–60).

  ii. Milo's subsequent actions since the killing show his confidence in his own innocence (*Mil.* 61–63).

  iii. Various rumors about Milo swirling in the air are untrue (*Mil.* 64–66).

  iv. Pompey is appealed to directly (*Mil.* 67–71).

V. *Pars extra causam* and beginning of *peroratio* (*Mil.* 72–91)

a. Milo was justified in killing Clodius in self-defense.

b. Even if, however, he were to lie and say that he ambushed Clodius deliberately, he would still be justified (*Mil.* 72–83).

c. In fact the killing was the work of the vengeful gods (*Mil.* 83–91).

VI. *Peroratio* (*Mil.* 92–105)

a. Milo's character is such that he cannot beg for pity (*Mil.* 92, 95).

b. Cicero thus tries to create pity for himself instead; he also shows Milo to be a man of singular courage and patriotism (*Mil.* 93–97).

c. Cicero imagines a dialogue between himself and Milo to showcase Milo's virtues and Cicero's misery if he should be condemned (*Mil.* 98–103).

    d.   Cicero imagines the dire situation had Clodius lived and held the praetorship (*Mil.* 104).

    e.   Cicero exhorts the jurors to courage and justice one last time (*Mil.* 105).

Quintilian on How to Read a Speech

So how did one in fact go about teaching a Ciceronian speech in the classroom? Quintilian gives us an idealized prescription for the method of instruction (*inst.* 2.5).[28] The *rhetor*, he says, will greatly contribute to his pupils' progress if he deigns to instruct them in history and, above all, in oratory. (This is to say, if he does not merely practice declamation with them and offer up his own compositions as models.) It would be beneath the *rhetor*'s dignity to explain the force of every word or to read the text aloud to the boys as they follow along, but it is quite consonant with his office to point out the *uitia* and *uirtutes* of a speech as they occur. The best method, he says, is to rotate the duties of reading out loud among the boys so that each becomes accustomed to public speaking in his turn; thus there may have been only one copy of the text circulating in the class, perhaps the teacher's own, which the rest of the pupils would have had to absorb aurally.[29] With a reader selected and silence established (*plus ça change* . . .), the teacher will explain the general background of the speech, providing a context that will help the students understand the oration itself. Then he proceeds to the detailed *enarratio* (*inst.* 2.5.7–9):

> . . . nihil otiosum pati quodque in inuentione quodque in elocutione adnotandum erit: quae in prohoemio conciliandi iudicis ratio, quae narrandi lux breuitas fides, quod aliquando consilium et quam occulta calliditas (namque ea sola in hoc ars est, quae intellegi nisi ab artifice non possit): quanta deinceps in diuidendo prudentia, quam subtilis et crebra argumentatio, quibus uiribus inspiret, qua iucunditate permulceat, quanta in maledictis asperitas, in iocis urbanitas, ut denique dominetur in adfectibus atque in pectora inrumpat animumque iudicum similem iis quae dicit efficiat; tum, in ratione eloquendi, quod uerbum proprium ornatum sublime, ubi

---

[28] Winterbottom (1982) 246–249 also discusses this section of Quintilian. For his further thoughts, see Reinhardt and Winterbottom (2006) xxviii–xxx along with their commentary ad loc. (cf. n. 3 above).

[29] Perhaps sometimes each student had his own book, but given the constraints around book production in the ancient world, it is hard to imagine every pupil always equipped with his own text. Students may also have copied down dictated excerpts for study and memorization; cf. Reinhardt and Winterbottom (2006) xxix.

amplificatio laudanda, quae uirtus ei contraria, quid speciose tralatum, quae figura uerborum, quae leuis et quadrata, uirilis tamen compositio.

> ... nothing must pass unnoticed: every noteworthy point of invention or elocution is to be observed – the way in which the judge is conciliated in the *prooemium*; the clarity, brevity, and credibility of the narrative; the speaker's plan and hidden artifice (in this business the only art is that which can only be seen by an artist!); the wisdom shown in dividing the materials; the delicate and dense argument; the vigor that stirs and the charm that delights; the sharpness of the invective, the wit of the jokes; and how finally the orator reigns over the jury's emotions, forces his way into their hearts, and makes their feelings reflect his words. As for elocution, he will point out the exact use, elegance, or sublimity of each word; where amplification is to be praised, and where the opposite quality is to be seen; the brilliance of the metaphors, the figures of speech, and how the composition is smooth and well-formed while remaining masculine. (trans. D. A. Russell, Loeb)

This is of course a counsel of perfection, but it does give an idea of the sort of comments a teacher might make in the classroom, and it is not mere idealism:[30] we will find that almost all of what Quintilian prescribes here in theory is reflected in the practice of the schoolroom.[31] The teacher is concerned above all to unpack each and every detail of the rhetoric so that it can serve as a model for his students' own oratory.

And the teacher is not merely to lecture to the class. He should constantly question the students, Quintilian emphasizes, and try to lead them to the desired answers as if of their own accord. Such a Socratic approach will both keep them on their toes and help them to retain the material that they are learning; indeed, as a result of this method of instruction they will begin to develop the ability to think for themselves – and this is the ultimate goal of all teaching. He feels that this active engagement with real speeches will bring more profit to the budding orator than studying "all the rhetorical textbooks of every author" (*omnes omnium artes, inst.* 2.5.14). Such textbooks are not without value, he continues, but since oratory is so various, knowledge of general principles will only go so far: "teaching is worth less than experience in just about every field" (*nam in*

---

[30] Winterbottom (1982) 247 calls it a "blueprint for a rhetorical commentary on a speech of Cicero" and notes that it also almost outlines the *Institutio* itself.

[31] "Almost all" because there are only a few remarks to be found about individual words (see n. 105 below). Such detailed verbal commentary was unsuitable for a general treatise on rhetorical education such as the *Institutio*; that is to say, had Quintilian been explicating the *Pro Milone* itself, he might have paused to dilate on one point or another, but the opportunity rarely would have arisen in what he was actually writing. For parallels to Quintilian's recommendations here, see the theorizing of Theon ch. 13 (above n. 3) as well as Gell. 2.27 and 11.13.

omnibus fere minus ualent praecepta quam experimenta, inst. 2.5.15).[32] And with time-tested and venerable models already to hand, why should the *rhetor* offer up his own declamations to his students? They could after all be reading Cicero and Demosthenes instead. Furthermore, the students will react better to adverse criticism of famous speeches past than they will to critique of their own efforts.

The advantages of this plan of instruction, Quintilian concludes, are manifest to all, and indeed one has the feeling that he must have run a very sensitive and humane classroom.[33] At this point, however, you might reasonably ask to what degree that classroom is unique. To what degree is Quintilian's idealized prescription in fact a Roman reality? This is an important issue, and it is doubtless in part in reaction to the errant teaching that he sees around him that Quintilian has created his utopian classroom. Some of his injunctions are plainly in direct contradiction of popular teaching methodology.[34] We thus cannot always take Quintilian at his word, and we must on occasion proceed with due skepticism. Nevertheless, despite his innovations in educational philosophy, when it comes to the practical business of instruction Quintilian is a traditionalist: as George Kennedy has put it, "Quintilian describes schools *as they existed through most of Hellenistic and Roman times*, with comments and suggestions growing out of his own experience."[35] Whenever we can see close parallels between his methods and comments and those of the Bobiensia, we are probably on safe ground, and in practice we simply must read carefully and tread with caution.

Having established the proper method, Quintilian goes on to consider the choice of authors for the rhetorical syllabus (*inst.* 2.5.18–26). He notes that opinions on this point have differed, with some preferring simple authors (as being easiest for beginners to understand),[36] while others

---

[32] Cf. Sen. *epist.* 6.5 *longum iter est per praecepta, breue et efficax per exempla,* as well as Quintilian's remarks on illustrating his precepts by example: *nam omnium quaecumque docemus hinc* [from reading and listening to the best models] *sunt exempla, potentiora etiam ipsis quae traduntur artibus . . . quia quae doctor praecepit orator ostendit (inst.* 10.1.15). For more on the very varied nature of oratory, see Quint. *inst.* 2.13.

[33] Cf. e.g. *inst.* 1.3 on the virtues of games and the vices of corporal punishment.

[34] For example, he does not believe that the boys should memorize all their own declamations, as was the contemporary custom: *illud ex consuetudine mutandum prorsus existimo in iis de quibus nunc disserimus aetatibus, ne omnia quae scripserint ediscant et certa, ut moris est, die dicant (inst.* 2.7.1). He would prefer that they memorize choice gobbets from good Latin authors instead. Quintilian likewise eschews corporal punishment (*inst.* 1.3.14–17).

[35] Kennedy (1969) 11 (my emphasis). Cf. Bloomer (2011) 82–84 on Quintilian's synthesis of educational theory and his own classroom practice.

[36] Cf. Theon ch. 13 (Patillon [1998] 102, preserved only in Armenian): "Le jeune homme devra l'aborder par les ouvrages les plus simples."

favored the *floridius genus*, which might be thought better suited to drawing out the talents of the budding orator. Quintilian recommends "the best" *et statim et semper*, and within the class of *optimi* those who are most accessible to the studious youth. For this reason Livy is to be preferred to Sallust, for example, but above all towers Cicero (*inst.* 2.5.20):

> Cicero, ut mihi quidem uidetur, et iucundus incipientibus quoque et apertus est satis, nec prodesse tantum sed etiam amari potest: tum, quem ad modum Liuius praecipit, ut quisque erit Ciceroni simillimus.

> Cicero, as it seems to me at any rate, is both pleasant to read even for beginners and easy enough to understand, nor is he merely useful but can even be loved. Next, as Livy advises,[37] whoever is most similar to Cicero.

Cicero's pride of place is further confirmed in book 10 of the *Institutio*. Quintilian's famous *elogium* is worth quoting here in its magisterial fullness (*inst.* 10.1.108–112):[38]

> nam mihi uidetur M. Tullius, cum se totum ad imitationem Graecorum contulisset, effinxisse uim Demosthenis, copiam Platonis, iucunditatem Isocratis. nec uero quod in quoque optimum fuit studio consecutus est tantum, sed plurimas uel potius omnes ex se ipso uirtutes extulit inmortalis ingenii beatissima ubertas. non enim pluuias, ut ait Pindarus, aquas colligit, sed uiuo gurgite exundat, dono quodam prouidentiae genitus in quo totas uires suas eloquentia experiretur. nam quis docere diligentius, mouere uehementius potest, cui tanta umquam iucunditas adfuit? – ut ipsa illa quae extorquet impetrare eum credas, et cum transuersum ui sua iudicem ferat, tamen ille non rapi uideatur sed sequi. iam in omnibus quae dicit tanta auctoritas inest ut dissentire pudeat, nec aduocati studium sed testis aut iudicis adferat fidem, cum interim haec omnia, quae uix singula quisquam intentissima cura consequi posset, fluunt inlaborata, et illa qua nihil pulchrius auditum est oratio prae se fert tamen felicissimam facilitatem. quare non inmerito ab hominibus aetatis suae regnare in iudiciis dictus est, apud posteros uero id consecutus ut Cicero iam non hominis nomen sed eloquentiae habeatur. hunc igitur spectemus, hoc propositum nobis sit exemplum, ille se profecisse sciat cui Cicero ualde placebit.

> For Cicero seems to me, since he devoted himself entirely to the imitation of Greek authors, to have achieved the force of Demosthenes, the abundance of Plato, and the charm of Isocrates. Nor did he just manage to achieve what

---

[37] Cf. *inst.* 10.1.39: *fuit igitur breuitas illa tutissima quae est apud Liuium in epistula ad filium scripta, legendos Demosthenen atque Ciceronem, tum ita ut quisque esset Demostheni et Ciceroni simillimus.*

[38] This sentiment is echoed by countless scattered remarks; to cite just one, when Quintilian discusses the various types of exempla and wants to provide some specifics, he says *singula igitur horum generum ex Cicerone (nam unde potius?) exempla ponamus* (*inst.* 5.11.11); shortly thereafter Cicero is described as the *optimus auctor ac magister eloquentiae* (*inst.* 5.11.17).

was best in each of them by studious imitation, but the most felicitous richness of his immortal genius produced most – or rather all! – of these virtues from itself alone. For he does not "collect the rain waters," as Pindar says, but rather swells with a rushing torrent,[39] born by a certain gift of Providence to be the man in whom eloquence might make full trial of her powers. For who can instruct more diligently, who can move more powerfully, who ever had such charm? As a result you would think that he has gained by entreaty the things which he has in fact wrested away by force, and when he carries the judge along by his own violence, the judge seems nevertheless not to be dragged but to follow of his own accord. In everything that he says there is such authority that it seems shameful to disagree, nor does he bring to bear the partisanship of an advocate but the trustworthiness of a witness or a judge. And all these things, any one of which scarcely anyone could achieve even with the most concentrated effort, flow from him effortlessly, and that speech which is the most beautiful anyone's ever heard nevertheless seems like it couldn't be easier. It's with good reason, then, that he was said by people of his own age to be the king of the law courts, and for posterity "Cicero" has come to be considered not the name of a man but eloquence personified. Therefore let us look to him, let us keep him before our eyes as an example, and let the student know that he has made real progress when Cicero delights him.

Cicero is the exemplum, combining the virtues of the greatest Greek prose stylists and exceeding them by his immortal genius. He is, simply put, the perfect orator. Note too that some of his qualities are the very points that Quintilian has earlier singled out for detailed explication by the *rhetor*: to say that Cicero has particular skill in "giving information" (*docere*) and "stirring up feelings" (*mouere*), for example, is just to say that he excels at *narratio* and *peroratio* (cf. *inst.* 8.1.7). Cicero's signal virtue, of course, is his ability to persuade, and this Quintilian dilates on at the greatest length, pairing it with his fluency (*facilitas*) as well. This is high praise indeed, and it need hardly be added that no other author is accorded such a favorable judgment. If we compare the case of Asinius Pollio, the famous anti-Ciceronian who immediately follows in Quintilian's list, we see that the decline has already set in. He is given credit for some good qualities, but he is so far removed from Cicero's elegance and eloquence that he could seem to belong to the previous century (*a nitore et iucunditate Ciceronis ita longe abest ut uideri possit saeculo prior*, *inst.* 10.1.113).[40] This

---

[39] Cicero's eloquence is often described in these metaphors from flooding. Cf. [Longinus] on p. 97 below and the less charitable assessment of Calenus in Cassius Dio on p. 184 n. 89, as well parallels in Juvenal (p. 100 n. 76) and perhaps Tac. *dial.* 30.5 (p. 262).

[40] Quintilian will elsewhere link Larcius Licinus, author of a *Ciceromastix*, with the decline of oratory (ap. Plin. *epist.* 2.14.9). This Licinus is mentioned by Gellius in the same breath as Pollio's son, the

description places Cicero at the very peak of oratory; the man who follows him chronologically seems to belong to the previous century, that is, to an inferior and pre-Ciceronian age. Cicero is, in sum, the ultimate model for posterity, no longer the name of a man but eloquence personified. This is programmatic for Quintilian's project in the *Institutio oratoria*, and it likewise undergirds everything that I will write about.

The tyro in Quintilian's rhetorical classroom therefore will have concentrated much of his effort on an attentive reading of Cicero's speeches, guided by a sage teacher keen to explicate them in the greatest detail. The focus will be firmly fixed on the rhetoric of the orations. Moreover, the student will not merely read the best speeches; he will also lay in a lasting store of such works by committing some to memory (*inst.* 2.7). This practice will benefit the memory as well as familiarize the pupil with the best models for imitation, leading him eventually to reproduce their excellences with unconscious ease. (Here again we see an emphasis on the Ciceronian virtue of *facilitas*.) Ultimately the diligent student will have at his fingertips an abundance of the best words and composition and rhetorical figures that seem to offer themselves up to him unbidden (*copia uerborum optimorum et compositione ac figuris iam non quaesitis sed sponte et ex reposito uelut thesauro se offerentibus, inst.* 2.7.4).

From this solid basis of Ciceronian knowledge the student will eventually be able to begin the process of *imitatio* (described in *inst.* 10.2). Quintilian explicitly notes that the *uerborum* ... *copia et uarietas figurarum et componendi ratio* must be taken from what the best models have established (*inst.* 10.2.1), and it will not escape the reader that these are some of the very things that the student was to gain by assiduous memorization. The Romans had a different conception of *imitatio* and *aemulatio* than we do today,[41] and Quintilian devotes much of the chapter to explaining these ideas. Not surprisingly, Cicero emerges as the primary model, albeit perhaps not the only one (*inst.* 10.2.25). Quintilian allows that there can be no harm in adding in a bit of Caesar's *uis* or Caelius' *asperitas* or Pollio's *diligentia* on occasion, but Cicero's example is plainly preeminent.

noted anti-Ciceronian Asinius Gallus (Gell. 17.1.1; cf. Quint. *inst.* 12.1.22, Suet. *Claud.* 41.3). Tacitus will point to Pollio himself (Tac. *dial.* 38.2). Cf. p. 282 below.

[41] The modern bibliography discussing *imitatio* and *aemulatio* is enormous, but on these as ancient notions see Russell (1979) and D'Ippolito (2000).

In the rhetorical school then, Cicero stands above all as a model to be studied, memorized, and imitated. For students of Quintilian's time, moreover, the first real acquaintance with Cicero would come from the instruction of the *rhetor*. Cicero had been dead now for well over a century, and living memory of the man had long since vanished. Prose writing was not felt suitable material for elementary instruction, and so the young men would have arrived at the *rhetor's* doorstep never having studied any of Cicero's speeches in detail. Their first impressions of Cicero will thus have been of the "rhetorical figure," the model who excelled all others, as presented by their teachers – and first impressions can last a lifetime.

Themes and Methods of Instruction

Quintilian's comments on the *Pro Milone* scattered throughout the *Institutio* show that he follows his own prescription. He is concerned above all to explicate the rhetoric of the speech, and in particular the strengths and weaknesses of Cicero's arguments. He also pays special attention to the *prooemium*, and dilates at some length on Cicero's excellence in the *narratio*. Finally, he is constantly concerned to point out various rhetorical figures as they arise in the course of the speech. All of Quintilian's comments ultimately serve one purpose: to make his pupils better orators.

The scholia Bobiensia show the same predilections and concerns. Even in their present mutilated state, we can see that they too are especially focused on the rhetoric of the speech.[42] Despite their gaps, they also help fill in some of what Quintilian lacks; the nature of the *Institutio*, for example, precluded any lengthy discussion of the background of a given speech, but we know from Quintilian's recommendations that he would have provided an introductory lecture on this material. Occasionally we can even see some traces of what he would have said in such a *praelectio* (e.g. *inst.* 2.20.8, see p. 31 below), but this is to be sure the exception. The scholia Bobiensia, by contrast, lead with an exposition of the background of the case and the issues at hand. They then proceed along similar lines to Quintilian: explication of argument, focus on rhetorical figures, attention to points of narrative detail, and so forth.

---

[42] Cf. Hildebrandt (1894) 50–53, arguing that the overriding goal of these scholia is to showcase Cicero's rhetorical artistry as a model for students.

Nor are the Bobbio scholia blind to historical detail, which they judiciously include throughout the course of the commentary.[43] We can only catch very fleeting glimpses of this in Quintilian – the end goal of the *Institutio* again left little room for these sorts of digressions – but historical exegesis was in any case not a primary concern of rhetorical education. Quintilian, for example, does not bother including anything about history in his description of how to read a speech. He seems to view history mostly as a mine for *exempla*, whose rhetorical usefulness he describes at length at *inst.* 5.11. The orator needed to have a ready supply of such *exempla*, and he would be hard pressed to acquire it without some help from his teachers.[44] The Bobiensia show that even the teacher focused primarily on rhetoric would dress up his teaching with some remarks on history, at least insofar as history was necessary to understand the force and argument of the speech itself and to stock the young orator's mind with usable *exempla*.

History only really comes into its own in the special case of Asconius. In contrast to Quintilian and the scholia, Asconius is much less concerned with rhetoric and much more concerned with *Geschichte* and *Realien*. This is in the first instance evidence of a pedagogical continuum. Just as no one would expect all teachers today to teach the same curriculum in exactly the same way – perhaps to the chagrin of some educational panjandrums – so too is it a mistake to expect that every teacher of the *Pro Milone* in the ancient world would have emphasized exactly the same points. All would have certainly included some discussion of rhetoric, some discussion of history, and so forth, but no doubt there was a bit of *à chacun son goût*.

Asconius' tastes, however, might seem in direct contradiction to the rhetorical emphasis of the established curriculum described by Quintilian and embodied by our corpus of scholia. It is very striking how little Asconius was attracted to rhetorical comment, and how exclusively he focuses on history. This does not appear to be just an accident of preservation, since we have Asconius complete for this speech as well as four others. I thus wonder whether Asconius' historical focus is a reaction against a perceived lack. That is to say, we might be able to read against the grain here and deduce that rhetorical teaching was "too much with us" and history was disproportionately excluded.[45] Perhaps Asconius is trying to

---

[43] See e.g. 113.27–114.2 St., 115.1–7 St., 117.32–118.17 St., etc. Cf. also p. 48 below.

[44] On historical exempla, see p. 47 below.

[45] Cf. the remarks of Marshall (1985) on Asconius' discussions of historical exempla: "they are ... necessary no doubt to supplement his sons' studies because history was not a subject taught in the schools" (37). Bishop (2015) 292–293, by contrast, thinks that Asconius may have patterned his work on contemporary commentaries on Demosthenes.

redress the balance. If you assume, as I have argued we must, that he was writing for a schoolroom audience, then you must either simply allow that he had his own tastes or try account for those tastes. This hypothesis certainly squares with the preserved evidence and would explain his otherwise unusual emphases, but ultimately it cannot be proven.

The Introductory *praelectio*

The teacher stands before a classroom of teenage boys. Doubtless he faces the perennial problems of the instructor in such a situation: the students' minds wander, their hands fidget, and they whisper incessantly. These details, alas, have gone for the most part unrecorded, although we do occasionally sight them from afar, for example in Quintilian's injunction toward silence (*inst.* 2.5.6). Did the students groan when they learned that the set text was to be yet more Cicero?[46] Perhaps, but the Roman schoolroom was not generally so kind as Quintilian's utopian vision: a Pompeian graffito records the menacing *si ti[bi] Cicero do[let], uap[u]labis* ("if you don't like Cicero, you will be beaten").[47] If you were a Roman student, the implication goes, you might not yet have reached that Quintilianic higher plane where Cicero "pleased you greatly," but you were to move in that direction whether you liked it or not, and a few good paddlings might speed you along the journey. The Roman schoolman evidently followed the model of "beatings will continue until morale improves."[48]

As we have seen, Quintilian first prescribes that the background to the case must be explained to the class (*inst.* 2.5.7; see p. 22 above). There was scant room for this in the *Institutio* itself, but we do catch glimpses once in a while: Quintilian declares, for example, that the orator must be courageous since he must sometimes speak in extremely unfavorable circumstances, often in the face of a threatening mob, or with the danger of offending the powerful, or even surrounded by armed soldiers

---

[46] Cf. Seneca the Elder's introduction to his cutting remarks on L. Cestius Pius (*contr.* 3 pr. 15): *pueri fere aut iuuenes scholas frequentant; hi non tantum disertissimis uiris, quos paulo ante rettuli, Cestium suum praeferunt sed etiam Ciceroni praeferrent, nisi lapides timerent.* Stoning is of course a humorously exaggerated punishment for truculent schoolboys.

[47] *CIL* IV.4208. For brief further remarks, see Gigante (1979) 160, who describes the inscription as probably "le parole di un *ludimagister*, emulo del *plagosus Orbilius*." Perhaps, but they seem more likely to be a schoolboy's scribbled aping of his teacher's threat.

[48] Magisterial beatings provided a physical impetus toward achievement in the typical ancient classroom; see Bloomer (2015b). An Egyptian wax tablet preserves a pupil's four-fold copying of the phrase "work hard, boy, lest you be beaten" (φιλοπόνει, ὦ παῖ, μὴ δαρῇς, cited with image by Bonner [1977] 61).

(*non fortitudinem postulat res eadem, cum saepe contra turbulentas populi minas, saepe cum periculosa potentium offensa, nonnumquam, ut iudicio Miloniano, inter circumfusa militum arma dicendum sit: ut, si uirtus non est, ne perfecta quidem esse possit oratio, inst.* 2.20.8). All of these perils were present for Cicero in the *Pro Milone*, and in Quintilian's final phrase about how in the absence of courage "a speech cannot even be completed" there may lurk a pointed allusion to Cicero's own failure in that oration. This is not the kind of comment Quintilian would have tied to any specific passage of the speech – although he might have mentioned it in various places[49] – but rather much more the sort of thing he would say by way of introduction to the speech. He also would doubtless have included some general information about how Cicero framed his defense, along the lines of *inst.* 3.6.93, where Cicero's theory of the case is contrasted with Brutus':

> pro Milone aliud Ciceroni agenti placuit, aliud Bruto cum exercitationis gratia componeret orationem, cum ille iure tamquam insidiatorem occisum et tamen non Milonis consilio dixerit, ille etiam gloriatus sit occiso malo ciue.

> When Cicero was defending Milo he took one approach; when Brutus was composing his speech as an exercise he took another. Cicero argued that Clodius had been justly killed as an ambusher and not by Milo's plan, whereas Brutus went so far as to boast about killing a wicked citizen.

This relates, of course, directly to the argument of the speech itself, which will be Quintilian's primary concern throughout, but it also serves well by way of preface. Quintilian says that there were several lines of defense that the pleader might have adopted, and that Cicero claimed simply that Milo had been ambushed and had not deliberately killed Clodius. Brutus, by contrast, actually boasts of the killing, basing his defense on the idea that by killing Clodius Milo had rendered signal service to the state. (The Brutus of the Ides of March would think this!)[50] Quintilian mentions at least a few

---

49 Most appositely in discussing the speech's *exordium*, since Cicero takes his beginning from the fact that the court is surrounded by an armed guard and attempts to calm the jurors (see p. 43 below). He will again attempt to reassure them in the *peroratio* (see p. 71 below).

50 For Brutus' philosophical bases, see Sedley (1997), not mentioning this speech. Cicero faced something of a sticky wicket here, having himself executed Roman citizens in service of the state. His *Pro Milone* as we have it does include a subsidiary argument about how Milo did not kill Clodius deliberately, *but if he had* it would have been right and proper (see p. 67 below); as Clark (1895) lvi speculates, this could have been included in the published speech in response to Brutus' pamphlet. (Fotheringham [2013b] 11–12 tries to make the case that the "if he had done it" argument was already in the delivered speech; cf. too Fotheringham [2007].) For more on Brutus' approach, see n. 25 above. We know that L. Cestius Pius also composed an *In Milonem* (Sen. *contr.* 3 pr. 16–17); a class

other key points of background; he acknowledges, for example, that the encounter between Milo and Clodius was entirely chance (*inst.* 6.5.10).

Nevertheless, we cannot really see what an introductory *praelectio* was like until we turn to our other two sources. The scholia Bobiensia are lacunose both at the beginning and at the end of their prefatory remarks on the speech, but enough is preserved to reveal the general tenor of the comments. (Based on what we see elsewhere, we might with some confidence speculate that in the lost portion we get basic information about who Milo and Clodius were and the history of their rivalry; some dates might also be included.) When our text begins we are in the middle of a summary of the events described in the speech (III.24–28 St.):

> utrimque inter seruos oborta est iurgiosa certatio et ad gladios usque processum, ut metu peragitatus ad Bouillas in cauponulam quandam P. Clodius fugiens concederet. quem secuti non sua sponte, ut in hac defensione Tullius loquitur pro sui officii necessitate, sed iussu domini qui hoc maxime praeoptauerat serui Milonis interemerunt.

> An obstreperous quarrel broke out among the slaves on both sides, and the matter escalated all the way into a sword-fight, so that P. Clodius was scared off and retreated into a small tavern near Bovillae. And Milo's slaves followed him and killed him not spontaneously, as Cicero says in this speech in keeping with the constraints of his duty [*sc.* as a defense advocate], but rather at the orders of their master, who desired this above all things.

Straightaway we observe that the preface does not merely summarize the contents of the speech in short compass.[51] We see instead immediate

---

might be instructed to compare prosecution and defense speeches (Quint. *inst.* 10.1.22–23), which is hardly surprising, since so much of declamatory rhetoric was dialectic in nature.

[51] I make this point because very often scholiastic comments simply parrot back what is already in the text itself. This tendency has influenced how modern scholars value scholia generally, and the Bobiensia too have come in for various forms of criticism, including that of simply rephrasing Cicero (e.g. Badian [1973] 125–130). Clark (1895) 119 takes a depreciating attitude in publishing some of the Bobiensia: "I give only a selection, since a number of these notes are quite valueless," and Hildebrandt (1894) 53 n. 7 already had to defend the scholia from the slings and arrows of outrageous fortune. What the modern detractors evidently mean is that the scholia are not of great value as witnesses for history "as it really happened," but this is to misunderstand their purpose. They are of capital importance for our understanding of how a speech would have been taught. Furthermore, their relatively high quality is clear from a comparison to the later scholia Gronoviana: the preface to the Gronoviana is written in the simplest of Latin, and even the basic version of events there presented contains serious errors of fact (see 322.19–323.13 St.). The Gronoviana do not seem to draw on other scholarship; for example, they contend that Clodius ambushed Milo (322.29–323.2 St.), presumably just because Cicero says so. (Compare the fact that all three of our scholars agree that the encounter was by chance; see p. 19.) And the notes themselves contain basic misunderstandings; see e.g. *"popa" quidam proprium nomen uolunt, quidam "coponem"* (323.21 St., on *Mil.* 65), where neither interpretation is correct. (Rightly Asconius *"sacrificulus"* [45C], i.e. a butcher attendant on a priest.)

interpretation that goes beyond the story that Cicero retails. The first remarkable detail is the comment that Clodius retreated *metu peragitatus*,[52] which is not to be found in Asconius or any other source. Even Cicero does not claim this.[53] The scholiast then shows again that he is no blind follower of Cicero's text, since he asserts that Milo's slaves did not follow and kill Clodius *sua sponte*, as Cicero would have it (*Mil.* 29), but at their master's command (*iussu domini*),[54] who indeed is said to have wanted Clodius' death above all other things. Cicero lied, and the teacher knows it, but the lie actually redounds to Cicero's credit. His defense runs along these lines, after all, *pro sui officii necessitate*. Thus from the teacher's opening monologue the rhetorical exigencies of the situation take center stage, and the pupils' eyes will be held firmly on the rhetoric of the speech throughout the course of their instruction.

The preface continues (III.28–II2.I St.):

> post quod facinus perpetratum et nuntio Romam perlato uehemens in Milonem inuidia commota est. adlato enim cadauere nobilissimi senatoris et popularis uiri, post denique iniecto in curiam Hostiliam faces subiectae sunt ab turbulenta et sordida multitudine, cui et uita P. Clodi nimium fructuosa in praeteritum fuerat et tunc mors acerba erat.

> After this crime was committed and news of it was brought to Rome, a vehement feeling of ill will toward Milo was stirred up. For when the corpse of the most noble senator and *popularis* man was brought (to Rome) and finally placed in the Curia Hostilia, the factious and base mob – for whom Publius Clodius' life had been very advantageous in the past and his death was a harsh blow at that time – threw torches into the Curia.

Here we have both factual reporting and some editorial comment. The bare outline of the facts could perhaps be gleaned or surmised from the speech itself, but the details appear the result of independent research.[55] Clodius' corpse was brought back to Rome, the people were mightily

---

[52] Into a *cauponula*, a vanishingly rare diminutive: *TLL* III.657.48–54 lists only Cic. *Phil.* 2.77 and the present passage, along with various glosses equating it with *taberna* or *tabernula*. This may relate to the date of composition of the Bobbio scholia, but it is also intriguing to wonder if we may here see a "didactic diminutive": could we be hearing the *ipsissima uerba* of the schoolteacher's voice?

[53] Cicero in fact wisely suppresses any detail of the killing, saying only that *fecerunt id serui Milonis . . . nec imperante nec sciente nec praesente domino, quod suos quisque seruos in tali re facere uoluisset* (*Mil.* 29). It is hard to guess why the scholia include this particular detail. Perhaps it comes from an unknown source, or perhaps it was added merely for color.

[54] Note that Asconius too uses the phrase *iussu Milonis* (53C) and also *exturbari taberna iussit* (32C).

[55] Cicero never explicitly mentions any *in Milonem inuidia*, nor does he specify how the body was brought back to Rome or how it was cremated or by whom. This all could be derived at some remove from Asconius. Nevertheless, even here there is some independence from Asconius; e.g. the scholia specify the *curia Hostilia* (III.30 St.), while Asconius refers to it as just the *curia* (33C).

wroth with Milo, and his body was burned in the Curia. The rather
significant fact that the Curia itself was destroyed in the conflagration is
oddly omitted. (It is mentioned later in the scholia: 115.5–9 St.) In any
event, beyond this simple factual narrative – true so far as we can tell –
there also lies a series of judgments expressed by evaluative adjectives.
Clodius is described as a *nobilissimus senator* and a *popularis uir*, and
Cicero himself would have agreed that Clodius was nothing if not *popularis*
(e.g. *har. resp.* 44). Cicero only could have described him as *nobilissimus*,
however, with dripping irony (as at *Mil.* 18). Since I see no particular irony
in the use of the word by the scholiast here, I take it that his description of
Clodius is again independently motivated.[56] The Clodian supporters, by
contrast, are nothing more than low-class rabble: they are a *turbulenta* and
sordida bunch, and they are actuated solely by the base motive that they
had profited during Clodius' lifetime. Perhaps it is not possible to describe
a mob who burned down the Senate House in neutral language, and we
should always bear in mind that the teacher has a duty to inculcate values in
his charges. That sort of rebellion and wanton destruction was obviously to
be deprecated.

Next we read (112.1–7 St.):

> quibus turbis et seditionibus aduersus Milonem flagrantibus conuocato dein
> senatu decretum est caedem in Appia uia contra rem p. esse commissam.
> Cn. etiam Pompeius, qui tunc sine collega tertium consulatum gerebat, tulit
> legem ut de eadem caede extra ordinem quaereretur. ac primo quidem
> iudices consederunt in aede Saturni. et cernendam causam pro debita
> necessitudine nec minus uoto quo inimici sui interitum gratulabatur,
> Cicero suscepit.

> While these seditious mobs burned with hatred against Milo, the Senate was
> summoned and it was decreed that the killing on the Appian Way had been
> committed *contra rem publicam*. Gnaeus Pompeius too, who at that time
> was, without a colleague, holding his third consulship, proposed a law that
> the killing be tried by an extraordinary commission. And so for the first time
> the judges heard a case in the Temple of Saturn. And Cicero took up the case
> both because of his close connection with Milo and more importantly
> because he was elated by the death of his enemy.

Here too we find factual reporting mixed with interpretation, not all of
which is to be derived from Cicero's speech itself. The Senate decreed that
the killing on the Appian Way was *contra rem publicam*: a fact admitted
even by Cicero (not mentioned by Asconius in his preface but discussed at

[56] Quintilian too calls Clodius a *uir nobilis* (*inst.* 6.1.25; quoted on p. 70 below).

44C), but his reasoning and the scholiast's differ. Cicero asks why the Senate passed this decree and answers his own question: because in a free state acts of violence among the citizenry are never not against the interests of the state (*quia nulla uis umquam est in libera ciuitate suscepta inter ciues non contra rem publicam, Mil.* 13). He goes on to say that although a defense against violence is never something to be desired, it is nevertheless on occasion necessary, and this was one of those occasions. The scholiast takes a more perceptive interpretative line: there was much ill feeling against Milo in the air, and this climate of discontent produced the decree. Again the teacher has seen through Cicero's somewhat feeble argument and struck closer to the truth of the matter.

Then back to facts: Pompey was sole consul in 52 BC, he created a special procedure to try this case, and the jury heard the case in the Temple of Saturn. The Bobbio scholia have been criticized for being inaccurate in their reporting here,[57] but this is to expect too much. They are providing a summary of the basic facts, and they need not elaborate that Pompey was elected to the sole consulship in the wake of the firing of the Senate House, nor do they need to deal with all the legal subtleties that surrounded Pompey's law and special commission. Did the *iudices* in fact sit *in aede Saturni*? Perhaps not literally, but there is no question that the Temple of Saturn was the setting for the trial. It may be the case that Pompey alone was actually within the temple precinct, but this is an overly pedantic level of detail to expect from the briefest schoolroom summary.

More interesting is the discussion of Cicero's reasons for taking the case. These are not given by Cicero himself, nor are they to be found elsewhere, and they are probably no more than the best guesses of the teacher. From our perspective today, they certainly seem logical. Cicero took the case in the first instance because Milo was his client and a man who had worked hard to bring him home from exile in 57. Furthermore, the scholia say, he felt a keen sense of *Schadenfreude* at his enemy's death and so was delighted to defend his killer – and this too is not hard to believe.

Then comes a narration of the events of the trial (112.7–10 St.):

> sed quoniam et turbulenta res erat et confessa[58] caedes et ad seditionem populus inflammatus et circumpositi iudicio milites et non longe praesidens consul ipse Pompeius obnixe studens in damnationem Milonis, perferri

---

[57] E.g. Clark (1895) x, Stangl (1964) ad loc.
[58] It is always tempting to press the scholiast's Latin to help settle questions of dating, but the perfect passive participle of *confiteor* is commonly passive from the XII Tables onwards (*TLL* iv.226.35 [Burger]), so this instance is not evidence for dating.

> defensio ista non potuit: nam metu consternatus et ipse Tullius pedem rettulit.

> But because it was a raucous affair and the killing had been admitted and the people were inflamed to the point of rebellion and soldiers were stationed around the tribunal and the consul Pompey himself was sitting not far off and was steadfast in his determination to condemn Milo, the defense could not be carried through: overcome by fear even Cicero himself beat a retreat.

Here is the account of Cicero's failure. The circumstances are briefly summarized: it was a turbulent affair, the killing was openly acknowledged, the people were inflamed to the point of rebellion, soldiers stood guard over the trial, and Pompey himself, clearly desiring a guilty verdict, presided. This all seems true enough, and some of it can be inferred from the speech, but a couple of points merit special mention. First, the teacher recognizes that Pompey was hostile to Milo and eager to secure his condemnation. Cicero would not acknowledge this in his speech, and indeed he insistently claims that Pompey is a neutral party,[59] but one cannot escape the impression that Cicero doth protest too much. The scholiast thus has made a perceptive comment. Perhaps more importantly, all these "facts" serve to excuse Cicero's failure. The teacher cannot change history, and for a class about to devote serious study to Cicero's defense speech, it is a point of some embarrassment that it failed. Some justification must be offered.[60]

The scholiast continues (112.10–14 St.):

> et exstat alius praeterea liber actorum pro Milone: in quo omnia interrupta et inpolita et rudia, plena denique maximi terroris agnoscas. hanc orationem postea legitimo opere et maiore cura, utpote iam confirmato animo et in securitate, conscribsit.

> And there also exists another version of the *Pro Milone*. In it everything is choppy and rough and unpolished, and in a word you can see that it is full of sheer terror. Cicero wrote the version of the speech that we're reading afterwards with proper attention and greater care, inasmuch as his confidence was restored and his person secure.

Here we find the compositional history of the text to be studied. The version of the speech that Cicero actually delivered is acknowledged to exist (and admitted to be bad), but the revised version is

---

[59] E.g. *Mil.* 15 and later 70–71.
[60] Asconius too will seek to vindicate Cicero at 41–42C. His defense of Cicero is much more strident; see p. 42 below.

thus pointed up as all the better.[61] It is perhaps fruitless to wonder exactly at what date the phrase *exstat alius praeterea liber* was written, but we would certainly like to know; we do not, after all, have the original speech ourselves.

Finally, just before the text breaks off for eight pages (encompassing the end of the preface and comment on the first six sections of the speech itself), we get a description of the defense strategy that Cicero adopts (112.14–18 St.):

> sed enim cum ratio defensionis huius ordinaretur, quonam modo et secundum quem potissimum statum agi pro Milone oporteret, M. Brutus existimauit κατὰ ἀντίστασιν pro eo esse dicendum, quae a nobis nominatur qualitas compensatiua. hoc enimuero Ciceroni uisum est parum salubre, nam maluit ἀντεγκλήματος specie, id est rela< . . . >

> For when the plan of this defense was being drawn up, in what way and under what heading of *status* theory it was most fitting that the case for Milo be argued, Marcus Brutus thought that he should be defended κατὰ ἀντίστασιν [i.e. by arguing that the benefit outweighed the injury done], which we call the *qualitas compensatiua*. It did not seem to Cicero that Milo would be saved under such a defense, for he preferred the method of ἀντέγκλημα [i.e. counter-claim or counter-charge], that is what we call . . .

Just as Quintilian and Asconius do, the scholiast acknowledges that there were various avenues of defense open to Cicero. Brutus chose one (see n. 25 above), Cicero another; perhaps in oral exposition in front of the classroom the teacher might spell out the possible reasons for these choices. Note in any event that the whole discussion presumes some knowledge of *status* theory, and it includes both Greek terms and their Latin equivalents. The students must have known a fair bit of Greek – or at least the teacher thinks that they should – since Greek is frequently integrated into the notes without further gloss, e.g. on just one page μυθῶδες (114.4 St.), βιαίως (114.13 St.), and ἐναντία (114.15 St.). The Greek words are sometimes technical terms (e.g. ἐνάργεια, 120.28 St. or ἐπανόρθωσις, 121.17 St.), but on other occasions seem to be introduced simply for variety (e.g. λεληθότως instead of *clam* or *occulte* at 121.7 St.). These Greek flourishes receive further explanation only when they are terms of art, which supports the commonsense notion that the *rhetor* had to steep his pupils in the

---

[61] Asconius is again more insistent in declaring the present speech very good indeed; again, see p. 42 below. Cf. Dio 40.54.2 on Cicero revising this speech "some time later at his leisure" (χρόνῳ ποθ' ὕστερον καὶ κατὰ σχολήν).

unfamiliar terminology of rhetoric in both Greek and Latin (see e.g. *egressio, quam* παρέκβασιν *Graeci uocant*, 121.12 St.).[62]

The preface breaks off here, but it was nearing its end in any case. We thus have a fairly accurate idea of how this particular teacher would have introduced the speech: necessary background information, factual reporting of the events of the speech and of the outcome of the speech itself, all intermingled with interpretation and analysis of its rhetoric.

Asconius' preface we have complete, and it is very full indeed, stretching over some twelve pages of Oxford text. A teacher would not have covered all of Asconius' points in such exhaustive detail, but he certainly could have followed the commentary in outline, and it would have furnished a stock of material to elaborate on points of particular interest. Moreover, some of what Asconius has put in his preface, such as his detailed description of the battle at Bovillae, could be treated *suo loco* by the teacher in discussing the speech.

The preface begins with the information we would expect to find in the scholia Bobiensia's opening lacuna. First the basics (Ascon. 30C): we are given the date of the speech and then the signal fact that Pompey had stationed his army all about the forum during the proceedings. In passing it is worth observing that Asconius, as is his practice, here cites another Ciceronian work to justify his assertion that the forum was packed with soldiers (*ex libro apparet qui Ciceronis nomine inscribitur de optimo genere oratorum*). Then comes the *argumentum* itself. Asconius starts by providing basic information on the background of the case (Ascon. 30C). We are told that Milo and Clodius were enemies with a long history, and we learn the reasons for their mutual hatred, namely that Milo was a staunch Ciceronian ally and had helped engineer his recall from exile. Their last encounter, it is revealed, was hardly their first; their factions had often brawled in the streets of Rome. All of this is necessary background for understanding the events of the speech.

Next comes an explanation of the immediate political situation preceding the skirmish at Bovillae. Clodius is seeking the praetorship in the same year in which Milo is seeking the consulship, and Asconius makes the observation that Clodius' praetorian powers would be lame in the face of Milo's superior status as consul (*in eundem annum consulatum Milo, Clodius praeturam petebat, quam debilem futuram consule Milone intellegebat*, Ascon. 30C).

---

[62] This practice is also reflected in the teaching of the late *rhetor* Fortunatianus; see *RLM* 81 with Bonner (1977) 304. It is interesting to note how often the Greek foxed the scribe of our palimpsest; this is evident from a glance at almost any page of Stangl's edition, which is sure to be marred by brief lacunas that should contain Greek.

This last observation demonstrates active interpretation only to a very limited degree, since it closely echoes Cicero's own words (*occurrebat ei mancam ac debilem praeturam futuram suam consule Milone, Mil.* 25). Asconius then summarizes the events leading up to the killing and the fatal skirmish itself. Much of this is done with reference – implicit or explicit – to the speech, but for his account of the fight Asconius is obviously drawing on other sources, and he makes particular mention of both the senatorial *acta* and Fenestella.[63] His description of the fight directly contradicts Cicero's own story, and he is quite well aware of this fact (Ascon. 41C):

> itaque cum insidias Milonem Clodio fecisse posuissent accusatores, quia falsum id erat – nam forte illa rixa commissa fuerat – Cicero apprehendit et contra Clodium Miloni fecisse insidias disputauit, eoque tota oratio eius spectauit. sed ita constitit ut diximus, nec utrius consilio pugnatum esse eo die, uerum et forte occurrisse et ex rixa seruorum ad eam denique caedem peruentum. notum tamen erat utrumque mortem alteri saepe minatum esse, et sicut suspectum Milonem maior quam Clodi familia faciebat, ita expeditior et paratior ad pugnam Clodianorum quam Milonis fuerat.

> Therefore when the accusers claimed that Milo had set the ambush for Clodius, since that wasn't true – for the brawl had broken out by chance – Cicero seized on the point and claimed instead that Clodius had set the ambush for Milo, and his whole speech looked to that point. But, as I've said, the fight actually happened that day without prior planning by either Milo or Clodius, but rather arose by chance and from a squabble among slaves it finally resulted in the killing. It was known, however, that both Clodius and Milo had often threatened each other with death, and although the larger size of Milo's retinue made him more suspect, the Clodians were less encumbered and more ready for battle than Milo's followers.

Asconius sees right through Cicero's defense and openly acknowledges that it was founded on a false pretense.[64] Just as with the scholia Bobiensia (see p. 33 above), however, this lie is actually a sign of Cicero's skill. Cicero grasped what the accusers were doing and so devised an ingenious counter-argument, toward which his entire speech was directed.[65] Truth is nowhere a concern.

---

[63] He later mentions Tiro as well (48C), although this is unique in his extant commentaries. For a very thorough treatment of Asconius' sources, see Marshall (1985) 39–61.

[64] The jurors apparently saw through it too, according to Asconius (53C): *uidebantur non ignorasse iudices inscio Milone initio uulneratum esse Clodium, sed compererant, postquam uulneratus esset, iussu Milonis occisum.*

[65] Gambet (1963) 194–195 believes that Asconius is embarrassed by Cicero's lies in the *Pro Milone*. I see no evidence of embarrassment, only of appreciative admiration for Cicero's skill. While Asconius is generally concerned to defend Cicero's accuracy and honesty (see esp. Marshall [1985] 46–47), those virtues can at times be trumped by sheer rhetorical brilliance. A Ciceronian lie, in the world of Asconius, will always be both *ben trovato* and persuasive.

Asconius tells a tale very different from Cicero's of how the skirmish broke out (Ascon. 31–32C). Milo went to Lanuvium in his official capacity as local dictator to appoint a *flamen*; Clodius happened to be returning from giving a speech at Aricia.[66] It was, Asconius says, "around the ninth hour" (*circa horam nonam*) – not the eleventh hour, as Cicero would have it (*Mil.* 29).[67] Two of Milo's gladiators, Eudamus and Birria, kicked up a ruckus with Clodius' slaves, and when Clodius got involved he was promptly hit with a spear in the shoulder. He retreated to the safety of a nearby tavern, whereupon,

> Milo ut cognouit uulneratum Clodium, cum sibi periculosius illud etiam uiuo eo futurum intellegeret, occiso autem magnum solacium esset habiturus, etiam si subeunda esset poena, exturbari taberna iussit. (Ascon. 32C)

> when Milo learned that Clodius had been wounded, since he understood that matters would be more dangerous for him if Clodius lived, but that if Clodius died he would have a great recompense, even if he had to be punished for it, he ordered Clodius to be rousted from the tavern.

Again, therefore, Asconius directly contradicts Cicero (*Mil.* 29). Asconius' Milo is a Machiavellian practitioner of *Realpolitik*, and since he judges Clodius' death to be in his best interests, he coldly orders his killing – regardless of the punishment. After all, better to be hanged for a sheep than a lamb.[68] This is a very prejudiced description indeed, and I suspect that it comes from one of the prosecution's own speeches, although Asconius never cites them explicitly. He has thus again demonstrated independence of Cicero in his evaluation of the *circumstantiae* of the case.

Après ça, le déluge: we are next nearly drowned in a welter of detail about the aftermath of the killing. Much of this is simply narrative, some parts found in the *Pro Milone* itself, others derived probably from the *acta* and perhaps the prosecution's speeches. All of this provides a valuable check on Cicero's own *narratio*, particularly when Asconius describes the devious machinations by which Milo first contrived to manumit his slaves and eliminate a source of adverse evidence, then distributed a bribe of some 1,000 *asses* per man to ward off negative publicity (Ascon. 35C). He dives into the nuances of Pompey's special laws governing the trial and various other things that Cicero does not bring up in the course of the speech. Why does he include so much detail? We can probably divine the general reason from his specific explanation of why he has discussed certain sensational

---

[66] All three of our commentators share this emphasis on the chance nature of the encounter: see p. 19 above.

[67] See Lewis (2006) ad loc.   [68] As Melchior (2008) 282 well puts it.

charges alleged by Lepidus' freedman Philemon: "Even though Cicero made no mention of these charges, nevertheless, because I'd investigated them, I thought that the results of my investigation should be put on record" (*haec, etsi nullam de his criminibus mentionem fecit Cicero, tamen, quia ita compereram, putaui exponenda*, 37C). He feels an obligation to report his own research, or perhaps a sense of pride in doing so.

Much of Asconius' independent research sheds a perceptive light on the gambits and power plays made by various political figures to stir up hatred against Milo in advance of the trial. Where the scholia Bobiensia are content to note that a violent ill will was stirred up against Milo (*uehemens in Milonem inuidia commota est*), Asconius spells out much of this in detail. The same can be said for Pompey's law: the scholia note that it was carried; Asconius describes all its various provisions (Ascon. 38C and 43–44C). Finally Asconius unfolds the specifics of the trial itself with the keen interest of a storyteller; for example, he recounts how on the last day of the trial taverns were closed throughout the city and Pompey took up a position in front of the treasury, surrounded by a select band of soldiers. There followed as great a silence as was ever heard in a forum (Ascon. 41C).

Asconius concludes by discussing Cicero's difficulties in delivering the speech (Ascon. 41–42C):

> Cicero cum inciperet dicere, exceptus <est> acclamatione Clodianorum, qui se continere ne metu quidem circumstantium militum potuerunt. itaque non ea qua solitus erat constantia dixit. manet autem illa quoque excepta eius oratio: scripsit uero hanc quam legimus ita perfecte ut iure prima haberi possit.

> Cicero, when he began to speak, was greeted by the jeers of the Clodians, who couldn't be restrained even by fear of the soldiers surrounding the tribunal. Therefore Cicero spoke without his customary constancy. Moreover that speech which he delivered is also extant; but he wrote this one, the one that we're reading, so perfectly that it can rightly be considered his very best.

The elegant meiosis of *non ea qua solitus erat constantia dixit* nearly leaps off the page: this is a very charitable description indeed of a halting and stammering speech that could barely be delivered! Asconius is plainly a partisan of Cicero, and he too, when faced with the awkwardness of explaining Cicero's failure, tries to make the best of a bad situation. He concludes by observing that while the delivered speech is still extant, the speech which "we are reading" (an address to his classroom?) was written so perfectly that it might rightly be held as Cicero's very best. Thus, despite Cicero's apparent failure, he is vindicated at the last. In the schoolroom environment, where Cicero is being held up as a paragon of excellence, this vindication is of sovereign importance.[69]

Asconius' preface is thus remarkably full. This in fact goes against his usual practice as seen elsewhere in his commentaries: his notes on the *In Pisonem* and the *In toga candida* have a preface of one and a half OCT pages each, the *Pro Scauro* of about three, the *Pro Cornelio* of five and a half. As R. G. Lewis speculated, perhaps it is because Asconius considered the *Pro Milone* such a fine speech that he lavished so much attention on its preface.[70] Nevertheless, his preface does not differ substantially in content from what Quintilian prescribes or from what the scholia Bobiensia practice. If it is longer and more detailed, then the teacher will have had the liberty of choosing what points to expound at length and what to treat in short compass.[71]

Our three sources thus present a clear picture of what it means to "explain the case" (*inst.* 2.5.7; see p. 22 above) to the class before the students turn their attention to the business of actual reading. The students would be given basic information: the date of the speech, the players and their history, salient *circumstantiae*, a recap of the *narratio*, the form of argument, and so forth, all mixed in with some interpretative remarks and preliminary rhetorical analysis. Cicero and his speech are not treated as Gospel truth: he is seen to be a liar and a cheat, but these vices are turned into virtues, since they show how he is able to play his cards to the greatest effect even when dealt a bad hand (cf. *inst.* 6.5.10). Of course, he did not actually win the game in this instance, and that fact creates some embarrassment for the Cicero-loving *rhetores*, but the failure finds an excuse in the extremely adverse circumstances under which he had to deliver his defense. More importantly, the revised version of the speech is seen as all the better: what actually happened in the courtroom is less important than the rhetoric of a well-constructed speech; rhetoric is, from first to last, the central concern. I have teased out the implications of these

---

[69] Cf. the Bobiensia's defense, p. 36 above.   [70] Lewis (2006) 232.

[71] Note that Asconius' work here cannot be classified as "history," since much of it is just too basic. It is targeted at the level of the schoolroom. The citations of Fenestella and the *acta* may strike us as unusual today, but they have clear comparanda both in the scholia Bobiensia and indeed in authors like Servius. We might draw the parallel of the modern teacher who justifies his or her authority on English usage with reference to the *Oxford English Dictionary*. Alternatively Asconius may have been writing *magistrorum in usum*. (The Bobiensia will also – independently of Asconius – cite Cicero's letters [122.24–25 St. on *Mil.* 37], the *Pro Tullio* [114.15–18 St.], and the *Philippics* [123.4–7 St. on *Mil.* 40], and Quintilian constantly instructs his pupils to compare speeches; cf. e.g. p. 44 below.)

prefatory remarks in some detail because the material is copious, and yet we should not forget that they are only a preface. The teacher would have spent vastly more time on the speech itself, and it is to commentary on the actual speech that we now turn our attention.

Exordium

I have one chance, dear reader, to try to get your attention and capture your good will: my *prooemium*. The first words you hear from me are perhaps the most important that I will utter in the course of my speech: will you listen carefully or twiddle your thumbs? Will you be looking to refute my every statement, or will you find me likable and persuasive? The orator's first task – conciliating his audience – is of such signal importance that if he should fail in it, no matter how well-reasoned or coruscating with rhetorical brilliance the argument that follows, his whole speech will be in vain: he will have lost the case before it has even gotten underway. This was no secret to the Romans, and their injunctions regarding the *prooemium* were clear.[72] It is thus hardly surprising that Quintilian should devote special attention to this portion of the speech in his teaching; well begun is half-done. While we have lost the scholia Bobiensia here, Quintilian will allow us to form a clear picture of how to teach the all-important opening of the speech.

Quintilian notes that there are as many forms to the *prooemium* as there are speeches, but that their aim remains constant: to render the listeners *beneuoli attenti dociles* (*inst.* 4.1.5). One might begin a speech by discussing the people or the issues involved in the case; on the other hand, one might discuss external circumstances related to the case but not themselves part of it. This, he says, is what Cicero does in the *Pro Milone*: he focuses on the fact that the court is surrounded by Pompey's armed guard (*inst.* 4.1.31). This salient circumstance cannot go unmentioned, and indeed Cicero must allay the judges' fears, striving to persuade them not to think that Pompey's soldiers represented a threat to them (*metus etiam nonnumquam est amouendus, ut Cicero pro Milone ne arma Pompei disposita contra se putarent laborauit, inst.* 4.1.20). Quintilian thus shows himself keenly aware of the particular circumstances that have shaped Cicero's entire proem, circumstances which will recur in the *peroratio* (see p. 71 below). Fear is a central concern of the *Pro Milone*.

Just as he is not blind to the *circumstantiae* of the proem, Quintilian also shows himself not deaf to its subtle rhythms and rhetoric. He notes that

---

[72] See Lausberg (1998) §§266–279.

a verse opening is cacophonous at the beginning of a sentence, but that a verse closing, especially that of a senarius, is in fact elegant: *ĕtsī uĕrĕōr, iūdĭcēs*, the opening of the *Pro Milone*, is a perfect example (*inst.* 9.4.74). His points can be very subtle indeed: clausulae, he claims (*inst.* 9.4.93), are *firmissimae* when they end with a long syllable, and a *breuis in longo* may not provide quite the same fullness; he compares *dicere incipientem timerĕ* (*Mil.* 1) with *ausus est confiterī* (*Lig.* 1). But different rhythms conduce to different ends, and so they too must be chosen according to the case at hand (*inst.* 9.4.133):

> nam iudicis animus uarie praeparatur: tum miserabiles esse uolumus, tum modesti, tum acres, tum graues, tum blandi, tum flectere, tum ad diligentiam hortari. haec ut sunt diuersa natura, ita dissimilem componendi quoque rationem desiderant. an similibus Cicero usus est numeris in exordio pro Milone, pro Cluentio, pro Ligario?

> For the judge's mind has to be prepared in various ways: sometimes we want to be pitiable, other times modest, or cutting, or authoritative, or flattering; sometimes we want to bend (the judges), other times to encourage them to pay attention. Just as these are different in nature, so they require different methods of composition. Did Cicero use a similar rhythm in the *exordium* of the *Pro Milone*, the *Pro Cluentio*, and the *Pro Ligario*?

We see here that a speech would not be read in complete isolation. The students might compare the *exordia* of three speeches to see how Cicero has employed different prose rhythm to different effects. Different cases call for different treatments, and rhetoric – even prose rhythm – must always be adapted to the demands of particular circumstances.

Finally Quintilian can combine all these nuances into a single continuous exposition of delivery. He stands before the class and gazes out, delivering the proem of the speech himself, now casting his eyes downward in mock fear, now staring forth proudly and boldly; a confidential whisper here, a confident roar there, all while his pupils watch with rapt attention (*inst.* 11.3.47–51):

> proponamus enim nobis illud Ciceronis in oratione nobilissima pro Milone principium: nonne ad singulas paene distinctiones quamuis in eadem facie tamen quasi uultus mutandus est? "etsi uereor, iudices, ne turpe sit pro fortissimo uiro dicere incipientem timere": etiam si est toto proposito contractum atque summissum, quia et exordium est et solliciti exordium, tamen fuerit necesse est aliquid plenius et erectius dum dicit "pro fortissimo uiro" quam cum "etsi uereor" et "turpe sit" et "timere." iam secunda respiratio increscat oportet et naturali quodam conatu, quo minus pauide dicimus quae secuntur, et quod magnitudo animi Milonis ostenditur:

"minimeque deceat, cum Titus Annius ipse magis de rei publicae salute quam de sua perturbetur." deinde quasi obiurgatio sui est: "me ad eius causam parem animi magnitudinem adferre non posse." tum inuidiosiora: "tamen haec noui iudicii noua forma terret oculos." illa uero iam paene apertis, ut aiunt, tibiis: "qui, quocumque inciderunt, consuetudinem fori et pristinum morem iudiciorum requirunt." nam sequens latum etiam atque fusum est: "non enim corona consessus uester cinctus est, ut solebat." quod notaui ut appareret non solum in membris causae sed etiam in articulis esse aliquam pronuntiandi uarietatem, sine qua nihil neque maius neque minus est.

Let us take as an example the beginning of Cicero's splendid *Pro Milone*. Is it not clear that, at almost every stop, the face (as it were) stays the same, but its expression has to change? "Although I fear, members of the jury, that it is discreditable, when beginning to speak on behalf of a very brave man, to feel afraid." Although the general tone of the passage is restrained and subdued (it is after all a *prooemium*, and the *prooemium* of a speaker conscious of his difficulties), nevertheless there must have been a fuller and prouder tone when he says *pro fortissimo uiro* than when he says *turpe sit* or *timere*. The second breath has now to be stronger, both because of the natural effort which makes us speak the following words less timidly, and because Milo's courage is now to be shown: "and that it is very unbecoming, when Titus Annius is more troubled for the state's security than for his own . . ." Then comes a sort of self-reproach: "that I should be unable to offer courage equal to his to serve his cause." And then something more hard-hitting: "Nevertheless, the unprecedented appearance of this unprecedented court strikes terror into my eyes." And now he opens practically every stop of his instrument: ". . . my eyes, which, wherever they fall, look in vain for the ordinary ways of the forum and the ancient procedures of our courts." What follows is positively ample and diffuse: "Your sitting is not, as it used to be, surrounded by a ring of spectators . . ." I note all this in order to make it clear that some variety of delivery is found not only in the longer units of the speech but also in the smaller ones, because without this nothing would seem either more or less important than anything else. (trans. D. A. Russell, Loeb)

What a spectacle this must have been! The emphasis on the smallest details of delivery is remarkable; Quintilian dilates on details as small as when to take a breath. He is well aware that *actio* is a vitally important part of a successful speech, and he is concerned to model it for his students with reference to the supreme exemplar of oratorical excellence. Throughout he shows sensitive insight into the particulars of the case, like the balance Cicero must strike between acknowledging his own fear and praising Milo's courage. He explains how the form of delivery must match its content in order to lead the jurors where the orator wants to take them.

In the course of this performative exposition the speech would have come alive before the class's very eyes and ears.

After such theatrics Quintilian's comments on specific rhetorical features must have savored more of the schoolroom's wax tablets than the dust of the forum, but he also would have pointed out that *equidem ceteras tempestates et procellas in illis dumtaxat fluctibus contionum semper Miloni putaui esse subeundas* ("I for my part always thought that Milo would have to endure the other storms and squalls amid the waves of the *contiones* alone," *Mil.* 5) is an example of a mixed allegory. (It would have been a true allegory, he says, had Cicero not added the *dumtaxat contionum*.) "In this type," he dutifully informs the class, "we get both splendor from the imported words, and intelligibility from those used literally" (*inst.* 8.6.48). Similarly it must not escape the students' attention that the expression *non modo ad salutem eius exstinguendam, sed etiam gloriam per tales uiros infringendam* (*Mil.* 50)[73] is an example of homoeoteleuton (*inst.* 9.3.77). Just as such observations are scattered throughout the *Institutio* on all parts of the *Pro Milone*, there can be no doubt that Quintilian peppered his discussion of the proem with elaboration of Cicero's various rhetorical excellences.

Dispelling *praeiudicia*

The proem treated, the teacher now faced a certain difficulty: Cicero "should" have proceeded directly to the *narratio*, but he does not.[74] It is difficult enough to inculcate the basic rules, one imagines the poor *rhetor* thinking, and already we are faced with exceptions! The way out, of course, is to say that speeches must always be adapted to the case at hand: this rule supersedes all others, as Cicero himself acknowledges in his own rhetorical works.[75] Thus, Quintilian says, while as a general rule the *narratio* ought to follow the *prooemium*,

> hoc quoque interim mutat condicio causarum, nisi forte M. Tullius in oratione pulcherrima quam pro Milone scriptam reliquit male distulisse

---

[73] Cicero's text actually runs: *ad eius non modo salutem exstinguendam* etc. Clark (1895) xlv–xlvi documents Quintilian's vagaries in quotation; if he was in fact often quoting from memory, he must have known the speech remarkably well.

[74] On the *narratio* as normally following the *exordium*, see Lausberg (1998) §289.

[75] Cf. too *inst.* 4.3.17, where Quintilian discusses how Cicero was forced by unfavorable circumstances (presumably the soldiers surrounding the court) to digress already in the *prooemium* of the speech that he actually delivered in defense of Milo. For Cicero's remarks on adaptability, see e.g. *inu.* 1.13 *non enim causa ad constitutionem, sed constitutio ad causam accommodatur; orat.* 123 *is erit ergo eloquens, qui ad id quodcumque decebit poterit accommodare orationem; de orat.* 2.146 and *passim*.

narrationem uidetur tribus praepositis quaestionibus, aut profuisset expo-
nere quo modo insidias Miloni fecisset Clodius si reum qui a se hominem
occisum fateretur defendi omnino fas non fuisset, aut si iam praeiudicio
senatus damnatus esset Milo, aut si Cn. Pompeius, qui praeter aliam gratiam
iudicium etiam militibus armatis cluserat, tamquam aduersus ei timeretur.
ergo hae quoque quaestiones uim prohoemii optinebant, cum omnes iudicem praepararent. (inst. 4.2.25–26)

this too is sometimes changed by the circumstances of the case at hand,
unless perhaps you think that Cicero, in the written version of his super-
lative *Pro Milone*, was wrong to put off the *narratio* by placing three
preliminary questions before it, or that it would have been useful to explain
how Clodius had set an ambush for Milo (a) if it had been altogether wrong
to defend a man who confessed that he had killed someone, or (b) if Milo
had already been condemned in advance by the Senate's judgment, or (c) if
Pompey, who beyond exerting influence in other ways had even encircled
the court with armed soldiers, was to be feared as Milo's enemy. Therefore
these preliminary questions also had the force of an *exordium*, since they all
served to prepare the judge.

The "circumstances of the case" have dictated that Cicero follow another
arrangement. Quintilian then explains exactly why the standard order
would have been wrong, demonstrating that three objections needed to
be cleared away before Cicero could begin the *narratio* proper.[76] Finally,
he notes that these *quaestiones* function somewhat like a *prooemium* in
that they prepare the judge to listen to what is to come, and thus Cicero's
whole excursus can indeed be recast as an extension of the proem itself.
This might be thought to appeal to the rule-bound mind of the schoolboy: it only *looks* as if Cicero is deviating from the prescription, the
teacher intimates. Thus, Quintilian says, while the essential conflict of
the case must be made crystal clear to the judge, it might not be the first
thing that the orator will say (*inst.* 3.6.12). Cicero's clever *dispositio* is in
fact considered one of the most admirable things about this speech (*inst.*
6.5.10).

Now we move on to the details of the *quaestiones* themselves. In the first
instance, of course, we find recurring mention of various rhetorical figures
(see p. 66 below). Quintilian will also illustrate different ways of introducing historical exempla: if a story is not well known, as that of the abused
military tribune in Marius' army, it must be narrated in full (*Mil.* 9, *inst.*
5.11.15), whereas if the audience is familiar with the story, an oblique

---

[76] Quintilian makes effectively the same observation in brief at *inst.* 5.2.1 in mentioning the Senate's
praeiudicia against Milo.

allusion may suffice, as in the case of Servius Ahala and the like (*Mil.* 9, *inst.* 5.11.16).

Here we can compare the scholia Bobiensia, which explain not only the purport of these exempla but also what they refer to and their rhetorical arrangement and effect. First, the scholia say, Cicero tries to refute the notion that anyone who confesses to a killing must be condemned; instead he argues that we must look to the reasons behind the act (*hoc primum adgressus refutare, in omnibus caedibus non confessiones esse damnandas, sed causas potissimum requirendas*, 113.10–11 St.).[77] To this end he offers the support of various historical and mythological exempla such as Horatius, whose story the scholia retell at length: the duel with the Curiatii, the killing of his sister, condemnation at trial, *prouocatio ad populum*, passing under the yoke or "Sister's beam" (113.11–22 St.). Introducing standard historical precedents to the students was a vital function of the *rhetor*; this process of cultural indoctrination took place in large part in his school, and students would in turn make use of such examples themselves both in declamation and later in the courts.[78]

The scholia, however, do not restrict themselves to a bare explanation of allusions. With the basics covered, they turn more importantly to the rhetorical effect of such exempla. Consider the case of Orestes (*eum qui patris ulciscendi causa matrem necauisset, Mil.* 8):[79]

> μυθῶδες hoc exemplum uideri poterat, de Oreste scilicet, a quo adultera mater occisa est: noluit id in primo constituere nec in postremo, sed in medio, ut utrimque firmitatem de exemplis uerioribus mutuetur: cui tamen et ipsi, quamuis aliquantum leui et fabuloso, consideremus quanto ingenio firmitatem pariat orator, ita inferens: "atque hoc, iudices, non sine causa etiam fictis fabulis." leuitatem habent summam fictiones fabularum, sed quid adiecit? "doctissimi homines memoriae prodiderunt": ut scriptorum peritia det exemplo quamuis minus idoneo firmitatem. (114.4–10 St.)

> This exemplum could seem to belong to the realm of fable; Cicero is of course referring to Orestes, who killed his adulterous mother. He didn't want to place this example first or last, but rather in the middle, so that it might borrow from the strength of the more factual examples that surround it. Nevertheless, let us observe how skillfully the orator has strengthened

---

[77] Cf. too the concluding comments (114.1–2 St.): *necessario igitur hanc enumerationem facit, qua plenius doceat nonnumquam caedes iure optimo fieri posse.*

[78] On the use of historical exempla in oratory, see e.g. *Rhet. Her.* 4.62, Cic. *inu.* 1.49, Bonner (1977) 283, Bloomer (1992) 4, 12 n. 1, and index s.v. *exempla*, and most comprehensively Alewell (1913).

[79] Cf. too Quintilian briefly on this same example at *inst.* 5.11.18.

even this example, even if it is of lesser substance and fantastic, by adding: "and this, judges, not without cause even in fictitious fables" – the fictions of fable do indeed altogether lack gravity, but what did he add? – "have the most learned men handed down to posterity." The expertise of the writers lends strength to even a less suitable exemplum.

The scholia make a number of astute observations here. First, they call attention to the proper location for a weak (in this case mythological) example: in between the strong ones so that it can draw on their strength. Furthermore, although fiction is perhaps a less reliable source of parallels, Cicero strengthens his case by describing it as fiction written by *doctissimi homines*, which implicitly adds to its reliability. Such comments are absolutely typical of the scholia Bobiensia: they first establish the basic interpretation of the text, and then they build on that foundation to show the inner workings of Cicero's rhetoric. The focus above all is on understanding what tactics Cicero uses to persuade the judges.

Another example from earlier in the speech will again shine a bright spotlight on this emphasis. In introducing his *quaestiones* Cicero says: *uidentur ea mihi esse refutanda quae et in senatu ab inimicis saepe iactata sunt* (*Mil.* 7). The scholia observe (112.20–113.7 St.):

> "ab inimicis" dixit: iam detraxit illi decreto auctoritatem cui potest propter simultates inesse studium maleuolentiae. et quod addidit statim "iactata sunt," non "decreta," non "statuta," non "iudicata": uerbo usus est efficaciter ad detrahendum pondus illi senatusconsulto quo reus grauabatur. post haec etiam significaturus legem Pompeiam "et in contione ab improbis" inquit. molestum namque fuisset, si "a populo" adiceret: "ab improbis" maluit, ut ne illud plebiscitum pro grauissimo ducendum sit quod inprobi et studentes iniuriae conceperunt. ad extremum tertio gradu in hunc exitum desinit: "et paulo ante ab accusatoribus." omne enim quod accusatores comminiscuntur non aequitatis iudicio, sed nocendi proposito moliuntur. haec itaque uiuacitas M. Tullio propria est, ut, antequam argumentationes impleat, uictoriam praelibet in ipsis propositionibus.

> He said "by his enemies" (*ab inimicis*): he has already undermined the authority of that decree in which there may be a desire for doing harm on account of animosity. And because he straightaway added "tossed about" (*iactata sunt*), not "decreed" (*decreta*), not "decided" (*statuta*), not "adjudged" (*iudicata*): he has used the word effectively to lessen the weight of the *senatusconsultum* under which the defendant was laboring. Also, moreover, in order to refer to the Pompeian law he says "and in a *contio* by the wicked" (*ab improbis*). For it would not have gone over well if he had added "by the people" (*a populo*); he preferred "by the wicked" (*ab improbis*), so that the decree of the people would not be considered of the greatest

weight because wicked people and those eager to do harm had thought it up. At the end in the third part of the tricolon he finishes thus: "and a short time ago by his accusers" (*et paulo ante ab accusatoribus*). For everything that his accusers contrive they endeavor not by a judgment of what is right but with the intention to do harm. Thus this liveliness is one of Cicero's traits, so that before he fills up the argumentative part of the speech, he already has a foretaste of victory in the very sketching out of his argument.

These are sensitive observations. The scholia are not simply glossing the meanings of words; they are instead focusing on their connotations. The Senate had passed a decree judging Clodius' killing to be *contra rem publicam* (*Mil.* 12), but Cicero adroitly weakens the authority of this proclamation by implying that it was no calm and reasoned judgment of the *patres conscripti* – nay, rather it was the ill will of Milo's enemies given the force of law (illegitimately, we are to understand). He subtly builds his case still further with *iactata sunt* rather than a more neutral or positive *decreta* or *statuta* or *iudicata*. Again, he will refuse to allow the *populus* any role in the anti-Milonian *contiones*; no, these *contiones* were the work of *improbi* who were desirous of injuring Milo. Finally, he finishes his tricolon with the *accusatores*, who are thus implicitly associated with those vile *inimici* and *improbi*: their every effort is given over not to justice and fairness but rather to harming Milo. The scholia observe that this liveliness is a Ciceronian characteristic, and that before he even makes any arguments he already seems to have a foretaste of victory in the way he presents his case – that is to say, his presentation of the *propositiones* clears the way for the judges to be persuaded by his arguments. This is another way of expressing what Quintilian said, namely that the placement of the *quaestiones* here acts as a kind of further *prooemium*.

In section 9 of the speech Cicero invokes the authority of the XII Tables to justify the notion that sometimes it may be right and proper to kill a man. The scholia observe that he does this βιαίως (114.13 St.), i.e. that it is somewhat forced, and that in the *Pro Tullio* he uses the XII Tables in the exact opposite way, to show how they hardly ever allowed homicide. But, as the scholia observe, there of course the circumstances of the case at hand demanded a different treatment (*aliud praesentis negotii condicio poscebat*, 114.16–17 St.). So again the necessity of the case is seen to be sovereign, and it is up to the skill and craft of the orator to shoehorn the argument to fit the evidence – or vice versa.

Quintilian too comments at length on the argumentation introduced by the passage about the XII Tables. He describes the technicalities of correct logic and reasoning in considerable detail. You might, he says, provide a major premise then a conclusion (*inst.* 5.14.17, *Mil.* 11), for example: "Laws are silent in the midst of arms, and they do not require that we wait for their approval, since a man who decides to wait will have to pay an unjust penalty before justice is served." You might on the other hand just state the bald proposition: *silent leges inter arma.* Or you might finally begin with a reason and then complete the argument, as in the XII Tables example, where indeed Cicero has put the reason both first and last (*inst.* 5.14.18, *Mil.* 9): "But if the XII Tables say that at night a thief can be killed for any reason, and by day if he defends himself with a weapon, who is there who would think that a killer should be punished in any circumstances, when he sees that sometimes a sword is extended to us by the laws themselves?" This same example, when slightly rephrased, fulfills the criteria for a proper syllogism: major premise, "What death can be unjust for an ambusher and a robber?"; minor premise, "Why is it that we have escorts, why is it that we have swords?"; conclusion, "If we were under no circumstances allowed to use them, surely we would not be allowed to have them" (*inst.* 5.14.19, *Mil.* 10). He then goes on to show with considerable care how you refute this same argument by attacking each of its constituent parts (*inst.* 5.14.20–23), both on technical grounds and with reference to the specific situation under discussion in the speech. He concludes, however, by noting that this bland diet of sophistic casuistry is best seasoned occasionally with spicier fare (*inst.* 5.14.35):

> quoque quid est natura magis asperum, hoc pluribus condiendum est uoluptatibus, et minus suspecta argumentatio dissimulatione, et multum ad fidem adiuuat audientis uoluptas: nisi forte existimamus Ciceronem haec ipsa male <in> argumentatione dixisse, "silere leges inter arma," et "gladium nobis interim ab ipsis porrigi legibus," is tamen habendus est modus ut sint ornamento, non impedimento.

> The more bitter a thing is by nature, the more it needs to be sweetened by pleasant bits. Furthermore, argumentation is less suspect when it is well disguised, and the audience's pleasure contributes quite a lot to making them believe the speaker. Unless perhaps we think that it was wrong for Cicero to say in the middle of one of his arguments, "laws are silent in the midst of arms" and "sometimes a sword is extended to us by the laws themselves." Nevertheless these things must be kept in moderation, so that they're an ornament and not an obstacle.

The focus is, as ever, on the effectiveness of the argumentation. What makes an argument effective is not just the airtight logic that Quintilian has unfolded in such detail; instead, the logic should lie concealed, and the audience should enjoy what they are listening to – *this* is what will persuade them.[80]

The Bobiensia, meanwhile, are not idle, but I will not discuss their every remark. A few samples will reveal their methods and aims, which are the same as Quintilian's: they are concerned above all to expound Cicero's rhetorical strategy. They explain, for example, as does Asconius, who the *ambustus tribunus plebis* (*Mil.* 12) is and why he is so called. The tribune is Titus Munatius Plancus, and he is called "singed" either because Cicero wants to make it seem that the Curia was burnt down at his instigation (a rhetorical interpretation) or because he was unable to continue his harangue in the *contio* on account of the fire (a historical alternative, and the only one considered by Asconius). Cicero mentions him in the first place, the scholia say, in order to emphasize how much the Senate in fact favored Milo, and how it was really only a few of his enemies who managed to stir up such a fuss against him (115.1–7 St.). In regard to the choice epithet *ambustus*,[81] Asconius is so far moved as to make one of his few remarks on Cicero's rhetoric: *fuit autem paratus ad dicendum* (Ascon. 42C), which I take to mean something like "Cicero was moreover always ready with a quip."[82]

Both the scholia and Asconius explain the other historical allusions among the *quaestiones*, Asconius content with a bare statement of the facts, the scholia usually offering further comments on their rhetorical force. When Cicero alludes to Clodius' involvement in the Bona Dea affair, for example, the scholia do indeed explain what supposedly happened in an introductory clause (*cum intra caerimonias Bonae Deae incestum cum pontificis uxore fecisset*, 115.23–24 St.), and so the teacher would have likewise explained this to his classroom, but that is just one brief part of a lengthy paragraph. They go on to analyze just why Cicero mentions the Bona Dea affair in the first place: it shows that the Senate had no desire to avenge Clodius' death, and it moreover heaps *inuidia* on Clodius, thus making the judges less likely to be sympathetic toward him. And so, the scholia conclude, in this part of the speech Cicero both confirms the authority of the traditional law – i.e., there is no need for a special new

---

[80] In this same vein he notes that the clinching clause of an argument can take the form of a pithy and pungent *sententia*, as in *Mil.* 9 *facere enim probus adulescens periculose quam perpeti turpiter maluit* (*inst.* 8.5.11).

[81] Perhaps unexpected as a description of a person, but cf. *TLL* 1.1877.26–1878.39 (Vollmer).

[82] Cf. Plutarch's comments about about Cicero's glib facility with (inappropriate!) jokes (*Cic.* 25–27). For the infamous remark about Octavian, who was *laudandus, ornandus, tollendus* (Cic. *fam.* 11.20.1), see p. 106 below.

procedure; the old standby would have been more than adequate – and shows that his opponent is still deserving of opprobrium for his lewd violation of religious ceremonies (*in hac parte Tullius et confirmat iuris ueteris auctoritatem et adhuc odio dignam facit <personam> eius qui de incesto fuerit infamis*, 115.25–27 St.).

Other comments large and small continue the laser-like focus on the rhetoric of the speech. A brief note on the emphatic pronunciation of *ego ipse* (116.25–27 St. ad *Mil.* 14) gives way to an analysis of Cicero's refutation of the second *praeiudicium* of the judges, viz. that Milo had already been condemned by Pompey's law (117.21–26 St.). First the scholia explain what Cicero is doing: he is dashing to pieces another possible prejudice, and he is doing it by turning the accusers' argument against them, repurposing for his own use the very motion of the Pompeian inquiry (*ad utilitatem suam reuocaturus ipsam rogationis Pompeianae lationem*, 117.21–22 St.). The prosecution claims that Milo is condemned in advance by this decree. But the killing was admitted by all, and so Pompey would never have introduced a special inquiry into the deed unless he realized that there was some equitable reason to hear Milo's side of the story (*Tullius in respondendo satis uiuaciter argumentatur, cum caedes in confesso teneretur, numquam laturum fuisse Cn. Pompeium consulem huiusmodi rogationem, ut de eodem facinore quaereretur, nisi animaduerteret aequitatem subesse*, 117.23–25 St.). All this, goes the scholiast's interpretation, ought to carry some weight for the defendant in the judges' eyes. So far from making Milo's condemnation a foregone conclusion, Pompey's law actually demonstrates that the case needs careful consideration. The prosecutors are thus seen vividly (*uiuaciter*) hoisted by their own petard.

Here is one final rhetorical comment on the *praeiudicia*. In section 17 of the speech Cicero mentions the Via Appia and Appius Claudius Caecus. The scholia insightfully explain why (118.20–24 St.):

> quoniam et augere poterat inuidiam Milonis et commendabilem facere memoriam P. Clodi Appiae uiae mentio in qua maiorum eius titulus eminebat, omnem hanc materiam cuiusdam taciti fauoris deflorauit orator, quasi ea non monumentum familiae suae P. Clodius habuerit, sed quoddam scelerum deuorsorium: in qua occidisse Marcum etiam Papirium uidebatur, equitem R.

> Because the mention of the Via Appia could both increase dislike of Milo and make the memory of Publius Clodius seem worthy of praise, bearing as it did the title of his ancestors, the orator has stripped bare this whole forest of material that could give rise to a certain tacit feeling of support for Clodius. He has made it seem that Publius Clodius did not consider it

a monument of his family, but some den of wickedness, in which he is alleged also to have killed Marcus Papirius, a Roman *eques*.

Cicero is seen to realize just how useful it had been for opposing counsel to expatiate on the virtues and public works of Clodius' storied antecedents, which could both hurt Milo and help Clodius,[83] and so he cleverly "strips bare this whole forest of material"[84] and renders it utterly useless to the prosecution: the road is no longer a monument of his family's glorious past but rather a site of wickedness where Clodius has apparently even murdered a Roman *eques* before. Perhaps Cicero's learned adversaries would have regretted bringing it up in the first place.

Before turning to the *narratio* we might also take note of Asconius' lengthy disquisition on *diuisio* of a senatorial proposal. Cicero insists that the Senate's intention was never to have this "new form of inquiry" (*noua quaestio*), but that they instead wanted a trial of Milo in line with existing laws (*Mil.* 14). A proposal was put forward to declare the killing on the Appian Way and the burning of the Senate House *contra rem publicam*, and at the same time to try the case in accordance with current laws. A rogue senator, however, called for a division of the proposal, and while the various acts were indeed declared *contra rem publicam*, the second part of the bill was voted down. Pompey was thus able to introduce his legislation creating a new type of trial. Asconius is concerned to explain the details of *diuisio* (Ascon. 43–44C):

> quid sit diuidere sententiam ut enarrandum sit uestra aetas, filii, facit. cum aliquis in dicenda sententia duas pluresue res complectitur, si non omnes eae probantur, postulatur ut diuidatur, id est de rebus singulis referatur. forsitan nunc hoc quoque uelitis scire qui fuerit qui id postulauerit. quod non fere adicitur: non enim ei qui hoc postulat oratione longa utendum ac ne consurgendum quidem utique est; multi enim sedentes hoc unum uerbum pronuntiant "diuide": quod cum auditum est, liberum <est> ei qui facit relationem diuidere.

> Your youth, my sons, means that I must explain what it means to divide a proposition. When someone in moving a proposition includes two or more issues, if they are not all approved of, there is a call for a division, that is, to consider each issue individually. Perhaps you'd now also like to know who it was who called for the division in this case, but this generally has not been added to the accounts. For the man who calls for a division does not

---

[83] Quintilian makes the same observation: *inst.* 5.10.41 *et Miloni inter cetera obiectum est quod Clodius in monumento ab eo maiorum suorum esset occisus.*

[84] *Defloro* is choice indeed, and it actually appears to be a favorite word of the scholiast. It may have implications for the dating of the commentary in its present form, since the word is not found before Symmachus. See *TLL* v.1.361.79–362.35 (Gudeman), esp. 362.24–29.

have to make a long speech and doesn't even have to stand up; many people while seated just say this one word, "divide," and when that word is heard, the man who introduced the motion is free to make a division.

Here we see Asconius address his fictive audience, his young sons, directly. They are envisioned as being utterly ignorant of basic senatorial procedure, but it is implied that they should be very interested, presumably since they are fitting themselves for a public career.[85] Asconius' discussion functions then, on the one hand, to explicate Cicero's speech, but it also plays the far more important role of preparing the young listeners for their future profession. The study of Ciceronian speeches in the classroom has thus become almost a *tirocinium fori*. Asconius goes on to explain how he has checked the senatorial *acta* and managed to determine who the rogue senator was ("Fufius") and adds some further details of the vote.[86]

Nor are the Bobiensia silent here. They too explain the procedure of *diuisio*, and they too provide further details of the vote, which in fact contradict Asconius' interpretation. First, on *diuisio* itself, they say (117.7–13 St.):

> hoc [i.e. *diuisio*] autem solebat accidere cum uidebatur aliquis per saturam de multis rebus unam sententiam dixisse; et habebat nonnumquam conexio huiusmodi rerum multarum fraudulentas captiones, ut rebus aequis res improbae miscerentur atque ita blandimentis quibusdam obreperent ad optinenda ea quae, si per se singulariter proponerentur, displicere deberent. desiderabatur itaque ut fieret sententiae diuisio, hoc est ut de singulis, non de pluribus una sententia diceretur.

> This (division), moreover, usually happened when someone seemed to have stuffed several things into one proposition; and sometimes this sort of yoking of many disparate things contained fraudulent deceptions, so that unjust things might be mixed in with the just, and so by means of a few pleasing things the proposers of the motion might manage to obtain things which, if they were proposed individually, would not meet with approval. There was a desire therefore that the proposition be divided, so that one proposition would be moved for each item, not for several.

Again the scholia spell out what exactly the procedure of *diuisio* is, but they go beyond Asconius' reporting of procedure to explain precisely why one might try to bundle multiple pieces of legislation together into one shiny

---

[85] Note that the basic nature of this note militates against Asconius pitching his commentary to a more "scholarly" audience. Cf. p. 17 above.

[86] See Marshall (1985) ad loc. for the uncertain evidence that leads to the identification of Q. Fufius Calenus, and cf. schol. Bob. 117.6–7 St., which mention Fufius Calenus as a possibility but are not sure. The details of the vote itself are actually contested: see Marshall (1985) ad loc. with references.

package: so that your *res improbae* might escape detection by being mixed in with *res aequae*. This is no moral judgment but rather a useful bit of *Realpolitik* for aspiring senators.

The scholia actually interpret the specific *diuisio* in question differently than Asconius. They do not here discuss any acts declared *contra rem publicam*; rather they claim that the two parts of the bill were that the trial should be conducted according to the traditional laws and that it should be given precedence on the docket (*ut et ueteribus legibus et extra ordinem quaereretur*, 117.15 St.). There is no possible way that the scholia could have misunderstood Asconius' lengthy and lucid note, and so this difference of opinion is a very strong piece of evidence that the scholia Bobiensia are not to be thought of as dependent on Asconius even in historical matters.[87]

Narratio

The obstacles cleared from his path, Cicero can now turn to the *narratio* proper, and here Quintilian will be seen in particularly fine fettle. The scholia observe that Cicero's transition from the *quaestiones* to the *narratio* is deftly handled, since he sums up as briefly as possible his various refutations in the *quaestiones* while preparing a transition to the *narratio*, a narrative which in this speech will be best placed here (119.22–24 St.). Moreover, Cicero has been very diligent in preparing his narrative; in a lacunose note we are informed (119.27–120.3 St.):

> uigilantissime praeparationibus instructa narratio est: cuius quidem secundum morem sibi familiarissimum a persona sumit exordium, quae disciplina habilior ad docilitatem, id est < …,> uidetur. consideremus itaque ad coniecturam duplicem sic praemunitam < …,> ut et personam P. Clodi ad locandas inimico insidias idoneam faciat et causas faciendi ualidissime instruat et alia semina futurarum quaestionum ad defensionem Milonis pertinentium ἐκ τοῦ <προσώπου … > praemuniat sollertissime, utque, ita moratus, nec ullo emolumento prouocatus existimetur illud facinus cogitasse. haec explorato per totum cursum narrationis istius, et multo altius adiecta cogitatione inuenies ita narrari, ut …

The *narratio* has been most diligently provided for in advance by Cicero's preparations. According to his very frequent practice he has begun his *exordium a persona*, which seems to be an approach better suited to teaching, i.e., < … >. Let us therefore examine carefully his double conjectural case thus prepared < … > so that he attributes to Publius Clodius a character

---

[87] Cf. also nn. 55 and 86 above; these examples can be multiplied.

likely to set up an ambush for an enemy and very diligently gives him good reason to do so and most cleverly plants in advance the seeds of his future *quaestiones* which pertain to the defence of Milo from his <character ... >, and so that, thus having delayed, and not led by any thought of profit he might be deemed to have thought up this crime. You'll find these things proved throughout the whole course of the *narratio* and thus told much more deeply with added thought so that ...

Cicero's *exordium* had begun from the respective characters of Clodius and Milo (*a persona*). This approach is noted to be quite apt for "teaching," or for the *narratio*,[88] into which the speech seamlessly flows. The scholia observe that Cicero tries to show that Clodius was the sort of person who would prepare an ambush for his enemy and that he had grounds to do so; at the same time he sows the seeds of *quaestiones* to come. Throughout the *narratio* Cicero will deliberately and ingeniously expand on these themes. The scholia are here concerned to explain the continuity of argumentation throughout the entirety of the speech, showing how hints and themes planted well in advance will eventually grow into centerpieces of the defense strategy. This is, as usual, a sensitive attempt to understand the rhetoric underlying the persuasive power of the speech as a whole.

Quintilian too is quite keen on Cicero's *praeparationes*, and in discussing the *narratio* he outdoes himself in his sensitive understanding of Cicero's rhetoric. He observes that grandeur (*magnificentia*) is often counted as a virtue of narratives, but sometimes it is out of place, as in this case (*inst.* 4.2.61). Here is how he interprets the *narratio* instead (*inst.* 4.2.57–59):

> optimae uero praeparationes erunt quae latuerint. ut a Cicerone sunt quidem utilissime praedicta omnia per quae Miloni Clodius, non Clodio Milo insidiatus esse uideatur, plurimum tamen facit illa callidissima simplicitatis imitatio: "Milo autem, cum in senatu fuisset eo die quoad senatus est dimissus, domum uenit, calceos et uestimenta mutauit, paulisper, dum se uxor, ut fit, comparat, commoratus est." quam nihil festinato, nihil praeparato fecisse uidetur Milo! quod non solum rebus ipsis uir eloquentissimus, quibus moras et lentum profectionis ordinem ducit, sed uerbis etiam uulgaribus et cotidianis et arte occulta consecutus est: quae si aliter dicta essent, strepitu ipso iudicem ad custodiendum patronum excitassent. frigida uidentur ista plerisque, sed hoc ipso manifestum est quo modo iudicem fefellerit, quod uix a lectore deprenditur.

The best preparatory remarks will be those which escape notice. Thus Cicero most profitably says in advance everything that makes it look as if

---

[88] *Docere* is the technical verb used for *narrationes*; cf. p. 22 above.

Clodius set an ambush for Milo, not Milo for Clodius. But it is his exceptionally clever imitation of simplicity that contributes the most to this impression: "Milo, however, since he had been in the Senate on that day until the Senate was dismissed, came home, changed his shoes and clothes, and waited for a bit while his wife got ready – you know how women are." How Milo seems to have done nothing hurriedly, nothing with premeditation! The most eloquent of men achieved this effect not just by including the details, by which he spins out the delays and the slow build-up to their departure, but also by his everyday and common language and well-concealed art. If these things had been put differently, the sound of the words would have alerted the judge to pay close attention to the advocate's defense of his client. This passage leaves most people cold, but the fact that the reader scarcely even notices it shows precisely how Cicero must have fooled the judge.

This is a remarkably sensitive passage of Quintilianic instruction. The best preparations are those that escape our notice, he says, as Cicero achieved in this speech – but at the same time as he claims the preparations eluded the judges, he implicitly revels in the fact that he has laid them bare. The most subtle detail – Milo's changing shoes, or waiting for his wife to complete her *toilette* (*ut fit*, spoken with a knowing and commiserating glance at the men surrounding him) – can be more convincing than volumes of argumentation. The form is seen to match the content, as Cicero "delays" his speech while speaking of Milo's delay, and the humble language is observed to be thoroughly appropriate to the passage, since the subject matter itself is the stuff of domestic life. By reining in his high-flown rhetoric and choosing this lower register instead, Cicero manages to slip his point under the judges' guard. They are thus persuaded without ever realizing that they were being influenced at all.[89] Quintilian takes his charges under his wing here, unraveling the mysterious power of this passage (which, he says, has eluded so many others who failed to understand it) and sleuthing out the true, hidden meaning behind Cicero's words.[90]

After such a purple patch of exegetic ecstasy, it may seem bathetic to plunge back into more workmanlike efforts. If in smaller compass, however, some of Quintilian's and the scholia's other remarks on the *narratio* are nonetheless impressive. For example, the scholia note that Cicero's *hora fere undecima aut non multo secus* (*Mil.* 29) was well calculated: he made his

---

[89] On this Ciceronian virtue, cf. the praise of Quint. *inst.* 10.1.110 *ut ipsa illa quae extorquet impetrare eum credas, et cum transuersum ui sua iudicem ferat, tamen ille non rapi uideatur sed sequi.* (See p. 25 above.)

[90] Quintilian excels at sensitive interpretation of *narrationes*. See too his comments on the details that make the *narratio* in the *Pro Ligario* persuasive (*inst.* 4.2.108–110; cf. 4.2.51).

statement seem quite plausible by injecting a little note of doubt, because he did not say "the eleventh hour" with earnest certainty; that addition of "or thereabouts" goes quite a long way toward ensuring a façade of truth (εὔπιστον *fecit ipsa addubitatione, quod non undecimam horam quasi pro certo dixit adseueranter; nam hoc additamentum "aut non multo secus" uerisimilitudini plurimum dedit,* 120.12–14 St.). The mention of both the time and place,[91] in fact,

> simul et ad innocentiam Milonis et ad cogitationem sceleratam P. Clodii ferenda praestructio est, quoniam facilius ille iuxta limitem possessionis suae potuerit caedem facere quam Milo in alienis regionibus deprehensus; cumque hora undecima dicat eum profectionem coepisse, magis deriua-bitur in eum suspicio insidiarum, quando eo tempore proficisci coeperit quo alii ad destinatum locum peruenire consuerunt, die paene finito. (120.5–10 St.)

is a foundation that leads at once both to Milo's innocence and to the wicked plotting of Publius Clodius, since Clodius, being along the border of his own property, was more easily able to carry out the killing than Milo, who was caught out in a strange place; and when Cicero says that Clodius began his journey at the eleventh hour, still more suspicion of responsibility for the ambush will be diverted onto him, since he began his journey at a time when other people are accustomed to have already arrived at their destinations, with the day nearly finished.

The scholia carefully unpack and explicate the full import of Cicero's words, as usual showing themselves fully alert to the rhetoric of his argument.

Argumentatio

As we move into the part of the speech given over to more overt argumentation, Quintilian well notes what Cicero does spell out. In a conjectural case, he says, we must look always to means and motive (*inst.* 5.10.50):

> haec et in deliberando intuemur et in iudiciis ad duas res solemus referre, an uoluerit quis, an potuerit; nam et uoluntatem spes facit. hinc illa apud Ciceronem coniectura: "insidiatus est Clodius Miloni, non Milo Clodio: ille cum seruis robustis, hic cum mulierum comitatu, ille equis, hic in raeda, ille expeditus, hic paenula inretitus."

---

[91] Note that Asconius gives a different time in his preface (*circa horam nonam,* Ascon. 31C), which appears to be more accurate. Thus what may have been an outright lie on Cicero's part is felt to be particularly persuasive. Quintilian too observes that Cicero emphasizes the place where the skirmish occurred (*inst.* 5.10.37).

We look to these things in both deliberate and forensic oratory, and in forensic cases we generally make reference to two questions, whether someone had the will to do something, and whether he had the power; for hope creates even the will. Hence the famous conjectural case in Cicero: "Clodius laid an ambush for Milo, not Milo for Clodius: Clodius was accompanied by strong slaves, Milo by a retinue of women; Clodius traveled by horseback, Milo in a carriage; Clodius was equipped as a lightly armed soldier, Milo encumbered by a traveling cloak."

He thus recaps the salient points of Cicero's narrative that pin the ambush on Clodius, not Milo. The whole argument rests on no more than pure conjecture, of course, and Quintilian sees this. He proceeds to break down in great detail how Cicero must have determined what arguments to use. The truth is not a consideration – rhetorical expediency trumps all (*inst.* 7.1.34):

> "Accusatur Milo quod Clodium occiderit." aut fecit aut non: optimum erat negare, sed non potest; occidit ergo. aut iure aut iniuria: utique iure; aut uoluntate aut necessitate (nam ignorantia praetendi non potest): uoluntas anceps est, sed, quia ita homines putant, attingenda defensio ut id pro republica fuerit. necessitate? subita igitur pugna, non praeparata: alter igitur insidiatus est. uter? profecto Clodius. uidesne ut ipsa rerum necessitas diducat defensionem? adhuc: aut utique uoluit occidere insidiatorem Clodium aut non. tutius si noluit: fecerunt ergo serui Milonis neque iubente neque sciente Milone. at haec tam timida defensio detrahit auctoritatem illi qua recte dicebamus occisum; adicietur: "quod suos quisque seruos in tali re facere uoluisset."

> "Milo is accused of killing Clodius." Either he did it or he did not: it would be best to deny the charge outright, but this can't be done. Therefore he killed him. It was either justifiable homicide or it was not. Of course it was justifiable! It was done either intentionally or out of necessity (for we can't claim ignorance): "intention" is risky, but, because this is the way people think, you have to touch on the defense that the killing was done on behalf of the Republic.[92] Out of necessity then? Therefore the fight was sudden, unplanned: thus one ambushed the other. Which one? Clodius, of course. Do you see how the very facts of the case lead to the division of the defense? Furthermore: either he wanted to kill Clodius the ambusher or he did not. It's safer if he didn't want to: thus it was Milo's servants who did it, without Milo's knowledge or orders. But this quite cautious form of defense takes away from the argument that he was rightly killed; this leads to the following addition: "that which everyone would have wanted his slaves to do in such a situation."

---

[92] Cf. Quintilian's later comments on this point, p. 67 below, as well as the various commentators' remarks on Brutus' pamphlet *Pro Milone* (p. 31 above).

Quintilian obviously does not believe a word of Cicero's defense.[93] Cicero would have preferred to deny the charge *tout court*, but he could not. Was it justifiable homicide? Cicero perforce takes the line that it was justified. And so on and so forth: the unavoidable necessity of the facts dictates the layout of the defense. Did Milo wish to kill Clodius? Well, it is "safer" if he did not, and so it must have been his slaves. But we would not want to blunt the force of our persistent pointed implication that Clodius' death was for the best in any event, and so we add a clever line at the end. Quintilian singles out this *sententia* for special praise: this sort of phrase, he says, can refresh the judge's tired mind (*Mil.* 29, *inst.* 4.2.121).[94]

The scholia show themselves here to be Quintilian's equal, for they are not willing simply to go along with Cicero's story either (120.16–19 St.):[95]

> pars haec narrationis aliquanto turbatior est: sine dubio in ea multa finguntur. uerum hanc omnem confusissimam permixtionem cursim praeteruolat: non enim debent cum mora protrahi quae uideri iudicibus possunt aliquod habere figmentum, ne orator, si laciniosus[96] sit, in mendacio deprehendatur.

> This part of the *narratio* is a bit more confused; doubtless much of it is pure fiction. But Cicero swiftly sails across this whole thoroughly jumbled mess: things shouldn't be dragged out by delays when they could seem to the judges to contain some elements of oratorical imagination, lest the orator, if he should become entangled in his own folds, be caught out in a lie.

They keenly observe that the confusion in this part of the narrative is deliberate, since without a doubt Cicero has conjured much of it from his own imagination! This, however, is hardly to his discredit. On the contrary, he is seen to be skillful at flying through the mess at breakneck speed so that the judges will not spot his inconsistencies or outright lies. This all goes back, of course, to the scholia's prefatory remark about Cicero speaking *pro sui officii necessitate* (p. 32 above). It is best to have the truth on your side, the teacher tells the class, but if you do not, you must lie, and here is

---

[93] Cf. his admiration of how Cicero *insidiarum inuidiam in Clodium uertit, quamquam re uera fuerat pugna fortuita* (*inst.* 6.5.10; cf. p. 19 above).

[94] Quintilian goes on to discuss *sententiae* in general, focusing on how they are overused in a world where speeches are no longer composed *ad utilitatem potius quam ostentationem*. Nevertheless he grants them some allowance, and it is interesting to note that rather than cite a sparkling epigram from one of his sententious contemporaries, he has again resorted to Cicero, who was not particularly conspicuous for these gems. For more of Quintilian's opinion on this sort of ornamentation, see *inst.* 8.3.7–15.

[95] In sharp contrast to the later and inferior scholia Gronoviana, which just take Cicero at his word: 322.29–323.2 St.

[96] Another piquant expression, meaning something like "entangled in his own folds." The word itself is used as early as Pliny the Elder, but in this metaphorical sense first in Apuleius and Tertullian; once elsewhere in the scholia Bobiensia (145.18 St.). See *TLL* vii.2.835.24–75 (Montefusco).

how to do it.[97] Quintilian again singles out this line of reasoning as one of the speech's high points, not despite its mendacity but rather because of it (*inst.* 6.5.10). The emphasis of the instruction, both here and in the scholia, is always and exclusively on Cicero's rhetorical brilliance.

After the *narratio* Cicero detours slightly for a brief digression, whose force the scholia explain in straightforward terms (121.12–15 St.):

> finita narratione subicitur egressio, quam Graeci παρέκβασιν uocant: quae quidem < . . . > miserationem conciliat reo, inuidiam grauissimam P. Clodio quamuis interempto. hic enim quasi destitutus misere et infeliciter uindicatus, ille quasi grassator et paene tyrannus inducitur.

> After he finishes the *narratio* he adds a digression (*egressio*), which the Greeks call a παρέκβασις. This < . . . > creates pity for the defendant and the most profound dislike for Publius Clodius, even though he's the one who was killed. For Milo is presented as wretchedly destitute and avenged to his own misfortune, while Clodius is cast as a street-robber and almost a tyrant.

Here we get a bit of Greek technical terminology, but this is leavened with a sensitive explication of Cicero's rhetorical reasoning. The digression, we are rightly told, serves a very specific function in the speech, stirring up dislike of Clodius and creating sympathy for Milo. Understanding and appreciating the full force of Cicero's argument remains the central classroom concern.

Cicero then sharpens the horns of a false dilemma on which he will base the entirety of his case. All that is at issue in this trial, he claims, is who set an ambush for whom (*num quid igitur aliud in iudicium uenit nisi uter utri insidias fecerit?, Mil.* 31). The scholia choose this comment on which to hang their discussion of Cicero's whole argument (121.23–122.3 St.):

> constituit in medio κεφάλαιον τοῦ κρινομένου et summam quaestionis breuissime comprehendit < . . . > diducens in utramque personam coniecturalem disceptationem, quae diuiditur secundum artis oratoriae legem locis duplicatis: < . . . >, id est uoluntatis, < . . . > facultatis, scilicet per comparationem. cumque sit in arte praeceptum ut nosmet ipsos ante purgemus, tunc aduersarium criminemur, quod est et antiquius sine dubio et magis naturale: in hac oratione Tullius ante arripit locum uoluntatis ad arguendum Clodium, post deinde transgreditur ad defendendum Milonem. nec istud inconsulte facit, sed necessario; quippe animaduertens plus sibi ipsi

---

[97] Quintilian too discusses how an orator can best lie, if necessary, at *inst.* 4.2.88–94, and provides a theoretical justification for oratorical deception at *inst.* 12.1.34–45.

fiduciae in illo accusando, maluit exordium confirmationis ab eo capere, ut in hominem sceleratissimum magis congruere insidiandi uoluntatem, et causas habuisse praecipuas eum potissimum diceret cui expediret interfici Milonem, ne in praetura gerenda haberet impedimento inimici sui consulatum.

He placed in the middle the main point of the issue at hand and embraced the whole of the case in very brief compass < ... >, splitting among both parties the conjectural dispute, which is divided according to the laws of oratory under two headings: < ... >, that is of will, < ....> of ability, obviously by means of comparison. And although it is laid down as a rule that we first clear ourselves of the charges, then we accuse our adversary (which is both doubtless the older and more natural approach), in this speech Cicero first seizes upon the heading of "will" to accuse Clodius, and only then passes over to the defense of Milo. And he didn't do this thoughtlessly, but rather by necessity; doubtless realizing that he would create more trust in his case by accusing Clodius, he preferred to begin his *confirmatio* from that point, so that he might claim that the will to commit an ambush better fit a most wicked man, and that Clodius especially had particular reason to benefit from Milo's death, namely so that in his praetorship he would not have to contend with the impediment of his enemy Milo holding the consulship.

The scholia explain how such a conjectural argument will work: just as Quintilian instructs, the speaker will focus on means and motive, comparing Clodius and Milo and appraising who was more likely to have done the deed. Furthermore, although the rhetorical handbooks prescribe that we should clear our good name before besmirching our opponent's, here Cicero immediately goes on the attack, focusing on how Clodius wanted Milo's death. This tactic was no chance move; on the contrary, Cicero realized that his case would seem more believable if it began thus. The rhetoric is all important; and within the rhetoric, one must never be bound by the handbooks: Cicero would prefer *ratio et res ipsa* to a thousand rhetorical manuals.

Both Quintilian and the scholia continue to develop the theme of how to argue a conjectural case. Quintilian, for example, says (*inst.* 7.2.43):[98]

post haec, an alio tempore et aliter facere uel facilius uel securius potuerit, ut dicit Cicero pro Milone enumerans plurimas occasiones quibus ab eo Clodius inpune occidi potuerit. praeterea cur potissimum illo loco, illo tempore, illo modo sit adgressus, qui et ipse diligentissime tractatur pro eodem locus.

---

[98] Cf. other comments at e.g. *inst.* 5.14.2–3.

Furthermore, could he have done it at another time or in another way or more easily or more safely? So Cicero in the *Pro Milone* says when he lists the many occasions when Clodius could have been killed by Milo with impunity. Furthermore, why of all places did he make his attack in that place, why of all times at that time, why of all methods that method? This topic itself is likewise handled most diligently in that same defense speech.

The scholia have a set of lengthy notes on a similar theme, e.g.: "He goes through a list of the more opportune occasions when it would have been easy for Milo to kill Clodius, since he had both good opportunities and just reasons. Since Milo refused to kill him then, it is hardly likely that he would have tried to do so at such an inopportune moment" (122.14–17 St.). This is another perfectly reasonable and correct summary explanation of Cicero's argument.

From here until the end of the *peroratio* the Bobiensia are badly lacunose (we have lost some thirty-four pages and have only two preserved, followed by a solitary leaf from the very end of the speech). Nevertheless, the tenor of the preserved comments is the same: a constant emphasis on Cicero's rhetorical strategy and tactics. On sections 47–48, for example, the scholia explain how Cicero continues to follow the form of the *coniectura duplex* by showing that Clodius' departure from his Alban villa was unmotivated – unless he had been informed of Milo's arrival and wanted to kill him. Clodius could not have been hastening to Rome at the news of a particular old man's death, because he had earlier left him as he lay dying, and he furthermore could not have been curious about the contents of his will, since it had been made openly and both Clodius and Cicero had been named as heirs. It was the tenth hour, a time more suitable for killing than for coming home (*hora decuma, quae opportunior esset magis caedi quam profectioni*, 123.33 St.). There can be no doubt that the missing portions of the commentary are similar in character.

Asconius for his part continues in his customary vein. When Cicero says *itaque illud Cassianum indicium*[99] *in his personis ualeat* ("therefore let the Cassian test apply to these people", *Mil.* 32), Asconius elucidates the "Cassian test" (Ascon. 45–46C). L. Cassius, he says, was a man of the utmost severity. In any murder trial he always used to advise the judges to

---

[99] There is an interesting textual issue here. First, Asconius' lemma actually reads *iudicium*; this was corrected by Purser to *indicium*. More problematically, the *Pro Milone* manuscripts read *cui bono fuerit* instead of *indicium*. While Cicero's editors print *cui bono* etc. as in the MSS, this seems to me a case where Asconius has preserved a genuine reading. The MSS once had *Cassianum indicium*, and this was eventually glossed by *cui bono fuerit*, which subsequently made its way into the text and expelled the more difficult and obscure *indicium*.

consider *cui bono?*, i.e., exactly what Cicero wants the jury to consider here. Asconius then goes on to describe some of Cassius' harsh judgments. For example, a case involving Vestal Virgins accused of actions unbecoming was once referred to Cassius. The *pontifex maximus* had earlier heard the case and judged only one guilty, letting two go free. Cassius condemned all three and several others besides!

In much the same way Asconius explains Cicero's punning innuendo about Sextus Cloelius being the *lumen Curiae* (*Mil.* 33): the obvious meaning is Cicero's ironic reference to Cloelius' good standing in the Senate, but the subtext hidden in plain sight is what Asconius picks up on, namely that it was Cloelius who cremated Clodius' body in the Curia and burned the building to the ground. He is thus the *lumen Curiae* in an entirely different sense as well (Ascon. 46C). If we had the Bobiensia here, they too surely would have given such an explanation.

Asconius occasionally comes across as more naïve than our other two commentators. When Cicero claims, for example, that Milo spent *tria patrimonia* in an attempt to placate the rampaging mobs of Clodians (*Mil.* 95), Asconius takes him literally and duly reports that the third inheritance seems to be that of his mother; he has not found another possibility (*tertium patrimonium uidetur significare matris; aliud enim quod fuerit non inueni*, Ascon. 53C). As Robert Tyrrell well observed, however, "Did any one ever hear of a man who had spent *two* or *four*?"[100] It is doubtless a chimerical quest to try to ferret out the true source of Milo's supposed inheritance, and this is not the sort of vain pursuit that a Quintilian would have busied himself with.[101]

Once in a while Asconius is likewise too clever for his own good. At one point Cicero accuses Clodius of being accompanied by "Greeklings" at every waking moment (*comites Graeculi quocumque ibat, etiam cum in castra Etrusca properabat, Mil.* 55), but Asconius espies a deeper insult lurking here (Ascon. 50C):

> saepe obiecit Clodio Cicero socium eum coniurationis Catilinae fuisse; quam rem nunc quoque reticens ostendit. fuerat enim opinio, ut Catilina

---

[100] Ap. Clark (1895) ad loc. (emphasis original).
[101] For similar examples of possible Asconian naïveté, see e.g. Clark (1895) ad *Mil.* 37 (cf. Marshall [1985] 46). Asconius (48C) "cannot be led to believe that Cicero has lied here, especially since he adds 'as you know' (*ut scitis*)," even though he cannot discover exactly what the orator is supposed to be referring to. Clark thinks that the parenthetical *ut scitis* "will suggest to a modern reader that the anecdote is apocryphal." When Cicero utters the phrase it is plainly supposed to be confirmatory, as Asconius takes it, but whether it is mere bluster and bravado to cover a hollow assertion is perhaps open to debate.

> ex urbe profugerat in castra Manli centurionis qui tum in Etruria ad Faesulas exercitum ei comparabat, Clodium subsequi eum uoluisse et coepisse, tum dein mutato consilio in urbem redisse.

> Cicero often reproaches Clodius with the charge that he had been a member of the Catilinarian conspiracy; and here he alludes silently to this same thing. For the belief had been that, when Catiline had fled from Rome to the camp of Manlius the centurion, who at that time had procured an army for him in Etruria near Faesulae, Clodius had wanted to follow him and began to do so, then changed his mind and returned to Rome.

Cicero, according to Asconius, implies by *castra Etrusca* that Clodius was a member of the Catilinarian conspiracy. This is doubtful in the extreme, and in Cicero's extant writings he never once charges Clodius with this offense, which he surely would have done with the greatest relish had it been even remotely plausible.[102] In reality, *castra Etrusca* probably just refers, as Lewis says, "to Clodian armed depredations in Etruria frequently alleged in the *Pro Milone*."[103] Nevertheless, even if Asconius got it wrong, he is shown to be reading the text closely to explicate its hidden nuances, and his precise wording shows that he does not accept the allegation uncritically: *fuerat enim opinio* implies that he himself may think differently and believe that Clodius had nothing whatsoever to do with Catiline.[104]

One category of comment that I have not dwelt on is the identification of rhetorical figures. While glossing the meaning of specific words is vanishingly rare,[105] pointing out rhetorical figures is extremely common. It is easy to believe that a teacher might at any time stop and ask the class

---

[102] Cicero does, however, eventually begin trying to present Clodius as a new Catiline; see Kaster (2006) ad *Sest.* 42 pp. 217–218.

[103] Lewis (2006) ad loc.; other instances include *Mil.* 26, 50, 55, 74, 87, 98. See too Marshall (1985) ad loc. and Clark (1895) ad *Mil.* 55, both of whom come to the same conclusion. For a similar mistake, cf. the Bobiensia on the *De aere alieno Milonis*, 172.14–15 St.

[104] Asconius also exercises his creativity, perhaps with more success, on Cicero's argument that Milo would have picked a better spot to ambush Clodius had he in fact desired to do so (*Mil.* 49): Asconius points out that there was an ideal spot for such an ambush near the monument of Basilus on the Via Appia near Rome (50C), where Clodius would have had to pass on his return to the city. (The monument of Basilus is not an anachronistic importation by Asconius: Cicero himself mentioned that his friend L. Quinctius was wounded and robbed there [*Att.* 7.9.1].)

[105] Although Quintilian does sanction discussions of words (see p. 22 above), he has just two such comments on our speech: at *inst.* 1.5.57 *raeda* is noted to be Gaulish in origin (*Mil.* 28), and at *inst.* 8.3.22 the phrase *heus tu Rufio* is observed to be just right for its context (*Mil.* 60). In the Bobiensia we can also mention two notes, 124.2–9 St.: *uerbum hoc "properandi" non sum nescius aput quosdam indifferenter accipi ac solere unum uideri "festinare" et "properare." uisum est igitur mihi propter eos quibus aliquod studium proprie loquendi est auctore ipso M. Catone haec uerba distinguere. quippe aliud esse "properare," aliud "festinare" ipse nos, ut dicebam, Cato docuit in oratione quae inscribitur "de uirtute sua contra Thermum"; eius igitur uerba ponamus. qui sic ait: "nam aliud est 'properare'*

what figure a particular passage exemplifies. At *inst.* 8.6.37, for example, Quintilian notes some of the metaphors Cicero uses to refer to Clodius in the speech (*fons gloriae eius* and *seges ac materia*).[106] Elsewhere he will address *amplificatio: nam et uerba geminantur, uel amplificandi gratia, ut "occidi, occidi non Spurium Maelium" (alterum est enim quod indicat, alterum quod adfirmat)* ... ("for words are doubled, either for the sake of amplification, e.g. *occidi, occidi non Spurium Maelium*, where the first states the fact and the second emphasizes it ...,"*inst.* 9.3.28, *Mil.* 72).[107] Other examples include parenthesis (*inst.* 9.3.23, *Mil.* 94), apostrophe (*inst.* 9.2.38, *Mil.* 85), forms of digression (*inst.* 9.2.56, *Mil.* 33), aposiopesis (*inst.* 9.2.54, a reference to the delivered *Pro Milone*), allegory (*inst.* 8.6.48, *Mil.* 5), homoeoteleuton (*inst.* 9.3.77, *Mil.* 5), antithesis (*inst.* 9.3.83, *Mil.* 10), μετάστασις[108] (*inst.* 9.2.41), and so forth. The scholia contain similar remarks, e.g. 119.11 St. on apostrophe (*Mil.* 22; cf. 124.12 St., *Mil.* 101), 120.28 St. on ἐνάργεια (*Mil.* 29), 121.17 St. on ἐπανόρθωσις (*Mil.* 30), 124.16 St. on αὔξησις (*Mil.* 102), and so forth.

Most of the commentary on the speech is focused on its main argument, namely that Clodius must have set an ambush for Milo, who only reacted in self-defense. Nevertheless, as we have seen, all three commentators are aware that other avenues of defense are available and indeed that Brutus took one such alternative approach.[109] Brutus' defense of Milo rests on positively boasting of the fact that Milo had killed a *malus ciuis* (Quint. *inst.* 3.6.93). Cicero, however, as Quintilian observes, tries to have it both ways. First he claims that Milo did not murder Clodius, but then he says that if he had, he would have acted rightly. This tactic surprises some, but, Quintilian says, it is in fact a specimen of brilliantly successful unorthodoxy (*inst.* 4.5.13–15):

---

aliud *'festinare'*: qui unumquodque mature transigit, prope<rat; qui multa simul incipit neque perficit, is festinat.*'*> (Similarly Fest. 254 Lindsay; cf. too e.g. Gell. 10.11 and esp. 16.14.) Also 120.21–26 St.: *quos nunc uulgo "muliones" dicimus, eos scilicet qui iumenta uehiculis subiuncta moderantur et regunt, eos ueteres, ut animaduertis, "redarios" dicebant, "muliones" autem proprie eos qui negotiationem lucri sui causa in huiusmodi iumentis exercebant. quamuis et in Filippicis "mulionem" Ventidium dixerit eapropter, quod de publico redemerat iumentorum praebitionem quae esset aput exercitum necessaria.* (Ventidius the muleteer is not found in the extant *Philippics*, but cf. schol. ad Iuu. 7.199 and perhaps Plin. *nat.* 7.135; see also Planc. Cic. *fam.* 10.18.3 *Ventidii* ... *mulionis castra despicio.* Further Manuwald [2007] 66–67.)

[106] For more on Milonian epithets and metaphors, see e.g. *inst.* 8.6.41.

[107] More Milonian *amplificatio* at *inst.* 9.3.30. Quintilian also uses the Spurius Maelius passage as an example of a comparison from lesser to greater (*inst.* 5.11.12).

[108] A Greek term for the description of a hypothetical future situation. (En route to the epilogue Cicero paints a vivid – but entirely imaginary – picture of the evils that would have befallen the Roman world had Clodius won the consulship, *Mil.* 88–90.)

[109] See p. 31 above.

de illo quoque genere defensionis plerique dubitant: "si occidi, recte feci, sed non occidi"; quo enim pertinere prius si sequens firmum sit? haec inuicem obstare et utroque utentibus in neutro haberi fidem. quod sane in parte uerum est, et illo sequenti, si modo indubitabile est, [sit] solo utendum; at si quid in eo quod est fortius timebimus, utraque probatione nitemur. alius enim alio moueri solet; et qui factum putabit, iustum credere potest, qui tamquam iusto non mouebitur, factum fortasse non credet: ut certa manus uno telo potest esse contenta, incerta plura spargenda sunt, ut sit et fortunae locus. egregie uero Cicero pro Milone insidiatorem primum Clodium ostendit, tum addidit ex abundanti, etiam si id non fuisset, talem tamen ciuem cum summa uirtute interfectoris et gloria necari potuisse.

Many are uncertain about the following sort of defense too: "If I killed him, I did so rightly, but I did not kill him." Because what's the point of claiming the former if the latter is true? These claims are not consistent, and those who make use of both should not be believed in either. Now admittedly this is partly true, and as long as the latter claim is beyond any doubt, it and it alone should be used. But if there is anything we're worried about in the stronger claim, we will rely on both proofs. For different people are persuaded in different ways: the one who thinks that the killing happened can believe that it was just, while the one who is not moved by the argument about justice perhaps will not believe that the killing even took place. In the same way a sure hand can be content with one shot, whereas an uncertain one must scatter many in the hope that he will get lucky. In his *Pro Milone* Cicero brilliantly first showed that Clodius was the ambusher, then added as an extra argument that even if he had not been the ambusher, nevertheless killing such a citizen would redound to the great glory and honor of his killer.

And so Cicero is able to have his cake and eat it too.[110] This trick is again thought of as one of the signal successes of the speech. Quintilian says that Cicero acted brilliantly (*egregie*) by introducing the second argument, and elsewhere he lists the tactic among his most praiseworthy innovations in the speech (*inst.* 6.5.10).[111] He thus maintains his unswerving focus on explicating Cicero's rhetorical virtues, which are found even in apparently misguided decisions.

Peroratio

Cicero has conciliated the judges' good will, dispelled their prejudices, told his story, and made his case with several arguments. All that remains is to make a final appeal to the jurors' sense of justice and outrage and pity.

---

[110] Cf. Fotheringham (2007).   [111] For yet another mention of the device, see *inst.* 5.14.2.

Before he moves into the epilogue proper, Cicero allows himself to be carried away to the loftiest heights of the grand style, hoping to sweep the jury up in the vortex following in his wake. Milo, he says, did not kill Clodius, nay, rather it was the very Alban hills and groves and altars that rose up and struck down Clodius that day. He prays to them directly: *uos enim iam, Albani tumuli atque luci, uos inquam, imploro atque testor* (*Mil.* 85), and Quintilian admires these lines a great deal. Cicero would have delivered them with his hands outstretched (*inst.* 11.3.115) and with a full-throated torrent of vocal emotion (*inst.* 11.3.167; cf. *inst.* 11.3.172). He will thus inspire both anger (against Clodius) and pity (for Milo) in the jurors. Indeed, hearing these lines, the juror will grow pale and weep and after being dragged through the whole gamut of emotions will follow wherever Cicero leads and have no need of explicit instruction (*iudex pallebit et flebit et per omnis adfectus tractus huc atque illuc sequetur nec doceri desiderabit, inst.* 12.10.62).[112] If Cicero can achieve this, it will be a true stroke of victory, because the jurors will stand persuaded regardless of the facts of the case, and Cicero will have no further need to convince them by reasoned argument (*docere*). This is one of Cicero's signal qualities, singled out for special praise by Quintilian in his eulogy of Cicero in book 10: even when Cicero is sweeping the listener along by brute force, he will feel not that he is being snatched away but that he is following of his own accord (*ut . . . ille non rapi uideatur sed sequi, inst.* 10.1.110; cf. p. 25 above).

Having roused the jurors' outrage against Clodius to a fever pitch, Cicero turns finally to stirring up their pity for his own client. Traditionally this would be done by presenting the defendant miserable and in rags, bewailing his fortune and fate. Here Cicero was faced with a problem: Milo had all the appearance of a burly mobster, and a reputation to match. Furthermore, Cicero had taken a proud line in the defense, and he has just finished by emphasizing what a great gift to the Roman people Clodius' death was. In these circumstances Milo could hardly beg for mercy. Instead, then, Cicero animates an imaginary dialogue between himself and Milo, in which Milo remains strong and constant while Cicero himself is seen to break down. He does not, of course, spell out the reasons for this approach, but Quintilian sensitively perceives and explains them (*inst.* 6.1.23–25):

> plurimum tamen ualet miseratio, quae iudicem non flecti tantum cogit, sed motum quoque animi sui lacrimis confiteri. haec petetur aut ex iis quae

---

[112] For yet more on this address, see *inst.* 9.2.38 and 11.1.34.

passus est reus, aut iis quae [quam] cum maxime patitur, aut iis quae damnatum manent: quae et ipsa duplicantur cum dicimus ex qua illi fortuna et in quam reccidendum sit … nonnumquam etiam ipse patronus has partes subit (ut Cicero pro Milone: "o me miserum! o me infelicem! reuocare me tu in patriam, Milo, potuisti per hos, ego te in patria per eosdem retinere <non potero>?") maximeque si, ut tum accidit, non conueniunt ei qui accusatur preces; nam quis ferret Milonem pro capite suo supplicantem qui a se uirum nobilem interfectum quia id fieri oportuisset fateretur? ergo et illi captauit ex ipsa praestantia animi fauorem et in locum lacrimarum eius ipse successit.

But pity carries the most weight, which not only compels the judge to bend, but also to show his own feelings by tears. Pity will be sought either on account of what the defendant has suffered, or what he is suffering at that very moment, or what remains for him to suffer if he is condemned. All of that will itself be doubled when we contrast his former good fortune with that to which he will be reduced … Sometimes even the advocate himself takes on this role, as Cicero did in the *Pro Milone*: "O miserable, o misfortunate me! You, Milo, were able to secure my recall to the fatherland with these men's help – I won't be able to keep you in that same land with these same men?" This is especially the case if, as happened then, pleas for mercy are not suitable for the man who is being accused. For who could tolerate a Milo begging for his life after he claimed that he had killed a man from a noble family because that was what was right and just? Thus Cicero sought favor for his client on the grounds of his high character and shed tears himself in Milo's place.

While Cicero sheds the tears, Milo remains stoic and courageous. He could not have done otherwise – who would have tolerated it? Although Milo does not beg, he is nevertheless given complaints appropriate to his character that will in their own way move the jurors: "So my labors were undertaken in vain! O my deceitful hopes! O my fruitless plans!" (*inst.* 6.1.27). Quintilian further specifies the appropriate delivery of these lines (*inst.* 11.3.172), namely with the greatest emotion, and one might again imagine Quintilian's own theatrical recitation before the class. This form of epilogue is the last of the unusual features of the speech to which Quintilian accords special praise (*inst.* 6.5.10). With the speech all but over, he quite likes Cicero's pretense of being overcome by grief and weariness at the end (*sed finis sit, neque enim prae lacrimis iam loqui possum, Mil.* 105), and believes it will be quite effective, provided that the delivery matches the words (*inst.* 11.3.174).

At this point the scholia Bobiensia resume very briefly, and they comment on some of the closing words of the speech as well. At 105 Cicero implores the jurors to be brave enough to voice their true opinion: *uos oro obtestorque, iudices, ut in sententiis ferendis quod sentietis id audeatis.* This is of course a topos of epilogues everywhere, and yet the scholia observe that it has special relevance in this case (125.3–4 St.):

> destiturus orator ibi finem posuit ubi maxime necessarium uidebatur: ne iudices in pronuntiando Pompeium timerent quem praesentem <int>uerentur.

> When Cicero was about to stop speaking he placed the end of the speech where it seemed most necessary, so that the judges, in rendering their verdict, would not fear Pompey who was there in person in plain view.

Thus Cicero is seen to end where he began in the very first section, urging the jurors not to be afraid in the face of a *corona* of armed soldiers and Rome's most powerful magistrate. The scholia do not simply explain the commonplace; they evince a keen desire to understand and appreciate the individual rhetorical details by reference to the speech as a whole.

Conclusion

Asconius, Quintilian, and the scholia Babiensia grant us a unique window into the Roman schoolroom. We have seen in great detail just how a teacher would have explicated a Ciceronian speech for his pupils. Servian grammatical commentary this was not, nor was Cicero put forward as a source of "pure" Latinity. There was rather an insistent and over-whelming focus on rhetoric and argumentation, buttressed as necessary by explanation of contemporary or historical allusions. These latter served primarily to aid the students to understand the rhetoric of the speech itself, but they also helped stock the budding orator's mind with ready anecdotes and exempla that he could insert into his own future orations.

The rhetorical focus is of the utmost importance for understanding Cicero's reception in the early Empire. Students would have come to the *rhetor* as raw recruits, young teenagers uninitiated into the arcana of oratory. They would doubtless have heard the name Cicero before, but they would not have read any of his speeches nor had much of an idea of the man himself. In the classroom they were not presented with a full picture of Cicero with all his complexities and contradictions, but rather studied him primarily as a rhetorical exemplar. His skillful strategy and tactics were to be analyzed, admired, and imitated. The details of his life and his complex political choices were not studied for their own sake but only insofar as they helped explain the persuasive power of a speech; they were thus flattened out or elided altogether. As Quintilian says, Cicero is *the* rhetorical model for the classroom, and so close study of his rhetoric becomes the primary form of engagement with the man. This is the effect of canonizing Cicero's oratory and enshrining it in the school curriculum. He was simplified and reduced to a rhetorical figure.

CHAPTER 2

Eloquence (Dis)embodied: The Textualization of Cicero

A Modern Syncrisis

One of the greatest political figures in history. Born into relatively modest circumstances away from the capital, he rose through the contemporary *cursus honorum* by dint of legal acumen and sterling oratory to the highest rank in the land. At a time of great peril he saved his country from self-destruction, but in the end he could not escape his political enemies and was murdered. Not all of his actions, perhaps, were deserving of unstinting praise: his poetry could not be said to have risen to the same level as his prose, and he violated key provisions of the constitution in his suppression of an armed rebellion. Of whom are we speaking – M. Tullius Cicero or Abraham Lincoln?

While this thought experiment may prove most profitable to the American reader, I believe nonetheless that it is a useful way to think about the reception of a political figure. In the case of both Cicero and Lincoln, the facts of their lives have always been available, and yet there has consistently been a tradition of limited engagement with only a partial version of the story. Moreover, the comparison also shows how easily half-truths become accepted as reality. "Every schoolboy knows" that Lincoln freed the slaves by the Emancipation Proclamation in 1863 – but in fact he thereby freed only the slaves of the reconquered Confederate states, saying nothing about the four slave-holding states that did not secede. Earlier in the war he had even explicitly opposed freeing the slaves in those states.[1] His own views on the details of emancipation were probably complex, tempered by both political expediency and contemporary prejudices, and he only advocated for a Thirteenth Amendment abolishing slavery after it had become a part of the Republican party platform.[2] This complex picture, however, is simplified into a familiar story with a kernel of truth.

[1] Thomas (2009) 275–277.
[2] See e.g. Thomas (2009) 494: "Except for secession, a Thirteenth Amendment forever *guaranteeing* slavery in the states might well have been enacted after Lincoln's inauguration" (my emphasis); cf.

It is in the schoolroom that certain key moments and stories about famous men become firmly ensconced in young minds, and the complex contours and rough edges of those figures' lives are simplified and smoothed out into a harmonious image. A once vibrant and full-bodied life is almost inevitably reduced to a few anecdotes and attributes, which in time come entirely to replace the actual person in the popular imagination.[3] This is certainly true of Cicero: the evidence of his life was abundantly recorded and available for those who cared to use it. There were biographies by Tiro and Nepos; there were Pollio's and Livy's histories; there was even Cicero's own *De consiliis suis*, a vindication of his political career; and eventually his letters.[4] Plutarch's full life of Cicero, quoting many of these sources, is a good witness to their continuing availability throughout the first century AD, as is the testimony of Asconius.[5] Nevertheless, certain elements are mentioned time and again, while others are neglected, and in this chapter and the next two I will attempt to isolate and identify these various themes. It is in the schoolroom and the declamatory tradition that we observe these particular elements crystallizing out of the swirling chaos that was Cicero's life. Before the

---

pp. 149–150 on Lincoln's position in the Great Debates with Stephen Douglas. Gates (2009) provides a comprehensive collection of Lincoln's statements on race relations.

[3] Kaster (1998) 250–251 notes that canonization of a classic is always reductive, but that we are better positioned to watch the process in action in the case of Cicero because of the declamations preserved in Seneca the Elder. I would also point out that, unlike the case of a Vergil, we have copious evidence of Cicero's life outside of his most canonical texts, and so we are uniquely able to see what has been stripped away.

[4] McDermott (1972) is comprehensive on Tiro the man and his work, with pp. 282–284 treating the biography of Cicero. It was lengthy (in at least four books, Ascon. 48C) and we can reasonably surmise that it was concerned to show Cicero's life and actions in a good light; see also *FRHist* 46. The biography of Nepos has left only the most exiguous traces (frr. 37–38 Marshall, from Gellius and Jerome), but one might imagine that it enjoyed a circulation in the company of Nepos' other biographies; see also *FRHist* 45. The evidence for Cicero's *De consiliis suis*, a sort of apologia for his political career published after his death, is collected in *RE* s.v. "M. Tullius Cicero" 1267–1269; in brief, Cicero speaks of the work in various letters to Atticus, and it is known to, among others, Cassius Dio (39.10.3), Plutarch (e.g. *Crass.* 13), and Asconius (e.g. 83C); see also *FRHist* 39. Cicero's letters do not seem to have circulated as early or as widely as one might have expected; see ch. 5 n. 34. On Pollio's and Livy's Cicero, see p. 131 below.

[5] Moles (1988) 28–31 summarizes the results of Plutarchean *Quellenforschung*. For the *Life of Cicero*, Plutarch primarily used "Cicero's *Brutus*, monograph on the consulship, *De consiliis suis*, speeches, and letters, Augustus' *Autobiography*, Tiro's biography and collection of jokes ... Though Plutarch did draw on some later material (some Augustan 'rhetoricians' history,' some oral tradition, Thrasea Paetus' biography of Cato), he did so sparingly; nor did he make much, if any, use of the major narrative historians" (Moles [1988] 30). I treat Plutarch's Latin abilities in n. 61 below; for a fuller discussion of source criticism, see *RE* s.v. "Plutarchos (2)" 911–914, Desideri (1992), Pelling (2002) chs. 1–4, and the outdated but still useful Gudeman (1902). Marshall (1985) 39–61 is comprehensive and detailed on Asconius' sources, of which the most notable – besides Cicero himself – include Fenestella, the senatorial *acta*, and Tiro's biography (note that he does not cite Cicero's letters).

declaimers there is only darkness and void, although we will be able to make deductions about the origins of various declamatory traditions. These favored elements will then reappear and be amplified further in other Latin literature ranging from historiography to satire: the image fashioned by declamation and the rhetorical schoolroom influenced and even shaped the reception of Cicero in later literature and the popular imagination.

This chapter and the next two will be organized by these key themes. After a brief introduction to the tradition of declamation in the Roman world, I will first consider Cicero as a model of eloquence. It was this reputation – not an inevitable one, as we shall see – that ensured his centrality to the rhetorical curriculum, a curriculum of course dedicated precisely to the teaching of eloquence. This school-room canonization comes to underly his entire *Nachleben*. Rather than simply accumulate testimony to Cicero's oratorical excellence, I will show some of the ways in which that excellence was presented in the classroom, including the persistent theme of the decline of eloquence from its peak in a Ciceronian Golden Age and comparisons between Cicero and his Greek "counterpart," Demosthenes. As will quickly become clear, these discussions have ramifications far beyond the classroom. Cicero's eloquence will furthermore be seen to be intimately bound up with the other event most significant for his later reception, his death, which I will treat in detail in the following chapter.

The Declamatory Classroom

The rhetorical schoolroom, as discussed in chapter 1, is where young Romans would have made their first acquaintance with Cicero. We have already seen how they read a Ciceronian speech, with a focus above all on the rhetorical skill of the supreme Roman orator. The *rhetor*'s most significant charge, of course, was to instruct his pupils in the art of eloquence. Passive reading of Cicero as a model did indeed conduce to this end, but active writing and declaiming was even more important. Cicero appeared as both a subject of and a model for declamations; that is to say, as a student you might be asked to write about Cicero, or you might be asked to write like Cicero.

The central role of declamatory rhetoric in Roman high culture cannot be overstated. Any upper-class youth with ambitions for a public career would have spent years in the *rhetor*'s tutelage, fundamentally shaping his attitude toward life and literature.[6] Successful oratory elevated a man from the common herd, leading not infrequently to positions of power and considerable emolument, and good rhetorical instruction led to successful oratory. This is the common educational background of essentially all preserved imperial literary authors. Furthermore, "professional" declamation was a common form of elite entertainment. Indeed, many of these so-called professionals were also teachers of rhetoric whose themes for declamation were likewise fixtures of the rhetorical school: when we look at the evidence preserved in Seneca the Elder, the schoolroom is never far away.[7] While there were certainly critics of the system, for the most part it reigned for centuries without significant change or challenge.[8]

The criticisms, in fact, often serve only to demonstrate how important and pervasive rhetorical teaching was in contemporary Roman society. Our meager remains of Petronius, for example, begin with one such critical discussion between the vagabond Encolpius and the *rhetor* Agamemnon (Petron. 1–5). Since by the Neronian period it had long since become conventional to lambaste the decline of oratory, what we have here is a parody of such complaints, or indeed perhaps even "parody on parody."[9] The upshot of the discussion is that Encolpius claims that oratory is in steep decline from its former lofty heights, principally because of the malign influence of declamatory education.[10] In sum, he says, addressing the tribe of rhetorical teachers, "it was you who first destroyed eloquence" (*primi omnium eloquentiam perdidistis*, Petron. 2.2).

Agamemnon in reply attempts to place the blame for this decline – and he does not dispute that there has been a decline – on parents, students, and anyone but the *rhetores* themselves. More importantly for my purposes, the whole conversation is shot through with Ciceronian reminiscences, sometimes misapplied, which help point up Cicero's central role in the

---

[6] Recent scholarship has rightly emphasized the fundamental role of declamatory education in inculcating young men with what it meant to be "Roman"; see e.g. Beard (1993), Bloomer (1997a), Bloomer (1997b) 110–153, Gunderson (2003), Migliario (2007) 17–22, Bloomer (2011) 170–191.

[7] For details, see ch. 3 n. 2.

[8] For example, as Winterbottom says s.v. "declamation" in the *OCD*, "Quintilian, though critical (*Inst.* 2. 10) of the unreality of contemporary practice, never questions the basis of declamation, and his book is a handbook for the declaimer as well as for the orator." Cf. *inst.* 10.5.14 for Quintilian's guarded praise of declamation. To be certain, there was some adverse criticism; see Bonner (1949) 71–83 and Berti (2007) 219–247 for the ancient evidence, as well as Clark (1953) 251–261, whose discussion extends into the Renaissance.

[9] Schmeling (2011) 1, who believes that already by this time "parodies of the poor state of rhetoric were becoming hackneyed."

[10] Cf. the discussion of the decline in eloquence after Cicero on p. 90 below, along with the more extensive treatment in ch. 6.

contemporary debate: Encolpius' *eloquentia ... obmutuit* ("eloquence fell silent," Petron. 2.7) reproduces Cicero's own *eloquentia obmutuit* (*Brut.* 22),[11] and his *sed omnia quasi eodem cibo pasta non potuerunt usque ad senectutem canescere* ("but everything ate the same food, as it were, and could not mature to a ripe old age," Petron. 2.8) is again modeled on the *Brutus* (*Brut.* 8): *cumque ipsa oratio iam nostra canesceret haberetque suam quandam maturitatem et quasi senectutem* ("when our speech had matured and had reached a certain ripeness and, as it were, an old age").[12] Agamemnon's response is also clothed in a patchwork of Ciceronian echoes. At Petron. 3.2, for example, he explicitly signals his borrowing: *nam nisi dixerint quae adulescentuli probent, ut ait Cicero, "soli in scholis relinquentur"* ("for unless they say what the youth approve of, they will be 'left alone in the schools,' as Cicero says"; ~ Cic. *Cael.* 41 *prope soli iam in scholis sunt relicti*, of Stoic philosophers),[13] and Gareth Schmeling may be right to see an allusion to Cicero in the phrase *cum insanientibus furere* ("to rave with the insane").[14] Moreover, in the poem laying out his educational curriculum, Cicero is the model for oratory, being also the only Latin author mentioned by name and representing the very summit of rhetorical instruction as the would-be orator is advised to study the mighty and menacing words of indomitable Cicero (*grandiaque indomiti Ciceronis uerba minentur*, Petron. 5.20). Both *indomitus* and *minari* might be thought to point particularly to the *Philippics* or *Catilinarians*. In sum, this brief satirical example from Petronius shows how central declamation was to Roman education and how central Cicero was to both its theory and practice.[15]

The procedural details of declamatory instruction are recorded in the standard handbooks and need not be rehearsed at length here,[16] but a brief

---

[11] Cf. the same allusion in Cornelius Severus' poem on Cicero, discussed on p. 140 below.

[12] These are the only two passages that the *TLL* (III.250.20–23 [Meister]) cites with this usage of *canescere* (i.e. used metaphorically of things to mean "to mature to a ripe old age") until a third in Ambrose (*uirg.* 3.4.16, of a *mens*).

[13] Cf. Sen. *contr.* 3 pr. 15 for this same line of reasoning.

[14] Schmeling (2011) ad loc. points to Cic. *orat.* 99 *uix satis sanus uideri* and says, "Both E. and Aga. paraphrase Cicero as a classic, but here Aga. reverses Cicero's meaning." But cf. Otto (1890) 744.1 s.v. *furere*; the phrase is proverbial.

[15] Casual allusions in other authors also bear witness to the close connection between Cicero and the *rhetores*. See e.g. Mart. 5.56.3–5 (advising Lupus on where to send his son to school): *omnes grammaticosque rhetorasque | deuites, moneo: nihil sit illi | cum libris Ciceronis aut Maronis* ("You should avoid all the *grammatici* and *rhetores*, I'm warning you! Don't let him have anything to do with the works of Cicero or Vergil.") Here Vergil and Cicero both stand as a kind of synecdoche for the main objects of study of the *grammatici* and *rhetores* respectively.

[16] Such treatments include Bonner (1977) 277–327, with details on all aspects of schoolroom declamation and further references, as well as Clark (1953) 213–250. Bonner (1949) 51–70 has discussion of declamation as handled at its highest levels.

description highlighting a few areas of particular importance will not be out of place. Roman declamations came in two flavors, the *suasoria* and the *controuersia*. *Suasoriae* were deliberative speeches, usually based on historical events, which were designed to persuade a famous figure to adopt a particular course of action. Seneca the Elder preserves two such themes involving Cicero: in *suas*. 6 the declaimer must advise Cicero whether to beg Antony's pardon, and in *suas*. 7, a very similar situation, he is to counsel Cicero on whether to burn his writings to secure Antony's forgiveness. The more advanced *controuersia*, by contrast, was supposed to be akin to a courtroom speech. The declaimer would give a speech for the prosecution or defense in some made-up case, often featuring rather outlandish particulars. We will look later at one of Seneca's *controuersiae* in which Cicero's supposed killer, Popillius, whom he had originally defended against a charge of parricide, is prosecuted "*de moribus*" for his role in the murder (*contr. 7.2*).

The *rhetor* would choose a theme and assign it to his pupils; depending on their age and experience, he might first dictate a model declamation of his own, he might give them a few useful ideas, or he might leave them entirely to their own devices.[17] The students would compose and memorize their speeches, which they then recited one after another in competition before the master. With a parade of students speaking in sequence on the same subject, there was inevitably much repetition, and thus there also grew up an arms race of pupils striving to come up with the most florid or pointed way of expressing the material under discussion. The most successful pupils were rewarded with preferment; others were relegated to the back benches of the classroom. And so instruction would proceed, day after day and year after year, until finally the *iuuenis* was deemed ready to try his voice in the forum.

Cicero as Model of Eloquence

The man who considered himself the pinnacle of Latin eloquence in his own lifetime continued to be so regarded after his death. We too have been conditioned by our classroom training and two millennia of reception to make this identification, but it was by no means a foregone conclusion that Cicero would become primarily a metonymy for eloquence, still less that he would become *the* metonymy for eloquence. As his life drew to a close, his style of speech was embroiled in a fierce controversy, and his political

---

[17] See e.g. Quint. *inst*. 2.6.

causes were faltering or lost.[18] He had led a richly varied existence as a political figure, and today we know more about him than any other person from antiquity. There would seem to be a variety of ways one could have chosen to engage with him, and yet the ancient world consistently looked to a circumscribed set of characteristics. Furthermore, he was surrounded by skilled contemporary orators whose speeches circulated and could have served as competing models. Consider the contrasting case of Julius Caesar. Caesar was a writer too, and a good one at that; he put his speeches into circulation, and they were read and admired by his coevals.[19] His writings, however, never became a staple of the imperial classroom. Caesar is thus remembered in completely different ways, as his reception was shaped by different forces.[20] It is Cicero and Cicero alone who was canonized as the patron saint of oratory and enshrined in the school curriculum. Much as Vergil drove Ennius out of circulation at about this same time, so Cicero became the authorative model for oratory and soon developed a sort of educational monopoly. (It is not just chance that we have no preserved Latin speeches between Cicero's *Philippics* and Pliny's *Panegyricus*.) Cicero's reputation as *the* orator was not inevitable: it developed out of his schoolroom canonization and all its various effects.

This classroom tradition lies at the heart of post-mortem evaluations of Cicero by those who had never known him or heard him speak. Numerous authors bear witness to Cicero's position as the *disertissimus Romuli nepotum*.[21] Indeed, whenever a writer gives Cicero only a brief mention, he seems invariably paired with some eloquence-inspired epithet. Lucan, for example, calls Cicero the *Romani maximus auctor | ... eloquii*

---

[18] Both points rightly noted by Kaster (1998) 249, who also observes how striking it is that the declaimers choose to focus almost exclusively on Cicero's death (252–253). Cicero's detractors attacked him while he was alive and were even quicker to pounce after he was killed in the proscriptions (Quint. *inst.* 12.10.12–13).

[19] See e.g. Cic. *Brut.* 252 (Atticus speaking) *de Caesare et ipse ita iudico et de hoc huius generis acerrimo existimatore saepissime audio, illum omnium fere oratorum Latine loqui eloquentissime* (cf. *Brut.* 261, where the character Cicero echoes the same praise, and 262, where Brutus claims to have read and approved some of his speeches). See similarly Quint. *inst.* 10.1.114 *C. uero Caesar si foro tantum uacasset, non alius ex nostris contra Ciceronem nominaretur.* Aper in Tacitus' *Dialogus* is more lukewarm in his praise (21.5), but he has his biases; Tacitus himself seems to have had a high opinion of Caesar's oratorical prowess (*ann.* 13.3): *dictator Caesar summis oratoribus aemulus.* See too Suet. *Iul.* 55. For modern speculations on Caesar's oratory, see Kennedy (1972) 283–292 and *ORF* 383–397; extensive discussion now in van der Blom (2016a) 146–180.

[20] This difference in reception is even more obviously true for other late Republican figures who were not great writers, like a Pompey.

[21] Cat. 49.1, whose prescient if sarcastic (?) judgment continues *quot sunt quotque fuere, Marce Tulli, | quotque post aliis erunt in annis* (49.1–2). Romans of the imperial era would have agreed completely and without irony.

(Lucan. 7.62–63). Likewise Manilius refers to Cicero as the man who won the consulship[22] by the "wealth of his mouth" (*censu Tullius oris | emeritus fasces*, 1.794–795), while Vitruvius cites him as the preeminent speaker whom later generations of orators will hark back to (9 pr. 17).[23] Even in brief fragments we find his eloquence praised; Tullius Laurea addresses him as the *Romanae uindex clarissime linguae* ("most renowned paladin of the Roman tongue," ap. Plin. *nat.* 31.8). These examples can be multiplied (e.g. Sil. Ital. 8.406–411), but they all clearly belong to the same tradition. Although imperial writers had never heard Cicero speak, they all grew up reading his speeches in the classroom and hearing him praised to the skies as the *facundiae Latiarumque litterarum parens* ("parent of eloquence and Latian letters," Plin. *nat.* 7.117). For all later Latin authors Cicero stands in the first instance as the *princeps eloquentiae*, the man whom Quintilian could describe as eloquence personified (*iam non hominis nomen sed eloquentiae, inst.* 10.1.112). Cicero's reputation was not inevitable, but once established it proved immovable.

We can surmise a fair amount about which speeches gained Cicero this reputation, all of which predictably turn out to be fixtures of the school curriculum. In Tacitus' *Dialogus* Maternus specifies them explicitly (37.6):[24]

> non, opinor, Demosthenem orationes inlustrant, quas adversus tutores suos composuit, nec Ciceronem magnum oratorem P. Quinctius defensus aut Licinius Archias faciunt: Catilina et Milo et Verres et Antonius hanc illi famam circumdederunt.

> It is not, in my opinion, the speeches which Demosthenes composed against his guardians that made his reputation, nor do Cicero's defense speeches for P. Quinctius or Licinius Archias make him a great orator: the *Catilinarians* and the *Pro Milone* and the *Verrines* and the *Philippics*, these speeches won him his fame.

The *Catilinarians*, the *Pro Milone*, the *Verrines*, and the *Philippics*: these are the speeches that won Cicero the greatest fame, and these are the ones we would have pointed to even without Tacitus' testimony.[25] The *Catilinarians* are hardly surprising, coming as they do at the summit of

---

[22] Or immortality: *caelum* rather than *fasces* is transmitted by the MSS and retained by Housman.

[23] Cf. too Colum. 1 pr. 30 for a similar sentiment. Iuu. 7.139 and 214 also use Cicero as the representative of supreme eloquence.

[24] There is an implicit comparison with Demosthenes here; on the tradition of syncrisis between Cicero and Demosthenes, see p. 93 below.

[25] Fairweather (1981) 85 well observes that these are the favorite speeches of the declaimers cited in Seneca the Elder as well; in more detail Kaster (1998) 253–254.

Cicero's political career, published by Cicero himself to be read by young orators, and remaining central to the Latin classroom even today. Nor would we look askance at the *Pro Milone*, having seen its schoolroom treatment and the praise accorded to it in chapter 1. The *Philippics* also represent another obvious high point, and they become closely linked with Cicero's death in the popular imagination. So Juvenal, for example, says that Cicero died because of his eloquence, and particularly because of his renowned and immortal second *Philippic* (10.125; see p. 99 below).

At first blush the *Verrines* might surprise the modern reader the most, but they should not. It was in these speeches that Cicero first made his reputation and dethroned Hortensius from the imaginary chair of Roman eloquence, and although they are rarely read today – especially in their entirety – in antiquity they proved quite popular. Of the thirteen Ciceronian papyri that are now known, fully five preserve parts of the *Verrines*.[26] As if that were not enough, we find allusions to them cropping up constantly in the most unexpected places. So, for example, as G. P. Goold pointed out, Manil. 5.619–630 is unmistakably a versified Cic. *Verr.* II 5.118:[27]

> patres hi quos uidetis iacebant in limine, matresque miserae pernoctabant ad ostium carceris ab extremo conspectu liberum exclusae; quae nihil aliud orabant nisi ut filiorum suorum postremum spiritum ore excipere liceret. aderat ianitor carceris, carnifex praetoris, mors terrorque sociorum et ciuium Romanorum, lictor Sextius, cui ex omni gemitu doloreque certa merces comparabatur.

> These fathers whom you look upon now were lying at the threshold, and wretched mothers were spending the night at the door of the jail denied a last look at their children; and they asked for nothing except to be allowed to receive the dying breath of their sons with their mouth. The doorman of

---

[26] M–P³ 2918 *Verr.* II 1.1–4, 7–9, 2.3, 2.12 (and *De imp. Cn. Pompei* 60–65, 68–69, 70–71; *Cael.* 26–55); M–P³ 2919 *diu. in Caec.* 33–37, 44–46 (with Greek and Latin scholia); M–P³ 2919.1 *Verr.* II 1.60–61, 62–63; M–P³ 2920 *Verr.* II 2.3–4 (1st cent. AD!); M–P³ 2920.1 *Verr.* II 5.39–40, 40–41. Of the other eight papyri, seven contain the *Catilinarians*: M–P³ 2921.001 *Cat* 1.3–4; M–P³ 2921.010 *Cat.* 1.5 (with Greek translation); M–P³ 2921.1 *Cat.* 1.6–8, 13–33; *Cat.* 2 (on this remarkable papyrus, see Roca-Puig [1977]); M–P³ 2922 *Cat.* 1.15–16, 17–19, 19–20 (with Greek translation); M–P³ 3026.2 *Cat.* 1.14–15, 27 (with Greek translation); M–P³ 2923 *Cat.* 2.14–15 (with Greek translation); M–P³ 2923.1 *Cat* 3.15–16 (with Greek translation, possibly part of the same codex as the preceding). The exceptional case is M–P³ 2924, with *Planc.* 27–28, 46–47. Most of these texts are conveniently assembled and edited in Cavenaile (1958) 70–96 (= *C.Pap.Lat.* 20–27). Sánchez-Ostiz (2013) is a useful discussion of the educational context of most of these papyri: some appear to have been used for basic Latin instruction; others for the relatively few who studied Latin speeches at an advanced level. The most recent addition to the corpus, M–P³ 3026.2, is identified and edited by Internullo (2016). On Latin learning by Greek speakers, see Dickey (2012) 4–15.

[27] Goold (1977) 350 n. a.

the jail was there, the praetor's <u>butcher</u>, death and terror for both the allies and the citizens of Rome, the lictor Sextius, <u>who</u> was provided with a <u>certain reward</u> from every instance of pain and suffering.

Cicero is describing the terrible executioner Sextius. Manilius, in turn, discusses the lot of the man born under the sign of Andromeda rising from the sea. He will be cruel and, in Goold's elegant turn, "a warden of dungeon dire" (Manil. 5.619–627):

> quisquis in Andromedae surgentis tempora ponto
> nascitur, immitis ueniet poenaeque minister   620
> <u>carceris</u> et duri custos, quo stante superbe
> prostratae iaceant miserorum in <u>limine matres</u>
> <u>pernoctesque patres cupiant extrema suorum</u>
> <u>oscula et in proprias animam transferre medullas.</u>
> <u>carnificisque uenit mortem uendentis imago</u>   625
> accensosque rogos, <u>cui</u> stricta saepe securi
> <u>supplicium uectigal erit.</u>

Whoever is born when Andromeda rises from the sea will be cruel and a dispenser of punishment and a guard <u>of the harsh jail</u>, and while he stands by arrogantly, <u>mothers of the wretched prisoners will</u> lie prostrate on the <u>threshold and fathers will stay awake through the night longing for the last kiss from their sons and to transfer their sons' dying breath into their own marrow. He will be the image of the butcher selling death</u> and the inflamed funeral pyre, <u>for whom punishment brings a payment</u> with his ax often bared.

It can of course be fraught with fallacy to try to peer inside the artist's workshop and watch him ply his trade, but it is hard not to imagine Manilius, when confronted with the need to describe a brutal executioner, thinking back to his school days and this most famous example. Just how well known was this particular scene in the Roman classroom? No paragraph from the *Verrines* is cited more often by Quintilian, and taken together with the sections immediately preceding and following it, it comprises one of the most cited Ciceronian passages in all of the *Institutio oratoria*.[28] It is used as an example of various rhetorical figures, of prose rhythm, of periodic construction, and of argumentative

---

[28] Quintilian cites our paragraph (5.118) at *inst.* 4.2.106, 8.4.27, 9.4.71, 9.4.108, 9.4.124, 11.1.40. He also cites *Verr.* II 5.117 at *inst.* 6.1.54, 8.4.19, 9.2.51, 9.4.70, and *Verr.* II 5.119 at *inst.* 9.3.34. The only other passage from the *Verrines* that receives this much attention is *Verr.* II 5.162 (*ciuis Romanus sum*), which is cited at *inst.* 4.2.113, 6.1.54, 9.4.102, 11.1.40, and 11.3.90. Elsewhere only Cic. *Phil.* 2.62–64 and Cic. *Lig.* 1–3 receive comparable treatment (the former cited 15 times, the latter 13 [16 if you include three mentions of *Lig.* 4]).

technique. There can thus be little doubt that Manilius would have read it in school. Furthermore, under the *rhetor*'s careful supervision he doubtless once paraphrased prose into poetry and vice versa, and now perhaps he has effortlessly slipped back into that declamatory mode.[29] Even if this scenario is thought too fanciful, it is nevertheless clear that Manilius had intimate knowledge of the *Verrines*, and that he was hardly alone. Indeed, even the graffiti of Pompeii may show knowledge of this famous speech.[30]

To turn now to declamatory rhetoric itself, Seneca the Elder furnishes a convenient starting point for evaluating how Cicero's eloquence was appraised in declamation. In Seneca's seventh *Suasoria*, for example, Cicero supposedly considers an offer from Antony to spare his life – on the condition that he burn his writings. Seneca knew of no declaimer who advised Cicero to consign his writings to the flames; "everyone was worried about Cicero's books, no one about the man himself" (*omnes pro libris Ciceronis solliciti fuerunt, nemo pro ipso, suas.* 7.10). This is clear evidence that Cicero, even shortly after his death, becomes "textualized" and equated with his writings.[31] After he dies his body is transmogrified into a written *corpus*, which itself becomes immortal. As living memory of the man began to fade, this static and canonical body of writing became people's primary connection to Cicero himself. Note that in these declamations Cicero was not only identified more with his writings than with his person, but indeed more valued for his writings than for anything else that he had done or could do in a hypothetical future. (It is not intuitively obvious that this should be so: I venture to say that Lincoln's supporters after his assassination would gladly have traded his writings in exchange for his continued life and leadership.) The declaimers' advice mostly rings variations on a theme: so Cestius Pius says that as long as his monuments of eloquence were intact, Cicero could not die (*saluis eloquentiae monumentis non posse Ciceronem mori, suas.* 7.2), and

---

[29] See e.g. Cic. *de orat.* 1.154 for the traditional exercise of versifying prose and prosifying verse; further Quint. *inst.* 10.5.4–11.

[30] For the fascinating Pompeiian instance of Verrine imitation, or rather parody, see Gigante (1979) 160–161 and Cugusi (1985) 27–28 (with further bibliography); on the literary qualities of the graffito see Millnor (2014) 122–124. The graffito runs (*CIL* iv.1261, orthography *sic*): *futebatur, inquam, futuebatur, ciuium Romanorum atractis pedibus cunus, inqua nule aliae ueces erant nisissei dulcisime et pissimae.* If we want to see a Ciceronian echo we must emend *ueces* to *uoces* (not, e.g., *uices*), but neither text nor interpretation is secure. The possible source is the famous *Verr.* ii 5.162: *caedebatur uirgis in medio foro Messanae ciuis Romanus, iudices, cum interea nullus gemitus, nulla uox alia illius miseri inter dolorem crepitumque plagarum audiebatur nisi haec, "ciuis Romanus sum."*

[31] On this process, "textualization," cf. the discussion of Cicero's canonization in Kaster (1998) and the criticisms of Wilson (2008) 322 n. 32.

this motif of immortality through eloquence is repeated over and over again.[32]

Cicero's tongue, itself a metonymy for his eloquence, is indeed singled out as uniquely valuable. Cestius Pius, for example, riffs and invents a new but parallel contrafactual: if Antony wanted to gouge out Cicero's eyes, he says, or to cripple his feet, or to commit any other such barbarous mutilation, those just might be tolerable, but addressing Cicero he declares with certainty, "You would have made an exception for your tongue" (*excepisses tamen linguam, suas. 7.3*).[33] Cicero's eloquence is not only his singular virtue, it becomes almost his *single* virtue, so far does it outstrip any others. His physical tongue is further associated with the metaphorical Latin tongue itself, for both Sextilius Ena and Cornelius Severus write hexameters in which they mourn Cicero's passing and the impoverishment of the Latin language in the same breath: *deflendus Cicero est Latiaeque silentia linguae* (*suas.* 6.27) and *conticuit Latiae tristis facundia linguae* (*suas.* 6.26). Cicero's eloquence is thus not his alone; he is indeed the very voice of the Roman people (*publica uox, suas.* 6.26).[34]

These judgments are echoed time and again by later writers, often in quite similar terms. We have already had occasion to quote Quintilian's judgment on Cicero's oratorical prowess,[35] but his is only one of many. Velleius Paterculus, for example, also calls Cicero the *publica uox* in a most declamatory passage to which I will return later (*abscisa ... scelere Antonii uox publica est*, 2.66).[36] This repeated insistence on Cicero's status as the *publica uox*, while perhaps at first blush unremarkable today, must have been a striking statement in the early Empire. On the one hand it means simply that Cicero has become *the* Roman voice, his eloquence canonized

---

[32] E.g. Publius Asprenas (*suas.* 7.4): <si> *scripta combusseris, Antonius paucos annos tibi promittit; at, si non combusseris,* [quam] *populus Romanus omnes*; Argentarius (*suas.* 7.7): *mortem tibi remittit ut id pereat quod in te solum immortale est ... sine durare post te ingenium tuum*; Arellius Fuscus Senior (*suas.* 7.8): *quoad humanum genus incolumne manserit, quamdiu suus literris honor, suum eloquentiae pretium erit, quamdiu rei publicae nostrae aut fortuna steterit aut memoria durauerit, admirabile posteris uigebit ingenium* <tuum>, *et uno proscriptus saeculo proscribes Antonium omnibus*. Later authors will talk about Cicero in the same way.

[33] If the last word of Cicero's infamous *cedant arma togae, concedat laurea linguae* was originally *laudi*, this would be a further interesting case of the centrality of Cicero's tongue to his reception, this time in an early parody. Cf. ch. 3 n. 67.

[34] Silius Italicus manages to mention both Cicero's tongue and his voice at the same time (Sil. Ital. 8. 409–410): *implebit terras uoce et furialia bella* | *fulmine compescet linguae*. He was a great admirer of Cicero, even owning one of Cicero's former estates (Mart. 11.48, where note Cicero and Vergil are again joined).

[35] See ch. 1 p. 25.

[36] See p. 118 below. For another passage ripped straight from the declaimers' playbook that praises Cicero's eloquence, see Plin. *nat.* 7.116–117, which is discussed on p. 127 below.

and put up on an unreachable pedestal.[37] But the phrase *uox publica*, "voice of the people," must have had another resonance. The mature Cicero was anything but the spokesman for the *populares*, the politicians advocating for the Roman people, instead inclined to represent himself as a staunch champion of the *optimates*, the aristocratic defenders of senatorial prerogative.[38] He was a conservative politician with a convert's zeal, having raised himself up to the consulship from a family that could boast no senators among its ancestors, and at least from his consulship on he could not easily have been described as the voice of the people. And yet scholars have been untroubled by such descriptions, a testimony to the success of the imperial rebranding campaign.

In general, when a Roman author talked about the voice of the people, he meant not "one man who speaks for the people," but rather "the people speaking with one voice." Cicero, for example, can say that he "was elected consul by the united voice of the entire Roman people" (*me . . . una uox uniuersi populi Romani consulem declarauit, leg. agr.* 2.4).[39] The conceit had always had political overtones, since the people usually come together in one voice for some political end; for Cicero, these overtones are often positive, an example of the people's unity in favor of some beneficial choice (such as Cicero himself as consul).[40] By Tacitus' day, however, the dark side was also exposed to view: when the writings of various dissidents were burned in the forum by Domitian's watchdogs, Tacitus writes: "they doubtless believed that the voice of the Roman people was being destroyed in that fire" (*scilicet illo igne uocem populi Romani . . . aboleri arbitrabantur, Agr.* 2.2). Commentators often refer this to the extinction of literature under Domitian,[41] which doubtless is one aspect of what Tacitus is talking about, but the much more sinister point is that the people's political power was suppressed.

Nevertheless, *uox* can be used of a single person as well. Cicero himself already had begun talking about his third-person voice by the time of the

[37] Cf. the description of a Ciceronian quotation as *sacra illa uox tua* (*suas.* 7.13).
[38] See Achard (1981) for copious detail. The bibliography on *populares* and *optimates* is immense and the issues controversial; for a guide to the literature, see Robb (2010) 15–33; also Arena (2012) 81–168 (on the concept of *libertas* in the *populares* and optimate traditions).
[39] *Vox* is quite often paired with *una* in this usage; see *OLD* s.v. *uox* 2a.
[40] Even Horace's rich man who despises the "voice of the people" implicitly highlights the people's right judgment, for Horace wants us to understand that the people have it right, while it is the Scrooge counting his coins at home who has gone astray: *ut quidam memoratur Athenis | sordidus ac diues, populi contemnere uoces | sic solitus: "populus me sibilat, at mihi plaudo | ipse domi, simul ac nummos contemplor in arca"* (*serm.* 1.1.64–67).
[41] E.g. Ogilvie and Richmond (1967) ad loc.: "Tacitus implies that creative originality died under Domitian"; cf. less narrowly Woodman (2014) ad loc.

Catilinarian speeches, referring to *mea uox, quae debet esse in re publica
princeps* ("my voice, which ought to be the foremost in the state," *Cat.*
4.19),[42] and later writers have perhaps picked up on this synecdoche,
especially as Cicero came to be valued as an orator above all. More apposite
for our purposes, Lucan describes Cicero's friend Curio, who had been
tribune of the plebs, as the one-time "voice of the people" and someone
who had "dared to defend liberty and to bring down the armed chiefs to
the level of the crowd" (<u>uox</u> *quondam* <u>populi</u> *libertatemque tueri* | *ausus et
armatos plebi miscere potentes*, 1.270–271) – before he sold his oratorical
talents for Caesar's gold. Here one man has become the *uox populi*, and he
is so described because he was a defender of freedom. This is, however,
a singularly appropriate way to describe a rhetorically gifted tribune of the
plebs; for the self-proclaimed leader of the *optimates*, it was not. Thus it
should be a surprising and unexpected move when Lucan goes on to make
Cicero a spokesman for all the Roman people, writing: "Cicero, the greatest source of Roman eloquence, spoke with <u>everyone's voice</u>" (*cunctorum
<u>uoces</u> Romani maximus auctor* | *Tullius eloquii . . . pertulit*, 7.62–65).[43]

   After his consulship Cicero unabashedly presented himself as an optimate politician. In a famous and programmatic digression in the *Pro Sestio*,
for example, he distinguishes between *optimates* and *populares* thus (*Sest.*
96; cf. *off.* 1.85):[44]

> duo genera semper in hac ciuitate fuerunt eorum qui uersari in re publica
> atque in ea se excellentius gerere studuerunt; quibus ex generibus alteri se
> populares, alteri optimates et haberi et esse uoluerunt. qui ea quae faciebant
> quaeque dicebant multitudini iucunda uolebant esse, populares, qui autem ita
> se gerebant ut sua consilia optimo cuique probarent, optimates habebantur.

> There have always been two kinds of people in this city who were eager to be
> involved with the commonwealth and to achieve eminence in it; of those
> two groups one wanted both to be and to be considered *populares*, the other
> *optimates*. Those who wanted what they said and did to be pleasing to the
> masses were considered *populares*; those, on the other hand, who behaved in
> such a way that their plans would be approved by the best people were
> considered *optimates*.

---

[42] Cf. *ad Q. fr.* 1.3.2 *nunc commisi ut . . . mea uox in domesticis periculis potissimum occideret, quae saepe
    alienissimis praesidio fuisset* and *off.* 3.121 *his uoluminibus ad te profecta uox est mea.*

[43] Described by Dahlmann (1975) 104 n. 150 as a paraphrase of the content of Cornelius Severus. Ahl
    (1976) 161–163 sees Cicero as the symbol of or stand-in for the Senate in this speech, which is further
    explored in Narducci (2003b) and Rolim de Moura (2010) 74–78. Cicero is also present elsewhere in
    Lucan, e.g. Lucan's echo of *Mil.* 1 (Lucan. 1.319–323), or Cato's eulogy of Pompey (*praetulit arma
    togae, sed pacem armatus amauit*, Lucan. 9.199).

[44] On this digression, see Kaster (2006) ad loc. and 31–37; Robb (2010) 55–64.

As Robin Seager points out, there is no room for doubt in this definition about which group the good citizen should belong to.[45] The standard distinction is made again and again in Cicero's writings; and often the very terms of the division – *boni* vs. *populares* – make the underlying values clear. Cicero tells Atticus, for example, that the good opinion of the *boni* and the *populares* alike bars him from defending his consular colleague Antonius (*res eius modi est ut ego nec per bonorum nec per popularem existimationem honeste possim hominem defendere*, *Att.* 1.12.1). Likewise when praising the tribunate of Marcus Caelius he can say: *talis tribunus plebis fuit, ut nemo contra ciuium perditorum popularem turbulentamque dementiam a senatu et a bonorum causa steterit constantius* ("he was such a tribune of the plebs that no one has ever stood more staunchly on the side of the Senate and the *boni* against the seditious and *popularis* madness of morally bankrupt citizens," *Brut.* 273). The contrast here between the "cause of the *boni*" and the "seditious and *popularis* madness of morally bankrupt citizens" is especially sharp. Elsewhere too the *populares* are described as *improbi* and *seditiosi* (*rep.* 4.11, Scipio speaking; they are also concerned with land redistribution and the forgiveness of debts at e.g. *off.* 2.78). In general, in the *De republica* and the *De legibus* Cicero is keen to set up a society governed by the "best people," with only the necessary concessions made to the masses. So, for example, he would allow the people to vote, but only on the condition that they show their ballots to the *optimates* (*optimatibus nota, plebi libera sunto* [sc. *suffragia*], *leg.* 3.39).[46] This appears to be Cicero's standard attitude toward the *populares*, and he assuredly counted himself an optimate.

And yet Cicero is a clever man, and he can adapt his definitions of these terms to suit the rhetorical exigencies of the case at hand. In the *Pro Sestio*, for example, he goes on to expand the definition of *optimates* to include everyone who is not a criminal or intrinsically evil or insane, in sum everyone who seeks *otium cum dignitate* (*Sest.* 97–98). In such a definition the typical distinctions of social class are thrown out the window: we can all be *optimates*, Cicero claims. Even more interestingly, on rare occasions he can redefine *popularis* to include himself as well. So in his first speech as consul, the *De lege agraria*, while opposing a "*popularis*" land bill he neatly maneuvers to present himself as the real *popularis*. He was elected consul by the people, after all, and he promises *pax, libertas,* and *otium*:

[45] Seager (1972) 328.
[46] On these notions in Cicero's political philosophy, see Zetzel (2013) 187–193.

quid enim est tam populare quam pax? . . . quid tam populare quam
libertas? . . . quid tam populare quam otium? . . . quare qui possum non
esse popularis, cum uideam haec omnia, Quirites, pacem externam, libertatem propriam generis ac nominis uestri, otium domesticum, denique
omnia quae uobis cara atque ampla sunt in fidem et quodam modo in
patrocinium mei consulatus esse conlata? (leg. agr. 2.9)[47]

What is so *popularis* as peace? . . . What is so *popularis* as liberty? . . . What is
so *popularis* as repose? . . . And so how can I not be *popularis* myself, citizens,
since I see that all these things – peace abroad, liberty appropriate to your
ancestral name, domestic tranquillity, in sum everything which is near and
dear to you – were entrusted to me and, so to speak, to the protection of my
consulship?

Cicero knows full well that he is playing fast and loose with definitions
here, and that this is a thoroughly tendentious – and frankly not very
believable – way for him to characterize himself. He will frequently use this
technique to deride his *popularis* opponents, claiming that they cannot
really be *populares*, since they do not actually act in the best interests of the
people,[48] but it is only on a few occasions that he has the cheek to claim to
be a *popularis* politician himself.[49]

When Cicero is described as the *publica uox*, then, there are at least
two meanings in play. In the first instance Cicero has become, simply
put, "the" Roman voice, the highest exemplar of eloquence. But on
another level we see a fundamentally partial appraisal of his role in late
Republican politics, perhaps adopting Cicero's own occasional, rhetorically expedient, and highly tendentious characterization of himself
while ignoring all of its problematic elements. Rather than presenting
a nuanced picture of Cicero's complex engagement with the varying
political currents of the day, these early imperial writers saw him, like
Curio, as a noble paladin of the people, arrayed in shining armor against
the dastardly tyrant Mark Antony. Cicero is not generally used a symbol
of Republican resistance;[50] his eloquence has rather been reappropriated
to champion a redefined cause of popular freedom, namely freedom
from Mark Antony. This simplified rhetoric neatly aligned with the

---

[47] Cf. *leg. agr.* 2.102 *ex quo intellegi, Quirites, potest nihil esse tam populare quam id quod ego uobis in
hunc annum consul popularis adfero, pacem, tranquillitatem, otium.* On Cicero's use of "populist
speech for anti-'popular' ends" in this oration, see esp. Morstein-Marx (2004) 194–202 and on
Cicero's adoption of the *popularis* stance 230–240. On *leg. agr.* 2 see also Vasaly (1993) 218–243.

[48] Cf. Seager (1972) 333–336.

[49] Also at *Phil.* 7.4, equally tendentiously: *me quidem semper, uti scitis, aduersarium multitudinis
temeritati haec fecit praeclarissima causa popularem.*

[50] Noted by Wirszubski (1950) 128–129; see too Gowing (2005) 110 and (2013) 246.

interests of Octavian and his successors, as I will discuss in the following chapter.

Cicero's eloquence, particularly as displayed in opposition to Antony in the *Philippics*, is time and again alleged to have led directly to his doom: this is, remember, the very premise of the declamation about whether Cicero should burn his writings in return for his life. An epigram of Martial sums it all up, with Cicero's eloquence intertwining with his death (5.69):[51]

> Antoni Phario nil obiecture Pothino
>   et leuius tabula quam Cicerone nocens:
> quid gladium demens Romana stringis in ora?
>   hoc admisisset nec Catilina nefas.
> impius infando miles corrumpitur auro,   5
>   et tantis opibus uox tacet una tibi.
> quid prosunt sacrae pretiosa silentia linguae?
>   incipient omnes pro Cicerone loqui.

> Antony, you've got no room to criticize Pharian Pothinus [i.e., the orchestrator of Pompey's murder], and you have done more harm by killing Cicero than by (the rest of) your proscription list (*tabula*). Why, you madman, do you draw sword against the voice of Rome (*Romana . . . ora*)? Not even Catiline would have committed this foul crime. A wicked soldier (*impius . . . miles*) is bribed by accursed gold, and at so great a price you buy the silence of a single voice (*uox . . . una*). How do you benefit from this costly silence of the sacred tongue (*sacrae silentia linguae*)? Everyone will begin to speak on behalf of Cicero (*pro Cicerone*).

Even the smallest details, like the word *tabula*, repeat arguments and motifs found in the declaimers.[52] Antony is exclusively responsible for the deed, a firm and fixed declamatory notion, as will become clear in the next chapter; indeed, just as we will see in Velleius Paterculus, Antony himself is rhetorically addressed. Martial makes this madman "draw his sword against the voice of Rome" (*Romana . . . ora*, a variant on the *publica uox* theme), a deed so heinous that not even Cicero's former arch-enemy, the conspirator Catiline, would have countenanced it. Martial's "impious soldier" is the infamous Popillius, a figment of declamatory imagination

---

[51] We will return to this intertwining in detail in the next chapter. Cf. e.g. Iuu. 10.118 *eloquio sed uterque perit orator* (of Cicero and Demosthenes; discussed on p. 99 below). On Cicero in Martial, see Mindt (2013) 31–69, with discussion of this poem at 37–41.

[52] Sen. *suas.* 6.3, Porcius Latro speaking: *unius tabellae* [*iniusta bella* codd.] *albo Pharsalica ac Mundensis Mutinensisque ruina uincitur, consularia capita auro rependuntur. Tabula* is the technical term for a proscription list (*OLD* s.v. 4), while Latro's diminutive *tabella* seems to add poignancy to the comparison: "a single tiny tablet" surpasses enormous military catastrophes.

whom I will discuss in detail in the next chapter. In line 6 we return to Cicero as *uox*, and the *silentia linguae* of 7 allusively echoes Sextilius Ena's line quoted above (p. 84). In the end, however, just as in the declaimers, Cicero is assured of immortality: once he was the *uox publica* who spoke on behalf of the people, but now it is the people who will speak for him, as if the people themselves have become an advocate and give a defense speech *pro Cicerone*. Indeed, it is precisely Cicero's own skill in speaking that will cause future generations to speak of him! From first to last, Antony stands accused not of murdering a great man, but of silencing a great voice. Here the identification between Cicero's writings and his person, begun in the declamatory classroom, has become total.[53]

Cicero and the Decline of Eloquence

So much for Cicero's rhetorical reputation and its foundation. If he represents the peak of oratory, it is unavoidable that after him must come a decline. Nevertheless, it would seem that there is more to this decline than mere mathematical inevitability: many early imperial writers seem to feel a sort of general oratorical malaise in the air. No new Latin stylist proved able to rival Cicero's achievements, and as a result the collective gaze remained firmly fixed on a bygone orator from a bygone

---

[53] With this poem should also be compared Mart. 3.66:

> Par scelus admisit Phariis Antonius armis:
>   abscidit uoltus ensis uterque sacros.
> illud, laurigeros ageres cum laeta triumphos,
>   hoc tibi, Roma, caput, cum loquereris, erat.
> Antoni tamen est peior, quam causa Pothini:
>   hic facinus domino praestitit, ille sibi.

Pierini (2003) 44–47 has some discussion of both of Martial's epigrams on Cicero's death; more in Mindt (2013) 36–42. This image continues beyond our period and into late antiquity. A ninth-century manuscript preserves twelve *hexasticha de titulo Ciceronis* (*Anth. Lat.* 603–614 Riese), where we find poems like the following (603, by one Euphorbius):

> Hic iacet Arpinas manibus tumulatus amici,
>   qui fuit orator summus et eximius,
> quem nece crudeli mactauit ciuis et hostis.
>   nil agis, Antoni: scripta diserta manent.
> uulnere nempe uno Ciceronem conficis, at te
>   Tullius aeternis uulneribus lacerat.

We will meet with all of these themes and indeed some of these very words again (cf. e.g. Vell. 2.66 *nihil tamen egisti, M. Antoni*, discussed p. 122 below). Friedrich (2002) 201–227 offers an introduction to and detailed commentary on this cycle of poems from the *Anthologia*.

era. The epigoni labored under a sense of belated inferiority, and they were obsessed with their relationship to Cicero and the Golden Age of the past. I will treat this theme more comprehensively in the light of Tacitus' *Dialogus* in chapter 6, but we should advert to its importance straightaway and at least glance at it. This message of decline was repeatedly and insistently hammered into students' heads by their conservative teachers; this was how their taste and literary judgment was formed at its earliest stage. An indoctrination into a declinist narrative of oratory with Cicero at its quondam peak was a central part of Roman education.

Seneca the Elder states the case particularly plainly (*contr.* 1 pr. 6–7):

> deinde ut possitis aestimare in quantum cotidie ingenia decrescant et nescio qua iniquitate naturae eloquentia se retro tulerit: quidquid Romana facundia habet quod insolenti Graeciae aut opponat aut praeferat circa Ciceronem effloruit; omnia ingenia quae lucem studiis nostris attulerunt tunc nata sunt. in deterius deinde cotidie data res est.

> Then, so that you can judge how much talent declines daily and by what injustice of nature eloquence has retreated: whatever the eloquence of Rome has to set opposite arrogant Greece or even to best, it flourished in Cicero's day; all the talents which have brought light to our studies were born at that time. Since then matters have grown worse by the day.

In Cicero's day Roman oratory could rival even the Greeks; since that time it has been all downhill. Seneca says this very much in his role as notional schoolmaster, addressing the dedicatees of the work, his sons. This is the sort of thing that schoolboys would have been bombarded with by their prescriptive and traditionally minded teachers. Predictably, such rhetoric had an effect. Velleius Paterculus, for example, passes the same judgment, writing that "oratory and forensic activity and the perfect glory of prose eloquence ... so completely burst forth under Cicero, the leader in the field, that before him you could enjoy only a very few orators and truly admire no one, unless he was one of Cicero's contemporaries" (*oratio ac uis forensis perfectumque prosae eloquentiae decus ... ita uniuersa sub principe operis sui erupit Tullio ut delectari ante eum paucissimis, mirari uero neminem possis, nisi aut ab illo uisum aut qui illum uiderit*, 1.17.3). Such was Cicero's perfection that you could scarcely be impressed by his predecessors or successors; this is Quintilian's verdict too (*inst.* 10.1.113), and it represents the *communis opinio* of the schoolmen. It is hardly surprising to find Seneca the Elder's son echoing the very thought of Velleius, that oratory "burst forth" under Cicero (*Cicero quoque noster, a quo Romana eloquentia exiluit*, Sen. *epist.* 40.11). We have already seen Petronius' discussion of the decline of oratory from Cicero's day and observed that rather than deny it or argue against it, the *rhetor* Agamemnon simply seeks to place the blame on someone else.[54] There is just no comparing the debased oratory of the present day, imperial writers claim, with the glory and grandeur that was Cicero.

The Elder Seneca himself considers three possible causes for the decline: the "luxury of the age," the loss of prestige of oratory and consequent transfer of energy to "sordid matters that bring fame and profit," or the dark hand of Fate (*contr.* 1 pr. 7). As Schmeling aptly puts it, "in other words, he has no idea why oratory has declined."[55] This is surely the right assessment of Seneca's contentions; after all, old men, Romans not least, have been lamenting the downfall of society because of decadent luxury since time immemorial, or at least since Cato the Elder.[56] Seneca goes on in the same crotchety vein: today's youth are lazy and shiftless; given over to sex and vice; effeminate and weak. It is easy to hear his voice even today, but it cannot be said to carry much conviction.[57]

A better analysis of the decline was perhaps provided by Quintilian in his lost *De causis corruptae eloquentiae*, and certainly we can see a much more sophisticated engagement by Tacitus in his *Dialogus de oratoribus*. These will be treated in greater detail in chapter 6, but for now I will simply again observe that this profound conservatism ensured a continuing retrospective focus on Cicero. There is a persistent failure to realize that times change and language changes with them, and so contemporary speech is always regarded as inadequate and inferior. When faced with such a barrage of adverse criticism, the budding orator could either work harder to emulate the master (Quintilian's view and to a degree that of his pupil Pliny) or punt and adopt a wholly different style, as did Seneca the Younger and, eventually, Tacitus. But in any event, we can note that the narrative of decline and the canonization of Cicero are in some sense simply two sides of the same coin, not only mutually consistent but in fact mutually reinforcing.

---

[54] See p. 76 above. One cannot help but wonder whether it was safer to talk about decline of oratory than decline of the political system – that is to say, perhaps a discussion of the decline of oratory can serve as a proxy for the discussion of a far more sensitive issue. Tacitus will address this topic directly in the *Dialogus*; see ch. 6.

[55] Schmeling (2011) 2. Similarly Kaster (1998) 259–260.

[56] Cf. e.g. Sen. *benef.* 1.10.1 *hoc maiores nostri questi sunt, hoc nos querimur, hoc posteri nostri querentur, euersos mores, regnare nequitiam, in deterius res humanas et omne nefas labi.*

[57] Cf. too the younger Seneca, *epist.* 114.1–3 on how style is a reflection of character, and the character of the times is debased. Contrast the sharply divergent opinion of Norden (1958) 12: "Der Stil war im Altertum nicht der Mensch selbst, sondern ein Gewand, das er nach Belieben wechseln konnte."

The Ancient Syncrisis: Cicero and Demosthenes

If no Roman writer could compete with Cicero, was there anyone who could? There was perhaps a Greek – Demosthenes. Already in his own lifetime Cicero began to set himself up as the Roman Demosthenes, most explicitly of course with the *Philippics*,[58] but also elsewhere, particularly in the rhetorical works composed in 46 BC.[59] This comparison continued after his death, particularly as the two came to be seen not only as the principal exponents of Greek and Roman oratory,[60] but also as political leaders with many other overlapping points of contact. As Plutarch says (*Dem.* 3.2–3):

Δημοσθένει γὰρ Κικέρωνα τὸν αὐτὸν ἔοικε πλάττων ἐξ ἀρχῆς ὁ δαίμων πολλὰς μὲν εἰς τὴν φύσιν ἐμβαλεῖν αὐτοῦ τῶν ὁμοιοτήτων, ὥσπερ τὸ φιλότιμον καὶ φιλελεύθερον ἐν τῇ πολιτείᾳ, πρὸς δὲ κινδύνους καὶ πολέμους ἄτολμον, πολλὰ δ' ἀναμεῖξαι καὶ τῶν τυχηρῶν. δύο γὰρ ἑτέρους οὐκ ἂν εὑρεθῆναι δοκῶ ῥήτορας ἐκ μὲν ἀδόξων καὶ μικρῶν ἰσχυροὺς καὶ μεγάλους γενομένους, προσκρούσαντας δὲ βασιλεῦσι καὶ τυράννοις, θυγατέρας δ' ἀποβαλόντας, ἐκπεσόντας δὲ τῶν πατρίδων, κατελθόντας δὲ μετὰ τιμῆς, ἀποδράντας δ' αὖθις καὶ ληφθέντας ὑπὸ τῶν πολεμίων, ἅμα δὲ παυσαμένῃ τῇ τῶν πολιτῶν ἐλευθερίᾳ τὸν βίον συγκαταστρέψαντας· ὥστ' εἰ γένοιτο τῇ φύσει καὶ τῇ τύχῃ καθάπερ τεχνίταις ἅμιλλα, χαλεπῶς ἂν διακριθῆναι, πότερον αὕτη τοῖς τρόποις ἢ τοῖς πράγμασιν ἐκείνη τοὺς ἄνδρας ὁμοιοτέρους ἀπείργασται.

For it seems that God originally created Cicero in the same fashion as Demosthenes and imparted to his nature many similarities, such as the

---

[58] See *Brut. Cic. ad Brut.* 3.4: *legi orationes duas tuas, quarum altera Kal. Ian. usus es, altera de litteris meis, quae habita est abs te contra Calenum. non scilicet hoc exspectas, dum eas laudem. nescio animi an ingeni tui maior in his libellis laus contineatur. iam concedo ut uel Philippici uocentur, quod tu quadam epistula iocans scripsisti.* Cf. *Cic. ad Brut.* 4.2 *haec ad te oratio perferetur, quoniam te uideo delectari Philippicis nostris.* On the title, see Manuwald (2007) 47–54.

[59] This identification began in earnest when Cicero was assailed by "Atticist" partisans in the stylistic kerfuffle of the mid 40s BC. Cicero compares himself explicitly with Demosthenes for the first time, for example, at *orat.* 105: *uides profecto illum* [= Demosthenen] *multa perficere, nos multa conari, illum posse, nos uelle quocumque modo causa postulet dicere*, and he claims that Demosthenes was the master of all three registers of speech, whereas Lysias could wield only the plain style (and so Demosthenes was the more desirable model). Wooten (1977) sketches Cicero's relationship with Demosthenes, and Wooten (1997) revisits some of the same questions from a different perspective; Leeman (1963) 136–167 discusses "Cicero and the Atticists" and provides an overview of the whole ancient debate between Attic and Asiatic oratory. Bishop (2016) suggests that in the *Brutus* and the *Orator* Cicero was not only setting himself stylistically as the Roman Demosthenes, but also in parallel to Demosthenes' opposition of the tyrant Philip as himself an opponent of Caesar. Cicero may already have harbored Demosthenic ambitions in 60 BC when publishing his consular orations; see *Att.* 2.1.3.

[60] See e.g. Quintilian on Demosthenes (*inst.* 10.1.76): *quorum* (i.e. *oratorum Graecorum*) *longe princeps Demosthenes ac paene lex orandi fuit: tanta uis in eo, tam densa omnia, ita quibusdam neruis intenta sunt, tam nihil otiosum, is dicendi modus, ut nec quod desit in eo nec quod redundet inuenias.*

desire for glory and a love of freedom in the state and a lack of courage in danger and war, and he mixed in together many similarities of fortune as well. For I don't think two other orators could be found who had risen from such small and humble beginnings to become so great and powerful, who had come into conflict with kings and tyrants, who had lost their daughters, been exiled from their fatherlands and then honorably recalled, who ran away from their enemies but were captured by them, and who brought their lives to an end as soon as the people lost their freedom. Thus if there should be a contest between nature and fortune, as there is among craftsmen, it would be hard to judge whether the one made the men more similar in their characters or the other in their actions.

For all the manifold similarities in life and circumstances that Plutarch mentions, he neglects the first comparison that any Latin-speaking Roman would make, that of speaking prowess. He indeed specifically disclaims this province, saying that he will compare his subjects' actions and political careers and characters, but he will not judge their speeches or their oratorical powers (*Dem.* 3.1). So too we can observe that Plutarch provides a full biography of Cicero and deals with his whole life, much different from the limited engagement that we see from the Romans. While some of these preferences will be due simply to the fact that Plutarch was a native speaker of Greek, to whom Latin stylistic concerns would have literally been foreign,[61] as well as to the fact that he was writing a biography, some perhaps may be due to the greater freedom felt by a Greek philosopher from Chaeronea as compared to a native born Roman citizen with political ambitions. Or they may simply be attributable to Plutarch's greater ability to detach himself from the dominant declamatory tradition; his own rhetorical education obviously did not feature Ciceronian Latin declamations, and so he was less subject to their immediate influence.[62]

Cicero and Demosthenes were read side by side in the Roman rhetorical classroom; Quintilian recommended that schoolteachers follow advice given as early as Livy, "to read Demosthenes and Cicero, and then others

---

[61] Plutarch *does* know Latin, as careful *Quellenforschung* would reveal even if he had not told us himself. By his own free admission, however, he does not have much of a sense for Latin stylistics, being an ὀψιμαθής: "to perceive the beauty and speed of the Latin style and its figures of speech and rhythms and all the other things which adorn a language, well, I think all of those things lovely and not devoid of pleasure, but practice and training in them isn't easy, and they are the province of those people who have more time and whose age still allows scope for such pursuits" (κάλλους δὲ Ῥωμαϊκῆς ἀπαγγελίας καὶ τάχους αἰσθάνεσθαι καὶ μεταφορᾶς ὀνομάτων καὶ ἁρμονίας καὶ τῶν ἄλλων, οἷς ὁ λόγος ἀγάλλεται, χαρίεν μὲν ἡγούμεθα καὶ οὐκ ἀτερπές· ἡ δὲ πρὸς τοῦτο μελέτη καὶ ἄσκησις οὐκ εὐχερής, ἀλλ' οἷστισι πλείων τε σχολὴ καὶ τὰ τῆς ὥρας ἔτι [πρὸς] τὰς τοιαύτας ἐπιχωρεῖ φιλοτιμίας, Plut. *Dem.* 2.4). See Pelling (2011a) 43–44 with n. 103 and Rochette (1997) 239–241 with n. 116 for discussion of Plutarch's Latin with further references.

[62] With Plutarch's comparison here cf. App. *BC* 2.15, quoted in ch. 4 n. 61.

as they are most like Demosthenes and Cicero" (*legendos Demosthenen atque Ciceronem, tum ita ut quisque esset Demostheni et Ciceroni simillimus, inst.* 10.1.39).[63] This pairing must have facilitated the inevitable comparisons, and debating the virtues and vices of the two orators inevitably became a standard school exercise.[64] Quintilian again provides the best example in short compass, but his is far from the only one (*inst.* 10.1.105–108):

> nam Ciceronem cuicumque eorum fortiter opposuerim. nec ignoro quantam mihi concitem pugnam, cum praesertim non id sit propositi, ut eum Demostheni comparem hoc tempore: neque enim attinet, cum Demosthenen in primis legendum uel ediscendum potius putem. quorum ego uirtutes plerasque arbitror similes, consilium, ordinem, diuidendi praeparandi probandi rationem, omnia denique quae sunt inuentionis. in eloquendo est aliqua diuersitas: densior ille, hic copiosior, ille concludit adstrictius, hic latius, pugnat ille acumine semper, hic frequenter et pondere, illic nihil detrahi potest, hic nihil adici, curae plus in illo, in hoc naturae. salibus certe et commiseratione, quae duo plurimum <in> adfectibus ualent, uincimus. et fortasse epilogos illi mos ciuitatis abstulerit, sed et nobis illa quae Attici mirantur diuersa Latini sermonis ratio minus permiserit. in epistulis quidem, quamquam sunt utriusque, dialogisue, quibus nihil ille, nulla contentio est. cedendum uero in hoc, quod et prior fuit et ex magna parte Ciceronem quantus est fecit.

I would happily pit Cicero against any of the Greeks. I know, of course, what a storm of opposition I am raising, especially as it is no part of my plan to compare him with Demosthenes – and anyway that is not relevant, since I regard Demosthenes as a primary author to be read, or rather to learn by heart. The excellences of the two are for the most part, I think, very similar: strategy, arrangement, principles of division, preparation, proof – in a word everything that comes under invention. In their elocution, there is some divergence: the one is more concentrated, the other more expansive; one has shorter periods, the other longer ones; one always fights with the sword point, the other often also puts his weight behind the blow; you cannot take anything away in the one, you cannot expand the other; one displays more care, the other more nature. In wit and pathos, the two most powerful elements in emotional writing, our man certainly wins. Perhaps it was the practice of his city that deprived Demosthenes of epilogues; but it may also be the case that the very different nature of the Latin language has robbed

---

[63] Cf. *inst.* 2.5.20, discussed in ch. 1 p. 25.

[64] On the σύγκρισις in general as school exercise, Russell (1970) ad [Long.] 12.4 notes that its rules are to be found in ancient rhetorical manuals like Theon's *progymnasmata* (Spengel 2.112) and Nicolaus' *progymnasmata* 59ff. Felten (= 485 Spengel). These are usefully translated by Kennedy (2003) 52–55 and 162–164. For other schoolroom-based comparisons of Cicero and Demosthenes, see e.g. Quint. *decl.* 268.20, along with Gell. 15.28.6–7 (similarly Tac. *dial.* 37.6).

Cicero of qualities which Attic speakers admire. In letters (which both of them wrote) and in dialogues (there are none by Demosthenes), there is no contest. We have to admit however that Demosthenes was the earlier and very largely made Cicero the great orator that he is. (trans. D. A. Russell, Loeb)

The discussion is largely stylistic, which of course suits everything that we have seen thus far about the rhetorical classroom. The two exhibit similar virtues in the various parts of a speech, but differ somewhat in how they express themselves. Cicero is, to be blunt, wordier, but this is not exactly presented as a fault; instead Cicero's virtue of *copia* is praised. Quintilian may be able to say this with a straight face to his pupils, but perhaps he spared a wry smile or a knowing glance at his assistant master when he said that "nothing could be taken away from the one [i.e. Demosthenes], nothing added to the other [i.e. Cicero]"[65] – or perhaps *copia* is simply that central to his conception of proper oratory. In any event, Cicero reigns undisputed in the *peroratio*, where his skill at stirring the jurors' emotions was recognized early on in his career as an advocate.[66] Still, Demosthenes is given credit for being Cicero's forerunner and paving the way; this ultimately, of course, redounds to Cicero's praise, as he is seen to be the greater of the two speakers. Quintilian goes on to say that Cicero has taken the best of all the great Greek orators and mixed them with the products of his own "immortal genius"; thus Cicero unquestionably wins, and not just over Demosthenes but over the sum total of all Greek literature.[67]

The first such widely circulating comparison between Demosthenes and Cicero was apparently made by the shadowy Caecilius of Calacte; Plutarch reports that it focused on their speeches and styles but was badly done (*Dem.* 3.2).[68] While Caecilius' comparison is lost, we do have another contemporary Greek stylistic syncrisis provided in the *De sublimitate* of [Longinus], which probably dates from roughly the same time and is certainly doing roughly the same thing.[69] The comparison is made on

---

[65] Cf. the (opposite) paradox of Val. Max. 8.10 ext. 1: *etsi operi illius adici nihil potest, tamen in Demosthene magna pars Demosthenis abest, quod legitur potius quam auditur.*

[66] Cicero always, or at least almost always, spoke last when the defense was conducted by multiple advocates; this allowed him to avoid tedious rehearsal of the facts and legal details of a case and focus instead on emotional appeal. See e.g. Cic. *Brut.* 190 with the notes of Douglas (1966).

[67] The rest of Quintilian's favorable judgment is quoted and discussed in ch. 1 p. 25.

[68] Also mentioned in the *Suda* K 1165; cf. Woerther (2015) T 1 and 6.

[69] Speculative scholarly industry has sometimes tried to find the lost Caecilius in [Longinus'] words; see Gambet (1963) 88 with n. 106. There is unfortunately no hard evidence for this claim (Russell [1970] ad loc. doubts it), but it is not impossible, and we certainly see in [Longinus] an imperial Greek rhetorician doing the same thing as a Caecilius. (The exact dating of [Longinus] is problematic: the first century AD is possible, and argued for in brief by Whitton [2015b] 220–222 with

the same terms as that of Quintilian above, focused on stylistic similarities and differences ([Longinus] 12.4–5):

οὐ κατ᾽ ἄλλα δέ τινα ἢ ταῦτα, ἐμοὶ δοκεῖ, φίλτατε Τερεντιανέ, (λέγω δέ, <εἰ> καὶ ἡμῖν ὡς "Ελλησιν ἐφεῖταί τι γινώσκειν) καὶ ὁ Κικέρων τοῦ Δημοσθένους ἐν τοῖς μεγέθεσι παραλλάττει. ὁ μὲν γὰρ ἐν ὕψει τὸ πλέον ἀποτόμῳ, ὁ δὲ Κικέρων ἐν χύσει, καὶ ὁ μὲν ἡμέτερος διὰ τὸ μετὰ βίας ἕκαστα, ἔτι δὲ τάχους ῥώμης δεινότητος, οἷον καίειν τε ἅμα καὶ διαρπάζειν σκηπτῷ τινι παρεικάζοιτ᾽ ἂν ἢ κεραυνῷ, ὁ δὲ Κικέρων ὡς ἀμφιλαφής τις ἐμπρησμός, οἶμαι, πάντη νέμεται καὶ ἀνειλεῖται, πολὺ ἔχων καὶ ἐπίμονον ἀεὶ τὸ καῖον καὶ διακληρονομούμενον ἄλλοτ᾽ ἀλλοίως ἐν αὐτῷ καὶ κατὰ διαδοχὰς ἀνατρεφόμενον. ἀλλὰ ταῦτα μὲν ὑμεῖς ἂν ἄμεινον ἐπικρίνοιτε, καιρὸς δὲ τοῦ Δημοσθενικοῦ μὲν ὕψους καὶ ὑπερτεταμένου ἔν τε ταῖς δεινώσεσι καὶ τοῖς σφοδροῖς πάθεσι καὶ ἔνθα δεῖ τὸν ἀκροατὴν τὸ σύνολον ἐκπλῆξαι, τῆς δὲ χύσεως ὅπου χρὴ καταντλῆσαι· τοπηγορίαις τε γὰρ καὶ ἐπιλόγοις κατὰ τὸ πλέον καὶ παρεκβάσεσι καὶ τοῖς φραστικοῖς ἅπασι καὶ ἐπιδεικτικοῖς, ἱστορίαις τε καὶ φυσιολογίαις, καὶ οὐκ ὀλίγοις ἄλλοις μέρεσιν ἁρμόδιος.

It seems to me, my dearest Terentianus – I mean, if we Greeks are allowed to venture an opinion on such things – that Cicero differs from Demosthenes in this very same way [i.e. as in a foregoing comparison between Demosthenes and Plato] when it comes to his sublime excellences. For Demosthenes is better in sharp and direct sublimity, while Cicero excels in abundance. And our Demosthenes, on account of doing everything with force, indeed with speed and strength and terribleness so as to burn and destroy all at once, might be compared to lightning or thunder, while Cicero, I think, rolls along and devours everything like some conflagration spreading in every direction; he has a long-lasting and ever-burning fire and scatters it now here and now there, keeping it well fed by a succession of fuel. But you [*sc.* Romans] could judge these things better than I [*sc.* a Greek]. Still, the right time for the Demosthenic sublime and his strained eloquence is in the moments of great intensity and strong emotions and where it's necessary to really hit the listener hard; the moment for abundance is where it's necessary to drown the listener in a flood of words. Abundant oratory is therefore generally more suited to commonplaces and perorations and digressions and descriptive and display passages of all sorts, and history and philosophy, and not a few other genres as well.

[Longinus] is concerned only with a small province of stylistic comparison, viz. how the two orators differ ἐν τοῖς μεγέθεσι, i.e. the περὶ τοῦ ὕψους with which the whole treatise is concerned.[70] Nevertheless, even in this restricted ambit we see clear similarities with Quintilian. Cicero's strength, [Longinus]

---

references. More generally on the questions of date and authorship, see Russell [1970] xxii–xxx, esp. xxviii–xxx, and cf. Heath [1999] and ch. 6 n. 46 below.)

[70] On the equivalency of μέγεθος and ὕψος in [Longinus], see Russell (1970) xxxi n. 7.

alleges, is "in diffusion" (ἐν χύσει), while Demosthenes favors a more "abrupt" (ἀποτόμῳ) style; this is clearly parallel to Quintilian's claim that Cicero is much fuller and more copious, while Demosthenes is sharper and more direct. Although the critical language is vague and metaphorical, this is the main thrust of both Quintilian's and [Longinus'] comparisons. Moreover, Quintilian emphasizes that Demosthenes has more natural eloquence, whereas Cicero's derives more from sedulous preparation (*cura*); so too does [Longinus] emphasize that Demosthenes is at his best when he can give free rein to his intensity and violent emotion, while the "strong and steady" Cicero does better with set-piece elements like commonplaces. Interestingly, while they both agree that Cicero is thus the clear winner in the *peroratio*, they seem to differ on the underlying reason for his superiority: Quintilian believes that the *peroratio* is the product of emotion, while [Longinus] contends that it is more along the lines of a prepared passage where the orator can overwhelm his audience with a well-timed torrent of rhetorical force.

When [Longinus] prefaces his remarks by saying "if we Greeks may venture an opinion," he is nodding to the fact that this comparison was already a stock topic of Roman debate. The prevalence of the theme is what makes Trimalchio's pretentiously fatuous question to the *rhetor* Agamemnon over dinner so funny: *"rogo" inquit "magister, quid putas inter Ciceronem et Pub<li>lium interesse?"* (Petron. 55.5). Publilius was a late Republican writer of mimes.[71] Thus Trimalchio knows enough to try to engage the schoolmaster in a literary comparison, but when he should have chosen Demosthenes to set against Cicero, he instead yokes the most inappropriate possible pair.[72] Trimalchio is yet again skewered as a pompous boor, but for our purposes it is more important to note that the joke only works because of how standard the "right" comparison had become as a topic of discussion, especially in a conversation with a schoolmaster.

These comparisons, however, do not merely live within the walls of the rhetorical classroom. Juvenal, for example, incorporates such a syncrisis in one of his poems that neatly ties together many of the strands of Ciceronian reception that we see throughout this chapter and the next.

---

[71] See Smith (1975) ad loc., more helpful in this instance than Schmeling (2011).

[72] Winterbottom (1982) 261 goes astray when he traces this comparison back to Sen. *contr.* 7.3.9. In that passage Seneca claimed that punning *sententiae* originated with Publilius, and then "spread by imitation first to Laberius, then to Cicero; and it was he who brought it to the level of a virtue" (*primum ad Laberium transisse hoc studium imitando* [*imitandi* codd.], *deinde ad Ciceronem, qui illud ad uirtutem transtulisset*). This is not a comparison between Cicero and Publilius. Petronius' "syncrisis" is original.

The whole passage is deeply influenced by the themes of the declamatory schoolroom,[73] and Juvenal weaves together a tapestry in which Cicero's eloquence intertwines with his politics and leads directly to his death, all of which is juxtaposed with his great Athenian predecessor (Iuu. 10.114–132):

> eloquium ac famam Demosthenis aut Ciceronis
> incipit optare et totis quinquatribus optat   115
> quisquis adhuc uno parcam colit asse Mineruam,
> quem sequitur custos angustae uernula capsae.
> eloquio sed uterque perit orator, utrumque
> largus et exundans leto dedit ingenii fons.
> ingenio manus est et ceruix caesa, nec umquam   120
> sanguine causidici maduerunt rostra pusilli.
> "o fortunatam natam me consule Romam":
> Antoni gladios potuit contemnere si sic
> omnia dixisset. ridenda poemata malo
> quam te, conspicuae diuina Philippica famae,   125
> uolueris a prima quae proxima. saeuus et illum
> exitus eripuit, quem mirabantur Athenae
> torrentem et pleni moderantem frena theatri.
> dis ille aduersis genitus fatoque sinistro,
> quem pater ardentis massae fuligine lippus   130
> a carbone et forcipibus gladiosque paranti
> incude et luteo Volcano ad rhetora misit.

That eloquence and fame of Demosthenes or Cicero – that's what every schoolboy starts to pray for and keeps on praying for through the whole of the festival of Minerva, every schoolboy who still pays tribute to thrifty Minerva with a single *as* and who is followed to school by a little home-born slave to guard his tiny backpack. But it was because of their eloquence that each orator met his end; that abundant and overflowing wellspring of talent handed each of them over to death. Because of his genius Cicero's head and hands were chopped off, but never did petty case-pleaders stain the rostra with their blood. "*O fortunatam natam me consule Romam*": he could have despised Antony's swords if he'd spoken everything like that. I prefer his laughable attempts at poetry to you, divine *Philippic* of glorious fame, you who are unrolled next to the first on the scroll [= the second *Philippic*]. A savage death snatched Demosthenes away too, the one whom Athens used to admire as he raged white-hot and guided the reins of a packed house. He was born with the gods against him and an unfortunate fate when he was sent by his father, a man half-blind from the smoke of fiery masses of ore,

---

[73] On this passage cf. Keane (2015) 136–137, where Juvenal is described as "a sort of poetic declaimer" (136). See too Uden (2015) 155–157 and briefly Winkler (1988) 85–86.

away from the coal and the tongs and the sword-making anvil and the filth
of the forge to the *rhetor*'s school.

The satire treats the "vanity of human wishes," among which the desire for
eloquence is included as a signal example. The educational context is clear
from the start (this eloquence is what *schoolboys* pray for), but I would go
even further and say that this whole passage is playing a subtle game with
the comparison genre. Juvenal's shifting tone is difficult to pin down, but
I suspect that he exhibits here the sort of comparison that these schoolboys
would themselves make, except he blends equal parts irony and logic in
order to arrive at a remarkable (and sarcastic) conclusion, one entirely
different from that of the youths in the rhetorical classroom: eloquence
results not in success, fame, or fortune, but rather in death. Juvenal, by
contrast, ironically claims to prefer Cicero's notoriously inferior poetry[74]
and alleges that the life of the *pusillus causidicus* is better than that of the
orator. The word *causidicus* itself is already fraught with negative
connotations,[75] and coupling it with *pusillus* removes any lingering
doubt about its implication. This is not the comparison that the schoolboys are supposed to make, or at any rate not the conclusion that they
should draw. Juvenal's provocative pose as devil's advocate clearly demonstrates that the contrary position is in fact the default.

Elsewhere Juvenal seems to play the comparison straight, simply following it all the way through. Demosthenes and Cicero are yoked together for
comparison as two eloquent orators who came to a disastrous end precisely
because of their oratory.[76] Cicero's death, as we shall see in the next
chapter, is absolutely central to declamatory rhetoric, and here those stories
are alluded to by mentioning how Cicero's head and hands were chopped
off and affixed to the *rostra*. Furthermore it is the *Philippics*, especially the
"immortal" second, which are seen to have led directly to his death. Line
123 *Antoni gladios potuit contemnere* even alludes directly to *Phil.* 2.118
contempsi Catilinae gladios, non pertimescam tuos, while at the same time
getting in a dig at Cicero's notorious poetry.[77] The *Philippics* also provide
the hinge for the comparison between Cicero and Demosthenes, as Juvenal
then pivots around the like-named speeches to return to Demosthenes and
his eloquence-induced demise. The comparison ends where it began, in the

---

[74] On Cicero's poetry, see ch. 4 n. 97.   [75] See *TLL* III.703.78–79 (Meister).
[76] Note that the phrase "overflowing wellspring of talent" (*exundans . . . ingenii fons*), i.e. the supposed
cause of their deaths, is remarkably similar to Quintilian's *uiuo gurgite* [sc. *Cicero*] *exundat* (*inst.*
10.1.109; cf. p. 25 above).
[77] Is it coincidence that Antony too is said to have mocked Cicero's poetry, citing the other infamous
line (*cedant arma togae*)? (See Cic. *Phil.* 2.20.)

classroom, as we see Demosthenes' banausic father pack him off to the *rhetor*'s school. When Juvenal thinks of Cicero, then, he thinks of him in terms completely inflected by his classroom training, but rather than be limited by this imposed matrix of ideas, he is able to step outside of it and exploit it. From the outside looking in, by a sort of *reductio ad absurdum* he turns the comparison against itself, arriving at the exact opposite conclusion from what he "should" have. He thus not only makes his readers smile but also forces them to question their cherished assumptions.[78]

Conclusion

Other "extracurricular" comparisons between Cicero and Demosthenes occur,[79] but the point is sufficiently made. They are an important element in the way the rhetorical classroom engages with one of the primary facets of its Cicero, namely Cicero as the embodiment of eloquence. This image of Cicero, as we have seen, while grounded in the schoolroom, exerts an influence that ranges far beyond the strictly educational context. Cicero the embodiment of eloquence is in fact the "textualized" Cicero, the once real man in a sense disembodied and replaced by his written corpus. Being remembered in this way might have suited Cicero, and yet he cannot really claim responsibility for controlling this aspect of his reception. Although he set the stage for such a posterity by careful self-fashioning, publishing his speeches for the edification of the studious youth, and thoughtfully theorizing about education, equally important was a constellation of factors over which he had no control. There were unforeseeable politics that aligned Octavian's interests after Actium with those of Cicero in the *Götterdämmerung* of 44–43 BC, a force which I will discuss in the next chapter; there was the conservatism that pervaded Roman education; and there was the fact that eloquence was the stock in trade of the rhetorical schools. In sum, for a variety of reasons Cicero's powers of speech lay at the heart of his reputation in the early Empire. Young students received this message early and often, and it stuck with them throughout their lives. The declaimers and their pupils believed that it was Cicero's tongue that first brought him success and the consulship, and that it would be his tongue that ultimately brought him his death – and immortality.

---

[78] The ability to extend beyond the essentials of the tradition will be seen again in the likes of Seneca the Younger and Tacitus and Pliny in chapters 5–7.

[79] E.g. Columella 1 pr. 29–30, Plin. *epist.* 1.20.4.

CHAPTER 3

Remaking Cicero in the Schoolroom: Cicero's Death

Popillius the Parricide

In the first century AD every schoolboy would have learned that Cicero was assassinated by one Popillius, whom he had earlier defended successfully against a charge of parricide. This Popillius shows up in the various declamations concerning Cicero's death, which was a tremendously popular topic for the declaimers. All three of the declamations in Seneca the Elder that touch on Cicero center around his final moments,[1] and no other theme in the Senecan corpus receives such repeated treatment; the same subject is mentioned by Quintilian (*inst.* 3.8.46), and Seneca likewise tells us that these themes were declaimed in the schools (*suas.* 6.14, 7.12).[2] In one *controuersia* Popillius even plays a starring role as the defendant in a trial "*de moribus*" after Cicero's slaying.[3] He is a useful figure: in the first place, if you assume that he was guilty of the charge of parricide – as our declaimers generally do – then Cicero sowed the seeds of his own destruction by

---

[1] On these three declamations in general, see Gunderson (2003) 79–89; Berti (2007) 106–109, 325–332; Wilson (2008); briefly Dugan (2005) 70–74; on the two *suasoriae*, see esp. Feddern (2013); on *contr.* 7.2, see now Lentano (2016). Lobur (2008) 140–158 focuses on the role of these declamations in building imperial *consensus* and *concordia*. Migliario (2007) 121–149 and Migliario (2008) are attempts to recover the political ideology of individual declaimers in *suas.* 6 and 7, but her approach is unsustainable (see n. 27 below; Lobur [2008] 152–158 proceeds along similar lines as Migliario). Pierini (2003) makes mention both of Seneca's declaimers and the historical fragments he cites; Noè (1984) 44–63 concentrates on the latter. For some Ciceronian themes in late antique declamations, see Kohl (1915) 105–107.

[2] The schools are never far away from the declamations reported in Seneca the Elder. Many of his declaimers are teachers; cf. his frequent use of the term *scholastici*, "teachers of rhetoric," e.g. *suas.* 6.14 *solent enim scholastici declamitare: deliberat Cicero an salutem promittente Antonio orationes suas comburat*. Seneca even heard his own teacher, Marullus, declaim on one of these Ciceronian themes (*contr.* 7.2.11). The distinction between *Schuldeklamation* and *Schaudeklamation* in Seneca is blurred at best; see Feddern (2013) 79–80, Bonner (1949) 39–41 (remarking that "nearly all these themes were invented for and debated in the schools"), Sussman (1978) 12, 15. Cf. similarly Stramaglia (2016) on the pseudo-Quintilianic *Declamationes maiores*.

[3] *Contr.* 7.2. The exact meaning of *de moribus* here is disputed, since *actiones de moribus* seem to have been confined to cases of divorce. Bonner (1949) 124–125 provides a full discussion, speculating that "the position envisaged may be that of the summoning of Popillius by the censors."

securing the acquittal of a guilty man. Furthermore, Popillius creates some choice dramatic irony in the closing act of Cicero's life, and declaimers delight in dwelling on its possibilities. As the rhetorician and historian Bruttedius Niger said, when Cicero was on the run and saw his old client Popillius approaching him, his face brightened – little did he know what fate held in store for him (*suas.* 6.20). So too do other declaimers have Cicero greet Popillius with friendly anticipation; in Cestius Pius' take, when Popillius is announced, Cicero cheerfully replies, "I've always got time for Popillius" (*Popillio semper uaco*, Sen. *contr.* 7.2.14). Indeed, Sabidienus Paulus even represents Cicero as reading the very speech he had once delivered on behalf of Popillius when the dastardly villain arrives in the flesh (Sen. *contr.* 7.2.14)!

Popillius is thus a useful invention, to be sure, but he is literally that, a product of declamatory *inuentio*, a non-existent entity created entirely out of the declaimers' imagination.[4] Seneca the Elder reports that "few of the historians have told us that Popillius was the killer of Cicero, and even they didn't represent him as having been defended by Cicero for parricide, but rather in a private suit. It was the declaimers who decided that he had been tried for parricide" (*Popillium pauci ex historicis tradiderunt interfectorem Ciceronis et hi quoque non parricidi reum a Cicerone defensum, sed in priuato iudicio: declamatoribus placuit parricidi reum fuisse, contr.* 7.2.8). We can go further: it is literally incredible that Cicero would have been killed by a man he once defended in court. Surely Livy, whose account of Cicero's death Seneca preserves, could not have resisted mentioning such a story if it had even a chance of being true.[5] In fact Popillius is nowhere

---

[4] Roller (1997) 124–128 and, in more detail, Wright (2001) independently each come to the same conclusion. This insight is prefigured by Gudeman (1902) 28: "the connection of Popillius with the death of Cicero is unhistorical, being an invention of rhetoricians which was subsequently improved upon for epideictic purposes"; so too Moles (1988) ad Plut. *Cic.* 48.1 p. 200: "C(icero) probably never even defended Popillius at all" (cf. his p. 38; he believes that Plutarch *knowingly* included this declamatory element) and Edwards (1928) 130. Fairweather (1981) 324 is uncertain on Popillius' status, but oddly believes that even if he is altogether an invention, declamation is not here influencing historiography. Roller, by contrast, rightly notes the importance of declamation for the development of the entire tradition surrounding Cicero's death (e.g. [1997] 110). Homeyer (1977), a detailed attempt to trace the traditions of Cicero's death back to Tiro, Nepos, and Asinius Pollio, remains a useful collection of the ancient evidence, but she does not discuss declamation in any detail, and Roller and Wright have rendered much of her argument obsolete.

[5] This claim is not changed by Liu. *per.* 120 *huius* [i.e. *Ciceronis*] *occisi a Popillio, legionario milite, cum haberet annos sexaginta tres, caput quoque cum dextra manu in rostris positum est*; this passage in the *Periochae* is probably *not* Livian. Wright (2001) 439–440 summarizes the reasons, including signally that Livy does not mention Popillius in the actual passage describing Cicero's death; the *periocha* states that Cicero's right hand was affixed to the *rostra* whereas Livy had said both hands; and Seneca the Elder would not have dismissed the Popillius story if it had been reported by Livy. Bingham (1978) 403, 475 had made the same arguments; he observes that "the *Periochae* are an intelligent

attested except in accounts of Cicero's death; that is to say, the trial does not have any independent existence.[6] The irony of the whole situation, Cicero being killed by the very man he had earlier saved, smacks much more of the declaimer's pen than of reality – this is really just too good to be true, and it is the sort of thing that turns up all the time in schoolroom compositions. Indeed, declaimers were positively encouraged to invent such creative twists, called *colores*, "rhetorical colors."[7] The *pater patriae* himself killed by a parricide – what could be better? Seneca knows that part of the story is pure fiction, and he plainly has doubts about the whole thing,[8] for which our only early source outside of declamation is a declaimer turned historian (Bruttedius Niger; see below). The whole Popillius saga is thus nothing other than declamatory *inuentio* in action.

At a distance of two millennia, the colorful story of Popillius seems to us to have no basis in historical reality – and yet it infiltrates the historiographic tradition and becomes accepted as fact by later writers. It shows up in authors from Valerius Maximus (5.3.4), the collector of anecdotes writing under Tiberius, to the Greek Plutarch writing a biography of Cicero more than half a century later, to Cassius Dio (47.11.1–2) and beyond (e.g. Hier. *chron.* p. 158 Helm). To take Plutarch as an example, when he describes Cicero's death, he numbers among the death squad one "Popillius, a tribune, <u>whom Cicero had once defended against a charge of parricide</u>" (Ποπίλλιος χιλίαρχος, ᾧ πατροκτονίας ποτὲ δίκην φεύγοντι συνεῖπεν ὁ Κικέρων, *Cic.* 48.1). Plutarch thus reports as historical fact the very charge that Seneca explicitly tells us the declaimers had made up. This

---

summary of the Livian books by a student of Roman history . . . He may have referred to outside sources for variant details, or he may have drawn on his own knowledge of a tradition different from that presented by Livy" (401) – or, in this instance, he may have drawn on his own experiences as a schoolboy in the Roman classroom and not been able to help himself from adding these cornerstone elements from declamatory exercises that were so well known.

[6] Well observed by Roller (1997) 125.

[7] *Colores* are details invented by a declaimer that are not found in the givens of a particular case; they serve generally to increase the guilt of the defendant in a prosecution or minimize it in a defense. For the details and a summary of some technical difficulties with the term, see Feddern (2013) 44–59 and Burkard (2016) 108–132. In the case of Popillius, the original declamation could simply have been a trial of Cicero's murderer; one *color* then made him a former client of Cicero's, and this was one-upped by making the charge against him parricide. So Roller (1997) 126 and already Gudeman (1902) 28.

[8] Seneca surely reports that "few historians" tell this tale in order to indicate his general skepticism. He concludes this digression with a slightly unclear epigram: *sic autem eum accusant tamquam defendi non possit, cum adeo possit absolui ut ne accusari quidem potuerit* (*contr.* 7.2.8). This seems to mean: "the declaimers accuse him as though he could not be defended, when in fact he can be so completely absolved from the crime that he could never even have been accused of it." Is this to say that "he could not have even have been accused" because he never did it and no one in "real life" ever thought that he had? Cf. Wright (2001) 438 n. 6.

figure, originally invented to add rhetorical color to a declamation, has taken on a life of his own in the historical imagination and assumed a canonical place in the mythology of Cicero's death. This is a small but telling example of how the schoolroom tradition shapes the way Romans remember their past; it is indeed fair to say that declamation is here constructing memories of a past that never was.[9] In this chapter I will explore the influence of declamation on the tradition of Cicero's death. But first, what are the forces shaping Cicero's image in the schoolroom itself? We will now try to peer into the black box of the years between Cicero's death and our earliest declamatory evidence.

Propaganda and Declamation

Cicero's death presented Octavian, the future Augustus, with a bit of a conundrum; after all, Cicero seems to have been preparing to take Caesar's youthful heir under his wing and provide him with a sort of *tirocinium fori*.[10] The possibility of a shared consulship may have even been mooted.[11] Octavian, for his part, went along at first, but soon changed his mind, and Cicero almost immediately landed on his proscription list, named as an enemy of the state who could be killed with impunity.[12] In the aftermath of Cicero's brutal death and dismemberment – his head and hand(s) were chopped off and nailed to the speaker's platform in the Roman forum – Octavian could hardly ignore what had happened: Cicero

---

[9] On "created memories," see Gowing (2005) 10.

[10] Cicero begins with complete confidence in Octavian, who he believes is entirely devoted to him (*mihi totus deditus, Att.* 14.11.2, 21 April 44 BC). He himself is willing to take responsibility for Octavian's actions (e.g. *Phil.* 3.19, 20 December 44 BC) and has no hesitation in vouching for the youth's good character (e.g. Cic. *Phil.* 5.42–51, 1 January 43 BC): *promitto, recipio, spondeo, patres conscripti, C. Caesarem talem semper fore ciuem qualis hodie sit qualemque eum maxime uelle esse et optare debemus.* He shows similar, if perhaps eroding, confidence in a letter to Brutus (18.3, June 43 BC): *sed Caesarem meis consiliis adhuc gubernatum, praeclara ipsum indole admirabilique constantia, improbissimis litteris quidam fallacibusque interpretibus ac nuntiis impulerunt in spem certissimam consulatus.* Six months later Cicero would be dead. On the development of Cicero's attitudes toward Octavian, see e.g. Achard (1981) 178–183; for an attempt at a historical evaluation of Cicero's contribution to Octavian's rise to power, see Bellen (1985).

[11] On the consular pact, see Plut. *Cic.* 45.5–6 with Moles (1988) ad loc. p. 197 and p. 52, who strongly defends its historicity. Similarly Appian (*BC* 3.92) and Cassius Dio (46.42.2). Cf. Plut. *Cic.* 44.1 with Moles (1988) ad loc. p. 194 for an earlier, "clearly historical," pact between Cicero and Octavian.

[12] See Plut. *Cic.* 45 on the whole sordid affair. It is not surprising to see that the later Augustus is completely silent about the proscriptions in his *Res Gestae*, although he is quick to note that in wars foreign and domestic he spared all citizens who asked for mercy (*R. gest. diu. Aug.* 3). Later, when the emperor Claudius turned his hand to writing a history from the death of Caesar, he too skipped over this whole period on the grounds that he would not be allowed to speak the truth freely (Suet. *Claud.* 41.2); cf. Dio on the difficulty of writing the history of this period (Cass. Dio 53.19).

was too famous and his murder too public to be simply swept under the rug. Octavian's own eventual conflict with Antony, however, brought about a serendipitous alignment of interests, since Cicero had been Antony's most fervent opponent at the end of his life. By happy and convenient coincidence, then, Octavian and the dead Cicero found themselves on the same side of a new ideological divide, and Augustan propaganda exploited this alliance as much as it could.

Cicero had positioned himself perfectly, albeit unconsciously, as the martyr-hero of the new regime with his *Philippics*, in which he pilloried Antony and praised Octavian. Thus when Antony became *persona non grata*, there was no difficulty in setting up Cicero as a hero who fell in the cause of freedom against this would-be tyrant. Ignored, of course, is Octavian's own role in Cicero's death, along with the fact that Cicero would have doubtless opposed what Augustus and his regime had become – Cicero was a stout defender of the traditional Roman constitution, a man who had sided with Pompey over Caesar. No mention can be made of problematic passages like this one from the *De re publica*, where *libertas* is defined: "liberty, which means not that we have a just master, but rather that we have none at all" (*libertas, quae non in eo est, ut iusto utamur domino, sed ut nul<lo>*, Scipio speaking, *rep.* 2.43).[13] Cicero's writings are full of such sentiments, all of which would have been inconvenient for Augustus. Likewise problematic are Cicero's various remarks at Octavian's expense, the young man who was *laudandus, ornandus, tollendus* – "to be given praise, honor, and the push."[14] The received truth was simply that Cicero had fought tooth and nail against Antony, author and prince of sin, in the *Philippics*, and the devil Antony, smarting and stung by their evident truth, had ruthlessly ordered Cicero's execution to assuage his own hurt feelings. Millennia of reception have made this tale seem believable, but we should be very skeptical of the victor's version of events. Plenty of Romans changed allegiances in the civil wars and found

---

[13] Cf. the whole passage. This is just one of many examples where Cicero's political feelings are made clear; these political and philosophical works seem roundly ignored in our period. Another one is *off.* 3.83: *ecce tibi, qui rex populi Romani dominusque omnium gentium esse concupiuerit idque perfecerit. hanc cupiditatem si honestam quis esse dicit, amens est; probat enim legum et libertatis interitum earumque oppressionem taetram et detestabilem gloriosam putat.* Plutarch seems to have recognized this as a reason for Octavian's hostility: Plut. *Ant.* 19.1 Καῖσαρ δὲ Κικέρωνι μὲν οὐκέτι προσεῖχε, τῆς ἐλευθερίας ὁρῶν περιεχόμενον; see Pelling (1988) ad loc.

[14] Cic. *fam.* 11.20.1 (from D. Brutus): *ipsum Caesarem nihil sane de te questum nisi dictum, quod diceret te dixisse laudandum adulescentem, ornandum, tollendum; se non esse commissurum ut tolli possit.* Cf. e.g. Cass. Dio 46.43.4–5 (with Gowing [1992] 152 n. 30), reporting another witty remark of Cicero's opposing Octavian's forcible seizure of the consulship; it is said to have "paved the way for his destruction." Likewise Octavian's sardonic comment reported by App. *BC* 3.92.

acceptance among their former foes, and Cicero himself had switched sides on more than one occasion over a long political career.[15] Antony was willing enough to forge an alliance with Octavian, the very man who had been sent with an army expressly to kill him. It seems incredible that the triumvirate would have proscribed Cicero solely because of the *Philippics*, but this was a very congenial fiction for the eventual Augustus to encourage.[16] By reading against the grain, however, we can see at least a little bit of a more conflicted story.[17]

After his death Cicero may have initially remained a delicate topic, perhaps best avoided by the prudent. While he was not himself a member of the conspiracy to assassinate Caesar, once the deed was done he fully supported it, and indeed Brutus, as he pulled his bloody dagger from Caesar's corpse and held it aloft, called out to Cicero in the Senate House and congratulated him on the restoration of liberty to the Republic (Cic. *Phil.* 2.30).[18] Cicero's ideology and behavior were thus potentially more than a little troubling for Caesar's great-nephew, heir, and eventual avenger. Contemporary writers like Vergil and Horace make no mention of him in their poetry, even though they had abundant opportunity to do so.[19] Nevertheless, Augustus was determined to paper

---

[15] A classic side-switcher is Messalla Corvinus, who was proscribed in 43; escaped and fought with Brutus at Philippi; went over to Antony; then finally allied himself with Octavian. His career culminated in a triumph in 27. He transforms his inconstancy into a virtue, claiming: "I was always on the better and more just side" (αὐτὸν δὲ τὸν Μεσσάλαν λέγουσιν ὕστερον ἐπαινούμενον ὑπὸ Καίσαρος, ὅτι καίπερ ἐν Φιλίπποις πολεμιώτατος αὐτοῖς γενόμενος διὰ Βροῦτον, ἐν Ἀκτίῳ προθυμότατον ἑαυτὸν παρέσχεν, "ἐγώ τοι" φάναι "ὦ Καῖσαρ ἀεὶ τῆς βελτίονος καὶ δικαιοτέρας [τιμῆς καὶ] μερίδος ἐγενόμην," Plut. *Brut.* 53.2). Cicero's *inconstantia* was one of his most notable vices (e.g. Sen. *contr.* 2.4.4). The hostile Pollio may even have suggested that he would have retracted his *Philippics* and published pro-Antony tracts if Antony had spared his life (Sen. *suas.* 6.15), and Seneca himself says that Cicero would have at least countenanced such a notion (*suas.* 7.10).

[16] Note too the insightful remark of Syme (1939) 146, that the survival of the *Philippics* "imperils historical judgement and wrecks historical perspective"; he also observes that the second *Philippic* would not have led to an irreparable feud: the Senate was used to much worse political invective (140). It might further be noted that Antony was in Rome only for the first and second *Philippics*; it is hardly clear – and might well be doubted – that he would have read the entire corpus as we have it today when he was in Gaul. For an extremely detailed discussion of the publication of the *Philippics*, see Manuwald (2007) 54–90.

[17] Cf. Tac. *ann.* 1.9.3–4 exonerating Octavian, followed by 1.10.2 blaming him for the proscriptions and other ills.

[18] Cf. Cass. Dio 46.22.4 (and 44.20.4).

[19] Most prominently on the shield of Aeneas, where both Catiline and Cato make an appearance (*Aen.* 8.666–670). One might argue that mention of Catiline evokes mention of Cicero (so Seru. ad 8.668), but then why not just mention Cicero outright? An absence need not necessarily imply hostility (so rightly Gambet [1963] 101, 279–280), but as Pierini (2003) 3 observes, "certo è che a volte anche i silenzi possono avere il loro peso"; similarly Gowing (2013) 235–236. Think too of the remarkable *alii* [i.e. *Graeci*] ... *orabunt causas melius* (*Aen.* 6.847–849), which directly contradicts what a Quintilian will eventually boast (cf. p. 95 above). The notion that Vergil's Drances = Cicero is

over the cracks. Plutarch ends his life of Cicero with two telling Augustan incidents (*Cic.* 49.3–4):[20]

πυνθάνομαι δὲ Καίσαρα χρόνοις πολλοῖς ὕστερον εἰσελθεῖν πρὸς ἕνα τῶν θυγατριδῶν· τὸν δὲ βιβλίον ἔχοντα Κικέρωνος ἐν ταῖς χερσίν, ἐκπλαγέντα τῷ ἱματίῳ περικαλύπτειν· ἰδόντα δὲ τὸν Καίσαρα λαβεῖν καὶ διελθεῖν ἑστῶτα μέρος πολὺ τοῦ βιβλίου, πάλιν δ᾽ ἀποδιδόντα τῷ μειρακίῳ φάναι "λόγιος ἀνήρ, ὦ παῖ, λόγιος καὶ φιλόπατρις." ἐπεὶ μέντοι τάχιστα κατεπολέμησεν ὁ Καῖσαρ Ἀντώνιον, ὑπατεύων αὐτὸς εἵλετο συνάρχοντα τοῦ Κικέρωνος τὸν υἱόν, ἐφ᾽ οὗ τάς τ᾽ εἰκόνας ἡ βουλὴ καθεῖλεν Ἀντωνίου, καὶ τὰς ἄλλας ἁπάσας ἠκύρωσε τιμάς, καὶ προσεψηφίσατο μηδενὶ τῶν Ἀντωνίων ὄνομα Μᾶρκον εἶναι. οὕτω τὸ δαιμόνιον εἰς τὸν Κικέρωνος οἶκον ἐπανήνεγκε τὸ τέλος τῆς Ἀντωνίου κολάσεως.

I learn that Caesar Augustus, a long time after Cicero's death, came upon one of his daughter's sons holding a book of Cicero in his hands. He was terrified and sought to hide it in his toga. When Caesar saw this he took the book and paged through a great part of it as he stood there, and when he gave it back again to the youth he said, "An eloquent man, my boy, an eloquent man and a lover of his country."

Moreover, as soon as Caesar had defeated Antony, when he himself was serving as consul he chose Cicero's son as his co-consul, and in his consulship the Senate took down the statues of Antony, and canceled all the other honors that he had been given, and decreed that no descendant of Antony could have the name Marcus. Thus the gods granted the house of Cicero the final steps in the punishment of Antony.

These are revealing anecdotes both. The first shows that at this time a prudent man, or even a callow youth, might fear Augustus' reaction to being found out as a Ciceronian partisan. Just as importantly, it shows that Augustus took pains to control those reactions and present Cicero in a positive light, implicitly aligned with himself as a "lover of his country." In his choice of co-consul Augustus showed further thoughtful image management.[21] He had

---

unpersuasive; see Horsfall (2003) ad *Aen.* 11.122 p. 116 with bibliography. For an even less plausible echo of Cicero in Vergil, see Seru. ad *Aen.* 6.623 (citing Donatus on the "incestuous" Cicero); note also Seru. ad *ecl.* 6.11 with Cicero attending one of Vergil's recitals! It is perhaps also worth observing that there is no Cicero in the Forum of Augustus (Gowing [2005] 145). For speculation on Ciceronian influence on Augustan poetry, see Feeney (2014), who must admit that there "are vanishingly few direct references to Cicero" (3).

20   Appian tells a similar tale at *BC* 4.6.51. Flower (2006) 116–117 is skeptical about Plutarch's story of the extirpation of Antony's memory, preferring Dio's account (Cass. Dio 51.19), but these two versions are not necessarily contradictory, just focused on different details. Even if Plutarch was embellishing, that would still be of interest for what it tells us about the prevalence of Augustan ideology and Cicero's reception. Cf. Yavetz (1990) 31–32.

21   So too a former associate of Brutus, C. Antistius Vetus, would replace Augustus that year as suffect consul. Cf. the choice of the Republican Cn. Calpurnius Piso in 23 BC and, again as suffect consul to

won the war and consolidated his power, and so he could afford to be magnanimous in life's smaller details. He thus extends an olive branch to Cicero *fils*, giving him the satisfaction of helping extirpate Antony's public memory and expelling "Marcus" from the Antonian onomasticon – implicitly perhaps reserving the name for the likes of the Ciceros. In any case, Augustus thereby not only made peace with Marcus the younger; he more importantly helped legitimize his own version of events. If Marcus acted as Augustus' co-consul and helped suppress Antony, then surely he agreed with the authorized version according to Augustus – and if, of all people, Cicero's only living descendant agreed and lent his *auctoritas* to this version, who was anyone else to disagree?

This attitude is entirely of a piece with Augustus' other efforts to co-opt Cicero's good name. For example, Augustus' birth is said to add luster to Cicero's *annus mirabilis*, 63 BC,[22] and in his autobiography Augustus claims that Cicero had a dream of him as the man who would end civil wars (*FRHist* 60 fr. 4 = Tert. *anim.* 46.7). This story and its congeners are widespread in the tradition.[23] Suetonius even reports that Octavian's father was late to a session of the Senate in which Cicero gave one of his speeches on the Catilinarian conspiracy precisely because Atia was giving birth; when Nigidius Figulus learned the reason for the delay, he supposedly declared that the ruler of the world had been born (Suet. *Aug.* 94.5). Is it coincidence that we have none of the letters between Octavian and Cicero, and no letters at all from the last five months of Cicero's life?[24] Augustus wants Cicero on his side and is keen to avoid even a whiff of suspicion that he had something to do with Cicero's demise.

The ideology and propaganda of the early Empire thus played a key role in creating the classroom Cicero. Since Ronald Syme's *Roman Revolution*, the concept of "Augustan propaganda" has been freighted with heavy and

---

replace Augustus, L. Sestius, a former quaestor to Brutus who "worshipped the memory of the Liberators" (Syme [1939] 335).

[22] Vell. 2.36.1 *consulatui Ciceronis non mediocre adiecit decus natus eo anno diuus Augustus ... omnibus omnium gentium uiris magnitudine sua inducturus caliginem*, discussed by Schmitzer (2000) 92–94; cf. Plut. *Cic.* 44.7.

[23] Cf. Plut. *Cic.* 44.3–7, Suet. *Aug.* 94.8–9, Cass. Dio 54.2.2–4. Moles (1988) ad *Cic.* 44.3–7 p. 195 and Lintott (2013) ad *Cic.* 44.3–7 pp. 202–203 collect and discuss the evidence for this dream.

[24] See Nicholson (1998) 85, who also notes that later Augustus did not scruple to stop the publication of the *acta senatus* and destroy 2,000 books of the Sibylline oracles (Suet. *Aug.* 31 and 36.1). Cf. damningly App. *BC* 5.132, where in 36 BC Octavian is said to have arranged the burning of all documents relating to the "civil strife" (στάσις) earlier in the triumvirate.

problematic scholarly cargo.[25] When I speak of ideology and propaganda, I do not mean systematic, top-down attempts to control the formation of public opinion, but rather the whole swirling combination of Augustus' own deliberate image management and the more and less willing collusion of those around him in promoting that image. The privileged place of rhetorical education and declamation in contemporary Roman culture meant that they were deeply imbricated in imperial politics. Many of the declaimers mentioned in Seneca the Elder, for example, were intimate associates of the imperial family, while they also played a vital role in shaping elite opinion by educating the aristocracy's sons.[26] It is hardly surprising that they should put forth a message that the emperor would approve of, with or without any additional nudges in the "right" direction.[27] Once they start promoting a certain version of events, a feedback loop takes over and that version begins to take on a life of its own, in the classroom and beyond.

[25] For some of its problems, see e.g. Kennedy (1992) and Galinsky (1996) 30–41. Recent treatments like Lobur (2008), esp. 2–8, and Levick (2010), esp. 10–15, both with further references, defend the careful application of the terms "ideology" and "propaganda" to the Augustan world. Cf. the nuanced approach of Zanker (1988), e.g. 89–98 on the "*res publica restituta.*" Scott (1933) remains a fundamental collection and discussion of political propaganda in the earlier triumviral period, now supplemented by the comprehensive Borgies (2016).

[26] A detailed prosopography of Seneca's declaimers is beyond the scope of my book (see Bornecque [1902] 143–201 for the basic collection of material; cf. Migliario [2007] 22–31 with more up to date discussion and references and Migliario [2008] with speculative conjectures on the declaimers of *suas.* 6 and 7). I will, however, point out that e.g. Porcius Latro (*contr.* 2.4.12–13), Lucius Vinicius (*contr.* 2.5.20), Varius Geminus (*contr.* 6.8), Gavius Silo (*contr.* 10 pr. 14), Quintus Haterius (*contr.* 4 pr. 7), and the Greeks Craton and Timagenes (*contr.* 10.5.21–22) all declaim before Augustus. This does not even begin to take into account the other networks of power that the declaimers were part of; Cestius Pius, for example, had among his pupils Quintilius Varus, son-in-law of Germanicus and son of the infamous losing general of the Teutoburg Forest, and felt so secure in his position that he could mock the unfortunate youth by saying, "It was by that sort of carelessness that your father lost his army" (*ista neglentia pater tuus exercitum perdidit, contr.* 1.3.10). Seneca generally promotes the expected imperial line: in discussing a declamation of Latro's before Augustus, Agrippa, and Maecenas, he says that he has no pity for those who would rather "lose their head than a choice remark" (*horum non possum misereri qui tanti putant caput potius quam dictum perdere, contr.* 2.4.13). On the declaimers as teachers, cf. n. 2 above. Note too, in a later era, that Quintilian is tutor to Domitian's possible successors (Quint. *inst.* 4 pr. 2; cf. Suet. *Dom.* 15).

[27] For a different take on the political dimensions of the Cicero declamations, cf. Miglario (2007) 121–149 and (2008); she tries to recover a lively political debate based on what Seneca's declaimers say and what she can surmise about their biographies. The weaknesses of this approach are well cataloged by Feddern (2013) 70–75; note esp. that the declaimers are speaking to persuade (and entertain) an audience, not to give voice to their true feelings, and that much of Migliario's detailed prosopographical speculation is dubious. We are on much safer ground when we look at the other side of the coin, i.e. not what the declaimers are really thinking, but what they say to persuade their audience.

The Death of Cicero: Declaimers Writing History

Virtually every declaimer places the blame for Cicero's death squarely at Antony's doorstep; no one criticizes Octavian. Consider Popillius again. Marcellus Aeserninus explains how he came to be sent on a mission to kill Cicero (Sen. *contr.* 7.2.10):

> cogitabat … secum Antonius: "quod Ciceroni excogitabo supplicium? occidi iussero? olim iam aduersus hunc metum emuniuit animum: scit mortem nec inmaturam esse consulari nec miseram sapienti. fiat aliquid noui, quod non expectat, quod non timet; non indignatur ceruicem hosti porrigere, indignabitur clienti. Popillium aliquis uocet, ut sciat quantum illi defensi rei profuerint."

> Antony was wondering: "What punishment shall I think up for Cicero? Shall I order him to be killed? But he has long since fortified his mind against fear of that: he knows that death is not premature for a man of consular rank nor wretched for a wise man. Let me devise something new, which he neither expects nor fears; he does not consider it beneath him to extend his neck for an enemy, but he will for a client. Let someone summon Popillius, so that he might learn how much the defense of a guilty man profited him."

This is savage criticism, but not of Popillius. It is instead Antony who is vicious and without scruple, and Popillius is merely the dumb instrument of his misguided sadism. Shunting blame onto Antony is the most common technique used to exculpate Octavian in this sorry affair. As a sidenote that will become more important in the next chapter, notice that this declaimer echoes and twists Cicero's own words: "No death can be shameful for a brave man or premature for a man of consular rank or miserable for a wise man" (*neque turpis mors forti uiro potest accidere neque immatura consulari nec misera sapienti*, Cic. *Cat.* 4.3). In the declamation the words are placed in Antony's mouth, and he presumably speaks them with derisive contempt, "remembering" the end of the second *Philippic*, where Cicero repeats them (*etenim si abhinc annos prope uiginti hoc ipso in templo negaui posse mortem immaturam esse consulari, quanto uerius nunc negabo seni?*, *Phil.* 2.119). But immediately after this verbatim quotation, our declaimer offers a meta-literary comment, saying, "Let me devise something new" (*fiat aliquid noui*): thus he self-consciously adverts to his own citation, only to trump Cicero's words with a novel twist, a savage punishment of his own. Such reworking of Ciceronianisms is a form of intertextuality that is absolutely standard for the declaimers when they talk about him, but virtually never used when they write about other subjects.

This very sentiment on death is in fact reiterated *ad uerbum* at Sen. *suas.* 6.12, and in general *contr.* 7.2 teems with echoes of Cicero. By stark contrast, the *Declamationes minores* ascribed to Quintilian almost completely lack such tags, as do Seneca's declamations that do not concern Cicero.[28] There seems to have been a strong feeling that when talking about Cicero it was right and proper to use his *ipsissima uerba*. This tendency reaches its zenith in the various pseudo-Ciceronian rhetorical exercises, in which the declaimer actually takes on the persona of Cicero himself and attempts to imitate his every quirk of thought and diction, as we will see in the next chapter, but the same allusive pattern recurs in authors as diverse as Velleius Paterculus and Juvenal.

Most of the remarks quoted by Seneca from this declamation are given over to *sententiae* bursting with rhetorical fireworks, virtually all intended to scorch and singe the morally bankrupt Popillius. "What luck Cicero had! Antony, who had proscribed him, he had accused; Popillius, who killed him, he had defended" (*fortunam Ciceronis! Antonius illum proscripsit, qui accusatus est, Popillius occidit, qui defensus est*); "the man who the living Cicero said was no parricide was shown to be one by Cicero's death" (*parricidam quem uiuos negarit Cicero, occisus ostendit*); "no one but Popillius could have killed Cicero – just as no one but Cicero could have defended Popillius" (*non magis quisquam alius occidere Ciceronem potuit praeter Popillium <quam quisquam alius Popillium> praeter Ciceronem defendere*); and so forth.[29]

Comments of this sort tend to tell us more about declamatory methods than about Cicero, but there are nevertheless some worthwhile gleanings to be had in the rhetorical harvest. First there is the obvious point that the theme heroizes Cicero's death and takes as a given the deficient character of his killer. After all, "could anyone kill Cicero who had heard him speak?" (*Ciceronem quisquam potuit occidere qui audiit?*, Sen. *contr.* 7.2.6).[30] Cicero's supreme virtue of eloquence is thus repeatedly emphasized,

---

[28] For echoes of Cicero in Sen. *contr.* 7.2, see: *contr.* 7.2.1 (Cic. *Verr.* 5.118), 7.2.3 (Cic. *S. Rosc.* 72), 7.2.5 (*bis*: Cic. *Phil.* 2.64 and *p. red. in sen.* 39 [*uel sim.*]), 7.2.6 (e.g. Cic. *Sest.* 49 and perhaps *Brut.* 230), 7.2.10 (Cic. *Cat.* 4.3 and *Phil.* 2.119). In the *Declamationes minores* ascribed to Quintilian the index of Winterbottom (1984) s.v. "Cicero, Master shows acquaintance with" contains only seven entries for 289 pages of Latin text. On these points, see Winterbottom (1982) 252–253, Kaster (1998) 253–254. For references to Cicero in the *Declamationes maiores*, again not frequent, see Håkanson (2014) 26–35. Many of even these are in the category of coincidence.

[29] All drawn from Mento's remarks at *contr.* 7.2.3. Cf. the "only a Cicero could adequately praise Cicero" motif, p. 134 below.

[30] Cf. Kaster (1998) 249, who is rather harsh on this typical declamatory paradox: "The question, when I first encountered it, stopped me in my tracks because of its sheer and compounded fatuousness: it is fatuous because it is asked with reference to Cicero's killers, who certainly *had* heard him speak;

sometimes in the form of his skill as an advocate – as we just read, "no one but Cicero could have defended (a man so guilty as) Popillius"!³¹ Other signal moments of Cicero's career come in for mention as well, if less frequently. Triarius, for example, reviews some Ciceronian highlights under the guise of begging Popillius to let him live, referring to Verres, Catiline, and perhaps Clodius (*contr.* 7.2.4).³² Catiline is also referred to by Capito, who claims that Cicero saved Rome from Catiline, an enemy who came closer to the city than any of her other historical foes (*contr.* 7.2.7). We will see some more of these highlights mentioned below.

The defense had a tough row to hoe, and few seem to have taken it up willingly; the declaimers, after all, accuse Popillius "as if he could not possibly be defended" (Sen. *contr.* 7.2.8). Romanius Hispo decided on a hard line and inveighed against Cicero, but he was apparently the only one (*solus ex declamatoribus in Ciceronem inuectus est, contr.* 7.2.13).³³ Once again we see that it is a fundamental premise of the case that Cicero's death was wrong in every possible way. The more common strategy for the defense was displacement, first using the age-old evasion "I was only following orders" (*necessitate coactum fecisse, contr.* 7.2.10). This excuse is repeated time and again, and what it really amounts to, of course, is not so much a defense of Popillius – the action is still admitted to be wrong – as an indictment of Antony. Sometimes this indictment remains implicit, but more often it is made explicit: "Send for that client and friend of Cicero," Buteo makes Antony say. "I have discovered how Cicero can die by his own hand" (*contr.* 7.2.12). Just so Cestius and Arellius Fuscus (*contr.* 7.2.13), or most brutally Marcellus Aeserninus (*contr.* 7.2.10, quoted above p. 111). Convicting Antony neatly absolves Octavian of responsibility.

Many of the themes and emphases that we have already met will be found in the other two declamations treating Cicero's death as well, a consistently

---

and it is fatuous because it is asked by a man who almost certainly could *not* himself have heard Cicero speak, for reasons of simple chronology." On p. 255 he criticizes another such sentiment, when Seneca laments that because of the civil wars he was prevented from hearing Cicero speak (*contr.* 1 pr. 11): *alioqui in illo atriolo in quo duos grandes praetextatos ait secum declamasse potui adesse, illudque ingenium quod solum populus Romanus par imperio suo habuit cognoscere.* Kaster comments that "it is of course the sheer extravagance of the conceit that is truly breath-taking, as Cicero's individual *ingenium* is equated with the value of the vast expanse of empire." In fact, however, this phrase is not simply praise of Cicero but also a clever allusion to Caesar's commendation of Cicero as quoted by Plin. *nat.* 7.117 (see p. 128 below).

³¹ Cf. other remarks *passim*, e.g. *contr.* 7.2.4, 7.2.5, etc.

³² There is a textual issue that prevents certainty about the mention of Clodius; see the apparatus of Håkanson (1989a) ad loc.

³³ Seneca admits that despite its intrinsic distaste, this approach was well handled by Hispo (*hic color prima specie asperior est, sed ab illo egregie tractatus est, contr.* 7.2.13). Earlier in the paragraph Seneca describes the *color* as *uehemens* and *durus*.

popular subject for the declamatory classroom (Quint. *inst.* 3.8.46). Each of these focuses on a similar dilemma, viz. whether Cicero should make some concession to Antony in order to save his own skin – in *suas.* 6 the declaimer advises him on whether to beg for forgiveness, in *suas.* 7 on whether to agree to burn his books. In the sixth *Suasoria* there is particular scope to praise Cicero's character, including some fascinating comparisons with Cato the Younger. Cicero's life and virtues are simplified, the gray ambiguities painted away by stark Catonian blacks and whites, and he is seen as a man who has lived too long, a *rei publicae superstes* (Sen. *suas.* 6.6).[34] The seventh *Suasoria* mostly revolves around Cicero's inimitable eloquence, which we have also already treated at some length. Cicero's moral virtues – as manifested by the fearless *cursus honorum* recounted by Cestius Pius[35] – produced his eloquence, and his eloquence led to his glorious death. Since in these scenarios Cicero is not yet looking up at the sharp edge of the executioner's blade, there is perforce less scope for elaboration on his final moments. Aside from this particular, however, most of the rest of the two declamations is of a piece with what we have seen so far.[36]

So consider only the universal condemnation of Antony. In his version of the blame game, Triarius soars to mythological heights on Cicero's own wings (Sen. *suas.* 6.5):

> "quae Charybdis est tam uorax? Charybdim dixi, quae, si fuit, animal unum fuit? uix me dius fidius Oceanus tot res tamque diuersas uno tempore absorbere potuisset." huic tu saeuienti putas Ciceronem posse subduci?

> "What Charybdis is so ravenous? Did I say 'Charybdis'? If she existed at all, she was just one creature. Good heavens, scarcely could the whole Ocean

---

[34] Cf. *suas.* 6.1 for the same theme of outliving the Republic. Cato likewise became a figure of schoolroom declamations (cf. e.g. Sen. *epist.* 24.6–7, Pers. *sat.* 3.45–47, and van der Poel [2009] 350). In *suas.* 6 Cicero is exhorted to follow Cato's example, which he himself had praised (*suas.* 6.4); Cestius instructs him to die bravely so that he might be counted with Cato, and Marcellus plays a variation on the theme (*suas.* 6.10). Quintus Haterius is most explicit (*suas.* 6.2): *M. Cato, solus maximum uiuendi moriendique exemplum, mori maluit quam rogare – nec erat Antonium rogaturus – et illas usque ad ultimum diem puras a ciuili sanguine manus in pectus sacerrimum armauit.* Velleius Paterculus also seems sometimes to intertwine Cicero and Cato; see Pelling (2011b) 165. Note that Cato seems eventually to be more remembered for his resolute way of life than his political views; so Gowing (2005) 79, Gallia (2012) 137–144.

[35] *Suas.* 7.2 *quid <referam> consulatum salutarem urbi, quid exilium consulatu honestius, quid prouocatam inter initia adulescentiae libertate tirocinii tui Sullanam potentiam, quid Antonium auulsum <a> Catilina, rei publicae redditum? ignosce, Cicero, <si> diu ista narrauero: forsitan hoc die nouissime audiuntur.*

[36] Indeed, we may even sometimes read significance into silences: *uide ut Cicero audiat Lepidum, Cicero audiat Antonium, nemo Ciceronem* (*suas.* 7.8) – why is there no mention of Octavian? Cf. Migliario (2008) 85–86, Feddern (2013) 75, ad loc. pp. 508–509 (including discussion of the textual difficulty with *uide ut*).

have swallowed up so many different things all at once." Do you think that Cicero could be saved from such a savage beast?

Triarius has reproduced Cic. *Phil.* 2.67 almost exactly. This was a popular schoolroom passage; Quintilian quotes it on several occasions and once adds that this is one of those famous passages well known even to students (*nota sunt enim etiam studiosis haec lumina, inst.* 12.10.62).[37] In these declamations too we find countless Ciceronian echoes and allusions. Pompeius Silo, for example, asks Cicero, "Will not even your groans be free?" This reworks Cicero's passage about the Roman people's last vestiges of freedom in Caesarian servitude, when Antony was auctioning off Pompey's property, *gemitus tamen populi Romani liber fuit* ("nevertheless, the groans of the Roman people were free," *Phil.* 2.64). Silo has neatly redirected the phrase at Cicero: once Cicero used this as a confident statement of the defiance of the Roman spirit; now it is turned into a forward-looking question that Cicero will answer by his choice to keep silent or to speak out bravely and freely, that is, by choosing to live or die.[38]

The second *Philippic* was a popular quarry for such phrases, and these examples are easily multiplied.[39] In Seneca's declaimers they are mostly small bits of direct quotation. For example, consider Sen. *suas.* 6.7: Argentarius, encouraging Cicero to resist Antony, says that when Antony, "reeling with wine and sleep" – an image straight out of the *Philippics* – raises his drooping eyes to look upon the heads of the men he has sentenced to death, "it is no longer enough for you, Cicero, just to say *hominem nequam!*" (Sen. *suas.* 6.7 and Cic. *Phil.* 2.77). The target is the same for both Argentarius and Cicero – Antony – but the meaning is different, for Argentarius uses Cicero's phrase not only to evoke the second *Philippic* but to show that speech is no longer sufficient. Cicero, Argentarius implies by his allusion, can no longer just talk: he must match deeds with words and act. Again then Cicero's own words are felt to be particularly appropriate when talking about Cicero himself, and none could be more apposite than those drawn from what Juvenal called

---

[37] Cf. *inst.* 8.4.25, 8.6.70.

[38] Cf. too Quintus Haterius' remark (Sen. *contr.* 7.2.5): *proposito in rostris capite Ciceronis, quamvis omnia metu tenerentur, gemitus tamen populi liber fuit*, where, as Winterbottom (1982) 252 remarks, "there is a sort of *aemulatio*," since (he feels) the phrase was better employed at the death of Cicero than at the auction of Antony. But it could also be observed that the phrase is more pointed when Antony is tearing apart the Republic than when he is running an auction.

[39] Cf. e.g. Sen. *suas.* 6.12 and Cic. *Phil.* 2.119 (likewise Sen. *contr.* 7.2.10, discussed on p. 111 above), *suas.* 7.2 and *Phil.* 2.24, *suas.* 7.5 and *Phil.* 2.20, 2.71, and perhaps 2.5.

"divine second *Philippic*." In the next chapter we will meet with more sophisticated allusive reworkings of these famous passages.

These declamations simply presuppose that Antony is uniquely responsible for Cicero's death, and the criticism is unrelenting. The declaimer Argentarius' opening remarks are typical: "Antony is in no way to be trusted. Do I lie? He is capable of anything if he is capable of killing Cicero and incapable of saving his life without greater cruelty than he would show in killing him" (*nihil Antonio credendum est. mentior? quid enim iste non potest qui occidere Ciceronem potest, qui seruare nisi crudelius quam occidat non potest?*, Sen. *suas.* 7.7). Antony is untrustworthy, he is cruel, he is a vomiting drunkard; see, for example, the words of Porcius Latro (*suas.* 6.3):

> uidebis ardentes crudelitate simul ac superbia oculos; uidebis illum non hominis sed belli ciuilis uultum; uidebis illas fauces per quas bona Cn. Pompei transierunt, illa latera, illam totius corporis gladiatoriam firmitatem; uidebis illum pro tribunali locum quem modo magister equitum, cui ructare turpe erat, uomitu foedauerat.

> You will see his eyes burning with both cruelty and arrogance; you will see the face not of a man but of civil war; you will see that gullet that gulped down the property of Pompey, those flanks, the gladiatorial strength of his whole body; you will see that place on the tribunal which just now, when he was Master of the Horse – for whom even a burp would have been shameful! – he polluted with his vomit.

The narrow focus on Antony and the repeated insistence on his multifarious vices aligns perfectly with Augustan values, and this piece of propaganda will become the standard line for later writers to follow. Any niggling doubts about Octavian's role are quickly swept aside; the declaimer Cornelius Hispanus, for example, contends that Octavian was forced to agree because his fellow triumvirs made concessions by sacrificing their own relatives: Antony proscribed his uncle and Lepidus his own brother; "so many parricides were committed so that Cicero might die!" (*alter fratrem proscribi, alter auunculum patitur . . . ut Cicero periret, tot parricidia facta sunt*, Sen. *suas.* 6.7). Conveniently both L. Aemilius Paulus and Lucius Caesar were later pardoned (Cass. Dio 47.8.1, 5); Cicero was not. Again we should be very skeptical of this rhetorical justification for Cicero's death. Cicero was a powerful man who, as we have seen, stood with the "Liberators" after Caesar's death; he was on the wrong side and could be counted on to oppose the dismantling of Republican institutions and the concentration of power in the hands of one man – or three. Only one declaimer dares try to give voice to this suspicion, Albucius: "if any of the triumvirs doesn't hate you, he still finds you a burden" (*solus ex declamatoribus temptauit dicere non unum illi esse Antonium infestum . . . "si cui ex triumuiris non es inuisus, grauis es, "*Sen. *suas.* 6.9).[40] Furthermore, as Syme observed, Cicero's wealth would have made him an attractive target.[41] But this supposed justification for Octavian's failure to protect Cicero enters the declamatory consciousness early, and it is then faithfully repeated by later writers.

Consider Plutarch again, who tells the same story. He records that for two whole days Octavian stoutly resisted including Cicero among the proscribed, but on the third the combined force of Antony and Lepidus overwhelmed him (Plut. *Cic.* 46.2–5):[42]

κατεγράφησαν ἄνδρες οὓς ἔδει θνῄσκειν ὑπὲρ διακοσίους. πλείστην δὲ τῶν ἀμφισβητημάτων αὐτοῖς ἔριν ἡ Κικέρωνος προγραφὴ παρέσχεν, Ἀντωνίου μὲν ἀσυμβάτως ἔχοντος, εἰ μὴ πρῶτος ἐκεῖνος ἀποθνήσκοι, Λεπίδου δ' Ἀντωνίῳ προστιθεμένου, <u>Καίσαρος δὲ πρὸς ἀμφοτέρους ἀντέχοντος</u> . . . <u>λέγεται δὲ τὰς πρώτας ἡμέρας διαγωνισάμενος ὑπὲρ τοῦ Κικέρωνος ὁ Καῖσαρ ἐνδοῦναι τῇ τρίτῃ καὶ προέσθαι τὸν ἄνδρα.</u> τὰ δὲ τῆς ἀντιδόσεως οὕτως εἶχεν. ἔδει Κικέρωνος μὲν ἐκστῆναι Καίσαρα, Παύλου δὲ τἀδελφοῦ Λέπιδον, Λευκίου δὲ Καίσαρος Ἀντώνιον, ὃς ἦν θεῖος αὐτῷ πρὸς μητρός.

They made out a list of men who must be put to death, more than two hundred in number. The proscription of Cicero, however, caused the most strife in their debates, Antony consenting to no terms unless Cicero should be the first man to be put to death, Lepidus siding with Antony, <u>and Caesar holding out against them both . . . It is said that for the first two days Caesar kept up his struggle to save Cicero, but yielded on the third day and gave him up.</u> The terms of their mutual concessions were as follows. Caesar was to abandon Cicero, Lepidus his brother Paulus, and Antony Lucius Caesar, who was his uncle on his mother's side.

Florus, the second-century Roman historian, says the same thing (*epit.* 2.16.1), as do writers like Cassius Dio, who, after claiming that Antony and Lepidus were responsible for the majority of the ills related to the proscriptions (47.7.1), goes so far as to insist that Octavian actually "saved as many as he could" from the lists (πολλούς, ὅσους γε καὶ ἠδυνήθη, διεσώσατο,

---

[40] Cf. e.g. the hostility found in or implied by the passages discussed in n. 14 above.

[41] Syme (1939) 195. App. *BC* 4.5 adverts to this motivation for the proscriptions more generally (cf. Cass. Dio 47.5–6); on this passage in Appian, see Gowing (1992) 249–250.

[42] Cf. the similar condemnation of Antony at Plut. *comp. Dem. et Ant.* 5.1: Ἀντώνιος δὲ τὸν ἀδελφὸν τῆς μητρὸς ἐξέδωκεν ἐπὶ τῷ Κικέρωνα ἀποκτεῖναι, πρᾶγμα καὶ καθ' ἑαυτὸ μιαρὸν καὶ ὠμόν, ὡς μόλις <ἂν> Ἀντώνιον ἐπ' αὐτῷ συγγνώμης τυχεῖν, εἰ σωτηρίας τοῦ θείου μισθὸς ἦν ὁ Κικέρωνος θάνατος.

47.8.1). This is simply the standard declamatory line repeated as historical fact. This voice of Augustan propaganda was amplified by the megaphone of the declamatory classroom almost to the point that it drowned out everything else, and was repeated again and again in the minds of young men over decades. When the political issues sensitive for the early imperial regime had long since perished, the tradition had already taken on a life of its own and continued to live on.

It is remarkable and cannot be coincidence that we have three declamations treating this one theme: this was a very popular and influential set of exercises in the rhetorical schools (cf. Quint. *inst.* 3.8.46), and I will underscore again the outsized influence of declamation on elite culture. The declaimers, taken as a body, present a fairly consistent picture of Cicero. He was a man of distinguished career and unmatched eloquence, the last bastion of heroic virtue, a Catonian holdout who had outlived his time. Set against the evil Antony in a struggle to the death, he ultimately lost the battle but won the war: he was cruelly murdered, but he lives on through his immortal eloquence as an icon of resistance to Antony's tyranny. The rough edges of a complex and inconsistent life are smoothed over into one coherent image. Such a process is no doubt necessary for canonization, especially in the schoolroom. Nevertheless, this image is hardly confined within the four walls of the rhetorical classroom: as we shall see presently, it is widely adopted by later writers. Moreover, these writers also adopt the declamatory mode when discussing Cicero: amid otherwise pedestrian prose they will suddenly take wing with flights of rhetorical force, they will quote Cicero and imitate him, and they will repeat all the sacred stories of his now-canonical mythology, assailing Antony and the perfidious Popillius while extolling the snow-white Octavian. When they think of Cicero, they think back to their school days and slip effortlessly into declamatory prose. The myths and messages set in motion by Augustan ideology were enshrined in young minds in the rhetorical schools and reinforced; through declamation they were amplified in a sort of feedback loop as the young men grew up and began writing themselves. First the declaimers wrote history; then the historians wrote declamation.

The Death of Cicero: Historians Writing Declamation

When reading Velleius Paterculus' description of Cicero's death, you could be forgiven for thinking that he was writing for the pages of Seneca's

Suasoriae.[43] He switches effortlessly (and self-consciously) into declamatory mode, and he reiterates many of the themes that we have seen emphasized by the declaimers. First he sets the stage (2.64.3–4):

> haec sunt tempora quibus M. Tullius continuis actionibus <u>aeternas Antonii memoriae inussit notas</u>, sed hic fulgentissimo et caelesti ore, at tribunus Cannutius canina rabie lacerabat Antonium. utrique uindicta libertatis morte stetit; sed tribuni sanguine commissa proscriptio, Ciceronis <u>uelut satiato Antonio</u> paene finita.

> This is the time when Cicero in a series of speeches <u>branded the memory of Antony with everlasting marks of infamy</u>. Cicero railed at Antony with eloquence like thunder raining down from the heavens, while Cannutius the tribune tore him to pieces with the ravening of a mad dog. For each man this defense of liberty was bought at the cost of his life; the proscription was begun with the blood of the tribune, and was nearly brought to an end with Cicero's, <u>as though Antony were now sated</u>.

Cicero's eloquence in the *Philippics* is yet again the centerpiece of the description. Velleius' language in the evocative phrase *fulgentissimo et caelesti ore* is paralleled in authors like Columella (Colum. 1 pr. 30; cf. Sil. Ital. 8.410), and Velleius himself will presently refer again to Cicero's *caelestissimi oris* (2.66.3). This must have been a typical way of talking about Cicero, and indeed descriptions of his eloquence in terms of thunder and lightning go back to Cicero's own lifetime.[44] Furthermore, Velleius adopts the declamatory trope of talking about Cicero in Cicero's own words; *inurere notas* ("to brand with a mark") is a common expression in Cicero, especially in the *Philippics*, where the memory of Antony is likewise stigmatized with eternal infamy: *quem ego inustum ... notis tradam hominum memoriae sempiternae* ("I shall <u>brand him with the truest marks of infamy</u> and hand him over to the <u>everlasting memory of posterity</u>," *Phil.* 13.40).[45] This phrase, however, virtually never occurs outside of Cicero in

---

[43] For detailed commentary on this passage, see Woodman (1983) ad loc., who rightly observes that Velleius "has produced what is essentially a suasorial speech; but it is cast in a historical mould" (144); cf. too the briefer remarks in the commentary of Elefante (1997) ad loc. pp. 367–369. Gowing (2005) 44–48 discusses this passage in the context of the continuity of Republic and Empire in Velleius' history; cf. Gowing (2005) 34–66 and Gowing (2010) on the ideological underpinnings of writing history under Tiberius, with reference to both Velleius and Valerius Maximus. The analysis of Schmitzer (2000) 184–189 places the passage in the context of Velleius' work as a whole. Velleius is also discussed by Pierini (2003) 33–37. Lobur (2008) 126, 147 notes that this passage significantly occurs almost exactly in the middle of the book.

[44] Cf. Cic. *fam.* 9.21.1, to Paetus: *insanire tibi uideris quod imitere uerborum meorum, ut scribis, fulmina?*

[45] Cf. *Phil.* 1.32 *haec inusta est a te (Antonio) ... mortuo Caesari nota ad ignominiam sempiternam, Phil.* 14.7 *quae sunt urbanarum maledicta litium, non inustae belli interneciui notae*, and *Cat.* 1.13

this sense – except here.[46] Velleius thus looks back to the very words of Cicero's *Philippics* when he wants to talk about Cicero's demise, following the declaimers, who, as we have seen, delight in matching Ciceronian form to Ciceronian content.

Besides emphasizing Cicero's eloquence and echoing his words, Velleius shows other tendencies that we have seen in Seneca the Elder. Consider his image of the bloodthirsty Antony being sated, and compare what Velleius says with this passage from Cremutius Cordus, a historian influenced by the declamatory tradition: "Antony was happy when he saw Cicero's death. He said that his proscription was finished, for he was not only sated with citizen slaughter, but indeed stuffed, and he displayed Cicero on the rostra" (*quibus uisis laetus Antonius, cum peractam proscriptionem suam dixisset esse, quippe non satiatus modo caedendis ciuibus sed differtus quoque, super rostra exponit,* Sen. *suas.* 6.19).[47] In both versions Cicero's death marks the end of the persecutions and Antony is said to be "sated"; the same ideas recur even in later Greek authors like Plutarch (p. 142 below) and Appian (p. 144). Moreover, Cicero is painted as a staunch champion of *libertas*, and its opposite, tyranny, is completely embodied in the person of Antony. Cicero good, Antony bad: this suits the simplified world of declamatory rhetoric perfectly, and, as we have seen, is in line with the Augustan ideology that the declaimers manifest. This "defense of liberty" led directly to Cicero's death – that is to say, Cicero's death is entirely due to Antony.

Antony's leading role and Octavian's innocence are made even plainer in the sequel. Velleius briefly describes the formation of the triumvirate – which Caesar's heir only acquiesced in, Velleius claims, because Antony threatened to join forces with Brutus and Cassius otherwise, and certainly only with a view toward avenging his father – and then he lets slip the dogs of declamation in full-throated growl (2.66.1–2):

> furente deinde Antonio simulque Lepido ... repugnante Caesare, sed frustra aduersus duos, instauratum Sullani exempli malum, proscriptio. nihil tam indignum illo tempore fuit quam quod aut Caesar aliquem proscribere coactus est aut ab ullo Cicero proscriptus est. abscisaque scelere

---

Woodman (1983) ad loc. adds *Pis.* 41 *sempiternas ... notas.* For more Ciceronian examples of *inuro notam*, see Merguet (1877–1884) s.v. *inuro.*

[46] *TLL* vii.2.270.16–19 (Hiltbrunner) cites no example of the phrase in this sense aside from Cicero until Lactantius, although Pliny the Younger does seem to offer one instance (*epist.* 9.13.17, nowhere cited in the *TLL* entry). Literally the phrase is used of branding animals (e.g. Verg. *georg.* 3.158), but even this usage is rather rare.

[47] Cordus (*FRHist* 71) seems to have been born shortly after 35 BC, and so he would have grown up with our Ciceronian declamations.

Antonii uox publica est, cum eius salutem nemo defendisset qui per tot annos et publicam ciuitatis et priuatam ciuium defenderat.

Then as Antony and Lepidus raged madly ... proscriptions, the wicked custom sanctioned by Sulla's precedent, were renewed, even though Caesar fought against it – but he fought in vain, being but one against two. Nothing was so unworthy at that time as the fact that Caesar was forced to proscribe anyone or that Cicero was proscribed by anyone. The voice of the people was cut off by Antony's wicked crime, when no one defended the safety of the man who for so many years had defended both the public safety of the state and the private safety of its citizens.

In case you were in any doubt about who was responsible for Cicero's death, Velleius again makes it abundantly clear: it was the mad Mark Antony. It was by Antony's crime that the *uox publica* was cut off from the *res publica*. And if you were to suspect Octavian's complicity, Velleius says, you would be entirely wrong. Caesar's heir fought manfully against such injustices, but he was simply outnumbered. He was forced against his will to go along with the shameful proscriptions – and this coercion of a noble and upright young man was the most shameful thing of all. This line of reasoning comes straight from the declaimers, as we saw above, and will be repeated by later historians as well. Florus, for example, says nearly the same thing (*epit.* 2.16.1):[48]

cum solus etiam grauis paci, grauis rei publicae esset Antonius, quasi ignis incendio Lepidus accessit. quid contra duos consules, duos exercitus? necesse fuit uenire in cruentissimi foederis societatem.

Although Antony alone was a grave threat to both peace and the Republic, Lepidus joined him and added fuel to the fire. What could he [i.e. Octavian] do against two consuls, against two armies? Necessity compelled him to join as a partner in the bloody pact.

Octavian is again coerced into acquiescence under duress and protest. With the proscriptions renewed, Florus goes on, each member of the triumvirate showed his true character: Lepidus acted out of greed, Antony out of hatred and vengeance, but Caesar out of the sincere desire to punish those who had murdered his father (*Caesarem inultus pater et manibus eius graues Cassius et Brutus agitabant*, 2.16.2). Antony and Lepidus proscribed their own relatives, but Caesar only his father's killers (2.16.4), and then only so that justice could be served (*Caesar percussoribus patris contentus fuit, ideo ne, si inulta fuisset, etiam iusta eius caedes haberetur*, 2.16.6).

---

[48] As does Orosius 6.18.10–12.

So it was all Antony's fault. Velleius again invokes the motif of Cicero as *uox publica*, identifying him with his eloquence and refashioning him as the people's champion who had fought for both the state and its citizens against Antony's tyranny (cf. p. 84 above). The choice of verb, *abscidere*, is also piquant: "to cut off a voice" is striking Latin. Anthony Woodman notes that *uox . . . abscisa* may be modeled on *abscidere linguam*,[49] and, as we have seen, Cicero is intimately identified with his *lingua*. At the same time, however, I would also point out that Cicero literally was beheaded, as Velleius says just a few lines later (*capitis abscisi*, 2.66.3), and so the resonance with the even more common *abscidere caput* must also be strong.[50] The polyvalent *abscisa . . . uox publica* further includes the notion that Cicero, the emblematic *uox* of the *res publica*, has been forcibly amputated from the body politic.[51]

Now, however, Velleius truly opens the full declamatory floodgates, and in a very self-aware and deliberate fashion (2.66.3–5):

> <u>nihil</u> tamen <u>egisti</u>, M. Antoni – cogit enim excedere propos="propositi" formam operis erumpens animo ac pectore indignatio – <u>nihil, inquam, egisti</u> mercedem caelestissimi oris et clarissimi capitis abscisi numerando auctoramentoque funebri ad <u>conseruatoris quondam rei publicae</u> tantique consulis irritando necem. <u>rapuisti tum Ciceroni lucem sollicitam et aetatem senilem et uitam</u> <u>miseriorem, te principe, quam sub te triumuiro mortem, famam uero</u> <u>gloriamque factorum atque dictorum adeo non abstulisti, ut auxeris. uiuit</u> <u>uiuetque per omnem saeculorum memoriam, dum</u>que hoc uel forte uel prouidentia uel utcumque constitutum rerum naturae corpus, quod ille paene solus Romanorum animo uidit, ingenio complexus est, eloquentia illuminauit, <u>manebit incolume</u>, comitem aeui sui laudem Ciceronis trahet <u>omnisque posteritas illius in te scripta mirabitur, tuum in eum factum</u> execrabitur citiusque [in] mundo genus hominum quam <M. Cicero> cedet.[52]

> But <u>you accomplished nothing</u>, Mark Antony – for the indignation bursting forth from the soul in my breast forces me to go beyond the limits of the work I've proposed for myself – <u>you accomplished nothing</u>, I say, by counting out a reward for the sealing of Cicero's godlike mouth and the severing of his most famous head and by provoking with a hit contract the death of <u>the man who once saved the republic</u> and who was so great a consul. <u>You snatched away from Cicero a few troubled days and senile years and</u> <u>a life that would have been more miserable under your power than was his</u>

---

[49] Woodman (1983) ad loc. Cf. *TLL* 1.147.83–148.6 (Lehnert) for instances of *abscidere linguam*.
[50] See *TLL* 1.148.6–15 (Lehnert) for a collection of the instances.
[51] Similar images of amputation of a part from the body politic are found at e.g. Cic. *Sest*. 135, *Phil*. 8.15.
[52] For the text, see Woodman (1983) ad loc.

death in your triumvirate. But you did not take away from him the fame and glory of his words and deeds; in fact you increased them. He lives and will live on in the memory of the ages, and as long as this universe (whether established by chance or divine providence or any other way), which he almost alone of all the Romans saw with his soul, grasped with his mind, illuminated with his eloquence, as long as this universe endures, it will carry with it as a companion for all time Cicero's fame, and all posterity will admire what he wrote against you, while what you did to him will be cursed, and sooner will the human race disappear from this world than Marcus Tullius Cicero.

The rhetorical fireworks are on full display as we are barraged by a flurry of figures.[53] Velleius apostrophizes Mark Antony directly – and straightaway interrupts himself with a deliberate anacoluthon in order to "excuse" his coming outburst, which, as he openly acknowledges, exceeds the bounds of narrative history and passes fully into the realm of declamation.[54] You can tell that he has done this sort of thing in school before. (Velleius' *indignatio*, which supposedly provokes this eruption of emotion, echoes the note sounded in 2.66.2 by the word *indignum* applied to the whole situation.) He then picks up his emphatic opening *nihil egisti* with anaphora, underscoring the repetition by *inquam*. No Roman reader could ever have been in any doubt that with this emotional opening sentence, crammed with rhetorical figures, we have moved from the more measured Muse of history to the loftier heights of epideictic oratory.

Velleius goes on, as he could not fail to do, to discuss Cicero's "godlike mouth" – again a metonymy for his eloquence – and his "most famous head" that has now been so ignobly amputated. This is a keynote for the declaimers too, providing as it does a pathos-packed picture – see Sen. *contr.* 7.2 *passim* – but Velleius layers in further Ciceronian reminiscences. The first is obvious enough even at this distance: Cicero is accorded the "title" *conseruator rei publicae*, just as he had so often styled himself in the *Philippics* and elsewhere (e.g. *Phil.* 2.51, 3.28).[55] That, however, was all of course *quondam*; the glorious past contrasts sharply with the current sad state of affairs. Velleius' second element is more subtle. The *auctoramentum funebre* ("death contract") manages to evoke Cicero's caricature of Antony as gladiator while at the same time characterizing the cold *quid pro quo* of the

---

[53] Rhetoric at these heights in Velleius is found only in this passage; see Schmitzer (2000) 186.

[54] For discussion of the work's "plan" (*forma*), see Rich (2011), with brief mention of this departure at pp. 73–74.

[55] See too e.g. *har. resp.* 58, *Vatin.* 7, *Pis.* 23, *Mil.* 73, etc. Comprehensively Merguet (1877–1884) s.v. *conseruator*. The phrase recurs in the pseudepigrapha discussed below, e.g. *epist. ad Oct.* 2.

slaying. As Woodman astutely notes, "*auctoramentum* ... is literally a contract or fee for gladiators ... and is doubly effective: its bluntness reflects the brutality of the murder, and Velleius no doubt remembered that Cicero had regularly abused Antony with the term *gladiator*."[56] The word furthermore has extremely negative connotations, which heaps additional scorn on Antony's whole gangster-like scheme.[57]

Velleius continues his direct address to Antony by allowing that he perhaps snatched away from Cicero a few years of miserable senility, but he goes on to boast that Antony could not rob him of his eternal fame and glory – in fact he increased them. Every single one of these themes is ripped from the pages of the declamatory playbook: Cicero's literary immortality is everywhere in Seneca the Elder's *Suasoriae* (e.g. *saluis eloquentiae monumentis non posse Ciceronem mori*, 7.2 or *si ad memoriam operum tuorum* [sc. *respicis*], *semper uicturus es*, 6.4; cf. n. 32 above). Moreover, Cestius Pius, among others, talks about how an old man can expect only a short span of further life before he must shuffle off this mortal coil (*breuem uitam esse homini, multo magis seni: itaque memoriae consulendum, quae magnis uiris aeternitatem promitteret, non qualibet mercede uitam redimendam esse. hic condiciones intolerabiles*, Sen. *suas.* 7.10). Indeed, Velleius adds, life under Antony's tyrant rule would hardly have been worth living: so too do the declaimers advise Cicero time and again (e.g. *non feres Antonium*, Sen. *suas.* 7.1; *uilis* [*illis*] *uita futura* <*est*> *et morte grauior detracta libertate, suas.* 6.8; cf. *suas.* 6.4, 6.6). Ultimately, then, in a favorite declamatory paradox, Cicero's inglorious death at the hands of Antony redounds to his undying glory.

Velleius dilates at some length on Cicero's sempiternal fame: *uiuit uiuetque per omnem saeculorum memoriam*, "he lives and will live on in the memory of the ages," so long as the universe itself exists. The insistently alliterative polyptoton of the first two words continues the high declamatory style of the passage, and the notion and language of a man living on in *omnis* [or *omnium*] *saeculorum memoria* is Ciceronian (*Phil.* 4.3 and *Marc.* 28); *uiuit uiuetque* is likewise a Ciceronianism (*Scipio quamquam est subito ereptus, uiuit tamen semperque uiuet, amic.* 102).[58] Thus this may be yet another instance of the declamatory technique of talking about Cicero

---

[56] Woodman (1983) ad loc.

[57] *TLL* II.1213.28 (Ihm). Note that Velleius had used the word earlier in the context of (Sullan) proscriptions at 2.28.3. Diliberto (1981), a comprehensive monograph devoted to the *auctoramentum* and the *auctorati*, treats neither of these passages.

[58] Admittedly *omnium saeculorum memoria* is found also in later authors, and *uiuit ... uiuetque semper* occurs at Plin. *epist* 2.1.11 and so may be a commonplace in obituaries.

with Ciceronian tags. Finally, Velleius' "so long as the universe endures" proviso is paralleled perfectly by what Arellius Fuscus says at Sen. *suas.* 7.8: "As long as the human race endures, as long as literature is valued and eloquence has its reward, as long as the fortune of our state stands firm or its memory remains, your genius will flourish and be admired by posterity, and although you've been proscribed in this age, you will proscribe Antony forever" (*quoad humanum genus incolume manserit, quamdiu suus litteris honor, suum eloquentiae pretium erit, quamdiu rei publicae nostrae aut fortuna steterit aut memoria durauerit, admirabile posteris uigebit ingenium <tuum>, et uno proscriptus saeculo proscribes Antonium omnibus*).

Just as Fuscus' Cicero proscribes Antony for all time, so too does Velleius' gain eternal glory for himself and eternal infamy for Antony by means of the *Philippics*. In Velleius' big finish, then, all the traditional elements come together: Cicero's eloquence, as manifested in the *Philippics*, leads to both his death and his immortality; Antony is painted as exclusively responsible for Cicero's death (*tuum in eum factum*, Vell. 2.66.5), and for this he has incurred all posterity's curses. This is the very picture that the declamations offer as well, and Velleius has likewise imitated a *declamatio* in his rhetoric and style. In a quiet concluding transition Velleius says that no one could mourn this period adequately (2.67.1); Florus makes the same statement in the form of a rhetorical question (*epit.* 2.16.4); so too Valerius Maximus (5.3.4, discussed immediately below). There is no doubt that Velleius' Cicero is the "rhetorical figure," cast in the image and likeness of what he had learned in the declamatory schoolroom.

Valerius Maximus presents us with this same image, if painted in somewhat more muted shades.[59] In 5.3 he is discussing *ingrati*, and once more that figment of declamatory *inuentio*, Popillius (now dignified with the cognomen Laenas),[60] appears to provide a signal example of the type. The story is the now-familiar one, with a few small twists (5.3.4):[61]

---

[59] Perhaps not surprising in an author who may have had declaimers specifically in mind as an audience; see Bloomer (1992) 255, but cf. Skidmore (1996) 103–112 and *passim*.

[60] The impossible prosopography of such a figure is well treated by Roller (1997) 126–128; cf. Wright (2001) 446–447. No one seems yet to have suggested the simplest explanation for the addition of the otherwise unattested cognomen, viz. that it is a semi-learned interpolation perhaps based on the occurence of a (different) Popillius Laenas twice elsewhere in Valerius Maximus (8.1 amb. 1: M. Popillius Laenas, consul of 139; 8.6.3: M. Popillius Laenas, consul 359, 356, ?354, 350, 348). See the index nominum of Briscoe (1998) 879.

[61] On Cicero in Valerius Maximus, see Bloomer (1992) 191–204, who observes that "the historical or historian's Cicero is not to be found" in Valerius' work (191). Bloomer remarks the influence of declamation on this account of Cicero's death (203), and the influence of the rhetorical schools on

sed ut ad alium consentaneum huic ingrati animi actum transgrediar,
M. Cicero C. Popillium Laenatem Picenae regionis rogatu M. Caeli non
minore cura quam eloquentia defendit eumque causa admodum dubia
fluctuantem saluum ad penates suos remisit. hic Popillius postea nec re
nec uerbo a Cicerone laesus ultro M. Antonium rogauit ut ad illum
proscriptum persequendum et iugulandum mitteretur, impetratisque
detestabilis ministerii partibus gaudio exultans Caietam cucurrit et uirum,
mitto quod amplissimae dignitatis, certe salutari studio praestantis officii
priuatim sibi uenerandum, iugulum praebere iussit ac protinus caput
Romanae eloquentiae et pacis clarissimam dexteram per summum et
securum otium amputauit eaque sarcina tamquam opimis spoliis alacer in
urbem reuersus est: neque enim scelestum portanti onus succurrit illud se
caput ferre, quod pro capite eius quondam peroraerat. inualidae ad hoc
monstrum suggillandum litterae, quoniam qui talem Ciceronis casum satis
digne deplorare possit, alius Cicero non extat.

But to turn to another act of an ungrateful soul not unlike the preceding
tale: at the prompting of Marcus Caelius, Marcus Cicero defended Gaius
Popillius Laenas from the region of Picenum with no less care than
eloquence, and sent him home safe even though the case was quite
a doubtful thing. Later on, this same Popillius, although he had not
been harmed by Cicero in word or deed, asked Mark Antony of his own
accord to be sent to hunt down the proscribed Cicero and cut his throat.
When he had been granted his wish to take part in this vile office, he
dashed off to Caieta jumping for joy and ordered Cicero to offer up his
throat – Cicero who, leaving aside the fact that he was a man of the highest
dignity, ought to have been at least privately respected by Popillius because
of his successful effort in Popillius' defense. Straightaway then in perfect
and utter tranquillity he cut off the head of Roman eloquence and the
most famous right hand of peace, and treating this bundle as if it were the
spolia opima he quickly returned to Rome. It did not occur to him as he
was carrying that vile burden that he was bearing the head which had once
spoken in defense of his own head. Words are not enough to vilify this
monster, since no other Cicero exists who could adequately lament an end
as wretched as Cicero's.

Valerius Maximus has bought the Popillius story hook, line, and sinker.
Cicero defended him successfully when he was in dire straits, and Popillius
repays his generosity with death. Indeed, Valerius' Popillius is particularly
sinister (and "ungrateful") because, although he had not been harmed by
Cicero in any way, he nevertheless asks Antony "of his own accord" (*ultro*)
to be allowed to carry out the execution. This wanton ingratitude may itself

Valerius more generally (e.g. 61, 153–154). Cicero in Valerius Maximus is also briefly discussed by
Pierini (2003) 32–33.

originate as a declamatory *color*.[62] Cicero again is mentioned as deserving
of both private and public honor, just as we have seen so often in the other
treatments of his death – he becomes once more a sort of *uox publica*.
In a declamatory move, Valerius has Popillius chop off the *caput Romanae
eloquentiae* and the *pacis clarissima dextera*: not only are the head and
hand(s) mentioned, as ever, but they are also rhetorically paired with
Cicero's greatest accomplishments, his eloquence and his upholding of
peace (presumably during his consulship, when, as he often reminds us, he
saved the Republic without bloodshed). Valerius caps the section with
a paradox lifted straight from the pages of declamation: he was carrying the
very *caput . . . quod pro capite eius quondam perorauerat*.[63] Finally there is
the rhetorical transition: no other Cicero exists who could adequately
lament an end as wretched as Cicero's (*qui talem Ciceronis casum satis
digne deplorare possit, alius Cicero non exstat*). This motif of futility is
sounded in both Velleius Paterculus (2.67.1), who states that no one
could mourn this period adequately, and Florus (2.16.4), who makes the
same statement in the form of a rhetorical question. All three, of course, go
back to the declamatory trope that we have seen several times, as exemplified by Mento's "no one but Popillius could have killed Cicero – just as no
one but Cicero could have defended Popillius" (Sen. *contr.* 7.2.3) and
Livy's lament that to praise Cicero with due justice one would need to be
a Cicero oneself (Sen. *suas.* 6.22; see p. 134 below).

Valerius Maximus, Florus, and Velleius Paterculus are not the only ones
taking their cues from the declamatory playbook. In one passage of Pliny the
Elder (7.114–117), for example, the omnivorous encyclopedist is describing
some of the great figures of Rome's literary past. Men like Ennius, Vergil,
and Varro come in for modest and restrained praise; Vergil gains a *maius
testimonium* to his genius from Augustus' ordering his books to be saved
from the flames and published than he would have if he had commended
them himself (7.115). Whether the story is true is unimportant; the moral, at
any rate, is unexceptionable. Ennius and Varro got statues, Varro's in
Rome's first public library, and while he was still alive at that. But then,
suddenly and out of nowhere, this outburst (Plin. *nat.* 7.116–117):

> sed quo te, M. Tulli, piaculo taceam, quoue maxime excellentem insigni
> praedicem? quo potius quam uniuersi populi illius genti<um> amplissimi

---

[62] So tentatively Feddern (2013) 382 n. 81.

[63] Cf. e.g. Sen. *contr.* 7.2.5 (Quintus Haterius): *qui modo Italiae umeris relatus est, nunc sic a Popillio
refertur?*; 7.2.14 (Murredius): *descripsit enim ferentem caput et manum Ciceronis Popillium et
Publilianum dedit: Popilli, quanto aliter reus Ciceronis <tangebas caput> et tenebas manum eius!*

testimonio, e tota uita tua consulatus tantum operibus electis? te dicente legem agrariam, hoc est alimenta sua, abdicarunt tribus; te suadente Roscio theatralis auctori legis ignouerunt notatasque se discrimine sedis aequo animo tulerunt; te orante proscriptorum liberos honores petere puduit; tuum Catilina fugit ingenium; tu M. Antonium proscripsisti. salue primus omnium parens patriae appellate, primus in toga triumphum linguaeque lauream merite et facundiae Latiarumque litterarum parensaeque (ut dictator Caesar, hostis quondam tuus, de te scripsit) omnium triumphorum laurea maiorem, quanto plus est ingenii Romani terminos in tantum promouisse quam imperii.[64]

But what excuse could I have for keeping silent about you, Marcus Tullius? What brilliant testimony could I render to your most outstanding preeminence? What could be better than the testimony of the whole Roman people, that most honorable of all nations, selecting from the whole course of your life only the accomplishments of your consulship? Because of your speech on the subject, the tribes rejected the agrarian law, that is, food for themselves; on your advice they forgave Roscius, who proposed the law concerning the theater, and tolerated with equanimity the distinctions imposed by segregated seating; because of your speech the children of the proscribed were ashamed to seek political office; it was your genius that Catiline fled; you proscribed Mark Antony. Hail Cicero, you who first of all were called the father of the fatherland, you who first earned a civilian triumph (*in toga triumphum*) and a laurel crown for your powers of speech (*linguaeque lauream*), you who are equally the father of eloquence and of Latin literature which – as the dictator Caesar, your one-time foe, wrote about you – is a greater honor than any triumph, since it is of much greater value to have advanced so far the frontiers of Rome's genius than its empire.

Pliny has abruptly switched into fully declamatory mode – precisely when it came time to talk about Cicero.[65] Apostrophe, anaphora, and rhetorical question are combined into an elaborate tricolon crescens opening, and the reader can have no doubt about what game is being played. Pliny has slipped effortlessly into the declamatory thought of his school days.[66] He

---

[64] The Latin of the passage is occasionally difficult and there is room for doubt about the text. The Budé edition of Schilling (1977) brackets *et facundiae . . . parens* as a gloss and reads *atque* rather than *aeque* following.

[65] And having ridden out his rhetorical horse, at the beginning of the next section he returns to his usual style. Pliny has typical declamatory praise for Cicero elsewhere too, e.g. in his preface: *M. Tullius extra omnem ingenii aleam positus* (6), a man who wrote *uolumina ediscenda, non modo in manibus cotidie habenda* (22).

[66] Beagon (2005) ad loc. p. 306 observes the pervasive rhetorical language but misses its declamatory resonances, writing instead: "P[liny]'s personal tribute to Cicero is couched in appropriately rhetorical language which both acts as a compliment to the subject and a means of achieving emphasis by varying the tone and texture of his own prose narrative." See too the discussion of Wolverton (1964), esp. 161–162, and now Volk and Zetzel (2015) 212–220, focusing on Pliny's

focuses throughout on Cicero the eloquent orator, the father of eloquence and Latin literature (*facundiae Latiarumque litterarum parens*), which is of course consonant with what we have already seen. His *facundia* serves him particularly well in the consulship, where he was "the first to earn a civilian triumph and a laurel crown for his eloquence" (*primus in toga triumphum linguaeque lauream merite*). This phrase must be evocative of Cicero's (in)famous line *cedant arma togae, concedat laurea linguae*,[67] and so follows the familiar declamatory pattern of talking about Cicero in Cicero's own words. Pliny also offers a Ciceronian tag with *uniuersi populi illius genti<um> amplissimi testimonio* (a periphrasis for Cicero's consulship), which echoes *leg. agr.* 2.7, where the orator describes himself as elected consul *uniuersi populi Romani iudicio*. Even though Pliny wants to confine himself to the events of Cicero's consulship,[68] he soon becomes swept away by his own rising declamatory tide, and having put Catiline to flight he cannot resist adding: *tu M. Antonium proscripsisti* ("you proscribed Mark Antony"). This is out of place, of course, in Pliny's own purported plan to limit himself to Cicero's consular achievements, but, just as was the case with Velleius Paterculus, perfectly in line with the declamatory tendencies that have overwhelmed him. So too does Argentarius, for example, exhort Cicero to allow his *ingenium* to survive as a *perpetua Antonii proscriptio* (Sen. *suas.* 7.8), and Arellius Fuscus boasts to Cicero, *uno proscriptus saeculo proscribes Antonium omnibus* ("although proscribed in this lifetime you will proscribe Antony for all time," *suas.* 7.8). Pliny closes with an elaborate hail and farewell to the *pater patriae* – as Cicero loved being described – who had done more for the Roman people by advancing the bounds of its *ingenium* than any general ever did by advancing the limits of its *imperium*. Making a virtue of necessity, Pliny thus cleverly turns Cicero's lack of military success into a positive to be praised and manages to finish with

---

language in an attempt to determine the extent of the embedded fragment of Caesar. For some reflections on Cicero's role in Pliny the Elder more generally, see Citroni Marchetti (2016).

[67] There is a long-standing debate over whether Cicero wrote *laudi* or *linguae*. The traditional arguments are summarized by Nisbet (1961) ad *Pis.* 74: *laudi* has "the best manuscript authority at *off.* 1.77," and at *Pis.* 24 is probably confirmed by the following *iudicasti non modo amplissimae sed etiam minimae laudi lauream concessisse*. Nevertheless, [Sall.] in *Tull.* 6, Quint. *inst.* 11.1.24, Plut. *comp. Dem. et Cic.* 2.1, and Pliny in our passage all knew *linguae*. Nisbet concludes that *concedat laurea linguae* is a satiric adaption of Cicero's original *concedat laurea laudi*; if so, it was established early, and may have something to do with the identification of Cicero with his tongue (see p. 84 above); similarly Courtney (2003) 172. An alternative hypothesis is that Cicero changed his original *linguae* to *laudi* to avoid censure; see the references in Volk and Zetzel (2015) 206 n. 10. Volk and Zetzel (2015) provide a new approach to the problem, proposing that Cicero's poem actually contained *both* verses (207). Volk (2013) 105–110 offers a novel take on this fragment and indeed the entire *De consulatu suo*.

[68] Especially in the light of Cicero's consular speeches (cf. Cic. *Att.* 2.1.3).

a final eulogy of his eloquence. Pliny shows some flair and originality in working within the declamatory framework, but, no less than for Velleius Paterculus or Valerius Maximus, declamation remains the dominant influence on his picture of Cicero.[69] We have already seen above that poets like Martial and Juvenal combine all these same motifs in their poems as well.[70] It is clear, then, that the rhetorical schoolroom has made an indelible impression on the Roman image of Cicero and his death in the early Empire.

The Death of Cicero: Livy *et al.*

We do have two early sources on Cicero's death that were largely uninfluenced by declamation, fragments from Livy's and Pollio's histories, since neither Pollio nor Livy could have grown up declaiming on Cicero's death.[71] In these accounts we get the basic facts that will be reworked by the declaimers with additional color and detail. We are singularly fortunate that Seneca the Elder has preserved for us these precious snatches on Cicero's demise, which allow us to go beyond mere speculation and actually to see the tradition found in the declaimers begin coalescing.[72] While this will reveal that some of the ideas that we see in the declaimers' speeches did not originate with them, it will nevertheless become clear that they did develop and amplify them significantly. On the other hand, we will see that the declaimers omit some parts of the story and emphasize

---

[69] It is no surprise to find that Seneca the Elder's own appraisal of Cicero was influenced by the declaimers whose praises he reports; see e.g. *contr.* 1 pr. 11 with Fairweather (1981) 88, noting a close parallel in one of Cestius' remarks at *suas.* 7.10.

[70] On Martial, see p. 89 above, on Juvenal p. 99.

[71] Pollio (*FRHist* 56) was born *ca.* 76 BC; Livy 64 or 59 BC. Roller (1997) 115–123 seems to me to go too far in claiming that these earliest accounts were already shaped by declamation. While he is right to insist that the declamations developed very early, both Pollio and Livy were simply born too soon to have been influenced in the fundamental way that we see just decades later. (Roller does not discuss the declamations' influence on later authors.) Wilson (2008) 313 n. 15 well criticizes some of the weaknesses in Roller's argument; cf. Wilson (2008) 316 n. 23, as well as Pierini (2003) 16 n. 68, 26 n. 111, Migliario (2007) 144–145, Migliario (2008) 79 n. 8.

[72] There is disagreement about the chronology of the declamatory and historical material. Roller (1997) 115–119 argues that the Ciceronian themes were already being declaimed in the triumviral period, so too Migliario (2008) 79. Feddern (2013) 484–486, by contrast, contends unpersuasively that the particulars of *suas.* 7 were devised after the burning of Labienus' books, perhaps no earlier than AD 5. The specific dating of Pollio's history is also very vexed; from allusions in Horace we can see that it was underway in the 20s BC, but a terminal date seems impossible to fix (*FRHist* 1. 436–438). The circulation of Livy, as well as his work's structure, are even more troublesome: Lamacchia (1975) 434 assumes that Livy wrote book 120, containing the death of Cicero, in AD 13, presumably since the *Periochae* note that book 121 was published after the death of Augustus (*editus post excessum Augusti dicitur*). And yet that need not imply that 120 was written in the preceding year, and indeed 121 could also have been written earlier but withheld.

others – and of course some elements will be shown as pure declamatory *inuentio*. Furthermore, historians of the generations immediately following Pollio and Livy already show signs of declamatory influence from the rhetorical training of their youth.

Seneca pretends to stumble into this particular digression, saying that, since he has happened upon the theme of Cicero's death, it might not be out of place to discuss how the historians treat these matters (*suas.* 6.14).[73] His grand point is that the declamations are at best fictionalized versions of the truth – none of the historians dared to make Cicero so base as to beg for mercy, not even the extremely hostile Pollio (*infestissimus famae Ciceronis, suas.* 6.14).[74] In any event, having fortuitously alighted upon the historians, Seneca cannot pass up the opportunity to quote some edifying extracts for the benefit of his sons. Livy's testimony features at the greatest length, and it is against his account that the others are measured.[75] On Cicero's death itself Livy says (*suas.* 6.17 = Liu. fr. 60 Weissenborn–Müller):

> M. Cicero sub aduentum triumuirorum urbe cesserat, pro certo habens, id quod erat, non magis Antonio eripi se quam Caesari Cassium et Brutum posse; primo in Tusculanum fugerat, inde transuersis itineribus in Formianum ut ab Caieta nauem conscensurus proficiscitur. unde aliquotiens in altum prouectum cum modo uenti aduersi rettulissent, modo ipse iactationem nauis caeco uoluente fluctu pati non posset, taedium tandem eum et fugae et uitae cepit, regressusque ad superiorem uillam, quae paulo plus mille passibus a mari abest, "moriar" inquit "in patria saepe seruata." satis constat seruos fortiter fideliterque paratos fuisse ad dimicandum; ipsum deponi lecticam et quietos pati quod sors iniqua cogeret iussisse. prominenti ex lectica praebentique inmotam ceruicem caput praecisum est. nec <id> satis stolidae crudelitati militum fuit: manus quoque scripsisse aliquid in Antonium exprobrantes praeciderunt. ita relatum caput ad Antonium iussuque eius inter duas manus in rostris positum, ubi ille consul, ubi saepe consularis, ubi eo ipso anno aduersus Antonium quanta nulla umquam humana uox cum admiratione eloquentiae auditus fuerat; uix attollentes lacrimis oculos humentes intueri truncata membra ciues poterant.

> Cicero had left the city at the arrival of the triumvirs, since he was certain – and in the event he was right – that he could no more be saved from Antony than Brutus and Cassius could be saved from Octavian. First he had fled to

---

[73] For a sophisticated take on the place of this digression in Seneca's work, as well as on the structure of *suas.* 6 and 7 more generally, see Wilson (2008) 316.

[74] In his historical work, at any rate. Supposedly in a published speech *Pro Lamia* he alleged that Cicero did promise to recant and produce pro-Antony speeches, but Seneca calls this a bald falsehood and claims that Pollio was not so bold as to include this passage in his history or in the speech he actually delivered (*suas.* 6.14–15).

[75] Livy's judgment of Cicero is discussed at length by Lamacchia (1975).

his Tusculan villa, then he set out cross-country to his estate at Formiae, where he intended to board a ship from Caieta. There he tried to set sail several times, but he was first brought back by unfavorable winds, then he himself couldn't stand the tossing of the ship in the blindly swirling swell, and at last he grew tired of both flight and life. Then he returned to the villa where he had been staying, which was a little more than a mile inland, and he said, "I shall die in the fatherland that I have often saved." It's generally agreed that his slaves had been bravely and faithfully prepared to fight, but that he himself ordered the litter to be put down and that his slaves suffer in silence what cruel fate forced him to endure. He leaned out of the litter and offered up his neck unflinchingly and was beheaded. And that wasn't enough for the stupid cruelty of the soldiers: they cut off his hands as well, reproaching them for having written something against Antony. Thus Cicero's head was brought to Antony and at his command was placed between the two hands on the rostra, where once as consul, and often as an ex-consul, and indeed in that very year speaking against Antony, he had been heard with admiration such as has never been felt for any other human voice. The citizens of Rome could scarcely lift their eyes overflowing with tears to look upon his butchered limbs.

This is the fundamental account of Cicero's death that has been preserved. It may have been based on Tiro's lost biography, or even on consultation with eyewitnesses, and there can be little doubt that it influenced subsequent historians who tell this tale.[76] It begins, however, with a key part of the story that the declaimers altogether omit: Cicero ran away at the approach of the triumvirs, fleeing for his life.[77] He betook himself to one villa then another, and tried on numerous occasions to put to sea, only to turn back because of foul weather or his own sea-sickness. This is an embarrassing accumulation of descriptive detail, and it is not exactly consonant with a heroic image. Nor was his choice to face his fate made out of a sense of bravery; he did not rage against the dying of the light. Instead, Livy tells us, *taedium* took hold of him and he simply seems to have given up: Cicero went gently into the dark night.

---

[76] Richter (1968) has intriguing speculations about the origins of Cicero's biographical tradition. He believes that the biographies of Tiro and Nepos were fundamental in shaping the earliest strands of Ciceronian reception (see esp. 179–181). This is ultimately an unprovable hypothesis (the biographies having vanished almost without a trace), and we should remember that a man like Pollio knew Cicero personally, while a Livy could have talked to plenty of eyewitness sources. Nevertheless, there can be no doubt that the biographies of Tiro and Nepos must have exerted some influence on the tradition; cf. Homeyer (1977), a study of the ancient testimony on Cicero's death, to be read only with the questions large and small raised by Roller (1997) and Wright (2001).

[77] Note that one declaimer urges Cicero to flee and save himself, implying that he did not in fact think that Cicero had actually fled (Varius Geminus: Sen. *suas.* 6.11 *omnia conplexus est quae a ceteris dicta erant; sed addidit et tertium; adhortatus est illum ad fugam: illic esse M. Brutum, illic C. Cassium, illic Sex. Pompeium*).

The declaimers, however, make a virtue of necessity, turning Cicero's resignation into a final act of grim defiance. Livy tells us that Cicero stretched out his own neck to the executioner's blade without flinching, and this the declaimers certainly pick up on. They also could not resist the conceit of Cicero's hands being chopped off as well, but where Livy attributes this to the excessive bloodlust of the soldiers, the declaimers are wont to assign the authorship of this deed to Antony himself (or to his wife, the insatiable Fulvia). The head and hands of Cicero displayed on the rostra became some of the most iconic elements of his death. Even for Livy, the responsibility for Cicero's death is placed squarely on Antony's shoulders, in line with imperial ideology, and the declaimers had no interest in a more equitable distribution of blame. Finally Cicero's death is tied in explicitly with his eloquence, particularly as expressed in the *Philippics*, where his *uox* – this word again! – had resounded with singular clarity and fame.

Seneca regards this account as evidence for Livy's unswerving commitment to Cicero's courage (*suas.* 6.18). The declaimers with their *utile*-tinted glasses certainly focused only on the good parts, but I would not describe this as a passage of unstinting praise.[78] Still less would I share Seneca's assessment of Livy's "epitaph" on Cicero, which he calls a *plenissimum Ciceroni testimonium*. Livy's summary judgment runs (Sen. *suas.* 6.22):

> uixit tres et sexaginta annos, ut, si uis afuisset, ne inmatura quidem mors uideri possit. ingenium et operibus et praemiis operum felix, ipse fortunae diu prosperae; sed in longo tenore felicitatis magnis interim ictus uulneribus, exilio, ruina partium pro quibus steterat, filiae morte, exitu tam tristi atque acerbo, omnium aduersorum nihil ut uiro dignum erat tulit praeter mortem, quae uere aestimanti minus indigna uideri potuit, quod a uictore inimico <nihil> crudelius passus erat quam quod eiusdem fortunae conpos ipse fecisset. si quis tamen uirtutibus uitia pensarit, uir magnus ac memorabilis fuit et in cuius laudes exequendas Cicerone laudatore opus fuerit.

> He lived 63 years, so that, if he hadn't been compelled to die by violence, his death wouldn't even seem premature. He had a genius that was fortunate in his works and in the rewards he merited for those works, and he himself enjoyed prosperity for quite some time; but in the long course of his good fortune he was sometimes struck by great blows: exile, the downfall of the party for which he had stood, the death of his daughter, and his own end so sad and bitter. Of all his adversities he faced none save death as a man

---

[78] Then again, Seneca the Elder was clearly a lover of Cicero. Cf. Fairweather (1981) 84–88 on Seneca's admiration of Cicero; she remarks, "it was normal in the schools of rhetoric to revere Cicero uncritically" (84).

should – but this death of his might seem to someone judging impartially not so unworthy, because he had suffered nothing more cruel from his victorious enemy than he would have done himself had he been in control of his own fortune. Nevertheless, if someone weighs up his virtues and his vices, he was a great and memorable man, and it would take a Cicero to praise Cicero adequately.

This is a remarkably neutral assessment, I should say. Cicero, Livy declares, had lived a long life by the time he died, and had he met his end through natural causes none would have judged it untimely.[79] He is given credit for his *opera*, presumably in the literary sense, but he also is shown as a failure, particularly in the phrase *ruina partium pro quibus steterat*: his cause ultimately failed utterly.[80] Moreover, he bore none of his misfortunes besides his death as befits a man (*ut uiro dignum erat*) – harsh words indeed, and not to be found in the declamatory tradition. The declaimers in fact skillfully elide the rest of Cicero's life so that they can focus on the one thing that he did do worthily: die. But for Livy even the praise of his death is not unmixed; after all, Cicero would have done the same thing to Antony had he come out on top, he says. This is an extraordinary claim – even after the vehemence of the *Philippics*, could Livy have really imagined Cicero nailing Antony's head and hands to the rostra? – but he may be harking back to the fate of the Catilinarian conspirators. In the end, nevertheless, after Livy computes the calculus of Cicero's virtues and vices, he is adjudged a *uir magnus ac memorabilis*, and Livy concludes with an epigrammatic *sententia* beloved of the declaimers: only a Cicero could praise Cicero adequately.[81] This may provide some evidence that Livy himself was occasionally influenced in style, if not substance, by the declamatory tradition. In his pointed paradox there lurks a none too concealed jibe at Cicero's penchant for self-praise; this clever ambiguity is transmuted into unalloyed praise in the rhetorical reproductions.[82]

---

[79] Does Livy's *ne inmatura quidem mors* allude to Cic. *Cat.* 4.3/*Phil.* 2.119 (*neque turpis mors forti uiro potest accidere neque immatura consulari*)?

[80] Livy's phrase is rather vague. *Partes pro quibus steterat* is clearly the language used to describe being a member of a political faction (see *TLL* x.1.477.30–32 [Teßmer]), but Cicero himself was neither an adherent to nor a founder of a political party. His goal was the *concordia ordinum*, which, as Syme (1939) 16 says, "was an ideal rather than a programme: there was no Ciceronian party." Is Livy alluding to the failure of this ideal, while cloaking it under the standard language of factionalism?

[81] Cf. the very similar remarks of Valerius Maximus (p. 126 above), as well as the "only a Cicero could have (successfully) defended a Popillius" motif (p. 113).

[82] Criticisms of Cicero's self-praise are a commonplace of declamation (see e.g. pp. 156, 193 below) and found as accepted truth in authors like Quintilian (*inst.* 11.1.17–28) and Plutarch (*Cic.* 6.5, 24.1, *comp. Dem. et Cic.* 2). Allen (1954) 136–143 argues that such criticisms were not found in Cicero's own lifetime except as concerns his poetry, but I am less certain: we only hear what Cicero himself tells us. (And even if his enemies did concentrate on his poetry, why should they not attack the vice in its

Seneca also recounts a few other early historians' judgments on Cicero's last moments, all supposedly favorable. We meet briefly the accounts of Aufidius Bassus, Cremutius Cordus, and Bruttedius Niger,[83] en route to a much more substantial discussion of Asinius Pollio, Cicero's harshest critic. Even Pollio finds favor with Seneca because of his supposedly generous assessment of Cicero's life. Seneca indeed judges this the most eloquent passage in all of Pollio, where he seems, in an imitative rivalry that is the sincerest form of ancient flattery, "not to have praised Cicero but to have competed with him [*sc.* for the palm of eloquence]" (*non laudasse Ciceronem sed certasse cum Cicerone*, Sen. *suas.* 6.25). This from a man who alone reported a negative judgment of Cicero's death (*Ciceronis mortem solus ex omnibus maligne narrat, suas.* 6.24); nevertheless, in Seneca's opinion, he was compelled by Cicero's greatness to give him his "full praise" (*testimonium quamuis inuitus plenum ei reddidit, suas.* 6.24; cf. Livy's *plenissimum ... testimonium, suas.* 6.22). Once again, I would judge Pollio's praise very grudging at best (*suas.* 6.24):

> huius ergo uiri tot tantisque operibus mansuris in omne aeuum praedicare de ingenio atque industria superuacuum <est>. natura autem atque fortuna pariter obsecuta est ei, si quidem facies decora ad senectutem prosperaque permansit ualetudo; tum pax diutina, cuius instructus erat artibus, contigit; namque ad priscam seueritatem iudiciis exactis maxima noxiorum multitudo prouenit, quos obstrictos patrocinio incolumes plerosque habebat; iam felicissima consulatus ei sors petendi et gerendi magno munere deum, consilio <suo> industriaque. utinam moderatius secundas res et fortius aduersas ferre potuisset![84] namque utraeque cum euenerant ei, mutari eas non posse rebatur. inde sunt inuidiae tempestates coortae graues in eum certiorque inimicis adgrediendi fiducia; maiore enim simultates adpetebat animo quam gerebat. sed quando mortalium nulli uirtus perfecta contigit, qua maior pars uitae atque ingenii stetit, ea iudicandum de homine est. atque ego ne miserandi quidem exitus eum fuisse iudicarem, nisi ipse tam miseram mortem putasset.

> Since this man's works, so many and so great, will last forever, it's hardly necessary to praise his genius and his hard work. But nature and good luck alike favored him: his decorous appearance and good health remained into

most egregious form?) Nevertheless, Allen is right to argue that Roman norms of self-promotion were more tolerant than our own. It should also be noted that mentions of Cicero's consulship in his later speeches would have had a far different effect on his contemporaries, who heard them individually in their immediate context as Cicero expressed them, than on posterity, who turn from one speech to another without pause and divorced from the heat of the moment.

[83] All probably influenced by declamation: Aufidius Bassus (*FRHist* 78) was born perhaps around 5 BC; Cremutius Cordus (*FRHist* 71) shortly after 35 BC; Bruttedius Niger (*FRHist* 72) *ca.* 6 BC or a bit before.

[84] Cf. Sen. *dial.* 10.5.1 *nec secundis rebus quietus nec aduersarum patiens.*

his old age. Furthermore, he lived during a lengthy period of peace, in whose arts he was well versed; and since the law courts had been returned to their former standards of severity, a vast crop of criminals was at hand, and he bound many of them to himself by defending them successfully in the courts. He had the very best of luck in seeking and carrying out the consulship, due to the kindness of the gods and his own intelligence and industry. I wish that he had been able to bear success more graciously and difficulties more bravely! For whichever of the two he was experiencing at any given moment, he believed that it could never change. That's whence those powerful storms of resentment rose up against him and gave a firmer sense of confidence to his enemies to attack him; he picked fights with greater enthusiasm than he carried them out. But since no man enjoys perfect virtue, we must judge men by the character and way of life that they have generally shown. And I wouldn't even say that he had a death worthy of pity, if he himself hadn't judged it so pitiable.

Pollio acknowledges Cicero's literary immortality, a theme that obviously resonated with the rhetoricians. He is even generous in describing his good looks, where the slanderer might have resorted to the standard topos of invective that Cicero was ugly.[85] Thereafter, however, we meet a series of left-handed compliments. Cicero was fortunate to meet with a long span of peace, for which he was well suited – one cannot help but read the subtext that Cicero was singularly *unsuited* for war, a much more reputable activity for a Roman man.[86] He was lucky enough to have a full stable of clients – because there were many guilty men to be defended. The image of the amoral advocate was already very much alive. He was supremely felicitous in his bid for the consulship and his tenure in office, but this is ascribed first and foremost to the kindness of the gods, and only secondarily to Cicero's own qualities. He was too elated by success and depressed by failure, and he was good at picking a fight but bad at fighting – hardly high praise. Only after this elaborate catalog of mixed goods and evils does Pollio appear to be about to concede that Cicero might be thought on the balance a virtuous man, but he then surprises by abstaining from actually saying so. "No one is perfect," he says, "and so we must judge a man as a whole" – he should have gone on to say, "And judged by these standards, Cicero was a fine and upstanding citizen." Instead he undercuts this message by his final

---

[85] See Opelt (1965) 152–153 on conventional criticisms of politicians' appearance. Perhaps he was simply considered to be genuinely handsome; images of Cicero would seem to indicate a dignified and imposing countenance. (Borda [1961] provides a comprehensive discussion of literary and iconographic testimonia to Cicero's appearance, complete with images of all surviving busts and coins.) Later slanderers, however, do resort to the ugliness topos; cf. p. 185 below.

[86] Cf. Liu. *per.* III *uir nihil minus quam ad bella natus.*

statement, so unlike Livy's epigrammatic tribute: "And I wouldn't even judge Cicero's death to be a bad one, except that he considered death so awful." It is hard to see how Seneca found this passage to be full of praise for Cicero; on the contrary, as we shall see in the next chapter, it begins to develop the declamatory template for how to criticize him.[87]

Seneca and the declaimers found a way to read the accounts of Livy and Pollio very reductively and simplistically as uniformly laudatory, whereas we have seen a far more nuanced picture. The declaimers' methodology was simply to amplify what they found attractive and to ignore any complicating factors. This tendency is already revealed in two other "historical" judgments quoted by Seneca, both of which are heavily influenced by declamatory thought.

The first such specimen is provided by Bruttedius Niger, a rhetor trained by Apollodorus of Pergamum.[88] Seneca elsewhere preserves a few snatches of his explicitly declamatory rhetoric (*contr.* 2.1.35–36), where he comes off as a sore loser at best. We know from Tacitus that Niger held the aedileship in AD 22 (*ann.* 3.66), and so he would have been born well after Cicero's death and subject to the influence of the rhetorical tradition as a young man. As a rhetorician educated at the height of Augustus' reign, Niger's brand of "history" was rather different from Livy's, and we see in him the explicit beginnings of the ahistorical declamatory tradition in historiography. Most notably Popillius, Cicero's supposed slayer, makes his first appearance here. Cicero is made to rejoice upon seeing a familiar and friendly face, for he had successfully defended Popillius against an unspecified charge. His good offices, however, proved unavailing, as Popillius mercilessly cuts him down in an attempt to curry favor with Antony. Indeed, Niger says, Popillius altogether forgot that Cicero had even defended him, so eager was he to please the new powers (*suas.* 6.20). As we have seen, however, this whole story is naught but fiction. Niger does not go so far

---

[87] Pomeroy (1991) 142–145 reads Seneca's citation of Pollio as ironic. This is highly unlikely: Seneca has said that Pollio provided a *testimonium quamuis inuitus plenum* to Cicero – hardly the way to introduce irony – and he has embedded this quotation in the midst of a sea of other *testimonia* that he plainly believes to be favorable to Cicero. Seneca furthermore suppresses Cordus' "unworthy" remarks about Cicero's demise; if he found Pollio's words similarly objectionable, he could have consigned them to the dustbin of history as well. Seneca is rather wearing a peculiar set of blinders because of his own love of Cicero. (For the textual problem at the end of *suas.* 6.25, see Håkanson [1989b] 18–19.)

[88] *FRHist* 72; cf. *RE* III/1.907 s.v. "Bruttedius." Gambet (1963) 137 n. 33, following Teuffel's literary history, denies that Bruttedius wrote history at all and sees him solely as a declaimer. This is going too far.

as to make Popillius a parricide – perhaps that was *de trop* even for a rhetorician in a work of history – but he does retail the story that he was the murderer.

Niger continues with the story of Cicero's head and hands, so beloved of the rhetoricians striving for *enargeia*. Antony ordered them displayed on the rostra, of course, but his supposed triumph was instead met with a flood of tears and wails as Cicero received spontaneous and unbidden funeral rites from the people. The gathering is described in pointed rhetorical paradox; for the people did not hear a eulogy for the dead man, as was the custom, but rather narrated it themselves.[89] There is a great emphasis on the public benefits that Cicero had rendered and the people had received; every part of the forum bore some trace of Cicero's famous speeches, and everyone had a story to tell of Cicero's good offices (*nulla non pars fori aliquo actionis inclutae signata uestigio erat; nemo non aliquod eius in se meritum fatebatur, suas.* 6.21). This theme tallies with the Cicero who was the *publica uox*, and it represents a distinct reimagining of a man who really had been in the service of the few, the proud, the *optimates*.[90] In sum, then, Bruttedius Niger is a rhetorician in historian's clothing, and in his "history" we see how declamatory traditions have already wrought an influence.

Now to declamation hidden under the veil of poetry. Having told us of the opinions of the historians, Seneca cannot resist adding the "finest tribute" to Cicero's life and death, that provided by the poet Cornelius Severus.[91] Severus was an Augustan poet who was still active under Tiberius; he wrote historical epics like a *Bellum Siculum*. As Adrian Hollis noted, "the fragments of Severus ... betray very strong rhetorical influence; the only long extracts which we possess are quoted to show how poets could compete with, and even outdo, declaimers and prose historians."[92] Our fragment cannot be dated more precisely, but the text betrays clear declamatory influences, taking its beginning from Cicero's head on the rostra. His head was not the only one, says Severus, for the heads of other "great-hearted men" (*magnanimum ... uirorum, suas.* 6.26.1) lay all but breathing (*spirantia paene*) alongside as well, but Cicero's image swept away all others, as if it were the only one.[93] Just as in Bruttedius Niger, there is then a poetic funeral eulogy placed in the minds of the gathered people: Cicero's glorious consulship, for example, is

---

[89] Cf. Martial's populace speaking *pro Cicerone*, p. 89 above.
[90] On the *uox publica* theme, cf. p. 84 above.
[91] For exhaustive commentary on this poem, see Dahlmann (1975) 74–119.   [92] Hollis (2007) 347.
[93] Note the extremely close parallel in Florus (2.16.5); for more on Florus, see p. 121 above.

recalled with nostalgia. Again Cicero is said to have found favor with the people (*fauor . . . coetūs*) and to have been

> unica sollicitis quondam tutela salusque,
> egregium semper patriae caput, ille senatus
> uindex, ille fori, legum ritusque togaeque,
> publica uox . . .   (suas. 6.26.12–15)

> once the sole guardian and savior for the distressed, always the outstanding head of the fatherland, the champion of the Senate, the forum, laws and religious and civil life, the voice of the people . . .

Thus here we see again Cicero's refashioning as the people's champion. Next we get a very vivid description of his blood-flecked white hair and his hands trampled under by his ungrateful countrymen, a passage quite at home in the display rhetoric of the declaimer. Finally, as usual in declamatory accounts, Antony is damned for his monstrous crimes, for which he will never be able to atone (*nullo luet hoc Antonius aeuo, suas.* 6.26.20).

Severus shows himself influenced by the declaimers in another way as well: he includes allusions to and echoes of Cicero's own works in his poetry. The declaimers, as we have seen and will see again in the next chapter, often include Ciceronian pastiche when they talk about Cicero, as if matching form to content, but they almost never seem to imitate Ciceronianisms otherwise. Severus, for example, refers to the Catilinarian conspirators as the *iuratae manus* (line 5); Cicero had spoken of the *coniuratorum manum* (*Cat.* 3.3). When these conspirators are uncovered, Severus talks about the *deprensa foedera* (line 5); *deprehendere* is how Cicero describes his own unmasking of the conspiracy (*sceleris manifesti atque deprensi, Cat.* 3.11).[94] There may be other assorted echoes of Cicero's *Catilinarians* as well, but the skeptical reader might retort that when talking about Catiline and the conspiracy Severus could hardly avoid using some of Cicero's words and themes. In line 11, however, Hollis detected an even more remarkable allusion. The line runs: *conticuit Latiae tristis facundia linguae* ("the eloquence of the Latin tongue fell silent with sadness"), and Seneca himself tells us that Severus was bettering Sextilius Ena's *deflendus Cicero est Latiaeque silentia linguae* ("Cicero is to be lamented, and the silence of the Latin tongue"), which he had once heard Ena recite at a dinner party. This is no doubt true, but the way in which he betters it is very clever, for he incorporates echoes of the *Brutus*, which is ostensibly written on the occasion of Hortensius' death and

---

[94] Cf. Hollis (2007) ad loc.

Cicero's withdrawal from public life. As Atticus tells Cicero in the dialogue, *iam pridem enim conticuerunt tuae litterae* ("for your letters have lain silent for some time," *Brut.* 19), and Cicero acknowledges that *ea ipsa . . . eloquentia obmutuit* ("that very eloquence itself has fallen silent," *Brut.* 22) and moreover *hoc studium . . . nostrum conticuit subito et obmutuit* ("this pursuit of ours suddenly fell silent and has stayed silent," *Brut.* 324). Severus has thus here reworked Ena's line with a view toward Cicero, substituting *facundia* for the unmetrical *eloquentia* while retaining Cicero's verbs (*conticuit* here and *obmutuit* in line 15 below). This is excellent one-up-manship, and the fact that it is done with evocative reminiscence of Cicero himself fits it directly into the declamatory mold.[95] While Livy and Pollio wrote histories that were largely uninfluenced by declamation and provided raw material for rhetorical elaboration, already in authors like Bruttedius Niger and Cornelius Severus we see creative adapation and refashioning in action.

Greek Historians on Cicero's Death

If the declamations of the Roman rhetorical schools genuinely influenced the "historical" version of Cicero, then we would expect to find traces of this influence in the Greek tradition as well. While rhetorical education was just as much a given in the Greek-speaking world as it was in the Latin, the extent to which Cicero's works were known in the East is less clear, to say nothing of whether Greek students declaimed on Ciceronian themes.[96] Plutarch, to be certain, did not grow up performing weekly Latin declamations on Cicero's death, and yet he tantalizingly remarks that Latin is the language "which just about everyone uses nowadays" (ὁ Ῥωμαίων ᾧ νῦν ὁμοῦ τι πάντες ἄνθρωποι χρῶνται, *mor.* 1010d).[97] The cases of Appian and

---

[95] This use of *conticesco* with speech or letters or the like as subject is not found at all before Cicero, is frequent in Cicero, and then appears only sporadically thereafter (see *TLL* IV.696.39–41 and 62–65 [Gudeman]). There is thus little doubt that Severus was thinking of Ciceronian usage here. Cf. too p. 77 above on the phrase *eloquentia obmutuit* in Petronius.

[96] On the Cicero papyri, our most direct evidence for knowledge of Cicero's Latin in the (later) Greek world, see ch. 2 n. 26. The question of Greek speakers' knowledge of Latin has so far generally foundered because of a collective Greek silence on the subject. For what little we know, see Rochette (1997), who treats all evidence of Latin education prior to the third century AD in two pages (166–167); see too Fisher (1982) on later Greek translations of Latin texts. (Note already the second-century Greek Sallust: *Suda* ζ 73.) Dickey (2012–2015) 1.4–15 is a lucid summary of Latin learning by Greek speakers. It is worth noting that already in Seneca the Elder we have numerous Greek declaimers, some specifically speechifying on Cicero's death; see Anderson (1993) 18–19.

[97] Cited by Dickey (2012–2015) 1.5; note that ὁ Ῥωμαίων ᾧ is a conjecture for the transmitted ὁρῶ μέλλω. By the fourth century Libanius was complaining that no one wanted to study Greek rhetoric anymore; everyone was learning Latin; see Rochette (1997) 133–135.

Cassius Dio would certainly seem to have room for direct influence: Dio was in Rome at the age of sixteen or seventeen and so could have been exposed to the typical Latin rhetorical training at its source; even if not, he still might have received this sort of training as the son of a Roman consul and a man destined for a distinguished public career – he eventually held two consulships himself.[98] Appian was an upper-class Alexandrian with legal training, and in addition to being a friend of Fronto he knew Latin well enough to plead cases before emperors and enjoy a successful administrative career (App. *praef.* 15.62).[99] But whether directly or indirectly, the declamatory tradition has left its mark on Plutarch, Appian, and Cassius Dio. In these authors the reception of Cicero cannot be divorced from the presentation of the late Republic more generally,[100] and declamation only furnishes part of the picture – but it is a marked and important part.

Plutarch's version (*Cic.* 46–49.4) exemplifies these tendencies. As we have seen, he proffers us Popillius the parricide whom Cicero had once defended; this figure, as we know, is cut from the whole cloth of declamatory fable. We have also seen him adopt the standard Augustan line that was repeated and amplified in the rhetorical schools, namely that Octavian resisted proscribing Cicero as long as he could, but that he was at last forced to give in to the combined force of Antony and Lepidus. Nevertheless, the Greek speaker from Chaeronea shows himself a bit more independent, for Plutarch opens the passage by saying that at that time in particular an old man was led on and deceived by a youth (ἐνταῦθα μέντοι μάλιστα Κικέρων ἐπαρθεὶς ὑπὸ νέου γέρων καὶ φενακισθείς, *Cic.* 46.1): Plutarch can see the treachery of Caesar's heir.

---

[98] See Millar (1964) 14–15, 42–43; Gowing (1992) 20–21 on the highlights of his career. Burden-Strevens (2015) 39–44 treats the question of Dio's knowledge of Latin; Rochette (1997) 246 takes it as a given. Jones (2016) 300 n. 19 provides comprehensive bibliography on Dio's rhetorical training. Detailed investigation of Dio's sources lies outside the scope of this book, but see reasonably Gowing (1992) 39–50. It seems clear that Dio was drawing on a plurality of sources (not just, say, Livy), some of which themselves could have been subject to rhetorical influence.

[99] See Gowing (1992) 15–18 (now too Brodersen [2015] on what may be Appian's sarcophagus); Rochette (1997) 242–243, with further references in n. 129. Roman law was a particular bastion of the Latin language in the East; see Dickey (2012–2015) 1.15. Again I disclaim detailed *Quellenforschung* on Appian; see the dueling accounts of Rich (2015) and Westall (2015), both with review of previous scholarship. At least in the *Civil Wars* Appian probably consulted a variety of sources – and certainly not just just Pollio, as maintained by Gabba (1955) – which may likewise have been influenced by declamatory rhetoric; see e.g. Gowing (1992) 41 n. 9. Westall (2015) 160 thus aptly describes the *Civil Wars* as "an original work of synthesis." Welch (2015b) 278 detects "at least two conflicting sources" for the period between the Ides of March and Philippi.

[100] For an attempt to discuss Dio's Cicero in the context of the fall of the Republic, see Rees (2011) 102–181; Burden-Strevens (2015) also tries to recover Dio's conception of the transition from Republic to Empire from his speeches, including the Ciceronian specimens.

The moment of Cicero's death is told without the elaborate rhetorical figures of the Latin tradition, and yet it repeats much of the declamatory sentiment and pathos. At the last his resolution hardens and he faces his fate with courage, staring stubbornly at his slayers (ἀτενὲς <ἐν>εώρα τοῖς σφαγεῦσιν, *Cic.* 48.4). He stretches out his neck to meet the blade, and the onlookers cannot bear to watch. Just as in the declaimers, Cicero's death is a signally heroic moment, and his slayers are condemned both explicitly and implicitly. Plutarch does not use a relatively neutral word like ἀποκτείνω to describe the killing; instead, he chooses loaded terms like σφάζω and its derivatives (used of slaughtering sacrificial victims by cutting the throat; his killers, Herennius and Popillius, are moreover σφαγεῖς, butchers or cut-throat murderers). Cicero is the innocent victim, while the savage and bloodthirsty nature of his killers is placed on full display.

Ultimately, of course, all of this barbarism can be traced back to the architect of evil, Antony, at whose command (Ἀντωνίου κελεύσαντος, *Cic.* 48.6) Cicero's head and hands are chopped off. This is the final brutality, and so Plutarch ends where he had begun, by ascribing blame for Cicero's slaughter to Antony and Antony alone. When Antony hears of Cicero's murder and, perhaps more importantly, sees the corpse, his bloodlust is at last sated and he says that the proscriptions are finished (ἀκούσας δὲ καὶ ἰδὼν ἀνεβόησεν, ὡς νῦν αἱ προγραφαὶ τέλος ἔχοιεν, *Cic.* 49.1).[101] We have seen this sentiment in Velleius Paterculus and others, and it again underscores Antony's blind rage directed against Cicero. He orders the severed head and hands to be displayed on the rostra, and Plutarch says that the Roman people shuddered at the sight, thinking that they were looking not upon the face of Cicero but the soul of Antony (θέαμα Ῥωμαίοις φρικτόν, οὐ τὸ Κικέρωνος ὁρᾶν πρόσωπον οἰομένοις, ἀλλὰ τῆς Ἀντωνίου ψυχῆς εἰκόνα, *Cic.* 49.2), an epigrammatic *sententia* worthy of any of the declaimers, coming at a moment – Cicero's head and hands on display – that they so favored.

Plutarch does us the favor of citing his sources for his account of Cicero's death, namely Cicero's slave and biographer Tiro and συγγραφεῖς ἱστορηκότες, i.e. "historians" (*Cic.* 49.4).[102] Tiro, of course, cannot have

---

[101] Cf. Plut. *Ant.* 20.2 for similar language about Antony rejoicing at Cicero's death until he felt sated: Κικέρωνος δὲ σφαγέντος ἐκέλευσεν Ἀντώνιος τήν τε κεφαλὴν ἀποκοπῆναι καὶ τὴν χεῖρα τὴν δεξιάν, ᾗ τοὺς κατ' αὐτοῦ λόγους ἔγραψε. καὶ κομισθέντων ἐθεᾶτο γεγηθὼς καὶ ἀνακαγχάζων ὑπὸ χαρᾶς πολλάκις· εἶτ' ἐμπλησθεὶς ἐκέλευσεν ὑπὲρ τοῦ βήματος ἐν ἀγορᾷ τεθῆναι, καθάπερ εἰς τὸν νεκρὸν ὑβρίζων.

[102] On these sources, see the detailed remarks of Wright (2001) 444 n. 30, with extensive further references. Contrast the certainty of Plutarch's account of Cicero's demise with the various explanations canvassed in *Dem.* 30 for where Demosthenes' poison was concealed, a discussion which results only in aporia.

been influenced by the declaimers in his version of the events, and some historians whom Plutarch might have consulted, like Livy, were substantially independent of the rhetorical schools as well. But other elements seem clearly to have descended from the declamatory tradition; the most obvious of these, although not the only one, is Popillius the parricide.[103] As I said above, however, I do not propose that Plutarch was personally influenced by performing and hearing declamations on Cicero's death in his own youth. When Plutarch adopts declamatory themes and motifs, he has probably been influenced by intermediaries who themselves had had such an upbringing. Once these myths and legends had infiltrated the historiographical tradition, they began to take on a life of their own, independent of the rhetorical schools. What started as Augustan propaganda was repeated *ad infinitum* to the schoolboys of Rome; when they themselves began peddling these counterfeit wares as the genuine article, perception became reality, and ideology by the alchemy of rhetoric was transmuted into historical fact.[104]

Appian paints a picture similar to Plutarch's (*BC* 4.19).[105] He insists that he visited Caieta in order to become personally acquainted with the sad saga of Cicero's end, but one wonders what he hoped to learn from the place some two centuries after the events transpired.[106] Be that as it may, he recounts many of the same details as Plutarch, and his account shows similar traces of declamatory influence. We meet again with Popillius, who is here described not as a parricide but merely as someone whom Cicero

---

[103] Plutarch's notion that Cicero contemplated sneaking into Octavian's house and killing himself on his hearth (*Cic.* 47.6) also has a fair claim to derive from a declamatory tradition; for the resolve to die, cf. *epist. ad Oct.* 10. So too the ominous ravens found at Plut. *Cic.* 47.8–10, among other places. On both of these possibilities, see Wright (2001) 448–449. See also Moles (1988) 30, who adds the story of Philologus and the fearful punishment he is visited with for his betrayal of Cicero (Plut. *Cic.* 48.2, 49. 2–3).

[104] If Lamberton (2001) 143–145 is right, Plutarch's audience for his parallel lives may have included pupils of rhetoric in his own school, and so these tales may be recycled yet again into the declamatory tradition, now fully in Greek.

[105] On the death of Cicero in Appian and Dio, see esp. Gowing (1992) 154–157, to be set in the wider context of his treatment of Cicero's last year (143–161) and of Appian's and Dio's accounts of the triumviral proscriptions as a whole (247–269). Gowing keenly remarks that "Appian's and Dio's portraits of Cicero are both disappointing and astonishing. Disappointing, because they fail to reveal or elaborate much that we would like to know. Astonishing, because there was such a wealth of material from which they could have drawn but did not" (157). For the death scene in Appian, see Westall (2015) 126–130, concerned principally to show that it does not derive from Pollio. His hypothesis that it derives instead from Seneca the Elder's *Historiae* is not impossible – there are few impossibilities when dealing with lost sources – and might even account for some of the declamatory influence, but some of Appian's details could not be deduced from a hypothetical text in which "Seneca . . . wove together the various reports that he relates in the *Controversiae*" (158).

[106] Gowing (1992) 156 n. 37 observes on the one hand that mention of such a visit lends pathos to Appian's narrative, but that he also would have had other good reasons to visit the area.

had once defended in court (*BC* 4.20). As is by now abundantly clear, this declamatory invention has taken on a life of its own. Appian also introduces a certain cobbler (σκυτότομος), supposedly a former client of Clodius, who from a long-festering hatred for his patron's enemy betrays Cicero's location to Popillius. No other source mentions this particular detail, and it too has the ring of declamatory rhetoric, even if this cannot be proven. The motif of Cicero being betrayed at the end is certainly part of the rhetorical tradition, and what Judas could be more fitting than the client of Cicero's arch-enemy, a man whom Cicero was happy to see dead and whose very killer he defended before Pompey's tribunal?[107]

Whatever we may think about the shoemaker's ontological status, there can be no doubt that Appian's insistent emphasis on Antony's savagery perfectly parallels the declaimers. It was of course Antony alone who had proscribed Cicero, and it was at his orders that Cicero's head and hands were crudely sawed off – the hands with which he had written the speeches accusing Antony of being a tyrant – and, as ever, placed on display. Antony is absolutely delighted (ἥσθη μάλιστα, *BC* 4.20), and he gives Popillius a crown and a cash bonus on top of the published fee in the death contract. He is indeed so barbaric that he would take his meals with the head of Cicero on the table, until at last he was sated with the awful sight (μέχρι κόρον ἔσχε τῆς θέας τοῦ κακοῦ)[108] – the motif of Antony being "sated" by Cicero's death is one we have often seen, and that again probably goes back to the rhetorical schools. Appian concludes with the standard tribute to Cicero: he is a man still renowned for his eloquence, who had served his country most meritoriously as consul, but who in the end was killed and outrageously mistreated (ὧδε μὲν δὴ Κικέρων, ἐπί τε λόγοις ἀοίδιμος ἐς ἔτι νῦν ἀνήρ, καὶ ὅτε ἦρχε τὴν ὕπατον ἀρχήν, ἐς τὰ μέγιστα τῇ πατρίδι γεγονὼς χρήσιμος, ἀνῄρητο καὶ ἀνῃρημένος ἐνυβρίζετο).

Cassius Dio provides our final point of comparison.[109] We again meet Popillius (47.11.1–2), but Dio alone of the sources does not choose to focus

---

[107] Gowing (1992) 254 rightly notes that the victims in the proscriptions "had provided material for the declamatory schools and for such moralizing compilers as Valerius Maximus"; there was thus no shortage of opportunity for declamatory influence (see the series of anecdotes in App. *BC* 4.17–45). Cf. Gowing (1992) 263–264, where it is pointed out that Appian and Dio would have used this material artfully for their own narrative purposes.

[108] On the "John the Baptist motif," see n. 110 below.

[109] When reading Dio's account we must bear in mind a certain tension: Dio was himself a Roman senator witness to political murders in his own day, and yet he was generally sympathetic to Augustus: see Gowing (1992) 266–267. For the entire picture of Cicero in Dio, such as it is, see Millar (1964) 46–55, who remarks that Dio "fails to deal adequately with Cicero" (46) and "does not begin to take into account the realities of politics at the end of the Republic" (49). Ultimately "Dio's handling of Cicero is a failure" (55) – that is to say, a partial version, or what we see in

on the last moments of Cicero's life, recounting them only with parenthetic brevity (φεύγων γὰρ καὶ καταληφθεὶς ἐσφάγη, 47.8.3). He instead focuses exclusively on Antony's cruelty and culpability. Dio's Octavian is especially innocent (47.7.1–4): Caesar's heir had no part in the proscriptions, being associated with them only because he happened to share power with Lepidus and Antony, who were the real culprits. Dio realizes that this claim might be thought controversial, and so he offers several proofs (σημεῖα and τεκμήρια): Octavian was not savage by nature, he says, having been brought up in his father's ways. He anyway hardly had political enemies and preferred to be loved rather than feared. Finally, when he assumed sole power, all proscriptions ceased.

So Dio introduces his description of Cicero's demise, capping his exculpation of Octavian with the rather extraordinary claim that Octavian saved many of the proscribed, as many in fact as he was able (πολλούς, ὅσους γε καὶ ἠδυνήθη, διεσώσατο, 47.8.1). While Octavian is busy saving lives, however, Antony gives his unbridled barbarity free rein, killing without mercy both the proscribed and any who dared aid and abet them (ὁ δὲ Ἀντώνιος ὠμῶς καὶ ἀνηλεῶς οὐχ ὅτι τοὺς ἐκτεθέντας ἀλλὰ καὶ τοὺς ἐπικουρῆσαί τινι αὐτῶν ἐπιχειρήσαντας ἔκτεινε, 48.8.1). He invariably viewed their decapitated heads, even, as in Appian, while eating, until he had his fill of this most disgusting spectacle (τῆς τε ἀνοσιωτάτης καὶ τῆς οἰκτροτάτης αὐτῶν ὄψεως ἐνεπίμπλατο, 48.8.2). Cicero, of course, is a special case, and Antony curses the corpse and orders the head and hands to be displayed on the rostra where Cicero had so often given speeches against him. Fulvia, indeed, goes so far as to yank out Cicero's tongue and use it as a pin-cushion.[110] If a declaimer had not invented this detail, he surely should have, for it is perfectly in line with the declamatory taste for graphic descriptions of savage violence.

Dio thus follows the declaimers in adducing Popillius as Cicero's killer and in the way he ascribes Cicero's death to Antony and Antony alone, heaping invective on Antony's cruelty while exculpating and indeed

---

virtually every ancient author who discusses Cicero. Cf. the avowedly revisionist account of Rees (2011) 102–181.

[110] Cf. Sen. *epist.* 83.25. Beheadings over the dinner table would make a Christian audience think immediately of King Herod and the execution of John the Baptist; Jerome, with characteristically mordant sarcasm, made the association explicit (*adu. Rufin.* 3.42): *sic te docuerunt magistri tui? talibus institutus es disciplinis ut cui respondere non potueris, caput auferas, et linguam quae tacere non potest seces? nec magnopere glorieris, si facias quod scorpiones possunt facere et cantharides. fecerunt hoc et Fuluia in Ciceronem et Herodias in Iohannem, quia ueritatem audire non poterant; et linguam ueriloquam crinali acu confodiebant.* Fromentin and Bertrand (2014) 69 n. 51 do not mention these passages but do add a parallel (and confused) notice in John of Antioch, fr. 152.

praising the young Octavian. Ancient historians talking about Cicero's death were ineluctably influenced by declamation. For a Velleius Paterculus or Valerius Maximus, the declamatory tradition surrounding Cicero's death determined both the form and content of their accounts. The same is true even for Roman poets like Martial and Juvenal. These men had all grown up declaiming and hearing declamations on this very theme under the *rhetor's* tutelage, and it left an indelible impression on their mental image of Cicero. This image, simplified and shaped in the schools, began to become historical reality. In the Greek tradition, direct influence is perhaps less clear. A Plutarch, at least, probably stood one remove from these classrooms, whereas Appian and Dio may have been exposed to Ciceronian declamation as young men. Regardless, we see in their versions of events a marked declamatory influence in themes and presentation. They may have had no sense that they were following the declamatory tradition; they could have been merely following their sources in good faith. These sources, however, had already been thoroughly dyed in declamation, which had by now assumed a bright and vivid existence in reality outside of the classroom. The picture of Cicero, and especially of his death, is thus painted with declamatory *colores*.

CHAPTER 4

Pro Cicerone/In Ciceronem: *How to Criticize Cicero*

The question of whether Cicero should burn his books in return for his life formed a unique subject for declamation: everyone was concerned about Cicero's books, no one about the man himself, and Seneca the Elder says that he knew of no one who argued the other side (*suas.* 7.10). This is the exception that proves the rule; in general, declaimers could make their case *in utramque partem.* The structure of the themes – argue for or against this course of action, prosecute or defend this case – naturally encouraged a dialectic approach. Other rhetorical productions surrounding Cicero well exemplify this tendency, and in this chapter we will see how Cicero is attacked and defended. After a brief discussion of sources, I will focus especially on a few key events from his life that come up again and again in his later reception: his consulship as a *nouus homo*, his exile, and his conflict with Mark Antony.

In the previous chapter I discussed declamations *about* Cicero, but now we will turn to prosopopoeiae, declamations written in Cicero's own persona, or in the persona of one of his contemporaries. These so-called pseudepigrapha have often been derided as inept forgeries, but in fact most of them were probably never intended to deceive anyone.[1] They are products of the rhetorical schools, and were meant to be read and appreciated on those terms. In a concluding section I will discuss one aspect of the declamatory aesthetic, namely its penchant for playful reuse of Ciceronian words and phrases. All of these compositions, in which someone puts words into Cicero's mouth or speaks into his ears, are of particular value in understanding his reception: nothing else shows so clearly how and what ancient audiences thought about him. Furthermore, as we have already seen, many of the themes and modes of thought found in these

---

[1] On Roman pseudepigrapha, see Peirano (2012); some of what I try to do here with prose texts parallels her work with Latin poetry. See esp. her pp. 12–19 on the influence of declamation and the rhetorical schools. Deufert (2013) 345 has also noted the importance of pseudo-Vergilianic texts for understanding the reception of Vergil.

rhetorical productions also appear in literary authors who have been trained in the declamatory schools. Ultimately there was no Manichean dichotomy between a positive and a negative tradition; all its variegated parts would have been available to subsequent Greeks and Romans, and they would choose to emphasize what suited their personal outlook or the rhetorical task at hand. That tradition comes into view in its fullness when we examine these texts.

Pseudepigraphic Sources

The pseudepigrapha that I will discuss stand in the same tradition as the declamatory rhetoric in Seneca the Elder. I will concentrate on various pseudonymous works that are almost certainly products of the rhetorical classroom: pseudo-Sallust's *In M. Tullium Ciceronem inuectiua* (= *in Tull.*) and pseudo-Cicero's counterblast, *In C. Sallustium Crispum inuectiua* (= *in Sall.*); the pseudo-Ciceronian *Oratio pridie quam in exilium iret* (= *exil.*) and *Epistula ad Octauianum* (= *epist. ad Oct.*); and pseudo-Brutus' violent epistolary outbursts to Cicero and Atticus (*Cic. ad Brut.* 1.16, 1.17).[2]

There are two main difficulties in working with these sources. The first is that scholars have occasionally maintained the authenticity of some of these texts: the pseudo-Sallustian invective, for example, has no faults of language or anachronisms so marked as to rule out entirely the possibility that Sallust wrote it himself, and Quintilian not once but twice cites it under Sallust's name (*inst.* 4.1.68, 9.3.89). One might expect Quintilian to be a good judge. The reader nevertheless cannot escape the impression that the whole thing smacks much more of the classroom than the Curia, and it is hard to countenance the idea that a junior senator would have let loose such a screed against a respected elder statesman in 54 BC, the dramatic date of the composition. There is furthermore not a single mention of the invective in Cicero's own writings. This speech, in sum, was almost certainly not written by the

---

[2] Shackleton Bailey (2002) 339 calls all of these exercises "essentially parallel to the *suasoriae* of which the elder Seneca has left us examples." He includes in this category all but one of the items which I will discuss here, omitting only the *Oratio pridie quam in exilium iret*. We know of the existence of still others, like a speech entitled *Si eum P. Clodius legibus interrogasset* (schol. Bob. 108.16 St.) and responses to Cicero's *Pro Milone* by Cestius Pius (Sen. *contr.* 3 pr. 15, Quint. 10.5.20) and Brutus (Quint. *inst.* 10.1.23, 10.5.20). There were also (probably) spurious anti-Cicero compositions circulating in Asconius' lifetime under the names of Catiline and Cicero's consular colleague Antonius (Ascon. 94C). I exclude the *Commentariolum petitionis* because of intractable problems of authenticity and dating, on which see recently Sillett (2016).

real Sallust.[3] Its companion piece is of even more dubious parentage. While the two may have always circulated as a pair, it is entirely possible – and perhaps even likely – that the pseudo-Ciceronian text is a later response to an earlier rhetorical exercise.[4]

Similarly vexing are the two letters ascribed to Brutus by our manuscripts and transmitted along with the corpus of genuine correspondence between Cicero and Brutus. Again we have ancient authority accepting them as genuine, this time Plutarch (*Cic.* 45 and *Brut.* 22). Plutarch himself, however, admits that some of Brutus' letters were probably spurious.[5] There had been further rumblings of discontent throughout the nineteenth and early twentieth centuries, but a critical consensus gradually coalesced that the letters must be authentic.[6] Nevertheless, good reasons to doubt them had long been adduced,[7] and D. R. Shackleton Bailey added several clinching arguments. Most importantly, he notes, it is beyond belief that Cicero would have criticized the assassination of Caesar and referred to Casca as a *sicarius*; elsewhere he invariably praises the assassins.[8] As Shackleton Bailey put it, "his only criticisms are that Antony was allowed to survive and that the conspirators failed to follow up their achievement."[9] In the coda to this chapter I will show that the unlikely word *sicarius* has its origin in the declamatory aesthetic of intertextuality. Further incongruities can also be

---

[3] For a brief summary of the arguments against authenticity, see Santangelo (2012) 29–32. Novokhatko (2009) 111–129 provides a comprehensive doxography of scholarly opinion from antiquity to the present; she believes firmly that the speech is a rhetorical production. Syme (1964) 314–318 is a particularly effective demolition of the case for Sallustian authorship.

[4] The fourth-century grammarian Diomedes attributes the composition to an unknown "Didius" (*GL* 1.387.6). Santangelo (2012) 37 points out that the dramatic date of the pseudo-Ciceronian response appears to be in the 40s BC, while the pseudo-Sallustian invective purports to be written in 54.

[5] Plut. *Brut.* 53 καίτοι φέρεταί τις ἐπιστολὴ Βρούτου πρὸς τοὺς φίλους ... εἴπερ ἄρα τῶν γνησίων ἐστίν.

[6] See Shackleton Bailey (1980) 10 n. 1, who quotes one recent editor's biting judgment: anyone who thinks that these letters are spurious is "stultus, immo sanitate vacans"!

[7] Summarized by Shackleton Bailey (1980) 11. Reasons include Brutus referring to Octavian as *Octauius* (in the genuine correspondence he calls him *Caesar*; see Shackleton Bailey [1980] ad 25.6) and the periodic style of the letters, which contrasts sharply with the style of the letters universally accepted as genuine. Meyer (1881) 150–160 attempts to collect the lexical and syntactical oddities of these letters, although he is an excessively skeptical judge of Latinity and also believes that the entire *Briefwechsel* is spurious. (Similarly but less usefully arranged are Becher [1882] and [1885].) Schmidt (1884) 632–634 is more impressionistic, and although Moles (1997) 152 objects that "our aesthetic response to the letters is necessarily to some extent subjective and does not allow of conclusive judgments," even he allows that there are "objective oddities of language and usage" in the Brutus collection which are "much more numerous and concentrated in the letters in question." See too Harvey (1991) 24–26, with a couple of additional observations; Beaujeu (1991) summarizes preceding work.

[8] See e.g. Cic. *Att.* 14.11.1 or 14.14.3; these examples can be multiplied.

[9] Shackleton Bailey (1980) 12.

detected, and in sum I am persuaded that the letters cannot have been written by Brutus.[10] The alternative hypothesis of composition in a rhetorical school accounts full well for their style, tone, and occasional errors.

None of the other pseudo-Ciceroniana that I shall treat is exposed to quite the same doubts about authorship; works like the *Oratio pridie quam in exilium iret*, for example, manifestly cannot have been written by Cicero. (To leave aside style and language, the historical Cicero simply never had the occasion to deliver such a speech.)[11] They are however liable to another question: when were they composed? The testimony of Quintilian and Plutarch provides a *terminus ante quem* for pseudo-Sallust's *Invective* and pseudo-Brutus' letters, but we have no such firm handles to grasp when we try to date the other works. In the absence of blatant anachronisms, we are reduced to relying on style and language – and since the authors are doing their best to imitate first-century Ciceronian Latin, this becomes a challenging task indeed.[12]

Let it be said up front that all of these works could date anywhere from the first to the fourth centuries AD, and different scholars plump for different dates within this range. It has been seriously argued, in fact, that the *Epistula ad Octauianum* was written before Cicero's death – by someone other than Cicero.[13] More reasonably, a recent editor has declared that she believes the author to be a *rhetor* who lived at some point between the first and fourth centuries AD.[14] The story is almost the same for the *Oratio pridie quam in exilium iret*. The text has attracted virtually no critical attention over the years,[15] but it was at last edited in 1991 for the first time in well over a century. On linguistic grounds Maria De Marco

---

[10] Shackleton Bailey (1980) 12–14. Moles (1997) tries to uphold the authenticity of these letters, and in so doing attempts to deal with Shackleton Bailey's arguments one by one. Although he makes some good points individually, overall he is not convincing, and he does not consider my additional observation about Ciceronian pastiche (p. 192 below).

[11] This fits what Peirano (2012) 12–24 has observed about "creative supplements"; that is to say, these "fakes" often fill in gaps, real or imagined, in an author's works or career.

[12] Cf. Gamberale (1998) 65 on dating the *Oratio pridie quam in exilium iret*: "Ora proprio questa gran quantità di debiti dal Cicerone autentico rende difficile un'indagine linguistica e stilistica che accerti l'epoca del falso."

[13] Romano (1965) 598–600. "Si inferisce che la lettera fu composta tra l'ottobre ed il novembre del 43, quando ancora Cicerone non era stato colpito, o non sapeva di essere stato colpito, dalla proscrizione" (599).

[14] Lamacchia (1967) 49–50: "Cum certa eius desint uestigia, inter saec. 1 p. Ch. n. . . . et saec. IV . . . rhetorem illum qui hanc Epistulam, uel potius declamatiunculam scripserit ponendum esse putamus." A year later she was inclined toward the latter end of this range (Lamacchia [1968] 22 n. 2). The most recent editor, by contrast, looks to the very beginning of this range (20 BC – AD 120): Grattarola (1988) 27–32.

[15] Richard Rouse and Michael Reeve in Reynolds (1983) 58 n. 11 observe that "altogether it has aroused remarkably little curiosity."

concludes in her preface that the text was probably written in the second century, but she assumes that the author of the text had read Plutarch's *Life of Cicero*.[16] This assumption is thoroughly questionable,[17] and so what De Marco is really saying is that the language betrays no telltale signs of late composition: for all we know it could be first century. Of course, the one other scholar to have devoted serious attention to it argues for a slightly later date than De Marco.[18] Once again, then, we are at an impasse.

I think that none of these texts was written by the author it claims for itself, and all either certainly or possibly fall within the period we are considering here. It must be confessed, however, that in any individual case we cannot be certain. Nevertheless, there is not only a great continuity in Roman education in general (see p. 15 above); there is a particular continuity of thought in these texts. Even if one or another is not actually from the first century or the early second century, they will all be seen to preserve a continuous and living tradition that dates back to that time. They can thus be used as later examples of earlier trends and can help fill in the gaps in our knowledge. They are above all of signal value for giving us direct insight into the minds of early Romans, telling us explicitly how they imagined Cicero speaking and being spoken to.[19]

---

[16] De Marco (1991) 5: "Quo autem tempore opusculum ille [*sc.* auctor ignotus] conscripserit plane ignoratur; attamen, si quis perattente consideret quam elocutionis rationem ille adhibuerit, ueterum rerum notitiam ostenderit, facile intelleget orationem saeculo II p.Ch.n. ... esse compositam." Similarly De Marco (1967) 37.

[17] And Gamberale (1998) 54 has gently questioned it: "questo forse non è strettamente necessario." I would go much further. Plut. *Cic.* 30.6 says that Cicero κινδυνεύων ... καὶ διωκόμενος, ἐσθῆτά τε μετήλλαξε καὶ κόμης ἀνάπλεως περιιὼν ἱκέτευε τὸν δῆμον; the inference then is that this speech is his "supplication to the people." But on any natural reading of Plutarch this passage means that Cicero "went around" (περιιών) and talked to people, probably individuals and certainly on multiple occasions. Here we are dealing instead with a set-piece oration. It seems much more likely that a fictitious situation was simply invented for the classroom: "Write a speech that Cicero would have given to the people on the eve of his exile." In any event, even if the present speech does allude to the historical situation mentioned in Plutarch, there is no need for our author to have gotten his information from Plutarch simply because Plutarch is the only source we have today who preserves the story. He was himself drawing on earlier sources, and so may be our declaimer.

[18] Gamberale (1997) 331 states that various oddities of language and style "mi inducono a ritinere che l'orazione sia stata composta in un periodo più tardo del II secolo d. C." A year later he offered a fuller treatment of the issue, concluding that the speech is a declamation from a rhetorical classroom of late antiquity – "sia pure con qualche margine di incertezza" (Gamberale [1998] 74). The "margin of uncertainty" consists of approximately four centuries.

[19] Texts of clearly medieval origin, such as the *Quinta Catilinaria*, the *Catilinae responsio*, and the *Oratio aduersus Valerium* are excluded here. For a convenient collection of these texts, which do provide evidence of Cicero's reception in a later age, see De Marco (1967); Glei (2002) gives a new critical edition and introduction to the *Catilinae responsio*. The *Declamatio in L. Sergium Catilinam* is perhaps a special case: it purports to be a courtroom speech from 63 BC, in which Cicero acts as a prosecutor against Catiline. Oddities of style and language rule out an early date, and indeed many have held it to be a Renaissance forgery. It may instead be late antique, but the nagging questions

Consul and *nouus homo*

If you asked Cicero what his most important achievement was, he would have answered without hesitation: "When I was consul I saved the Republic from Catiline's conspiracy."[20] Indeed, you would not have had to ask him; he would have gladly told you unbidden. Seneca the Younger's pithy epigram about Cicero's view of his consulship might fairly encapsulate the salient aspects; the consulship was praised, he says, *non sine causa sed sine fine* ("not without cause but without end," Sen. *dial.* 10.5.1).[21] Now the consulship was the summit of the *cursus honorum* and so would represent the pinnacle of any Roman's political career, but circumstances rendered it especially prominent for Cicero. After 63 BC he declined to take a province – although more than a decade later Pompey's new regulations forced him to assume the governorship of Cilicia unwillingly – and so he had no further political or military triumphs to speak of. Moreover, until Caesar's assassination he was buffeted almost constantly by the winds of adverse fortune: exile, backing the wrong horse in the race between Pompey and Caesar, and finally an ignominious reprieve from Caesar coupled with a forced withdrawal from free political activity. But all of this pales by comparison with Cicero's real reason for pride in his consulship: he crushed Catiline's uprising. When he or anyone else talks about his consulship, they are little concerned with what happened before the month of November. Cicero's consulship was in an objective sense quite extraordinary, and it is fair to say that it is *non sine causa* the best known in Roman history.

Cicero's self-promotion of the events of his consulship was helped immensely by the canonization of the Catilinarian orations as school texts. He published them in a body along with his other consular speeches as models for aspiring young orators (*Att.* 2.1.3), and while most of his other speeches of 63 were eventually lost or but little read, the

---

about its date have led me to exclude it. This is not a great loss: although there are numerous Ciceronian echoes and quotations in the composition, it does not otherwise tell us much about Cicero beyond the fact that the Catilinarian conspiracy might figure in a declamation, and the work would instead be more useful in a study of the afterlife of Catiline. Schurgacz (2004) is a helpful introduction and commentary to the speech, which can still be usefully supplemented by the extensive list of parallels in Kristofferson (1928).

[20] Citations for this point are almost superfluous; see virtually anything written by Cicero after 63 BC. An example is his famous oath on leaving office: *ego cum in contione abiens magistratu dicere a tribuno pl. prohiberer quae constitueram, cumque is mihi tantum modo ut iurarem permitteret, sine ulla dubitatione iuraui rem publicam atque hanc urbem mea unius opera esse saluam* (*Pis.* 6; cf. *fam.* 5.2.7). Cicero's consulship is a key element in his own self-fashioning; see e.g. Steel (2005) 49–63.

[21] Cicero's ceaseless boasting about his consulship is a declamatory theme; cf. e.g. [Sall.] *in Tull.* 6.

Catilinarians immediately took up a firm place in the classroom curriculum, where they stayed until just about yesterday. As we have already seen, authors from the Senecas to Petronius to Quintilian and Tacitus all bear witness to the primacy of the *Catilinarians* in the schoolroom, and the Ciceronian papyri tell the same story: alongside the *Verrines*, the *Catilinarians* are the speeches of Cicero best represented by papyri.[22] Their echoes show up throughout later Latin literature, and it would be supererogatory to cite instances of phrases like *quo usque tandem* from Sallust (*Cat.* 20.9 – spoken *by* Catiline!) to Apuleius (*met.* 3.27).[23] A particularly delightful bronze statue of a schoolteacher, dating probably from the third or fourth century, even has Cicero's *quo usque tandem* inscribed on its base.[24]

Rather than bludgeoning you with such obvious examples of such a manifest phenomenon, I will point to a somewhat more subtle instance of allusion to the *Catilinarians* that shows how well known they must have been to the educated. In Seneca's *Medea*, Creon gives a speech in favor of expelling the title character. He concludes his rhesis with the following brief epilogue (*Med.* 266–271):[25]

> tu, tu malorum machinatrix facinorum,
> cui feminae nequitia, ad audendum omnia
> robur uirile est, nulla famae memoria,
> egredere, purga regna, letales simul
> tecum aufer herbas, libera ciues metu,   270
> alia sedens tellure sollicita deos.

> You, you inventress of evil deeds, you who have both a woman's wickedness and a man's strength to dare anything and everything, you who take no heed of your reputation – leave, cleanse the kingdom, and take away all your fatal poisons with you, free the citizens from fear, and taking up residence in another land trouble the gods.

Creon's situation parallels that of Cicero in 63. Each wishes to expel from his city what he views as a noxious bane. Indeed, Seneca's Creon speaks directly to Medea, just as Cicero had addressed Catiline himself before the Senate in the first *Catilinarian*. Seneca, moreover, clearly echoes Cicero's own words in those speeches. Medea is the *malorum machinatrix facinorum*; Cicero describes one of Catiline's co-conspirators as the *omnium*

---

[22] See p. 81 above.   [23] On Sall. *Cat.* 20.9, see Feldherr (2013).   [24] See Passelac (1972).
[25] The parallels with Ciceronian language here are registered but not discussed by Costa (1973) and Boyle (2014). Seneca also channels the first *Catilinarian* in a speech of Jocasta's in the *Phoenissae* (632–643); see Ginsberg (2016).

scelerum improbissimum machinatorem (*Cat.* 3.6).[26] Medea has the strength *ad audendum omnia*; Cicero's Catiline <u>omnia</u> *norat, omnium aditus tenebat; appellare, temptare, sollicitare poterat,* <u>audebat</u> (*Cat.* 3.16).[27] Creon commands Medea, *egredere . . . libera ciues metu*; Cicero had spoken almost the same words: *egredere ex urbe, Catilina, libera rem publicam metu* (*Cat.* 1.20). In sum, this brief *peroratio* is shot through with allusions to Cicero's *Catilinarians*. This is the school exercise of turning prose into verse that we have already seen, but deployed with considerable sophistication. Beyond the situational parallels, Seneca may be characterizing Medea as a Catiline and Creon as, while not unjustified, a bit pompous in his rhetoric, as Seneca perhaps views the Cicero of 63 (the consulship praised *non sine causa sed sine fine!*). In any event, for our present purposes the references themselves are the most interesting point: they suggest that the Catilinarian orations would have been easily recognized by literate contemporaries. Cicero's speeches and Cicero's version of the events of 63 established an early hold on the Roman consciousness and hung on tenaciously.

Cicero's consulship is simply a given for later Romans. The declaimer Cestius Pius, for example, poses the rhetorical question, "What need is there for me to speak of your consulship that saved the city?" (*quid <referam> consulatum salutarem urbi?*, Sen. *suas.* 7.2), and other declaimers likewise speak constantly of 63 BC, the *annus mirabilis*.[28] It is similarly the subject of countless incidental mentions in other authors. Take Manilius: Cicero won the consulship,[29] he says, by the wealth of his oratory (*censu Tullius oris | emeritus fasces*, 1.794–795). This makes Cicero's highest political achievement the product of his highest achievement *tout court*, his eloquence. There is little point to multiplying such examples.

But Cicero's enemies also found fertile ground to plow in his consulship. In his own lifetime, of course, Cicero faced the slings and arrows of Clodius regarding his consular activities, and men like Asinius Pollio continued such criticisms in historical writing and declamation after his death. Much of this early tradition remains shrouded in obscurity, but we have a sterling example of early rhetorical criticism of Cicero in the pseudo-Sallustian

[26] Seneca's reference is in no doubt, and it is only strengthened by the fact that *machinatrix* is a hapax legomenon (*TLL* VIII.16.81–83 [Dietzfelbinger]).
[27] Catiline's *audacia* is indeed one of his signal attributes, referred to time and again both in Cicero's speeches (e.g. found seventeen times in the *Catilinarians*, beginning with *Cat.* 1.1 [see Dyck (2008) ad loc.]) and in Sallust (see e.g. Vretska [1976] ad Sall. *Cat.* 5.4 *animus audax*).
[28] E.g. Sen. *contr.* 7.2.4, 7.2.6, 7.2.7, *suas.* 6.3, 6.7. Augustus was himself born this year, another happy coincidence for Augustan ideology: see p. 109 above.
[29] If Bentley's bold emendation *fasces* for the transmitted *caelum* is correct.

Inuectiua in Ciceronem and its response, the pseudo-Ciceronian *Inuectiua in Sallustium.*[30] Taken together, these two productions of the rhetorical schools give us unique insight into early criticism and defense of Cicero and his consulship – and it is no surprise to find that they emanate precisely from the declamatory tradition. Other critical accounts, like the speech of Calenus in Cassius Dio, will parallel these criticisms in almost every detail.[31]

The fundamental premise of the pseudo-Sallustian *Invective*, purportedly written *ca.* 54 BC, is that Cicero's consulship was bad. Not only, pseudo-Sallust alleges, was it in Cicero's consulship that the Roman Republic was rent asunder by conspiracy and revolution, but indeed his consulship was its very cause (*in Tull.* 3). The key charge, of course, is that he put Roman citizens to death without trial. For example, pseudo-Sallust says (*in Tull.* 5–6):

> atque is cum eius modi sit, tamen audet dicere: "o fortunatam natam me consule Romam"! <Romam> te consule fortunatam, Cicero? immo uero infelicem et miseram, quae crudelissimam proscriptionem eam perpessa est, cum tu perturbata re publica metu perculsos omnes bonos parere crudelitati tuae cogebas, cum omnia iudicia, omnes leges in tua libidine erant, cum tu sublata lege Porcia, erepta libertate omnium nostrum uitae necisque potestatem ad te unum reuocaueras. atque parum quod impune fecisti, uerum etiam commemorando exprobras neque licet obliuisci his seruitutis suae. egeris, oro te, Cicero, profeceris quidlibet: satis est perpessos esse: etiamne aures nostras odio tuo onerabis, etiamne molestissimis uerbis insectabere? "cedant arma togae, concedat laurea linguae." quasi uero togatus et non armatus ea, quae gloriaris, confeceris, atque inter te Sullamque dictatorem praeter nomen imperii quicquam interfuerit.

> And although he's that sort of person, he still dares to say: "Fortunate Rome, born when I was consul"! Rome, fortunate when you were consul, Cicero? Try "unfortunate and wretched"! She endured the cruelest proscription when you forced all honest men, cast down as they were by fear in a republic thrown into confusion, to submit to your cruelty; when all the law courts, all the laws were subject to your arbitrary judgment; when, with the *lex Porcia* abolished and freedom snatched away, you had brought the power of life and death over us all into your hands alone. And the fact that

---

[30] The commentary of Novokhakto (2009) on the two *Inuectiuae* is very sparse; Vretska (1961) is very full, but only treats the pseudo-Sallustian speech. A connected reading of both speeches is provided by Koster (1980) 177–200. See also the useful notes in the Budé text of Ernout (1962).

[31] See p. 182 below. The account of Zielinski (1929) 280–288 remains fundamental, although he focused on reconstructing a lost common source for pseudo-Sallust and Dio. I see no need to look for a *single* source; these texts and others can best be read as representing a whole tradition shaped by the rhetorical schools.

you did this with impunity is not enough; you continually throw it in our faces, and these people [i.e. the Romans] are not allowed to forget their servitude. You've done it – please, Cicero – you've accomplished whatever you wished. It is enough that we have suffered through it. Will you also burden our ears with your insolence, will you keep assaulting us with your unbelievably annoying phrases? "Let arms yield to the toga, let the laurel bow to the tongue." As though you accomplished what you're bragging about in a toga and not in arms, as though there were any difference between you and Sulla the dictator besides the word *imperium*.

Scathing rhetoric. Cicero is a second Sulla, and he is charged with sole responsibility for the executions, which pseudo-Sallust calls "proscriptions" – a harsh depiction of the executions in any event, but particularly cutting to apply to a man who will one day fall victim to a proscription himself.[32] The fundamental reason that Cicero's consulship was bad is that he executed Roman citizens without trial, in clear violation of the *lex Porcia*, but our rhetorician uses this theme as a hook on which he can hang related charges as well. Not only, for example, did Cicero have the audacity to *do* these things, but he has the face to boast about them continually – and in atrocious verse at that.[33] Indeed, the infamous *o fortunatam natam* line will be on pseudo-Sallust's mind elsewhere too; when he addresses Cicero as *Romule Arpinas* (7), he must be thinking of the "birth of Rome" in Cicero's consulship.

The consulship also leads into a discussion of Cicero's venality: he is alleged to have held trials prosecuting the conspirators under the *lex Plautia*, which punished disruptive public violence. Those who could afford to bribe him were let off with slaps on the wrist, but as for anyone else, he was alleged to have been "Catiline's closest associate; he either had come to assault [Cicero's] house or had plotted against the Senate; and in sum [Cicero] knew all there was to know about him" (*is erat Catilinae proximus, is aut domum tuam oppugnatum uenerat aut insidias senatui fecerat, denique de eo tibi compertum erat, in Tull.* 3). The verb *comperire* is piquant: this was Cicero's own word of choice when reporting on the Catilinarian conspiracy (e.g. *haec ego omnia . . . comperi, Cat.* 1.10), and it was likewise used as a reproach in his own lifetime.[34] Our declaimer uses Cicero's own words against him. And, pseudo-Sallust continues, if these things are not true, then how did Cicero buy his house on the Palatine?

---

[32] An instance of dramatic irony; on this declamatory trope, see p. 176 below.

[33] On Cicero's poetry, see p. 186 with n. 97 below.

[34] E.g. Cic. *Att.* 1.14.5 (cited by Koster [1980] 182 n. 615), *fam.* 5.5.2 with Shackleton Bailey (1977) ad loc. p. 284 "a catchword with Cicero's enemies."

In reality these things were not true; Cicero held no such trials, and his house was financed by loans. But the slanders are founded on legitimate reproaches: he did prosecute some of the accused conspirators and defend others, and the loans for his home came from clients who included Sulla, an alleged conspirator whom Cicero had defended.[35]

The charge of venality is intimately associated with the charge of inconstancy. Cicero would now pursue the conspirators with fire and sword, now back them to the hilt. Moreover, both Cicero's venality and his inconstancy are tied in with his status as a *nouus homo*.[36] In the very first paragraph of the speech Cicero is referred to as a man *reperticius, accitus, ac paulo ante insitus huic urbi ciuis* ("a newly discovered citizen, imported from abroad, and just recently grafted on to this city,"*in Tull.* 1),[37] and several sections later his *nouitas* is raised again. Cicero, pseudo-Sallust says, is a *homo nouus Arpinas* ("new man from Arpinum," *in Tull.* 4; cf. 7 *Romule Arpinas*). And yet so far from following the example of the most famous Arpinate *nouus homo*, Gaius Marius, Cicero is

> homo leuissimus, supplex inimicis, amicis contumeliosus, modo harum, modo illarum partium, fidus nemini, leuissimus senator, mercennarius patronus, cuius nulla pars corporis a turpitudine uacat: lingua uana, manus rapacissimae, gula immensa, pedes fugaces, quae honeste nominari non possunt inhonestissima. (in Tull. 5)

> a most fickle man, a suppliant to his enemies, reproachful to his friends, now on this side and now on that, loyal to no one, a most capricious senator, an advocate for hire, whose every body part is defiled with shame: his tongue is deceitful, his hands are most rapacious, his gullet is ravenous, his feet are fleet, and those parts of his body which can't be decently named are most indecent.[38]

Each of these reproaches is cutting: Cicero's services as an advocate were for hire; his tongue, usually considered his most prized virtue, is here *uana*; his hands, which will one day be cut off, are grasping and greedy; his fleeing feet delivered him speedily into exile. Above all, he is a man without loyalty. Next to the crime of executing Roman citizens, Cicero's inconstancy is plainly seen as his most serious failing. While a Valerius Maximus might occasionally attempt to turn this into a virtue, talking about how

---

[35] On the question "Was Sulla guilty?" and the morality of Cicero's defense, see Berry (1996) 33–42.

[36] For the theme of *nouitas* in invective, see Opelt (1965) 149–151.

[37] Twisting Sall. *Cat.* 31.7 *M. Tullius, inquilinus ciuis urbis Romae.*

[38] For parallels to these reproaches, see Ernout (1962) 55 and Opelt (1965) 148. Vretska (1961) ad loc. p. 42 notes that *homo leuissimus* may well be a parody of Cicero, who likes to use *leuis* in this sense; ditto for *mercennarius patronus*.

Cicero had the magnanimity to put aside old hatreds and defend Gabinius against a charge of extortion and Vatinius on two separate occasions (4.2.4), almost everyone else found flip-flopping a grave fault. Our "Sallust" has the bit between his teeth now and is off to the races: he too mentions Vatinius as a signal example of Cicero's waffling, along with his ever-changing relations with Pompey and Caesar; in sum, "when you're standing you feel one way about the state, when you're sitting you feel something else, you faithless deserter, loyal neither to this side nor to that" (*aliud stans, aliud sedens sentis de re publica . . . leuissime transfuga, neque in hac neque in illa parte fidem habens, in Tull.* 7).

These reproaches are all staples of the declamatory diet of Ciceronian criticism. Dio's Calenus will reproduce all of them, including pseudo-Sallust's slanderous charges about Cicero's incest with his daughter and prostitution of his wife (*in Tull.* 2; cf. Seru. ad *Aen.* 6.623). Others are found scattered throughout texts like pseudo-Brutus' letters to Cicero and Atticus. These diverse sources, considered synoptically, present a remarkably consistent and coherent picture of how to criticize Cicero in the declamatory classroom. And yet again such criticisms will pass from the rhetorical school into the literary and historical tradition in writers like Dio.

Such an attack could not go unanswered. Most declaimers, like most of our literary authors, prefer to praise Cicero's consulship, and we have a rhetorical response to pseudo-Sallust's vituperative outburst. In the *Inuectiua in Sallustium*, "Cicero" spends two lengthy sections defending his status as a *nouus homo* (*in Sall.* 4–5). Someone has to be the first to win glory for his family, he says, even among the Scipios or Metelli. Why should his own ennoblement, the result of virtuous deeds and a virtuous life, be viewed any differently? Moreover, he continues,

> ego meis maioribus uirtute mea praeluxi, ut, si prius noti non fuerunt, a me accipiant initium memoriae suae: tu tuis uita quam turpiter egisti magnas offudisti tenebras, ut, etiamsi fuerint egregii ciues, per te uenerint in obliuionem. quare noli mihi antiquos uiros obiectare; satius est enim me meis rebus gestis florere quam maiorum opinione niti et ita uiuere ut ego sim posteris meis nobilitatis initium et uirtutis exemplum. (*in Sall.* 5)

> I have outshone my ancestors in virtue so that, if they weren't known before, they'll receive the beginning of their fame from me: you have cast your ancestors into shadowy obscurity by your life, which you've led disgracefully, so that even if they were outstanding citizens, because of you they'll be forgotten entirely. Therefore don't cast the men of old in my teeth; for it's

better for me to prosper in the deeds that I've done than to rely on the reputation of my ancestors, and to live in such a way that I am the first stage of nobility for my descendants and an exemplar of virtue.

None of this is particularly surprising. "Cicero" must play the cards that he has been dealt, and he plays them well, managing both to defend himself and to counterattack his adversary at the same time. There was a lively dialectic tradition in the declamatory classroom, in which declaimers competed against one another and vied to one-up each other's arguments. Here Cicero speaks second and so has the advantage. Whatever his real insecurities on his *nouitas*, when pressed on the point he must simply make a virtue of necessity (e.g. *Verr.* ii 5.180–182, *Sest.* 136–138).[39]

So too does pseudo-Cicero speak of his consulship, combining vigorous defense of his own actions with the harshest insults for his opponent (*in Sall.* 6–7):

> quam tu proscriptionem uocas, credo, quod non omnes tui similes inco-lumes in urbe uixissent: at quanto meliore loco res publica staret, si tu par ac similis scelestorum ciuium una cum illis adnumeratus esses? an ego tunc falso scripsi "cedant arma togae," qui togatus armatos et pace bellum oppressi? an illud mentitus sum "fortunatam me consule Romam," qui tantum intestinum bellum ac domesticum urbis incendium exstinxi? neque te tui piget, homo leuissime, cum ea culpas, quae historiis mihi gloriae ducis?

> You call it a proscription, I believe, because not all of those of your ilk survived in the city unscathed: but how much better off would the Republic be now if you had been counted together with them as the equal and compatriot of the wicked citizens? Was I wrong to write then *cedant arma togae*, I who wearing the toga put down armed men and with peace suppressed a war? Did I lie with the line *fortunatam me consule Romam*, I who extinguished so great a civil war and the domestic conflagration of the city? Aren't you ashamed, you worthless man, when you blame me for the very things which you consider my glory in your *Histories*?

Just as pseudo-Sallust had linked Cicero's poetry and his consulship, so pseudo-Cicero defends them in the same breath. His line of reasoning? "It's not boasting if it's true, and it's all true" – he crushed the conspiracy without military force, and even pseudo-Sallust must admit that (as the real

---

[39] Cicero feels compelled to report criticism of his *nouitas* even in the Catilinarians (*Cat.* 1.28); see the note of Dyck (2008) ad loc. For the reproaches of Catiline and Cicero's eventual colleague Antonius in 64 BC, see Ascon. 93–94C (cf. Quint. *inst.* 9.3.94, schol. Bob. 80 St., App. *BC* 2.2), 86C, and more generally e.g. Sall. *Catil.* 23.5–6. On the rhetoric and ideology of *nouitas*, see Wiseman (1971) 107–116, Dugan (2005) 6–13, and van der Blom (2010).

Sallust is said to have done in his *Historiae*).[40] Furthermore, he does all this with vocabulary characteristic of the declamatory Cicero; the phrase *qui tantum intestinum bellum ac domesticum urbis incendium exstinxi* smacks of Cicero in almost every way: e.g. *Cat.* 2.28 *bellum intestinum ac domesticum*, *Cat.* 2.11 *urbis incendia*, *Pis.* 6. *ego faces iam accensas ad huius* <u>urbis incendium</u> ... <u>exstinxi</u>.[41] So too *qui togatus armatos et pace bellum oppressi* is easily paralleled: *dom.* 99 *qui consul togatus armatos uicerim*. Similarities abound elsewhere too: at *har. resp.* 49 Cicero describes himself as the *togatum domestici belli exstinctorem*, contrasted with Pompey, the *externorum bellorum hostiumque uictorem*, the same constrast as in the infamous *cedant arma togae*. The tenor of the defense, moreover, is almost precisely that of *off.* 1.77–78. Such recombined Ciceronianisms are the hallmark of these compositions.

"Cicero" defends his riches in the same way that Socrates proposes free maintenance for life as a punishment for himself: "My wealth," he says, "is far less than what I deserve." He hastens to add that it mostly came from inheritances, and he professes that he would rather have his friends still alive than enjoy their empty wealth (*in Sall.* 9). This is a bold and tendentious claim. It was not only pseudo-Sallust who attributed Cicero's wealth to his oratory (e.g. *in Tull.* 4); even Dio's Philiscus states as simple fact that he did not acquire his riches as inheritances but rather through his eloquent speeches (οὐδὲ πατρῷά σοι τὰ πολλὰ αὐτῶν γέγονεν ... ἀλλὰ ὑπό τε τῆς γλώττης καὶ ὑπὸ τῶν λόγων σου πεπόρισται, 38.20.3). "Cicero" is also quick to defend his supposed fickle nature. He himself has always been constant, he claims, in his defense of the Republic and its principles – it is others who have now promoted its interests, now worked against it. His is true steadfastness of purpose.

The declaimer also imitates Ciceronianisms. Addressing Sallust, for example, he says that he could have "branded you for all time with marks that the remainder of your life could not wash away" (*tibi ... aeternas inurere maculas, quas reliqua uita tua eluere non posset, in Sall.* 16); this notion of "branding" with a mark is an extremely Ciceronian touch, found commonly in Cicero and very rarely elsewhere (see p. 119 above). He describes Sallust's joining Caesar's side in the civil war as "flinging himself into that army into which all of the sewage (*sentina*) of the Republic had flowed" (*in Sall.* 16), doubtless evocative of the

---

[40] Sallust's *Histories* treated 78–67 BC, and so critics have been troubled by this point (see e.g. Novokhatko [2009] 173 n. 20). In the absence of the *Historiae* themselves, it is hard to know what to make of this, but a forward-looking comment in the work itself is hardly to be excluded.
[41] Cf. *Cael.* 70, *Sull.* 83, *Mil.* 103, *Marcell.* 29, *fam.* 4.13.2.

Catilinarians, where Cicero uses *sentina* twice to describe the conspirators (*Cat.* 1.12, 2.7). So too when describing his exile pseudo-Cicero says *furori tribuni plebis cessi* ("I yielded to the madness of the tribune of the plebs," 10); Cicero himself had said *cessi tribuni plebis, despicatissimi hominis, furori* ("I yielded to the madness of the tribune of the plebs, a most despicable man," *Sest.* 36; cf. pp. 165 and 169 below for further development of these themes). These echoes can be multiplied *ad libitum*; as we have now so often seen, when writing about Cicero the declaimers love to imitate his *ipsissima uerba*, and nowhere is this more appropriate than when writing as Cicero himself.

Literary authors take a similar line. We have already seen Pliny the Elder's remarks on the glorious events of 63 BC and the likewise laudatory poem of Cornelius Severus (pp. 127 and 138). It will be worthwhile to look at two more extended treatments of the consulship, one in prose and one in verse, both of which will also throw into sharp relief the countervailing tradition that criticizes Cicero's consular conduct. Here is part of Velleius Paterculus' epitome of the year (2.34.3–4):

> per haec tempora, M. Cicero, qui omnia incrementa sua sibi debuit, uir nouitatis nobilissimae et, ut uita clarus, ita ingenio maximus, qui effecit ne, quorum arma uiceramus, eorum ingenio uinceremur, consul Sergii Catilinae Lentulique et Cethegi et aliorum utriusque ordinis uirorum coniurationem singulari uirtute, constantia, uigilia curaque aperuit. Catilina metu consularis imperii urbe pulsus est; Lentulus, consularis et praetor iterum, Cethegusque et alii clari nominis uiri, auctore senatu, iussu consulis, in carcere necati sunt.

> At this time Marcus Cicero – a man who had pulled himself up entirely by his own bootstraps, a man of most noble newness and as famous for his way of life as he was outstanding in his genius, a man who ensured that we would not be conquered in intellectual achievement by those whom we had conquered in war – was serving as consul and exposed the conspiracy of Sergius Catiline and Lentulus and Cethegus and other men of both orders by his singular bravery, steadfastness, vigilance, and care. Catiline was driven from the city out of fear of the consul's power; Lentulus, a former consul and a twice a praetor, and Cethegus and other men of noble descent were executed in jail at the order of the consul and with the Senate's full backing.

This is a typical passage concerned to praise and defend Cicero, similar to the Plinian remarks that we have already seen, and it is also of a piece with Velleius' description of Cicero's death.[42] As so often, the rhetorical focus

---

[42] Schmitzer (2000) 187 observes Velleius' unified picture of Cicero, not however noting its rhetorical basis.

is on display, with pointed paradox and careful constructions abounding.[43] But Velleius also takes a quietly polemical stand on several important issues. The most obvious, of course, is simply that the consulship is seen in a positive light – this is by no means always the case. More interestingly, Velleius makes repeated and positive reference to Cicero's status as a *nouus homo*, both implicitly by observing that the execrable conspirators included men of the highest status and explicitly with the marvelous oxymoron *uir nouitatis nobilissimae*. Cicero's lack of noble blood was a sore spot for him during his own lifetime, being mentioned several times with evident insecurity even in the *Catilinarians* themselves (cf. n. 39 above). Both contemporaries and later generations would criticize Cicero's upstart status, but Velleius, as Cicero had done before him, makes a virtue of necessity, admiring him for pulling himself up by his own bootstraps. Cicero and Velleius both would probably have preferred that he had simply come from a distinguished family, but Velleius was himself a new man, and so this may be a point of particular poignancy.[44] Declamatory paradox continues in the phrase *qui effecit ne, quorum arma uiceramus, eorum ingenio uinceremur* ("who brought it about that we would not be conquered in literary achievement by those whom we had conquered in arms"). Here Cicero's literary genius forestalls Horace's famous verdict that *Graecia capta ferum uictorem cepit et artes | intulit agresti Latio* (*epist.* 2.1.156–157); Velleius' allusion has a corrective bite. Here again, just as in Manilius and the declaimers, we see Cicero's political success linked with his sparkling eloquence. Finally and most tellingly, Velleius includes a seemingly innocuous ablative of attendant circumstances: the conspirators were indeed executed on Cicero's orders, but with the Senate's full backing (*auctore senatu*; cf. *senatus auctoritate*, p. 168 below). Here Velleius is plainly staving off the criticism that dogged Cicero throughout his life and continued unabated in the adverse declamatory tradition after his death, namely that he had executed Roman citizens without trial. This is the template for the defense.

Finally there is Juvenal's evocation of the consular Cicero as an exemplum in the eighth *Satire*, in which he criticizes noble families who rely on

---

[43] Elefante (1997) ad loc. p. 289 notes also some parallels with Cicero's own language.

[44] For Velleius' biography, see Levick (2011); admittedly his *nouitas* may be somewhat problematic, since he may have had family connections of senatorial rank and his ancestry is not entirely clear (ibid., p. 14 n. 4). But regardless, his father was not a senator. Somewhat surprisingly, there is no ancient definition of either *nouitas* or *nobilitas*; see Burckhardt (1990) 77–78, van der Blom (2010) 35.

their bloodlines rather than their virtue (*stemmata quid faciunt?*, 8.1).[45] After noting that Catiline's lofty birth did not stop him from acting like a pants-wearing Gaul and trying to set fire to Rome, Juvenal contrasts the behavior of the new man from Arpinum (Iuu. 8.236–244):

> sed uigilat consul uexillaque uestra coercet.
> hic nouus Arpinas, ignobilis et modo Romae
> municipalis eques, galeatum ponit ubique
> praesidium attonitis et in omni monte laborat.
> tantum igitur muros intra toga contulit illi   240
> nominis ac tituli, quantum †in† Leucade, quantum
> Thessaliae campis Octauius abstulit udo
> caedibus adsiduis gladio; sed Roma parentem,
> Roma patrem patriae Ciceronem libera dixit.

But the consul is vigilant and halts your troops. This new man from Arpinum – not a noble, just arrived in Rome, an *eques* from a *municipium* – he blankets the city with helmed warriors for the protection of the stunned citizenry and toils on every hill. Thus within the city walls the toga brought him as much fame and reputation as Octavian snatched for himself at Leucas and the Thessalian fields with his sword dripping wet from constant slaughter; but Rome, free Rome, called Cicero its parent, the father of the fatherland.

Juvenal's description of Cicero the consul should sound familiar: we have again the pseudo-Sallustian *homo nouus Arpinas* (*in Tull.* 4), the man who is *reperticius, accitus, ac paulo ante insitus huic urbi ciuis* (*in Tull.* 1). Juvenal likewise plays with the declamatory trope of talking about Cicero in his own words. The "vigilant consul" calls to mind Cicero's boasts in the *Catilinarians* (e.g. *iam intelleges . . . me uigilare*, *Cat.* 1.8), as does perhaps the word *praesidium* (e.g. *meis praesidiis, Cat.* 1.7), and of course the *toga* that brought Cicero his fame – contrasted with Octavian's bloody military action – alludes again to that infamous *cedant arma togae*.[46] It is hard to gauge the valence of the last two lines: are the repetitions (*Roma . . . Roma, parentem . . . patrem*), alliteration (*parentem . . . patrem patriae*), and assonance (*parentem . . . patrem . . . Ciceronem*) deliberately clumsy and designed to mock Cicero's own poetry?[47] It is in any case tempting to think that Juvenal may be alluding to something in the *De consulatu suo*

---

[45] On Cicero in this passage, see esp. Uden (2015) 126–128, as well as Winkler (1988) 86–87.

[46] There may likewise be an allusion in line 232–233 *arma . . . et flammas domibus templisque paratis* to Cicero's *De consulatu suo* fr. 10.64 Courtney *et clades patriae flamma ferroque parata*.

[47] Winkler (1988) 87 sees parody here. Juvenal certainly mocks Cicero's poetry in the tenth *Satire*; see p. 99 above.

here, whether sincerely or not.[48] Where does Juvenal stand in this passage? He plainly criticizes Catiline and praises Cicero's achievement in stopping him, but he may perhaps be taking some shots at Cicero along the way. Regardless, he is following in the footsteps of the same declamatory tradition found in the pseudo-Sallustian invective.

Few of the stories about Cicero's consulship or the give and take of Ciceronian criticism actually *originate* in the declamatory schoolroom. Most of these sentiments find their origins in Cicero's own lifetime, some reported by Cicero himself, others by enemies like Clodius. But just as is the case with his death, the declaimers amplified particular voices – and repeated them again and again in the minds of young men over decades. When Cicero's real enemies had long since perished, the tradition of Ciceronian praise and blame was kept alive in the declamatory classroom. This flourishing and unbroken tradition can be seen in the continuity of themes and emphases from the earliest declaimers through Cassius Dio.

Exile

Cicero's consulship brought about his exile. His flight from Rome did not show him to good effect – it was a low point in his political career, and he cannot be said to have taken it standing up. As anyone even slightly familiar with Cicero's letters from this time can testify, he is by turns morose and reproachful, despondent and distrusting of even his staunchest friends.[49] All of this means that those favorable to him tended not to dwell on the exile period, and it is relatively rarely mentioned in later authors. Nevertheless, since it provides ammunition for the critical tradition, it is abundantly present in pseudo-Sallust and those of his ilk. Cicero himself tried to rewrite his exile narrative in the *post reditum* speeches, and it is this revised story that is picked up by his later defenders. The cornerstone of the revisionist version is Cicero's triumphant return to Italy, which shows how beloved he was of the Roman people and at the same time ascribes blame for the exile to Clodius alone – who, as the argument goes, was hardly of upstanding moral character.[50]

---

[48] If Courtney (1980) ad loc. p. 420 is right that *libera* means "republican" then this might be less likely, but Cicero also rendered Rome "free" by his detection of the conspiracy (see e.g. Cic. *Cat.* 3.15), and it would hardly be surprising to find him boasting of that fact in his *De consulatu suo*.

[49] See e.g. Shackleton Bailey (1971) 64–72, stringing together the correspondence into a more or less continuous narrative.

[50] Kaster (2006) 11–14 well interrogates the truth of this "standard version" of events. The later tradition could have picked up on different elements, but it did not. For Cicero's self-presentation in his *post reditum* speeches, see May (1988) 88–127.

The exile was easy for the likes of a pseudo-Sallust to criticize. He makes casual reference to Cicero's *pedes fugaces* (*in Tull.* 5); so too does Dio's Calenus say (Cass. Dio 46.21.1–2):

ταῦτα γάρ σου τὰ λαμπρὰ ἔργα ἐστί, ταῦτα τὰ μεγάλα στρατηγήματα· ἐφ' οἷς οὕτως οὐχ ὅπως ὑπὸ τῶν ἄλλων κατεγνώσθης, ἀλλὰ καὶ αὐτὸς σαυτοῦ κατεψηφίσω, ὥστε πρὶν καὶ κριθῆναι φυγεῖν. καίτοι τίς ἂν ἑτέρα μείζων ἀπόδειξις τῆς σῆς μιαιφονίας γένοιτο ἢ ὅτι καὶ ἐκινδύνευσας ἀπολέσθαι ὑπ' αὐτῶν ἐκείνων ὑπὲρ ὧν ἐσκήπτου ταῦτα πεποιηκέναι, καὶ ἐφοβήθης αὐτοὺς ἐκείνους οὓς ἔλεγες ἐκ τούτων εὐηργετηκέναι, καὶ οὐχ ὑπέμεινας οὔτ' ἀκοῦσαί τι αὐτῶν οὔτ' εἰπεῖν τι αὐτοῖς ὁ δεινός, ὁ περιττός, ὁ καὶ τοῖς ἄλλοις βοηθῶν, ἀλλὰ φυγῇ τὴν σωτηρίαν ὥσπερ ἐκ μάχης ἐπορίσω;

These are your brilliant achievements [i.e. the execution of Roman citizens], these your great exploits as a general. For these acts you were not only condemned by others, you condemned yourself, and so you fled into exile before even coming to trial. And yet what greater show of your blood-guilt could there be than the fact that you were very nearly killed by those very people for whom you alleged that you had done all this, and that you were terrified of the very people who you kept saying had benefited from these things? And that you didn't even stick around to hear what they had to say or to say anything to them, you the remarkably clever man, the one who defends everyone else, but provided for your own safety by flight as if from a battle?

If you do not like Cicero, you perforce take the view that his consulship was a disgrace. His exile, then, was condign punishment. Salt is rubbed into the wound when Cicero is said to have been driven off by the very Roman people whom he claims he saved; this calls into question whether his consulship even served their interests at all. The critic will also be quick to seize on Cicero's *pedes fugaces*, that is, the fact that he did not stick around to decide the issue in a court of law but rather fled in advance – this can be read as a plain admission of guilt, and cowardice to boot. The run-up to the exile and the moment of exile itself are the points of emphasis for this tradition.

The countervailing argument, by contrast, sought to mitigate these initial circumstances and focus on Cicero's return. Pseudo-Cicero replies to the charges as follows (*in Sall.* 10):

ego fugax, C. Sallusti? furori tribuni plebis cessi: utilius duxi quamuis fortunam unus experiri, quam uniuerso populo Romano ciuilis essem dissensionis causa. qui postea quam ille suum annum in re publica perbacchatus est omniaque, quae commouerat, pace et otio resederunt, hoc ordine reuocante atque ipsa re publica manu retrahente me reuerti. qui mihi dies, si cum omni reliqua uita conferatur, animo quidem meo superet, cum uniuersi uos populusque Romanus frequens aduentu meo gratulatus est: tanti me, fugacem, mercennarium patronum, hi aestimauerunt.

I a runaway, Gaius Sallustius? I yielded to the madness of a tribune of the people: I considered it better to endure any misfortune myself than to be the cause of civil strife for the whole Roman people. I who, after that man had caroused through his year in office and everything which he had stirred up had settled down again in peace and tranquillity, returned to the city when this order recalled me and the very Republic of Rome was dragging me back by the hand. That day, if it were compared with the entire rest of my life, in my opinion at any rate would top them all, when all of you and the Roman people assembled together and rejoiced at my return: so highly did they esteem me, "the runaway," "the mercenary advocate"!

Pseudo-Cicero blunts the reproach of *fugax* with, as we have seen, the real Cicero's defense: he "yielded to the madness of a tribune" (cf. p. 169 below). He then adopts the standard line of Cicero's *post reditum* speeches, claiming that he preferred to suffer the storms of unjust misfortune himself rather than be the cause of strife and discord to the Republic.[51] (Dio's consoling Philiscus will take the same line at 38.26.)[52] But the exile was of course Clodius' doing, and after his turbulent year in office the Roman people, "Cicero" says, recalled him straightaway, joyously waiting to greet him upon his return.

Other declaimers make use of these points as well. Cestius Pius calls Cicero's exile "more honorable than his consulship" (*exilium consulatu honestius*, Sen. *suas.* 7.2), presumably because Cicero supposedly entered into it voluntarily to save the Republic from being rent asunder by dissension. Quintus Haterius focuses on Cicero's recall, echoing Cicero's words when claiming that he "was carried back on the shoulders of Italy" (*Italiae umeris relatus est*, Sen. *contr.* 7.2.4 ~ Cic. *post red. in sen.* 39 *Italia cuncta paene suis umeris reportarit*) – admittedly this very phrase could be turned against Cicero, as in pseudo-Sallust's sarcastic quotation designed to deflate Cicero's *insolentia*.[53] Velleius Paterculus makes the same declamatory apologia: Cicero was exiled at the instigation of his enemy Publius Clodius, whose character is painted in the blackest terms (e.g. *malorum*

---

[51] See for example the whole argument of Cic. *dom.* 53–92, esp. 62–64, and *Sest.* 42–53.
[52] See p. 174 below. Dio himself seems to agree with these sentiments at 38.17.4.
[53] [Sall.] *in Tull.* 7 *sed quid ego plura de tua insolentia commemorem? quem Minerua omnis artis edocuit, Iuppiter Optimus Maximus in concilio deorum admisit, Italia exulem humeris suis reportauit.* Note that both declaimers drop Cicero's apologetic *paene.*

propositorum executor acerrimus, 2.45.1). The exile was a terribly unjust reward for a man who had saved the state (*ita uir optime meritus de re publica conseruatae patriae pretium calamitatem exilii tulit*, 2.45.2), but within a short time Cicero was restored to his rightful status at Rome. Since the exile and return of Numidicus, Velleius avows, no one had been exiled with greater disapproval or welcomed back with greater rejoicing (*neque post Numidici exilium aut reditum quisquam aut expulsus inuidiosius aut receptus est laetius*, 2.45.3).

Even Valerius Maximus, in his one mention of Cicero's exile, speaks only of his return: Cicero was "driven out of Rome by a conspiracy of his enemies" (*inimicorum conspiratione urbe pulsus*, 1.7.5), but one night he saw a vision of Gaius Marius in his sleep. Marius asks him why he looks so glum – here we catch a glimpse of Cicero's bitter depression during the period – and tells him to go to the Marian Temple of Jupiter, where better things will await him. And indeed, says Valerius, "in Marius' temple of Jupiter the Senate passed its decree for his return." The yoking of the two sons of Arpinum who had saved Rome in their different ways made for symbolism that was, as Kaster puts it, "not subtle."[54]

One of the most fascinating productions of the rhetorical classroom that reflects on Cicero's exile is the pseudo-Ciceronian *Oratio pridie quam in exilium iret*. As the title implies, the text is an imaginary speech that Cicero could have given the day before he went into exile. All of the typical declamatory themes and motifs are on full display here, and there is much flowery rhetoric and Ciceronian pastiche to be seen. The Ciceronian echoes have been cataloged at length by Leopoldo Gamberale, and I will not reprise his work here: suffice it to say that he believes that the reminiscences are so extensive that the text becomes at points almost a Ciceronian cento.[55] "Cento" may be going a bit far, but this is to quibble over semantics, because it is plain that there is a lot of Cicero in our [Cicero].

The content of the composition is as declamatory as its form. After a brief *captatio beneuolentiae*, "Cicero" begins by reminding the listeners of his signal services as consul. "If your illustrious forebears ever honored those generals who shattered the madness of the enemy by force of arms," he says, "then you should think it right to retain in the state a consul who not by force of arms but rather by the outstanding virtue of his soul, with

---

[54] Kaster (2006) 10; for Cicero's telling of this story, see e.g. *Sest.* 129.

[55] Gamberale (1998) *passim*, e.g. 55: "Ritengo ... che la *facies* linguistica e stilistica del testo sia fortemente condizionata dalla riproduzione, a volte quasi centonaria, di moduli e frasi del Cicerone autentico." Gamberale's careful work supersedes the sparse testimonial apparatus of De Marco (1991).

the full authority of the Senate, defended you from the plotting of hostile citizens" (*tum uos eum consulem, qui non militum praesenti fortitudine, sed sua eximia animi uirtute hostilem ciuium mentem senatus auctoritate uindicauit, existimate uobis retinendum esse in ciuitate, exil.* 3). By now this is all quite familiar. "Cicero" extols his civilian triumph over military success, he carefully avoids saying that he actually put anyone to death, and he avers that his suppression of the conspiracy was done with the backing of the Senate (*senatus auctoritate*).[56] He continues by boasting that if ever anyone is given credit for good deeds done privately for individual citizens, he himself can rightly summon the entire citizenry to his defense, since he saved them all (*si quae beneficia singulis ciuibus priuatimque dantur ... iure et merito possum ego uos ad defensionem meae salutis adhortari, quos conseruaui uniuersos, exil.* 4). The rhetorical figures are plain to see, as we observe pointed pairings between *singulis* and *uniuersos* and *salutis* and *conseruaui*. Moreover, of course, these are precisely the sorts of things that our declamatory Ciceros say time and again.

"Cicero" emphasizes that he has done nothing wrong and that his exile is entirely the result of his enemies' willful misconduct. He alleges that he is really on trial because of his virtue (*uirtutis reus, exil.* 6), that he stands accused not because he attacked the Republic, but because he, a new man, extinguished the ruinous madness of the nobles (*non ... quod rem publicam oppugnarit, sed quod homo nouus perniciosum nobilium restinxerit furorem*).[57] In a speech supposedly delivered to the Roman *equites* (*nunc uos, equites Romani, optestor, exil.* 29), he makes hay of the fact that his enemies hate him because he is a *nouus homo*, a deft invention for the rhetorical context. Later on in the speech he is more explicit: "they reproach us for our humble origins" (*humilitatem generis obiciunt nobis, exil.* 15), where we might read the first-person plural not simply as a "royal we" but as including the imaginary *corona* as well. In any event, this defensiveness about his *nouitas* is entirely of a piece with what we have already seen in Ciceronian declamation.

Furthermore, in that same quote "Cicero" calls the conspiracy a *furor* that he has extinguished. We have already seen that the *furor* motif has a pedigree stretching continuously back through the declaimers to Cicero

---

[56] Cf. p. 161 above; *senatus auctoritate* itself is strongly Ciceronian: cf. *dom.* 94, 114, and *Phil.* 4.15, where it is used of the execution of the conspirators.

[57] On *restinguere*, cf. Cic. *Sull.* 83 *adeo oblitus constantiae meae, adeo immemor rerum a me gestarum esse uideor ut, cum consul bellum gesserim cum coniuratis, nunc eorum ducem seruare cupiam et animum inducam, cuius nuper ferrum rettuderim flammamque restinxerim, eiusdem nunc causam uitamque defendere?* The word recurs in the *exil.* as well (14); see too p. 160 above.

himself, and our "Cicero" here takes full advantage of the theme. It is crucial for him to underscore the fact that he is not fleeing the city, as pseudo-Sallust had charged, but departing unwillingly (*cedo inuitus, exil.* 7)[58] and yielding to the tribune's madness.[59] This figures prominently in pseudo-Cicero's response to pseudo-Sallust (see p. 165 above), and is hammered home repeatedly by this declaimer: *decedam pro omnibus unus tribunicio furori* ("on behalf of all, I shall take it upon myself alone to yield before the tribune's <u>madness</u>," *exil.* 13), *me ... tribuni furor exagitatus depellit ad calamitatem* ("the tribune's <u>madness</u> was stirred up and drives me off into ruin," *exil.* 14), *cedam inermus armatis, innocens nocentibus, priuatus furibundo magistratui* ("I shall yield unarmed to the armed, as an innocent man to those doing harm, as a private citizen to a <u>mad</u> public official," *exil.* 27).[60] The responsibility for Cicero's exile is thus placed squarely at the feet of the rogue Clodius, whose sole motives are personal enmity seasoned perhaps with some jealousy. Cicero's enemy, by extension, is made an enemy of the people (*qui nunc se mihi inimicum ostendit, se prius esse uestrum professus est inimicum, exil.* 14).

And whence this enmity? From Cicero's constant and unchanging custom of serving the Republic and fighting for the innocent against wrong-doers (*exil.* 11). He predictably defends his consulship as being blameless but as having provoked the enmity of the worst kind of people, the dregs of the Catiline conspiracy. Although innocent, god-fearing, and good, he is being driven into exile by a hostile and wicked enemy (*innocens ab inimico, religiosus a scelerato, beniuolus huic ciuitati ab hoste*). As he continues, *egone inimicus huic ciuitati? quam ob rem? quia inimicos necaui. egone hostis? quid ita? quia hostes interfeci. heu condicionem huius temporis!* ("I a private enemy of this city? For what reason? Because I killed its private enemies. I a public enemy? Why? Because I killed its public enemies. Alas, the plight of the times!," *exil.* 30). This is the last section of the speech, and our "Cicero" is determined to go out with guns blazing, defending himself and criticizing Clodius to the last – and including a not very convincing declamatory reworking of the famous *o tempora! o mores!* tag.

---

[58] The modern reader cannot but think of Verg. *Aen.* 6.440 *inuitus, regina, tuo de litore cessi* and Catull. 66.39 *inuita, o regina, tuo de uertice cessi.* Was our declaimer playing with such allusions as well? On the Vergilian phrase, see the massive article of Pelliccia (2010–2011), not discussing this later echo.

[59] *Furor* is one of Cicero's favorite words of character assassination, occurring *ca.* 180× in his extant corpus. Used of all his enemies, from Catiline (e.g. *Cat.* 1.1 *quam diu etiam furor iste tuus nos eludet?*) to Antony (9× in the *Philippics*), it is an almost constant description of Clodius. See too Achard (1981) 239–247, Taldone (1993) 8–16.

[60] Cf. *exil.* 18, 19, 21, and 24 for more instances of Clodius' (and Catiline's) *furor.*

But pseudo-Cicero must also of course justify why he does not stay to fight. He is prepared for this criticism (leveled by pseudo-Sallust and Dio's Calenus, among others),[61] saying (*exil.* 20):

> quas ob res ego amentiae cupiditatique paucorum omnium salutis causa decedam, neque in eum locum <rem> deducam aut progredi patiar ut opera mea manus inter uos conseratis caedesque ciuium inter se fiant, multo-que potius ipse patria liberisque meis carebo quam propter unum me uos de fortunis uestris reique publicae dimicetis. sic enim ab initio fui animatus, ut non magis mea causa putarem me esse natum quam rei publicae procreatum.

> For these reasons I shall yield to the madness and greed of the few in order to save everyone, and I shall not bring the matter or allow it to progress to such a point that because of me you join in battle and citizen be slaughtered by citizen, and I shall prefer to do without my fatherland and my children rather than for you to fight on account of me alone for your future and that of the Republic. For I have always been inclined to believe that I was not born more for my sake than created for the Republic.

This is the standard line. Cicero's exile is a supreme act of self-sacrifice, undertaken not to save his own skin but rather to preserve the very Republic of Rome. The line about doing without his *patria* cleverly reworks one of Cicero's short letters to Atticus about his recall from exile, in which he says that he would rather die than do without his fatherland: *potius uita quam patria carebo* (*Att.* 3.26.1). In the event, of course, he did just the opposite, and our declaimer, while echoing Cicero's phrasing, has completely changed its meaning to redound to Cicero's credit. Similarly, his phrase about being *non magis mea causa . . . natum quam . . . rei publicae procreatum* plays on the same theme that we see in Aufidius Bassus, who describes Cicero as *uir natus ad rei publicae salutem* ("a man born for the salvation of the Republic," Sen. *suas.* 6.23).[62] In the same virtuous vein he adds that death in the service of the state is not to be pitied – shades of the "future" *Philippics* – nor is an exile brought about by

---

[61] Cf. App. *BC* 2.15, who alleges that Cicero lost his composure, despite being accustomed to defending others so well, and fled voluntarily because of Clodius' harassment (ἐς τοσοῦτο δειλίας περὶ μίαν οἰκείαν δίκην κατέπεσεν, ὃς τὸν ὅλον βίον ἐν ἀλλοτρίαις ἐξήταστο λαμπρῶς, οἷόν τι καὶ Δημοσθένη φασὶ τὸν Ἀθηναῖον οὐδ' ὑποστῆναι τὴν ἑαυτοῦ δίκην, ἀλλὰ πρὸ τοῦ ἀγῶνος φυγεῖν. Κλωδίου δὲ καὶ τὰς παρακλήσεις αὐτῷ σὺν ὕβρει διακόπτοντος ἐν τοῖς στενωποῖς, ἀπέγνω πάνθ' ὁ Κικέρων καὶ ἔφευγεν ἑκούσιον). Observe too that Appian manages to work in a comparison with Demosthenes, who likewise fled into exile before his trial. (On comparisons between Cicero and Demosthenes, see p. 93 above.)

[62] These phrases may ultimately go back to Cicero's own description of Marius (*Sest.* 50): *memineram, iudices, diuinum illum uirum atque ex isdem quibus nos radicibus natum ad salutem huius imperi, C. Marium.*

virtue a matter for shame (*neque ... mors miseranda est, quae ob rem publicam capitur, neque exilium turpe est, quod uirtute suscipitur, exil.* 22). His exile is honorable and here even placed on the same rhetorical level as dying for the Republic – which, as our declaimer knows full well, he will later do.

Thus the declaimers impose a revisionist reading on Cicero's exile that is very favorable to his motives and circumstances. The exile came about because of the enmity of Clodius and the despicable remains of the Catilinarian conspiracy, they say, and Cicero incurred their hatred for his eminently just actions as consul. In a noble act of self-sacrifice he chose to go into exile rather than to allow the state to be torn apart by violence and discord. Finally, when Clodius' term of office expired, all of Italy united in recalling him in triumph. These declaimers conveniently ignore Cicero's swings between despondent depression and manic tantrums while actually in exile: in the case of the *Oratio pridie quam in exilium iret*, this is by fictive chronological necessity; in the case of the pseudo-Ciceronian *Invective*, it is by rhetorically convenient selective memory. This revisionist tradition, begun by Cicero himself *post reditum*, hardens into a consistent set of themes and emphases in the declamatory schools.

Those who wished to present a less charitable image of Cicero, however, were not so kind as to ignore the less reputable aspects of his exile. We have seen pseudo-Sallust and Dio's Calenus criticizing Cicero's willing flight, and his exilic tantrums managed not just to be heard in Rome at the time but indeed to reecho through the centuries. Already Livy, more objective than most, would number the exile among the "great wounds" that Cicero suffered in his career (Sen. *suas.* 6.22; see p. 131 above), adding that he did not face any of these disasters – including the exile – "like a man" (*ut uiro dignum*). Pollio likewise bemoans his lack of stoutness in adversity (Sen. *suas.* 6.24; see p. 135 above), a complaint that probably looks particularly, albeit not exclusively, to the exile. In both Livy's and Pollio's remarks there lurks too a criticism of Cicero's lifelong inconstancy and tendency toward emotional extremes.

The most interesting rhetorical reflection on Cicero's exile is found in Cassius Dio. Dio's Philiscus (an otherwise unknown character)[63] happens upon the morose and reproachful Cicero in exile and offers a fairly

---

[63] See Millar (1964) 49–50 for the interesting hypothesis that this Philiscus is a complimentary allusion to a rhetor contemporary with Dio; cf. however Bowersock (1965) 472. Further Fechner (1986) 49–50 with references. Rees (2011) 168–169 is one of the very few to think that Philiscus could be a genuine coeval of Cicero.

conventional *consolatio* to solace his suffering (38.18–29).[64] This speech is pure *inuentio*, and in it we see clearly the influence of declamatory education.[65] Amid the philosophical platitudes we find remarks specifically tailored to Cicero's situation and, more importantly, the simple acknowledgement that his behavior in exile was a disgrace for a right-thinking Roman: "Are you not ashamed, Cicero," he says, "at your weeping and carrying on like a woman? I at any rate never would have expected that you would grow so soft, inasmuch as you have partaken of so great and varied an education and have acted as defense advocate for many a person" ("οὐκ αἰσχύνῃ," ἔφη, "ὦ Κικέρων, θρηνῶν καὶ γυναικείως διακείμενος; ὡς ἔγωγε οὔποτ᾽ ἄν σε προσεδόκησα οὕτω μαλακισθήσεσθαι, πολλῆς μὲν παιδείας καὶ παντοδαπῆς μετεσχηκότα, πολλοῖς δὲ καὶ συνηγορηκότα," 38.18.1). Here we find the reproach stated bluntly and openly.[66]

Philiscus and Cicero proceed to engage in a sort of dialogue. In theory this is almost a dialectic engagement between two *suasoriae*, (1) "Philiscus tries to persuade Cicero that exile is not all that bad" and (2) "Cicero argues that nothing could be worse than his exile." In practice Cicero speaks less and less as the dialogue unfolds, leaving Philiscus a free hand to make lengthy set-piece speeches. After Philiscus reproaches Cicero for his unseemly depression, Cicero replies that his mind has been overcome by a dark affliction from which he sees no escape. Philiscus then launches into his *consolatio* proper.

Much of this, to be sure, is merely conventional philosophy.[67] "Cicero," Philiscus says, "you have good health and life's necessities in sufficient

---

[64] On this passage, see esp. Gowing (1998) and, with comprehensive bibliography, Rees (2011) 164–180; also Millar (1961) 15–17, Millar (1964) 49–51, Stekelenburg (1971) 21–28, Fechner (1986) 48–58, Gowing (1992) 144–145, Burden-Strevens (2015) 129–135. The notes in the Budé edition of Lachenaud and Coudry (2011) are especially useful. Kemezis (2014) 289–290, contending that Philiscus' arguments are a sort of coded reference to Dio's own "exile" at the end of his career, does not seem convincing, although I would not deny some connection between Philiscus' advice and Dio's own worldview (Gowing [1998] 381–383).

[65] See e.g. Gowing (1998) 378: "a product of the Greco-Roman declamatory tradition"; on this speech more generally, Lachenaud and Coudry (2011) lvii–lxi. Stekelenburg (1971) 14–16 notes the importance of declamation for all of Dio's speeches.

[66] So Plutarch as well: despite receiving countless friendly visitors, he says, Cicero was generally depressed and sorely aggrieved during his exile, forever staring forlornly toward Italy like some disconsolate lover, becoming small and petty as a result of his misfortune. None of this was to be expected in a man of his education (*Cic.* 32.4 πολλῶν δὲ φοιτώντων ἀνδρῶν ὑπ᾽ εὐνοίας καὶ τῶν Ἑλληνίδων πόλεων διαμιλλωμένων ἀεὶ ταῖς πρεσβείαις πρὸς αὐτόν, ὅμως ἀθυμῶν καὶ περίλυπος διῆγε τὰ πολλά, πρὸς τὴν Ἰταλίαν ὥσπερ οἱ δυσέρωτες ἀφορῶν, καὶ τῷ φρονήματι μικρὸς ἄγαν καὶ ταπεινὸς ὑπὸ τῆς συμφορᾶς γεγονὼς καὶ συνεσταλμένος, ὡς οὐκ ἄν τις ἄνδρα παιδείᾳ συμβεβιωκότα τοσαύτῃ προσεδόκησε). Cf. App. *BC* 2.15, quoted in n. 61 above.

[67] In addition to a large Stoic and Cynic element, there are significant Platonic reminiscences: see Lachenaud and Coudry (2011) lviii–lix and Jones (2016) 300.

quantities (τὰ ἐπιτήδεια αὐτάρκη) – your situation really isn't bad at all" (38.19.2). Cicero retorts, as might be expected, that the cares tugging at his soul far outweigh all these natural boons, and so he cannot help but be depressed. Philiscus does not hesitate to add other incidental criticisms *en passant*; for example, he claims that Cicero's material goods were not his by inheritance (πατρῶια), but were acquired by his tongue and his eloquence – the very things which caused him to lose them (ἀλλὰ ὑπό τε τῆς γλώττης καὶ ὑπὸ τῶν λόγων σου πεπόρισται, δι᾽ οὓς καὶ ἀπόλωλεν, 38.20.3). Here we get an allusion to Cicero the arriviste along with an identification of the man with his tongue, but the equation is hardly an unmixed blessing: just as we have seen in other declaimers, Cicero's tongue raised him high, but it also brought him low. Furthermore, such a claim for the origin of Cicero's wealth contradicts the story that Cicero or a pseudo-Cicero might like to tell.[68]

Nevertheless, the predominant tone of Philiscus' remarks is not derisive – nattering negativism would hardly have been effective in a *consolatio*. There are, as we have seen, the occasional ancient equivalents to a slap in the face coupled with a firm "pull yourself together, man," but Philiscus works best by adding some honey to the cup. He calls Cicero a "man of the greatest sagacity" (ὁρῶ τοίνυν ἔγωγε πρῶτον μὲν φρονιμώτατόν σε ἀνθρώπων ὄντα, 38.22.1) and "most just" (δικαιότατον, 38.22.2) and says that he had considered him "most brave" (ἐγὼ μέν σε καὶ ἀνδρειότατον ᾤμην εἶναι, 38.22.4) – but he has now fallen short of those lofty ideals. These are compliments laced with criticisms: either Cicero is not in fact any of those things, or his conduct in exile is utterly inconsonant with his character. Philiscus cleverly turns these negative judgments to good use in exhorting Cicero to courage and constancy, in sum to be consistent with his supposed earlier good character. There is thus here too an implied censure of Cicero's inconstancy, but this is all mentioned – ostensibly – only in order to persuade Cicero to steer a straight course.

In consoling Cicero, Philiscus also uses some of the standard declamatory defenses. The reason for Cicero's exile, for example, is simply that he defended the state with ceaseless energy against enemies who plotted against it (πανταχοῦ γοῦν ὑπέρ τε τῆς πατρίδος καὶ τῶν φίλων ἀνταγωνιζόμενος τοῖς ἐπιβουλεύουσιν αὐτοῖς ἐξήτασαι· καὶ αὐτά γε

---

[68] [Cic.] *in Sall.* 9 (p. 160 above), claiming that Cicero's wealth came mostly from inheritances, in response to the scathing comments of *in Tull.* 3–4, e.g. *opulentiam istam ex sanguine et miseriis ciuium parasti.* See too the criticisms of Calenus in Cass. Dio 46.4.1, 46.6.2–46.7.1 (p. 183 below).

ταῦτα ἃ νῦν πέπονθας, οὐ δι᾽ ἄλλο τι συμβέβηκέ σοι ἢ ὅτι πάνθ᾽ ὑπὲρ τῶν νόμων καὶ τῆς πολιτείας καὶ λέγων καὶ πράττων διετέλεις, 38.22.2–3). His innocence is repeatedly emphasized. After some general philosophizing and abstract reflections on the nature of the body and soul (38.23.2–38.24), Philiscus dilates on the particulars of the case at hand. Cicero has done no wrong, Philiscus avers, and it is better for a man to endure wrongful punishment than to do wrong himself. He defends Cicero's conduct as consul and claims that he was driven out by his enemies (38.25.1–5). Here we find both balanced rhetorical antithesis paired with Gorgianic jingles (οὐκ ἰδιωτεύων ἀλλ᾽ ὑπατεύων, "not as a private citizen but as consul") and some phrases that seem designed specifically to forestall the criticisms we see in a pseudo-Sallust. So Cicero acted not as a private citizen of his own initiative, but in accordance with the Senate's decrees (τοῖς τῆς βουλῆς δόγμασι πειθόμενος), i.e., with the *auctoritas senatus* that we have so often seen. Moreover, those decrees were passed οὐ κατὰ στάσιν ("not along the factional lines"), the very opposite of pseudo-Sallust's claim that Cicero's consulship caused the disintegration of the state into factionalism and civil war (*in Tull.* 3).

Philiscus is furthermore keen to defend Cicero from the reproach that he fled into exile before his case was heard (Cass. Dio 38.26.1–2):

κ
And yet I at any rate heard that you did not leave for exile unwillingly nor after being convicted of a crime, but that you volunteered to go and hated your life among them, since you couldn't make them better people nor stomach staying behind to perish along with them, and you fled not from your fatherland but from those plotting against it. Thus those men would be dishonored and banished, having cast out all good things from their souls, while you remain honored and blessed and free from disgraceful servitude and in possession of everything that you need.

The criticism that Cicero fled from Rome like a coward is found in pseudo-Sallust and the speech of Calenus, but Philiscus cleverly turns Cicero's voluntary departure into a virtue. The "as I at any rate hear" (ἔγωγε ἀκούω) may draw further, ironic attention to the reproach, implicitly acknowledging that there is another side to the story.[69] Cicero simply could not stand living among such people at Rome. What he fled, Philiscus claims, was not his fatherland but his enemies; this is the standard line of defense. Furthermore, in the notion that Cicero avoided disgraceful servitude, we may see an echo of the declamatory Cicero's last days, where he likewise refuses to serve an unjust master (cf. n. 80).

Philiscus continues with more commonplaces, eventually adducing historical exempla of successful Greek and Roman exiles past – which of course leads him ineluctably to talk about the possibility of restoration. This is a particularly pregnant section, since writer and reader both know that Cicero will eventually be restored. Philiscus parrots the usual notion that everyone wants Cicero to come back (38.27.4), but he advises him instead to be content with a quiet life in the country rather than to seek renewed political power. If he wants to become genuinely immortal (ὄντως ἀθάνατος), Philiscus says, he should retire and devote himself to writing. Here we see shades of the textualized Cicero from the declamatory classroom: he is a man remembered above all for his writings, a man who gained immortality through his immortal works.[70] On the other hand, Philiscus prophesies a baleful future if Cicero should return to the active life (Cass. Dio 38.29):

ἂν δὲ δὴ τήν τε κάθοδον σπουδάσῃς καὶ τὴν ἐν τῇ πολιτείᾳ λαμπρότητα ζηλώσῃς, δυσχερὲς μὲν οὐδὲν εἰπεῖν βούλομαι, φοβοῦμαι δέ, ἔς τε τὰ πράγματα ἀποβλέπων καὶ τὴν σὴν παρρησίαν ἐννοῶν, τήν τε δύναμιν καὶ τὸ πλῆθος τῶν ἀντιστασιωτῶν σου θεωρῶν, μήποτέ τι καὶ αὖθις σφαλῇς. καὶ εἰ μὲν ἐν φυγῇ γένοιο, μεταγνώσῃ μόνον, εἰ δέ τι ἕτερον ἀνήκεστον πάθοις, οὐδὲ μετανοῆσαι δυνήσῃ. καίτοι πῶς μὲν οὐ δεινόν, πῶς δ’ οὐκ αἰσχρὸν ἀποτμηθῆναί τέ τινος τὴν κεφαλὴν καὶ ἐς τὴν ἀγορὰν τεθῆναι, κἂν οὕτω τύχῃ, καὶ ἄνδρα τινὰ αὐτῇ καὶ γυναῖκα ἐνυβρίσαι; καί με μὴ ὡς φαῦλά σοι οἰωνιζόμενον μισήσῃς, ἀλλ’ ὡς διοσημίαν τινὰ προδεικνύντα φύλαξαι. μηδέ σε ἐξαπατάτω τοῦθ’, ὅτι καὶ φίλους τινὰς τῶν δυνατῶν ἔχεις· οὐδὲν γάρ σε ὠφελήσουσιν οἱ δοκοῦντες φιλεῖν πρὸς τοὺς ἐχθρῶς διακειμένους, ὥσπερ που καὶ πεπείρασαι. οἱ γὰρ δυναστείας ἐρῶντες παρ’ οὐδὲν πάντα τἆλλα, πρὸς τὸ τυχεῖν ὧν βούλονται, τίθενται, ἀλλὰ καὶ τοὺς φιλτάτους καὶ τοὺς συγγενεστάτους πολλάκις ἀντὶ τῶν ἐχθίστων ἀντικαταλλάσσονται.

But if you are eager to return and desirous of glory in politics, well, I don't mean to sound negative, but when I look at things and consider your outspokenness and see the power and number of those who oppose you,

---

[69] Similarly Rees (2011) 173.
[70] Perhaps there is also a nod to Dio's own activities at his Campanian villa; see Millar (1964) 51.

I'm afraid that you'll take a tumble again. And if you should end up in exile again, you'll just regret your course of action, but if you should suffer something irremediable, you won't even be able to change your mind. And yet how is it not terrible and shameful for someone's head to be cut off and set up in the forum so that any man or woman passing by can cast scorn upon it? And don't hate me on the grounds that I'm uttering some baleful prophecy for you, but take what I say to heart as if I've received a sign from Zeus himself. So you have some friends in high places – don't be deceived by that. These people who seem to be your friends won't help you one bit against those who bear you ill will, just as you've doubtless already experienced. Those who love power set everything else at naught by comparison with the chance to obtain what they want, and they will often give up in exchange both their best friends and their family in return for their bitterest enemies.

This dark foreboding, of course, will prove "eerily" correct in all its particulars – it is a *uaticinium ex euentu*. This species of dramatic irony is a common declamatory trope (see e.g. pp. 156 above, 181 below); it both increases the pathos of a situation and grabs the audience's attention.[71] Cicero will return and he will embark, at least at the last, on a shining political career. In the end, however, he will come a cropper; his head will be chopped off and displayed in the forum; his powerful friends will desert him (a particularly dark allusion to Octavian); and, as the declamatory story goes, Antony and Lepidus will trade the lives of their close relatives to convince Octavian to add Cicero to the proscription lists. What will be the cause of Cicero's demise? His outspokenness (παρρησία), of course; this is the typical reason adduced by the declaimers in discussions of Cicero's downfall. Philiscus' declamatory speech, for all its philosophical overtones, returns eventually to the best-known aspect of Cicero in the rhetorical tradition, his death.

Cicero's exile was a thorn in the side of his defenders, just as it was for him in his own lifetime. Nevertheless, we can see in the declamatory tradition a clear prescription for dealing with its unpleasant concomitants: defend Cicero's actions as consul; ascribe the blame for his exile to his enemies, especially Clodius, who of course acted out of only the basest of motives; present Cicero's voluntary departure as the ultimate act of

---

[71] Barchiesi (1993) terms this kind of allusion to a future known to the audience but unknown to the speaker the "future reflexive." As an example he offers the Polyphemus of Theocritus' *Idyll* 11, who in addressing his love, the nymph Galatea, says (*Id.* 11.60–62): "But now, my girl, even now I will at least learn to swim: may somebody (τις) arrive here in a ship, a stranger, so that I may know how sweet it is to live in your deep-sea dwelling!" That "τις" – or as it turns out, "οὔτις" – is of course Odysseus, and the Cyclops will not be so happy at his arrival.

self-sacrifice, done solely to save the city from being torn apart by Clodius' ravening dogs; and ignore his disreputable depression during the exile itself, all the while accentuating the glory of the return to Rome. All of these motifs, as we have seen, repeat Cicero's own propaganda as developed in his *post reditum* speeches. It is, however, yet again in the declamatory classroom that this propaganda hardens into reality, as countless generations of young Romans write and rewrite these themes which have long since been divorced from their original social and political context.

The *"Philippics"* of Appian and Dio

Appian and Dio also make rhetorical comment on Cicero's role in his tumultuous twilight of 44–43 BC, in the form of speeches given to Cicero himself and his adversaries. These speeches too are fashioned in the image of a continuous declamatory tradition. Admittedly we must tread carefully here, since there is great historiographic license in manufacturing appropriate speeches, and we lack a Thucydidean preface explaining what "appropriate" meant for a Dio.[72] For my purposes, however, issues like the historicity of the speeches are of much less moment: rhetorical reconstructions fashioned from a historian's imagination shed more light on Cicero's ancient reception than a simple Greek translation of a Ciceronian oration would. Both Dio and Appian present versions of Cicero's *Philippics* and a counterbalancing speech, each of which gives insight into the rhetorical influence shaping the early understanding of Cicero.

Appian's invented *Philippic* and the speech to which it is a response are rather less interesting (*BC* 3.52–53).[73] In his *"Philippic"* reminiscences of Cicero are conspicuous by their absence, and his version is more akin to a brief epitome than a rhetorical reworking.[74] Piso's speech in reply, however, is developed at much greater length. Each of the charges that Cicero had leveled – Antony misappropriated public funds, decimated his

---

[72] Thuc. 1.22; cf. Burden-Strevens (2015) 14. The bibliography on speeches in ancient historiography is immense; for an introduction see Marincola (2007) and the essays in Pausch (2010). On speeches in Appian and Dio, Gowing (1992) 225–246 is fundamental; for Dio, see further Millar (1964) 78–83, Millar (1961), Stekelenburg (1971), and now Burden-Strevens (2015). Appian's speeches have not attracted the same interest, but Gabba (1955) makes various remarks (e.g. 145) and Hahn (1968) provides a brief overview.

[73] For brief remarks on this speech, see the Budé introduction (Goukowsky and Torrens [2010]) lxxviii–lxxix, and also Gabba (1955) 167–168, Gabba (1957) 327–339, Gowing (1992) 235–236.

[74] So the Loeb editor comments that the actual *Philippics* "bear only a slight resemblance to [Appian's] speech" (White [1912] IV.57 n. 1); Gowing (1992) 235 notes "the degree to which Cicero's speech in Appian does *not* resemble its ostensible model," so too Hahn (1968) 199.

army without cause, and committed various and sundry other sins – Piso refutes painstakingly and at some length. He keeps anti-Cicero slander to a minimum (e.g., Cicero is again accused of "fickleness," μεταβολή [*BC* 3.59]), and says almost nothing against Octavian, preferring to present a sober and rational defense of Antony and his policies. Declamatory influence here seems muted.

Cassius Dio, by contrast, has imbibed deeply from the rhetorical cup. He too has a version of a *Philippic* and its response, presenting lengthy speeches from Cicero (45.18–47) and Calenus (46.1–29) which spell out the opposing viewpoints on Antony in elaborate and slanderous detail.[75] As Fergus Millar has pointed out, these two competing speeches are constructed "using historical material almost certainly through the medium of early Imperial rhetorical elaborations"[76] – that is to say, elaborations stemming from the declamatory schools. Dio's Cicero draws on the *Philippics*, but his speech is a patchwork that more breathes their spirit than reproduces their words, as was perhaps inevitable in a Greek version.[77] What we have is precisely the sort of rhetorical reworking that we have seen in various pseudo-Ciceronian texts, where an assortment of Ciceronian bits and bobs are joined together to create a new speech.[78] Dio's Cicero sounds all the typical anti-Antony notes, and faithfully reproduces the rhetorically enhanced tradition of Augustan ideology. The speech is long, and a few brief examples will suffice to prove the point.

One persistent point of emphasis is Antony's wastrel lifestyle. He is the epitome of the drunk and debauched lout, a man devoid of any moral feeling whatsoever. At 45.26, for example, Cicero makes use of the rhetorical figure of *praeteritio* and says that he will not talk about Antony's

---

[75] In Appian Cicero is the respondent; in Dio he speaks first. On Dio's pair of speeches, see Gabba (1957) 319–327, Millar (1961) 18–22, Stekelenburg (1971) 78–88, 91, Fechner (1986) 63–69, Gowing (1992) 237–239, Rees (2011) 149–162, and now Burden-Strevens (2015) 58–70.

[76] Millar (1961) 22; cf. Gowing (1992) 235 "a showcase for the historian's rhetorical talents" and, disapprovingly, Lintott (1997) 2517 "the baleful influence of later declamatory invective."

[77] *Quellenforschung* dates to Fischer (1870); see further Stekelenburg (1971) 80, Gowing (1992) 238 n. 34, and Burden-Strevens (2015) 59–64. Burden-Strevens argues that Dio's source was the *Philippics* themselves, while others, like Zielinski (1929) 280–288 and Gabba (1957), have seen an intermediary, perhaps Asinius Pollio or the Greek Cestius Pius or even one of his students. Greek puns (46.18.1) and the occasional odd misunderstanding (46.22.4) would seem to suggest an influence beyond just Cicero's Latin text. It is clear that Dio does know the *Philippics*, but I think the parallels with the rhetorical tradition (esp. the pseudo-Sallustian invective) show that he was influenced by something else – not necessarily a common written source, but rather the common declamatory tradition.

[78] This is also in line with the standard educational prescription to translate from Greek to Latin (and vice versa) and to try to outdo your model; see e.g. Plin. *epist.* 7.9.2–4, Quint. *inst.* 10.5.2–3, Cic. *de orat.* 1.155. This is thus another way of interpreting what Gowing (1992) 238 calls "a faithful if motley imitation of the originals."

licentiousness and avarice (τὸν γὰρ δὴ ἴδιον αὐτοῦ βίον τάς τε ἰδίας ἀσελγείας καὶ πλεονεξίας ἑκὼν παραλείψω, 45.26.1; cf. Cic. *Phil.* 2.47). He then of course proceeds to dilate on that very theme (45.26.1–4; cf. the parallel move of Calenus at 46.8.2):

αἰδοῦμαι νὴ τὸν Ἡρακλέα ἀκριβῶς καθ᾽ ἕκαστον, ἄλλως τε <καὶ> πρὸς οὐδὲν ἧττον εἰδότας ὑμᾶς, λέγειν ὅπως μὲν τὴν ὥραν τὴν ἐν παισὶν ὑμῖν διέθετο, ὅπως δὲ τὴν ἀκμὴν τὴν ἐφ᾽ ἥβης ἀπεκήρυξε, τὰς ἑταιρήσεις αὐτοῦ τὰς λαθραίας, τὰς πορνείας τὰς ἐμφανεῖς, ὅσα ἔπαθεν ἕως ἐνεδέχετο, ὅσα ἔδρασεν ἀφ᾽ οὗπερ ἠδυνήθη, τοὺς κώμους, τὰς μέθας, τἄλλα πάντα τὰ τούτοις ἑπόμενα. ἀδύνατον γάρ ἐστιν ἄνθρωπον ἔν τε ἀσελγείᾳ καὶ ἐν ἀναισχυντίᾳ τοσαύτῃ τραφέντα μὴ οὐ πάντα τὸν ἑαυτοῦ βίον μιᾶναι· ὅθενπερ καὶ ἐπὶ τὰ κοινὰ ἀπὸ τῶν ἰδίων καὶ τὴν κιναιδίαν καὶ τὴν πλεονεξίαν προήγαγε. ταῦτα μὲν οὖν ἐάσω.

I'm ashamed, by Heracles, to enumerate in detail – especially to you who already know all this just as well as I do – just how he spent his youth among you when you were boys, how he auctioned off the flower of his youth, his unchaste acts done in secret, his open whoring, what he let be done to him as long as he could, what he did himself from the earliest age he was able, the drunken debaucheries and all the other things that go along with them. It's impossible for a person raised in such shameless licentiousness not to pollute his entire life. Thus he led out his wanton lusts and greed from his private life to the public sphere. But I'll let all this go.

The rhetorical character assassination continues in this vein for pages. Two sections later, for example, Cicero is hammering away again at Antony's drunkenness, culminating in a comparison that the declaimers make as well: Antony has squandered all his ill-gotten gains, gorging himself on wine and women, swallowing down money and food alike as a "second Charybdis" (καὶ πάνθ᾽ ὅσαπερ ἐκτήσατο, παμπληθῆ τε γενόμενα καὶ ἐκ παντὸς τρόπου ἀργυρολογηθέντα, κατακεκύβευκε καὶ καταπεπόρνευκε καὶ καταβέβρωκε καὶ καταπέπωκεν ὥσπερ ἡ Χάρυβδις, 45.28.4). As we have seen, this Ciceronian tag (*Phil.* 2.67) is a declamatory favorite, and Calenus too will pick up on it in his answering speech.[79]

The matter and manner of Dio's Cicero speech are declamatory. It is at this point superfluous to recount the standard tropes in detail, but I will mention one more passage in which Dio manages to tick a slew of declamatory boxes in just a few sentences. Cicero here proclaims that he shall resolutely choose death over dishonor and slavery in thrall to the tyrant Antony (45.46.2–5):

---

[79] See Triarius at Sen. *suas.* 6.5 (p. 114 above); the motif also recurs in e.g. Sen. *suas.* 6.3 (Porcius Latro) *uidebis illas fauces per quas bona Cn. Pompei transierunt.* For Calenus, see p. 185 below.

ὡς ἔγωγε οὕτω γνώμης, ὦ πατέρες, ἔχω ὥστ', ἂν μὲν πεισθῆτέ μοι, καὶ
πάνυ ἂν ἡδέως καὶ τῆς ἐλευθερίας καὶ τῆς σωτηρίας μεθ' ὑμῶν ἀπολαῦσαι,
ἂν δ' ἄλλο τι ψηφίσησθε, τεθνάναι μᾶλλον ἢ ζῆν ἑλέσθαι. οὔτε γὰρ ἄλλως
τὸν θάνατόν ποτε τὸν ἐκ τῆς παρρησίας ἐφοβήθην (καὶ διὰ τοῦτο καὶ
κατώρθωσα πλεῖστον· τεκμήριον δὲ ὅτι καὶ θῦσαι καὶ ἑορτάσαι ἐφ' οἷς
ὑπατεύων ἐποίησα ἐψηφίσασθε, ὅπερ οὐδενὶ πώποτε ἄλλῳ μὴ οὐκ ἐν
πολέμῳ γέ τι καταπράξαντι ἐγένετο), νῦν δὲ καὶ ἥκιστα. καὶ γὰρ ὁ μὲν
θάνατος οὐκ ἂν ἄωρος ἄλλως τε καὶ πρὸ τοσούτων ἐτῶν ὑπατευκότι μοι
γένοιτο (καίτοι μνημονεύετε ὅτι τοῦτο καὶ ἐν αὐτῇ τῇ ὑπατείᾳ ὑμῖν εἶπον,
ἵνα μοι πρὸς πάντα ὡς καταφρονοῦντι αὐτοῦ προσέχητε)· τὸ δὲ δὴ
φοβηθῆναί τινα καθ' ὑμῶν καὶ τὸ δουλεῦσαί τινι μεθ' ὑμῶν καὶ πάνυ ἂν
μοι ἀωρότατον συμβαίη. ὅθενπερ τοῦτο μὲν καὶ συμφορὰν καὶ ὄλεθρον, οὐ
τοῦ σώματος μόνον ἀλλὰ καὶ τῆς ψυχῆς τῆς τε δόξης, ὑφ' ἧς που καὶ μόνης
ἀίδιοι τρόπον τινὰ γιγνόμεθα, εἶναι νομίζω· τὸ δὲ δὴ λέγοντά τε καὶ
πράττοντα ὑπὲρ ὑμῶν ἀποθανεῖν ἰσοστάσιον ἀθανασίᾳ ἄγω.

For my part, senators, I feel that if you listen to me, I would quite gladly
enjoy freedom and safety with you, but if you decree otherwise, I would
choose to die rather than live. For I have never feared death as a consequence
of my forthright speech – and it is on account of this that I have accomplished so much; the proof is that you decreed a sacrifice and festival
celebration for the things I accomplished as consul, which has never happened to anyone except those who have accomplished something in war –
and now least of all. For death could not be unseasonable for me, especially
since I served as consul so many years ago; and yet remember that I said this
during my very consulship as well, so that you might pay attention to me in
every matter, knowing that I despise death. But fearing what someone might
do to you and serving someone along with you would be the most unseasonable thing of all for me. Therefore I judge this to be the downfall and
destruction not just of the body but of the soul and the reputation, which is,
I think, the only thing that can make us immortal in any way. But dying
while speaking and acting on your behalf I consider to be the same thing as
immortality.

This is Greek Ciceronian pastiche filtered through the declamatory tradition. The Ciceronian *Urbild* is the famous close of the second *Philippic*
(2.119). As Dio's Cicero starts into his *peroratio*, he addresses the πατέρες,
just as the real Cicero had in fact invoked the *patres conscripti*. Dio's Cicero
declares that he is not afraid of death, as we have heard the declamatory
Cicero avow, but he goes beyond what the real Cicero said in the *Philippics* in
several ways. First, the real Cicero only states that death cannot ever be
immatura for a consular. This Cicero by contrast – after first saying the same
thing, that death cannot be ἄωρος for a man of his accomplishments – goes
on to say that he does not fear death on account of his παρρησία. This

"outspokenness" is of course precisely what the declaimers claim precipitated his death, in the form of the very *Philippics* that he is even now purporting to speak in Dio. Furthermore, while the real Cicero vaunted that he would face death unafraid, Dio's Cicero is seen positively to *choose* death. This aligns precisely with the declamatory tradition in which he is seen as a martyr who freely embraces death rather than submit to servitude.[80] This is the resolute Cicero of, for example, the *Epistula ad Octauianum*, determined to die rather than see the domination of tyranny.[81] Moreover, where the real Cicero has a brief reference to his constancy of opinion over the past two decades, Dio's Cicero seizes this opening to hang a keyword-packed digression on Cicero's consulship: "it was great, it was glorious, and I can't stop talking about it," his Cicero says. We even get a Greek paraphrase of Cicero's *togatus triumphus* (καὶ θῦσαι καὶ ἑορτάσαι ἐφ᾽ οἷς ὑπατεύων ἐποίησα ἐψηφίσασθε, ὅπερ οὐδενὶ πώποτε ἄλλῳ μὴ οὐκ ἐν πολέμῳ γέ τι καταπράξαντι ἐγένετο), declamatory embroidery stitched in from elsewhere in the *Philippics* (2.13) and the rhetorical tradition.

Finally, Dio's Cicero rounds out this paragraph by saying that while death would not be ἄωρος ("untimely," Cicero's *mors immatura*), life as Antony's slave would be ἀωρότατον. Such slavery would mean destruction of the reputation (δόξα) by which a man becomes immortal (ἀίδιος): this is of course precisely the line of reasoning by which the declaimers urge Cicero not to compromise with Antony.[82] For all his braggadocio, the real Cicero was not so bold as to forecast his own immortality in the *Philippics*; this was left to later generations, who, following in the declaimers' wake, did so with enthusiasm. Moreover, Dio's Cicero secures his immortality precisely as the declaimers so often said, by his eloquence (λέγοντα) and by his courageous action against Antony (πράττοντα), a concrete case of the ancient obsession with word and deed. This is all declamatory *uaticinium ex euentu* (cf. p. 176 above).

The Cicero found in Dio's pages is silent for the vast majority of his political career until near its very end – it is striking that Dio gives Cicero a speech, and a polished and lengthy one at that, precisely when he comes to the Ciceronian events treated so often by the declaimers.[83] The brief

---

[80] Cf. Sen. *suas.* 6 and 7 *passim*, e.g. 6.1 *sciant posteri potuisse Antonio seruire rem publicam, non potuisse Ciceronem*. The theme is prefigured by Cicero himself: see *Phil.* 3.29, 7.14, 10.19–20.

[81] Cf. pseudo-Brutus' resolve and exhortations to Cicero at e.g. [Brut.] *Cic. ad Brut.* 1.16.1.

[82] See again Sen. *suas.* 6 and 7 *passim*, where Cicero's reputation is particularly embodied in his writings.

[83] Cicero's other major speech in Dio likewise dates to after Caesar's death, when he advocates amnesty for the assassins (Cass. Dio 44.23–33). Sallust's Cicero likewise delivers no *Catilinarians*.

analysis conducted here can be repeated for the other sections of the speech with similar results. The conclusion is simple: while the speech is of course influenced by Cicero's actual *Philippics*, Dio's rhetorical rewrite, combining Ciceronian elements from diverse speeches and adding bits of declamatory color, is determined in form and content by the declamatory tradition surrounding Cicero's life and death.

Cicero's speech is in turn met with a reply, spoken by a known opponent, Calenus (cf. Cic. *Phil.* 8.11–19). Calenus' rejoinder both defends Antony and attacks Cicero. It fits the same declamatory mold: in the assault on Cicero, almost all of the stock topics of criticism of Cicero in the rhetorical classroom make an appearance. Again and again we find parallels for Calenus' barbs in the declamatory tradition, especially in the pseudo-Sallustian invective. Taken together, they present the alternative vision of Cicero that Zielinski called *Cicerokarikatur*.[84] This too is a remarkably clear and coherent picture: the way you criticized Cicero in a first-century Latin declamation again became embedded in the historical tradition, and so we meet the same criticisms in a Greek historian of the third century. Since this speech is also quite lengthy, I will again discuss only selected points of interest.

Calenus launches into his assault with the inevitable references to Cicero's consulship (cf. [Sall.] *in Tull.* 5–6): he is the one who made Catiline hostile to the Roman people and who executed Lentulus without trial (ἄκριτος, 46.2.3).[85] The Romans, Calenus says, rightly punished Cicero at that time – i.e. with exile – and it would be astonishing for them to listen to him now, when he is rehashing all the same arguments that he made twenty years ago. This is a clever way of turning Cicero's emphasis on his constancy of opinion against him.

Typical too is the next reproach. Cicero, Calenus claims, fled Rome after Caesar's death, but then changed his mind and returned. He used to love Antony, but now hates him; he allies himself with Caesar's heir, having killed his father. "And if fate so decrees, he shall soon attack Octavian as well." Why?

ἄπιστός τε γὰρ φύσει καὶ ταραχώδης ἐστί, καὶ οὔτε τι ἕρμα ἐν τῇ ψυχῇ ἔχει καὶ πάντα ἀεὶ κυκᾷ καὶ στρέφει, πλείονας μὲν τροπὰς τρεπόμενος τοῦ πορθμοῦ πρὸς ὃν ἔφυγεν, ἐφ᾽ ᾧπερ καὶ αὐτόμολος ἐπωνομάσθη,

---

[84] Zielinski (1929) 280–288; cf. n. 31 above.

[85] This charge is repeated even more vehemently at 46.25.5, where Calenus, accusing Cicero of stirring up such trouble as a consul by "antitheses" alone – i.e., by words and not arms – claims to fear what he might have done at the head of an army. For a parallel to these charges in another context, see the description of Cicero as *turbator oti* at Sen. *contr.* 7.2.13.

πάντας δὲ ὑμᾶς ἀξιῶν καὶ φίλον καὶ ἐχθρὸν νομίζειν ὃν ἂν αὐτὸς κελεύσῃ. (46.3.4)

Because he is faithless by nature and a confused man, and he has no ballast in his soul, and he constantly stirs everything up and turns it upside down, turning about in more directions than the strait to which he fled – for this reason he was given the name "deserter." And he thinks it right and proper that you all should adjudge whomsoever he himself commands as a friend or an enemy!

This charge against Cicero's constancy is one of the most common that we find leveled against him, and indeed the persistent declamatory theme of urging him to be steadfast of purpose is simply the other side of this coin. Here Calenus refers pointedly to Cicero's exile and gives him the painful nickname αὐτόμολος ("deserter"), precisely paralleled in pseudo-Sallust's *transfuga* and indeed in his entire complaint about Cicero's fickle faith: "when you're standing you feel one way about the state, when you're sitting you feel something else, you faithless deserter, loyal neither to this side nor to that" (*in Tull.* 7).

Cicero, Calenus continues, is greedy and venal. He has made himself rich by defending the guilty and slandering the innocent (46.4.1, 46.6.2–46.7.1). This reproach too we have seen before in the declaimers, both acknowledged openly and hinted at (see e.g. p. 111 above), and it is emphasized by pseudo-Sallust as well (*in Tull.* 3–4, e.g. *opulentiam istam ex sanguine et miseriis ciuium parasti*). For how else could he have become rich? His father was a fuller who defiled himself daily with the foulest of filth (καθ' ἑκάστην ἡμέραν καὶ νύκτα τῶν αἰσχίστων ἀναπιμπλάμενος, 46.4.3). Slander about a person's ancestry is a standard feature of invective,[86] but in Cicero's case the criticism of him as a *nouus homo* touches a particularly sensitive nerve. Already in his own lifetime he had to defend his upstart status, and scurrilous attacks continued unabated in the declamatory tradition after his death, including repeatedly in pseudo-Sallust.[87] Even the opening words of the paragraph, εἶτα τοιοῦτος αὐτὸς ὤν ... ἐτόλμησας may be paralleled by a phrase in the pseudo-Sallustian text: *atque is cum eius modi sit, tamen audet dicere* (*in Tull.* 5).[88] All this is supposedly in the service of rebutting Cicero's

---

[86] Opelt (1965) 149–151.

[87] Such criticism is sounded as one of the opening notes of [Sall.] *in Tull.* (1): *reperticius, accitus ac paulo ante insitus huic urbi ciuis*; later *homo nouus Arpinas* (4) and *Romule Arpinas* (7). [Cic.] *in Sall.* 4–5 responds by making a virtue of necessity; cf. too Vell. 2.34.3–4, who takes a similar tack. See above on Cicero as consul and *nouus homo*.

[88] Cf. Cass. Dio 46.12.1 εἶτα τούτων οὕτως ἐχόντων τολμᾷς λέγειν ~ [Sall.] *in Tull.* 3 *atque haec cum ita sint, tamen Cicero dicit*.

charges about Antony's indiscretions as a young man; pseudo-Sallust likewise is keen to point out the corresponding faults in Cicero's youthful morals (*in Tull.* 2).

Cicero is moreover not only a turncoat but also a coward, being afraid to take a firm stand in court or in life (46.7.2–4). Our mercenary advocate sells his speech for any client, innocent or guilty, a common reproach found in pseudo-Sallust and other declaimers (*in Tull.* 4–5; cf. e.g. Sen. *contr.* 7.2.10). And his much-vaunted eloquence? A mere figment of the imagination, for Cicero never actually delivered any of those speeches that he so carefully polished and published.[89] (This criticism could arise from comparing the disastrous *Pro Milone* as delivered with the elegant and compelling *Pro Milone* as revised and published.)[90] This abuse culminates in the scurrilous charge that Cicero wetted his toga when speaking against Verres – fitting, of course, for the son of a fuller (46.7.4).

Indeed, Calenus goes on to say, Cicero has achieved nothing worthy of a man in either war or peace (πρᾶξιν μὲν οὐδεμίαν πώποτε ἐλλογίμου ἀνδρὸς ἀξίαν, οὔτ' ἐν πολέμῳ οὔτε ἐν εἰρήνῃ, πέπραχας, 46.9.1). "What wars did we win under your leadership?" he asks. This too strikes at a real chink in Cicero's armor, because he was very much not a military man. If one can successfully cast aspersions upon his civilian triumph, then he really is left with no political achievement of note. The slight echoes Livy's judgment: Cicero was a man utterly unsuited to war (*uir nihil minus quam ad bella natus*, per. 111), someone who bore none of his adversity as befits a man (*ut uiro dignum erat*, ap. Sen. *suas.* 6.22). Calenus then doubles down by claiming that Cicero does not even do a worthy job as an orator. In the same breath he mocks his excessive παρρησία, a biting reproach in the declamatory tradition which valorizes Cicero's free speech as the cause of his death (46.9.4).

After ten sections of unremitting criticism, Calenus finally breaks off the attack in order to defend Antony. This defense, of course, is again refracted through the lens of Ciceronian criticism. Cicero is still called out as

---

[89] Later on Cicero's oratorical prowess is reduced to mere glibness: he pours out with utter abandon whatever comes to his tongue (οὕτω μὲν οὖν οὐδ' ὁτιοῦν αὐτῷ διαφέρει πᾶν ὅ τι ποτ' ἂν ἐπὶ τὴν γλῶτταν αὐτοῦ ἐπέλθῃ, καθάπερ τι πνεῦμα, ἐκχέαι, 46.15.3). For good or ill, Cicero's tongue is always a point of emphasis.

[90] Cicero's commentators and critics both show themselves well aware of his failure in the *Pro Milone* (see ch. 1 p. 36). It is nevertheless striking that we do not find this charge of revisionism leveled against him elsewhere; indeed, revising a speech for publication seems to have been entirely expected (see e.g. Pliny's comments on revising the *Panegyricus* at *epist.* 3.18.1). I would thus associate the allegation with specific instances of failure and revision rather than with the general practice of revision for publication.

a traitor (46.12.3–4) and suffers from the besetting vice of cowardice (δειλία, 46.13.2–3). Indeed, Calenus even repeats some of Cicero's famous phrases in order to turn them against him. So Antony swallows everything up "like Charybdis"? Well, Cicero is always using some Sicilian comparison, he says, as if we had forgotten that he had tried to flee there during his exile (ἀεὶ γάρ τι ἡμῖν ἐκ τῆς Σικελίας, καθάπερ ἐπιλελησμένοις ὅτι ἐς αὐτὴν ἔφυγε, παραφέρει, 46.14.4; on the Charybdis motif, see p. 179 with n. 79 above). So too does Calenus again mock Cicero's παρρησία and patriotic pretensions (φιλόπολις; cf. 46.10.3), culminating in a sarcastic prosopopoeia in which Cicero cannot be restrained by favor or fear from speaking for the good of the Republic (ἐμὲ οὔτε χάρις φίλων οὔτε φόβος ἐχθρῶν ἀπείργει τοῦ μὴ οὐ τὰ συμφέροντα ὑμῖν προσκοπεῖν, 46.16.4). These are almost exactly the words of pseudo-Sallust (*in Tull.* 4): *neque terrore neque gratia remouetur* [*sc. Cicero*] *a uero*. But throughout these sections Calenus is really more concerned to devote himself to defending Antony's conduct on the points where Cicero had impugned it.

When Calenus is satisfied that he has proved the righteousness of Antony's conduct, he turns again to savaging Cicero. The insults descend to the puerile, beginning with name-calling: ὦ Κικέρων ἢ Κικέρκουλε ἢ Κικεράκιε ἢ Κικέριθε ἢ Γραίκουλε (46.18.1).[91] The belitting diminutive Γραίκουλε points of course to Cicero's excessive familiarity with Greek,[92] and Κικέρκουλε looks like a halfway point between the legitimate vocative Κικέρων and the reproach of Γραίκουλε; it was a nonce word created for sarcastic effect. Κικεράκιε and Κικέριθε, by contrast, seem to refer to the supposed profession of Cicero's father, who was – according to Calenus and Cicero's detractors – a fuller (ῥάκος = "rag, tattered garment," ἔριθοι = "workers in wool").[93] We then hear some standard topics of invective: Cicero's legs are ugly,[94] he is overly fastidious, he reeks of midnight oil[95] and drinks naught but water. These generally find their parallels elsewhere in the tradition, but we alight upon some of the most striking correspondences when Calenus complains about Cicero's sexual mores. Cicero, he claims, prostituted his own wife and defiled his own daughter (τοσαύτη ἀσελγείᾳ καὶ ἀκαθαρσίᾳ παρὰ πάντα τὸν βίον χρώμενος ὥστε ... τήν τε

---

[91] On this passage, see Zielinski (1929) 284, whose explanation I largely follow. The Greek puns suggest that this insult at least cannot be drawn directly from a Latin source. More declamatory jingles follow, e.g. ὁ καὶ μέχρι τῶν σφυρῶν τὴν ἐσθῆτα σύρων (note too the isocola).

[92] Cf. Plut. *Cic.* 5.2 Γραικὸς καὶ σχολαστικὸς ἀκούων.

[93] Cf. e.g. Plut. *Cic.* 1.1 οἱ μὲν γὰρ ἐν γναφείῳ τινὶ καὶ γενέσθαι καὶ τραφῆναι τὸν ἄνδρα λέγουσιν.

[94] Opelt (1965) 152–153 discusses conventional criticisms of politicians' appearances, but why Calenus has chosen to focus on Cicero's *legs* is a mystery to me. Is it because he uses them to run away?

[95] Cicero's association with *lucubratio* is discussed in Ker (2004) 228–229.

γυναῖκα προαγωγεύειν καὶ τὴν θυγατέρα μοιχεύειν, 46.18.6). A mere generic topos? Perhaps, but a very similar charge occurs in the Sallustian invective (*uxor sacrilega ac periuriis delibuta, filia matris paelex, tibi iucundior atque obsequentior quam parenti par est*, [Sall.] *in Tull.* 2).[96] That this is all the basest slander need hardly be said; but the same base slander is repeated in the same terms over great distances of time and space. The declamatory tradition, as exemplified in pseudo-Sallust, had a long and influential afterlife.

Calenus soon returns again to Cicero's consulship, lambasting it in a lengthy purple passage studded with rhetorical gems (46.20.1–21.3). "What did you accomplish in your consulship," he asks, "I will not say that was wise and good, but that was not deserving of the greatest punishment?" (σὺ δ', ὦ Κικέρων, τί ἐν τῇ ὑπατείᾳ σου οὐχ ὅτι σοφὸν ἢ ἀγαθόν, ἀλλ' οὐ καὶ τιμωρίας τῆς μεγίστης ἄξιον ἔπραξας;, 46.20.1). The sum of his accomplishments was his summary execution of Roman citizens without trial, and for that he got his just deserts when he was exiled, indeed admitting his crime by fleeing before the trial (cf. e.g. the remarks of Philiscus at 38.26.1–2 and [Cic.] *exil.* 7). And that is not all: just as pseudo-Sallust complains that not only did Cicero execute Roman citizens, he also had the effrontery to brag about it ceaselessly (*in Tull.* 6), so too Dio's Calenus. Cicero is so bold that he has written up his "accomplishments" *himself*, whereas he should have prayed that no one else ever decided to record them so that his infamy could perish when he died (καὶ οὕτω γε ἀναίσχυντος εἶ ὥστε καὶ συγγράψαι ταῦτα τοιαῦτα ὄντα ἐπεχείρησας· ὃν ἐχρῆν εὔχεσθαι μηδὲ τῶν ἄλλων τινὰ αὐτὰ συνθεῖναι, ἵνα ἀλλὰ τοῦτό γε κερδάνῃς, τὸ συναπολέσθαι σοι τὰ πεπραγμένα καὶ μηδεμίαν αὐτῶν μνήμην τοῖς ἔπειτα παραδοθῆναι, 46.21.3). Even worse, Cicero is a hypocrite, since he is always and everywhere prating about the laws and the courts (πολλὰ μὲν περὶ τῶν νόμων πολλὰ δὲ καὶ περὶ τῶν δικαστηρίων ἀεὶ καὶ πανταχοῦ θρυλῶν, 46.20.2; cf. [Sall.] *in Tull.* 1 *leges iudicia rem publicam defendit*).

The tenor of Calenus' speech is by now abundantly clear, but one last jibe is worth recording. Cicero had to defend his poetry even during his own lifetime, and criticism only intensified after his death. We have seen this in abundance already, not least in pseudo-Sallust (*in Tull.* 5–7) and

---

[96] The motif of the *filia matris paelex* (where *matris* is "the genitive of the wronged wife") is found, in reverse, already in Cic. *Cluent.* 199 *filiae paelex*, where it is the mother who usurps the daughter's rightful place.

pseudo-Cicero's reply (*in Sall.* 7).[97] Particularly notorious was the line *o fortunatam natam me consule Romam*, which Juvenal too singles out for mention (10.122; see p. 99 above). Even in Greek Calenus finds a way to deflate this particular bombast (46.21.4):

> καὶ ὅπως γε καὶ γελάσητε, ἀκούσατε τὴν σοφίαν αὐτοῦ. προθέμενος γὰρ
> πάντα τὰ τῇ πόλει πεπραγμένα συγγράψαι (καὶ γὰρ σοφιστὴς καὶ
> ποιητὴς καὶ φιλόσοφος καὶ ῥήτωρ καὶ συγγραφεὺς εἶναι πλάττεται)
> ἔπειτ᾽ οὐκ ἀπὸ τῆς κτίσεως αὐτῆς, ὥσπερ οἱ ἄλλοι οἱ τοῦτο ποιοῦντες,
> ἀλλὰ ἀπὸ τῆς ὑπατείας τῆς ἑαυτοῦ ἤρξατο, ἵνα ἀνάπαλιν προχωρῶν
> ἀρχὴν μὲν τοῦ λόγου ἐκείνην, τελευτὴν δὲ τὴν τοῦ Ῥωμύλου βασιλείαν
> ποιήσηται.

And so that you might have a bit of a laugh as well, listen to this specimen of brilliance. He decided to compose a history of everything that Rome had accomplished (he fancies himself a rhetorician and a poet and a philosopher and an orator and a historian). He, however, didn't begin "from the founding of the city," as everyone else does who undertakes this sort of project, but from his own consulship, so that he might go backwards and make that the beginning of his account, and the kingship of Romulus the end!

Calenus has taken Cicero's line literally. If Rome was born during his consulship and he is the *Romulus Arpinas* ([Sall.] *in Tull.* 7), then he must intend to work backwards from that birth to the time of the original Romulus! This is of course utterly fantastic; Cicero had no intention of writing a "history of all the achievements of the city," but rather of glorifying himself and his consulship. Fantastic or not, however, it is certainly a novel and amusing variation on the declamatory theme of mocking Cicero's poetry.[98]

Having poured out this torrent of abuse, Calenus again returns to defending Antony's conduct for the remainder of the speech – not, of course, without throwing in a few incidental jibes at Cicero's expense as well.[99] One of the more interesting of these passing remarks comes in Calenus' *peroratio*,

---

[97] Such criticism could be very casual; see e.g. Sen. *contr.* 3 pr. 8 *Ciceronem eloquentia sua in carminibus destituit*, or Mart. 2.89.3–4: *carmina quod scribis Musis et Apolline nullo, | laudari debes: hoc Ciceronis habes*. It proved persistent and pervasive (e.g. schol. Bob. 137 St.). See also ch. 5 n. 19, ch. 6 n. 86, and ch. 7 n. 88. Soubiran (2002) and Courtney (2003) 149–178 are the standard editions Cicero's poetry, although the latter omits the *Aratea*. Ewbank (1933) remains a useful commentary on all the fragments; his introduction also discusses their ancient criticism. Cf. Gee (2013) for a more positive evaluation of Cicero's poetic reception in Lucretius and Vergil, as well as Volk (2013), who also takes Cicero seriously as a genre-bending poet.

[98] Zielinski (1929) 285 misses the joke when he takes this passage as a genuine misinterpretation of Cic. *leg.* 1.8 (discussing the point in time at which the *exordium* should begin).

[99] E.g. 46.22.2, Cicero is better at rebuking others than at setting himself straight: a charge that Cicero admits to in his dialogue with Philiscus (38.18.2); he is a quarrelsome busybody (46.27.1 φιλαπεχθήμων; πολυπραγμονεῖν); he brags like a woman (46.28.1 γυναικείως θρασύνεσθαι); etc.

where Cicero is urged not to let his "private grudge" against Antony place the entire city at risk "again" (μήτε διὰ τὴν ἰδίαν πρὸς τὸν Ἀντώνιον ἔχθραν δημοσίᾳ πᾶσαν τὴν πόλιν ἐς κίνδυνον αὖθις καθιστάναι, 46.28.1). This sentence is jam-packed with meaning. Even the smallest details, like the word αὖθις ("again") are pointed barbs, this one linking back to criticism of Cicero's consulship, when, Calenus has said, he likewise put the city and the citizenry in jeopardy. More importantly, contrary to Cicero's insistence that Antony is a *hostis*, a "public enemy" (or πολέμιος), here he is alleged only to be on the wrong side of Cicero's "private feud" (ἰδία ἔχθρα). This private vendetta is then seen to put the entire city in danger "at the public expense" (δημοσίᾳ) – thus Cicero, so far from defending the common interest, in fact threatens its ruin by his insistence on a personal vendetta.[100] This is a fascinating way to neutralize the standard Augustan line that Cicero was battling for freedom against the tyrant Antony: that he was fighting against Antony cannot be denied, but his reasons can be debated. So too does pseudo-Brutus question Cicero's motives, wondering if perhaps he was really just animated by personal hatred for Antony (*Cic. ad Brut.* 1.17.2). Thus this line too has a history in the declamatory tradition. Even Cicero's supposed – ὥς γε καὶ φής (46.26.2) – fearlessness in the face of death is at the last turned into a vice, threatening death for the citizenry as well, and so Calenus ends by undercutting the boast of Cicero's most defiant words (46.28.4–6).

In sum, then, in Dio both Cicero's and Calenus' speeches reflect the form and content of the tradition found in the rhetorical classroom. With these speeches we come in a sense full circle. We first hear about Cicero's last days and months from the declaimers, who have taken elements of an existing tradition influenced by propaganda and refashioned and amplified them. These declamatory versions eventually become canonical, influencing even the writing of narrative history. By Dio's day, these elements have simply become reality. Dio himself then fully embraces this tradition, giving his characters lengthy set-piece speeches that would have done any declaimer proud. The tradition is thus in continuous declamatory dialogue with itself, reflecting common matter and manner back and forth in an ever-intensifying cycle of reinforcement.

Coda: The Intertextual Declamatory Aesthetic

There is a story, perhaps apocryphal, that Richard Porson was once asked his opinion on some specimens of schoolboy verse composition.

---

[100] This line of reasoning was actually present from the very beginning of Calenus' speech (46.1.1–2).

"I see in them much Horace and Vergil," he is said to have replied, "but nothing either Horatian or Vergilian."[101] Students throughout history have larded their compositions, both prose and verse, with a generous supply of such quotations lifted ready-made from ancient authors. Indeed, their use and abuse was a lively issue of schoolroom controversy well into the twentieth century. Thomas Higham, in his lengthy and discursive introduction to *Some Oxford Compositions* (published in 1949), includes eight pages on "tips and tags," inveighing against the practice of plucking choice flowers from the fields of Latin literature to transplant into one's own compositions: "tags," he pronounces, "are as a general rule best avoided."[102] A composition should not be allowed to "sink into mere quotation."[103] And yet even he has to concede that examiners will look with favor on a well-chosen tag recalled under the watchful eye of the invigilators in the exam room. We still ask students in advanced composition classes to imitate the style of various ancient authors, and with the proliferation of searchable databases, assignments in such classes are perhaps more apt to be strewn with *flosculi* than ever before. After all, a student might reason, what can be more Ciceronian than Cicero's *ipsissima uerba*?

As we have seen, neither this reasoning nor these assignments are anything new. When students in the Roman rhetorical classroom wrote about or in imitation of Cicero, they packed their compositions with Ciceronian phrases. I want to conclude by claiming that it is no more correct to classify these sorts of compositions as "forgeries" than it would be to call a modern prose composition assignment a forgery: I do not believe that they were intended to deceive anyone, but rather to be recognized and appreciated for their rhetorical skill and self-conscious reworking of their sources.[104] A scholarly prejudice has long asserted or implied that the declaimers were incompetent,[105] but whatever one thinks of their literary or artistic abilities,

---

[101] An anecdote recounted by Potts (1886) 26.

[102] Higham (1949) xxix–xxxvi, quote from p. xxxiii.

[103] Higham (1949) xxxii – itself a quotation of Jacob Burckhardt!

[104] Peirano (2012) 24–31 likewise deprecates the term "forgery" as anachronistic and contends that "fraud and deception" are not suitable terms for discussing these texts.

[105] Even editors of this material have had little good to say about it. In his Loeb edition of Seneca the Elder, Winterbottom (1974) xxiii offers this evaluation: "The modern will find a good deal of the elder Seneca's material unreal, unfamiliar, and even tedious. He will skip many of the epigrams, and concentrate on the lively prefaces and the incidental anecdote. But anyone, lay or scholar, who wishes to understand the essence of Silver Latin will have to take the rough with the smooth and nerve himself to read at least a fair sample of the whole." Cf. Winterbottom (1984) vii for more on the long history of scholarly neglect.

their allusive practices deserve to be recognized on their own merits and are in fact a show of competence.[106]

We have seen various examples of intertextual play in Seneca's declaimers, including at least one speaker making a meta-literary comment at the moment of citation (Sen. *contr.* 7.2.10; cf. p. 111 above): when Aeserninus channels Antony coming up with a punishment for Cicero, he makes him mockingly quote the end of the second *Philippic*. Immediately after this reminiscence, however, he says *fiat aliquid noui*, "let me devise something new"; he then outdoes Cicero's words with a novel way of putting Cicero to death. Such sophistication is not confined to Seneca's pages. Take the *Epistula ad Octauianum*, which purports to be a letter from Cicero to the young Octavian from very near the end of Cicero's life.[107] Cicero's illusions about Caesar's heir have been shattered; no longer Cicero's protégé, he is now a full-fledged member of the ruling triumvirate. The letter thus represents the last words of Cicero, his final complaint against the youth who had led him on only to betray him. In this rhetorical production "Cicero" is made to refashion against Octavian barbs that were originally intended for Antony. He begins the letter, for example, by saying that the senators can only cower in fear, the Senate being "surrounded by armed cohorts" (*sed quoniam cohortibus circumsaeptus senatus nihil aliud libere potest [decernere] nisi timere, epist. ad Oct.* 1). This phrase echoes Cicero's criticism of Antony, asking him to defend his conduct (*Phil.* 2.112):

> cur armatorum corona senatus saeptus est, cur me tui satellites cum gladiis audiunt, cur ualuae Concordiae non patent, cur homines omnium gentium maxime barbaros, Ituraeos, cum sagittis deducis in forum?

> Why is the Senate surrounded by a circle of armed men, why does your retinue listen to me with drawn swords, why are the doors of the Temple of Concord not open, why do you lead the most barbaric of all tribes, the Ituraeans, into the forum armed with arrows?

Our declaimer, having resolved to make Octavian the target of Cicero's ire, found a ready supply of ammunition in his invectives against Antony.

---

[106] Indeed, a web of such allusions helps to create the self-contained world of declamation where many of these speeches are most at home, engaged in *imitatio* and *aemulatio* with their declamatory rivals. After long neglect, prose intertextuality has received dramatically increased attention in recent years, especially in historiography. See e.g. Levene (2010) 82–163 on Livy's allusions and reworking of his Polybian source material in his third decade, and van den Berg and Baraz (2013) more generally. Peirano (2012) 15–18 discusses the varying use of citations or near-citations in declamatory texts. van Mal-Maeder (2007) makes keen observations on the self-contained and intertextual world of declamation *passim*, esp. 82–93.

[107] On this text, see the commentaries of Lamacchia (1968) and Grattarola (1988).

Additional examples can be found on every page of the *Epistula*. So the text continues: *Italia tota legionibus ad libertatem nostram conscriptis ad seruitutem adductis ... distinetur* ("the whole of Italy is split apart/held down by legions that were enlisted to free us but now led to enslave us," *epist. ad Oct.* 1), which neatly repurposes Cic. *Phil.* 3.32 *Italia tota ad libertatem reciperandam excitata*, redirecting an exhortation to resist Mark Antony into a criticism of Octavian's miscarriages of justice. Indeed, the programmatic role of intertextuality in this epistle is made clear from its opening sentence, *si per tuas legiones mihi licitum fuisset, quae nomini meo populoque Romano sunt inimicissimae, uenire in senatum* ("if your legions, which are bitterly hostile to me personally and to the Roman people, had allowed me to enter the Senate," *epist. ad Oct.* 1), which plays with Cic. *Phil.* 5.20 *si per amicos mihi cupienti in senatum uenire licuisset.* The real Cicero was prevented by his friends (*amici*) from coming to the Senate; he claims that they saved his life from Mark Antony and his gang of armed thugs. In our declaimer, by contrast, he is prevented from coming to the Senate by Octavian's armed thugs, who are anything but friendly (*inimicissimae*). Octavian has become the new Antony, the true enemy of the *res publica*, and this persistent theme of the text is reinforced by its persistent intertextuality.

This allusive pattern is what we see in so many Latin authors who discuss Cicero. So when a rhetorician takes on the persona of Brutus reproaching Cicero, he writes ([Brut.] *Cic. ad Brut.* 1.17.1):

> nescio quid scribam tibi nisi unum: pueri et cupiditatem et licentiam potius esse irritatam quam repressam a Cicerone, tantumque eum tribuere huic indulgentiae ut se maledictis non abstineat iis quidem quae in ipsum dupliciter reccidunt, quod et pluris occidit uno seque prius oportet fateatur <u>sicarium</u> quam obiciat Cascae quod obicit et imitetur in Casca Bestiam. <u>an quia non omnibus horis iactamus Idus Martias similiter atque ille Nonas Decembris suas in ore habet</u>, eo meliore condicione Cicero <u>pulcherrimum factum</u> uituperabit quam Bestia et Clodius reprehendere illius consulatum soliti sunt?

> I don't know what to write except this: Cicero has stirred up the boy's [= Octavian's] lust for power and lawlessness, not checked it, and he has so practiced this indulgence that he does not refrain from the sort of offensive language which redounds twofold to his own discredit, because he has both killed more than one man and ought sooner to confess himself an <u>assassin</u> (*sicarius*) than reproach Casca as he does and become a second Bestia against him. <u>What? Because we don't spend every minute boasting about the "Ides of March" the way he has the "Nones of December" ever on his lips,</u> for that reason is Cicero in a better position to criticize the <u>most beautiful deed</u>

(*pulcherrimum factum*) than Bestia and Clodius were when they reproached his own consulship?

As is well known, Cicero supported those who had assassinated Caesar. Indeed, his only criticism of the Caesaricides was that they had not gone far enough – "'twas a fine deed, but half done," he writes to Atticus[108] – and so in arguing that this letter was not written by the real Brutus, Shackleton Bailey rightly objected to Cicero being made to call Casca the highly pejorative *sicarius* ("assassin"; cf. p. 149 above). Cicero would not have hurled such an insult about a deed that he so thoroughly approved of, nor would he have criticized "the most beautiful deed."

The very phrase *pulcherrimum factum*, in fact, is itself a marker of declamatory *imitatio*. The *iunctura* is peculiarly Ciceronian, entirely absent from other Latin authors but frequent in Cicero, including in particular as a euphemism for Caesar's assassination.[109] Furthermore, it is twice found yoked with *sicarius*, including in the famous second *Philippic*: "if Caesar's killers were not liberators and saviors, they were worse than assassins" (*plus quam sicarios*, *Phil.* 2.31), followed by "the Republic has as authors of that most beautiful deed the most illustrious men" (*habet istius pulcherrimi facti clarissimos uiros res publica auctores*, 2.36). There is also a letter from Cicero to Cassius that features both phrases (Cic. *fam.* 12.3.1, October 44):

> auget tuus amicus [i.e. Antonius] furorem in dies. primum in statua quam posuit in rostris inscripsit "parenti optime merito," ut non modo sicarii sed iam etiam parricidae iudicemini. quid dico "iudicemini"? iudicemur potius. uestri enim pulcherrimi facti ille furiosus me principem dicit fuisse. utinam quidem fuissem!

> That friend of yours [i.e. Antony] gets crazier by the day. First, on the statue (of Caesar) which he erected on the *rostra* he added the inscription, "for a most deserving parent," so that you are judged not just assassins (*sicarii*) but indeed parricides! But why do I say "*you* are judged"? I ought to say "*we* are judged," because that madman claims that I was in charge of that most beautiful deed (*pulcherrimi facti*). I wish I had been!

Cicero here uses both *sicarius* and *pulcherrimum factum* in almost the same breath. So too the "Brutus" of our disputed letter, right after the unexpected *sicarius*, equally unexpectedly accuses Cicero of reviling that same

---

[108] Cic. *Att.* 14.12.1 *o mi Attice, uereor ne nobis Idus Martiae nihil dederint praeter laetitiam et odi poenam ac doloris. quae mihi istim adferuntur! quae hic uideo!* "ὦ πράξεως καλῆς μέν, ἀτελοῦς δέ." (The translation here is Shackleton Bailey's in his Loeb.)

[109] The "exception" is not: Quint. *inst.* 9.3.40 quotes Cicero. For the euphemism, in addition to the two passages discussed in the text, see Cic. *Phil.* 1.9, 2.114, *off.* 3.19.

pulcherrimum factum. This double coincidence of phrases in immediate succession, neither of which Brutus would have written in such a context, suggests that the author had Ciceronian language in mind. This is precisely the language that Cicero – but only Cicero – uses to talk about the assassination. The declaimer has tried to twist Cicero's own words against him.

Much of the rest of pseudo-Brutus' letter is likewise a tissue of declamatory *sententiae*. The pungent opposition of the Ides of March and Cicero's Nones, for example, is absolutely of a piece with declamatory thought and rhetoric, and it is nigh impossible to picture the real Brutus reproaching Cicero with such a conceit, especially since the real Cicero gives precious little evidence that he was still banging on about this topic in 43 BC.[110] The author also evokes Cicero's besetting vice of self-praise and casts aspersions on his consulship, invariably the first ports of call for declaimers who wish to criticize him; compare, for example, pseudo-Sallust's similar complaint about Cicero's constant harping on the zenith – or nadir, depending on your perspective – of his consulship. Is it not enough, he says, that we have suffered through your consulship?

> etiamne aures nostras odio tuo onerabis, etiamne molestissimis uerbis insectabere? "cedant arma togae, concedat laurea linguae." quasi uero togatus et non armatus ea, quae gloriaris, confeceris. ([Sall.] *in Tull.* 6)

> Will you also burden our ears with your insolence, will you keep assaulting (*insectabere*) us with your unbelievably annoying phrases? "Let arms yield to the toga, let the laurel bow to the tongue." As though you accomplished what you're bragging about (*gloriaris*) in a toga (*togatus*) and not in arms.

When our "Brutus" continues in his letter to note that "our Cicero in his toga (*togatus*) brags (*gloriatur*) to me that he's borne the brunt of Antony's war" (*sustinuisse mihi gloriatur bellum Antoni togatus Cicero noster*, Brut. *Cic. ad Brut.* 1.17.2), the *togatus* also looks to this same critical tradition that we see at the end of our pseudo-Sallust passage, where we likewise find a double coincidence of *togatus* and *gloriatur*. The real Cicero would not have been making such a boast to the real Brutus in 43 BC; this was once Cicero's way of talking about the Catilinarian conspiracy, not Mark Antony, and our declaimer has simply picked up on the reproach in the

---

[110] Shackleton Bailey (1980) 13 notes that although he was wont to boast about his consulship in its immediate aftermath, "it is highly improbable that in 43 Cicero was trying his friends' patience in this fashion." Moles (1997) 158 replies that there are references to it in the *Philippics*, but for the most part these occur when Cicero is being forced to defend his consulship. This is plainly the later critical tradition speaking.

critical tradition and applied it to the fictitious present situation.[111] Elsewhere our letter also appears to play with motifs found in the pseudo-Sallustian invective; see, for example, yet another of Brutus' complaints about Cicero's boasting, which is worded very similarly to what we have just read (*desinat igitur gloriando etiam insectari dolores nostros*, [Brut.] *Cic. ad Brut.* 1.17.5).

The key thing to observe in all of these pseudepigrapha is that their authors positively *want* their allusions to be recognized. They want the reader to say, "I see what you did there," and so to appreciate the authors' skill. This is not the behavior of a forger trying to cover his tracks; indeed, to use Seneca's famous formulation, this is deliberate and open borrowing designed to be recognized (Sen. *suas.* 3.7).[112] When we find a Ciceronian tag in the disputed letter of "Brutus" – something that the real Brutus would not have written – we can place the letter squarely in this declamatory tradition. Again, however, it is wrong to think of the incongruence as incompetence: taking Cicero's words out of context and twisting them or repurposing them is likewise very much a part of the declamatory aesthetic.[113] These are not forgeries; they are compositions produced according to their own set of allusive and intertextual standards.

John Moles wrote that "many scholars, both rejectionists and believers, think that these letters [*sc.* the two pseudo-Brutus letters] have little or no historical value,"[114] but that is to confine "history" solely to the eyewitness accounts of the political events of 43 BC. In fact such recreations are precious artifacts of cultural memory, and these letters are a vital document in studying the reception of Cicero: they, along with other "spurious" products of the rhetorical classroom, give us direct insight into how a later age thought and wrote about him. Moreover, the ideas about Cicero that

---

[111] Cicero does frequently refer to his suppression of the Catilinarian conspiracy while *togatus* (Cic. *Cat.* 2.28, 3.15, 3.23, 4.5; *Mur.* 84; also occasionally in its immediate aftermath and elsewhere, e.g. *Sull.* 85, *dom.* 99), but he does not so describe his duel with Antony. In the *Philippics* he uses the word when forced to defend his consulship (*Phil.* 2.14) and his poetry (*Phil.* 2.20; cf. *Pis.* 73), but these instances again concern Catiline. The only contemporary reference to Cicero's togate status vis-à-vis Antony is to be found in *fam.* 12.13.1, a letter from Cassius (Parmensis, not Longinus) to Cicero, in which Cassius is trying to flatter Cicero: *cum rei publicae uel salute uel uictoria gaudemus tum instauratione tuarum laudum, quod maximus consularis maximum consulem te ipse uicisti, et laetamur et mirari satis non possumus. fatale nescio quid tuae uirtuti datum, id quod saepe iam experti sumus. est enim tua toga omnium armis felicior; quae nunc quoque nobis paene uictam rem publicam ex manibus hostium eripuit ac reddidit. nunc ergo uiuemus liberi.* This is a complimentary reference to Cicero's poetry, admirably calculated to please, but unusual in every respect; see Hall (2009) 99–103.

[112] On this passage, see McGill (2012) 163–167; his pp. 146–177 treat accusations of and defenses against plagiarism in Seneca's declaimers.

[113] Cf. Peirano (2012) 22–23 on Sen. *suas.* 6.13.

[114] Moles (1997) 161; similarly Shackleton Bailey (1980) 10.

were drummed into the heads of young Romans in their school days continued to permeate their thought and writing as adults, and so studying these compositions helps us to better understand writers from Velleius Paterculus to Tacitus to Juvenal to Cassius Dio. I would thus strongly disagree with those who disparage this and other examples of pseudo-Ciceroniana: these works are in fact of considerable historical value, for the early imperial image of Cicero was dyed deeply in declamation.

CHAPTER 5

Seneca the Younger and Cicero

In Seneca the Younger Cicero is conspicuous by his absence. He is generally absent in name, absent in quotation, absent in stylistic and philosophical influence – but he "should" have been there. Seneca, as a writer of epistles and philosophy, as a stylistic and educational theorist, and as a man out to make his bones in the world of Roman politics and literature, could not avoid Cicero's towering influence. And yet he seems to try to do just that. In this chapter I will study Seneca's engagement with Cicero, discussing both Cicero's occasional presences and his striking absences in Seneca's writings.[1] I will focus on the one hand on the influence of rhetorical education and declamation on Seneca's conception of Cicero, but also on how Seneca goes beyond that basis in his generic innovations in epistolography and in his vision for an ideal education, which contrasts sharply with Cicero's.

Seneca the Younger is without doubt the most consequential Latin prose author between Cicero and Tacitus. Born in Corduba shortly before the beginning of the Common Era, he came to Rome as a young boy and received his education there.[2] He was the son of a celebrated *littérateur*, the connoisseur of declamation *par excellence*, and so he will have been well trained in the art of rhetoric, even if his own interests inclined more to philosophy than oratory. He is thus in one sense the ideal representative of

---

[1] The most helpful treatment of Cicero in Seneca remains Gambet (1970); see also his p. 171 n. 2 for earlier bibliography. Since Gambet there have been several useful discussions. First Grimal (1984), who unconvincingly argues that Seneca viewed Cicero as a typical exemplum before his own exile, while judging him to fall short of Stoic ideals after his recall. Then Setaioli (2003), who includes discussion of Cicero as a philosophical source for Seneca as well as a treatment of Senecan and Ciceronian prose style. Finally Fedeli (2004), going beyond "Cicero in Seneca" to include later judgments on the two from Quintilian to Petrarch to Carlo Emilio Gadda. In a different vein Griffin (1987) compares the role of philosophy in the careers of Cicero and Seneca and the importance of philosophy in the life of a Roman statesman. Gowing (2013) 240–244 explores an instance of Seneca's implicit engagement with an absent Cicero in *epist.* 51.

[2] See Griffin (1976) 29–66 on Seneca's life before becoming Nero's minister; at p. 34 she rightly cautions that the evidence for the earliest period is exiguous.

the kind of rhetorical training that I have been discussing up until now; he has drunk deeply from the fount of declamatory education. The declamatory version of Cicero does indeed appear in his writings, and so far he plays the game by the rules that we have seen. And yet in another sense Seneca has plainly gone his own way and chosen to reject Cicero and all his works and empty promises: he rejects him as a stylist, as a philosopher, as a generic model, and as an educational theorist. Indeed, when Cicero is introduced it is often only so that he can be explicitly rejected. It is against this very Senecan attitude that Quintilian will react a generation later, as I will discuss in the next chapter. A study of Cicero in Seneca the Younger thus bridges the gap both chronologically and thematically between the world of the Augustan and Tiberian declaimers that his father represents, as discussed in the preceding chapters, and the reactionary neo-Ciceronianism of Quintilian a generation after his death, which I will discuss in the chapters that follow. It moreover shows Seneca, the premier prose author of his day, making a deliberate choice to stake out his intellectual and artistic claims in a different way from his most influential predecessor – and this very choice is itself a form of engagement with Cicero.

Declamatory Ciceronian Presences

Seneca cites Cicero on about two dozen occasions in his prose writings, hardly as often as you might expect.[3] That other paragon of the Roman schoolroom, Vergil, is cited some 119 times, and he did not even write philosophy.[4] And yet Seneca is intimately familiar with the full range of Cicero's writings, referring with equal facility to the details of Cicero's dealings with Clodius (*epist.* 97.2–9), his insults of Vatinius (*dial.* 2.17.3), and his work *De re publica* (*epist.* 108.30–35). A subtle but extremely telling sign of Seneca's close acquaintance with the Ciceronian corpus comes not from his citations of Cicero, but rather of Ennius, whom Seneca quotes ten times, comprising six short fragments. Five of those six fragments are also found in our extant texts of Cicero, and furthermore Cicero's versions are sometimes fuller than those found in Seneca, while the converse is never the case.[5] Indeed, the sixth citation too certainly depends on a lost part of

---

[3] Martín Sanchez (1989) 117 notes twenty-five passages, all of which I discuss here. This surprising lack of attention has often been remarked, e.g. Gambet (1970) 172, Fedeli (2004) 217. Moreschini (1977) 528 thinks that while Cicero was not a "source" for Seneca, he was nevertheless "read and pondered" ("letto e meditato").

[4] See Mazzoli (1970) 215–232, as well as Setaioli (1965).

[5] Mazzoli (1964) 309 makes these insightful observations.

the *De re publica*.[6] In Cicero the citations occur in the *Brutus, De officiis, De senectute, De re publica, De diuinatione,* and *Disputationes Tusculanae.* In addition to the standard bits remembered from the Ciceronian grammar grind, Seneca clearly had made a close study of most or all of Cicero's writings. His choices in mentioning or not mentioning Cicero are thus deliberate and significant.

The declamatory Cicero who appears so often elsewhere is well known to Seneca.[7] So he can observe that "we often seem to get angry at Clodius for driving Cicero into exile and at Antony for killing him" (*saepe Clodio Ciceronem expellenti et Antonio occidenti uidemur irasci, dial.* 4.2.3); these are the signal events of Cicero's career as mapped out by the declaimers.[8] Seneca accepts uncritically the tradition that ascribes responsibility for Cicero's death to Antony alone. Antony himself, as throughout the declamatory tradition, is represented as unable to slake his drunken thirst with anything but blood, having the heads of the proscribed – i.e., Cicero's head – brought to his dinner table (*epist.* 83.25).[9] Furthermore, when speaking of Cicero's death, Seneca echoes both the themes and the words of the declaimers: Pompey and Cicero were forced "to proffer their necks to their own clients" (*clientibus suis praebere ceruicem, dial.* 9.16.1). Cicero's "client" is the notorious Popillius, whom he supposedly had earlier defended against a charge of parricide (p. 102 above), while the motif of Cicero bravely extending his neck can be traced through declamatory accounts to that of Livy (Sen. *suas.* 6.17; cf. *TLL* III.948.45–50 [Probst]). When Cicero is said to have been *nec secundis rebus quietus nec aduersarum patiens* ("neither quiet in prosperity nor patient in adversity," *dial.* 10.5.1),

---

[6] Seneca attributes it to the *De re publica* in the midst of a detailed discussion of the work at *epist.* 108.34; see p. 204 below.

[7] Because of Seneca's parentage, this has been recognized, especially as regards his impression of Cicero's death, since at least Gambet (1970), e.g. 178. So too Grimal (1984) 658–659, Setaioli (2003) 57–59, Fedeli (2004) 219. Some aspects of these scholars' treatments may be doubted (e.g. Gambet [1970] 179 "Seneca, then, clearly minimizes Cicero's efforts against Antony" – there is no evidence of this), but the fundamental observation, viz. that in his death Cicero "non è l'uomo reale, ma piuttosto il personaggio delle declamazioni" (Setaioli [2003] 57), is indisputably correct.

[8] Catiline is added to the mix at *dial.* 6.20.5: *M. Cicero si illo tempore quo Catilinae sicas deuitauit, quibus pariter cum patria petitus est, concidisset, liberata re publica seruator eius, si denique filiae suae funus secutus esset, etiamtunc felix mori potuit. non uidisset strictos in ciuilia capita mucrones nec diuisa percussoribus occisorum bona, ut etiam de suo perirent, non hastam consularia spolia uendentem nec caedes locatas publice nec latrocinia, bella, rapinas, tantum Catilinarum.*

[9] Cf. p. 145 above. These less direct mentions of Cicero are found elsewhere too. So when speaking of men undone by their outspoken eloquence Seneca says *quam multorum eloquentia . . . sanguinem educit* (*dial.* 10.2.4), a nod to Cicero's *Philippics* as the supposed cause of his death. These words presage Juvenal's tenth *Satire* (cf. p. 99 above). The patronizing reference to Cicero *fils* (*benef.* 4.30.2, consul only because Cicero *père* had been) is likewise of a piece with the stories recounted in Seneca the Elder (*suas.* 7.13–14).

this too could come directly from his father's compendium (*Pollio ap. Sen. suas.* 6.24 *utinam moderatius secundas res et fortius aduersas ferre potuisset*), and Seneca's damning *sententia* on Cicero's consulship (*non sine causa sed sine fine laudatum, dial.* 10.5.1) is worthy of declamatory immortality itself.

Cicero is often combined with Cato in this exemplary role.[10] So when his disgraceful death is conjoined with that of Pompey (above), these are in fact only steps in a climactic series that will culminate with Cato (*dial.* 9.16.1):

> ubi bonorum exitus mali sunt, ubi Socrates cogitur in carcere mori, Rutilius in exilio uiuere, Pompeius et Cicero clientibus suis praebere ceruicem, Cato ille, uirtutium uiua imago, incumbens gladio simul de se ac de re publica palam facere, necesse est torqueri tam iniqua praemia fortunam persoluere; et quid sibi quisque tunc speret, cum uideat pessima optimos pati?

> When good men suffer disgraceful deaths, when Socrates is forced to die in jail, Rutilius to live in exile, Pompey and Cicero to proffer their necks to their own clients, and Cato, that living embodiment of virtue, to fall on his sword and make known both his own death and that of the Republic at the same time, one must be tormented by the knowledge that Fortune repays her debts with such unjust payments. What then could anyone hope for himself, when he sees that the very best men suffer the very worst things?

Cicero is an exemplum, but Cato is *the* exemplum of a great man faced with an unjust death. This image of Cato too is drawn from the schoolroom, as Seneca elsewhere acknowledges (*epist.* 24.6–7; cf. p. 114 above). In such implicit comparisons between Seneca's great Stoic forebear and the unfortunately inconstant Cicero, Cato always wins: here he stands rhetorically last, is given a laudatory description ("that living embodiment of virtue"), and is made to announce his own death and that of the Republic at a single stroke. Cicero's death is only wretched and pitiable, like Pompey cut down on the Egyptian shore, whereas Cato's, however undesirable, brings with it a certain defiant glory. Cicero is even denied any special virtue at the end: Livy had said that he stretched out his neck "without trembling" (*immotam,* ap. Sen. *suas.* 6.17) to the executioner's blade; others, like Aufidius Bassus, recount that he made some witty remark. None of that for Seneca.

---

[10] Gambet (1970) 180, 182 and Setaioli (2003) 60 rightly observe Seneca's idolizing of an idealized Cato and the implicit contrast with Cicero, but they do not mention the repeated and explicit juxtaposition of Cicero and Cato throughout Seneca's writings. Gowing (2005) 79 notes that Cato becomes a moral icon, and Gowing (2013) 249 points out that Cicero would have had more trouble fulfilling that role for Seneca.

We see this pairing of Cicero and Cato throughout the Senecan corpus. Pompey's, Cicero's, and Cato's deaths are again juxtaposed at *dial.* 6.20.4–6,[11] where again Cicero forms the middle member in a climactic series that culminates in Cato. Likewise in *De beneficiis* Seneca wishes to discuss those whose ingratitude brought about the ruin of their country. Cicero's unjust exile is briefly mentioned (*exulauit post Catilinam Cicero, diruti eius penates, bona derepta, factum, quidquid uictor Catilina fecisset, benef.* 5.17.2), but again only builds to the unjust treatment of Cato, who suffered constant political setback at the hands of the foolish Roman people (*Catoni populus Romanus praeturam negauit, consulatum pernegauit,* 5.17.2). Likewise the two are joined as generic types in *epist.* 58 (58.12, 16; cf. *benef.* 7.6.1). Indeed, even in *epist.* 97, when Seneca quotes at length one of Cicero's letters on Clodius and the Bona Dea scandal (Cic. *Att.* 1.16.5), he caps his discussion with a description of Cato's virtue (*epist.* 97.8) and a *sententia* where Cato plays the starring role: *omne tempus Clodios, non omne Catones feret* ("every age will produce men like Clodius, but not every age a Cato," *epist.* 97.10).

Thus, while Seneca does make a certain use of the declamatory image of Cicero, he tends to undercut it by explicit or implicit comparison with his idol Cato. Cicero, after all, humbled himself to receive Caesar's *clementia* (*clem.* 1.10.1), whereas Cato did not survive the death of liberty, nor did liberty survive the death of Cato (*neque ... Cato post libertatem uixit, nec libertas post Catonem, dial.* 2.2.2).[12] Cicero, simply put, cannot be a model for a proper Stoic like Seneca.[13] Cato is. And yet in an interesting wrinkle, Seneca acknowledges that Cato may be too hard for most to follow: if that should be the case, he recommends Laelius (*epist.* 11.10). This pairing is pointed and significant; Seneca repeats it several times elsewhere.[14] Laelius Sapiens, friend of Scipio Africanus and adherent of Stoic philosophy, gained an outsized literary reputation thanks precisely to Cicero.[15] Seneca thus first replaces a possibly exemplary Cicero with Cato, and then makes sure that even in second place Cicero is implicitly evoked only to be dismissed.

Seneca also grapples with that other facet of the schoolroom Cicero, viz. Cicero as master of Latin prose. He has no hesitation in claiming that

[11] Partially quoted in n. 8 above.

[12] Cf. Val. Max. 6.2.5 *quid ergo? libertas sine Catone? non magis quam Cato sine libertate.*

[13] Cf. Setaioli (2003) 66–67; note also Gowing (2013) 249: "For Seneca, Cicero's questionable moral authority still matters, and thus he excludes him from the canon of acceptable *exempla*."

[14] *Epist.* 25.6, 95.69–73, and 104.21.

[15] Most prominently in the *De re publica* and the dialogues *Laelius de amicitia* and *Cato Maior de senectute*, but also through incidental mentions throughout Cicero's works; cf. e.g. *fam.* 5.7.3, where Cicero makes himself Laelius to Pompey's Scipio.

Roman eloquence "burst forth" in "our Cicero" (*Cicero quoque noster, a quo Romana eloquentia exiluit, epist.* 40.11), and speaks generously of Cicero the stylist on more than one occasion. In a discussion of philosophical style, for example, Lucilius is instructed to read Cicero: his writing has a certain unity, and its pace, like the love of beauty in Periclean Athens, is moderate without being decadent (*lege Ciceronem: compositio eius una est, pedem curuat lenta et sine infamia mollis, epist.* 100.7).[16] His periods usually come to an appropriate close, unlike those of a Pollio (*omnia apud Ciceronem desinunt, apud Pollionem cadunt, epist.* 100.7). In this letter Seneca is keen to defend his teacher Fabianus from Lucilius' stylistic assault, but even with those interests in mind he yields pride of place to Cicero (*epist.* 100.9):

> adfer quem Fabiano possis praeponere. dic Ciceronem, cuius libri ad philosophiam pertinentes paene totidem sunt quot Fabiani: cedam, sed non statim pusillum est si quid maximo minus est.

> Tell me whom you'd rank before Fabianus. Cicero, you say, who wrote almost as many philosophical treatises as Fabianus did. I'll grant you that, but it's by no means a trivial thing to be inferior to the greatest.

Seneca openly acknowledges Cicero as the greatest writer of philosophical prose in Latin.[17] He goes on to list Asinius Pollio and Livy as holding the second and third place in his rankings, and sums them all up as being the "three most eloquent" of Latin philosophers (*tribus eloquentissimis, epist.* 100.9). Elsewhere Cicero is described as *disertissimus* (*epist.* 107.10, 118.1), *summus orator* (ap. Gell. 12.2.5), and the man in whose shadow other orators must stand (*Caecinam ... facundum uirum et qui habuisset aliquando in eloquentia nomen, nisi illum Ciceronis umbra pressisset, nat. quaest.* 2.56.1). Seneca here dutifully parrots what he had learned in school.[18]

---

[16] Cf. *epist.* 40.11 *Cicero ... gradarius fuit* and 114.16 *quid illa in exitu lenta, qualis Ciceronis est, deuexa et molliter detinens nec aliter quam solet ad morem suum pedemque respondens.* Note Seneca's aping of Ciceronian prose rhythm in the latter passage (double cretic and cretic-trochaic clausulae), matching form to content as he discusses Cicero's period ends. Setaioli (2003) 70–73 would see in Seneca's judgments a distinction between Cicero's own time, to which such a style was appropriate, and his own, to which it was not; cf. Fedeli (2004) 225.

[17] He could hardly do otherwise. There were certainly no Latin writers before Cicero who could compare; so Nepos fr. 58 Marshall *quippe qui ... philosophiam ante eum* [= *Ciceronem*] *incomptam Latinam sua conformarit oratione.* For what little we know of such predecessors to Cicero, see Rawson (1985) 282–297.

[18] He may try to undercut this praise somewhat in passages on philosophical style like *epist.* 75.3 *multum tamen operae inpendi uerbis non oportet:* has Cicero then wasted his time in gussying up supposed philosophical truth in rhetorical finery? Since Seneca himself cultivated such an exquisite

Now all this is high praise indeed, and even if Seneca himself did not believe it, a lot of his contemporaries certainly did. It is not then surprising that Seneca occasionally cites the eloquent Cicero as an authoritative precedent for word usage.[19] (In an odd twist, none of the words that Seneca cites is found in Cicero's extant writings, but it seems rather a stretch to think that he invented these passages out of whole cloth.) So Seneca, in describing the great benefits of philosophy, claims that Lucilius has not grokked how helpful it is and how, "to quote Cicero, it 'succors' us in the most important things and descends even to the smallest things" (*quemadmodum et in maximis, ut Ciceronis utar uerbo, "opituletur" <et> in minima descendat, epist.* 17.2). A Ciceronian passage in defense of philosophy naturally makes one think of the *Hortensius* as a possible source, and if that were the case Seneca might be importing some of the *auctoritas* of that canonical defense into his own apology. Likewise Seneca relies on Cicero's authority to use the word *essentia* (*epist.* 58.6):[20] *Ciceronem auctorem huius uerbi habeo, puto locupletem.* The humorous "afterthought" of "I think him sufficient surety" – a bit of legal language – underscores just how powerful that authority really was: who indeed could be a more reputable source?[21] So too is Cicero's word *cauillationes* said to be *aptissimum* (*epist.* 111.2). It is remarkable, however, that these three words (*opituletur, essentia,* and *cauillationes*) comprise an exhaustive list of Seneca's avowed borrowings from the man whom

---

prose style, it is hard to give these statements much credence, especially since he goes on to say that if a philosopher happens to be eloquent, he should make full use of his talent.

[19] And, although he expresses a certain skepticism about Cicero's poetry, Seneca also relies on Cicero's authority to introduce verses and verse translations into his philosophical prose (*epist.* 107.10–11). He jokingly disclaims all responsibility for this practice, avowing that he has only "followed Cicero's example." For his judgment on Cicero the poet, see *dial.* 5.37.5 and, with cutting sarcasm, ap. Gell. 12.2.6, where Cicero is said perhaps to have cited Ennius' verses only to make his own poetry look good by comparison. In this latter passage he also criticizes some of Cicero's Ennianisms in prose (*ponit deinde quae Ciceronem reprehendat quasi Enniana,* Gell. 12.2.7), but he immediately excuses Cicero on the grounds that he had to talk that way at a time when such verses were being read (12.2.8).

[20] Cf. Quint. *inst.* 2.14.2 *haec interpretatio non minus dura est quam illa Plauti "essentia" et "queentia"* (cf. *inst.* 3.6.23, 8.3.33), apparently implying that Sergius Plautus, a Stoic philosopher of perhaps Augustan date, coined the word. On the exiguous evidence for such a philosopher, including difficulties in the manuscript tradition of the relevant evidence, see Kroll and Skutsch (1910) §266.9 p. 163. It is hard to know what to make of this testimony.

[21] Cf. *OLD* s.v. 4, citing e.g. *CIL* 1.592.2.23. *TLL* VII.2.1572.82–1573.4 (Kemper) brings home just how Ciceronian this usage of *locuples* was (e.g. *rep.* 1.16 *quem enim auctorem de illo locupletiorem Platone laudare possumus, Att.* 8.2.4 *aut locupletior mihi sit quaerendus auctor quam Socrates*), and so perhaps Seneca is here referring to Cicero in Ciceronian terms. On *epist.* 58, see also McElduff (2013) 162–164, where Seneca is described as "trying to shuffle out from under the heavy shadow of Cicero" (164); she reads the citations of Cicero as an attack that points up Cicero's inadequacy as a translator of Greek philosophy.

Seneca himself describes as the most important philosophical stylist writing in Latin.[22]

Seneca has followed his own path as a prose stylist.[23] Out are the rolling Ciceronian periods; in are a staccato series of short sentences, each packing a pithy punch. The judgments on this style are legion: "sand without lime," according to Caligula (*harena sine calce*, ap. Suet. *Cal.* 53.2); more acerbically Fronto: Seneca's eloquence is like "soft little plums liable to produce a fever" (*mollibus et febriculosis prunuleis*, Fronto p. 153.12 van den Hout) and it should be pulled out of the ground root and branch. He may be a man abounding in *sententiae*, but these *sententiae* trot along and never rise to a gallop (Fronto p. 153.14–16 van den Hout).[24] Thomas Babington Macaulay famously said that reading Seneca straight through was like dining on nothing but anchovy sauce.[25] These verdicts aim at a feeling we all have when reading Seneca, namely that this is definitely not Cicero. Seneca has taken the declamatory style found in his father to a sort of perfection, beyond which it could go no further. The stage was set for a reaction, which, as we shall see, Quintilian will provide.

Philosophical Ciceronian Absences

Seneca simply does not often engage with Cicero's actual ideas. On occasion he will refer to some passage or other; for example, he quotes Cicero's opinion that gladiators who appeared to be protecting their lives were held in contempt, whereas those who held their lives in contempt were honored (Sen. *dial.* 9.11.4 ~ Cic. *Mil.* 92). He likewise mentions Cicero's cutting remark that even if his lifespan were doubled, he still would not be able to find the time to read lyric poetry (Sen. *epist.* 49.5 = Cic. *Hort.* fr. 12 Gr.). Once again, however, it is striking how rare these

---

[22] In *epist.* 58.1 Seneca complains about the *paupertas, immo egestas* of the Latin philosophical language as compared to Greek. He might here be engaging with the Cicero represented by e.g. *fin.* 1.10 *sed ita sentio et saepe disserui, Latinam linguam non modo non inopem, ut uulgo putarent, sed locupletiorem etiam esse quam Graecam.* But it must be admitted that his is a traditional complaint, most famously found at Lucr. 1.136–139, 1.832, and 3.260 (*patrii sermonis egestas*).

[23] Leeman (1963) 1.260: "There is no more striking contrast than that between the styles of the philosophical writings of Cicero and those of Seneca." On Seneca's innovative philosophical vocabulary, see Setaioli (2003) 68–69; Setaioli (2000) 111–217 is an invaluable and thorough discussion of Seneca's style in general. A more concise overview is provided by Williams (2015), and detailed lists of stylistic features are collected in the introduction to Summers (1910).

[24] In van den Hout's first edition this judgment was attributed to Laberius (*ut ait Laberius* follows). In his second edition he decided that *ut ait Laberius* refers only to the subsequent word *dictabolaria*. See van den Hout (1999) ad loc. p. 361 for justification.

[25] Pinney (1974–1981) III.178; cf. Pinney (1974–1981) III.180: "I have read through Seneca – and an affected empty scribbler he is."

passages are in comparison to what you might expect. Cicero was by Seneca's own acknowledgement his most important philosophical predecessor writing in Latin, and Seneca knew his work in great detail, but Cicero is damned by sustained silence.

It need not have been so. Consider Seneca's most explicit and detailed engagement, where he discusses how in the same material different readers will find very different things. It is worth quoting in full (*epist.* 108.30–35):

> cum Ciceronis librum de re publica prendit hinc philologus aliquis, hinc grammaticus, hinc philosophiae deditus, alius alio curam suam mittit.
>
> philosophus admiratur contra iustitiam dici tam multa potuisse.
>
> cum ad hanc eandem lectionem philologus accessit, hoc subnotat: duos Romanos reges esse quorum alter patrem non habet, alter matrem. nam de Serui matre dubitatur; Anci pater nullus, Numae nepos dicitur. praeterea notat eum quem nos dictatorem dicimus et in historiis ita nominari legimus apud antiquos "magistrum populi" uocatum. hodieque id extat in augur-alibus libris, et testimonium est quod qui ab illo nominatur "magister equitum" est. aeque notat Romulum perisse solis defectione; prouocationem ad populum etiam a regibus fuisse; id ita in pontificalibus libris †et aliqui qui† putant et Fenestella.
>
> eosdem libros cum grammaticus explicuit, primum [uerba expresse] "reapse" dici a Cicerone, id est "re ipsa," in commentarium refert, nec minus "sepse," id est "se ipse." deinde transit ad ea quae consuetudo saeculi mutauit, tamquam ait Cicero "quoniam sumus ab ipsa calce eius interpellatione reuocati." hanc quam nunc in circo "cretam" uocamus "calcem" antiqui dicebant. deinde Ennianos colligit uersus et in primis illos de Africano scriptos:
>
>> cui nemo ciuis neque hostis
>> quibit pro factis reddere opis pretium.
>
> ex eo se ait intellegere <opem> apud antiquos non tantum auxilium sig-nificasse sed operam. ait [opera] enim Ennius neminem potuisse Scipioni neque ciuem neque hostem reddere operae pretium. felicem deinde se putat quod inuenerit unde uisum sit Vergilio dicere
>
>> quem super ingens
>> porta tonat caeli.
>
> Ennium hoc ait Homero [se] subripuisse, Ennio Vergilium; esse enim apud Ciceronem in his ipsis de re publica hoc epigramma Enni:
>
>> si fas endo plagas caelestum ascendere cuiquam est,
>> mi soli caeli maxima porta patet.
>
> sed ne et ipse, dum aliud ago, in philologum aut grammaticum delabar, illud admoneo, auditionem philosophorum lectionemque ad propositum beatae uitae trahendam, non ut uerba prisca aut ficta captemus et transla-tiones inprobas figurasque dicendi, sed ut profutura praecepta et magnificas uoces et animosas quae mox in rem transferantur.

When a scholar, a schoolteacher, and a philosopher each picks up Cicero's book *De re publica*, they direct their attention to different things.

The philosopher marvels that so many things could have been said against justice.

When the scholar approaches this same text, he notes the following: there are two Roman kings of whom the one lacks a father, the other a mother. For there are doubts about the mother of Servius; Ancus had no father, he is said to be the grandson of Numa. Furthermore, he observes that the man whom we call *dictator* and in historical works is so named was called the *magister populi* by our ancestors. Today too that name exists in the augural books, and a proof is the fact that the man appointed by the *dictator* is the *magister equitum*. Likewise he notes that Romulus died during an eclipse of the sun; that the right of *prouocatio ad populum* already existed in the time of the kings; thus it stands in the pontifical books and so think Fenestella and others (?).

When a schoolteacher opens [or: explains] these same books, first he observes in his commentary that Cicero says *reapse*, i.e. *re ipsa*, as well as *sepse*, i.e. *se ipse*. Then he passes on to usages which the passage of time has changed; for example, Cicero says "since we have been called back by his interruption from the very *calx*." What in the circus we now call the *creta* earlier generations called the *calx*. Then he collects some Ennian verses, especially those written about Africanus:

A man whose deeds no citizen or enemy will be able to rightly repay.

From this he says that he understands that *ops* in earlier generations did not only signify *auxilium* ("help") but also *opera* ("work"). For Ennius says that no citizen or enemy could have adequately repaid Scipio's works. Then he congratulates himself because he thinks he has discovered why Vergil thought it was fitting to say:

above whom the vast gate of heaven thunders.

He says that Ennius stole this from Homer, and Vergil from Ennius; for (he says) that this epigram is found in these very books of Cicero's *De re publica*:

If it is right for anyone to ascend to the realms of the gods above, for me alone does the huge gate of heaven open.

But lest I too, while I'm really engaged in other business, slip into the mode of the scholar or the schoolteacher, I advise the following: listening to philosophers and reading their works must be directed to the goal of living a good life, not for snatching at old or invented words and unsuitable metaphors and figures of speech, but for gleaning beneficial precepts and marvelous and spirited expressions which can soon be brought to bear on the matter at hand.

This is a remarkable passage in which we see what could have been. Seneca demonstrates an intimate familiarity with the full range of details in Cicero's text. He is shown to be a master of antiquarian lore who can not only discuss the parentage of rulers in the Regal Period but can also cite other scholars on principles of Roman law. He knows the *De re publica* down to the level of individual words like *reapse* and *sepse* and has noted archaic usages like *calx* for "finish line (marked with chalk)." Such reflections lead him to consider the poetry of Ennius, where he not only explicates the word *ops* but also traces the literary history of "the vast gate of heaven" from Homer through Ennius to Vergil, all as mediated by Cicero's text. This is the sustained engagement with his illustrious predecessor that you might have expected from Seneca, and he plainly takes a certain delight in showing off his knowledge.[26] But no sooner has he given free rein to his inner scholar than he pulls back, claiming that philosophy should conduce to practical ends. As to the learned paragraphs he has just poured forth – what are they to him? The philosopher's engagement with the text has already been summarized: he is amazed that so much can be said *contra iustitiam*. Seneca is a philosopher, and so by rights he should content himself with that dismissal; the rest is presented as a satiric take on how Cicero can be read. In fact this curt dismissal is representative of Seneca's limited engagement with Cicero throughout his philosophical corpus.

Seneca knows that Cicero has written almost as many treatises as Fabianus (*epist.* 100.9), but he has nary a word about their philosophical content. He cannot even be bothered to refute Cicero's views; he simply ignores them entirely. There is occasional evidence that Seneca may be engaged in discreet borrowing from one or another of Cicero's works, but the evidence is sparse and hard to evaluate – a shared source can never be excluded and is at least sometimes likely.[27] By and large Seneca damns Cicero by silence. This silent treatment could spring from a number of causes, but there are a couple of notions that we can immediately discount. First, as is by now abundantly clear, Seneca did not ignore Cicero's *philosophica* out of ignorance. Second, Cicero had written plenty that was directly pertinent to Seneca's own discussions – think only of *amicitia*, for example – and so it cannot be the case that Seneca simply did not find

---

[26] Just before this passage he had explicated Vergil in a similar way (*epist.* 108.24–29), but he elsewhere quotes Vergil on scores of occasions, even though Vergil had very little to say of philosophical import. The contrast with Cicero is clear.

[27] To consider just one case, Cic. *Tusc.* 4.54 *sic iracundus non semper iratus est* ~ Sen. *ira* 1.4.1 *iratus potest non esse iracundus; iracundus potest aliquando iratus non esse.* The ideas are certainly similar, but the language is not so close as to make dependency certain, and a common source or even a commonplace cannot be excluded. For a good collection of such possibilities, see Moreschini (1977) (this example taken from p. 529); cf. too the very speculative Grilli (2002). More general similarities are documented in Evenepoel (2007), so p. 181: "Both Cicero and Seneca are opposed to the Epicurean theory of friendship and deny that true friendship can be pursued out of self-interest."

anything relevant in Cicero. There were plainly things that Seneca "should have" referred to, things that he doubtless knew about, but that he actively chose not to mention.

Perhaps while Seneca valued Cicero as a pioneer philosophical stylist, he did not value him as a philosopher. Cicero was, by his own admission, more a translator and interpreter of Greek philosophy in Latin than an original thinker, his *philosophica* being mere copies of Hellenistic originals (ἀπόγραφα *sunt, minore labore fiunt; uerba tantum adfero, quibus abundo, Att.* 12.52.3). Even if some of us today think he is being disingenuous, Seneca may have found this believable or true. As a first-century Roman with an excellent knowledge of Greek, he had no need for Cicero's translations; he could betake himself to Cicero's undiluted sources. Furthermore, Cicero and Seneca had fundamentally different philosophical missions. Cicero had already done the path-breaking work of importing Greek philosophy into the Latin language; Seneca just wanted to do philosophy.[28] He was a philosopher, not an interpreter, and he is writing practical, "self-help" treatises. Finally and perhaps most importantly, Seneca wanted to establish his independence from and indeed superiority to his most famous predecessor. If you spend much of your time and energy engaging with Cicero, even if you consistently strive to refute him, you are inevitably playing the game on his terms rather than your own. The more hostile version of this idea is that Seneca feared that if he allowed Cicero to speak in his own voice, his readers would recognize Cicero as the superior writer and philosopher.[29] And so Seneca instead follows his own path, not restricting himself to the well-trodden routes of the predecessors (cf. *epist.* 80.1 *licebit tuto uadere, quod magis necessarium est per se eunti et suam sequenti uiam*).

Senecan Form and Function

There remains one programmatic area where Seneca introduces Cicero only to reject him. He was well aware of following in Cicero's footsteps as a writer of a published collection of letters, and he refers to them

---

[28] Cicero is very concerned to justify the project of doing philosophy in Latin at all (e.g. *fin.* 1.1–10). Seneca is not. On differences in philosophical mission and environment between Cicero and Seneca, see also Inwood (1995) 66–67.

[29] Quintilian, with some prejudice, comes close to expressing this view (*inst.* 10.1.126): *sed potioribus [= Ciceroni] praeferri [sc. Senecam] non sinebam, quos ille non destiterat incessere, cum diuersi sibi conscius generis placere se in dicendo posse quibus illi placerent diffideret.*

explicitly.[30] They are in one sense a model. Writing to Lucilius he observes that Cicero's *epistulae* preserve the name and fame of Atticus, which otherwise would have perished (*nomen Attici perire Ciceronis epistulae non sinunt, epist.* 21.4).[31] So too had Epicurus immortalized Idomeneus in his letters. This is the promise he holds out to Lucilius: because of his letters he is going to be famous with posterity, and he can make Lucilius famous too (*habebo apud posteros gratiam, possum mecum duratura nomina educere, epist.* 21.5).[32] Cicero must be the primary model here, since Epicurus' letters – as well as Plato's, for that matter – were addressed to multiple correspondents, whereas Seneca has chosen a single "Atticus" as silent interlocutor.[33] The fact that Atticus does not speak in the preserved corpus – in sharp distinction to correspondents in Cicero's other letter collections – provided Seneca with a particular model. Indeed it is tempting to speculate that it was the recent dissemination of Cicero's correspondence with Atticus that spurred Seneca to his own literary creation in the first place.[34]

So far, then, Cicero is exemplary, and yet Seneca is also very keen to dissociate himself from Cicero's letters. He intends to go his own way, and Cicero thus serves more importantly as an "anti-model." In *epist.* 118, in response to that standard epistolary reproach that he is not sending frequent enough letters, Seneca tells Lucilius that he will not do what Cicero tells Atticus to do: he will not just write whatever comes to mind (*nec faciam quod Cicero, uir disertissimus, facere Atticum iubet, ut etiam "si*

---

[30] On one occasion perhaps even referring to a letter now lost, although he may be misremembering (*dial.* 10.5.3); cf. Williams (2003) ad loc. pp. 146–147 and Setaioli (2003) 59.

[31] His prophecy appears fulfilled by Suet. *Tib.* 7.2 *Agrippinam, Marco Agrippa genitam, neptem Caecili Attici equitis R., ad quem sunt Ciceronis epistulae, duxit uxorem.* Cf. too Plin. *nat.* 35.11 *Atticus ille Ciceronis.*

[32] Note too that this passage, unless it was added in revision, implies Seneca always intended to publish the correspondence, which supports the idea that it is a literary creation: he could not otherwise have known in *epist.* 21 that he would write enough to Lucilius to produce a publishable corpus. Cf. n. 37 below.

[33] Inwood (2007) 142 thinks that Epicurus is the more important model, despite the pointed formal correspondences between Seneca's and Cicero's letters and Seneca's explicit allusions to Cicero's epistles. I am skeptical, but it is a moot point in any case, because everyone must acknowledge the powerful influence of Cicero on Seneca's project.

[34] So Wilson (2001) 186 proposes. The dating of the "publication" of Cicero's letters to Atticus relies almost exclusively on an argument from silence. Nepos had famously seen them when writing his biography of Atticus at some point in the 30s BC (Nep. *Att.* 16.2–4), and obviously Seneca knew them by AD 62 or 63. And yet Asconius, commenting on all of Cicero's speeches around AD 55, seems to have no idea of their existence in what remains of his work. If they were available, he should have known them. For the complete evidence, such as it is, see Shackleton Bailey (1965) 1.59–74 and cf. Setaioli (1976); more recent treatments include Beard (2002) 116–119 and the extremely skeptical Nicholson (1998).

rem nullam habebit, quod in buccam uenerit scribat", epist. 118.1, also *apoc.*
1.2; cf. Cic. *Att.* 1.12.4). Why? He explains (*epist.* 118.2):

> numquam potest deesse quod scribam, ut omnia illa quae Ciceronis
> implent epistulas transeam: quis candidatus laboret; quis alienis, quis
> suis uiribus pugnet; quis consulatum fiducia Caesaris, quis Pompei, quis
> arcae petat; quam durus sit fenerator Caecilius, a quo minoris centesimis
> propinqui nummum mouere non possint. sua satius est mala quam aliena
> tractare.

> I can never lack for things to write, even ignoring everything that fills the
> letters of Cicero: what candidate is struggling; who is reliant on the strength
> of others, who on his own; who is seeking the consulship with Caesar's
> backing, who with Pompey's, who with a pile of gold; how harsh a usurer
> Caecilius is, from whom even his relatives can't borrow a dime at less than
> 1 percent monthly interest. It's much better to discuss one's own ills than
> those of others.

Here again there is, on the one hand, the closest possible engagement with
Cicero. Not only did Seneca quote Cicero's closing of *Att.* 1.12.4; he also
imports its beginning, where Cicero had written *nam a Caecilio propinqui
minore centesimis nummum mouere non possunt* (*Att.* 1.12.1). He quotes these
passages, showing off his knowledge of the details of Cicero for a readership
that appears to be expected to recognize those details too, only to reject
decisively the content of Cicero's letters as a model for his own. His mind is
turned to loftier and more important things than the grubby trivialities of
life in Romulus' cesspool. This is a programmatic repudiation: Seneca has
chosen to march to the beat of a different drummer, and he is certain that
his way is better.[35]

Seneca has never been afraid to find his own philosophical path (*epist.*
33.11):

> quid ergo? non ibo per priorum uestigia? ego uero utar uia uetere, sed si
> propiorem planioremque inuenero, hanc muniam.

> What then? Will I not follow the tracks of my predecessors? I will indeed use
> the old path, but if I find a closer and better one, that's what I'll pursue.

Although he is not referring directly to Cicero here, this bold statement
neatly encapsulates his relationship to that predecessor too. Cicero, however illustrious he may be as a Latin philosopher, is of little consequence to
Seneca because Seneca believes that he has found a new and better path to
philosophical truth.

---

[35] On Pliny's reaction to these letters, see. p. 308 below.

Cicero famously wrote letters to Atticus; Seneca famously wrote letters to Lucilius – and there the similarity seems to end. Cicero did not use his letters as a vehicle for philosophical instruction, and Seneca explicitly rejects writing Ciceronian letters filled with tawdry twaddle from Rome. Cicero's Atticus correspondence was never supposed to see the light of day, whereas Seneca's letters were destined for a broader reading public from the moment of their composition. Cicero's missives span more than twenty years; Seneca's perhaps two. Conversely, Cicero's philosophizing was done in dialogue guise, while Seneca's so-called *Dialogi* often seem more like extended philosophical essays.

Consider for a moment, however, the notion that Seneca's letters are actually a sophisticated blending of genres, a radical innovation in philosophical instruction.[36] I believe that the letters to Lucilius are a fictional creation; they are an epistolary form for Seneca's philosophical output.[37] Seneca has at any rate stripped Lucilius of all individuality, part and parcel of his rejection of trivial business in favor of universal philosophy. What if he has chosen to rework the traditional philosophical dialogue in the form of a record of extended correspondence?[38] An epistolary exchange allows Seneca to return to earlier topics and to have long excursuses at will. He is often keen to note how similar letters are to a conversation. He says, for example, that he wants his letters to be just as his conversation would be if he and Lucilius were sitting or walking together and conversing, easy and

---

[36] From the time of Montaigne and Bacon until fairly recently there was a tendency to ignore the letters' epistolary form altogether; they were seen as "essays in epistolary guise" (Edwards [2015] 41). Wilson (1987), among others, helped restore an appreciation of the letters' epistolary nature.

[37] The bibliography on this issue is immense, but Griffin (1976) 416–419 remains the most convincing summary of the reasons for believing that the correspondence is fictional. The most important point is that the letters are presented in a seemingly impossible chronology: they are supposedly written from winter 62 or 63 through autumn 64 (see Griffin [1976] 400), which would have required Seneca on occasion to perform such prodigies as sending thirty-two letters in forty days – and yet each letter could have taken months to reach Lucilius. He thus often could not have waited for a reply and would have had to send multiple letters at the same time, which, as Griffin says, "is to take all meaning out of the phrase 'genuine correspondence'" (418). (Subsidiary points include, for example, Lucilius' astonishingly swift spiritual progress from Epicurean [*epist.* 23.9 *Epicuri tui*] to Stoic sage; see Griffin [1976] 350–353). Other scholars, however, do continue to maintain that the letters are a genuine record of correspondence; see e.g. Setaioli (2014) 193–194 with references to previous scholarship, along with the bibliography collected in Wilson (1987) 119 n. 3.

[38] The dialogic character of the letters has been noted by scholars from Maurach (1970) 198–199 to Griffin (1976) 419 (with earlier references) to Inwood (2007) 146 and Williams (2015) 135–136. None of them, however, develops this observation as I do here. They tend to see the "dialogue" aspects of the correspondence as a mere rhetorical device within individual letters, not as a deliberate generic choice that has fundamental implications for Seneca's entire epistolary project. Roller (2015) goes a long way to putting the "dialogue" back in Seneca's *Dialogi*, making some similar arguments to mine here, but he deliberately segregates the *Epistulae* (pp. 65–66).

natural (*qualis sermo meus esset si una desideremus aut ambularemus, inlaboratus et facilis, tales esse epistulas meas uolo, epist.* 75.1).

The idea of a letter as a conversation between absent friends was not new; Cicero himself claims that when he reads his brother's letters he seems to hear him, and when he writes he seems to speak to him (*cum tua lego, te audire ... cum ad te scribo, tecum loqui uideor, ad Q. fr.* 1.1.45). So already Artemon (2nd cent. BC), the editor of Aristotle's correspondence, had contended that letters should be written in the same way as a dialogue, since, he said, a letter is one half of a dialogue (δεῖ ἐν τῷ αὐτῷ τρόπῳ διάλογόν τε γράφειν καὶ ἐπιστολάς· εἶναι γὰρ τὴν ἐπιστολὴν οἷον τὸ ἕτερον μέρος τοῦ διαλόγου, ap. Dem. 223). Seneca thus had good precedent for this idea, which he expresses again in *epist.* 67.2:

> cum libellis mihi plurimus sermo est. si quando interuenerunt epistulae tuae, tecum esse mihi uideor et sic adficior animo tamquam tibi non rescribam sed respondeam. itaque et de hoc quod quaeris, quasi conloquar tecum, quale sit una scrutabimur.

> I am absorbed in conversation with my books. But whenever your letters arrive, I seem to myself to be there with you and I feel as if I'm not writing back to you but replying. And so we'll investigate this thing you're asking about together, as if I were talking with you.

The whole conceit of Seneca's letter collection is that it represents an extended series of conversations between himself and his correspondent Lucilius. Lucilius is in Sicily and Seneca is not, and so, although Seneca urges Lucilius to come to him (*epist.* 6.6, 35.3), letters are the best available substitute for face-to-face conversation (*epist.* 40.1; cf. *epist.* 38). They show a constant awareness of their own nature as near-dialogues. Seneca speaks directly to Lucilius, and often refers to what Lucilius had written, especially in the beginning of a letter (*epist.* 3.1):

> SENECA LVCILIO SVO SALVTEM
> epistulas ad me perferendas tradidisti, ut scribis, amico tuo; deinde admones me ne omnia cum eo ad te pertinentia communicem, quia non soleas ne ipse quidem id facere: ita eadem epistula illum et dixisti amicum et negasti.

> Dear Lucilius,
> You write that you entrusted letters to a friend to give to me; then you warn me not to share with him everything that pertains to you, because, you say, even you don't usually do that. Thus in one and the same letter you said that he both was a friend and wasn't.

The second-person verbs bring the absent Lucilius before our very eyes, and we learn precise details about the contents of Lucilius' own letter. The reported subjunctive in *quia non soleas ne ipse quidem id facere* should mean that Lucilius himself had written something like *ne ipse quidem id facere soleo*, which Seneca here quotes back to him to demonstrate the contradiction latent in his own words. This is a fairly typical opening to a Senecan letter. He does not simply begin to discourse on his theme – friendship – but rather maintains the fiction that he only happens to be writing about this subject because Lucilius had asked him to do so.

It is not surprising that second-person verbs litter the correspondence; Seneca is, after all, writing to a "you." It is perhaps more surprising how often Lucilius and others are given a voice of their own. Nearly a hundred times, for example, words are put into Lucilius' mouth with *inquis*, particularly objections: *"difficile est" inquis "animum perducere ad contemptionem animae"* ("'it is difficult,' you say, 'to bring the mind to the point that it can despise life,'" *epist.* 4.4). Seneca shoots back that if lesser men can bring themselves to commit suicide for frivolous reasons (think of the spurned lover!), the virtuous man should have no difficulty in banishing fear of death. Or: *"sed modo" inquis "hunc librum euoluere uolo, modo illum"* ("'but now,' you say, 'I want to read this book, and now that one,'" *epist.* 2.4) – Seneca counters that it is the haughty man who flits from dish to dish, which corrupt him rather than nourish him. Later Seneca recommends that Lucilius leave behind money and power, but *"moratur" inquis "me res familiaris"* ("'what delays me,' you say, 'is my estate,'" *epist.* 17.1) – Seneca replies that philosophy is more enriching than any material estate. So on and on throughout the correspondence, from the first letter (*interrogabis fortasse . . ., epist.* 1.4) to the last (*"quid ergo" inquis . . ., epist.* 124.19), Seneca constantly ventriloquizes Lucilius and so creates a dialogic effect. In his 124 transmitted letters, Seneca uses *inquis* some 73 times.[39] In the vastly larger Ciceronian letter corpus, the word occurs only 23 times; indeed, in the entire corpus of Cicero's writings there are only 42 instances of *inquis*.[40]

Seneca allows yet other voices into the conversation as well. More than 150 times he introduces someone else's words with *inquit*, and he quotes both to approve (e.g. *"satis sunt" inquit "mihi pauci, satis est unus, satis est nullus"* is introduced by *bene et ille, epist.* 7.11) and to refute (*"sed ego" inquit*

---

[39] *Dicis, scribis*, and other similar verbs are also found.

[40] *Inquis* seems generally to introduce an imagined objection, while *dicis* and *scribis* report what Lucilius had supposedly written.

"uiuere uolo ... inuitus relinquo officia uitae" is met by the response that *unum esse ex uitae officiis et mori, epist.* 77.19). Seneca's epistolary dialogue thus incorporates a variety of viewpoints, but he has complete control over their presentation. Of course the writer of a traditional dialogue also has complete control over what its characters say, and yet such authors are more constrained by the form to mimic a natural conversation, or if they choose not to do so the literary flaw is more obvious. Seneca, on the other hand, plays a much more clever game: he talks only about what he wants to discuss, and only allows those objections to be voiced that he would like to refute.

This tendency reaches its apex in a letter like *epist.* 66, where Seneca says that he recently ran into his old *condiscipulus* Claranus. Claranus has grown old and frail over the years, but his soul is strong, and Seneca spent several days with him engaged in conversation. He writes now to Lucilius eager to pour forth and pass on those conversations to him (*multi nobis sermones fuerunt, quos subinde egeram et ad te permittam, epist.* 66.5). On the first day they investigated the philosophical question of how *bona* can be equal if they have a *triplex condicio*, and Seneca reports their results in great detail. He allows Lucilius to "interrupt" and "object" periodically: *"quid ergo? nihil interest inter gaudium et dolorum inflexibilem patientiam?"* ("What then? Is there no difference between joy and steadfast suffering of pain?," *epist.* 66.14), and of course responds to such objections (*nihil, quantum ad ipsas uirtutes*, "none at all, as far as the virtues themselves are concerned"). He even allows for interjections from a generic "other," e.g.: *scio quid mihi responderi hoc loco possit "hoc nobis persuadere conaris ...?"* ("I know what someone might respond to me at this point: 'Are you trying to persuade us that ...?,'" *epist.* 66.18), and then retorts *sed hoc respondeo* ("but this is my response," *epist.* 66.19). There are frequent questions to drive the argument forward (e.g. *quorsus haec pertinent?, epist.* 66.27). He veers between reporting the conversation with Claranus and direct address to Lucilius (e.g. *hoc ut scias ita esse, epist.* 66.21). In the lengthy compass of this letter (some thirteen pages), Seneca deploys in a novel way all the techniques of the Ciceronian dialogue: there is a narrative frame where we learn about Claranus, then Seneca reports their conversation to Lucilius, and Lucilius is allowed to "intervene" and question Seneca.

Now you might object that this is merely a rhetorical technique, the sort of thing I am doing right now when I claim that "you might object." It is indeed a rhetorical technique – who would deny that? – and yet if I were to present all my arguments as I have in this sentence and the one before it, you would quickly notice that something unusual is going on. Seneca uses *inquis* more than any other preserved Latin writer of antiquity; in fact, of the 233 instances of the word in the PHI corpus, nearly a third belong to him. Such a preponderance goes beyond a mere rhetorical technique; Seneca is plainly aiming for an extraordinary effect – and he achieves it.

This effect is perfectly paired with the novel form of Seneca's letter collection. As John Schafer has argued, the letters dramatize Lucilius' moral education and improvement over the course of his friendship with Seneca.[41] The earlier letters have a particularly lively and chatty style, and Seneca closes each one with a choice philosophical quotation drawn from his daily reading. By letter 31, Seneca begins to see Lucilius progressing (*epist.* 31.1; cf. 32), and so he stops his old practice of concluding his correspondence with his "thought of the day." Lucilius remonstrates with him; Seneca remains firm (*epist.* 33). The letters become longer and increasingly technical, especially after Lucilius' apparent retirement from public life (*epist.* 68, or at least by *epist.* 82),[42] culminating in the treatises on *decreta* and *praecepta* in 94 and 95. The remainder of the letters are "both idiosyncratic in their interests and technical in their exposition: Lucilius has reached the stage where he is competently absorbing a wide range of philosophical texts on his own, and need only trouble Seneca on certain difficulties."[43] By the end of the extant correspondence, Lucilius is fully a convert and well on his way to being a true Stoic philosopher.

Such a conversion is, writ large, precisely what the writer of a philosophical dialogue aims at in a smaller compass. It is, in fact, the way these things are supposed to happen in real life. Two philosophers walk into a bar, diametrically opposed foes. They drink and they debate, and in the end one prevails and the other gratefully acknowledges that he now sees the truth. (Or perhaps it just ends in aporia and a hangover.) But the writer of a dialogue is constrained to a conversation stretching over a few hours, or at most a few days. A character may be convinced of this or that proposition, but the proposition in question will be relatively restricted in scope: is a rhapsode divinely inspired or simply a skilled craftsman? Should an orator confine his studies to speaking or embrace law and philosophy as well? What is the nature of love? These are important topics, broad and expansive even, but they are limited. By spreading his own dialogic letters out over a period of fictional months and years, Seneca can expound an entire philosophical system. He can treat of individual questions in single

---

[41] Schafer (2011); the idea *in nuce* goes back at least to Griffin (1976) 351.
[42] On Lucilius' retirement narrative, see Wilson (1987) 112.
[43] Schafer (2011) 39; so too Griffin (1976) 353.

letters; he can take extended detours and excursuses; he can refer to earlier discussions and deepen or nuance them.[44] He can also return to the same topics again and again. By the end he has managed to present the whole of his doctrine, as much as possible through *exempla* rather than *praecepta* (*longum iter est per praecepta, breue et efficax per exempla, epist.* 6.5), and Lucilius has been entirely won over.

To mount a very imperfect analogy, a philosophical dialogue is like a two-hour feature film. There is a lot that can be done over the course of a such a film, but it is an inherently limited form because of its time restriction. The traditional letter, on the other hand, is like a typical television program. It is short and episodic, and stringing a series of them together often creates a whole that is simply the sum of its parts. Seneca's innovative approach is more like a big-budget miniseries. He combines the best of the thoughtfulness and production values of a film with the more expansive time horizon of the television series, and by following the plot through to the end we are taken along Lucilius' spiritual journey.

In creating this novel form, Seneca is engaging with Cicero in a wholly unexpected way. From reading Cicero's letters to Atticus he must have understood the possibilities of the genre (cf. Nep. *Att.* 16.4), but he rejects letters in a Ciceronian vein. He instead chooses to create a mosaic of philosophical conversations in epistolary form, which, when put together, create an all-encompassing philosophical dialogue tending toward the complete conversion of its interlocutor. Here, of course, Seneca can play a double game. When he writes in the second person, he nominally addresses Lucilius. But since we never read Lucilius' letters, he remains a creation of our imagination, and it is very easy to picture Seneca addressing *us* in his second-person exhortations. The dialogue can thus be realigned along an entirely new conversational axis: Seneca speaks to us.

Seneca's letters invite such a reading because they are so exquisitely self-aware. He is not, as Schafer observes, especially innovative in doctrine.[45] What he presents is traditional Stoic philosophy. And yet he arranges it in an entirely new fashion. As he himself says, the late-comer is in the best position of all (*epist.* 64.8):[46]

---

[44] For a collection of cross-references in the *Epistulae*, see Setaioli (2014) 193 n. 20. To these add *epist.* 121.18 and note that *epist.* 10 develops *epist.* 8, which in turn had cited *epist.* 7. See also Wilson (1987) 110–111, 115, 117 for some examples of recurring themes across the *Epistles*.

[45] Schafer (2011) 33.

[46] Quoted by Schafer (2011) 33 n. 5. Cf. Seneca's famous words to Lucilius as the latter contemplates writing a poem on the well-worn subject of Mount Aetna (*epist.* 79.6): *multum interest utrum ad*

sed etiam si omnia a ueteribus inuenta sunt, hoc semper nouum erit, usus et inuentorum ab aliis scientia ac dispositio ... animi remedia inuenta sunt ab antiquis; quomodo autem admoueantur aut quando nostri operis est quaerere.

But even if everything has already been discovered by our predecessors, this will always be novel, how to use and understand and present what others have discovered ... The remedies of the soul have been discovered by our predecessors; but it is our business to find out how and when they should be applied.

This is the very project of Seneca's letters. So too Seneca can propose a reading program to Lucilius in such a way that he cannot but imply that he himself, the author of the very text that Lucilius – and we, by extension – are reading right now, should have a prominent place in the canon (*epist.* 2).[47] Such sophisticated meta-gestures should persuade us that Seneca could likewise be aiming at a similarly sophisticated blending of genres in his epistolary project as a whole. In this project he has drawn inspiration from both Cicero's letters and his dialogues, but through a kind of generic alchemy he has transmuted the Ciceronian elements into his own unique literary creation. Seneca again looks back to Cicero but follows his own path.

Senecan Educational Theory

In *epist.* 88 Seneca lays out his vision for a proper education.[48] The letter is long and programmatic, introduced, as usual, at the supposed request of Lucilius (*de liberalibus studiis quid sentiam scire desideras, epist.* 88.1). Unlike modern critics of a liberal arts education, Seneca first actually rejects any pursuit that conduces to the making of money. He goes on to say that liberal studies are useful only insofar as they serve a propaedeutic role, preparing the mind for the higher pursuit of philosophy. Philosophy, he avows, is the only true "liberal art" (*unum studium uerum liberale est, quod liberum facit, hoc est sapientiae, epist.* 88.2). Other studies are therefore only to be cultivated as long as a man cannot attend to the sublimities of philosophical inquiry.

---

consumptam materiam an ad subactam accedas: crescit in dies, et inuenturis inuenta non obstant. praeterea condicio optima est ultimi: parata uerba inuenit, quae aliter instructa nouam faciem habent.

[47] Schafer (2011) 42. Likewise he instructs Lucilius to read a philosophical text in its entirety (*epist.* 100.8 *sed totum corpus uideris*), which seems plainly to point to his own epistolary corpus as well; so Wilson (1987) 110.

[48] Cf. e.g. *dial.* 10.13 for similar reflections on literary studies.

Seneca carries out his refutation of the so-called liberal arts at some length. Noting first that some have thought that one must investigate whether such pursuits make a man good (*quidam ... quaerendum iudicauerunt, an uirum bonum facerent, epist.* 88.2), he claims that this is self-evidently a ridiculous inquiry. The liberal arts do not even profess to aim at such a goal: the *grammaticus* is concerned with language, or if he ventures beyond that, perhaps with history or even poetry. But what do these have to do with *uirtus* (*epist.* 88.3)? Only the philosopher can teach virtue. Neither Homer nor music nor geometry nor astronomy avail a whit (*epist.* 88.5–17), to say nothing of such nonsense as painting or wrestling, which do not even merit admission into the canon of what others define as liberal arts (*epist.* 88.18–19). The liberal arts may contribute much in other areas, but nothing to virtue (*ad alia multum, ad uirtutem nihil, epist.* 88.20). Seneca reiterates his main point: *liberales artes non perducunt animum ad uirtutem* ("the liberal arts do not lead the soul to virtue," *epist.* 88.20). It is no objection to say that there is a part of philosophy which is aided by mathematics – it would be equally ridiculous to claim that food is a part of philosophy just because it is a necessity for a philosopher to eat (*epist.* 88.24–25). There follows a survey of the virtues various: *fortitudo, fides, temperantia, humanitas, modestia, moderatio, frugalitas, clementia* – the liberal arts do not form a man's character (*epist.* 88.29–30). Still other objections are heard, only to be refuted (*epist.* 88.31–42), and then Seneca concludes by acknowledging that much of what passes for philosophy is itself just as much a waste of time as the liberal arts (*epist.* 88.43–46).

Cicero, by contrast, is concerned to defend the liberal arts jointly and severally. This defense takes on many forms. For example, whereas Seneca mocks the connoisseur of astronomical phenomena in some detail (*epist.* 88.14–17; *hoc scire quid proderit?*, 88.14), Cicero emphasizes the importance of astronomical knowledge for a philosopher and a man of state. In the *De re publica* he notes that Socrates too studied *numeros ... et geometriam et harmoniam*, and after Socrates' death Plato traveled around the Mediterranean seeking such "Pythagorean knowledge" (*rep.* 1.16). Now we cannot take the words of a character in Cicero's dialogue as providing untrammeled access to the thoughts and opinions of Cicero himself, and yet Cicero's narrative frame for the entire dialogue revolves around the appearance of a "parhelion" (a "double sun") and a discussion of its causes and significance. Furthermore, Cicero closes the final book of the dialogue with the "celestial eschatalogy" of the *Somnium Scipionis*.[49] I could

---

[49] Zetzel (1995) III.

mention other examples, such as Cicero's own *Aratea*, but perhaps most telling are a few remarks in book 5 of the *De finibus*. Cicero here is describing Academic philosophy, the view which he himself – albeit not without reservations – espouses. Piso, the representative of the Academic position, claims (*fin.* 5.58):

> actionum autem genera plura ... maximae autem sunt primum ... consideratio cognitioque rerum caelestium et earum quas a natura occultatas et latentes indagare ratio potest, deinde rerum publicarum administratio aut administrandi scientia, tum prudens, temperata, fortis, iusta ratio reliquaeque uirtutes et actiones uirtutibus congruentes, quae uno uerbo complexi omnia honesta dicimus.

> There are many kinds of actions ... but the most important are, first, ... the study and contemplation of astronomy and those secret and hidden branches of natural knowledge which reason can penetrate; then the practice and theory of politics; and then prudence, temperance, courage, justice and all the other virtues and actions that match the virtues, which taken together we can, in a word, call *honesta*.

In this remarkable passage the most important activity is said to be *consideratio cognitioque rerum caelestium*. Moreover, the very virtues that Seneca names are listed here by Cicero, and he clearly implies that the study of astronomy conduces to them – the very opposite of Seneca's position. Cicero's philosophical school greatly valued "natural philosophy" as a stepping-stone to virtue; Seneca does not.

For a more general Ciceronian defense of the liberal arts, think only of the *Pro Archia*, in which Cicero asks the judges to allow him to speak with unaccustomed freedom about literature and *humanitas* (*patiamini de studiis humanitatis ac litterarum paulo loqui liberius, Arch.* 3). The whole speech is a stirring vindication of a liberal arts education, studded with memorable passages. If someone should ask whether all those virtuous men of days of yore were educated with such studies (*illi ipsi summi uiri quorum uirtutes litteris proditae sunt istane doctrina ... eruditi fuerunt?, Arch.* 15), Cicero confesses that he cannot be sure about every single one of them. A man can be virtuous without them, he admits, and nature without instruction more often arrives at virtue than instruction without a suitable nature. And yet, he adds, when *natura* and *doctrina* are combined, a truly special perfection results. Scipio Africanus, after all, and Gaius Laelius and Lucius Furius and Marcus Cato would never have devoted themselves to such studies unless they helped in the pursuit and cultivation of virtues (*qui profecto si nihil ad percipiendam colendamque*

uirtutem litteris adiuuarentur, numquam se ad earum studium contulissent,
Arch. 16). Even if no such practical gain were to be had, however, Cicero
claims that such studies would still rightly be esteemed a most suitable
occupation (*Arch.* 16):

> nam ceterae neque temporum sunt neque aetatum omnium neque locorum;
> at haec studia adulescentiam acuunt, senectutem oblectant, secundas res
> ornant, aduersis perfugium ac solacium praebent, delectant domi, non
> impediunt foris, pernoctant nobiscum, peregrinantur, rusticantur.

> For other occupations are not well suited to every time or age or place; but
> these studies sharpen the mind of the young man, delight the old man, are
> an adornment to prosperity, offer a refuge and comfort in times of difficulty,
> delight at home, are no hindrance abroad, are our companions by night, on
> travels, in the country.

It is hard to imagine a paean to the liberal arts more distinctly opposed to
Seneca's outlook.

Now a lawyer pleading for his client is perhaps not under oath to proffer
his true feelings – although I suspect that Cicero has done so here – but
when writing a philosophical dialogue at leisure he is more likely to have
done so. In the *De oratore*, which Cicero labored over with the greatest care
and diligence (*Att.* 4.13.2), we see his vision of ideal education in perhaps its
most perfect form. Cicero's own views are not far to seek:[50] the orator must
have wide and all-encompassing learning. He says this in his own words at
de orat. 1.17: successful oratory comprises all manner of knowledge, without which it is just empty verbiage (*est enim ... scientia comprehendenda*
rerum plurimarum, sine qua uerborum uolubilitas inanis atque irridenda est).
It demands familiarity with everything from jurisprudence to the liberal
arts (*eruditio libero digna*, 1.17). He reaffirms this same position a few
sentences later, saying that in his opinion the perfect orator must have
knowledge of every *ars* (*mea quidem sententia nemo poterit esse omni laude*
cumulatus orator, nisi erit omnium rerum magnarum atque artium scientiam
consecutus, 1.20). Seneca might perhaps grant that an orator in this sub-
lunary world must concern himself with such trifles, but the philosopher
need have no truck with them. Cicero, however, disagrees (*de orat.* 1.9):

> neque enim te fugit omnium laudatarum artium procreatricem quandam et
> quasi parentem eam, quam φιλοσοφίαν Graeci uocant, ab hominibus doc-
> tissimis iudicari; in qua difficile est enumerare quot uiri quanta scientia

---

[50] So e.g. Wisse (2002) 337 with n. 4: "The majority of his readers ... will have interpreted the dialogue
as an expression of Cicero's own ideas"; Fantham (2004) 106, Mankin (2011) 2.

quantaque in suis studiis uarietate et copia fuerint, qui non una aliqua in re separatim elaborarint, sed omnia, quaecumque possent, uel scientiae per-uestigatione uel disserendi ratione comprehenderint.

Nor does it escape you that what the Greeks call philosophy is judged by the most learned men to be, as it were, the creator and parent of all praiseworthy arts. In the field of philosophy it is difficult to enumerate how great and varied and comprehensive has been the erudition of so many men, who did not labor in isolation on some single matter, but rather embraced everything they could in their scientific inquiries and reasoned investigations.

Philosophy is here explicitly said to embrace as wide a field as possible, not to be confined to some narrow set of investigations. Moreover, if philosophy is the parent of all worthy arts, then perforce it is the parent of oratory, and so the orator must have a grounding in philosophy. After all, as Cicero will later say, no one can achieve eloquence without knowledge of both speaking and of philosophy (*neminem eloquentia non modo sine dicendi doctrina, sed ne sine omni quidem sapientia florere umquam et praestare potuisse*, where *sapientia* = philosophy, *de orat.* 2.5).

This is a cornerstone of the doctrine that Crassus will expound in the dialogue itself. The ideal orator, he claims, unites in himself a knowledge of rhetoric and of philosophy (e.g. *de orat.* 1.75–79)[51] – such a man does not now exist, perhaps, but he will be coming soon (*de orat.* 1.95, Antonius speaking, implicitly of Cicero himself). Indeed, this orator must possess a kind of "universal knowledge,"[52] being well versed in rhetoric, philosophy, poetry, history, jurisprudence, humor – the list goes on and on. (Note that in effect Cicero subordinates philosophy to oratory, while Seneca does just the opposite.) Everything that Crassus says in the first book of the *De oratore* argues for such a combination; as he says later (*de orat.* 3.21):

> est enim illa Platonis uera . . . uox, omnem doctrinam harum ingenuarum et humanarum artium uno quodam societatis uinculo contineri. ubi enim perspecta uis est rationis eius, qua causae rerum atque exitus cognoscuntur, mirus quidam omnium quasi consensus doctrinarum concentusque reperitur.

> For that saying of Plato is true, that all knowledge of these liberal arts and humanistic studies is joined together by a certain common bond. For when

---

[51] As Rawson (1985) 282 puts it, citing *de orat.* 3.56ff. (i.e. 3.56–62), for Cicero "oratory and philosophy . . . are the two parts, now sadly split, of a single whole, to which the earliest philosophers had devoted themselves" (cf. Leeman *et al.* [1996] ad loc. pp. 209–223 along with *de orat.* 3.132–143).

[52] Leeman and Pinkster (1981) 42–43, May and Wisse (2001) 10–11, Wisse (2002) 378, 383, 390. For references to this ideal in the *Brutus*, see Douglas (1966) xli.

the power of reason is seen clearly, by which we recognize the causes of outcomes of things, a marvelous and harmonious agreement of all knowledge is found.

This echoes the language of the *Pro Archia* (a *uinculum* binds all knowledge together) and again marks a strident defense of a "liberal arts education," here bolstered too with the authority of a Plato. Throughout we cannot but think of Cicero himself, who elsewhere describes his own time spent *in omnium doctrinarum meditatione* (*Brut.* 308): he practiced what he preaches.

More can be said, but the point has been sufficiently made: in both theory and practice, Cicero believes in the value of a wide-ranging education.[53] Seneca claims repeatedly that such a thing is superfluous (although he had obviously received just such an education himself), and he dismisses Cicero's arguments without a word. There is a cutting and polemical edge to Seneca's silence: while we cannot pretend that no one thought about education between Cicero and Seneca, Cicero was a dominant forerunner in this field for Seneca, and Seneca yet again chooses roundly to ignore him.

Conclusion

When Quintilian finally gets around to discussing Seneca, whom he deliberately postpones to the end of his "reading list" for the studious youth (*inst.* 10.1.125–131), he notes that he himself is widely but falsely believed to be hostile to Seneca (*propter uulgatam falso de me opinionem qua damnare eum et inuisum quoque habere sum creditus, inst.* 10.1.125). He subsequently insists that he was not in fact opposed to Seneca, just opposed to how Seneca had driven other, better writers out of circulation. He goes on, however, to damn Seneca with faint praise, noting that Seneca's followers had fallen short of him just as he had fallen short of the *antiqui*. His style is decadent and teems with vice calculated to ensnare the unsuspecting student. The implicit contrast, of course, is with Cicero.[54] While most of Quintilian's discussion is cast in terms of style, his project in the *Institutio oratoria* is also an explicit revival of the Ciceronian educational ideal (see next chapter). Insofar as that is true, what Quintilian rejects

---

[53] In theory we have seen; in practice he does not scruple, say, to read a Tyrannion's learned treatise on Greek accentuation (Cic. *Att.* 12.6.2), and he is proud of his *doctrina* in all manner of contexts.

[54] Cf. Leeman (1963) 1.278: "Cicero is the salutary example, Seneca the corruptor of youth, whose enormous and exclusive influence has created a vicious and corrupt way of speaking and writing."

about Seneca goes beyond just stylistics.[55] Seneca's knowledge of Cicero is grounded in the schoolroom tradition, but as we have seen, Seneca struck out on his own and dismissed Cicero as a model for life, philosophy, prose style, and education – and his view had apparently carried the day. Quintilian the neo-Ciceronian, on the other hand, will put Cicero forward as an exemplary model for these very things, and so he has every reason to condemn Seneca, particularly if he saw himself as Seneca's successor in the role of imperial tutor (*inst.* 4 pr. 2). It is to Quintilian and his circle that we turn in the following chapters.

---

[55] Even Quintilian's lengthy reading list itself is an implicit rebuke to the very selective approach to reading advocated by Sen. *epist.* 2.

CHAPTER 6

Tacitus: Dialogus de Cicerone?

The specter of Cicero haunted later ages, whispering incessantly, "Your prose is very pretty, but you are an epigone and you mustn't think that you can live up to my standards." And indeed, no one seemed to think that he could: everyone agreed that oratory had declined from Cicero's day.[1] The fixed and highest point of reference in their self-abasement is always Cicero himself, the acme of eloquence by universal assent.[2] This fact is itself quite remarkable, since in Cicero's own day no similar paragon of excellence existed. Cicero's *Brutus* surveys the whole history of Latin oratory, but despite allowing various luminaries to dot the Roman firmament (Cotta, Crassus, Antonius, Hortensius), Cicero can claim no one model.[3] You might object that this serves his own teleological ends, where he himself is the summit of Latin prose, and I would not deny that this is true. His narrative of self-promotion is in fact hungrily devoured by later generations. Nevertheless, it must also be true that there really was no such single exemplary figure until Cicero stepped into the breach.

Indeed, from our perspective there need be no such figure. Quick: who is the best writer of English prose? *Suum cuique* and *de gustibus* and all that, you might well respond. Thomas Babington Macaulay was a great prose stylist, but there are those who would prefer Ernest Hemingway's terseness, or the self-conscious brilliance of a David Foster Wallace. So, presumably, might a Roman have responded in 75 BC: he might have favored Cato's coarse vigor, or the stylings of an Antonius, or the ultra-modern Hortensius. In AD 75 the answer was Cicero.

---

[1] See e.g. Seneca the Elder (*contr.* 1 pr. 6–10), Velleius Paterculus (1.16–18), and Petronius (Petron. 1–2), discussed in ch. 2 above, pp. 76–91 (Petronius) and 000–000 (Seneca and Velleius); Luce (1993) 13 collects more disgruntled complainers. Modern discussions include Caplan (1970) 160–195, Kennedy (1972) 446–464, Fantham (1978) 111–116, and Williams (1978) 6–51. Van den Berg (2014) is the most prominent skeptic of the decline narrative (cf. n. 47 below); others, like Gowing (2005) 109–117, also note that the perceived change in oratory's place can reflect positive changes in the political situation.

[2] See ch. 2 p. 78 above.

[3] He does admit that he was particularly keen to imitate Cotta and Hortensius (*Brut.* 317).

Having filled this role, moreover, Cicero need hardly have kept it. Of orators active in 75 BC, he allows that Hortensius was the most distinguished (*princeps et erat et habebatur, Brut.* 318), but he goes on to recount Hortensius' decline and his own ascent. Cicero's own oratorical star, even if he had his critics, was in the ascendant all the way up until his death in 43 – whereupon, unlike the meteoric genius of his predecessors, it was never to dip below the horizon. He has maintained that position of supremacy virtually unchallenged right up to the present. Indeed, a sensitive commentator like Alan Douglas, having printed a mere nine pages of fragments from Cicero's contemporaries in an appendix to his edition of the *Brutus*, felt able to write:

> It would be unwise to generalize from a record so random and scanty, yet this much may be said. Some of these fragments . . . show a measure of rude vigour; a few are genuinely moving or amusing . . . Beyond this I see little to justify the often-heard cry that we would gladly surrender much of Cicero's surviving oratory for speeches of Hortensius, Caesar, Calvus, and others, except simply for the sake of variety and an increase of our knowledge of political or literary *history*. In terms of literary *merit* there is no escaping Cicero's supremacy.[4]

Perhaps, and so the Romans themselves certainly thought, but we have not a single word of Hortensius preserved for us to read today. I think it would be unwise to generalize about Hortensius' literary merit on the basis of dead and utter silence.

Cicero, in the *Brutus* and elsewhere, set himself up as the exemplary model that the Romans had not yet realized they needed. While insisting that he is not talking about himself, he likewise insists that no other Roman has even begun to approach the ideal orator (*Brut.* 322) – and no one can fail to realize that here he doth protest too much, for even as he speaks he is directly engaged in self-promotion.[5] Cicero was of course very good, and the Roman world, always eager for authoritative *exempla*, latched on to him as the pinnacle of oratory and never let go. The schoolroom, above all, needs models: you cannot very well just tell students, "Speak eloquently." You must show them what it means to speak eloquently, and "Cicero," as embodied in his writings, became a shorthand for that expression; he was

---

[4] Douglas (1966) 235 (emphasis original).
[5] Cf. his remarks about the perfect orator in the *De oratore* (1.95), where Antonius prophesies a future perfect orator who looks suspiciously like Cicero. On other occasions Cicero put himself forth unhesitatingly as an exemplar, as when he published his consular speeches in the service of the *adulescentulorum studia* (*Att.* 2.1.3). On Ciceronian self-fashioning generally, see Dugan (2005), Steel (2005), Kurczyk (2006), van der Blom (2010), Pieper (2014), Scheidegger Lämmle (2017).

no longer the name of a man, but eloquence personified (*non hominis nomen sed eloquentiae*, Quint. *inst.* 10.1.112). Moreover, the schoolroom perpetuates models. If you tell a classroom that Cicero is the unassailable apogee of oratory, and the students tell themselves and each other the same thing, and this goes on for generations, eventually everyone not only accepts it as the truth but indeed cannot see any other possibilities. And at that point it is more firmly fixed in the collective consciousness than even genuine truth could be.

Quintilian

Quintilian certainly agreed that oratory had gone into a precipitous decline; in fact, he went so far as to write a work *De causis corruptae eloquentiae.*[6] While the work itself has not survived, even the title speaks volumes about the lost volumes: not "On whether eloquence has gotten worse" or the like, since it is simply a shared assumption that, relative to the Golden Age past, contemporary Romans were living not in the Silver Age but rather in a time of oratorical iron.[7] The real issue was twofold: first, what were the causes of the decline? To this Quintilian plainly addressed himself in the lost *De causis*. Second, what can be done about it? Can oratory rise again, or must the Roman simply adapt himself to a life in diminished circumstances? Quintilian turns to these questions in the *Institutio oratoria*, published in AD 95 or 96,[8] and he comes up with a defiant program of educational reform to prevent the contagion from spreading.

Quintilian believes firmly that oratory's best days need not lie in the past. He says, for example, that even now the *orandi facultas* can be increased (*et adhuc augeri potest, inst.* 2.16.18), and similar optimism is scattered throughout the work.[9] In the twelfth book of the *Institutio* he states his view most clearly, and it is hardly surprising that he stakes out his position here with particular reference to Cicero (*inst.* 12.1.19–21):

---

[6] See the dissertation of Reuters (1887) for what little we know about this work, all of which is deduced from scattered statements in the *Institutio oratoria*. Barwick (1954) 10–14 speculates a bit more broadly; he believes that the causes for the decline of eloquence that Messalla adduces in the *Dialogus* can be paralleled in the *De causis corruptae eloquentiae*. I would be happy with this conclusion, but it rests on thin air alone, since we have not a word of the *De causis* with which to compare it.

[7] The implications of the title are plain, and van den Berg (2014) 246 n. 14 and 254 n. 37 is too cautious in questioning Quintilian's intent.

[8] Russell (2001) 3.

[9] See e.g. *inst.* 10.1.122 or 12.11.30 (the penultimate sentence of the last book).

ego tamen secundum communem loquendi consuetudinem saepe dixi dicamque perfectum oratorem esse Ciceronem, ut amicos et bonos uiros et prudentissimos dicimus uulgo, quorum nihil nisi perfecte sapienti datur: sed cum proprie et ad legem ipsam ueritatis loquendum erit, eum quaeram oratorem quem et ille quaerebat. quamquam enim stetisse ipsum in fastigio eloquentiae fateor, ac uix quid adici potuerit inuenio, fortasse inuenturus quid adhuc abscisurum putem fuisse (nam et fere sic docti iudicauerunt plurimum in eo uirtutum, nonnihil fuisse uitiorum, et se ipse multa ex illa iuuenili abundantia coercuisse testatur): tamen, quando nec sapientis sibi nomen minime sui contemptor adseruit et melius dicere certe data longiore uita et tempore ad componendum securiore potuisset, non maligne crediderim defuisse ei summam illam ad quam nemo propius accessit. et licebat, si aliter sentirem, fortius id liberiusque defendere. an uero M. Antonius neminem a se uisum eloquentem, quod tanto minus erat, professus est, ipse etiam M. Tullius quaerit adhuc eum et tantum imaginatur ac fingit: ego non audeam dicere aliquid in hac quae superest aeternitate inueniri posse eo quod fuerit perfectius?

Nevertheless, according to the usual way of talking, I for my part have often said and will keep saying that Cicero was the perfect orator, in the way that we commonly say that our friends are "good men" and "very prudent," even though none of these traits is given except to the perfect sage. But if I have to speak strictly and in conformance with the absolute standard of truth, I will continue seeking that orator whom even Cicero was looking for. I confess, to be certain, that he stood at the peak of eloquence, and I scarcely find anything that could be added to his virtues, although perhaps I might find something that I think he would have been going to prune away (for this is more or less how learned men have judged him, believing that he had an abundance of virtues along with a few vices, and he himself testifies that he restrained much of his youthful exuber- ance). Nevertheless, since he never claimed the title "wise man" for himself – and he was not given to modesty – and he certainly could have spoken better if he had been given a longer life and a more secure age in which to write,[10] I might think without reproach that he did not attain that summit that no one has approached more closely than he. And if I felt differently, I could argue more strenuously and freely for this position. Marcus Antonius claimed that he had never seen an eloquent man, which is a much lesser thing, and Cicero himself is still seeking such a man and only imagines him and creates him in his mind. Should I not be so bold as to say that something might be found in the limitless future even more perfect than what has come before?

---

[10] This line of reasoning agrees with Cicero's own thoughts; cf. *Brut.* 45 *pacis est comes otique socia et iam bene constitutae ciuitatis quasi alumna quaedam eloquentia.* Tacitus, however, will disagree vehemently: see pp. 270–273 below.

Quintilian is very much at pains to have his cake and eat it too: Cicero is indisputably the best, he is indeed "perfect" – but someone else could one day be "more perfect." How? The answer, implicit but clear, is by following Quintilian's educational program.

Contemporary education, Quintilian thought, plainly was not producing new Ciceros; it was indeed not even stanching the continued bleeding of oratorical vim and vigor. His educational program is thus conceived as a reform – and yet the reader of the *Institutio* will soon realize that much of Quintilian's prescription is hardly revolutionary.[11] After all, the careful study of Cicero's speeches with close attention to their rhetorical tactics and strategy must have been a classroom staple ever since Cicero published his consular speeches for the edification of Rome's studious youth.[12] Moreover, much of Quintilian's treatment of the technical points of rhetoric is entirely tralatitious, being merely a very skilled distillation and codification of well-known principles.[13] For generations Roman *rhetores* had labored to compile and organize the knowledge of rhetoric, like scholars carefully piling up notecards in neat stacks on the tables of some dim and dusty library. A true reformer would perhaps have flung open the windows, letting in light and a fresh breeze that would have swept all the established stacks of cards to the ground in disarray – only to pick them up again and reorder them in his own way. This Quintilian did not do; he merely wished to redecorate a bit and think about why the stacks were arranged as they were.

The most radical reform was in fact a neo-conservative move, a return to Cicero's own educational ideals, especially as enunciated in the *De oratore, Brutus*, and *Orator*.[14] There is a certain logic to this, of course: if Cicero is the best orator, and we want to be good orators (i.e. like Cicero), and Cicero has forged a path to the summit of eloquence, should we not do what the great man himself prescribes and follow in his educational

---

[11] Cf. Kennedy (1969) 11: "Quintilian describes schools *as they existed through most of Hellenistic and Roman times*, with comments and suggestions growing out of his own experience" (my emphasis).

[12] See n. 5 above.

[13] He admits this himself when he claims, in book 12, to be advancing beyond his predecessors (Quint. *inst.* 12 pr. 2): his work up to that point had been relatively straightforward, *dum tamen nota illa et plerisque artium scriptoribus tractata praecipimus*. While this is a rather self-deprecatory way for Quintilian to describe his contribution, comparison with other rhetorical manuals does show that other authors were treating these topics too.

[14] Sometimes very explicitly, as in the quotations of Cic. *de orat.* 3.201–208 and *orat.* 134–139 that begin at *inst.* 9.1.26. Quintilian proceeds to provide a detailed exposition of these texts – Russell calls it nearly a commentary – in the rest of the book. The magnitude of Quintilian's debt to Cicero is made especially clear in Cousin (1967), a massive study of Quintilian's sources, in the first volume of which it is only a slight exaggeration to say that Cicero appears on every page.

footsteps? This Quintilian does, and does very consciously; only in the twelfth book does he claim that he sails further out into the deep than Cicero had (*inst.* 12 pr. 4).[15] Thus Quintilian insists on the moral dimension of eloquence – the orator is a *uir bonus, dicendi peritus* ("a good man, skilled in speaking," *inst.* 12.1.1)[16] – and a thorough grounding not just in the technicalities of rhetoric, but also in the full range of the liberal arts. The whole person, Quintilian believes, must be educated in order to produce the perfect orator.[17] This stands in stark contrast both to Seneca's narrow insistence on philosophy (see p. 216 above) and to the typical manuals of rhetoric and the declamatory classroom, which seemed to focus exclusively on sententious fireworks and pretty points.

Cicero had proposed these same ideals,[18] but for him they were only ideals, and no one of his own time had ever managed to live up to them, with the possible exception of Cicero himself. Quintilian seems much more interested in implementing these ideals in reality. Cicero's dialogues were theoretical works that, although intended to grapple with serious issues and engage in contemporary cultural debates, did not lend themselves to easy transmutation via educational alchemy into classroom practice. Quintilian, on the other hand, has written a much more practical manual of instruction: he is a real teacher, and he speaks with the authoritative voice of experience. There is no evidence that anyone else between Cicero's death and Quintilian's floruit took the Ciceronian educational program so seriously; presumably other teachers had recognized it as merely an ideal, perhaps even an undesirable one. Quintilian, by contrast, sets out to describe in concrete and practical terms how the ideal Ciceronian orator should be trained and live from the cradle to the grave.

---

[15] On this passage, see Gowing (2013) 244–249.

[16] Cf. *inst.* 1 pr. 9 *oratorem autem instituimus illum perfectum, qui esse nisi uir bonus non potest, ideoque non dicendi modo eximiam in eo facultatem sed omnis animi uirtutes exigimus.*

[17] The description of Bloomer (2011) 83 is apt: "Education is wholly contained here; it is not preliminary to philosophy or later life; it alone is responsible for the most important transformation, that of boy into man, in fact, the ideal man, the orator."

[18] On Cicero's broad educational vision all would agree, but Winterbottom (1964) contends that "there was no doubt that Cicero was not concerned primarily with the moral aspect [of oratory]" in his rhetorical treatises (90). Nevertheless he himself cites *de orat.* 3.55 *quarum uirtutum experitibus si dicendi copiam tradiderimus, non eos quidem oratores effecerimus, sed furentibus quaedam arma dederimus,* and one need only think of the preface to the *De inuentione* (1.1–5) to see that Cicero was very concerned with the orator's moral character. The persistent emphasis on the importance of philosophy in the *De oratore* presumably conduced to a moral end. (May and Wisse [2001] 11–12 acknowledge that this is the *communis opinio*, but nonetheless dissent, saying that "high moral qualities . . . are part of the *prerequisites* for becoming a speaker worthy of the high name of 'orator'" [emphasis original]. Such a formulation, however, amounts to the same thing: it is important to be a *uir bonus* if one wants to be a *bonus orator*, and one becomes a *uir bonus* through philosophy.)

Once Cicero has been taken as a theoretical model, certain knock-on effects come about almost inevitably. For example, if Cicero's style is the *ne plus ultra* in eloquence, it is only natural that Quintilian should write relatively Ciceronian prose. (There are admittedly more than a few silver threads among the gold, but no one would mistake the Quintilian of the *Institutio* for a Seneca or a Tacitus.) Moreover, Cicero must assume pride of place as a practical example of eloquence: he is quoted more than 700 times in the course of the *Institutio*; Vergil is *longo sed proximus interuallo* with a shade over 150 quotations.[19] To understand just how outsized these numbers are, consider two other canonical poets with large corpora, Horace and Ovid: Horace is cited only 27 times, and Ovid a mere 13 times. Indeed, the sum total of all citations of orators not named Cicero is just 54. Even if we confine ourselves to Cicero's speeches, they are cited nearly 500 times – and Quintilian can only find excuse on 54 occasions to cite any other orator from any part of Roman history up until his own day! This shows how sincerely he practiced what he preached, and there can be no doubt that these emphases directly reflect his own classroom teaching.

Quintilian's revolutionary agenda was thus to revive Cicero's theoretical program of education for the ideal orator and to put it into practice. Why were these reforms necessary? Because contemporary Romans agreed that oratory had declined from Cicero's day, and Quintilian believed that by restoring Ciceronian ideals, he could also restore the standard of Ciceronian eloquence to Flavian Rome. It was an ambitious program, to be sure, but Quintilian was in a remarkable position to make ambitious *ex cathedra* pronouncements, and the ripple effect of his teaching spread far and wide. In this chapter and the next, I will investigate the contrasting responses of two well-known Romans who were influenced by his instruction, Tacitus and Pliny. Pliny was taught by Quintilian himself, and Tacitus may have been as well; Tacitus and Pliny were of course also friends and correspondents.[20] All three moved in the same circles and

---

[19] The numbers are based on Russell's (2001) Loeb index of "Authors and Passages Quoted." My rough count has Cicero cited 735 times. Rhetorical works: 195; speeches (extant): 426; speeches (lost): 62; letters (extant): 11; letters (lost): 16; philosophical works: 10; poems: 5; other (*commentarii, communes loci*, and unidentified works): 10. Note that for Quintilian, as for everyone else in the early Empire, Cicero was clearly not a philosopher: he is above all the orator *par excellence*. Cf. ch 5. on Seneca's rejection of Cicero's philosophy and the Epilogue on the late antique embrace of Cicero *philosophus*.

[20] Pliny tells us that Quintilian was his teacher (*Quintiliano praeceptore meo, epist.* 2.14.9; see too *epist.* 6.6.3), and some eleven letters addressed to Tacitus testify to their friendship; indeed no other addressee receives more letters in Pliny's collection (*epist.* 1.6, 1.20, 4.13, 6.9, 6.16, 6.20, 7.20, 7.33, 8.7, 9.10, 9.14; Tacitus is also mentioned in passing at *epist.* 2.11.2 and 2.11.17, 4.15.1, 9.23.2–3). The question whether Tacitus was actually Quintilian's student founders on lack of firm evidence;

must have known each other well, and it is entirely plausible to believe that the reactions we see played out in their writings arise as a direct result of these personal interactions and discussions.

In the *Dialogus de oratoribus*, Tacitus mounts a sophisticated theoretical rejection of Quintilian's ideas.[21] He accepts without demur the notion that oratory has fallen from its lofty Ciceronian heights and, like Quintilian, sets himself the task of determining the *causae* for this decline. Although the diagnosis is the same, Tacitus finds a rather different etiology for the disease than Quintilian and his contemporaries had: the reasons for the change, says Tacitus, lie not in the laziness or moral depravity of Rome's degenerate youth, but rather in the changed political circumstances of post-Republican reality. The successive strokes of doom that consigned Cato and Cicero to the grave also tolled the death knell for oratory: under the one-man rule of the Empire there was simply no scope for forensic or deliberative speech. There was nothing that an educational reformer or moral crusader could do to turn back time, no possible hope for revanche. Eloquence was dead, and the man of talent and energy would need to look elsewhere to win the fame and renown that were once to be found in political oratory.[22]

For Tacitus these were no mere academic ruminations. He himself, though a *nouus homo*, rose with a sure-footed step through the *cursus honorum* all the way to the proconsulship of Asia.[23] He moved in the very highest political circles under three or four successive emperors. It would be simplistic to point to a single cause for his success, and yet among the constellation of factors that enabled his rise, one, as for the *nouus homo* from Arpinum before him, was surely his eloquence. He was a well-known pleader at the centumviral court, and his oratory won superlatives from Pliny: Pliny gushes that in his successful prosecution of

---

as Syme (1958) 114 tersely put it, "Quintilian had a number of pupils, Pliny among them. Tacitus may, or may not, have belonged to the company."

[21] The view that Tacitus is writing to refute Quintilian is most forcefully expressed by Barwick (1954), but it goes back to Dienel (1915) and is picked up by e.g. Bringmann (1970). (It is far from universally accepted: see e.g. Heubner in Güngerich [1980] 207; van den Berg [2014] 246 n. 14.) None of these scholars, however, notices the sophistication and nuance of *how* Tacitus rejects Quintilian; unpacking and analyzing this "how" will be a major focus of this chapter.

[22] Cf. Barwick (1954) 21: "Für Tacitus war die Erkenntnis, dass zu seiner Zeit Höchstleistungen in der Beredsamkeit nicht mehr zu erreichen sind, wohl aber auf anderen Gebieten geistigen Schaffens, ein aufregendes und für seine weitere literarische Produktion entscheidendes Erlebnis."

[23] Syme (1958) 58–74 treats the career of Tacitus, to be supplemented by Birley (2000a) with further epigraphic evidence. Sherwin-White (1966) 100 goes too far in trying to redress the scholarly prejudice in favor of Tacitus over Pliny when he says that Tacitus' career was "of moderate distinction": it is hard to see what more a Roman senator could achieve in the political arena of the time, short of becoming emperor himself.

Marius Priscus, Tacitus spoke "most eloquently" and "in the grand style" (*eloquentissime* and σεμνῶς, *epist.* 2.11.17), and he elsewhere describes Tacitus as *eloquentissimus* (*epist.* 2.1.6). Tacitus was thus a man who could achieve conventional success by conventional means.

Nevertheless, although he could follow the traditional Roman career path as well as anyone else, Tacitus ultimately chooses to reject it. He does not seem to have published any of his speeches, and he eventually devotes himself instead to an entirely different sort of literary production. His theoretical rejection of Quintilian's Ciceronian revival is in fact reflected in the practice of his own life. Not only does he eschew publishing his speeches, he rejects the Ciceronian style wholesale – but only after showing, in the *Dialogus*, that he is the consummate master of that style. He chooses to engage deeply with contemporary theoretical debates on their own terms, only to say, while "doing" them perfectly, that they can no longer be done. Thus, while working entirely within the confines of the tradition, he manages to step outside and rise above that tradition, beating Cicero and his Quintilianic successors at their own game. His complex intertextual relationship of *imitatio* and *aemulatio* with his Ciceronian predecessors will be the focus of this chapter.

Pliny, by contrast, does not engage much at a theoretical level with Quintilian's teachings. Having sat at the master's feet and having drunk deeply of his precepts, Pliny focuses on becoming the perfect embodiment of the Ciceronian revival that Quintilian had instituted in the classroom. In the *Panegyricus, Epistulae,* and even – to a degree – in his own legal and political career, he tries to put into practice what Quintilian preaches and in various ways to become a Cicero *rediuiuus*. In the next chapter I will examine Pliny's relationship and rivalry with Cicero.

Tacitus and Pliny thus form a complementary pair exemplifying the bifurcated response to Quintilian's teachings.[24] One can imagine the three of them strolling beneath the covered portico of some Roman academy and hashing out these issues in their own dialogue on oratory, and it is not far-fetched at all to assume that each was making decisions that were both very self-aware and acutely conscious of the positions and arguments of the other two. Tacitus' *Dialogus* is in large part in dialogue with Quintilian and his ideas, and Pliny's literary works are likewise an implicit contribution to the debate. Nevertheless, while Quintilian is the immediate point about which Tacitus and Pliny pivot, Cicero is always the true fulcrum: he is simply foundational to any consideration, practical or theoretical, of

---

[24] On the intertextual relationship of Quintilian, Pliny, and Tacitus, see also Whitton (2018).

oratorical excellence, and as we have seen, Quintilian's educational program really just represents a repackaged version of Cicero's own ideals.
The fourth member of this imaginary dialogue, then, ever-present in the
mind even if absent in the flesh, is Cicero. Furthermore, the whole
discussion, as we have so often seen in Cicero's reception, is grounded in
the classroom, the place where young orators must be trained. And yet we
shall also see that, although Cicero's reception in later ages always has
a foundation in the schoolroom, it need hardly remain there: as in the case
of Seneca, both Tacitus and Pliny are able to rise above the classroom
tradition and make decisions in their own political and literary lives based
on a sophisticated and reflective engagement with their image of old Tully.

Dialogus de oratoribus: Authorship, Date, and Lacuna

The *Dialogus de oratoribus* is bedeviled by a variety of controversies,
including questions over its authorship, its date, and a potentially significant lacuna of indeterminate size – and all of this before one even begins to
consider problems of text and interpretation. I will briefly state my position
on these issues as a necessary preliminary to serious exegesis.

While the attribution to Tacitus hangs by a thinner thread than many of
its defenders might wish to acknowledge, the thread will hold. The *Dialogus*
survived into the Renaissance in one manuscript, the Hersfeldensis, discovered by the intrepid Poggio in 1425.[25] The manuscript contained three works
of Tacitus that were theretofore unknown, never having been mentioned by
any extant ancient author: the *Agricola, Germania,* and *Dialogus de
oratoribus.*[26] And how did Poggio know that all these mysterious texts
were Tacitean? An educated guess, since the manuscript itself attributed
the *Agricola* and *Germania* to Tacitus – but it was apparently silent about the
origin of the *Dialogus.*[27] Poggio's inference is not of the sort to comfort
skeptical scholars, and learned Taciteans of the stature of Beatus Rhenanus

---

[25] The story of the rediscovery of the Hersfeldensis is told with a marvelous combination of concision
and detail by Heubner in Güngerich (1980) 186–188, where most of the relevant passages from the
letters of Poggio *et al.* are also cited. For a leisurely stroll through the manuscript's history, see Krebs
(2011) 64–80; more details in Bo (1993) 11–41, 82–85.

[26] Some medieval writers may have known the *Agricola* and *Germania,* but we can only deduce this
because we ourselves know the works. See Winterbottom's account in Reynolds (1983) 410.

[27] The Hersfeldensis itself, as so often happened, soon disappeared from sight, and our text is founded
on its apographs. We deduce nevertheless that it did *not* specify the author of the *Dialogus* since
Antonio Beccadelli Panormita, writing to Guarino early in 1426, names Tacitus as the author of the
Agricola and *Germania,* and then goes on to say: "et inuentus est quidam dyalogus de oratore et est,
ut coniectamus, Corn. Taciti, atque ita ita incipit: 'Saepe ex me requirunt [*sic*, not *requiris*]' et
caetera" (cited by Heubner in Güngerich [1980] 186).

and Justus Lipsius doubted, primarily on stylistic grounds, that the Tacitus of the *Historiae* and the *Annales* could ever have composed such a work. A few scholars have in fact continued to question the attribution right up to the present day.[28]

If there were no other evidence, it would indeed be wishful imprudence to hope that Tacitus was the author of the *Dialogus*. Fortunately, however, there is one key allusion, first noticed by Adolph Lange in the nineteenth century, that disposes of all serious doubt.[29] At *dial.* 9.6 Aper says that one of the great downsides of poetry is that poets must leave behind the city and, as they themselves say, retreat *in nemora et lucos* if they are to produce anything of value. Pliny, writing to Tacitus himself, unmistakably echoes this very phrase and puts it in Tacitus' mouth, or at least his head: *itaque poemata quiescunt, quae tu inter nemora et lucos commodissime perfici putas* ("and so poetry is at rest, which you think can be most profitably produced among woods and groves," *epist.* 9.10.3). The thread is slender, but it will bear the weight of the attribution; the implied testimony of the Hersfeldensis and Pliny's reference, taken together, are convincing. Tacitus wrote the *Dialogus*, and this nets us considerable interpretive gains.

Tacitus wrote the *Dialogus*, but when did he write it? The work's dating poses the next – and somewhat more serious – problem.[30] The dramatic date of the work is reasonably clear: Aper claims Cicero should hardly be classed with the *antiqui*, calculating that it is some 120 years since his death, and concluding his reckoning of the lengths of the reigns of the intervening emperors with *adice . . . sextam iam felicis huius principatus stationem, qua Vespasianus rem publicam fouet* ("add in . . . that it's now the sixth stage of the happy reign in which Vespasian nurtures the Republic").[31] Although the precise meaning of *statio* has sometimes been disputed, in the context it seems clear that Aper must be referring to the sixth year of Vespasian's

---

[28] Most prominently Haß-von Reitzenstein (1970) 7–10, who followed Bardon (1953). Cf. too the thorough if fanciful Paratore (1951) 145–238, who would attribute the work to Titinius Capito (pp. 232–238). In some quarters skepticism persists, albeit apologetically: e.g. Crook (1995) 10, "I confess to an idiosyncrasy that some will find tiresome: I have never been totally convinced that the *Dialogus de Oratoribus* is by Tacitus."

[29] See Lange (1832) 5–8, reprinted from Dronke (1828) xviii–xx.

[30] Brink (1994) is a useful orientation to the debate, reviewing and discussing the evidence for various possible dates. I do not, however, agree with his end result, namely a date between 99 and 103 (p. 280). For some further reflections, see Edwards (2008), van den Berg (2014) 31–33, and Whitton (2018) 57–59.

[31] Note that the beginning of the Empire is in effect dated to the death of Cicero; not coincidentally, the Empire will also be said to have caused the death of eloquence. Eloquence, the death of Cicero, and imperial politics are forever intertwined. Cf. p. 272 below.

reign, viz. AD 75.[32] Now admittedly Cicero died in 43 BC, and so if it has been 120 years from his death to the dialogue's present, an arithmetical error of two or three years has been introduced. But it would be misplaced pedantry to press Aper about the extra couple of years; he has surely given the precise date with the Vespasian reference, and merely provided a round number here.

Tacitus was born in the mid to late 50s.[33] He claims that he heard this conversation when he was *iuuenis admodum* (*dial.* 1.2), which seems to imply that he was rather older at the time he wrote it down. While it is mere convention to claim that such a dialogue is the record of a real conversation, it must nevertheless have had the air of plausibility about it, and so a piece of juvenilia composed in the reign of Vespasian himself or Titus is a priori to be excluded. Furthermore, Tacitus himself strongly implies that he wrote nothing under Domitian (*Agr.* 3.2–3), and there are more subtle reasons to reject the hypothesis of authorship under Domitian as well.[34]

We are left with the possibility of authorship under Nerva or Trajan. The already mentioned allusion in Pliny to the *nemora et lucos* of the *Dialogus* provides a *terminus ante quem* of 109 or perhaps 110, the year of the letter's publication.[35] The *Dialogus* then probably saw the light of publication at some point between late AD 96 and 110. In the end there can be no absolute certainty about the date of composition, but the earlier the *Dialogus* was published, the more likely that it represents a direct and deliberate response to Quintilian's *Institutio oratoria*, which appeared shortly before the death of Domitian.[36] I believe that the *Dialogus* was probably the first of the *opera*

[32] The scholarly literature on the meaning of *statio* here is immense, and the entire issue is surveyed at length in van den Berg (2006) 210–236, who proposes a solution of his own, namely that *sexta statio* refers to Vespasian's reign in general (similarly Beck [2001] 168). There had been, by his reckoning, five "legitimate" emperors prior to Vespasian: Augustus, Tiberius, Gaius, Claudius, and Nero – that is to say, the three unsuccessful usurpers in the year of the four emperors are excluded (232). I find this much less convincing than assuming that Aper was simply giving an approximate number; nevertheless, it makes no difference for my purposes whether the dramatic date is AD 75 or 77.

[33] Syme (1958) 62 plumps for 56 or 57; Birley (2000a) 236 infers that he "should have been born not earlier than c. AD 58," but this is based on clever guesswork atop certain assumptions.

[34] Tacitus shows a knowledge of Quintilian's *Institutio oratoria*, published in 95 or 96 (see Güngerich [1951] 159–161 for the surest example, *dial.* 20.1, misremembering or deliberately varying *inst.* 4.1.8), and does not hesitate to give a prominent place to Eprius Marcellus, a supposed plotter against Vespasian who was subjected to *damnatio* by the Senate and eventually committed suicide. Quintilian, by contrast, had suppressed mention of Marcellus, perhaps in order to avoid offending Vespasian's son. For further discussion and references, see Mayer (2001) 23 with nn. 62 and 63.

[35] The dating of the publication of individual books of Pliny's letters is enormously complex; see the helpful tables in Bodel (2015) 106–108.

[36] The danger of divergent chronology is illustrated by Heubner in Güngerich (1980) 207, who, having plumped for a date *ca.* 101 (p. 195), feels that "der zeitliche Abstand zwischen beiden Werken" militates against the hypothesis that Tacitus is responding directly to Quintilian.

minora to be written, for reasons that I hope to explore elsewhere. Although the *Agricola* is usually assumed to fill that role, Charles Murgia showed that the work's famous preface need imply no such thing.[37] He then attempted to work out an internal chronology of the *opera minora* based on echoes and allusions, concluding that the order of composition was first the *Dialogus*, then the *Agricola*, and finally the *Germania*.[38] While I reject much of his evidence, I believe that with some refinements his argument is ultimately right. Regardless, there is no need to assume outright that the *Agricola* was the first of Tacitus' publications, and there may be at least some grounds for thinking that the *Dialogus* was the first to be written. This point matters because I am keen not to leave these works floating in some imagined literary universe, but rather to embed them in their cultural context. Tacitus of course could have been writing in response to Quintilian even in AD 109 (and I doubt that the terms of the debate changed much over the intervening decade), and yet it is more plausible to believe that he was responding soon after the *Institutio* began to circulate. Moreover, if the *Dialogus* genuinely has bearing on Tacitus' own career trajectory, as I believe it does, it makes most sense for it to have been written first. Still, as long as it was written before the *opera maiora* took shape, it will serve in part as intellectual justification. My main arguments will remain entirely the same whether the reader accepts an early date for the *Dialogus* or remains agnostic on the issue, but they will have slightly more cogency and explanatory power if the early date is right.

The last preliminary problem that must be dealt with is the length of the lacuna at *dial.* 35.5. The size of this gap is of real significance for our understanding and interpretation of the text, for if it is long, we may be missing a whole speech by an otherwise silent character, Secundus, which could radically alter our understanding of the work. In the fifteenth century Pier Decembrio claimed that the lacuna in the Hersfeldensis was of six folios, which would amount to about a third of the extant work. Fortunately, we appear to be on safe ground in believing that the lacuna was actually short and "contained little more than the end of Messalla's speech, and the beginning of Maternus', with some intervening chit-chat."[39] Structurally

---

[37] Murgia (1980) 101–102.

[38] More in Murgia (1985). I do not here take into account the argument of Beck (1998) 63–101, who believes that the *Germania* was written before the *Agricola*. He deals entirely in vague implication and inference, avoiding detailed examination of the texts themselves. (Indeed he dismisses the entire problem of the dating of the *Dialogus* in a few sentences on p. 79.)

[39] Mayer (2001) 50.

there are good reasons for believing that Secundus should not have made a speech,[40] and codicological arguments have shown that the lacuna is probably either of six columns, i.e. one and a half folios,[41] or a single folio.[42] Either way, there would be no space for another speech, and so we have the work more or less intact. We are therefore safe to interpret the text as we have it without excessive handwringing over known unknowns.

Dialogus de oratoribus: Structure and Characters

The details of the *Dialogus* will be discussed *suo loco*, but I provide here a short overview of the work's structure and characters. Tacitus introduces the dialogue as a response to Fabius Iustus' repeated inquiries about the reasons for the decline of eloquence. Claiming that he would be unequal to responding himself, Tacitus instead puts forward a dialogue on the subject that he says he heard as a young man. The three speakers are Curiatus Maternus, Marcus Aper, and Vipstanus Messalla; Iulius Secundus acts as judge; and Tacitus is silent. Aper and Secundus have come to Maternus' home the day after he had recited his *Cato*, a tragedy which had caused a stir in the city. They wish to warn him to be careful lest he offend those in power and come a cropper himself.[43]

Aper is keen to convince Maternus that he should abandon poetry and return to oratory, and here, with preliminaries dispatched, we reach the heart of the dialogue. Its structure is three pairs of opposing set-piece speeches. First Aper, champion of modernity, extols the virtues of oratory by comparison with poetry. Maternus responds with a defense of poetry. Just as he

---

[40] Haß-von Reitzenstein (1970) 106–130 provides a comprehensive discussion.

[41] Barwick (1929), which remains the *communis opinio*. In the MSS we are told variously *hic desunt sex pagelle; deerant in exemplari sex pagelle uetustate consumptae; multum deficit in exemplaribus quae reperiuntur; hic multum deficit; hic deficiunt quatuor parue pagelle; hic est defectus unius folii cum dimidio; hic deest multum: in exemplari dicitur deesse sex paginas* (Heubner in Güngerich [1980] 193).

[42] Murgia (1979), who argued that 1.5 folios are intrinsically unlikely to fall out of a manuscript – if you lose the front of a page, you should lose its back as well. His view has nevertheless not met with wide acceptance. Häussler (1986) 73–77, esp. 75–76, and Merklin (1991) 2271–2275 have undertaken a strong rebuttal, pointing out first that, despite the variety in the MSS testimony, none claims a lacuna of one folio, and furthermore that the Hersfeldensis itself may be preserving a notice found in its exemplar – which may have had a very different codicological structure from that of the Hersfeldensis, which we know something about from humanist letters – that reports a loss of six pages, i.e. perhaps a ternion. The question is enormously vexed (detailed bibliography in Bo [1993] 164–191) and of no consequence for my present purposes: the important point is that the lacuna is small.

[43] I take this warning seriously, because I see no indication in the text that we should not, but Gowing (2005) 112–114 has provocatively questioned how subversive Cato or a *Cato* could be in AD 75. Gallia (2012) 170 thinks that Cato might have been more dangerous as a philosophical than as a political symbol by this time; cf. his pp. 137–144.

finishes, however, Messalla arrives and, seeing them all intent on a serious conversation, jokingly asks whether he has interrupted some secret deliberation. When he learns the topic of conversation, he makes a chance comment about how Aper prefers to pass his leisure in the fashion of contemporary rhetoricians rather than the orators of old (*nouorum rhetorum more quam ueterum oratorum, dial.* 14.4). This leads directly to the second pair of speeches, in which Aper sallies forth on behalf of modern eloquence against the orators of yore. Messalla replies in a brief speech defending the ancients; then, admonished to keep to his brief to discuss the causes of the decline of eloquence rather than to prove that orators used to be more eloquent, he opens up his second speech with a long discussion about the decline of morals and the Ciceronian educational ideal, along with the pernicious influence of declamation. To this second speech Maternus, the final speaker, replies. He asserts that the decline has nothing to do with morals or education, but rather is predicated on the changed political climate: oratory can have no scope under an all-powerful emperor. After he says his piece, Messalla convivially notes that there are some things he might disagree with or add, if they had more time, but the sun is setting, and so they promise to continue the discussion anon and depart with a laugh.

If we strip out the interstitial matter – which will in fact be closely integrated in my argument[44] – the core of the *Dialogus* looks like this:

I. First pair of speeches: oratory vs. poetry.
    a. Aper: defender of oratory (5.3–10.8).
    b. Maternus: defender of poetry (11–13).
II. Second pair of speeches: modernity vs. antiquity.
    a. Aper: defender of modernity (16.4–23).
    b. Messalla: defender of antiquity (25–26).
III. Third pair of speeches: educational/moral vs. political causes of decline of eloquence.
    a. Messalla: oratory has declined because of corruption in morals, education, and declamation (28–32, 34–35).
    b. Maternus: oratory has declined because of a change in political circumstances. There is no room for oratory in the Empire (36–41).

It is worth observing that, as befits the dialogue form, no one character here has a complete monopoly on "truth." Nevertheless, while Maternus

---

[44] Van den Berg (2014) is right to emphasize the importance of treating the work as an organic whole; see esp. 98–123 on "reading around the speeches," i.e., the often-overlooked transitional matter.

cannot simply be thought of as the mouthpiece of Tacitus,[45] his final speech, presenting a radically new explanation for the decline of eloquence and coming at the culmination of the work, where it remains unchallenged by the other speakers, must have a position of special prominence.[46]

Cicero in the *Dialogus:* Formal Elements

The premise of the *Dialogus* is that oratory has declined from Cicero's day.[47] Given this premise and Cicero's acknowledged primacy in matters oratorical, it is hardly surprising that he is mentioned throughout the work. But Tacitus in fact goes far beyond the mandatory academic discussion of Cicero and a sprinkling of Ciceronian tags half-remembered

---

[45] So thought Barwick (1954) 17–22; see too e.g. 30: "Kein Zweifel, dass Tacitus sich hinter Maternus verbirgt." He also believed that Messalla was simply Quintilian (8–14). Güngerich (1980) 202 adopts a more moderate position that I would agree with: "Maternus ist . . . zweifellos der Protagonist und steht Tac. am nächsten, aber darüber sollte man . . . nicht hinausgehen." Cf. van den Berg (2014) 58–66 and, on similar themes in Cicero, Fox (2007).

[46] Only [Longinus] *subl.* 44 is parallel, but its dating is problematic. I suspect that Longinus is in fact responding to Tacitus (cf. Heldmann [1982] 286–293), but this is unprovable. Heath (1999) has made a strong argument against assigning the *De sublimitate* to the first century AD, pointing out that a prime reason to put it there is in fact its discussion of *corrupta eloquentia*, but this is circumstantial at best and circular at worst (cf. however Whitton [2015b] 220–222); Williams (1978) 17–25 makes some of the same points. (We obviously cannot say that the work is first-century because it resembles Tacitus, and then go on to say that Tacitus has an antecedent in [Longinus]!) Note that while there might seem to be some vague foreshadowing of Maternus' explanation at Cic. *Brut.* 6–7, 330, on the diminished place of oratory under Caesar, Cicero blames civil war and violence rather than one-man rule for the extinction of eloquence: cf. *Brut.* 45, discussed below p. 270.

[47] Van den Berg (2014) has mounted a challenge to this assertion, which until this point virtually all scholars would have accepted without demur. (The few exceptions include Goldberg [1999], Dominik [2007], and Goldberg [2009]. Gowing [2005] 109–117 agrees that the *Dialogus* is about decline, but contends that it also showcases the benefits of political stability. The redirection of Gallia [2012] 146 changes the terms only slightly; he claims that the work is "not concerned with the decline of rhetoric per se" but "the disappearance of a particular kind of speaker.") Van den Berg argues with great subtlety, but ultimately I cannot overcome the plain impression that the work gives: from the first sentence onwards – where Tacitus is speaking not as a character but as himself – we are told repeatedly that oratory has declined. (Even van den Berg seems to acknowledge this, e.g. [2014] 209: "Tacitus' text . . . seems resolute about the vacancy of the oratorical arena.") It is hard for me to see why Tacitus would have created this impression if he did not mean it. When we see pessimism or ambivalence in the ostensibly pro-Augustan *Aeneid*, we immediately understand why Vergil could not just come out and criticize the regime. By contrast, what motivation would Tacitus have had to cloak his optimism and praise for contemporary oratory under the guise of criticism? And so I propose no such radical rereading here. (Another recent radical reading of the *Dialogus* is Levene [2004], who sees in the contradictory speeches a complementary account of Roman literary history; his argument is subtle and may be able to coexist with other interpretations. Clearly literary history is a concern of the *Dialogus*, but I doubt that it is *the* concern. We each detect a [different] paradoxical tension between form and content.)

from his school days;[48] he instead engages in a sophisticated game of intertextual *imitatio* and *aemulatio* with Cicero and his followers, and after trouncing them on their own turf, he calmly picks up the ball and says that he will not play the game ever again.[49]

The intertextual relationship is one of both form and content. In terms of form, we can point to the Ciceronian style of the *Dialogus*, as well as the dialogue genre itself. As concerns content, there are both explicit discussions of Cicero placed in the mouths of all three of the main interlocutors, and countless implicit echoes of and allusions to Cicero's works.[50] In the *Dialogus* itself, all of these coexist and ultimately coalesce, and they both rely on each other and combine to create the work's various effects and, indeed, its overall effect. An analysis that teases out the various strands of this interwoven braid must necessarily be reductive at some level, and yet I hope that by picking apart these threads we might actually gain a greater insight into the work as a whole. Tacitus' audience, with their native-speaker *Sprachgefühl* and traditional Roman education, would have felt these effects almost unconsciously; today we can only hope to recapture them through close reading and diligent philology. In this section and the next I will trace Cicero's reception in the *Dialogus*, first at a high level in formal terms, then more specifically in matters of content, culminating with an analysis of Cicero as an explicit leitmotif running through the series of speeches delivered by the three main characters.[51]

[48] I imagine that Tacitus must have interwoven these allusions not from memory but after reading through and excerpting Cicero's rhetorical works, which, unlike Cicero's speeches, he probably did not have thrashed into his head at that age when memory was best. Compare the reading practice of Pliny the Elder (Plin. *epist.* 3.5.7–13).

[49] For theoretical reflections on Tacitus' prose intertextuality, see van den Berg (2014) 212–215, 231–233. There remains much work still to be done in transferring and adapting the established methods of approaching intertextuality in Latin verse to the related but distinct category of Latin prose.

[50] A small scholarly industry of collecting Tacitus' Ciceronian *Quellen* dates back over a century, when the similarly named but different Kleiber (1883) and Klaiber (1914–1916) both addressed the issue; Gudeman (1914) also made important contributions. Since that time commentators have treated most of this material as common property, and so except in rare instances of remarkable discovery I do not give a doxography of who noticed or did not notice the various allusions that I discuss below. The synthesis and interpretation of the allusions, by contrast, can be assumed to be my own unless otherwise noted, for while there has been much diligence in collecting *Quellen*, there has been very little interest in analysis of their purpose and effects. (A beginning has been made by Döpp [1986] 16–22, who rightly noted that Tacitus shows "ein tieferes und fruchtbareres Cicero-Verständnis, als es sich sonst je in der heidnischen Antike findet" [22]; one might expect such a treatment from Michel [1962] as well, but I have not found much of direct relevance in his theoretical arguments.) As Heubner in Güngerich (1980) 68 put it, "Eine in die Tiefe gehende Untersuchung der Ciceronähe des Tac[itus] im Dialogus fehlt." I hope that my chapter helps to fill that gap.

[51] Van den Berg (2014) is also concerned with the presence of Cicero in the *Dialogus*, albeit from a different perspective and with a different style of analysis from my own; see esp. his pp. 208–240. See too Gowing (2005) 109–120.

The relatively Ciceronian style of the *Dialogus* is plain from a glance at any of its pages, and for a long time cast a shadow of doubt on its authorship – how could the author of the *Historiae* and *Annales* write such prose?[52] Various unsatisfactory answers were put forth. Perhaps it was a work of the young Tacitus, before he had fully formed his mature style, and yet Tacitus' own words seem to rule out an early date of composition.[53] Or perhaps he simply did not write the work at all; maybe, say, Quintilian did – could this be his lost *De causis corruptae eloquentiae?* In 1898, in a review of Alfred Gudeman's commentary on the *Dialogus*, Friedrich Leo seemed to put a stop to such fanciful building of castles in the air. Gudeman had plumped for an early date of composition on stylistic grounds; Leo shot back that the style was simply determined by the content, that in a work on oratory, a Ciceronian style was mandatory.[54] This view has been faithfully repeated ever since, first by Eduard Norden a few years later, then by many a twentieth-century scholar, and eventually, through dutiful parroting, it has become the firm and fixed *communis opinio.*[55]

Unfortunately the *communis opinio* in this case is simply wrong. One could perfectly well discuss oratory and its decline in any style at all; think only of Seneca's *epist.* 114, which opens in a way remarkably similar to the *Dialogus* (*epist.* 114.1):

> quare quibusdam temporibus prouenerit corrupti generis oratio quaeris et quomodo in quaedam uitia inclinatio ingeniorum facta sit, ut aliquando inflata explicatio uigeret, aliquando infracta et in morem cantici ducta.

> You ask why certain times produce a corrupt sort of oratory, and how it is that *ingenia* have slid into certain vices, so that sometimes a puffed-up exposition was preferred, sometimes a choppy one that was reduced to the fashion of a song.

Compare the beginning of the *Dialogus* (1.1):

> saepe ex me requiris, Iuste Fabi, cur, cum priora saecula tot eminentium oratorum ingeniis gloriaque floruerint, nostra potissimum aetas deserta et laude eloquentiae orbata uix nomen ipsum oratoris retineat.

---

[52] See p. 233 above.   [53] See p. 234 above.

[54] Leo (1960) II.285: "Die Gattung erfordert ihren Stil, wer verschiedene Gattungen behandelt, muss in verschiedenen Stilen schreiben." Cf. 284–291, esp. 291, "Es war gewiss eine Hinneigung zu Quintilians Prinzipien, dass Tacitus die ciceronische Form als die der Gattung zukommende anerkannte. Sobald er aber das that, war er gezwungen, wenn er in dieser Gattung producierte, es in ciceronischem Stile zu thun."

[55] Goldberg (1999) 224 takes it as a given; and Mayer (2001) 19–21 likewise states it as a fact with very little argument beyond citing E. Löfstedt stating it as a fact (Mayer [2001] 20 n. 52). Cf. Norden (1958) 322–326.

> You often ask me, Iustus Fabius, why, although past ages flourished with the *ingenia* and glory of so many eminent orators, our own age is particularly barren and deprived of distinction in eloquence; it scarcely retains even the word "orator."

Seneca and Tacitus each address someone who has asked them why oratory, which once flourished, has now declined, and the two works have many other similarities as well. Each canvasses the causes of the decline, each provides a sort of literary history of eloquence, and each mentions Cicero. And yet Tacitus will go on to adopt a Ciceronian style and the dialogue form; Seneca, on the other hand, will respond in his own typical and distinctive style. Short, paratactic sentences studded with anaphora, antithesis, paradox, *sententiae*, and all the other characteristic accoutrements of the Senecan style – this letter is stylistically no different from the other epistles in the Senecan corpus.

It is thus clear that a Roman could write about oratory and its decline without becoming a *simia Ciceronis*; indeed he could do so without deviating a jot from his customary stylistic norms. Tacitus, however, has very much deviated from his usual practice. His style in the *Dialogus* is therefore not mere adherence to generic convention, but rather demands to be read as a conscious and deliberate choice. While many of the individual moves are small – twenty instances of *autem* in the *Dialogus* compared to six in all of the *Historiae* and *Annales*,[56] the postponement of *igitur* to second position,[57] an inclination toward synonymous doublets,[58] and so forth[59] – they combine to make a bold statement of eristic imitation. For the ancient audience, the work would have breathed an unmistakable Ciceronian spirit, adding resonances and additional meaning to its every sentence.

The Ciceronian style is in fact inseparable from the dialogue form in which Tacitus has chosen to cast it. We know precious little about the fate of the dialogue genre between Cicero and Tacitus; no specimen has survived for study,[60] and there are only a couple of scattered notices that

---

[56] Cf. Mayer (2001) 28, whose figures are slightly off.

[57] The table in *TLL* v.2.760–761 (Rehm, s.v. *ergo*) makes the preferences of Cicero and Tacitus crystal clear: Cicero uses *igitur* 2,304 times, but only 34 times in first position (27 of those instances occur in the *philosophica* and the correspondence with Atticus), while Tacitus uses *igitur* 177 times – of which 170 are in first position. Thus Tac. *dial.* 8.4, 10.7, and 20.6, where *igitur* is in second position, are a striking deviation from his regular practice and a clear attempt to follow Ciceronian tendencies.

[58] See Gudeman (1914) 22. Cf. p. 247 below.

[59] Many observations can be subsumed under this "and so forth." See e.g. Güngerich (1980) ad *dial.* 16.6 *si referas . . . uideatur*, who notes that such "future less vivid" conditionals are common in Cicero but very rare in Tacitus (cf. *ALL* ix.34 [Blase]).

[60] Seneca's "*Dialogi*," despite their title, are not dialogues. The title is presumably ancient, for Quintilian says that Seneca's works included *et orationes . . . et poemata et epistulae et dialogi* (*inst.*

attest to Maecenas and Livy having written them.[61] Since we have nothing to compare the *Dialogus* with, it is impossible to know for sure whether writers of dialogues in general favored a Ciceronian style, although I would suspect that they did not – it is hard to picture a Maecenas being Ciceronian.[62] More importantly, however, Tacitus' choice of genre was not predetermined either; he did not *have* to write a dialogue – none of his predecessors who discussed the decline of oratory seem to have adopted the form. This too is a direct challenge to Cicero and his successors on very Ciceronian territory.

Tacitus may have been familiar with all of Cicero's dialogues, and the careful work of Ute Haß-von Reitzenstein has shown possible thematic parallels between the *Dialogus* and most of the Ciceronian dialogues that survive.[63] There is nevertheless a certain danger in assuming that no writer can ever have an independent thought or that every element in Tacitus that could possibly be paralleled by something in Cicero must necessarily derive from him. The two are both writing dialogues, and some similarities will simply occur because of the general similarity of all dialogues. There is no particularly obvious reason to think that Tacitus has chosen to engage closely with, say, the *De natura deorum*:[64] the subject matter of the two works is simply far too different. Supposed allusions to the non-rhetorical dialogues of Cicero must be viewed with some skepticism; they are not necessarily to be ruled out, but they require a higher standard of proof for admission. On the other hand, a close engagement with Cicero's rhetorical dialogues is exactly what we would expect, and it is in fact exactly what we see.

We might characterize Cicero's *De oratore* as a general course of education and self-culture for the ideal orator, the *Brutus* as a history of oratory,

10.1.129), but as Williams (2003) 3 observes, "By *dialogi* Quintilian apparently means all of S[eneca]'s prose works apart from his speeches and letters; but none of those works is a *dialogus* in the conventional Platonic or Ciceronian sense of a 'real' conversation or debate between named characters in a social setting." Cf. Roller (2015), who does find dialogic elements in these texts. On Seneca's generic experimentation, see the previous chapter p. 207.

[61] *GL* 1.146 *"uolucrum" Maecenas in dialogo* ii; Sen. *epist.* 100.9 *nomina adhuc T. Liuium; scripsit enim et dialogos, quos non magis philosophiae adnumerare possis quam historiae, et ex professo philosophiam continentis libros: huic quoque dabo locum.* Hirzel (1895) ii.1–46 is a somewhat speculative account of what else we might surmise.

[62] See Seneca's damning description of Maecenas' "effeminate" stylistic improprieties at *epist.* 114.4–8.

[63] Haß-von Reitzenstein (1970), who seeks a "gattungsgeschichtliche Analyse" of the *Dialogus* (6). She is not concerned with individual allusions or their effects taken jointly or severally, focusing instead on comparing, say, the prooemium of the *Dialogus* to all the prooemia of Cicero's dialogues and noting the generic similarities. Her work is also useful for its comprehensive survey of earlier scholarship (e.g. 5–6 on Cicero in the *Dialogus* in general, and *passim* on individual issues).

[64] As Haß-von Reitzenstein (1970) thinks; see e.g. p. 34, where she finds many "Anklänge an Ciceros De natura deorum" in the prooemium to the *Dialogus*. So too van den Berg (2014) 61–65.

and the *Orator* as a portrait of the ideal orator in his finished form.[65] Tacitus neatly subsumes all three of these discussions into the *Dialogus*, all while managing to drastically shrink the length of the exposition.[66] Here again, then, the ancient reader will have constantly been thinking of Cicero and Tacitus' relationship to him. The rarer the use of the dialogue form in the first century AD, the more striking all of these points would have been to a contemporary audience. Moreover, as I shall show below, Tacitus not only alludes to Cicero, but also infuses his own words with added punch by reworking his Ciceronian exemplar.

A few examples will make the point clear. The very first words of the *Dialogus, saepe ex me requiris* (*dial.* 1.1), immediately establish a Ciceronian patina: in the first three paragraphs of the *Orator*, Cicero has *saepius idem roganti, saepius rogas,* and *quaeris . . . saepius* (*orat.* 1–3).[67] And yet almost immediately Tacitus begins to deviate from his model. Later in that same sentence he claims that *horum . . . temporum diserti* are nowadays case-pleaders or advocates or, in a word, anything other than "orators." The word *disertus* is doubtless deliberately chosen instead of *eloquens*; after all, if the present age is *laude eloquentiae orbata* (*dial.* 1.1), there can scarcely be anyone who is *eloquens.*[68] In Cicero, moreover, *disertus* very much carries pejorative associations. As he reports at *Or.* 18 (cf. *de orat.* 1.94), Antonius said that he had seen many good speakers (*disertos*), but no one truly eloquent (*eloquentem*), and Douglas has neatly summarized the word's Ciceronian connotations: "It often means 'glib' . . . or in other contexts reflects the condition of Roman oratory before (*a*) the impact of Greek rhetoric, (*b*) the emergence of orators capable of a genuinely elevated style . . . Hence C[icero] uses it (i) of undeveloped and unpolished oratory . . . (ii) of mediocrities generally."[69] Already, then, Ciceronian usage has informed Tacitus' choice of words, but there is more. In the

---

[65] So Sandys (1885) l; cf. similarly Döpp (1986) 8–11.

[66] Is this shrinking (at least partly) in line with Aper's advice toward brevity? Cf. *dial.* 19.2–20.2.

[67] *Quaeris . . .* is indeed a prefatory topos, as the collection of examples in Gudeman (1914) 41 n. 1 makes clear, and yet in none of those instances is it found with a form of *saepe.* This fact, combined with the similarity of subject matter between the *Dialogus* and the *Orator*, persuades me to see a direct connection.

[68] Güngerich (1980) ad loc., while acknowledging that there is originally a distinction between *disertus* and *eloquens,* thinks that *disertus* "entspricht aber bei Tac[itus] als Adjektiv etwa dem Nomen eloquentia." It seems much more likely to me that Tacitus is here, as throughout the *Dialogus,* an extremely close and careful reader of Ciceronian nuance. The word *eloquens* was still common in Tacitus' day (e.g. Quint. *inst.* 1.1.21 and *passim* or Plin. *epist.* 2.1.6, of Tacitus himself), and so it was perfectly available for him to use. Nowhere does he call someone like Cicero *disertus,* and indeed, everywhere he uses the word, a depreciating connotation seems implied. If Tacitus avoids the word *eloquens,* it is probably because he genuinely believes that *eloquentia* has died.

[69] Douglas (1966) ad *Brut.* 27 pp. 29–30 (quotation from p. 30).

very next sentence he says that he would scarcely dare to proffer his own opinion in response to the question of why oratory has declined, but (how fortunate!) he can report the *disertissimorum, ut nostris temporibus, hominum sermo* (*dial.* 1.2). So too had Cicero shrunk from repeating commonplaces in the *De oratore*, retailing instead what he once heard in a debate *hominum eloquentissimorum* (*de orat.* 1.23). Tacitus is plainly alluding to the *De oratore*,[70] but with an important twist, for he implicitly denigrates his own interlocutors by saying that they are *disertissimi*, not, as Cicero's had been, *eloquentissimi*. In order to draw further attention to this downgrading deviation from Cicero, he adds the limiting phrase *ut nostris temporibus* – by common consent, after all, eloquence no longer existed. Tacitus' introductory sentences thus take on a whole new level of meaning when read in light of the Ciceronian intertexts.

The formal similarities between Tacitus' *Dialogus* and the dialogues of Cicero are often especially visible in the transitions between set-piece speeches. After Aper has delivered his first speech, *subridens Maternus "parantem" inquit "me non minus diu accusare oratores quam Aper laudauerat . . . arte quadam mitigauit, concedendo iis qui causas agere non possent ut uersus facerent"* ("smiling slightly, Maternus said, 'I was preparing to inveigh against orators just as much as Aper had praised them . . . but he's somehow artfully soothed me by granting that those who can't plead cases be allowed to write verses,'" *dial.* 11.1). This unmistakably reproduces the beginning of Scaevola's response to Crassus' speech in the first book of the *De oratore* (1.74): *ridens Scaeuola "non luctabor tecum," inquit "Crasse, amplius; id enim ipsum, quod contra me locutus es, artificio quodam es consecutus, ut et mihi, quae ego uellem non esse oratoris, concederes . . ."* ("smiling, Scaevola said, 'I won't fight with you any more, Crassus; for in the very speech which you've spoken against me, you've somehow artfully brought it about that you both concede to me what I claimed did not belong to an orator . . .'"). A transitional moment in a dialogue about oratory, a participle *(sub)ridens,*[71] *arte quadam* and *artificio quodam*, forms of *concedere* – the allusion is plain to see.

---

[70] In addition to the echoes already noted, in *dial.* 1.2 Tacitus also has *repetendus esset* and *audiui*; Cic. *de orat.* 1.23 has both *repetam* and *audiui*. The certainty of the allusion is further clear from the similarity of subject matter between Cicero's and Tacitus' dialogues and the placement of this phrase at the end of the introduction in each.

[71] Smiling and laughter are topoi in the dialogues of Cicero (see Gudeman [1914] ad loc. p. 260); an atmosphere of bonhomie must always be maintained, even when there is disagreement among the speakers. The rest of the points of contact here, however, cannot be merely coincidental.

After Maternus' speech in reply to Aper, we are again met with a transitional allusion, this one a bit more sophisticated. Messalla promises that he will provide his own thoughts, *si illud a uobis ante impetrauero, ut uos quoque sermonem hunc nostrum adiuuetis* ("<u>if I first obtain your promise</u> that you too will assist in this conversation of ours," *dial.* 16.2). Maternus responds for both himself and Aper: *"pro duobus" Maternus "promitto"* ("'<u>I promise</u>,' said Maternus, '<u>for both of us</u>,'" *dial.* 16.3). This passage echoes *de orat.* 2.27, where Crassus says, *neque Antonium uerbum facere patiar et ipse obmutescam, <u>nisi prius a uobis impetraro</u> . . . ut hic sitis* [sc. *Catulus et Iulius*] *hodie* ("I won't stop talking myself and let Antonius say a word unless <u>I've first obtained your promise</u> that . . . you, Catulus and Iulius, will stay here today"), to which Iulius replies, *<u>pro utroque respondeo</u>: sic faciemus* ("<u>I'll respond for both of us</u>: we shall do so"). These precise verbal echoes, moreover, are redeployed here to introduce a further Ciceronian claim, as Maternus goes on to promise that he and Secundus will pursue any points that Messalla has not so much overlooked as left to them (*dial.* 16.3 *nam et ego et Secundus exsequemur eas partes quas intellexerimus te non tam omisisse quam nobis reliquisse*). This flatteringly polite notion of supplying any deficiencies in another's presentation is exactly what we find at *de orat.* 2.126, where Catulus says that Crassus will expound anything that Antonius has not and claims that these will not be interpreted as omissions but as things that Antonius preferred to have Crassus say (*qua re, Crasse, neque tu tua suauitate nos priuabis, ut, si quid ab Antonio aut praetermissum aut relictum sit, non explices; neque te, Antoni, si quid non dixeris, existimabimus non potuisse potius quam a Crasso dici maluisse*).

Such echoes in transitional moments can be multiplied. Sometimes they are obvious, as at *dial.* 28.1: *<u>non reconditas, Materne, causas requiris, nec aut tibi ipsi aut huic Secundo uel huic Apro ignotas</u>* ("<u>the causes that you're seeking, Maternus, are not obscure, nor are they unknown to you</u> yourself or to our friends Secundus or Aper"), which pretty well reproduces *de orat.* 3.148 *<u>peruolgatas res requiris</u> . . . et <u>tibi non incognitas</u>* ("<u>the things you're seeking are quite well known</u>, and <u>not unknown to you</u>"), albeit with noticeable and deliberate *uariatio*. At other points they are more subtle. When Messalla resumes his second speech after an interruption, Tacitus introduces it as follows: *deinde cum Aper quoque et Secundus idem adnuissent, Messalla quasi rursus incipiens* . . . ("then when both Aper and Secundus had nodded in agreement, Messalla, beginning again, as it were . . .," *dial.* 33.4). At *Brut.* 201 Cicero had written *uterque adsensus est; et ego tamquam de integro ordiens* . . . ("each nodded in agreement, and I,

beginning again, as it were ...”): as Roland Mayer notes, “T[acitus] characteristically offers synonyms for Cicero's expression, and omits a verb of
speaking (Cicero goes on to add *inquam*).”[72] The formal parallel is very close,
but it is remarkable how Cicero's every word has been transmuted – and yet
their essential meaning has been preserved. This passage of the *Brutus* was on
Tacitus' mind elsewhere as well, for at 9.1 he made Aper say (of Maternus'
focus on poetry) *inde enim omnis fluxit oratio*, which closely parallels the way
Brut. 201 continues: *a Cotta et Sulpicio haec omnis fluxit oratio*.

These echoes of Cicero in the interstices between the speeches serve to
keep him ever in the reader's mind. The outer form of Tacitus' *Dialogus* is
very much a composite of Ciceronian elements. The speeches too, however, are also replete with Ciceronianisms. I will provide an extended
analysis of the second and third pairs of speeches, tracing Cicero and
Ciceronianisms throughout, but even in the first pair of speeches, where
Cicero is not explicitly under discussion, he is ever present. Aper, for
example, describes the utility of oratory as follows (*dial.* 5.5):

> nam si ad utilitatem uitae omnia consilia factaque nostra derigenda sunt,
> quid est tutius quam eam exercere artem, qua semper armatus praesidium
> amicis, opem alienis, salutem periclitantibus, inuidis uero et inimicis
> metum et terrorem ultro feras, ipse securus et uelut quadam perpetua
> potentia ac potestate munitus?

> For if all our plans and actions are to be directed toward practical utility,
> what is safer than to practice the art (of oratory), armed with which you can
> always bring succor to your friends, help to strangers, safety to those in
> danger, but fear and terror to your envious enemies, all while you are safe
> yourself and protected as it were by a certain authority and power?

This precisely replicates the thought of Crassus in the *De oratore* (1.32):

> quid tam porro regium, tam liberale, tam munificum, quam opem ferre
> supplicibus, excitare adflictos, dare salutem, liberare periculis, retinere
> homines in ciuitate? quid autem tam necessarium, quam tenere semper
> arma, quibus uel tectus ipse esse possis uel prouocare integer uel te ulcisci
> lacessitus?

> What is so regal, so suited to a free man, so magnificent as to bring succor to
> suppliants, to stir up the afflicted, to bring safety, to free people from
> dangers, to keep them from exile? What, moreover, is so necessary as always
> having the weapons by which you can either be protected yourself or safely
> challenge another or avenge yourself when harmed?

---

[72] Mayer (2001) ad loc.

And yet while Tacitus' passage replicates the thought of Cicero's, it replicates very few of the words: *opem ferre* is repeated, but the *tenere semper arma* of Cicero has become simply *armatus*, the *quibus tectus* and *integer* have become *munitus* and *securus*, and so forth. Variation is the order of the day.

The imitations extend all the way to very small verbal reminiscences. Aper, for example, uses the phrase *ceteris aliarum artium studiis* (*dial.* 10.4), echoing and perhaps outdoing Cicero's *ceterarum artium studia* (*de orat.* 1.12). Maternus says *efficere . . . et eniti* (*dial.* 11.2), a common Ciceronian pair, but in Cicero always – as logic would dictate – *eniti et efficere* (e.g. Cic. *Lael.* 59 or *Phil.* 4.16).[73] While such Ciceronian doublets are foreign to Tacitus' typical style, they are common in the *Dialogus* (Gudeman counts sixty-three),[74] where he often reverses their order, as is the case above.[75] It would take an exhaustive line-by-line commentary to trace every echo and allusion of Cicero in the *Dialogus*, and I think that the general point has been sufficiently made. Cicero's voice, even though he is not explicitly a contributor to the debate, is constantly being heard. He is present in the style and the genre of the *Dialogus*, and he is present in the work's smallest details. In the next section I will trace his presence as a leitmotif in the main speeches that focus on the decline of oratory, and then I will try to draw together all these different threads to discuss the overall effect they create within the work.

Cicero as Leitmotif

Cicero's presence is felt everywhere in the *Dialogus*, but perhaps nowhere more so than in the series of speeches that focus directly on the work's main question, viz. the causes for the decline of oratory. Cicero is a continuous thread that links these speeches together, as each speaker makes his arguments with particular reference to Cicero's place at the summit of oratorical excellence. Aper, the champion of modernity, explicitly invokes Cicero and attacks him and his primacy. In a Quintilianic rejoinder, Messalla defends Cicero and puts forward a traditional explanation for the decline of eloquence. It is Maternus, in the end, who decisively rejects this Quintilianic argument and its Ciceronian antecedents, but on entirely revolutionary grounds, which are expressed, unsurprisingly, with a twist on

[73] Not mentioned in Wölfflin's (1933) collection of alliterative pairs.   [74] Gudeman (1914) 24.
[75] See too Mayer (2001) 28 and his General Index s.v. "doublet." This may also be a foretaste of Tacitean *uariatio*.

words Cicero himself had spoken. This is, in microcosm, Tacitus' project in the entire *Dialogus*: Tacitus rejects Ciceronianism by subverting Cicero's own words. His paradoxical point in this masterpiece of Ciceronian eloquence is that Ciceronian eloquence is dead under the imperial dispensation.

First Aper. He wishes, at least ostensibly, to dispute the apparent consensus that there has been a decline in oratory. While I think that he is in fact merely playing the devil's advocate, a role with a noble history in Cicero's dialogues,[76] it must be confessed that he never admits to this himself. If he is merely playing a role, he never breaks character, and so I will take what he says on its own merits as a genuine contribution to the debate. Even if Tacitus wants to imply that no one could possibly believe Aper's claims, he nevertheless must be making the best possible argument that can be made for the assertion that oratory is as healthy as it ever was. And the whole argument revolves around Cicero, as Aper first tries to separate him from the *antiqui* and claim him for the present age, then, perhaps sensing that this line of reasoning is specious at best, tacks against the wind and moves to denigrate Cicero's oratorical abilities. The beginning of the speech is chock full of implicit echoes of Cicero's thoughts and words, but these abruptly (and appropriately) stop when Aper turns to a sustained criticism of his style.

Aper begins his speech by caviling about who is really an *antiquus auctor*. When he thinks of antiquity, he says, he thinks of Ulysses and Nestor, men who lived some 1,300 years ago, not Demosthenes and Hyperides, who flourished as recently as Philip and Alexander the Great (*dial.* 16.5) – a mere 300 years in the past. Such a length of time is nothing in the grand scheme of things. He then cites Cicero's famous *Hortensius* (*dial.* 16.7):

> nam si, ut Cicero in Hortensio scribit, is est magnus et uerus annus, quo eadem positio caeli siderumque, quae cum maxime est, rursum existet, isque annus horum quos nos uocamus annorum duodecim milia nongentos quinquaginta quattuor complectitur, incipit Demosthenes uester, quem

---

[76] Haß-von Reitzenstein (1970) 131–143 has the most detailed demonstration that Aper is an *aduocatus diaboli*. The key statements in the *Dialogus* itself come at 1.4, where Tacitus himself says that one of the characters took the "other side," mocking antiquity and defending modernity, and at 15.2, 16.3, 24.2, and 28.1, where Messalla or Maternus allege that Aper does not really believe what he is saying. I add an argument of my own for the devil's advocate position in n. 121 below. The most vigorous defendant of Aper's sincerity is Goldberg (1999); he attempts to deal with the devil's advocate argument at 233–234. Cf. van den Berg (2014) 65–66 with comprehensive bibliography; he himself seems somewhat conflicted on Aper's case, writing: "The following arguments are not intended as a defense of Aper's positions *per se* even if they may be read along those lines" (216).

uos ueterem et antiquum fingitis, non solum eodem anno quo nos, sed etiam eodem mense exstitisse.

For if, as Cicero writes in the *Hortensius*, the "great and true year" is the one in which the same position of the heavenly bodies which exists at this very moment exists again, and such a year consists of 12,954 of what we call years, that Demosthenes of yours, who you claim is old and ancient, not only lived in the same year as us, but in fact in the very same month!

Cicero elsewhere discussed the Platonic "great year" and the vexed problem of its length,[77] and in the *Hortensius* he evidently claimed that it lasted 12,954 normal years (fr. 80 Gr.). By this reckoning, then, Demosthenes is neatly severed from the *antiqui* and turned into a contemporary orator! Hermann Usener speculated about the context of the *Hortensius* fragment, wondering whether it can be linked with *Hort*. fr. 52 Gr., in which Thales, who had flourished some five centuries before Hortensius, is called *recens* – did Hortensius use the "great year" argument to justify this claim?[78] If so, then Aper's citation gains added point, since he would be imitating not just the words but also the strategy of Hortensius, as both, in order to undercut an opponent's argument, would be trying to show that someone who lived hundreds of years ago in fact lived quite recently. This is an attractive but unprovable hypothesis. The allusion in fact has several other salient features to commend it even without this possible parallel. First, Aper knows that his interlocutors recognize Cicero as the supreme authority, and so by using Cicero as the basis for his claim he makes it harder for them to disagree with him. Furthermore, he is about to claim that Cicero ought to be considered a contemporary – what could be more elegant than to justify this claim about Cicero by reference to Cicero himself?

The *Hortensius* was a protreptic toward philosophy, best known today from Augustine's eloquent testimony about its salutary effect on him as a young man.[79] The preserved fragments, however, indicate that Cicero's philosophical exhortations took as their jumping-off point a debate about the relative merits of poetry, history, oratory, and philosophy.[80] Catulus discussed the pleasures of poetry (frr. 8–10 Gr.), to which Lucullus

---

[77] E.g. Cic. *nat. deor.* 2.51 *ex disparibus motionibus magnum annum mathematici nominauerunt, qui tum efficitur cum solis et lunae et quinque errantium ad eandem inter se comparationem confectis omnium spatiis est facta conuersio; quae quam longa sit magna quaestio est, esse uero certam et definitam necesse est.*

[78] Usener (1873) 394–395; cf. Mayer (2001) 140 for a very similar conjecture.

[79] See esp. Aug. *conf.* 3.4.7–8; also *soliloq.* 1.10.17, *beat. uit.* 1.4, and the Epilogue.

[80] I have followed the reconstruction of Grilli (1962) below, which of course cannot be certain in every detail. Nevertheless, the essential terms of the debate in the *Hortensius* seem clear; see further Plasberg (1892) 27–35.

countered that he preferred history (frr. 11–16 Gr.), and Hortensius made the case for oratory (frr. 17–18 Gr. and *passim*). Catulus then seems to reevaluate his position: if they are to talk about what is the best in absolute terms, the answer must surely be philosophy (frr. 19–22 Gr.), and Cicero's defense of philosophy against Hortensius' praise of oratory occupies the remainder of the dialogue. In the end, Hortensius is won over: philosophy is acknowledged to be the queen of *studia*. A dialogue on the merits of various literary pursuits is of obvious relevance to Tacitus' project in his own *Dialogus*, particularly to the debate between Aper and Maternus, where Aper extols the virtues of oratory and Maternus argues in favor of poetry. This is thus precisely the right dialogue for Aper to be alluding to at this moment, when he is still speaking in riposte to Maternus' praise of poetry.[81] I also have no doubt that there is much more of the *Hortensius* in the *Dialogus* than we are able to recognize today. Tacitus is very good at alluding to the Ciceronian works that he "should" allude to – the *De oratore*, the *Brutus*, and the *Orator* – and, because of its subject matter, he should likewise allude to the *Hortensius*. He does so explicitly here, and by coincidence we can recognize a couple of other cases,[82] but there are doubtless many more that we can no longer uncover. Finally, I note in passing that philosophy finds no advocate in the *Dialogus*, perhaps a pointed omission.[83]

Aper then amplifies his point that Cicero is not really to be classed with the *antiqui* (*dial.* 17.1):

> sed transeo ad Latinos oratores, in quibus non Menenium, ut puto, Agrippam, qui potest uideri antiquus, nostrorum temporum disertis anteponere soletis, sed Ciceronem et Caesarem et Caelium et Caluum et Brutum et Asinium et Messallam: quos quid antiquis potius temporibus adscribatis quam nostris, non uideo.

---

[81] When Maternus talks about poetry's venerable age compared to oratory's relative youth (*dial.* 12. 4–5), could he also be taking a page from the *Hortensius*? Cf. the already cited fr. 52 Gr., where philosophy is said to be of much more recent vintage than oratory.

[82] There may be another allusion to the *Hortensius* at *dial.* 16.6 *quod spatium temporis si ad infirmitatem corporum nostrorum referas*; see Helm (1908) 494 and Gudeman (1914) 89. There is definitely an allusion at *dial.* 41.3; see n. 111 below. For a very brief sketch of some other possible Hortensian echoes in the *Dialogus*, see Alfonsi (1965) and his n. 3 on p. 41 with further references.

[83] I might wonder if this reflects Tacitus' own attitude toward philosophy, but this is of course fundamentally unknowable (cf. suggestively *Agr.* 4.4 *memoria teneo solitum ipsum narrare se prima in iuuenta studium philosophiae acrius, ultra quam concessum Romano ac senatori, hausisse, ni prudentia matris incensum ac flagrantem animum coercuisset*). Van den Berg (2014) 172–174, 223–227 argues that, in contrast to Cicero's day, philosophy had become an accepted part of imperial education. I think instead that the prejudice against philosophy enunciated at *Agr.* 4.4 and instantiated by Domitian's expulsion of the philosophers (Suet. *Dom.* 10.4) was still very real.

But I pass to Latin orators, among whom I don't think you're accustomed to put Menenius Agrippa – who might rightly be classed as ancient – ahead of the polished speakers of our day, but Cicero and Caesar and Caelius and Calvus and Brutus and Asinius and Messalla. But I don't see why you class them as ancient rather than contemporary.

I think that the commentators have not fully understood what Aper is doing in this piece of his argument. He acknowledges that a class of *antiqui* does exist, and assigns the likes of Menenius Agrippa, consul of 503 BC, to it, but implies that nobody would prefer orators of that sort.[84] He claims that he cannot see why Cicero and Caesar and all the rest should be relegated to the past – and if they are instead considered contemporary orators, then there can be no decline from Cicero, since Aper and co. would be still living in a Ciceronian age. He is scraping the bottom of the argumentative barrel here: he goes on to discuss when Cicero died, citing Tiro, and calculates that it has only been some 120 years from that date to the present. Whether that makes Cicero *antiquus* or not is debatable, but he can hardly be considered a contemporary. If it is only through casuistry and quibbling over definitions that modernity's champions can vindicate themselves, they are in a very weak position indeed.

Aper must realize this, because he gradually changes his tactics. He would like to appropriate Cicero for the present, but failing that, he will claim that

> haec ideo praedixi ut si qua ex horum oratorum [*sc.* Ciceronis et Caesaris *et al.*] fama gloriaque laus temporibus acquiritur, eam docerem in medio sitam et propiorem nobis quam Seruio Galbae aut C. Carboni quosque alios merito antiquos uocauerimus. (*dial.* 18.1)
>
> I said these things for this reason, so that if any praise accrues to the times from these orators' reputation and glory, I might demonstrate that this glory is common property and closer to us than to Servius Galba or Gaius Carbo and others whom we might rightly call ancient.

That is to say, Cicero might not be our contemporary, but he is closer to us than he is to the *antiqui*. The *antiqui*, after all, are crude and barbarous and entirely lacking in polish. This leads Aper into his main thesis, namely that oratory has not declined, merely changed with the times (*agere enim fortius iam et audentius uolo si illud ante praedixero, mutari cum temporibus formas quoque et genera dicendi, dial.* 18.2).

---

[84] Cf. Liu. 2.32.9, of one of Agrippa's speeches delivered *ad plebem: prisco illo dicendi et horrido modo.* Agrippa does not appear in the *Brutus*.

To illustrate this point, Aper presents a brief history of oratory that is very much inspired by Cicero's *Brutus*, indeed almost literally inspired, for it breathes Cicero's *ipsissima uerba* in judging orators past. Compared with Cato, for example, C. Gracchus is *plenior et uberior* ("fuller and more copious," *dial.* 18.2), echoing Cicero's verdict *noli enim putare quemquam <u>pleniorem aut uberiorem</u> ad dicendum fuisse* ("don't think that anyone was <u>fuller or more copious</u> in speech," *Brut.* 125). Calvus is *exsanguis* ("bloodless," *dial.* 18.5), just as Cicero had said that *uerum sanguinem deperdebat* ("he lost his true blood," *Brut.* 283). Caesar was prevented from attaining the heights of eloquence by his *occupationes* ("activities," *dial.* 21.5); Cicero said that he was embroiled *in maximis occupationibus* ("in the most important activities," *Brut.* 82). Caelius' speeches *redolent antiquitatem* ("savor of antiquity," *dial.* 21.4); the phrase is used by Cicero of Galba (*Brut.* 82). Sometimes Aper will blend disparate passages from the *Brutus*, as in the phrase *equidem fatebor uobis simpliciter me in quibusdam antiquorum uix risum, in quibusdam autem uix somnum tenere* ("I'll admit to you frankly that with some of the old writers I can scarcely contain my laughter, with others I can scarcely stay awake," *dial.* 21.1), which yokes *somnum uix tenebamus* (*Brut.* 278) with *equidem in quibusdam risum uix tenebam* (*Brut.* 293).

Aper thus seems to follow Cicero's progress through the *Brutus* quite closely, but he ends his catalog with a radical deviation. The *Brutus* obviously tends toward Cicero as its teleological end, which was both a chronological necessity – Cicero could only talk about orators up until his own time – and a matter of conscious self-promotion.[85] Nevertheless, Cicero stops short of explicitly making himself the model orator: he simply implies it in such a way that no one could possibly fail to see it. Aper had already given some indication that he might not share that opinion, for he began to criticize Cicero earlier, only to check himself (*dial.* 18.5–6):

> satis constat ne Ciceroni quidem obtrectatores defuisse, quibus inflatus et tumens nec satis pressus, sed supra modum exsultans et superfluens et parum Atticus uideretur. legistis utique et Calui et Bruti ad Ciceronem missas epistulas, ex quibus facile est deprehendere Caluum quidem Ciceroni uisum exsanguem et aridum, Brutum autem otiosum atque diiunctum; rursusque Ciceronem a Caluo quidem male audisse tamquam solutum et eneruem, a Bruto autem, ut ipsius uerbis utar, tamquam "fractum atque elumbem." si me interroges, omnes mihi uidentur uerum dixisse: sed mox ad singulos ueniam, nunc mihi cum uniuersis negotium est.

---

[85] Fox (2007) 186–188 is unnecessarily and unconvincingly skeptical of this; cf. e.g. Dugan (2005) 248–250.

There is general agreement that not even Cicero lacked for detractors. To them he seemed puffed up and bloated and not sufficiently concise, but rather excessively exuberant and redundant and insufficiently Attic. You've doubtless read the letters that both Calvus and Brutus sent to Cicero, from which it's easy to see that Calvus seemed dry and bloodless to Cicero, and Brutus seemed to him listless and choppy; while Cicero was rebuked by Calvus as dissolute and lacking in vigor, and by Brutus, if I may borrow his own words, as "weak and enervated." If you ask me, they all seem to have spoken the truth: but soon I will come to treating the individual orators in detail, for now my business is with them in general.

Even as Aper implicitly acknowledges Cicero's primacy ("not even Cicero lacked detractors"), he makes the rounds of the standard reproaches: Cicero is bloated and wordy and *parum Atticus*, as his contemporaries Calvus and Brutus attest. "If you ask me," Aper says, "they were right." And yet he stops short, saying that this is not the right moment in his exposition to discuss such things, and so he puts it off.[86]

At *dial.* 22.1 the time has come: *ad Ciceronem uenio*, says Aper. This is the last part of his speech, what his catalog of orators had been leading up to. He makes explicit what Cicero in the *Brutus* could not; he makes Cicero the τέλος of oratory. And yet where Cicero had implied with all his might that this was a great and glorious end, Aper does precisely the opposite. In the final part of his "*Brutus*," he tears Cicero to shreds. Here as well, it should be noted, all allusions to Cicero's rhetorical writings abruptly cease: on the one hand, of course, Aper cannot imitate the *Brutus* anymore because he has now gone beyond it, but form also matches content, as Aper does not cloak his criticisms of Cicero in Ciceronianisms. The only bits of Cicero that are mentioned are singled out to be mocked.

Aper begins by tracing Cicero's development as an orator. He had some virtues, Aper must admit, but even they are given only tempered praise and immediately undermined (*dial.* 22.2–3):

primus enim excoluit orationem, primus et uerbis dilectum adhibuit et compositioni artem, locos quoque laetiores attemptauit et quasdam sententias inuenit, utique in iis orationibus, quas senior iam et iuxta finem uitae composuit, id est, postquam magis profecerat usuque et experimentis didicerat quod optimum dicendi genus esset. nam priores eius orationes non carent uitiis antiquitatis: lentus est in principiis, longus in narrationibus,

---

[86] He also takes a shot *en passant* at *dial.* 21.6, where, while ostensibly insulting the verse of Brutus and Caesar, he in fact puts a twist on the standard criticism of Cicero's poetic effusions: *fecerunt enim* [sc. Brutus et Caesar] *et carmina et in bibliothecas rettulerunt, non melius quam Cicero, sed felicius, quia illos fecisse pauciores sciunt.* On Cicero's poetry and its critics, cf. ch. 4 n. 97.

otiosus circa excessus; tarde commouetur, raro incalescit; pauci sensus apte et cum quodam lumine terminantur. nihil excerpere, nihil referre possis, et uelut in rudi aedificio, firmus sane paries et duraturus, sed non satis expolitus et splendens.

For he was the first to cultivate oratory, he was the first to apply both discriminating selection to words and artistry to composition; he also tried his hand at flowery passages and he came up with a few *sententiae*, at any rate in those speeches which he composed as an older man toward the end of his life, that is, after he had become more advanced and had learned by practice and experiment what the best style of speaking was. For his earlier speeches are not lacking in the vices of antiquity: he is slow in his introductions, long-winded in his narrations, fatiguing in his digressions; he gets worked up too late, and he rarely burns with feeling; few thoughts are concluded aptly and with some sort of ornamental phrase. You couldn't excerpt or quote any-thing, and he is just like a wall in a primitive building – solid, to be certain, and built to last, but insufficiently polished and shining.

The anaphoric *primus* could seem to praise Cicero as πρῶτος εὑρετής, but it also serves to undercut him as the "end" of oratory – far from being the end, he is in fact only the beginning! He "tried his hand" (*attemptauit*) at some more florid passages, perhaps implying a lack of success, and he came up with *quasdam sententias*, and that only toward the end of his career. His early speeches are thoroughly damned, stained as they are with the vices of antiquity (*uitiis antiquitatis*), which are then cataloged in detail: he is slow to get started, long-winded in *narrationes*, prone to superfluous digressions, hardly suitable for excerpting purple passages and quotable quotes. The best that can be said about his speeches is that they are "solid" (*firmus*) – a bit of damning with faint praise.

As if this recitation of Cicero's sins were not enough, Aper goes on to find yet more faults. He wants an oration to be studded with gemstones of rhetorical brilliance that gleam now this way, now that way in the light. He certainly does not want someone who ends every sentence with one and the same clausula (*nec omnes clausulas uno et eodem modo determinet, dial.* 22.5)! Ciceronian examples inevitably follow (*dial.* 23.1–2):

nolo inridere "rotam Fortunae" et "ius uerrinum" et illud tertio quoque sensu in omnibus orationibus pro sententia positum "esse uideatur." nam et haec inuitus rettuli et plura omisi, quae tamen sola mirantur atque expri-munt ii, qui se antiquos oratores uocitant. neminem nominabo, genus hominum significasse contentus.

I don't want to mock phrases like his *rotam Fortunae* and *ius uerrinum* and that *esse uideatur* which he tacks on to the end of every other sentence in all his speeches instead of a *sententia*. Indeed even these I've cited unwillingly, and I omit many more – and yet it is these things alone that those who fancy themselves "ancient" orators admire and imitate. I shall name no names, being content merely to have mentioned the type.

Aper claims that he does not wish to make fun of various Ciceronian phrases, but of course that is exactly what he does want to do, and his denial only serves to draw particular attention to it (the *praeteritio* is further emphasized by *inuitus rettuli* and *plura omisi*, which gives the impression of a vast store of such examples). His mockery in fact implies a very close reading of Cicero's speeches, for it is assumed that a phrase like *rotam Fortunae* – a commonplace idea in Latin literature[87] – will immediately evoke the Ciceronian pun and its context for the audience. "What pun?" you might well say – which rather proves the point. The tag is in fact just a throwaway barb from Cicero's invective *In Pisonem*, and not even directed at the main target of the speech: Gabinius, Piso's colleague, even while dancing naked at a feast and spinning a *saltatorius orbis*, had no fear of the *Fortunae rota* (*cumque ipse nudus in conuiuio saltaret, in quo cum illum saltatorium uersaret orbem, ne tum quidem Fortunae rotam*[88] *pertimescebat*, Cic. *Pis.* 22).[89] Presumably Aper felt that the comparison between the "wheel of fortune" and the "dancing hoop" was too far-fetched to be tolerable, and he certainly has singled out a nice example of Cicero straining for a point (although one might be forgiven for thinking that such a point would have suited Aper's taste).

The play on *ius Verrinum* in the *Verrines* was probably better known; after all, Cicero resorts to it several times in those speeches. The primary instance is *Verr.* II 1.121:

> hinc illi homines erant qui etiam ridiculi inueniebantur ex dolore; quorum alii, id quod saepe audistis, negabant mirandum esse ius tam nequam esse uerrinum; alii etiam frigidiores erant, sed quia stomachabantur ridiculi uidebantur esse, cum Sacerdotem exsecrabantur qui uerrem tam nequam reliquisset.

---

[87] See Otto (1890) 142.

[88] I do not make much of the differing word orders in Tacitus (*rotam Fortunae*) and Cicero (*Fortunae rotam*). Either the words have been exchanged in one of the traditions in the course of transmission, or Tacitus slipped up slightly in quoting from memory, or he deliberately misquoted so as to make Aper look less pedantic. If Tacitus has in fact misremembered, the fact that he could (more or less) trust himself to quote from memory is all the more evidence that Cicero's speeches were studied with exceptional intensity.

[89] Perhaps the scandalous and titillating nature of nude male dancing would have helped jog the readers' collective memory; cf. too *Verr.* II 3.24 *ille erat in tribunali proximus, in cubiculo solus, in conuiuio dominus, ac tum maxime cum accubante praetextato praetoris filio saltare in conuiuio nudus coeperat*; *Cat.* 2.23.

Hence there were even people who became comedians because of their anger. Some of them, as you have often heard, said that it was no wonder that *ius uerrinum* was so worthless; others were more insipid still, but because they were angry they seemed funny, when they cursed Sacerdos because he had left such a worthless *uerres* behind him.

Ius uerrinum of course means either "the justice of Verres" or "the juice of a boar," but Cicero rings variations on the theme on several further occasions (*Verr.* II 3.18, 3.191, 4.22, 5.5, 5.57, 5.95), and even Plutarch makes reference to it, claiming that Cicero, in defending one Caecilius against suspicion of Jewish practices, remarked (*Cic.* 7): "What does a Jew have to do with a pig?" (τί Ἰουδαίωι πρὸς χοῖρον;). Plutarch's mention is somewhat surprising, because in Greek there is no pun between Βέρρης and χοῖρος, but this merely underscores how well known Cicero's joke must have been. Quintilian was rather touchy on the whole Verres-the-pig point, saying, *nos quis ferat, si Verrem suem . . . nominemus?* ("Who would put up with us, if we were to call Verres 'Pig'?," *inst.* 8.6.37), but elsewhere he defends Cicero's impeccable taste by redirecting the blame. According to Quintilian, in telling these jokes Cicero merely reports the words on everyone's lips, words which his audience has already heard and which he acknowledges are somewhat lame: "It seems to me," Quintilian says,

> whether I judge rightly or am carried away by my love for the chief of eloquence, that Cicero was possessed of a remarkable *urbanitas* . . . for even those very things which were said somewhat lamely against Verres, those he attributed to others and employed for the purpose of evidence. The more banal these jokes were, the more reason there is to believe that they were common talk everywhere and not just invented by the speaker. (*inst.* 6.3.3–4; cf. 6.3.55)

Nevertheless, the fact that Quintilian must defend Cicero on this point on several occasions shows that it was a sore spot and a frequent target for Cicero's detractors – and one particularly apt for a detractor named *Aper*!

Finally there is the infamous *esse uideatur*. It is not actually found "in every other sentence in all his speeches," as Aper would have it, but Cicero certainly worked it hard,[90] and his imitators must have as well. Quintilian,

---

[90] Kinsey (1971) ad *Quinct.* 68 says that in Cicero's speeches *esse uideatur* occurs in clausular position "some eighty times." The distribution, however, is of interest; as Gudeman (1914) ad loc. p. 367 notes, it is much more common in early speeches (fifteen occurrences in the *Verrines*, for example), but it is altogether lacking in eighteen orations. It occurs moreover some seventy times in the *philosophica* and *rhetorica*, including thirty-one instances in the *De oratore* alone. (The letters furnish only twenty examples.) While Aper does exaggerate, the combination of the two words, plus their clausular position, plus their heavy rotation in places like the *De oratore*, plus the fact that the phrase

although he himself uses the clausula fourteen times, reports that it is *iam nimis frequens* (*inst.* 9.4.73) and that he knew some who thought that they had expressed themselves remarkably well if they concluded a sentence with that Ciceronian phrase (*noueram quosdam qui se pulchre expressisse genus illud caelestis huius in dicendo uiri sibi uiderentur si in clausula posuissent "esse uideatur,"* *inst.* 10.2.18).[91] This too, then, must have been a common criticism for a Ciceromastix to make, and Aper twists the knife just a little deeper by claiming that Cicero uses this phrase *pro sententia*, i.e. instead of the bit of sententious sparkle with which he should have rounded off a remark.

Aper is also keen to point out the neo-Ciceronians who ape Cicero's words in vain. We can deduce therefore that not only were Cicero's speeches read and studied so intensely that the mere mention of a tag was expected to jog the memory of the cognoscenti, but moreover sedulously imitated, doubtless as a result of training in the rhetorical classroom. Aper will have none of this.

Two sentences of exhortation to the other interlocutors follow (oddly not to Tacitus, who is roundly ignored), and so ends Aper's speech. Since Cicero is the acknowledged authority, virtually every point that Aper makes is expressed with reference to him. First Aper tries to claim Cicero's eloquence for the present age, which would sidestep the entire argument. Realizing perhaps the intrinsic weaknesses of this approach, however, he decides to make a virtue of necessity: he reworks Cicero's *Brutus*, following it to its apparent teleological end – Cicero himself – only to subvert our expectations and make Cicero the *beginning*. This allows him to have his cake and eat it too, because the looming specter of Cicero can fundamentally be rejected, while any of his good points can be refashioned as a mere prefiguration of the better things to come. One may feel that the argument relies as much on sophistry as on logic, but Aper simply cannot avoid dealing with Cicero's preeminence, and his solution is actually rather clever.

Messalla then essays a vigorous counter-attack in reply. He first dismantles Aper's casuistical chronology. Cicero and co. seem to be *antiqui* to him, but it really does not matter: Aper can call them whatever he would like, as long as all agree that eloquence has declined (*siue illos antiquos siue*

is often just a periphrasis for *sit* all make it stand out. (It is no coincidence that [Cic.] *in Sall.* 2 includes the tag.)

[91] Cf. Catullus' (H)Arrius: *et tum mirifice sperabat se esse locutum cum quantum poterat dixerat hinsidias* (84.3), where the Catullan commentators do not note the parallel. On this stigmatization of the hypercorrect aspirate, see Adams (2013) 125–127 with further references.

maiores siue quo alio mauult nomine appellet, dummodo in confesso sit eminentiorem illorum temporum eloquentiam fuisse, dial. 25.2). The next order of business is to respond to Aper's revisionist literary history, which Messalla does with the calm assurance of one with the full weight of Roman educational *auctoritas* on his side (*dial.* 25.3–4):

> sed quo modo inter Atticos oratores primae Demostheni tribuuntur, prox- imum [autem] locum Aeschines et Hyperides et Lysias et Lycurgus obti- nent, omnium autem concessu haec oratorum aetas maxime probatur, sic apud nos Cicero quidem ceteros eorundem temporum disertos antecessit, Caluus autem et Asinius et Caesar et Caelius et Brutus iure et prioribus et sequentibus anteponuntur. nec refert quod inter se specie differunt, cum genere consentiant. adstrictior Caluus, numerosior Asinius, splendidior Caesar, amarior Caelius, grauior Brutus, uehementior et plenior et ualentior Cicero: omnes tamen eandem sanitatem eloquentiae <prae se> ferunt.

> But just as among the Attic orators pride of place is given to Demosthenes, while Aeschines and Hyperides and Lysias and Lycurgus follow, and this era of oratory is by common consent considered the very best, so for us Cicero of course outpaces the rest of the speakers of his time, while Calvus and Asinius and Caesar and Caelius and Brutus rightly are ranked ahead of both those who came before them and those who followed them. And it doesn't matter that they differ from each other in points of detail, since they agree in general. Calvus is more concise, Asinius more rhythmical, Caesar more splendid, Caelius more bitter, Brutus more weighty, Cicero more vehement and fuller and more powerful: they all nevertheless exhibit the same vigorous type of eloquence.

Messalla begins with the typical comparison of Demosthenes and Cicero.[92] Demosthenes was the best of the Greeks, followed by various other con- temporary Attic orators; Cicero was the best Roman, again orbited by various lesser lights. They are all "rightly" (*iure*) preeminent compared to both their predecessors and successors. Messalla adjudicates among their various virtues, again with language and form reminiscent of the *Brutus* (e.g. *splendidior Caesar ~ Brut.* 261), but his catalog culminates in Cicero triumphant. The other members of the parade of names are assigned a single adjective, but Cicero merits three. He is undisputedly at the head of the procession.

Messalla next replies to Aper's criticism that Cicero and his contempor- aries constantly carped at each other. True enough, he says, but they have this fault because they are humans, not because they are orators. He would never claim that Cicero lacked jealousy or other human vices (perhaps

---

[92] See ch. 2 p. 93 and p. 267 below.

a necessary concession to the detractors?), but such flaws do not affect his oratorical prowess (*dial.* 25.5–6). Messalla then rebuts some of Aper's other characterizations in his history of eloquence, and finally trumps his argument entirely by pointing out that he has named no contemporary orators who could hold a candle to the best of the halcyon days of yore (*dial.* 26.6):

> ego autem exspectabam, ut incusato Asinio et Caelio et Caluo aliud nobis agmen produceret, plurisque uel certe totidem nominaret, ex quibus alium Ciceroni, alium Caesari, singulis deinde singulos opponeremus.

> I had been expecting that, after he had reproached Asinius and Caelius and Calvus, he would lead forth another column of orators for us and name more, or at any rate at least as many, from whom we might pit one against Cicero, another against Caesar, and in general man against man from the whole bunch.

Who is the modern Cicero? Messalla neatly demonstrates that Aper's catalog is not just incomplete; it is in fact fundamentally flawed. Cicero cannot be repurposed as the beginning of modern oratory if Aper cannot name his successors. He gives a sarcastic reason why Aper has refrained from naming names, namely that Aper was afraid of causing offense by an invidious selection (*ueritus credo ne multos offenderet, si paucos excerpsisset, dial.* 26.7). The parenthetical *credo* marks the irony. And yet even here he is playing with the *Brutus*, because in that dialogue Brutus claims in all seriousness that this is Cicero's real reason for not discussing his contemporaries: he alleges that Cicero is afraid that word of their conversation might get out and those whom he had passed over might get angry with him (*uereri te, inquit, arbitror ne per nos hic sermo tuus emanet et ii tibi suscenseant, quos praeterieris, Brut.* 231). Messalla's jibe is thus an elegant adaptation of the Ciceronian original with a tonal variation. Contemporary *scholastici*, he continues with further sarcasm (not *oratores*!), do not fear to rank themselves "before Cicero – but of course after Gabinianus" (*ante Ciceronem – sed plane post Gabinianum, dial.* 26.8). Gabinianus was a contemporary *rhetor* from Gaul, and so Messalla plainly implies that such a failure of judgment is completely ridiculous.[93] He himself is prepared to get down to brass tacks and name names to show

---

[93] This passage has often been misunderstood by commentators. Mayer (2001) ad loc. seems to take it too seriously, i.e. as reporting the fact that contemporary *rhetores* think this way. Whether any actually do or not is beside the point; the passage is dripping with sarcasm, and would be inexplicable otherwise. As Shackleton Bailey (1982) 255–256 points out, it makes no sense for boastful *rhetores* to think that they are better than Cicero but worse than Gabinianus. And yet that is precisely the point: they are fools devoid of sense. (And so Shackleton Bailey is wrong to emend *post Gabinianum* to *ante Gabinianum*; he has missed the sarcasm in his quest for logic.)

how far eloquence has fallen in the contemporary world when he is abruptly interrupted by Maternus. "We all agree that the *antiqui* were better. The question is why. Stick to the point!" In a clever move, then, Tacitus is saved from having to name names himself, which, while it would not have caused offense in the small circle of the imagined debate, certainly would have caused offense in the real world of Tacitus himself.

Thus prodded back into line, Messalla no longer kicks against the traces but rather sets out immediately to expound the causes of the decline. His reasoning is that of a cantankerous conservative, centering around the laziness of the youth and the failings of their parents and teachers and a collective forgetfulness of the morals of the good old days (*quis enim ignorat et eloquentiam et ceteras artes desciuisse ab illa uetere gloria non inopia hominum, sed desidia iuuentutis et neglegentia parentum et inscientia praecipientium et obliuione moris antiqui?, dial.* 28.2). Once, he says, free children were brought up by their own mothers, not raised in a servant's chamber by some rented nurse (*suus cuique filius … non in cella emptae nutricis, sed gremio ac sinu matris educabatur, dial.* 28.4). This recalls *Brut.* 211, and yet seems to flip its meaning, for there the Gracchi are described as <u>non tam in gremio educatos</u> quam in sermone matris – they were nourished by their mother's speech, not her bosom! Perhaps this is a subtle signal from Tacitus, coming right at the beginning of Messalla's disquisition on *causae*, that Messalla may not know what he is talking about. Messalla continues by decrying the *Graeculae* to whom child-raising is now entrusted (*dial.* 29.1), and he rails against lax discipline at home (29.2) and in the schools (29.4).

Indeed, Messalla avers, today's schools are simply entirely inadequate (*dial.* 30.1–2). We now hear the voice of the Quintilianic reformer speaking; it is tempting to wonder further whether the foregoing discussion of *causae* reproduces the argument of Quintilian's lost *De causis corruptae eloquentiae*. Whether that be the case or not, at this point Messalla again explicitly invokes the figure most central to the whole discussion, Cicero (*dial.* 30.3–4):

> notus est uobis utique Ciceronis liber, qui Brutus inscribitur, in cuius extrema parte (nam prior commemorationem ueterum oratorum habet)[94] sua initia, suos gradus, suae eloquentiae uelut quandam educationem refert:

---

[94] This parenthesis smacks of the glossator's pen to me. A parenthetical *nam*-clause can be Tacitean (see Gerber and Greef [1877–1902] 891–892), but if this one is genuine, it must be intended to characterize Messalla as exceptionally pedantic. (Editors generally agree that glosses have crept into the *Dialogus* at various places; *uirides* at 29.1 is followed by a superfluous *teneri*, for example. I would go further in expelling them than the current consensus: at 23.3, for example, *qui rhetorum nostrorum*

se apud Q. Mucium ius ciuile didicisse, apud Philonem Academicum, apud
Diodotum Stoicum omnis philosophiae partis penitus hausisse; neque iis
doctoribus contentum, quorum ei copia in urbe contigerat, Achaiam quoque et Asiam peragrasse, ut omnem omnium artium uarietatem complecteretur. itaque hercule in libris Ciceronis deprehendere licet, non
geometriae, non musicae, non grammaticae, non denique ullius ingenuae
artis scientiam ei defuisse. ille dialecticae subtilitatem, ille moralis partis
utilitatem, ille rerum motus causasque cognouerat.

Doubtless you know Cicero's book called the *Brutus*, in whose final part –
for the first part recounts the orators of old – he describes his beginnings and
his first steps, the education, as it were, of his eloquence. He studied civil law
with Quintus Mucius, he drank deep draughts of all parts of philosophy
with Philo the Academic and Diodotus the Stoic, and, not content with
those teachers whom he could hear easily in Rome, he traveled through
Greece and Asia in order to embrace every variety of every art. Therefore
indeed one can see from Cicero's works that he was not lacking in knowledge of geometry, or music, or grammar – in a word, not deficient in any art
befitting a free man. He knew the intricacies of dialectic, the utility of
morality, the motions of natural things and their causes.

The *Brutus* is cited by name – indeed, the whole phrase *notus est uobis
utique Ciceronis liber, qui Brutus inscribitur* might be thought a meta-
gesture to the dialogue's audience, who are supposed to recognize the
countless allusions to that work – and Cicero's educational *cursus* as
described therein is retailed. Civil law with Mucius, philosophy with
Philo the Academic and Diodotus the Stoic, a *Bildungsreise* through
Greece and Asia, geometry, music, grammar. Cicero devours every form
of learning with his insatiable appetite for knowledge. The point?
No branch of human knowledge is foreign to him; he did all this to
embrace the full range of learning (*ut omnem omnium artium uarietatem
complecteretur*). The polyptoton and the "holy of holies" construction
emphasize Cicero's vast range, but the phrase also alludes to *de orat.* 3.72,
where in a prelapsarian past philosophers pursued universal knowledge
(*ueteres illi usque ad Socratem* omnem omnium rerum*, quae ad mores hominum, quae ad uitam, quae ad uirtutem, quae ad rem publicam pertinebant,
cognitionem et scientiam* cum dicendi ratione iungebant*). This is the ideal
with which the present superficial focus on the *dicendi ratio* alone is being
contrasted, and the implicit argument is what we find in Quintilian (e.g.
inst. 12.2.6–7): if we want to be eloquent again as Cicero once was, we must

commentarios fastidiunt, oderunt, Calui *mirantur*, surely *oderunt* is a gloss? [Hor. *epist.* 2.1.22 *fastidit
et odit* is no defense.])

follow his prescription and embrace the full range of a liberal arts education (*dial.* 30.5):

> ita est enim, optimi uiri, ita: ex multa eruditione et plurimis artibus et omnium rerum scientia exundat et exuberat illa admirabilis eloquentia; neque oratoris uis et facultas, sicut ceterarum rerum, angustis et breuibus terminis cluditur, sed is est orator, qui de omni quaestione pulchre et ornate et ad persuadendum apte dicere pro dignitate rerum, ad utilitatem temporum, cum uoluptate audientium possit.

> Yes indeed, you wonderful fellows, yes indeed: that marvelous eloquence of his welled up and flowed forth from his great store of erudition and his mastery of so many skills and his knowledge of all things; nor is the orator's force and skill, as is the case with other things, closed off by narrow boundaries, but rather an orator is a man who can speak with beauty and grace on any issue, in a manner such as to persuade and befitting the dignity of the matter and suited to the needs of the moment and the pleasure of his audience.

Cicero's eloquence (*illa admirabilis eloquentia*) – and hence any eloquence – relies on much learning and a comprehensive knowledge; the orator's field is not narrow, but rather he must be able to speak appropriately on any topic as the occasion requires. While Messalla has linked his discussion to the *Brutus*, he has really been advocating a return to the ideals of the *De oratore*, and here, in this crowning moment, he weaves together several disparate strands from that treatise into one unified tapestry. The first part of the sentence reworks *de orat.* 1.20, where it is claimed that no one can be a perfect orator *nisi erit omnium rerum magnarum atque artium scientiam consecutus: etenim ex rerum cognitione efflorescat et redundet oportet oratio* ("unless he has gained a knowledge of every worthwhile subject and art: for a speech ought to flower and flow forth from a knowledge of things"). Tacitus has not only varied some of the vocabulary (e.g. *exundat et exuberat* instead of *efflorescat et redundet*), but he has also even outdone Cicero with an elegant tricolon crescens whose content matches its form: *ex multa eruditione et plurimis artibus et omnium rerum scientia.*[95] The next phrase, *oratoris uis et facultas*, derives directly from *de*

---

[95] Such tricola are infinitely more typical of Cicero's style than that of Tacitus. In the *Dialogus* Messalla particularly favors them; cf. e.g. *dial.* 34.3 *magnus ex hoc usus, multum constantiae, plurimum iudicii* (also 32.4, 32.9, 33.8). This matching of Ciceronian form to Ciceronian tendencies may help characterize Messalla in particular, but I would not push this point too hard: it does not seem to have been the convention of Roman dialogues to make sharp linguistic distinctions among the interlocutors. If Tacitus had really intended to do this, he presumably would have made Aper's speeches much *less* Ciceronian than they actually appear to be in the work.

orat. 1.142 (cf. *de orat.* 1.245, 2.125), but also picks up on *de orat.* 1.21 *uis oratoris*, which immediately follows the sentence discussed above. Messalla concludes his thought, finally, with a definition blended from a trio of Ciceronian ingredients. *De orat.* 1.21 again provides the immediate impetus: *ut omni de re, quaecumque sit proposita, ornate ab eo* [sc. *oratore*] *copioseque dicatur* ("so that every subject, whatever might be proposed, can be the theme of the orator's elegant and full speech"), but *de orat.* 1.64 is closer in form: *is orator erit mea sententia hoc tam graui dignus nomine qui, quaecumque res inciderit quae sit dictione explicanda, prudenter et composite et ornate et memoriter dicet cum quadam actionis etiam dignitate* ("the one who will be an orator worthy of this weighty name, in my opinion, will speak prudently and in an orderly way, with elegance and accuracy and a certain dignity of delivery as well, on whatever subject happens to arise that requires discussion"), and *de orat.* 1.138 *ad persuadendum accommodate* ("suitable for persuasion") provides a key phrase as well. In returning to these Ciceronian ideals, then, Messalla expresses himself in variations on Cicero's own thoughts.

Such Ciceronian frolics continue throughout the next section, where Messalla treats Cicero's program for training the orator. In Cicero's day, he says, students did not waste time declaiming in the rhetorical schools to train their tongues in nonsense exercises that bore no relation to reality, but rather tried to imbue their minds with discussions about things which really mattered: *nec ut fictis nec ullo modo ad ueritatem accedentibus controuersiis linguam modo et uocem exercerent, sed ut* [*in*] *iis artibus pectus implerent in quibus de bonis ac malis, de honesto et turpi, de iusto et iniusto disputatur; haec enim est oratori subiecta ad dicendum materia* ("not just to exercise their tongue and their voice in fictitious *controuersiae* that in no way resembled true court cases, but rather to fill their breasts with those arts by which one discusses good and evil, virtue and vice, justice and injustice; for this is the subject matter that an orator will speak about," *dial.* 31.1). The first part of this complaint neatly flips Crassus' praise of declamations that are spoken *quam maxime ad ueritatem accommodate* ("resembling true court cases as much as possible"),[96] and amplifies his criticism of those who *uocem modo . . . exercent et linguae celeritatem incitant* ("just exercise their voice and stimulate the speed of their tongue," *de orat.* 1.149). The students of yore sought to fill their breasts with knowledge of good and evil and other commendable things; the contrast between exercising one's *lingua* and filling one's *pectus* may also rework *de orat.* 1.121 *non enim solum*

---

[96] On this notion of *ueritas*, see Brink (1989) 476 n. 24.

acuenda nobis neque procudenda <u>*lingua*</u> *est, sed onerandum complendumque* <u>*pectus*</u> *maximarum rerum et plurimarum suauitate, copia, uarietate* ("for the <u>tongue</u> is not just to be forged to a keen edge, but the <u>breast</u> too is to be stocked and filled with a charming and varied supply of the most important things in the greatest number"). Finally, the phrase *subiecta . . . materia* is often used by Cicero (*de orat.* 1.201, 2.116, 3.54), but always with *materies*, not *materia* – Mayer speculates that "T[acitus'] feel for the language did not allow him to borrow Cicero's form of the word . . . for it probably seemed to him somewhat archaic."[97] In such matters there is little reason to trust the orthographic evidence of the manuscripts, and so I am reluctant to push this evidence very far, but the Ciceronian tag is unmistakable.[98]

So too no one can speak *copiose et uarie et ornate* in the various genres of oratory *nisi qui cognouit naturam humanam et uim uirtutum prauitatemque uitiorum et intellectum eorum quae nec in uirtutibus nec in uitiis numerantur* ("<u>unless he has formed an acquaintance with human nature and the meaning of the virtues</u> and the wickedness of vices and the understanding of those things which are counted as neither virtues nor vices," *dial.* 31.2). The three adverbs are linked by Cicero at *de orat.* 2.120 (although various pairs of this triad are found yoked elsewhere as well), and the conditional protasis reproduces *de orat.* 1.53 *nisi qui naturas hominum uimque omnem humanitatis . . . perspexerit* ("unless he has explored human nature and the entire meaning of humanity"). The echoes continue throughout this part of the speech, and I will forbear to detail them all. I will only add that the *Orator* is sometimes invoked too, as at *dial.* 32.5 *Demosthenen . . . studiosissimum Platonis auditorem* ("Demosthenes . . . the most eager listener of Plato"), which appears to blend *de orat.* 1.89 *Platonis studiosus audiendi* ("eager to listen to Plato") and *orat.* 15 *Platonis auditor* (a listener of Plato), both likewise of Demosthenes. Indeed, at *dial.* 32.6 Messalla even cites the *Orator*, if only vaguely out of a concern for the appearance of pedantry, to support his view that excessive interest in fantastic declamation is a chief cause of the decline in oratory. After all, he claims, Cicero himself had said that whatever he had achieved as an orator derived not from the workshops of the rhetoricians but from the promenades of the Academy: *et Cicero his ut opinor uerbis refert, quidquid in eloquentia effecerit, id se non "rhetorum <officinis>," sed Academiae spatiis consecutum* ("and Cicero reports, with these words, I think, that whatever he accomplished in the field of

---

[97] Mayer (2001) ad loc.

[98] Outside of Cicero, *TLL* viii.459.47–51 (Bömer) cites only our Tacitus passage and Quintilian, who is of course himself being Ciceronian. *Subiecta material/materies* does appear to become a more common phrase in the late antique grammarians.

eloquence, he achieved not 'from the workshops of the *rhetores*,' but from the grounds of the Academy"). Cicero had written *fateor me oratorem . . . non ex rhetorum officinis sed ex Academiae spatiis exstitisse* ("I confess that I became an orator not from the workshops of the *rhetores* but from the grounds of the Academy," *orat.* 12).[99]

Here Messalla brings his speech to a conclusion. From head to toe his Ciceronian thoughts are clothed in Ciceronian language. He, like Quintilian, believes that oratory can be restored to its former glory if only today's youth would follow sedulously in Cicero's footsteps on the path to eloquence. The essential point is that there must be a return to the Ciceronian ideals of the *De oratore*, and those ideals must be made reality. (He also never acknowledges that they were merely ideals in the first place; he treats what he presents as the way things actually were.) It may go too far to say that Messalla equals Quintilian *tout court*,[100] but he certainly represents Quintilian's ideals.[101] Interestingly, Messalla's speech makes Quintilian's argument afresh and returns *ad fontes*, that is, to Cicero's various works, rather than to their distillation in the *Institutio oratoria*. There is perhaps not a single verbal allusion to Quintilian in the speech,[102] and yet it seems to breathe the Quintilianic spirit. This is doubtless at some level simply because Cicero's spirit had been reborn in Quintilian, but

---

[99] Whitton (2018) 43–45 reads this citation as a window reference through Quint. *inst.* 12.2.23 *nam M. Tullius non tantum se debere scholis rhetorum quantum Academiae spatiis frequenter ipse testatus est.* Messalla's *his ut opinor uerbis* would thus be corrective of Quintilian's slight misquotation. But Tacitus' *officinis* is itself conjectural, and so the suggestion remains uncertain, although Whitton supports it with another suggestive connection between Demosthenes in the two texts.

[100] As Barwick thought; see n. 45 above. On the relationship between Messalla and Quintilian, see also the discussion and references collected in van den Berg (2014) 210 n. 6, and now Whitton (2018) 41–45.

[101] There has been a surprising amount of controversy on this point, which I altogether fail to understand; see the detailed doxography in Brink (1989) 485 nn. 46, 47, and 48. Brink himself sees Messalla as being Quintilianic, while noting that this does not imply that Tacitus himself holds the same positions – I of course agree. I am, however, mystified by Brink's notion (not unique to him; cf. e.g. Mayer [2001] 175) that Messalla, unlike Quintilian, believes that oratory cannot be revived (e.g. 485 n. 48, 493). Messalla never says such a thing, and I should think the whole point of his detailed description of the philosophy and training of the *antiqui* is precisely that of Quintilian, namely that it can be put into practice today and turn the tide. (So too Williams [1978] 31 and Döpp [1986] 16.) An explicit statement to this effect may have perished in the lacuna after *dial.* 35.5.

[102] None is adduced by Güngerich (1951), and I see only one possible candidate in Mayer (2001) (ad *dial.* 26.4 p. 173, comparing the brawling oratory of Cassius Severus, who *ipsis etiam quibus utitur armis incompositus et studio feriendi plerumque deiectus . . . rixatur*, with *inst.* 2.12.2, of the untrained speaker hoisting himself by his own petard: *nam et gladiator qui armorum inscius in rixam ruit et luctator qui totius corporis nisu in id quod semel inuasit incumbit . . . frequenter suis uiribus ipse prosternitur*; there is to be certain a similarity between the two passages, but it may well be a commonplace idea). Cf. Whitton (2018) 42 on possible structural allusions to Quintilian in Messalla's speech.

perhaps there is more to it than that. I might speculate that Tacitus'
Messalla out-Quintilians even Quintilian by returning to the pure and
untainted wellsprings of his thought.

Messalla thus appears successful in countering Aper's arguments, and to
such an extent his view seems at least "more right" than that of the radical
modernists. Nevertheless, Maternus is not satisfied. Messalla has only made
a beginning of the task, he says, by discussing the comprehensiveness of the
old educational system and the degeneracy of today's youth (*dial.* 33.1).
Maternus wants to know more about the practice of the old educational
system, not just its theoretical basis.[103] This may be a subtle dig at the notion
that these pie-in-the-sky ideals were ever a lived reality, but Messalla does not
flinch. He calmly takes up the task, claiming that he has sufficiently
demonstrated the first beginnings and the seeds of the eloquence of yore
by discussing how ancient orators were educated and instructed, and so he
will now discuss their exercises (*quoniam initia et semina ueteris eloquentiae
satis demonstrasse uideor docendo quibus artibus antiqui oratores institui erudirique soliti sint, persequar nunc exercitationes eorum, dial.* 33.4). Both *initia et
semina* and *institui erudirique* are Ciceronian pairs,[104] and this opening
sentence comes after a Ciceronian transition,[105] and so there can be little
doubt that more Cicero is on tap. Messalla begins to discuss the *tirocinium
fori*, but is quickly sidetracked by criticism of the declamation with which
modern youth occupy themselves. Cicero is of course again the reference
point and authority (*dial.* 35.1):

> at nunc adulescentuli nostri deducuntur in scholas istorum, qui rhetores
> uocantur, quos paulo ante Ciceronis tempora exstitisse nec placuisse maior-
> ibus nostris ex eo manifestum est, quod a Crasso et Domitio censoribus
> claudere, ut ait Cicero, "ludum impudentiae" iussi sunt.

> But now our young men are led off to the schools of those people who call
> themselves *rhetores*. It's clear that these people did not even exist a short time
> before Cicero's day, nor did they win the approval of our ancestors, for they
> were ordered by the censors Crassus and Domitius to close, as Cicero says,
> the "school of impudence."

---

[103] Bringmann (1970) 171 and n. 40 reads Maternus' emphasis on practice over theory as undercutting
Messalla's Ciceronianism, but it is oversubtle to think that Maternus here adopts Quintus Cicero's
position that eloquence is founded on natural talent and practice, not wide learning (*de orat.* 1.5 *tu
autem illam ab elegantia doctrinae segregandam putes et in quodam ingeni atque exercitationis genere
ponendam*). Such a view is moreover inconsistent with Maternus' following speech.

[104] Cic. *Tusc.* 5.69 *initiorum et tamquam seminum* (cf. Quint. *inst.* 2.20.6 *initia quaedam ac semina*), *de
orat.* 3.35 *qui instituunt aliquos atque erudiunt*, *Verr.* ii 3.161 *instituere atque erudire ad maiorum
instituta*.

[105] Discussed on p. 245 above.

Messalla's voice drips with contempt. He refuses even to acknowledge that such a category as *rhetores* exists ("so called," he says), referring to them with a depreciatory "those people" (*istorum*) – this nonsense was scarcely to be found in Cicero's day, and such places were of the lowest possible repute. His argument is supported by Cicero's own words: Cicero's Crassus had called these schools *ludi impudentiae* at *de orat.* 3.94. It is also plain that Tacitus has derived his whole knowledge of the situation from that passage of the *De oratore*, for in reality the schools were not closed, only formally censured (see Suet. *gramm.* 25.2 for the edict), but in the *De oratore* Crassus says that as censor he did away with Latin teachers of rhetoric (*quos* [sc. *Latinos magistros dicendi*] *ego censor edicto meo sustuleram*, 3.93). Tacitus – or just possibly the character Messalla – must have believed this meant that the schools were shut down.[106] In light of all this, we would doubtless expect more Ciceronian words and spirit to come, but these have disappeared into the lacuna after *dial.* 35.5.[107]

When the text resumes, Maternus is speaking. His explanation for the decline of oratory is entirely novel: in the Empire, unlike in the Republic, there is simply no scope for oratory. He thus sweeps aside both the notion of a moral decline and the possibility of a rebirth of eloquence. In some ways his speech is the least concerned with Cicero, because for him Cicero no longer matters – eloquent oratory is no longer possible, and so Cicero becomes an inimitable model and therefore irrelevant. And yet he too casts his argument in a Ciceronian mold, mentioning him several times explicitly and alluding to various passages from his works. The most remarkable of these, as we shall see, comes at the climax of his speech, when he expresses the kernel of his argument in language that unmistakably subverts Cicero's own: he rejects Cicero using Cicero's own words. This is, writ small, exactly what Tacitus has done in the larger project of the *Dialogus*.

Cicero remains, of course, the pinnacle of eloquence. Thus Maternus briefly makes the standard comparison with Demosthenes,[108] and uses Cicero's speeches to illustrate his contention that political oratory is preeminent (*dial.* 37.6):

> non, opinor, Demosthenem orationes inlustrant, quas aduersus tutores suos composuit, nec Ciceronem magnum oratorem P. Quinctius defensus aut Licinius Archias faciunt: Catilina et Milo et Verres et Antonius hanc illi famam circumdederunt, non quia tanti fuerit rei publicae malos ferre ciues,

---

[106] This point is well made by Mayer (2001) ad loc. p. 196.   [107] See p. 235 above.
[108] Cf. ch. 2 p. 93 as well as p. 258 above.

ut uberem ad dicendum materiam oratores haberent, sed, ut subinde admoneo, quaestionis meminerimus sciamusque nos de ea re loqui, quae facilius turbidis et inquietis temporibus existit.

It is not, in my opinion, the speeches which Demosthenes composed against his guardians that made his reputation, nor do Cicero's defense speeches for P. Quinctius or Licinius Archias make him a great orator: the *Catilinarians* and the *Pro Milone* and the *Verrines* and the *Philippics*, these speeches won him his fame – not that it was worthwhile for the Republic to bear bad citizens just so that orators might have material for their speeches, but, as I keep reminding you, let us remember the point at issue and acknowledge that we are talking about the sort of thing which is more easily produced in times of trouble and discord.

Cicero made his reputation in his most important public cases; the smaller private affairs were of little consequence. The point, of course, is that for orators in the imperial age, the small-scale disputes of the centumviral court were all that remained. It is not surprising that the most famous Attic orator and his Roman counterpart are the ones singled out to make this point: who better could be chosen? This is the central Ciceronian syncrisis of the schoolroom.[109] Maternus goes on to point out that the centumviral court, which in his day is the most important court in the land, was for Cicero of so little consequence that not a single speech delivered before that body by him or any of his contemporaries is read anymore (*dial.* 38.2). Nothing could be better calculated to humiliate contemporary orators and show up the poor state of oratory.

Maternus also mentions Cicero's death, that quintessential piece of his life for the imperial audience (*dial.* 40.4):

nostra quoque ciuitas, donec errauit, donec se partibus et dissensionibus et discordiis confecit . . . . tulit sine dubio ualentiorem eloquentiam . . . sed nec tanti rei publicae Gracchorum eloquentia fuit ut pateretur et leges, nec bene famam eloquentiae Cicero tali exitu pensauit.

Our state too, while it was unsettled, while it was rent by factions and disagreements and discord . . . without a doubt brought forth a stronger species of eloquence . . . but the eloquence of the Gracchi was not enough to make the Republic tolerate their laws as well, nor did Cicero's reputation for eloquence make up for that death of his.

The Gracchi's eloquence was not enough to make the Republic put up with their controversial laws, and Cicero's reputation for eloquence was

---

[109] Some of the comparison is left implicit here. So note that Demosthenes' speeches against his tutors were his first, as was Cicero's *Pro Quinctio*; the point is made explicitly by Gell. 15.28.6–7.

a poor recompense for his death. This death had of course long since become a stock declamatory theme (see ch. 3), and Maternus alludes to its fame (or notoriety) in the phrase _tali exitu,_ "such an end – you all know the one I'm talking about." He closely links the political climate of the late Republic, Cicero's eloquence, and his death, as so many declaimers had before him, and yet he ostensibly takes a very different line from them. The declaimers were wont to claim that Cicero's eloquence more than compensated for his death, and so they tried to console him and advise him not to bargain with the devil Antony for his life. Maternus, like Juvenal,[110] seems to be saying that it simply was not worth it. But can he mean this seriously? Juvenal was being satirical, and I think Maternus must likewise be speaking ironically here: he cannot possibly believe that Cicero should have forgone his eloquence and fame and lived to a ripe old age in comfortable obscurity. He himself, after all, courts a similar fate by unapologetically writing pointed political tragedies. As I shall show presently, the irony here is very much of a piece with the tenor of Maternus' speech as a whole.

Maternus' entire speech is shot through with Ciceronian tags. From the moment that the speech as we have it begins, there are numerous Ciceronian doublets: _nihil humile, nihil abiectum_ (*dial.* 36.1 ~ *orat.* 192; cf. *fin.* 5.57), _ingenio et eloquentia_ (*dial.* 36.7 ~ *Brut.* 318), _spoliatam uexatamque_ (*dial.* 41.2 ~ *Verr.* II 3.29 and *passim*), and so forth. As always, these help maintain the uniform veneer of Ciceronian style. So too are there various longer borrowings. Contemporary orators, Maternus says, often must plead their case with only two or three others looking on, but the orator in fact requires a large and boisterous audience of the sort that was de rigueur for the ancients: _oratori autem clamore plausuque opus est et uelut quodam theatro_ ("an orator needs shouting and applause and, so to speak, a theater," *dial.* 39.4). Cicero had emphasized this point as well: _orator sine multitudine audiente eloquens esse non possit_ ("an orator cannot be eloquent without a large audience," *de orat.* 2.338), which he precedes with the same theatrical metaphor, describing a *contio* as the _maxima quasi oratoris scaena_ ("the greatest stage, as it were, for the orator," ibid.; cf. too *Brut.* 6 _forum ... quasi theatrum ... ingeni_). Such borrowings again bespeak a close engagement with Cicero's corpus throughout the argument.[111]

---

[110] See ch. 2 p. 99.

[111] Cf. too e.g. *dial.* 36.3 _hinc contiones magistratuum paene pernoctantium in rostris_ and *Brut.* 305 _hi quidem habitabant in rostris._ The allusion to the fragmentary *Hortensius* at 41.3 (_quod si inueniretur aliqua ciuitas in qua nemo peccaret, superuacuus esset inter innocentes orator sicut inter sanos medicus_; cf. *Hort.* fr. 110 Gr. _quid opus esset eloquentia, cum iudicia nulla fierent,_ of the Isles of the Blest) is

Most interesting, however, is a case where Maternus resorts to Cicero at the very height of his argument. Toward the end of his speech he summarizes his main contention, that a fractious Republic provides fertile ground for oratory, whereas a well-ordered state like the current Empire does not (*dial.* 42.2–3):

> non de otiosa et quieta re loquimur et quae probitate et modestia gaudeat, sed est magna illa et notabilis eloquentia alumna licentiae, quam stulti libertatem uocitant, comes seditionum, effrenati populi incitamentum, sine obsequio, sine seueritate, contumax, temeraria, adrogans, quae in bene constitutis ciuitatibus non oritur. quem enim oratorem Lacedaemonium, quem Cretensem accepimus? quarum ciuitatum seuerissima disciplina et seuerissimae leges traduntur. ne Macedonum quidem ac Persarum aut ullius gentis, quae certo imperio contenta fuerit, eloquentiam nouimus. Rhodii quidam, plurimi Athenienses oratores exstiterunt, apud quos omnia populus, omnia imperiti, omnia, ut sic dixerim, omnes poterant.

> We're not talking about a quiet and peaceful thing here, one that rejoices in good and upright conduct – no, great and noteworthy eloquence is the child of *licentia*, what foolish men call *libertas*, the companion of sedition, a goad for the unbridled people, devoid of allegiance or respect, insolent, bold, arrogant, the sort of thing that does not arise in well-ordered states. For what Spartan orator have you ever heard of, what Cretan? In those cities the strictest discipline and the strictest laws are the tradition. Eloquence is unknown even in Macedonia and Persia, and in any other nation which is constrained by fixed *imperium*. There were some orators at Rhodes, and many at Athens – in those places the people, the ignorant mass, governed everything; "everyone," so to speak, "could do everything."

These sentences pack in so much Cicero that they nearly burst apart at the seams – and yet to a word it is disagreed with and subverted. "We're not talking about a quiet and peaceful thing here," says Maternus, "one that rejoices in good and upright conduct" – but in fact that is precisely what Cicero had claimed was required for oratory! At *Brut.* 45 he had said that *pacis est comes otique socia et iam bene constitutae ciuitatis quasi alumna quaedam eloquentia* ("eloquence is the companion of peace and the ally of tranquillity and, as it were, the child of an already well-ordered state"). Could Maternus have disagreed any more vehemently? His eloquence, by

---

intriguing, and we can only recognize it because Augustine has coincidentally preserved the fragment (*trin.* 14.9.12). In the absence of more context, however, we cannot press the allusion much further.

contrast, is the *alumna licentiae*, and *in bene constitutis ciuitatibus non oritur* ("does not arise in well-ordered states").[112]

Maternus moreover denigrates this *licentia, quam stulti libertatem uocitant*[113], plainly evoking Scipio's words in *rep.* 1.68 *ex hac nimia licentia, quam illi solam libertatem putant*,[114] and yet everything about this phrase should make us uneasy. Is Maternus really so in favor of the imperial system? Is he happy to live in a world with no scope for oratory? Or is there perhaps some irony here? "License which fools keep calling liberty." It is hardly consonant with the rest of Tacitus' oeuvre for him to decry *libertas*, but of course you might object that these are only the words of a character in a dialogue, not necessarily Tacitus' own opinion. Fair enough. And yet they are completely inconsistent with the Maternus who had dared to offend the powerful in his tragedy *Cato* (the ostensible cause for the *Dialogus* in the first place), who defiantly boasted that if his *Cato* had left anything out, this deficiency would be made good in his *Thyestes* (*dial.* 3.3)![115] It is, moreover, striking that Maternus has chosen *this* passage of the *De re publica* to allude to, for it describes how a tyranny develops out of a democracy. It is not hard to see a parallel development unfolding as the paragraph continues and shows the evolution of the Principate from the wild days of the dying Republic. Just when Maternus appears to be praising

[112] Güngerich (1980) ad loc. p. 176 makes an interesting observation on the usage of *alumna* here: "bei Tac[itus] und bei Cicero wird *alumnus* sonst stets von einer Person im eigentlichen Sinne gebraucht."

[113] *uocabant* codd., *uocant* Heumann, *uocitant* Hess. The imperfect cannot stand, and I prefer *uocitant*, since (1) it is used elsewhere in the *Dialogus* (23.2), (2) it is very easy to see how *uocitant* could have been misrecognized and replaced by *uocabant*, and (3) the frequentative makes a stronger point about the supposed fools of the present day.

[114] Köstermann (1930) 415–417 was the first to notice the echo of the *De re publica* sandwiched between the *Brutus* allusions.

[115] This inconsistency has been dealt with in various ways. Bartsch (1994) 98–125, esp. 110–119, has made a sophisticated argument about Maternus' use of "double-speak" to criticize the imperial regime, and some earlier scholars have likewise regarded Maternus' final speech as ironic (see Mayer [2001] 43 n. 98). Nevertheless, no one has yet brought the Ciceronian intertextuality into play as evidence to support such an interpretation. Of those who do *not* view Maternus' speech as ironic, the most interesting explanations for his contradictions have been put forth by Williams (1978) 33–42, who regards Maternus' first speech as being given "in character" in AD 75, but his second speech as instead applying to Tacitus' contemporary world *ca.* AD 102; Luce (1993), who regards each individual speech as a declamation complete unto itself and concerned only with presenting the strongest possible argument for the current topic of discussion, not with consistency with the characters' earlier utterances; and Gowing (2005) 109–117, who attacks the very premise of the problem, arguing that a *Cato* could pose no political threat to Vespasian. The positions of Williams and Luce strike me as special pleading, while the contention of Gowing relies on questioning the implication of Tacitus and the statements of Aper and Secundus that the *Cato* was in fact dangerous. Cf. too Barnes (1986) 238–244 on the possible literary ramifications of Maternus' prosopographical identity. Van den Berg (2014) 55–57 and *passim* (300–301 on this speech) argues for allowing the work's inconsistencies to stand productively unresolved.

the Principate, then, this intertext allows for a subversive ideological reading.

Maternus is far from finished with subverting his Cicero. He calls oratory the *effrenati populi incitamentum* ("a goad for the unbridled people"), which precisely reverses *de orat.* 2.35 *et languentis populi incitatio et effrenati moderatio* ("a stimulus for the listless and a check on the unbridled people"). He continues by saying, *quem enim oratorem Lacedaemonium, quem Cretensem accepimus? quarum ciuitatum seuerissima disciplina et seuerissimae leges traduntur* ("For what Spartan orator have you ever heard of, what Cretan? In those cities the strictest discipline and the strictest laws are the tradition"). So too Cicero continues in the *Brutus* (45): *quis enim aut Argiuum oratorem aut Corinthium aut Thebanum scit fuisse temporibus illis? ... Lacedaemonium uero usque ad hoc tempus audiui fuisse neminem* ("Who ever heard of an Argive or a Corinthian or a Theban orator in those days? ... and as for a Spartan orator, right up until today I've never heard of a single one"). And yet Cicero's precise point was to praise unruly Athens as the birthplace of oratory; Sparta and the other places are but barren fields being singled out for criticism. And why are they barren? Because they are governed by *imperium*, of all things, which certainly ought to ring a bell for Tacitus' readership. Again we might suspect that Maternus is not telling us how he really feels – or that he is, but only if we look closely enough at his allusions and inconsistencies.

Minor points of contact (e.g. *Rhodii quidam* < *Brut.* 51) are maintained throughout the rest of the sentence, but the allusive texture is already clear. At this climactic moment of his speech, and indeed of the entire *Dialogus*, Maternus has chosen to engage deeply with Cicero. In melting down several pieces of Ciceronian metal, he has forged a new alloy that seems to serve at least two purposes. First, he genuinely disagrees with Cicero about the right conditions for oratory. Cicero is simply wrong, he thinks, to believe that oratory is a product of peace and leisure. This disagreement leads him to reject Cicero as a model and to leave oratory behind, for it is no longer possible in the pacified and subdued Roman Empire. And yet, just because Maternus recognizes the inevitability and irreversibility of the predicament (i.e., he rejects both Aper's and Messalla's arguments), that hardly means that he has to like it. Throughout this section Maternus' apparent inconsistencies and subversive allusions to Cicero allow us to read into his words a real criticism of the imperial system that has engineered the end of oratory and the end of freedom.

Tacitus has united Cicero, eloquence, and politics into one interwoven braid. Earlier in the *Dialogus*, in a very unusual move, he had in effect dated the beginning of the Empire to Cicero's death.[116] The switch to an imperial government is thus heralded by the slaying of Cicero, which extinguished not just the voice of Rome's greatest orator, but indeed oratory itself. Silencing Cicero, as Cicero's proscribers sought to do, is made equivalent to the end of both eloquence and the Republic, for Cicero was both "eloquence personified" and "the voice of the people." For Tacitus, then, Cicero, eloquence, and the Republican political system are all snuffed out in one fell swoop on 7 December 43 BC.

Cicero is thus absolutely central to the *Dialogus* from its opening through its various speeches and all the way up to its last words.[117] Tacitus does not merely parrot a few half-remembered tags or worn-out stories from his school days; his Cicero helps shape both form and content; he is discussed explicitly by each of the speakers, and even when they are not speaking his name, their words show that they are constantly thinking about him. Since Cicero had become a byword for eloquence, it makes sense that the whole *Dialogus* is essentially framed around the question "What do we do with Cicero?" Aper tries to appropriate the parts he likes and reject the rest; Messalla, the Quintilianic reformer, says that if we want to be eloquent we must retrace Cicero's steps to the summit of eloquence; Maternus rejects Cicero with Cicero's own words and declares that eloquence is not just dying, it is dead and cannot be brought back to life. One might almost have entitled the work *Dialogus de Cicerone* – or perhaps *Dialogus cum Cicerone*?

Conclusion

So much for the arguments and allusions as seen from the perspective of the personae of their speakers. Ultimately, of course, the work is the unified product of a single mind, composed as a supremely skilled artistic master-piece, not a transcript of a historical conversation, and so we would like to understand the intertextual agenda of our elusively allusive author. What does Tacitus himself get out of all the Cicero and Ciceronianisms in his *Dialogus*? What is the overall impression of the work, and how does the intertextuality contribute to it?

The overall impression is unquestionably that not only has oratory declined, but the decline, owing to the changed political circumstances

---

[116] *Dial.* 17.2–3. According to Mayer (2001) 21, only Suetonius (*Aug.* 8.3) and Tacitus (here and *ann.* 1.9.1) date the beginning of the Empire to 43. Dio, for example, points to Actium (61.30.5). See further Sion-Jenkis (2000) 53–64.

[117] *Cum arrisissent, discessimus* (*dial.* 42.2): laughter often ends a day of Ciceronian dialogue (e.g. *de orat.* 1.265 *arridens*), and *discessimus* is the last word of *fin.* 3.80.

that Maternus outlines, is irreversible. Ronald Martin was nonetheless right to caution that "in Ciceronian dialogues one is rarely in doubt what the author's own opinion is: in the *Dialogus* it would be very unwise to think that any one character is exclusively the author's mouthpiece,"[118] and the equation Maternus = Tacitus is probably untenable.[119] Each speaker makes genuine contributions to the debate, and in Aper especially, the supposed *bête noire* of the bunch, we may hear some echoes of the voice of Tacitus. Aper, after all, fully embraces the brevity and point of contemporary Latinity and acknowledges that style changes with the times (e.g. *dial.* 18.2), all of which should sound rather familiar to a reader of Tacitus' other works.[120] We also cannot forget that the real-life Tacitus served out his *tirocinium fori* under Aper's watchful eye (*dial.* 2.1), which not only would have exerted some influence on his intellectual formation, but also makes it unlikely that he would have set up Aper as a character totally in the wrong.[121]

And yet while each speaker may reflect one facet of the prism that represents Tacitus' own thoughts and feelings, and while there is of course an epistemological problem with presuming to know too much about our author's inner workings, there is likewise a danger of ignoring the plain impression that the work gives. Tacitus himself, speaking *in propria persona*, acknowledges the decline of oratory (*dial.* 1.1–4), and so he cannot really be on Aper's supposed side. It would furthermore be perverse, from the perspective of ancient rhetorical training, to place Aper's arguments first and then allow not one but two speakers to refute them without challenge, if in fact they represented Tacitus' true beliefs. Indeed, the work seems to advance ineluctably toward Maternus' concluding speech, which provides an explanation for the decline of oratory heretofore unheard in the Roman world. His speech is allowed to stand unchallenged at the culmination of the work. His character, furthermore, is the most self-assured; he is the one who has dared to speak truth to power, writing political tragedies that have set the city abuzz. Aper and Messalla may be right in various diagnostic observations, but it is hard to escape the conclusion that it is Maternus who has identified the correct cause of the

---

[118] Martin (1972) 357. Van den Berg (2014) 58–66 also argues strongly against "character-oriented readings." Fox (2007) likewise fights against seeing characters in Cicero's dialogues as their author's mouthpieces, but much less successfully, sometimes perhaps even allowing for such a reading (e.g. 218). Cf. more reasonably Dugan (2005).

[119] Cf. Barwick (1954) and n. 45 above.   [120] Cf. Costa (1969) 31.

[121] This is in fact another reason (and one that I have not seen elsewhere adduced) to believe that Aper is playing the devil's advocate with his more extreme views. Cf. n. 76 above.

disease and issued the authoritative prognosis – oratory is dead and cannot be revived.

What, then, is Cicero's role in all this? As I have shown throughout this chapter, he is central to the entire discussion. Not only is he the fixed and highest point of reference on the scale of eloquence, his death also marks both the beginning of imperial rule and the decline of eloquence (a neat connection between oratory and politics), and he is moreover the most prominent educational theorist on oratory (if sometimes filtered through Quintilian). Thus at some level the various allusions to Cicero are simply how one plays this particular game, just as we saw the declaimers constantly citing Cicero when talking about him. Sometimes, as is the case with Messalla the neo-Ciceronian, Ciceronian diction is especially suited to the character and adds an extra level of meaning to his words. Moreover, Cicero was Tacitus' most important generic antecedent in writing dialogues, especially dialogues on matters oratorical, and so by his allusions Tacitus can take his place in the genre and pay homage to his great predecessor.

Beneath the surface of this adulatory *imitatio*, however, lies a keen edge of eristic *aemulatio*. Tacitus is engaged in a pitched struggle with both Cicero and the successor to Cicero's oratorical teaching, Quintilian. He has in a sense let them dictate the battlefield, a dialogue in the Ciceronian tradition, fully Ciceronian in style; so much the more glorious, perhaps, will his triumph be if he can best them on their home turf. Thus we see time and again subtle markers of independence in Tacitus' allusions, as he unmistakably echoes Cicero and yet one-ups him with changed words or even changed word order. More importantly still, Tacitus' interlocutors employ subversive allusions that change the meaning of Cicero's original at key moments in the argument. This is all the classic cut and thrust of learned rivalry that pervades much of Latin literature.

Tacitus, however, goes far beyond the typical correction of an errant predecessor. In a particularly delicious specimen of Tacitean irony, he actually explodes the entire genre that he is working within: while playing by its rules and conventions, he claims that the game can no longer be played and won. His whole point in this masterpiece of Ciceronian eloquence is that Ciceronian eloquence is no longer possible. This paradoxical proposition is perhaps the most destructive specimen of *aemulatio* to survive from antiquity, and an example of sheer intertextual brilliance. Having shattered his contemporaries' illusions with allusions in their own language, he leaves them to pick up the pieces and strikes out in a different direction of his own.

This sophisticated theoretical rejection of Cicero and all his holy works was no mere ivory tower rodomontade. Although Tacitus was a famous and successful orator, he spurned publishing any of his speeches, perhaps deeming such products of an age bereft of eloquence unworthy of the attention of future generations – quite unlike his contemporary Pliny. Instead, just as Maternus forsakes oratory for poetry, Tacitus betakes himself to another genre, history, and there makes his name. He altogether rejects the Ciceronian style, even though, as the *Dialogus* attests, he could obviously do it perfectly. Cicero the man is in fact mentioned only once in the rest of Tacitus' extant corpus.[122] In sum, he renounces Cicero and Ciceronianism in both theory and practice. This was a very self-conscious decision; Cicero was, as has been made abundantly clear, of central importance, but Tacitus, after pondering deeply the issues raised by Quintilian and putting forth his own analysis, which serves almost as a sort of self-justification, has chosen to go his own way. Pliny, by contrast, will try to follow his teacher.

---

[122] Admittedly in a fascinating context, *ann.* 4.34.4, the defense speech of Cremutius Cordus. Cordus stands accused of publishing *annales*, praising Brutus, and calling Cassius the "last of the Romans" (*Cremutius Cordus postulatur nouo ac tunc primum audito crimine, quod editis annalibus laudatoque M. Bruto C. Cassium Romanorum ultimum dixisset*, *ann.* 4.34.1). He vigorously defends both historiography and free speech, and invokes Cicero as an example: *Marci Ciceronis libro, quo Catonem caelo aequauit, quid aliud dictator Caesar quam rescripta oratione, uelut apud iudices, respondit?* (i.e., Caesar did not prosecute him on some trumped-up charge!). Tacitus is thus hardly blind to Cicero's symbolic value as a champion of liberty, a role in which, as we have seen before, Cicero can be joined with Cato (cf. p. 114 above). It is very tempting to hear the voice of Tacitus himself speaking here (cf. Martin and Woodman [1989] ad loc. p. 177). For comprehensive discussion of the Cremutius Cordus incident, see Moles (1998) and, ranging even more widely, Sailor (2008) 250–313.

CHAPTER 7

Est ... mihi cum Cicerone aemulatio: *Pliny's Cicero*

143 years after the death of the *conseruator rei publicae*, Pliny the Younger took the oath of consular office and delivered his speech of thanksgiving to Trajan and the assembled imperial Senate. His uneventful two months[1] as suffect consul in AD 100 could not confer upon him the greatness of Cicero's Nones of December, but they did mark an important step in his *imitatio* and *aemulatio* of his illustrious predecessor: not only did he arrive at the summit of the Ciceronian *cursus honorum*, he achieved this feat at a much younger age than had Cicero himself.[2] Just a few years later he was enrolled in the college of augurs, as Cicero once had been, again at a younger age.[3] Both Pliny and Cicero had been born into the equestrian class in small Italian towns outside Rome. They were both, moreover, public orators and case-pleaders, *littérateurs* and poets, epistolographers, and, eventually, provincial governors – indeed, with so many similarities,[4] how could Pliny not compare himself with his more famous predecessor?

Pliny had certainly been educated to make such comparisons. As a student of Quintilian, he had drunk deep draughts from the font of neo-Ciceronianism during years spent on the benches in his classroom.[5] There can be no doubt that Pliny was intimately familiar with Cicero's

---

[1] Or perhaps just one: see Sherwin-White (1966) 78. On Pliny's career in general, see Birley (2000b) 5–17 = Birley (2016) 55–66 with the most up-to-date evidence (but a controversial view on its Domitianic phase; see the discussion of Whitton [2015c]).

[2] So he informs us; see *epist.* 4.8.5 *consulatum multo etiam iuuenior quam ille sum consecutus*, discussed on p. 306 below.

[3] Again, see *epist.* 4.8.5 (p. 306 below). The date of the augurate is probably around AD 103; see Birley (2000b) 16 = Birley (2016) 65.

[4] On these similarities, see briefly Gibson and Steel (2010) 118, Wolff (2004) 441–442, and the occasionally whimsical Nutting (1926). Some features of this profile were common to many upper-class Roman men, but Pliny differs from his contemporaries both in the rapidity of his rise (emphasized by Syme [1958] 81–85 and [1991]) and, more importantly, because he chose to publish his speeches and letters.

[5] See *epist.* 2.14.9 *Quintiliano praeceptore meo* as well as *epist.* 6.6.3.

career and had devoted vast swaths of time to the study of his sacred texts; the process of studying a Ciceronian speech described in chapter one, while representative for Romans generally, is particularly the experience of one of Quintilian's pupils. Quintilian, moreover, would have impressed upon his young pupil the exemplary status of Cicero as prose stylist and hence the best possible model for imitation. As we have observed, Quintilian saw with singular clarity a remedy for the decline of eloquence in the years since Cicero's demise:[6] Cicero was the best orator; we want to be good orators (i.e. like Cicero); Cicero has forged a path to the summit of eloquence; thus we are to do what the great man himself prescribes and follow in his educational footsteps. Pliny proves the perfect guinea pig to test Quintilian's academic theories in the rough and tumble world of Roman life and letters.

In large part Pliny does what he is "supposed" to do. His own prose style, for example, is not that of a Seneca or a Tacitus, but rather Quintilian's carefully polished neo-Ciceronianism (admittedly, like Quintilian, with "silver" features intruding on the Ciceronian veneer). He delivers and publishes speeches – and not just the *Panegyricus*, it should be remembered[7] – and makes the conscious decision to redact and publish his letters. Indeed, although he is not much given to reflecting publicly on education, when he does, he seems unapologetically and unproblematically Quintilianic. In *epist.* 7.9 he lays out his own programmatic *ratio studiorum*, virtually every sentence of which can be paralleled in Quintilian.[8] For example, as Pliny begins to dispense advice to his protégé Fuscus Salinator, he first says (*epist.* 7.9.2):

> utile in primis, et multi praecipiunt, <u>uel ex Graeco in Latinum uel ex Latino uertere in Graecum</u>. quo genere exercitationis proprietas splendorque uerborum, <u>copia figurarum</u>, uis explicandi, praeterea imitatione optimorum similia inueniendi facultas paratur; simul quae legentem fefellissent, transferentem fugere non possunt.

---

[6] See p. 227 above.

[7] Only the *Panegyricus* happens to survive, perhaps because of the late antique taste for panegyric, but Pliny tells us of a number of speeches that he has revised for publication. He mentions at least a *Sermo de bibliotheca* (*epist.* 1.8), *De Heluidi ultione* (*epist.* 4.21, 7.30, 9.13), *Pro patria* (? *epist.* 2.5 with Sherwin-White), *In Marium Priscum* (*epist.* 2.19), *Pro Basso* (*epist.* 4.9), *Pro Vareno* (*epist.* 6.29.11), *Pro Attia Viriola* (*epist.* 6.33), *Pro Clario* (*epist.* 9.28.5; the reading *Clario* is uncertain) and of course the *Panegyricus* (*epist.* 3.13, 3.18). Schanz–Hosius 658–660 compiles all mentions of possible Plinian speeches, including seven "die in Buchform vorhanden waren" and nine "andere gehaltene Reden" (a more dubious category). The figure in the *RE* of "sechsehn ... Buchreden" is presumably a misinference from this account (*RE* xxi/1.447). Many of these speeches are discussed by Kennedy (1972) 529–543.

[8] On this letter, see Keeline (2013).

In the first place a useful practice, and one which many commend, is <u>to translate either from Greek into Latin or from Latin into Greek</u>. Through this sort of exercise you'll acquire propriety and splendor in diction, <u>a ready supply of rhetorical figures</u>, forcefulness in exposition; moreover, through the imitation of the best models you'll acquire skill in devising similar speeches yourself. At the same time, what would have eluded a reader cannot escape the translator's attention.

Pliny hardly strikes out on his own here, for many advise (*multi praecipiunt*) what he is suggesting. These include Quintilian above all, who approvingly reported that orators of an older generation judged translating from Greek into Latin to be the best exercise (*uertere Graeca in Latinum ueteres nostri oratores optimum iudicabant, inst.* 10.5.2), citing the testimony of Crassus in Cicero's *De oratore* (*de orat.* 1.155) as well as Messalla and the practice of Cicero himself. Quintilian goes on to emphasize that this exercise helps the student develop facility in coming up with *figurae*, a point that Pliny likewise emphasizes (*copia figurarum*). This is thus thoroughly Quintilianic advice, which is furthermore implicitly grounded in Cicero's own writings.

So Pliny continues by discussing the virtues of paraphrase of Latin speeches, particularly as concerns *imitatio* and *aemulatio*, just as Quintilian does in his subsequent paragraphs (*inst.* 10.5.4–8). Indeed, even in very minor points of detail Pliny may be looking to Quintilian. At one point, in verse, he compares the *ingenium* of men to wax (*epist.* 7.9.11):

> ut laus est cerae, mollis cedensque sequatur
>   si doctos digitos iussaque fiat opus
> et nunc informet Martem castamue Mineruam,
>   nunc Venerem effingat, nunc Veneris puerum;
> [utque sacri fontes non sola incendia sistunt,   5
>   saepe etiam flores uernaque prata iuuant,][9]
> sic hominum ingenium flecti ducique per artes
>   non rigida doctas mobilitate decet.

Just as it is the virtue of wax that it follows learned fingers, soft and yielding, and becomes whatever work of art is commanded, and now forms a Mars or a chaste Minerva, now a Venus, now Venus' son; [and just as sacred springs stanch not fires alone, they also often benefit flowers and spring meadows,] so too it is fitting that men's talents be guided and led by means of learned arts with flexible mobility.

Here Pliny is probably thinking of *inst.* 10.5.10, where Quintilian recommends expressing the same *sententiae* in a variety of ways in order to

---

[9] I believe these lines are a later interpolation; see Keeline (2013) 217.

develop oratorical *facilitas*, also with a comparison to wax: *uelut eādem cerā aliae aliaeque formae duci solent* ("just as all manner of shapes can be produced from the same piece of wax"). Moreover, this passage shows Pliny putting his own advice into practice, as he paraphrases Quintilian with copious *uariatio*, going so far as to transpose him into verse in order to support his own agenda of encouraging amateur versification. Indeed, Pliny may even play with the wording of Quintilian's advice *ut ex industria sumamus sententias quasdam easque uersemus <u>quam numerosissime</u>* ("to deliberately take up certain *sententiae* and turn them <u>in as many ways as possible</u>") – what "turn" could be more *numerosus* than rewriting this *sententia* as verse? This is not mere imitation; it rises to rivalry.

Nevertheless, both here and throughout the letter, the rivalry is respectful and Quintilian is the unacknowledged but obvious preceptor.[10] Nowhere in this letter does Pliny suggest the dark and cynical musings of a Tacitus, who, as we saw in the previous chapter, says in the *Dialogus* that oratory is dead and cannot be brought back to life. Pliny, by contrast, happily implies that if Fuscus Salinator follows his instructions, he will become an eloquent writer. Such cheerful optimism is a page right out of Quintilian's book[11] and represents the sunny side of Pliny's public persona.

Pliny himself is completely imbued with Quintilian's educational ideals, and on the surface at least he does not seem to regard them as particularly problematic. He knows full well that he "should" be Ciceronian in both his life and his literature. It is no surprise, therefore, that Cicero is a pervasive theme in Pliny. He serves particularly as a stylistic precedent, used to justify Pliny's own approach to oratory and poetry, while – as in Quintilian – there is an attempt to neutralize his potentially problematic political dimension by simply ignoring it. Nowhere in Pliny do we find mention of Cicero's death, for example, which is otherwise so central to his reception. And yet, as we shall see, Pliny's political anxieties break through on more than one occasion, both in what he says and in what he leaves unsaid. He mentions Cicero explicitly in some ten letters, and other letters allude to or are modeled on published letters of his. Indeed, as Ilaria Marchesi has rightly emphasized, Pliny's very project of publishing his letters is itself an act of homage to and rivalry with his most famous epistolary antecedent.[12] The *Panegyricus*, too, may bear occasional Ciceronian traces, and in his project of revising and publishing the speech Pliny positions himself

---

[10] So when Pliny closes the letter by disclaiming the need to provide a reading list since the "best authors" in each genre are so well known, he is obviously thinking of Quintilian's own list in book 10 of the *Institutio*. See Keeline (2013) 260–261, Whitton (2018) 52.

[11] See p. 225 above. [12] See Marchesi (2008) 207–240 *passim*.

particularly in relation to Cicero.[13] Cicero, in sum, is an important part of Pliny's self-fashioning.

And yet Pliny knew Tacitus too, and he knew full well that times had changed; life under Trajan was not life in Cicero's dying Republic. Just beneath his cheerful façade lurk Pliny's anxieties and tensions (*epist.* 9.2.2, to Sabinus):[14]

> neque enim eadem nostra condicio quae M. Tulli, ad cuius exemplum nos uocas. illi enim et copiosissimum ingenium, et par ingenio qua uarietas rerum qua magnitudo largissime suppetebat; nos quam angustis terminis claudamur etiam tacente me perspicis, nisi forte uolumus scholasticas tibi atque, ut ita dicam, umbraticas litteras mittere.

> You want me to follow Cicero's example, but our situation is not the same as his. For he had both a peerless intellect and an abundant supply of varied and important topics to match it. You see, however, even without my telling you, within what narrow bounds I am hemmed in, unless perhaps I wish to send you letters from the schoolroom and composed, so to speak, out of the public eye.

Pliny was all too painfully aware of his own belatedness. He could not but feel that he fell short of Cicero both in intellect and in opportunities to use it. He is plainly sensitive about that lack of opportunity, since he alludes to it but refuses to describe it explicitly (*etiam tacente me perspicis*); it is a condition shared by all his contemporaries (*nostra condicio* may not simply reflect the "royal we"). Pliny's lament finds a neat parallel in Tacitus' *Dialogus*. There Maternus describes the orators of old, who had noble defendants and important cases, both of which contribute mightily to eloquence: *his accedebat splendor reorum et magnitudo causarum, quae et ipsa plurimum eloquentiae praestant* (*dial.* 37.4). As in Pliny, Maternus is discussing the *condicio* of Cicero and co. (*dial.* 37.8) and contrasting it with the forensic arena of the present day. So too Pliny elsewhere sardonically describes his own activities in the centumviral court, which keep him busy but hardly delight him: he takes on small and trivial cases, and it is rare to find one distinguished by the fame of the people involved or the importance of the matter at hand (*distringor centumuiralibus causis, quae me exercent magis quam delectant. sunt enim pleraeque paruae et exiles; raro incidit uel personarum claritate uel negoti magnitudine insignis, epist. 2.14.1).*[15] Tacitus

---

[13] Cf. nn. 24 and 90 below.

[14] For more on this letter, see p. 308 below, as well as Morello (2003) 187–195, who also treats 3.20.

[15] Cf. *epist.* 2.11.1 for the exceptional case that is *personae claritate famosum … rei magnitudine aeternum.*

had similarly denigrated the centumviral courts, claiming that no speeches delivered by the *antiqui* before the centumviral court are read anymore, a damning verdict on the only speaking outlet left to contemporary orators (*dial.* 38.2). Pliny indeed goes on in his letter to acknowledge a decline in eloquence more generally, a view which he expresses by quoting Quintilian himself (*epist.* 2.14.9). Quintilian implicitly marks the decline as a failure to adhere to Ciceronian standards, reporting a story that pins the blame for the downturn on Larcius Licinus, a noted anti-Ciceronian whom Gellius mentions in the same breath as Asinius Gallus as author of a work entitled *Ciceromastix* (Gell. 17.1.1). Even this is perhaps paralleled by the *Dialogus*, for Tacitus observes that the first speeches in the centumviral court that are still read today are those of Asinius Pollio, father of Asinius Gallus and another staunch opponent of Cicero; he thus marks an anti-Ciceronian as the beginning of the decline. Finally, we will return to Pliny's "narrow bounds" and *scholasticae et umbraticae litterae* below.

Again and again Pliny is forced to acknowledge these diminished circumstances (*epist.* 3.20.10–12):

> haec tibi scripsi, primum ut aliquid noui scriberem, deinde ut non numquam de re publica loquerer, cuius materiae nobis quanto rarior quam ueteribus occasio, tanto minus omittenda est. et hercule quousque illa uulgaria? "quid agis? ecquid commode uales?" habeant nostrae quoque litterae aliquid non humile nec sordidum, nec priuatis rebus inclusum. sunt quidem cuncta sub unius arbitrio …

> I wrote this to you first in order to tell you something new, but also in order to speak for once about matters political. Our opportunities for talking about such things are so much more limited than they were for the men of old, and therefore they are all the more eagerly to be seized upon. And anyway, what's the point of those trite phrases? "How are you? Are you well?"[16] Our letters too should contain something that rises above the mundane, something not confined within the limits of private affairs. Everything does indeed depend on the will of one man …

He lives under the Empire, with everything dependent on the will of a single man (*cuncta sub unius arbitrio*), and he is deeply conscious of how different this is from the situation of the *ueteres* (like Cicero) of Republican times. His scope for action is much more limited, and so limited too is the ambit of his letters, even though he would like desperately to rise above the trivialities of domestic life and its banal pleasantries. Ever the apparent optimist, he finishes this letter by saying that Trajan is an

---

[16] Cf. the somewhat similar Sen. *epist.* 15.1 on the old *si uales, bene est* formula.

emperor who takes good care of his subjects, but we have already seen the cracks in Pliny's calm and contented mask.

These political tensions simmer throughout the collection, steam periodically escaping with a hiss. So at *epist.* 3.7.14, in the obituary notice of Silius Italicus, we read:

> sed tanto magis hoc, quidquid est temporis futilis et caduci, si non datur factis (nam horum materia in aliena manu), certe studiis proferamus, et quatenus nobis denegatur diu uiuere, relinquamus aliquid, quo nos uixisse testemur.

> All the more reason then for us to extend whatever bit of fragile and fleeting time is given to us, if not by action – for the opportunity to take action is now in the hands of another – at any rate by our literary work, and inasmuch as we cannot live for a long time, let us leave behind something to testify that we have lived.

If Pliny can no longer match deed with word – since the opportunity for action rests entirely with the emperor – he can at least produce words that aim at undying glory.[17] Beyond the acknowledgement of his inferior status relative to a more glorious past, there lurks too an implicit anxiety in the privileging of words over deeds; the latter are clearly felt to be superior.[18] The ideal, of course, was to combine both, as Cicero had done. Pliny, however, is denied the chance to do anything and is forced to resort to nothing but speaking, and to speaking, both in the centumviral court and in his own letters, about unimportant things at that.

The self-consciously epigonal Pliny resembles no one so much as his friend Tacitus, and not just in the *Dialogus*. So, for example, *ann.* 4.32, where Tacitus digresses from his Tiberian narrative for a moment:

> pleraque eorum quae rettuli quaeque referam parua forsitan et leuia memoratu uideri non nescius sum: sed nemo annalis nostros cum scriptura eorum contenderit qui ueteres populi Romani res composuere. ingentia illi bella, expugnationes urbium, fusos captosque reges, aut si quando ad interna praeuerterent, discordias consulum aduersum tribunos, agrarias frumentariasque leges, plebis et optimatium certamina libero egressu memorabant: nobis in arto et inglorius labor; immota quippe aut modice lacessita pax, maestae urbis res et princeps proferendi imperi incuriosus erat.

> I am not unaware that most of what I have related and most of what I will relate might seem trifles not worth the telling – but let no one compare my

---

[17] See too e.g. *epist.* 4.25.5, where no Roman except Trajan – who is all but assimilated to a god by a repurposed quote from Plato's *Phaedo* 95b – can provide effective remedies for what ails Roman society.

[18] Cf. e.g. Sall. *Cat.* 4.

Annales with the writing of those who wrote the earlier history of the Roman people. With unrestricted elaboration they could tell of great wars, stormings of cities, kings driven to flight and taken prisoner; when they looked to internal affairs, there were feuds between consuls and tribunes, land laws and grain laws, the struggles between the *plebs* and the *optimates*. We, by contrast, have only inglorious toil in a confined field: a peace that was undisturbed or at any rate barely touched, the pathetic affairs of the city and a *princeps* who neglected expanding the Empire.

Tacitus contrasts the staid affairs of imperial life with the excitement of the late Republic, and preemptively apologizes for the seeming triviality of much of his history. The language of being confined in narrow bounds is exactly what we find in Pliny (*quam angustis terminis claudamur ... perspicis, epist.* 9.2.2),[19] and the cause, of course, is also the same: the *princeps* and the Empire.[20] Pliny and Tacitus share some of the same very real political anxieties, although they choose to express them in rather different form.

It need hardly be reemphasized that Pliny was a close friend of Tacitus and would have been intimately familiar with Tacitus' thoughts on the Empire. He knew the *Dialogus* well enough to allude to it in his correspondence with Tacitus, and he may even have believed that Maternus acted as Tacitus' mouthpiece in the work.[21] Here, then, is Pliny's unresolved and unresolvable tension: he has been educated in Quintilian's classroom to believe that Cicero is the One True Model who must be imitated, especially for someone writing speeches and letters, and so he knows full well that he *should* imitate Cicero. He also knows, however, that he *cannot*: his own *ingenium* may not be able to match Cicero's, but even if it could, the times have changed too much and it would simply be impossible. This twin anxiety, bound up with both talent and politics, is inescapable and the hallmark of Pliny's relationship with Cicero.[22] At one moment he will be humble and deferential to his great predecessor, while the next he will try to rival him, and he can never quite resign himself to

---

[19] Cf. too the slightly different *dial.* 30.5 *neque oratoris uis et facultas ... angustis et breuibus terminis cluditur.*

[20] On this passage in Tacitus, see Woodman (1988) 180–186, and, at length, Moles (1998) and Sailor (2008) 250–313.

[21] See p. 233 above. Marchesi (2008) 134 floats the idea that Pliny himself saw Maternus as Tacitus' mouthpiece.

[22] My approach here is fundamentally influenced by Hoffer (1999), whose book, starting from the premise that "the leading trait in Pliny's epistolary self-portrait is his confidence," sets out "to look at the opposite side of the picture, at Pliny's anxieties, to help us understand his aims in putting together and publishing his letters" (1). Hoffer does not, however, discuss Pliny's Ciceronian anxieties.

inferiority or fully rise to the challenge of *aemulatio*.[23] His struggle to negotiate this relationship and integrate it into his careful self-presentation will be the central theme of this chapter. I will discuss all of Pliny's explicit mentions of Cicero in the *Epistulae*, and then consider various letters that deliberately evoke Cicero's own life or writings.[24] By probing beneath Pliny's cheery and confident exterior, I hope to show just how anxious he is to get this relationship "right."

Genre and Plinian Artistry

The standard histories of epistolography jump from Cicero to Seneca to Pliny to Fronto and beyond, perhaps with a detour for the poetic epistles of Horace or Ovid along the way.[25] Such an approach is understandable; with the exception of a few papyri and imperial rescripts, we have no other Latin letters preserved until late antiquity. But consider the case of oratory: we likewise have only exiguous fragments between the death of Cicero and Pliny's *Panegyricus*, but no one would dare leap from 43 BC to AD 100 in a single bound, still less claim that Cicero was Pliny's only possible model in the speech. We know full well that there must have been other letter collections in the early Empire; Tacitus, for example, mentions in passing the three books of letters published by one Mucianus, a "paladin of

---

[23] I thus stand between the two poles of Marchesi (2008), esp. 207–240, who thinks that Pliny confidently takes up the gauntlet thrown down by Cicero and attempts to outdo him (e.g. 212–213), and Lefèvre (2009) 111–122, who believes that Pliny is too afraid to accept the challenge. (Rudd [1992] 26–32 also observes Pliny's general seesawing between self-praise and self-doubt, not centered on Cicero.) Marchesi and Lefèvre, along with Gibson and Morello (2012) 74–103, have set the tone for the recent scholarly discussion of Pliny's Cicero, and my own contribution is very much in dialogue with them. For earlier pioneers in this field, see Guillemin (1929) 67–99, 113–117, Weische (1989), and Riggsby (1995). Sensitive on individual echoes of Cicero in *epist.* 2 is Whitton (2013a); see his index s.v. "Cicero" and commentary *passim*.

[24] I will not discuss the *Panegyricus* here, simply because there are few significant reminiscences of Cicero to be found (most interestingly Cic. *Marcell.* 8 *eum* [sc. *Caesarem*] . . . *simillimum deo iudico* – Plin. *paneg.* 1.3 *dis simillimus princeps*, 7.6 *dis simillimum*, where, in the wake of Domitian the *dominus et deus*, Pliny may be glad of Ciceronian precedent for a divine comparison). For a variety of reasons, a *gratiarum actio* is simply not the place to play an elaborate intertextual game or to show off your rivalry with Cicero. Still less, I imagine, were speeches before the centumviral court, where the orator was in the real business of persuasion. The *Epistulae* are the site of Pliny's *imitatio* and *aemulatio*. The testimonial apparatus of Moreno Soldevila (2010) lists possible verbal parallels of various probability between the *Panegyricus* and Cicero; cf. too Suster (1890), Durry (1938) 29–30, and Manuwald (2011).

[25] See e.g. Peter (1901), who has a brief pre-Ciceronian history of the genre, then goes from Cicero to Pliny, Fronto, Symmachus, and Sidonius Apollinaris before returning to verse epistles and "der amtliche Brief" (e.g. imperial correspondence). Cugusi (1983) 176–182 does briefly mention other collections after discussing Cicero, but then passes from Seneca to Pliny to Fronto, returning to discuss imperial correspondence and the papyri while excluding verse epistles (cf. his pp. 8–9).

Vespasian"[26] who died before AD 77 (*dial.* 37.3). More famous collections included the letters of Julius Caesar,[27] which apparently even attracted a learned commentary by Valerius Probus on their abstruse secret codes and were still circulating for Gellius to read,[28] and the letters of Augustus, which Tacitus again cites casually (*testes Augusti epistulae, dial.* 13.3) and from which Suetonius quotes liberally.[29] Plutarch had access to the letters of Cato the Elder (*Cat. ma.* 20; *Moralia* 273f = *quaest. Rom.* 39); Cornelia's letters to her son Gaius Gracchus famously survive in Cornelius Nepos (fr. 59 Marshall);[30] Quintilian can quote from Livy's letters (*inst.* 10.1.39). When we know of so many letter collections today – even if we do not have them to read ourselves – there can be no doubt that the epistolary landscape was dotted with the anthologies of numerous lesser lights.

All this is to say nothing of Greek letter collections, which were plentiful and in at least one case even written by a native speaker of Latin.[31] Already in the fourth century BC Greek rhetoricians had set to work on codifying the rules of the epistolary genre, beginning with Demetrius of Phalerum,[32] and Cicero himself seems to have taken such theories for granted (*fam.* 2.4.1, to Curio, from the first half of 53 BC):

> epistularum genera multa esse non ignoras sed unum illud certissimum, cuius causa inuenta res ipsa est, ut certiores faceremus absentis si quid esset quod eos scire aut nostra aut ipsorum interesset. huius generis litteras a me profecto non exspectas. tuarum enim rerum domesticos habes et scriptores et nuntios, in meis autem rebus nihil est sane noui. reliqua sunt epistularum genera duo, quae me magno opere delectant, unum familiare et iocosum, alterum seuerum et graue.

---

[26] Gudeman (1914) ad *dial.* 37.2 p. 473.

[27] Suet. *Iul.* 56.6 *epistulae quoque eius ad senatum extant ... extant et ad Ciceronem, item ad familiares domesticis de rebus.* Cf. too Gell. 17.9.1 *libri sunt epistularum C. Caesaris ad C. Oppium et Balbum Cornelium, qui rebus eius absentis curabant.*

[28] Gell. 17.9.5 *est adeo Probi grammatici commentarius satis curiose factus de occulta litterarum significatione in epistularum C. Caesaris scriptura*; cf. Suet. *Iul.* 56.7.

[29] Again, still circulating in the Antonine age; see Gell. 15.7.3 *librum epistularum diui Augusti, quas ad Gaium nepotem suum scripsit*; cf. too Quint. *inst.* 1.6.19 *Augustus ... in epistulis ad C. Caesarem scriptis.* Wallace-Hadrill (1984) 91–95 discusses Suetonius' habit of quoting these letters; for the fragments, which are considerable, see Malcovati (1945) 6–49.

[30] Whether these fragments are Cornelia's *ipsissima uerba* remains controversial; see Horsfall (1989) 41–42, who judges that "these texts are not exact citations of virgin second-century BC originals, though they fit irreproachably into a context of (say) 125–124 BC." Cornelia's letters certainly survived to be read and admired by Cicero (*Brut.* 211).

[31] The Greek letters of Brutus, edited and translated by Torraca (1959). These are commonly believed to be spurious, but Jones (2015) argues that they should be considered genuine.

[32] See Hercher (1873) 1–16 for the Greek treatises with (modern) Latin translations, along with Cugusi (1983) 27–41; cf. p. 211 above.

You know that there are many types of letters. But the one that is the most genuine, for the sake of which letter-writing was invented, is this: to inform those who are not present of anything that is in their interest or ours for them to know. Of course you don't expect that type of letter from me. You've got your own correspondents and messengers to cover your affairs, and in mine there is not much new. There remain two types of letters which I quite enjoy, the one familiar and jocular, the other serious and grave.

Such a division into categories was absolutely typical of the doctrine of the rhetorical schools, and here Cicero presumes that his correspondent is equally *au fait* on the various conventions. He likewise makes mention of different epistolary subgenres in other letters (*fam.* 4.13.1 to Nigidius Figulus, 6.10.4 to Trebianus), and even if Quintilian has little to say about such matters, it seems clear that epistolary theory was well-trodden ground by Pliny's day.[33]

Moreover, literate and even illiterate Romans of all sorts would have constantly been exchanging letters. (Slaves and professional scribes facilitated letter-writing even for those who could not write themselves.)[34] The endless flow of correspondence that must have passed beneath Pliny's watchful eyes would have also exerted a real influence on the formation of his epistolary taste. The papyri preserve ample evidence that Romans of every stripe were familiar with the rules and customs of epistolary exchange.[35]

The upshot of all this is that we cannot assume, as Marchesi does, that epistolography was a "fluid genre" whose rules had not yet been fixed.[36] Still less can we assume that Pliny's choices are always in reaction to Cicero's letters, or perhaps to Seneca's: we have simply lost far too many Roman letter collections – to say nothing of individual letters – to be sure. We must always remember that Pliny was probably reading and writing correspondence on an almost daily basis. This is not to say, of course, that he did not react to Cicero's letters, or that they did not occupy a special place in the Roman epistolary consciousness. From Nepos through Seneca down to Quintilian, we see Roman writers treating Cicero's letters as

---

[33] On all these passages from Cicero, see Peter (1901) 23–24; cf. Cugusi (1983) 27–28 and, more generally, 105–135.

[34] And even those who could write often employed amanuenses. To say nothing of the Ciceronian evidence, consider the birthday invitation from Claudia Severa to Sulpicia Lepidina (*Tab. Vindol.* 291), the body of which is in an elegant scribal hand, while the valediction seems to have been written (with noticeably less elegance) by Severa herself.

[35] For Latin letters on papyrus, see Cugusi (1983) 271–284; cf. too the ongoing publication of the Vindolanda Tablets.

[36] Marchesi (2008) 7; cf. xi, 241, and *passim*.

exemplary models.[37] We simply must always be mindful of what we have lost, and we must resist the urge to draw straight lines between the dots of preserved evidence.

The most recent scholarship on Pliny's letters, moving away from social and historical readings, also has a tendency to treat them as existing in an imaginary literary universe. Marchesi spells out her position with particular clarity:

> Pliny's autobiographical practices are still the focus of Ludolph, Hoffer, and Henderson, and Pliny's letters emerge from their readings as the tool through which the author effected change in his status either with his contemporaries or posterity. This kind of instrumental analysis still subjects Pliny's text to readings that find their validation in the extra-textual reality of authorial agency. In my reading, on the contrary, it is not the texts that are in the service of the author, but rather the author … who, in the Aristotelian sense, provides the efficient cause for the coming into existence of these texts. My approach thus insists on advancing an hypothesis of autonomy, not only in the generally accepted sense that the author is necessarily the artificial and fictional by-product of philological inference (since no direct, extra-textual access to his real intentions is available to the reader), but also in the more radical sense that authorial intention and strategies are subordinate to the functioning of the texts. If it is true that the self-reflexivity of literary texts is what produces a literary author, and not vice versa, it is also true that one should not locate in the author the final object of interpretation.[38]

While such an approach may be justifiable for a theoretical study of Plinian intertextuality – and I should emphasize just how useful Marchesi's study is – I take a very different tack. "My" Pliny was a real person, deeply embedded in Roman society, a friend of Tacitus and a student of Quintilian. He was a consul and an orator, a correspondent of Trajan and a provincial governor. His letters absolutely have an author, and they have real recipients as well: that is to say, I believe that while the private letters have been revised for publication, they were originally sent as genuine pieces of correspondence.[39] They are, to be

---

[37] E.g. Nep. *Att.* 16.3, Sen. *epist.* 21.4 and 118.1–2 (see p. 208 above), Quint. *inst.* 10.1.107.

[38] Marchesi (2008) 5.

[39] See the thorough and convincing discussion of Sherwin-White (1966) 11–20, along with Gamberini (1983) 122–136 for a full history of the question. While critics today have an inclination to dismiss this issue, it remains fundamental for determining our approach to the text. So even as Whitton (2013a) 4 calls the debate "sterile," he acknowledges that "we have no reason to doubt that Pliny wrote off a debt for Calvina (2.4)" etc. If we thought that Pliny just sat ensconced in his villa imagining all of this, the *Epistles* would have a very different status indeed. But Whitton is right to emphasize that Pliny's publication of his letters "opens an interpretive chasm" and that the primary audience

certain, carefully selected from a larger corpus and diligently edited to produce a particular picture, but they have a foundation in reality as well as a literary function.

More complex is the issue of "cycles" of letters, a term quite popular of late but usually left undefined.[40] Even the most conservative of today's Plinian scholars will emphasize the artful composition of individual letters,[41] and it is not too much of a leap to believe in careful construction of individual books of letters – Pliny would not have arranged his correspondence completely at random. And yet here too the natural tendency to find patterns in everything is pernicious, since juxtaposed letters are seen to be significant, as are letters separated by gaps large and small; indeed, it often feels as if any arrangement is significant if a critic would like it to be so.[42] The really sticky wicket, however, arises when scholars see deliberate links stretching throughout the entirety of the corpus. Since I believe that these letters were real, and since they were originally not published *en masse* in nine (or ten) books but rather in smaller chunks over a period of years, there would seem to be no way for the Pliny of book 1 to be looking forward to the Pliny of book 9. When he published the earlier books, he simply may not have yet written the letters in the later books.

Except – what about revision and republication? That is to say, what if Pliny did originally circulate smaller units, but ultimately published a collected and revised edition of all his *Epistles*? John Bodel has made the most detailed case for Pliny's process of revision and reissuing, and while it can be questioned in almost every particular, it does raise a real possibility.[43] But again, the procedure tends ineluctably to the arbitrary and capricious: in book 1, for example, Bodel detects two "partially consonant, partially conflicting" schemes of arrangement, and then argues that

---

becomes "a readership of eavesdroppers such as us." Gibson and Whitton (2016) 28–29 now pull back slightly from the notion that the debate over authenticity is a "critical dead end."

[40] See e.g Gibson and Morello (2012) 3: "We believe that we do a disservice to Pliny by stripping his most attractive letters from their original context, namely as part of a deliberately sequenced and artistically constructed book or *cycle of letters*" (my emphasis), and *passim*. Cf. Whitton (2013a) 17–20 on possible connections between book 2 and the rest of the corpus, acknowledging that such connections are often evanescent.

[41] E.g. Lefèvre (2009) *passim*.

[42] Whitton (2015a) is both the most persuasive and the most self-aware of critics who postulate such an arrangement, which he can argue for in detail in the case of book 2 (cf. Whitton [2013a]). For the dangers, see esp. his pp. 118–119 on circularity and subjectivity; p. 121 on whether a reader could notice such putative placements; p. 129 "accident or design?"; p. 130 "(misplaced?) readerly ingeniousness," etc.

[43] Bodel (2015), which influentially circulated in samizdat form for years before publication.

we do not need to pick between them.[44] But of the finding of such patterns there will be no end; scholars are after all an ingenious tribe, and if even contradictory interpretations are allowed to stand, then the door is open for almost anything.[45] While each case must be judged on its own merits, I suspect that we are questing after the unknown and unknowable at best, or a chimera at worst. When Roy Gibson and Ruth Morello talk about the "Cicero cycle," they mean simply all the letters in which Cicero is mentioned by name (as their discussion makes clear), and yet they imply that mentions scattered across various books come together with a grand unified purpose.[46] While this possibility cannot be excluded, it seems to me that Gibson and Morello are privileging particular points of interest far too much. I think it is more likely that Pliny, in responding to and writing letters over a period of years, simply has occasion at various times and places to discuss Cicero. I will try to use these instances to reconstruct Pliny's Cicero, but I will not assume a complex web of Ciceronian links that has been carefully built up to carry some extraordinary meaning.

The tendency to search after hidden patterns reaches its zenith in the notion that Pliny edited and published the tenth book of the *Epistulae* himself. Gibson and Morello see this book "as a kind of Ciceronian coda and as the climax of a collection in which Pliny began as the lazy pleasure seeker and ended up on the Black Sea as not only a new and better prose Ovid, but a new and better Cicero, trumping both his predecessors by getting on well with the sole ruler, and documenting his service to the state in the short letters for which he seemed to apologize in 1.10 and 9.2."[47] Although they are not the first to believe that "Book 10 was designed and published by Pliny himself,"[48] such a claim seems exceptionally unlikely to

---

[44] Bodel (2015) 56. For another example of the arbitrary and contradictory, consider that Bodel (2015) 68 makes heavy weather of *epist.* 2.10 as being in the "center" of book 2 and books 1–3 as a whole; while sixty pages later in the same volume Whitton (2015a) 126–127 emphasizes (somewhat more persuasively) that 2.11 is the central letter. Bodel (2015) 19–20 acknowledges the speculative nature of much of his argument. In rejecting many of the proposals advanced by Merwald (1964), his pattern-finding predecessor, he seems hoisted by his own petard (see e.g. p. 86).

[45] Whitton (2013b) is a sympathetic guide to one subset of such interpretations and their implications: on pp. 46–51 he finds (false?) closural elements throughout the Plinian corpus and shows how slippery such "endings" are, acutely remarking on the "(over-)refined structural play which fascinates current criticism" and asking rhetorically whether some of this is "fantasy creating meaning?" (p. 55).

[46] Gibson and Morello (2012) 83–99. So, for example, they believe that to understand Pliny's Ciceronian intertexts readers must be willing to "re-read earlier letters in the light of later more strongly marked allusions" (p. 75).

[47] Gibson and Morello (2012) 263–264.

[48] Gibson and Morello (2012) 251. Their most prominent predecessor is Noreña (2007) 261–271 (who emphasizes that "this thesis is speculative and cannot be proven by any explicit testimony," 262); see also Stadter (2006), and Woolf (2006) and (2015), the latter responding to some of the objections.

be true. The language is markedly different from books 1–9 and particularly bureaucratic,[49] Trajan's replies are included, Pliny often ends up
looking bad, and the book breaks off sharply and for no apparent reason.
I do not believe that Pliny could possibly have published these letters
himself. As a result, when Gibson and Morello spend fourteen pages
tracing the subtle connections between the earlier books and the letters
to Trajan, they call into question the methodology of the entire enterprise.

None of this is to deny Pliny's consummate artistry throughout books
1–9 of the *Epistulae*; I believe that he is a very self-consciously literary
author and deserves to be treated as such. The misplaced condescension of
much earlier Plinian scholarship has now been replaced by a welcome
willingness to meet the man on his own terms.[50] I would emphasize,
however, that scholars who read too much into Pliny are not meeting
him on his terms – they are, just as much as the detractors, meeting him on
their own.[51]

Cicero in the *Epistulae*

Cicero, then, is not Pliny's only model, but he is his most important one.
Sallust's Cato may have preferred actually being a good man to merely
appearing to be one, but Pliny is very concerned not just to negotiate his
relationship with Cicero successfully, but to be seen doing so. Cicero thus
plays a key role in Pliny's self-fashioning.[52] He is mentioned in letters from
all across the collection, particularly in his Quintilianic role as the master of
Latin style. And yet it is in these scattered discussions that we see most

---

[49] See Coleman (2012) on bureaucratic language in book 10, esp. pp. 233–235 on the hypothesis of
deliberate publication; cf. too Gamberini (1983) 332–376 for a copious collection of material
illustrating the style of the Trajanic correspondence.

[50] And this is one of the many strengths of Gibson and Morello (2012): they take Pliny seriously as
a literary artist. This same virtue is to be found in Marchesi (2008) and (2015), and in the various
publications of Whitton, e.g. (2013a), (2013b), (2015a), (2015b). Condescension still arises in
unexpected quarters; even Bodel (2015) 104 writes in his conclusion: "Pliny the Younger is not in
the first rank of Roman authors, nor even, perhaps, the second."

[51] A view presciently and trenchantly expressed by Henderson (2011) 315: "the gathering contemporary
respect for ordering within relatively discrete book units promises to extend ultimately towards an
overdeterminedly unified simulacrum of an unhistorical, counter-generic, pseudoorganic final
'design' (for nine books, or for ten); and *this* represents force applied to the element of relatively
detached, semi-autarchic, quasi-casual multiplicity so salient in this epistolography" (emphasis
original). Of course individuals will differ on what constitutes "reading too much into" their Pliny.

[52] On Pliny's Ciceronian self-fashioning, see Weische (1989) 381–383 and, not always persuasively,
Riggsby (1995). The notion that a primary project of Pliny's *Epistulae* is self-fashioning underpins
the studies of Leach (1990), Ludolph (1997), Hoffer (1999), Henderson (2002), Méthy (2007), and
Carlon (2009), and is likewise central to my understanding of the letters. See now too Häger (2015)
and Gibson and Whitton (2016) 32–33.

clearly the tension in Pliny's relationship with Cicero, as he vacillates between humility and boasting, keen both to follow behind "Cicero the unsurpassable example"[53] and to surpass him.

The first letter of the first book of the *Epistulae* is a dedicatory epistle that introduces the collection and explains its rationale; it is the closest thing Pliny gives us to a preface. In a few short lines he lays out some important principles: the letters are not necessarily arranged in chronological order; they are not the full record of his correspondence, since he is publishing only the letters which he wrote with particular care; he may publish more letters in the future. It is therefore the second letter, addressed to Maturus Arrianus, that functions as the real first letter of the collection.[54] Here, with programmatic intent, Pliny presents himself to the world as a man of letters, so to speak, and an orator who publishes speeches. He asks Arrianus to read and correct the book that he attaches (*hunc* [sc. *librum*] *rogo ex consuetudine tua et legas et emendes, epist.* 1.2.1), and carefully stakes out his position in contemporary stylistic debates (*epist.* 1.2.2):

> temptaui enim imitari Demosthenen semper tuum, Caluum nuper meum, dumtaxat figuris orationis; nam uim tantorum uirorum, "pauci quos aequus . . . " adsequi possunt.

> For I tried to imitate that Demosthenes who has always been your model, and that Calvus who has recently become mine, at least as concerns figures of speech; for "only the favored few" can achieve the force of men so great.

Pliny wants to present himself as a "pure" and "Attic" orator, not given to the florid Asiatic style so beloved of the declaimers and their followers. All this name-dropping, however, situates him as a moderate Atticist: he is not

---

[53] "Cicero das unerreichbare Vorbild," the title of Lefèvre's (2009) chapter on Pliny's relationship with Cicero; Lefèvre believes that Pliny, all too conscious of his epigonal status, never even makes the attempt to challenge his great predecessor.

[54] Arrianus was an equestrian from Altinum (see Birley [2000b] 38–39 and Sherwin-White [1966] 86 with Jones [1968] 113 on his nomenclature and career), presumably inferior in station to Pliny, since Pliny writes a letter of recommendation to secure his advancement (perhaps to a position in Egypt – see *epist.* 3.2, addressed to Vibius Maximus, prefect of Egypt 103–107). He later receives another letter with Cicero as its focus (*epist.* 4.8; see p. 305 below), and he is also the recipient of the perhaps "Ciceronian" 2.11 (see p. 332 below). It is hard to discern any patterns in the prosopography of who receives letters discussing Cicero. Many of the recipients are, to be certain, "literary friends" who receive other letters discussing oratory or poetry or stylistics (e.g. Lupercus: *epist.* 9.26 [with Cicero] and 3.5; or indeed Tacitus himself), and some who are unknown must fall into the same category (we know, for example, that the Silius Proculus of *epist.* 3.15 was a poet, but no more). Still, many of Pliny's letters deal with matters belletristic, and so this observation is not especially helpful. His attitude toward Cicero seems the same no matter who his addressee is, and so I will comment on the specifics of prosopography only in cases of particular interest. For Plinian prosopography, Birley (2000b) summarizes the most recent evidence; Sherwin-White (1966) is corrected and supplemented in great detail by Syme (1968), esp. 146–151, and Jones (1968), esp. 112–131.

so astringent as to prefer Lysias, but rather adopts Demosthenes, whom Cicero himself had favored.[55] Calvus, nonetheless, tends toward the *attenuata oratio* and indeed achieved with conscious effort a sort of *exilitas* (cf. Cic. *Brut.* 283–284, a discussion which revolves around Calvus' Atticism), and so the *nuper meum* perhaps implies that Pliny is showing a newfound restraint. The whole allusive discussion is itself cloaked in an allusion, for *pauci quos aequus* cites a famous passage in Vergil (*Aen.* 6.126–131):

> . . . facilis descensus Auerno:
> noctes atque dies patet atri ianua Ditis;
> sed reuocare gradum superasque euadere ad auras,
> hoc opus, hic labor est. <u>pauci, quos aequus</u> amauit
> Iuppiter aut ardens euexit ad aethera uirtus, 130
> dis geniti potuere.

> . . . the descent to Avernus is easy; the entryway to the house of black Dis lies open day and night – but to retrace your steps and reach fresh air again, that's the challenge, that's the real work. Only <u>a few</u>, sprung from the stock of gods, <u>whom Jupiter favored</u> and loved or whose burning virtue carried them up into heaven, have been able to do it.

We are of course meant to recognize the Vergilian tag and appreciate that Pliny has injected yet another canonical author into the discussion. Marchesi is also doubtless right to understand such an explicit allusion, coming in this first "real" letter of the corpus, as signaling Pliny's own allusive program in the *Epistulae*.[56] But we can push the force of the allusion further. *Hoc opus, hic labor est*: if we remember the Vergilian context, we can almost feel Pliny's difficulty in striking just the right Atticist tone in the speech. He implies that it is so hard that it can be compared to returning from the dead, i.e., it is well-nigh impossible.

Demosthenes and Calvus, however, were not Pliny's only models (*epist.* 1.2.4):

> non tamen omnino Marci nostri ληκύθους fugimus, quotiens paulum itinere decedere non intempestiuis amoenitatibus admonebamur: acres enim esse non tristes uolebamus.

> Nevertheless I didn't altogether avoid the λήκυθοι of our Marcus whenever it seemed right to digress a bit from the journey in pleasant and comfortable surroundings: I wanted to be cutting, not cut and dried.

---

[55] On Pliny and Demosthenes, see Tzounakas (2015), who argues that Pliny presents himself, not Cicero, as the Roman Demosthenes.
[56] Marchesi (2008) 29–30.

This apparently simple sentence is in fact freighted with heavy cargo. Pliny had earlier referred to *Demosthenen semper tuum* and *Caluum nuper meum*, but here we have simply *Marci nostri*. Cicero is Pliny's; he always has been and always will be; Pliny is literally on a "first name basis" with old Tully. Using this *praenomen* is the least formal and most familiar way to refer to a Roman man, and so Pliny gives the impression of being on intimate terms with Cicero.[57] Thus in this first, programmatic letter he claims Cicero as his own special province, and he stakes his claim with no hesitation. The reader is simply to accept it.

Non tamen omnino Marci nostri ληκύθους *fugimus*: "the λήκυθοι of our Marcus" again constitute a programmatic allusion, this time to Cicero himself (Cic. *Att.* 1.14.3, 13 February 61 BC):

> Crassus, postea quam uidit illum excepisse laudem ex eo quod [hi] suspicar-
> entur homines ei consulatum meum placere, surrexit ornatissimeque de
> meo consulatu locutus est, ut ita diceret, se quod esset senator, quod ciuis,
> quod liber, quod uiueret, mihi acceptum referre; quotiens coniugem, quo-
> tiens domum, quotiens patriam uideret, totiens se beneficium meum uidere.
> quid multa? totum hunc locum, quem ego uarie meis orationibus, quarum
> tu Aristarchus es, soleo pingere, de flamma, de ferro (nosti illas ληκύθους),
> ualde grauiter pertexuit.

> When Crassus saw that Pompey had netted some credit from the general
> impression that he approved of my consulship, he got to his feet and held
> forth on the subject in most encomiastic terms, going so far as to say that it
> was to me he owed his status as a Senator and a citizen, his freedom and his
> very life. Whenever he saw his wife or his house or the city of his birth, he
> saw a gift of mine. In short, he worked up the whole theme which I am in
> the habit of embroidering in my speeches one way and another, all about
> fire, sword, etc. (you are their Aristarchus and know my color-box), really
> most impressively. (trans. D. R. Shackleton Bailey, Loeb)

There is no doubt that Pliny was thinking of precisely this passage when he wrote about "Cicero's λήκυθοι," and again such an allusion is ideally suited to Pliny's programmatic context. In the first letter of his collection, he alludes to a letter of Cicero's, telling the reader very explicitly that his letters bear some relation to those of his great forebear. Cicero had called Atticus the Aristarchus of his *orationes*, that is to say, the pinnacle of critical acumen who goes over his speeches with a fine-tooth comb to emend every fault. Pliny thus makes Arrianus his Atticus/Aristarchus – and so by

---

[57] See e.g. Adams (1978) 161: "The *praenomen* was the most intimate of the *tria nomina*. It was mainly used within the family and between close friends." Jones (1996) 92 adverts to this striking usage in Pliny; on naming conventions in Pliny's letters more generally, see Jones (1996) 86–96.

implication makes himself Cicero. More than just being on intimate terms with Cicero, then, Pliny in fact subtly positions himself as a Cicero *rediuiuus.*[58]

We have not yet exhausted the interpretive possibilities of this sentence. In all of extant Greek and Latin literature, the word λήκυθος as a term of stylistic criticism occurs only in these two passages. Literally a λήκυθος is an "oil-flask," or a container for holding "unguents, cosmetics, etc."[59] The usage of Cicero and Pliny, however, is more mysterious; as A. N. Sherwin-White puts it, "[t]he metaphor is not quite clear ... The formal rendering 'paint-pots' seems adequate."[60] This is not especially helpful. Shackleton Bailey takes a firmer line, claiming that "the context shows that Pliny understood λήκυθοι as 'embellishments.'"[61] Pliny's context, however, does not necessarily show any such thing, and I think another interpretation is to be preferred, namely "passages of high/bombastic style."

Although λήκυθοι = bombast occurs only in these two passages, related Greek words make this meaning plain.[62] Callimachus fr. 215 Pf. (*Iamb.* inc. sed.), for example, is preserved among other places in a scholion to the metrical treatise by Hephaestion on a passage that discusses the trochaic heptheimer. This metrical form is also known as a ληκύθιον, the diminutive of λήκυθος made infamous by Aeschylus and Dionysus in Aristophanes' *Frogs.* The reason: "They call it a ληκύθιον either because Aristophanes made fun of Euripides' trochaic heptheimer θοαῖς ἵπποιειν– ληκύθιον ἀπώλεσεν [*Ran.* 1233] or because of its tragic booming sound (βόμβος), for such a sound is produced by a ληκύθιον when the air surrounding it is put in motion either because someone blows on it or for some other reason. This is why Callimachus too calls tragedy the μοῦσαν ληκυθίαν."[63] The scholiast, we may allow, is unsure of himself and perhaps cannot be trusted with the interpretation of Callimachus. But Horace seems to have read the Callimachus passage the same way; at *ars*

---

[58] I thus disagree with Bodel (2015) 77 and Gibson and Morello (2012) 76, 98 on the "belated placement" of reference in Pliny's collection to Cicero's letters (*epist.* 9.2 contains the first explicit mention of them): Pliny's relationship to Cicero's *epistulae* is signaled almost from the very start; cf. Gibson and Morello (2012) 85.

[59] LSJ s.v.   [60] Sherwin-White (1966) ad loc. p. 90.

[61] Shackleton Bailey (1965–1970) ad *Att.* 1.14.3 p. 308.

[62] On these related words, see briefly O'Sullivan (1992) 110, 125.

[63] ληκύθιον δέ φασιν αὐτὸ ἢ δι᾽ Ἀριστοφάνην σκώπτοντα τὸ μέτρον τὸ ἐφθημιμερὲς Εὐριπίδου τὸ "θοαῖς ἵπποιειν – ληκύθιον ἀπώλεσεν" ἢ διὰ τὸν βόμβον τὸν τραγικόν· βόμβος γὰρ γίνεται περὶ τὸ ληκύθιον ἐκ τοῦ ἐμπεριεχομένου αὐτῶι ἀέρος κινουμένου ἢ ὑπὸ πνεύματος ἀνδρὸς ἢ ὑπὸ ἄλλου. διὸ καὶ Καλλίμαχος "μοῦσαν ληκυθίαν" λέγει τὴν τραγωιδίαν, scholia A in MSS AC(D)I ad Hephaest. 6 περὶ τροχαικοῦ, cited from Consbruch (1906) p. 122, lines 17–25.

95–97 he allows that in tragedy a grieving hero will often cast aside the bombast and sesquipedalian words associated with the genre: *tragicus … proicit ampullas et sesquipedalia uerba*. Commenting on these lines, Porphyrio tells us that "he lifted this from Callimachus, who said" (*hoc a Callimacho sustulit, qui dixit*) – followed, unfortunately, by a lacuna, but one that doubtless contained the fragment preserved in the scholia to Hephaestion. An *ampulla* is simply the Latin calque of λήκυθος, and in the Horatian context clearly refers to "bombast";[64] pseudo-Acro ad loc. nicely explains, "that is, angry, bloated, lofty words; he eschews over-wrought and bloated speech" (*id est irata uerba, inflata, grandia; omittit orationem tumidam et inflatam*). Other passages from Sophocles to Strabo seem to confirm this meaning.[65]

Back then to Cicero: is there any reason to suppose that, when Cicero talks about "embroidering his speeches this way and that" and says to Atticus *nosti illas* ληκύθους, he does not simply mean "you know that high style of mine"? He is being humorously self-deprecating, self-consciously undercutting himself as he describes Crassus' overheated rhetoric – it is, he jokes, even more overdone than his own, and we all know how worked up he tends to get about his consulship!

If Pliny understood Cicero's passage this way, then he is continuing his astute self-positioning in the stylistic debate. He has, he claims, mostly stuck to Calvus' plainer style, but he has not hesitated, when circumstances called for it, to embroider his speech with more florid and bombastic passages. He thus has the best of both worlds: he is simple and Attic when he should be, and he can use high style too, particularly in digressions, which had long been associated with Cicero.[66] After all, he says, *acres … esse non tristes uolebamus*.

The letter concludes with Pliny's firm intent to publish (*est enim plane aliquid edendum*, epist. 1.2.6). He mixes self-praise with self-deprecation, claiming that his old works still find readers – or so the booksellers flatter him, at any rate. And so here, in one letter, we catch a glimpse of Pliny exactly as he wants to be seen: an orator, a *littérateur*, a man well versed in

---

[64] Cf. Brink (1963–1982) ad loc. p. 180, as well as Hor. *epist.* 1.3.14 *an tragica desaeuit et ampullatur in arte?* I do not understand why Brink thinks there must be "two metaphorical notions in Latin as well as in Greek," i.e., one referring to painted "embellishments," the other to "bombast." It seems remarkably improbable that so unusual a word could develop not one but two metaphorical senses concerning style.

[65] Strabo 13.1.54; Sophocles fr. 1063 Radt with notes (see esp. Hesych. λ 856 Latte ληκυθιστής [Musurus: -ηστής codd.]: κοιλόφωνος). See Bill (1941) for a collection of the instances and for conclusions that agree for the most part with my own.

[66] See e.g. ch. 6 p. 254 for Aper's biting comment on Cicero's digressive tendencies (Tac. *dial.* 22.3).

contemporary stylistic debates who strikes just the right balance between models like Demosthenes, Calvus, and – above all – "his" Cicero, a man of learning who can casually make profound allusions, which, if we follow them through, position him as someone laboring mightily to get his style just right and, indeed, as a second Cicero.[67] This last, however, is precisely what he cannot ever come out and say – he can only imply it.

Pliny is no stranger to trying to associate himself with Cicero in very subtle ways. In *epist.* 9.23, he reports a story that he had heard from Tacitus. Supposedly a circus-goer, on learning that he was sitting next to a famous literary man, guessed that it must be either Tacitus or Pliny. Pliny is delighted that "our names are ascribed to literature as if they belonged to literature, not people" (*nomina nostra quasi litterarum propria, non hominum, litteris redduntur, epist.* 9.23.3). For the cognoscenti, this is irresistibly evocative of Quintilian's famous description of Cicero as "not the name of a man but of eloquence personified" (*ut Cicero iam non hominis nomen sed eloquentiae habeatur, inst.* 10.1.112). Pliny thus subtly positions himself as a Ciceronian successor – without, of course, ever explicitly saying so. Such an allusion may have been understandable only to a small readership, but Tacitus certainly would have understood, and as Christopher Whitton points out, this is a particularly piquant compliment to pay to a man who contended that the age in which he was living "scarcely retained the name 'orator'" (*uix nomen ipsum oratoris retineat, dial.* 1.1).[68]

In *epist.* 1.5 we meet Pliny's arch-nemesis Regulus for the first time. Regulus is everything that Pliny claims not to be: a malfeasant *delator*, a political opportunist, a man of low morals and lower style. This *bête noire* is destined to be a theme of the *Epistulae* until his abrupt death in the sixth book, whereupon Pliny wryly remarks, "Regulus did a good deed by dying: he would have done a better one had he died sooner" (*epist.* 6.2.4 *bene fecit Regulus quod est mortuus: melius, si ante*). They clash time and again in the centumviral court, but Pliny, as he happily reports, always comes out on top.

Pliny also easily outdoes Regulus in the field of speech and style. He contemptuously cites a few of Regulus' choicer *sententiae* – *Stoicorum simiam* ("the Stoics' ape"), *Vitelliana cicatrice stigmosum* ("branded with the scar of Vitellius," of Arulenus Rusticus) – and dismisses them with an

---

[67] And if we fail to follow them through, we may miss the point entirely; cf. Vogt-Spira (2003) 54, who focuses on the mentions of Demosthenes and Calvus and writes "daß [Plinius] Ciceronianer sei, ist offenbar nicht das Signal dieses ersten Programmbriefes," believing that Pliny seriously engages with Cicero only in later letters (55).

[68] Whitton (2018) 61–62.

offhand *agnoscis eloquentiam Reguli* ("you recognize the 'eloquence' of Regulus," *epist*. 1.5.2), where we are plainly to understand that his "*eloquentia*" is anything but eloquent. In this letter, Regulus, terrified after the death of Domitian, desperately wants a reconciliation with Pliny, and visits him to apologize for one of his many insults in the centumviral court (*epist*. 1.5.11–12):

> paucos post dies ipse me Regulus conuenit in praetoris officio; illuc persecutus secretum petit; ait timere se ne animo meo penitus haereret, quod in centumuirali iudicio aliquando dixisset, cum responderet mihi et Satrio Rufo: "Satrius Rufus, cui non est cum Cicerone aemulatio et qui contentus est eloquentia saeculi nostri." respondi nunc me intellegere maligne dictum quia ipse confiteretur, ceterum potuisse honorificum existimari. "est enim" inquam "mihi cum Cicerone aemulatio, nec sum contentus eloquentia saeculi nostri; nam stultissimum credo ad imitandum non optima quaeque proponere."

> A few days later Regulus himself met me when I was attending the inauguration of the praetor;[69] he followed me there and tried to get me alone. He said that he was afraid that something he had once said in the centumviral court in a speech against me and Satrius Rufus was still bothering me: "Satrius Rufus, who does not attempt any rivalry (*aemulatio*) with Cicero and who is content with the eloquence of our age." I responded that I now understood that he meant it as an insult because he admitted it himself, but that it could have been taken as a compliment. "For there is," I said, "a rivalry (*aemulatio*) between me and Cicero, nor am I content with the eloquence of our age; for I believe it's the dumbest thing imaginable not to put forward the best possible models for imitation (*ad imitandum*)."

Regulus' comment about Satrius is evidently supposed to imply that Pliny himself, i.e. the other half of this dynamic duo, is *not* "content with the eloquence of our age." Regulus means this as an insult, but Pliny claims that he had not until just now understood it as such – he had thought it was a compliment! He is, after all, a Quintilianic neo-Ciceronian, and he rejects the debased style of the declaimers and *delatores*. Indeed, Pliny would have been insulted had he *not* been thought Ciceronian, and he thus reverses the insult by implying what he had earlier said explicitly, namely that Regulus' un-Ciceronian "eloquence" is not worth the name.

In this letter, then, Pliny aligns himself closely with the uncorrupted style of Cicero. He shows that other people, even his own enemies, compare him with Cicero, and he takes the comparison seriously. And yet his enemies here made the comparison to insult him, insinuating that it

---

[69] For this understanding of *in praetoris officio*, see Sherwin-White (1966) ad loc. p. 98.

was ridiculous for Pliny to aspire to rise so far above his oratorical station in life. We thus see a hint here that this Ciceronian self-fashioning could be a point of anxiety. Pliny determines to brazen it out, defusing the insult by pretending that he had not understood it as such, but rather as praise of his stylistic choices – but he could not possibly have failed to understand Regulus' original intent. Furthermore, he justifies his Ciceronianism just as Quintilian so often had: Cicero is simply the best orator that ever lived, and one ought to model oneself on the best examples; therefore he has taken Cicero for his model. This is, in fact, Pliny at his boldest, because Regulus had not called him an *imitator Ciceronis*, but rather claimed that he had a relationship of *aemulatio* with Cicero – the implication being that this is simply absurd. But Pliny seizes on this as an opportunity to present himself publicly as a Ciceronian. And as ever, this element of presentation – the fact that Pliny has chosen to report this story – is of considerable importance.

In *epist.* 1.20 Pliny writes to Tacitus in a similar vein, reporting an ongoing debate on proper style with "a certain skilled and learned man" (1.20.1). He criticizes the modish tendency toward *breuitas* in oratory – except when a case genuinely permits it – and claims that a good speech should be long and written in high style. The letter itself is a brilliant example of form matching content, as it stretches over six pages of Oxford text and is studded with Greek quotations, but its linchpin is again Cicero (*epist.* 1.20.4):

> hic ille mecum auctoritatibus agit ac mihi ex Graecis orationes Lysiae ostentat, ex nostris Gracchorum Catonisque, quorum sane plurimae sunt circumcisae et breues: ego Lysiae Demosthenen Aeschinen Hyperiden multosque praeterea, Gracchis et Catoni Pollionem Caesarem Caelium, in primis M. Tullium oppono, cuius oratio optima fertur esse quae maxima. et hercule ut aliae bonae res ita bonus liber melior est quisque quo maior.

> At this point the learned man begins to argue with me with recourse to authority figures, and he holds up the speeches of Lysias on the Greek side, and those of the Gracchi and Cato from our own; they are, to be certain, almost invariably short and concise. I counter by opposing Demosthenes, Aeschines, and Hyperides – and many others besides – to Lysias, and to the Gracchi and Cato I oppose Pollio, Caesar, Caelius, and above all Marcus Tullius Cicero, whose longest speech is considered his best. And by Hercules, just like other good things, so the bigger a good book the better.

Here again Cicero is the supreme exemplum: he is "above all" (*in primis*) the refutation of the foolish claims of Pliny's interlocutor. Cicero is indeed a sort of shorthand here, for it is simply taken as self-evident that no one can compare with him; he is not just Pliny's preferred model, but the preferred model full stop, Quintilian's "eloquence personified." And furthermore Cicero at his best is Cicero at his longest – again not just Pliny's opinion, but presented as a truth universally acknowledged. What does this mean? Sherwin-White is silent, while Betty Radice has a two-word footnote: *Pro Cluentio*.[70] I cannot imagine that Pliny seriously means to imply that of all Cicero's speeches, competent critics are accustomed to rate the *Pro Cluentio* his best. I think it much more likely that he is making a general statement ("the more Cicero speaks, the better"),[71] or just possibly referring to the *Verrines* as a whole, which are both remarkably long and first made Cicero's reputation. Yet again Pliny here plays ono-mastic games with Cicero, referring to Gaius Asinius Pollio, Gaius Julius Caesar, and Marcus Caelius Rufus by a single name, either cognomen or nomen. This was the standard form of "informal reference."[72] Cicero, by contrast, is distinguished by the more formal praenomen + nomen, *M. Tullius*, not so much because Pliny wants to be formal, but because a more elevated reference better suits his rhetoric: "W, X, Y, and above all Mr. Z" is the effect.

Pliny is not yet finished with Cicero. His anonymous interlocutor alleges that Pliny's named predecessors, in working up their speeches for publication, greatly increased their bulk. Pliny begs to differ (*epist.* 1.20.6–7):

> haec ille multaque alia, quae a me in eandem sententiam solent dici, ut est in disputando incomprehensibilis et lubricus, ita eludit ut contendat hos ipsos, quorum orationibus nitar, pauciora dixisse quam ediderint. ego contra puto. testes sunt multae multorum orationes et Ciceronis pro Murena pro Vareno, in quibus breuis et nuda quasi subscriptio quorundam criminum solis titulis indicatur. ex his adparet illum permulta dixisse, cum ederet omisisse. idem pro Cluentio ait se totam causam uetere instituto solum perorasse, et pro C. Cornelio quadriduo egisse, ne dubitare possimus, quae per plures dies (ut necesse erat) latius dixerit, postea recisa ac repurgata in unum librum grandem quidem unum tamen coartasse.

He dodges these examples and the many others that I usually adduce in support of my position – he's a slippery fellow and impossible to get

---

[70] Radice (1969) 58 n. 1.

[71] Cf. Plin. *epist.* 9.20.1, Cic. *Att.* 16.11.2, and most interestingly Plut. *Cic.* 24.6: Cicero, when asked which of the speeches of Demosthenes he thought was the best, replied "the longest" (περὶ δὲ τῶν Δημοσθένους λόγων ἐρωτηθείς, τίνα δοκοίη κάλλιστον εἶναι, τὸν μέγιστον εἶπε). Perhaps then Pliny is echoing Cicero's own words in discussing him. Cugusi (2003) 99–100 suggests that Pliny in this letter is conditioned by Cicero's stylistic theories.

[72] Adams (1978) 145.

a handle on in a debate. Indeed, he claims that these very men whose speeches I was relying on as my examples actually said fewer things in the oral version of their speech than in the published version. I think the opposite. Many speeches of many orators bear me out on this point, including the *Pro Murena* and the *Pro Vareno* of Cicero, in which a brief and bare sort of subscription to certain accusations is indicated by section headings alone. From these speeches it is plain that Cicero said a great deal that he omitted when he published the speech. He also says in the *Pro Cluentio* that he conducted the whole case himself, following the old custom [i.e. Cic. *Clu.* 199], and that he spoke for four days in the *Pro Cornelio*. Thus we cannot doubt that what he said at length over many days (as was necessary) was afterwards pruned and trimmed and compressed into a single book – a large one, admittedly, but still a single book.

Again Pliny resorts to Cicero to defend his position. Although "many speeches of many orators" support his claim, it is to Cicero that he turns first, and he cites various specific examples where Cicero must have shortened his speeches in the revision process. Cicero is for Pliny the ultimate authority figure, and he knows a variety of his speeches – not just the greatest hits – like the back of his hand. He is able to produce relevant passages from obscure portions of these speeches *ex tempore*. Pliny has plainly studied his Cicero in some detail.

When Pliny's learned friend contends that there is a difference between a good oral speech and a good written one, Pliny is again quick to look to Cicero. First (*epist.* 1.20.9) he echoes Quintilian, who had said, "it seems to me that speaking well and writing well are the same thing, nor is a written speech anything other than a record of the speech as delivered" (*inst.* 12.10.51 *idem uidetur bene dicere ac bene scribere neque aliud esse oratio scripta quam monumentum actionis habitae*). Quintilian then summons Cicero as a witness, observing that he is known by his written texts alone, not his delivery.[73] So Pliny (*epist.* 1.20.9):

> persuasum habeo posse fieri ut sit actio bona quae non sit bona oratio, non posse non bonam actionem esse quae sit bona oratio. est enim oratio actionis exemplar et quasi ἀρχέτυπον.

> I am convinced that while it's possible for a speech to sound better than it reads, it's not possible for a good oral speech not to be a good written speech too. For the written speech is the model and, as it were, the archetype of the oral version.

---

[73] The implications of not hearing Cicero's voice are explored in Butler (2015) 185–187.

Examples? Cicero, of course. Written speeches, Pliny says, are full of rhetorical figures, even when they were not in fact ever delivered orally. Witness the *Verrines*: *ut in Verrem, "artificem quem? quemnam? recte admones; Polyclitum esse dicebant"* ("as, for example, in the *Verrines*: 'An artist – who in the world was it? Ah, thank you for reminding me; they said that it was Polyclitus,'" *epist.* 1.20.10 = Cic. *Verr.* II 4.3). Cicero again serves as the cornerstone of Pliny's argument. Here indeed Pliny continues to show off his Ciceronian range, not merely referring to another speech but quoting its actual words. Perhaps not coincidentally, Quintilian cites this same passage as a clever example of feigned ignorance (*inst.* 9.2.61). We may thus see here another instance of Quintilian's stamp on Pliny's Ciceronian outlook.

The letter continues with further arguments supporting a copious and grand style, but Pliny's point has already been sufficiently made. Cicero is the ultimate defense for Pliny's volubility, because everyone agrees that he was the best orator, and everyone also agrees that the more he spoke, the better he was. Indeed, when Pliny revisits this topic in *epist.* 9.26, Cicero is again the first orator he turns to.[74] His correspondent, Lupercus, had impugned Pliny's high style. In reply Pliny proffers examples of lofty language from Homer, but then imagines Lupercus objecting, "But oratory and poetry are completely different things!" (*at enim alia condicio oratorum, alia poetarum, epist.* 9.26.8). And so Pliny shoots back (*epist.* 9.26.8):

> quasi uero M. Tullius minus audeat! quamquam hunc omitto; neque enim ambigi puto. sed Demosthenes ipse ...

> As if Marcus Tullius Cicero were less daring! Nevertheless, I won't use him as my example; for about him there can be no doubt. But Demosthenes himself ...

Cicero is again cited first, and again referred to as *M. Tullius*, but rather than develop his Ciceronian case as he had in *epist.* 1.20, Pliny instead makes a deliberate *praeteritio*. "There's no need to talk about him," he insists, "because you'll already agree with everything I would say." This is a clever way of forcing his opponent's consent – Lupercus is given no chance to object – and forestalling argument, but it only works because Pliny considers Cicero's exemplary status so absolutely certain that his readers could not possibly doubt or deny it.

In these examples Pliny has followed Quintilian's lead, adopting Cicero as the ultimate stylistic model apparently without any uneasy tuggings at

---

[74] For a reading of the allusive texture of this letter, see Schenk (1999) 116–123 = (2016) 335–342.

his conscience. He has not yet dared to compare himself directly to Cicero, however, and nowhere in the *Epistulae* does he work up enough courage to do so. He hints, he suggests, and – above all – he lets others do it for him.[75]

For example, in *epist.* 3.15 Pliny replies to Silius Proculus, who had asked him to comment on his poetry. The letter begins (*epist.* 3.15.1–2):

> petis ut libellos tuos in secessu legam examinem, an editione sint digni; adhibes preces, adlegas exemplum: rogas enim, ut aliquid subsicui temporis studiis meis subtraham, impertiam tuis, adicis M. Tullium mira benignitate poetarum ingenia fouisse. sed ego nec rogandus sum nec hortandus; nam et poeticen ipsam religiosissime ueneror et te ualdissime diligo.

> You ask me to read your books of poetry while I'm on vacation to determine whether they are worth publishing; you implore me, you adduce a precedent: for you ask that I take a bit of my free time away from my own literary work and devote it to yours, and you add that Cicero encouraged the talent of poets with marvelous generosity. But I need hardly be asked or exhorted; for I both venerate the poetic art itself with an almost religious fervor and I have the deepest affection for you.

Silius Proculus had evidently compared Pliny with Cicero, a bit of flattery well calculated to win over Pliny's good will. Pliny is keen to turn this to his own advantage, and very deliberately writes back that such a comparison was unnecessary, because he himself already values both Proculus and poetry so much. Pliny's reiteration of the compliment is thus entirely superfluous, but it clearly serves his own self-fashioning. It might be unduly boastful for him to make the comparison himself, but if someone else makes it, it is entirely within the bounds of modesty. And yet it is not really someone else making the comparison, because we are not reading Proculus' original letter, but rather Pliny's supposed quoting – he is thus able to control every aspect of his message, and yet appear to be merely replying to an inquiry. Furthermore, Pliny's apparent downplaying of the comparison ("come now, Proculus, this really wasn't necessary") fits in perfectly with the pattern we shall soon see. It is finally significant that this is the only part of Proculus' letter that Pliny sees fit to repeat; one can hardly imagine that Proculus simply wrote, "Dear Pliny, please have a look at my poetry and see what you think of it. You know Cicero did the same

---

[75] Cf. *epist.* 9.23.6. On Pliny putting praise of himself in the mouths of others, see Ludolph (1997) 115 (coining the term "iudicium alienum"), Mayer (2003) 229–230, and Gibson and Morello (2012), e.g. 90, 97.

thing. Yours sincerely, Proculus." Pliny echoes only what serves his own self-image.[76]

Pliny is really very good at self-serving echoes. In the last epistle of book 3, he writes to Cornelius Priscus about Martial's death.[77] *Audio Valerium Martialem decessisse et moleste fero* ("I hear that Valerius Martial has died, and I'm taking it hard"), he begins, although we might doubt just how upset he is – *moleste fero* bespeaks something more along the lines of mild discomfort than profound grief.[78] He begins by giving the poet credit – he was a clever man, sharp, penetrating; he could wield both wit and an acid-tipped pen, and he wrote with sincerity (*epist.* 3.21.1) – but then immediately turns to his own role in promoting Martial's career. Upon Martial's retirement, as a gesture of thanks for some laudatory verses that Martial had written, Pliny rewarded him with the *uiaticum* for the trip back to his native Spain. He explains (*epist.* 3.21.4–5):

> quaeris, qui sint uersiculi quibus gratiam rettuli? remitterem te ad ipsum uolumen, nisi quosdam tenerem; tu, si placuerint hi, ceteros in libro requires. adloquitur Musam, mandat ut domum meam Esquilîs quaerat, adeat reuerenter:
>
> > sed ne tempore non tuo disertam
> > pulses ebria ianuam, uideto.
> > totos dat tetricae dies Mineruae,
> > dum centum studet auribus uirorum
> > hoc, quod saecula posterique possint
> > Arpinis quoque comparare chartis.
> > seras tutior ibis ad lucernas:
> > haec hora est tua, cum furit Lyaeus,
> > cum regnat rosa, cum madent capilli.
> > tunc me uel rigidi legant Catones.
>
> You ask what these little verses are that I have rewarded? I'd refer you to the book itself, if I didn't have some of the verses off by heart. If you like these,

---

[76] This is not to say that Pliny is being entirely selfish here; after all, he goes on to say that Proculus is a magnificent reciter of poetry. Sherwin-White (1966) ad loc. p. 248 thinks that "Pliny is rather cool in his praise for once, avoiding praise of the verses by praising the delivery." Perhaps, but Pliny should then deserve a place in the diplomatic hall of fame, for he is nothing but complimentary and gives every impression of a favorable judgment of the poems' content, even if he does not actually say so.

[77] *Epist.* 3.21 has attracted much recent critical attention. See the foundational Henderson (2001) and (2002) 44–58; more recently Tzounakas (2013), Neger (2015) 132–138.

[78] So e.g. Sen. *epist.* 61.1; see *OLD* s.v. *moleste* and *TLL* VIII.1355.27–62 (Lumpe). When Pliny is genuinely upset by someone's death, he says so; cf. e.g. *epist.* 5.16, where Pliny writes to Aefulanus Marcellinus on the death of the daughter of a mutual acquaintance.

you'll find the rest in the book. He's addressing his Muse; he orders her to seek out my home on the Esquiline and tells her to approach respectfully:

> But see to it that you don't knock drunkenly on that learned door at an unseasonable hour. He devotes his entire days to morose Minerva, preparing something for the ears of the centumviral court which future generations will be able to compare with the works of even the man from Arpinum. You will go more safely by the evening lamps: this is your time, when Lyaeus runs riot, when the garland reigns supreme and hair is oiled with perfume. Then let even stiff Catos read me.

Priscus had not actually asked what Martial's verses were; Pliny, after all, has initiated this particular epistolary exchange. Still, Pliny pretends that Priscus has asked or doubtless would ask (*quaeris*), and so he undertakes to answer in advance. He pretends that he just happens to have memorized part of the epigram – he does not quote the entire poem, which makes this fiction slightly more plausible, preferring to preface a sentence of paraphrase – while the modern reader feels certain that Pliny has been preening himself on having garnered this praise ever since he first laid eyes on it. And at the heart of Martial's encomium of Pliny lies a comparison with Cicero, predicting that future ages will judge Pliny's speeches for the centumviral court the equal of Cicero's orations. Pliny is only too delighted that his contemporaries are again making such comparisons, which must be the highest possible compliment, and he can of course report it without the impropriety of actually making the comparison himself. In his eulogy of Martial, then, Pliny does not extol Martial's virtues or tell us anything about his life; instead, he devotes the centerpiece and the bulk of the letter to praise of himself. This self-promotion thus constitutes the real theme of the critical last letter of the book, which will be all the more significant if Sherwin-White is correct in hypothesizing that book 3 was published independently, or if there were at some point a three-book edition of the *Epistles*.[79] Indeed, Pliny's last sentence even borders on insult in its condescension toward Martial's posthumous reputation (*at non erunt aeterna quae scripsit: non erunt, fortasse, ille tamen scripsit tamquam essent futura, epist.* 3.21.6), which also helps explain why he has had the boldness to quote Martial's verses here: he wants to take out an insurance policy on this particular bid for immortality.

Pliny plays a similar game in *epist.* 4.8, a reply to Maturus Arrianus, who had congratulated him on being inducted into the College of Augurs.

---

[79] Sherwin-White (1966) 32, who is skeptical of the three-book edition. Bodel (2015) 68 seems to accept Sherwin-White's conclusion, but goes on to discuss in detail the (in his view) interrelated structure of the first three books; cf. Whitton (2013b) 47. I consider Cicero's prominence at the beginnings and ends of books and letters in n. 115 below.

Cicero too had been an augur, and Arrianus evidently complimented Pliny on following in his role model's footsteps (*epist.* 4.8.4–5):

> te quidem, ut scribis, ob hoc maxime delectat auguratus meus, quod M. Tullius augur fuit. laetaris enim quod honoribus eius insistam, quem aemulari in studiis cupio. sed utinam ut sacerdotium idem, ut consulatum multo etiam iuuenior quam ille sum consecutus, ita senex saltem ingenium eius aliqua ex parte adsequi possim! sed nimirum quae sunt in manu hominum et mihi et multis contigerunt; illud uero ut adipisci arduum sic etiam sperare nimium est, quod dari non nisi a dis potest.

> My co-option as augur pleases you especially, as you write, for this reason, because Cicero was an augur. You are happy that I'm retracing the political *cursus honorum* of the one whom I desire to rival in literary pursuits (*aemulari in studiis*). But I wish that as I achieved this same priesthood and indeed the consulate at a much younger age than he, so too I might be able, at least as an old man, to attain some small part of his genius (*ingenium*)! But of course the things which are in the power of men have fallen to my lot just as they have to others; but not only is such genius difficult to achieve, it is too much even to hope for, since it cannot be bestowed except by the gods.

This passage enunciates Pliny's paradox in a nutshell. Again a correspondent has compared him favorably with Cicero, and again he is without doubt delighted by such a comparison. He takes advantage of the opportunity to allow this association to be bruited abroad, diligently reiterating Arrianus' words for the ears of posterity. And yet again he is very careful to specify that this is the opinion of Arrianus: *te quidem, ut scribis,* … *delectat … laetaris … quod honoribus eius insistam.* Pliny has fronted the *te*, giving it a special prominence in the sentence, and added unmistakable further emphasis with the particle *quidem*: it is as if Pliny takes a step back from Arrianus, leans away, and putting up his hands defensively avows, "This is why you are happy, not why I am." He immediately clarifies this with the parenthetical *ut scribis*, i.e., "Everyone who's reading this, you need to understand, these are Arrianus' words, not mine." The phrase *ut scribis* is in fact common in Cicero's letters and probably a regular feature of Roman correspondence,[80] but Pliny uses it only here and at *epist.* 7.30.1, where again it may bear some emphasis. It is thus a highly marked piece of Plinian diction in the *Epistulae*, and so he must be very keen to stress that this is Arrianus speaking.

---

[80] It occurs more than a hundred times in Cicero; Trajan uses it three times in *epist.* 10: 10.20.2, 10.32.1, 10.40.3.

Arrianus says that Pliny is retracing Cicero's path through the political *cursus honorum*, and we know full well that these are Arrianus' words, for Pliny reports them in the subjunctive: *laetaris . . . quod honoribus eius insistam.* Thus Pliny is able to distance himself from this compliment, while of course reporting it for all to read. He continues, however, by defining *eius* as *quem aemulari in studiis cupio.* This is still to be taken as part of Arrianus' original praise – the run of the sentence makes it unmistakable – but here Pliny vouches for the assertion himself, reporting it in the indicative. Whatever he may think about his political progress, Pliny really does want to rival Cicero in the literary sphere.

Pliny continues with what at first appears to be a bit of braggadocio, claiming that he achieved the consulship and the augurate at a younger age than Cicero. Such a claim is all the more remarkable because Cicero, as he loves to tell us (e.g. *leg. agr.* 2.3–4, *Brut.* 323), was consul in his earliest year of eligibility.[81] And yet this also points implicitly to the changed political circumstances, for Pliny could only beat out a man made consul *anno suo* because laws governing minimum ages had changed under the Empire. By reading against the grain, we may detect a subtext of anxiety here. Regardless, Pliny only makes this boastful statement in order to undercut himself in the next breath: *utinam . . . senex saltem ingenium eius aliqua ex parte adsequi possim!* He confesses frankly that he falls far short of matching Cicero's *ingenium*, and he hedges his hopes for ever doing so in the future with the greatest possible caution. His political successes were achieved as a *iuuenis*; he hopes to rise to Cicero's intellectual standard only as a *senex* (qualified by *saltem*) and only then *aliqua ex parte*, "in some small way." He differentiates between the two spheres of achievement. Men can grant and receive political office, but only the gods can bestow the gift of *ingenium*, and to hope for such a gift is simply too much. Cicero's singular talents are thus appropriated to the realm of the divine.

In this letter Pliny is at his most anxious to paint the perfect picture of his relationship with Cicero. He reports somebody else's complimentary comparison of him and Cicero, deliberately making it available for the world to see, but consciously distancing himself from it and emphasizing that the words are someone else's. The one aspect of the relationship that he will admit to – his desire to rival Cicero not in politics but in the Quintilianic realm of *studia* – he immediately undercuts by a self-deprecating comparison of *ingenia*. He knows that, by the standards of Quintilian, he should be a second Cicero; at the same time, he feels that he

---

[81] Rightly noted by Gibson and Morello (2012) 90 n. 41.

cannot be; and torn between the two poles he tries desperately to have it both ways and not make a misstep.

This is likewise the Pliny of *epist.* 9.2, whose political dimensions we glanced at briefly above (p. 281). Here his correspondent Sabinus has written to ask for more and longer letters, citing Ciceronian precedent, but Pliny demurs (*epist.* 9.2.1–2):

> praeterea nec materia plura scribendi dabatur. neque enim eadem nostra condicio quae M. Tulli, ad cuius exemplum nos uocas. illi enim et copiosissimum ingenium, et par ingenio qua uarietas rerum qua magnitudo largissime suppetebat; nos quam angustis terminis claudamur etiam tacente me perspicis, nisi forte uolumus scholasticas tibi atque, ut ita dicam, umbraticas litteras mittere.

> Furthermore I didn't have suitable material for writing more. You want me to follow Cicero's example, but our situation is not the same as his. For he had both a peerless intellect and an abundant supply of varied and important topics to match it. You see, however, even without my telling you, within what narrow bounds I am hemmed in, unless perhaps I wish to send you letters from the schoolroom and composed, so to speak, out of the public eye.

Here is our familiar mixture of diffidence and confidence. Sabinus compares Pliny to Cicero; Pliny repeats the comparison and then immediately denies that he is worthy of it. Cicero's *ingenium* far surpasses his own, he says, and the political circumstances of life under one-man rule are altogether changed from Cicero's Republic. Pliny is thus trapped within narrow bounds and simply cannot write the kind of letters that Cicero once wrote.

There may, however, be more going on here. Marchesi has astutely pointed out that *epist.* 9.2 reverses the complaint of *epist.* 2.2 while echoing much of its language. In *epist.* 2.2 it is *Pliny* who complains that his addressee, Paulinus, has not been sending him enough letters, and avows that the only remedy is *si nunc saltem plurimas et longissimas miseris* ("if now at least you send me <u>very many</u> and <u>very lengthy</u> letters," *epist.* 2.2.2). So too does Pliny's correspondent in *epist* 9.2 apparently complain: *facis iucunde, quod non solum plurimas epistulas meas, uerum etiam longissimas flagitas* ("it is kind of you to demand from me not only <u>very many</u> but also <u>very lengthy</u> letters," *epist.* 9.2.1).[82] I think Pliny may even signal the allusion with his opening *facis*

---

[82] Marchesi ignores a slight textual problem that could complicate this allusion: manuscript M reads *non solum epistulas uerum etiam plurimas*, while the lost γ (reconstructable from apographs) had *non solum plurimas epistulas meas uerum etiam longissimas*. The two MSS are independent and of roughly equal authority, and so their readings must be judged on their own merits. But Mynors and other

iucunde, which perhaps means not only "it is kind of you," but also "you write in a playful way" or even "you make me happy, writing that ..."[83] There are other, less certain, echoes of *epist.* 2.2 in *epist.* 9.2 as well.[84] Marchesi believes that Pliny here feels superior to Cicero, since "among Cicero's accomplishments there was not the joy of having his published letters quoted back to him."[85] Rather than such an optimistic reading, however, I think *scholasticae* and *umbraticae epistulae* are perhaps exactly the sort of game that Pliny and his correspondent might be playing in this very epistle, which ultimately falls short by comparison with a Sabinus doing real stuff in the field as a man of action. This letter, after all, is devoid of content (in Cicero's sense) and makes a self-referential gesture back to another Plinian letter; it is disconnected from the real world and lives in a universe constructed out of other correspondence. And so Pliny's allusions, far from demonstrating a defiant spirit of rivalry, may actually add a further layer of self-deprecation. As we saw above, Pliny is reduced to words with no scope for deeds, and to insignificant words at that.

The whole topic of unfaithful correspondents is a commonplace of letter-writers at all times and places, but Pliny here enters into the tradition in a particularly self-conscious way.[86] Cicero himself apologizes to Atticus, saying *quid praeterea ad te scribam non habeo* ("I don't have anything further to write to you about," *Att.* 1.12.4), and one could believe that Pliny's *praeterea nec materia plura scribendi dabatur* ("furthermore I didn't have anything more to write about," *epist.* 9.2.1) looks to such a phrase. This letter to Atticus was well known to Romans complaining about indolent pen-pals; Cicero concluded by exhorting Atticus: *tu uelim saepe ad nos scribas. si rem nullam habebis, quod in buccam uenerit scribito* ("Please write to us often. If you have nothing to say, just write whatever pops into your head," *Att.* 1.12.4). Seneca explicitly cites this very phrase, only to disown it, when chiding Lucilius for keeping up his end of the epistolary conversation (Sen. *epist.* 118.1–2):[87]

> exigis a me frequentiores epistulas. rationes conferamus: soluendo non eris. conuenerat quidem ut tua priora essent: tu scriberes, ego rescriberem. sed

---

editors must be right to prefer γ here, which seems both more forceful and confirmed by the reference to <u>breuibus epistulis</u> at 9.2.5.

[83] For this sense, see *TLL* VII.2.595.22–25 s.v. *iucundus* (Lossau).

[84] See Marchesi (2008) 231. She is perhaps too confident in claiming that every possible echo is in fact a deliberate allusion, but the overall texture is persuasive.

[85] Marchesi (2008) 232. Gibson and Morello (2012) 98–99 pick up on and amplify this interpretation.

[86] Note too that *epist.* 9.18 is a follow-up letter to Sabinus on the same topic.

[87] On this letter of Seneca, cf. p. 209 above.

non ero difficilis: bene credi tibi scio. itaque in anticessum dabo nec faciam quod Cicero, uir disertissimus, facere Atticum iubet, ut etiam <u>si rem nullam habebit, quod in buccam uenerit scribat</u>. numquam potest deesse quod scribam, ut omnia illa quae Ciceronis implent epistulas transeam: quis candidatus laboret; quis alienis, quis suis uiribus pugnet; quis consulatum fiducia Caesaris, quis Pompei, quis arcae petat; quam durus sit fenerator Caecilius, a quo minoris centesimis propinqui nummum mouere non possint. sua satius est mala quam aliena tractare.

You demand more frequent letters from me. Well, let's tally up our accounts; you will be found the one in debt. We had agreed that your letters would come first: you would write, I would reply. But I won't be difficult: I know that you can be trusted with a loan; therefore I shall pay in advance. Moreover, I won't do what Cicero, that most eloquent man, ordered Atticus to do, namely <u>even if he had nothing to write, that he write whatever happens to come to mind</u>. I can never lack for things to write, even ignoring everything that fills the letters of Cicero: what candidate is struggling; who is reliant on the strength of others, who on his own; who is seeking the consulship with Caesar's backing, who with Pompey's, who with a pile of gold; how harsh a usurer Caecilius is, from whom even his relatives can't borrow a dime at less than 1 percent monthly interest. It's much better to discuss one's own ills than those of others.

Seneca here alleges that he always has plenty of material to write about, even leaving out the late Republican tittle-tattle that Cicero stuffed his letters with. I think Pliny must be looking to Seneca's letter as well (both asked for more letters, both adduce Cicero), but he takes the opposite line. Seneca will indeed write more often in the future, but Pliny cannot. He is rejecting the Senecan type of letter – he has no interest in philosophical dialogues cloaked in epistolary garb – and claiming that the right and proper style for letters is the one that Seneca expressly disavows, namely the Ciceronian letter bursting with the latest news from Rome. And yet he himself, by his own acknowledgement a belated epigone, can do no such thing, because there are no current events worth reporting. It has often been observed that Pliny's letters omit details and focus on the general as opposed to the particular; I would suggest that in so doing he is making a virtue of an unpleasant necessity. He is again trapped between knowing what he should do and the limits of what he can actually achieve.

Cicero also seems to serve as Pliny's primary precedent for writing poetry. This should strike us as rather remarkable today, since Pliny's contemporaries were keen to lambaste Cicero's verses, and theirs has been the dominant tradition from antiquity to the present. Why, then, has Pliny chosen such an apparently inept model? It is of course possible that he is heir to a different tradition; Plutarch, after all, could say that Cicero "seemed not only the best orator, but also the best poet of the Romans" (ἔδοξεν οὐ μόνον ῥήτωρ, ἀλλὰ καὶ ποιητὴς ἄριστος εἶναι Ῥωμαίων, *Cic.* 2.3). Even Plutarch, however, acknowledges that Cicero's poetic reputation has gone into a decline – unlike his oratorical reputation, which despite innovations has apparently remained unbesmirched – and he attributes this decline to the continued flourishing of poetic genius after Cicero's death (ἡ μὲν οὖν ἐπὶ τῇ ῥητορικῇ δόξα μέχρι νῦν διαμένει, καίπερ οὐ μικρᾶς γεγενημένης περὶ τοὺς λόγους καινοτομίας, τὴν δὲ ποιητικὴν αὐτοῦ, πολλῶν εὐφυῶν ἐπιγενομένων, παντάπασιν ἀκλεῆ καὶ ἄτιμον ἔρρειν συμβέβηκεν, *Cic.* 2.5). Thus even Cicero's most stalwart poetic allies must confess that he is no longer held in high regard as a poet, and this is to say nothing of those like Pliny's friends Tacitus and Martial, who pull no punches in describing Cicero's poetic output.[88] Pliny plainly knew, although he never breathes a word of it, that people held Cicero's poetry in no great esteem.[89]

Why does Pliny bring up Cicero's verses? It is not for their quality. Pliny does not seem to harbor any anxieties about the quality of his own verse, which he nowhere feels compelled to defend – although he cleverly cites very little of it, despite talking about it at length.[90] What he worries about is the project of a Roman consular writing poetry at all, and especially writing the kind of light verse that he so enjoys. Thus in *epist.* 5.3 Pliny

---

[88] Even Pliny's teacher wished that Cicero had been a bit more sparing in his poetic output, which, he says, has provided boundless material for his detractors: *in carminibus utinam pepercisset, quae non desierunt carpere maligni: "cedant arma togae, concedat laurea linguae" et "o fortunatam natam me consule Romam!" et Iouem illum a quo in concilium deorum aduocatur, et Mineruam quae artes eum edocuit: quae sibi ille secutus quaedam Graecorum exempla permiserat* (Quint. *inst.* 11.1.24). For Tacitus' cutting comment on Cicero's poetry, see ch. 6 n. 86 (*dial.* 21.6); for Martial (2.89) and more generally, see ch. 4 n. 97.

[89] Gibson and Morello (2012) 95 believe that Pliny has deliberately aligned himself with "a statesman-poet who became synonymous with limited poetic talent" and that this "suggests the playful self-awareness of the man who knows that verse is not the foundation of his career but who knows, too, that the quality of Cicero's verse was a topic of great interest among his contemporaries and the *littérateurs* of the previous generation." This strikes me as unlikely, and I emphasize again that Pliny says not a word about the quality of Cicero's verses or his own.

[90] This is likewise his technique in discussing his own speeches. Pliny knows that he cannot compete with Cicero as an orator (cf. e.g. *epist.* 2.14.1, 9.2, p. 281 above), but he uses his letters to burnish his oratorical reputation (so too Mayer [2003]). With astonishing vagueness (cf. Morello [2003]) he shows himself again and again in the process of revising his speeches, reaping all the benefits of being seen engaging in communal revision (on these benefits, see Gurd [2012] 4 and *passim*), without enduring any of the unpleasantness that inevitably ensues in the face of negative critiques. He appears to have an unending flow of faultless literary production, and yet we can say almost nothing about its specifics. In the face of an anxiety about having nothing to say, he says a lot without really saying anything.

writes in reply to Titius Aristo, who claimed that a dispute had arisen after
Pliny had recited his verses (5.3.1):

> me celandum non putasti, fuisse apud te de uersiculis meis multum copio-
> sumque sermonem ... exstitisse etiam quosdam, qui scripta quidem ipsa
> non improbarent, me tamen amice simpliciterque reprehenderent, quod
> haec scriberem recitaremque.

> You thought that I ought to know that there was a lengthy and lively
> discussion about my verses at your house ... that there were also some
> people who didn't criticize the writings themselves, but nevertheless in
> a frank and friendly way reproved me because I wrote and recited them.

The competence of the verse is a non-issue (no one criticized the *scripta
ipsa*; although this very statement could be a prophylactic against criticism), but the idea that Pliny of all people should stoop to these trifles –
and to recite them at that! In *epist.* 4.14 Pliny also preemptively defends
himself against such charges (4.14.4):

> Ex quibus tamen si non nulla tibi petulantiora paulo uidebuntur, erit
> eruditionis tuae cogitare summos illos et grauissimos uiros qui talia scripser-
> unt non modo lasciuia rerum, sed ne uerbis quidem nudis abstinuisse.

> Nevertheless if some bits of these poems seem to you a trifle saucy, your
> learning and education will lead you to recall that those most excellent and
> serious men who wrote about such things not only didn't hold back from
> risqué topics, but wrote about them in unclothed[91] language.

In *epist.* 4.14 he continues by citing the (in)famous precedent of Catullus
16, where the poet must be chaste himself – but his verse need not be (*nam
castum esse decet pium poetam | ipsum, uersiculos nihil necesse est*, Cat. 16.
5–6). Catullus, however, might not be the best point of reference for the
chaste lifestyle. Writing to Aristo in *epist.* 5.3, then, Pliny summons Cicero
as a witness for the defense (5.3.5):

> nec uero moleste fero hanc esse de moribus meis existimationem, ut qui
> nesciunt talia doctissimos grauissimos sanctissimos homines scriptitasse, me
> scribere mirentur. ab illis autem quibus notum est, quos quantosque auctores
> sequar, facile impetrari posse confido, ut errare me sed cum illis sinant, quorum
> non seria modo uerum etiam lusus exprimere laudabile est. an ego uerear
> (neminem uiuentium, ne quam in speciem adulationis incidam, nominabo),
> sed ego uerear ne me non satis deceat, quod decuit M. Tullium, C. Caluum,
> Asinium Pollionem, M. Messalam, Q. Hortensium, M. Brutum, L. Sullam,

---

[91] Pliny's playful protestation here includes a clever pun on *nudus*: those excellent and serious men used
"plain" and "risqué" language all at once.

Q. Catulum, Q. Scaeuolam, Seruium Sulpicium, Varronem, Torquatum, immo Torquatos, C. Memmium, Lentulum Gaetulicum, Annaeum Senecam et proxime Verginium Rufum et, si non sufficiunt exempla priuata, diuum Iulium, diuum Augustum, diuum Neruam, Tiberium Caesarem?

It doesn't bother me that people so esteem my character that, altogether unaware that the most learned and serious and revered men have often written such things, they are all agog that I'm writing this sort of poetry. But I trust that, from those who know how great the precedents are whom I now follow, I will easily be able to gain permission to go astray with such authorities, whose trifles are no less worthy of imitation than their serious writings. Surely *I'm* not supposed to be afraid – I will name none of the living, lest I seem to speak merely to flatter – surely *I'm* not supposed to be afraid that what was right for Cicero, Calvus, Asinius Pollio, Messalla, Hortensius, Brutus, Sulla, Catulus, Scaevola, Servius Sulpicius, Varro, Torquatus (indeed several of the Torquati), Memmius, Lentulus Gaetulicus, Annaeus Seneca, and most recently Verginius Rufus and, if private individuals are not enough, the deified Julius Caesar, the deified Augustus, the deified Nerva, and Tiberius Caesar isn't appropriate for me?

This is a distinguished list of precedents, and Cicero leads the parade.[92] He is endowed with the full measure of *doctrina, grauitas,* and *sanctitas,* and yet he too put his hand to light verse, and thus he is perfectly suited to be one of Pliny's *auctores* for the practice. Pliny's list, moreover, is not chronological, and so Cicero in first place bears particular emphasis (as do, of course, the row of emperors to close out the serried ranks).[93] This is the man whom Pliny is so keen to imitate in all things.

Having defended himself against the charge of writing light verse in the first place, Pliny must then justify his practice of public recitation. He does so chiefly on the grounds of utility and does not here cite distinguished predecessors, but elsewhere he will rework a Ciceronian tag to support recitations. Once again he has received a report that he has been adversely criticized for reciting; he professes to be surprised (*miror quod scribis fuisse quosdam qui reprehenderent quod orationes omnino recitarem, epist.* 7.17.2). In the course of a lengthy apologia for the practice, he cites Cicero, saying (*epist.* 7.17.13):

nam, quod M. Cicero de stilo, ego de metu sentio: timor est, timor emendator asperrimus. hoc ipsum quod nos recitaturos cogitamus emendat;

---

[92] So too does Seneca use Cicero as a precedent for poetry; see ch. 5 n. 19.

[93] Tiberius is placed last, out of chronological order, presumably because Pliny is separating deified from non-deified emperors.

quod auditorium ingredimur emendat; quod pallemus horrescimus circum-
spicimus emendat.

For what Cicero felt about the practice of writing, I feel about fear: it is fear
that is the harshest corrector. The fact that we are thinking about giving
a recitation; the fact that we are entering the auditorium; the fact that we are
pale and shudder and glance about nervously – all these force us to correct
our work.

At *de orat.* 1.150 Cicero had written *stilus <est, stilus>*[94] *optimus et praestan-
tissimus dicendi effector ac magister*, the "pen" – that is, regular practice in
writing – is the best and most outstanding teacher of eloquence. Pliny, in
modifying the tag to suit his own context, subtly imports Cicero's authority in defending the practice as well. Cicero thus serves to justify Pliny's
decisions at every step.

Cicero is, in fact, the very reason that Pliny first turned his hand to light
verse. In *epist.* 7.4 he replies to Pontius Allifanus, who had apparently asked
how a man as serious as Pliny came to write such things (*requiris etiam
quemadmodum coeperim scribere* [sc. *hendecasyllabos*], *homo ut tibi uideor
seuerus, ut ipse fateor non ineptus*, 7.4.1). The theme is thus yet again the
same: Pliny, a *homo seuerus*, must justify his choice to write *uersiculi*. He
says that he has always been interested in poetry, and had experimented in
other genres before, but these hendecasyllables are his first foray into that
meter (*epist.* 7.4.3–4):

> expertus sum me aliquando et heroo, hendecasyllabis nunc primum,
> quorum hic natalis haec causa est. legebantur in Laurentino mihi libri
> Asini Galli de comparatione patris et Ciceronis. incidit epigramma
> Ciceronis in Tironem suum. dein cum meridie (erat enim aestas) dormi-
> turus me recepissem, nec obreperet somnus, coepi reputare maximos ora-
> tores hoc studii genus et in oblectationibus habuisse et in laude posuisse.

I had occasionally tried writing epic verse, but this is my first attempt at
hendecasyllables, and this is the reason I wrote them. In my Laurentian
villa I had Asinius Gallus' books comparing his father and Cicero read to
me. An epigram of Cicero's on his favorite Tiro came up. Then when at
midday (for it was summer) I had retreated to take a nap and sleep refused
to come, I began to think that the greatest orators considered this form of
literary activity pleasurable and reckoned it praiseworthy.

---

[94] The addition is found in the manuscripts of Iulius Victorinus (*RLM* 444.3) and defended by Stangl
(1886) 222. For Cicero to omit *est* is not impossible, of course, particularly if the saying is proverbial
(cf. Wilkins [1888] ad loc. p. 147), but it is a bit strained, and the testimony of Victorinus and Pliny
combined with an easy *saut du même au même* makes the emendation seem all but certain.

Even on vacation at one of his country villas, Pliny is constantly thinking
about the great man from Arpinum. Cicero wrote epigrams, Cicero was the
greatest of orators, Cicero thought it was right and proper to write
epigrams – and Cicero, of course, is Pliny's model in many other things
besides. Pliny should thus follow his model (*epist.* 7.4.6):

> cum libros Galli legerem, quibus ille parenti
> ausus de Cicerone dare est palmamque decusque,
> lasciuum inueni lusum Ciceronis et illo
> spectandum ingenio, quo seria condidit et quo
> humanis salibus multo uarioque lepore
> magnorum ostendit mentes gaudere uirorum.
> nam queritur quod fraude mala frustratus amantem
> paucula cenato sibi debita sauia Tiro
> tempore nocturno subtraxerit. his ego lectis
> "cur post haec" inquam "nostros celamus amores
> nullumque in medium timidi damus atque fatemur
> Tironisque dolos, Tironis nosse fugaces
> blanditias et furta nouas addentia flammas?"

When I was reading the works of Gallus, in which he dared to give to his
father the palm of victory over Cicero, I found a lascivious little poem of
Cicero, to be marveled at for that genius of his, by which he both wrote on
serious matters and showed that the minds of great men rejoice in human
wit and charming variety. For he complains that Tiro deceives his lover by
a wicked trick and denies him the handful of kisses owed for a dinner when
night draws on. When I read these verses, I said to myself, "After this, why
should I conceal my own love affairs and fearfully publish nothing and not
confess that I know the tricks of my Tiro, that I know my Tiro's fleeting
favors and thefts which add new flames to my fire?"

Cicero furnishes Pliny's poetic initiation. Pliny does not scale the summit
of Mount Parnassus or drink from the fount of the Hippocrene; it is
instead a "lascivious little poem" of Cicero's that sets him on the path to
poetry. *Cum libros Galli legerem* – the reader will immediately think of
other poetic initiations where such a *cum*-clause sets the scene, like Verg.
ecl. 6.3–4 *cum canerem reges et proelia, Cynthius aurem* | *uellit et admonuit*
("when I was singing of kings and battles, Cynthian [Apollo] tugged on my
ear and admonished me").[95] Indeed, Pliny continues to play with the
Vergilian scene, for Vergil had contrasted the fact that his Syracusan

---

[95] The tradition, of course, stretches back through Callimachus (καὶ γὰρ ὅτ͵ε πρͺώͺτιστον ἐμοῖς ἐπὶ
δέλτον ἔθηκα | γούνασιͺν, Ἀ[πό]λλων εἶπεν ὅ μοι Λύκιος, *Aetia* fr. 1.21–22 Pf./Harder) to Hesiod
(*theog.* 22–25); see Kambylis (1965).

Muse had deigned to indulge in *lusus* (*ludere, ecl.* 6.1) with the *seria* represented by *reges et proelia*.[96] Pliny intends to have the best of both worlds, because Cicero both wrote this *lusum ... spectandum* and *seria condidit*. He thus provides the perfect precedent for Pliny: he is a *uir magnus* endowed with a remarkable *ingenium*, he wrote *seria*, and yet he could also delight in humane wit (*humanus sal*) and charming variety (*uarius lepor*).

What is the effect of Pliny's Ciceronian poetic initiation? No god plucks him by the ear or speaks to him; in a thoroughly bookish baptism it is rather Cicero addressing him from the page. And yet the Cicero of Pliny's poem is hardly some grave and dignified figure – he is a frustrated lover complaining that his slave, of all people, is withholding the kisses that are his due.[97] Cicero is thus set up on a pedestal only to be subverted, at least implicitly. (It is not surprising that this story is found in the pages of Asinius Gallus; the Asinii were notoriously hostile to Cicero.)[98] One might suspect that Pliny's own poetry does not place him in quite so compromising a position. But if the great Cicero feels no shame at such a thing, why should Pliny be bashful about his own erotic verses? He will not be. Having aligned himself securely with his favorite model in all matters of life and literature, he can proceed with confidence to write his saucy hendecasyllables.[99]

So end the explicit mentions of Cicero in Pliny's *Epistulae*. He everywhere serves Pliny in his Quintilianic role as the ultimate stylistic model and precedent, and yet Pliny tries to ignore uncomfortable political issues. Nevertheless, when politics do come up, we can see that Pliny is uneasy about the contemporary imperial system and his diminished role within it. While he would like to aspire to be a new Cicero – as Quintilian had trained him – he is all too conscious of his relative inferiority and belatedness; he simply feels that he cannot be Gaius Plinius Caecilianus Secundus Ciceronianus. Thus we see him always torn between what he wants to be (and feels he should be), and the reality of what he actually is. He delights in being compared with Cicero, but does not dare to put such a comparison in his own mouth; when he responds to such positive comparisons, it is invariably with a bit of self-deprecatory humility as he

---

[96] Cf. Clausen (1994) ad loc. p. 179 and Coleman (1977) ad loc. pp. 175–176 ("contrast ... between *ludus* and *seria*").

[97] Although this motif is a literary commonplace; see Kroll (1959) ad Catull. 99 p. 272.

[98] See e.g. pp. 131 and 135 above.

[99] In the total loss of Pliny's hendecasyllables and the near-total loss of Cicero's poetic oeuvre, it is probably impossible to say whether Pliny wished to challenge Cicero as a poet.

professes to fall short. Pliny very much labors under the anxiety of Cicero's influence.

Echoes of Ciceronian Letters in the *Epistulae*

In Pliny's collection of *Epistulae*, specific verbal allusions to Cicero are not as frequent as one might expect. Marchesi has compiled an appendix of "the most relevant passages in Pliny's letters in which scholars have detected potential links to Cicero, both literal references and thematic echoes."[100] This was a valuable service, but rather than indicating that these parallels are "so numerous,"[101] I think her list shows how scattered and inconsistent such allusions are – and Marchesi, rightly noting that many of them are tenuous, rejects not a few in a detailed series of footnotes.[102] It is remarkable how seldom Ciceronian tags are mentioned in her very thorough collection, and those that do find a place are often dubious at best.[103]

It seems to me that there is much that is Ciceronian in Pliny's *Epistulae*, but relatively little Cicero – that is to say that Pliny breathes the Ciceronian spirit, not Cicero's *ipsissima uerba*.[104] He does not compose Ciceronian pastiche like some of the declaimers whom we have seen, nor does he evoke Cicero in the foundational way that Tacitus does in the *Dialogus*. He is too self-consciously sophisticated to follow the declamatory pattern, but his insecurities in his rivalry with Cicero do not usually allow him to challenge the great man's *ipsissima uerba* à la Tacitus. And yet although Pliny does not allude to Cicero constantly, he is present in Pliny's collection in

---

[100] Marchesi (2008) 252–256. Whitton (2013a) adds some new possibilities; see his index s.v. "Cicero." Doubtless as detailed commentaries continue to be written on individual books, more reminiscences will be uncovered, but the very fact that we have to work so hard to find them makes the point that they are relatively rare.

[101] Marchesi (2008) 252.

[102] I would reject even more. For example, Marchesi mentions *epist.* 1.3.1 *euripus* as pointing to Cic. *leg.* 2.2.2, supposedly on the testimony of Sherwin-White. Sherwin-White (1966) ad loc. p. 92 has a note that runs: "euripus. A water-course, Cic. *de Leg.* 2.2; Sen. *Ep.* 83.5." This hardly indicates an allusion to Cicero, who also uses the word several times elsewhere, as do Livy and Pliny the Elder. In fact, if any allusion is to be detected, it would be to another passage in Seneca (*epist.* 55.6): *platanona medius riuus . . . euripi modo diuidit*; Pliny's passage runs: *quid platanon opacissimus? quid euripus uiridis et gemmeus?* The word Greek word *platanon*, "grove of plane trees," is exceptionally rare in Latin literature, occurring otherwise first in Vitruvius (5.11.4, by probable conjecture), then twice each in Petronius (126.12, 131.1) and Martial (3.19.2, 12.50.1). Such doubts can be voiced about many of the examples in Marchesi's list.

[103] E.g. on *epist.* 5.5.4 *in diem uiuunt*, the comment of Bütler (1970) 21 is cited: "schon bei Cicero öfters." Bütler hardly intended to imply that Pliny was alluding to Cicero here; on the contrary, he was pointing out that the expression was proverbial, going on to cite Otto (1890) no. 530. This Marchesi tacitly acknowledges in a footnote ([2008] 257 n. 15).

[104] Marchesi (2008) 214 suggestively calls Cicero the "background music" to Pliny's *Epistles*.

a variety of significant ways.[105] Pliny's Ciceronianism is subtle. In this last section I will examine a few letters that seem unmistakably designed to evoke memories of a Ciceronian model. Once again Pliny's very careful game of self-presentation will be on full display as he tries to associate himself with the great Cicero without ever explicitly saying so.

In such matters it is again very difficult to be certain. When Pliny writes to Valerius Paulinus about the illness of his literary *libertus* Zosimus (*epist.* 5.19), could he be thinking of Cicero's letters about his own sick *seruus* – and eventual *libertus* – Tiro (e.g. *Att.* 6.7 or *fam.* 16.9–11, 13, 15)?[106] There are some definite similarities in sentiment between the two cases. Pliny undoubtedly wishes to position himself as a man who treats his household with great indulgence (*epist.* 5.19.1), perhaps at odds with the practice of the times,[107] but there is no need to seek a literary antecedent for his kindness. We postulate a supremely cynical Pliny if we believe that his primary motive in tending to the health of those in his care was to align himself with Cicero. And yet when publishing such a letter for posterity, some thought of Tiro and Cicero may well have crossed his mind.[108]

Likewise we hear in *epist.* 9.6 of Pliny's profound dislike for circus races. His description of these spectacles is thoroughly damning, and may of course originate in his own genuine feelings. Here, however, there are particular parallels with one of Cicero's letters (*fam.* 7.1, to M. Marius) – and at least one salient difference. Pliny writes that he has been able to spend a few quiet days engaged in his literary work because the circus races were being held, which he altogether spurns (*omne hoc tempus inter pugillares ac libellos iucundissima quiete transmisi ... circenses erant, quo genere spectaculi ne leuissime quidem teneor*, *epist.* 9.6.1). The rest of the

---

[105] And absent. Consider e.g. *epist.* 2.17 (on Pliny's Laurentian villa), which Guillemin (1929) 116 regarded as a response to Cic. *Att.* 12.9, where Cicero is enjoying himself at his villa but says that such matters are not worthy of a lengthy letter: *epist.* 2.17 is nothing if not lengthy! But Whitton (2013a) 221 rightly observes that there is precious little engagement with Ciceronian villa culture in this letter. Pliny can have independent thoughts.

[106] Carlon (2009) 166–167 likewise suggests that *epist.* 6.4, on the health of Pliny's wife Calpurnia, could look to Cicero's Tiro letters. It has also been suggested that *epist.* 6.4, 6.7, and 7.5 were modeled on Cicero's letters to Terentia (Guillemin [1929] 138; cf. Nicholson [1998] 92–93).

[107] Cf. Sherwin-White (1966) ad loc. p. 350: "Pliny and Paulinus were exceptional in giving their household freedmen a standard of life approaching their own."

[108] Another potential antecedent is Cic. *Att.* 1.12.4 *puer festiuus, anagnostes noster Sositheus, decesserat meque plus quam serui mors debere uidebatur commouerat*. With this letter Bütler (1970) 112–113 compares Plin. *epist.* 8.16, also on the illnesses and deaths of Pliny's slaves, noting a possible verbal echo in Pliny's *de his plura fortasse quam debui, sed pauciora quam uolui* (8.16.5). Cicero's letter contains only a brief mention of his grief, however, while Pliny's epistle is given over entirely to that topic.

letter details the reasons why such spectacles hold no attraction for him (*epist.* 9.6.1–3):

> nihil nouum nihil uarium, nihil quod non semel spectasse sufficiat. quo magis miror tot milia uirorum tam pueriliter identidem cupere currentes equos, insistentes curribus homines uidere . . . tanta gratia tanta auctoritas in una uilissima tunica, mitto apud uulgus, quod uilius tunica, sed apud quosdam graues homines; quos ego cum recordor, in re inani frigida adsidua, tam insatiabiliter desidere, capio aliquam uoluptatem, quod hac uoluptate non capior.

> There is nothing new or different in these spectacles, nothing that it isn't enough to have seen once. Thus I am all the more astonished that so many thousands of men long like boys to see the horses a-running, the drivers pressing behind them in their chariots . . . So great is the popularity and authority of a single worthless shirt – I don't mean among the common mob, which itself is worth less than the shirt, but even among certain men of substance. When I think about how they sit there with insatiable eagerness for something so pointless and tedious and monotonous, I take some pleasure from the fact that I am not taken with their pleasure.

Shows of this sort, Pliny says, are but pablum for the masses. Such vitriol and such a biting tone seem unusual for Pliny, a man whose letters strive to give the uniform impression of contented good cheer. Cicero, however, had adopted the same sarcastic tone in his letter to M. Marius, and Pliny's arguments and language find parallels in that letter as well.

Marius had evidently written to Cicero for details about Pompey's inaugural show in his new theater, the first such permanent structure in Rome. Unlike Pliny, however, Cicero had actually attended this show, while it is his correspondent who spent the morning at his Stabian villa pleasantly buried in his books (*tu in illo cubiculo tuo, ex quo tibi Stabianum perforando patefecisti sinum, per eos dies matutina tempora lectiunculis consumpseris, fam.* 7.1.1). The spectacle, Cicero assures Marius, would not have been to his taste (*non tui stomachi, fam.* 7.1.2). Of course the unwashed masses delighted in such things, but they would have brought Marius not a jot of pleasure (*quae popularem admirationem habuerunt, delectationem tibi nullam attulissent, fam.* 7.1.3). Again, far better that Marius was listening to his slave recite good literature (*fam.* 7.1.3). In any event, Marius has seen such spectacles before, and this one held nothing new (*quae tamen, si uidenda sunt, saepe uidisti, neque nos qui haec spectauimus quicquam noui uidimus, fam.* 7.1.3).

The argument of the two letters is thus very similar, even down to the level of verbal correspondences like *nihil nouum*/*neque . . . quicquam noui*. Pliny's purpose here seems to be to align himself with a higher calling – *studia* – than the mindless pleasures of the crowds. The criticisms that Pliny levels are not those of a Seneca, who had complained that the crowd disturbs one's hard-won philosophical self-control and that the spectacles themselves are immoral (Sen. *epist.* 7); Pliny, by contrast, shows only contempt for the crowd and indifference to the spectacles. It is not that chariot racing is immoral – it is simply, for a man of substance, pointless and a waste of time. Pliny, however, neatly reverses a key element of Cicero's letter. While Cicero claims that one's time is better spent in *studia* than in the stadium, he himself went to the theater; it was his correspondent who wisely stayed home. Pliny, by contrast, stayed far away from the races, doing as Cicero said, not as he had done. Pliny thus manages to one-up Cicero here, outdoing him by following his own prescription. Never, of course, does Pliny actually mention Cicero, but the parallels between the two letters are so striking and so unusual – it is better to avoid public spectacles in order to devote oneself to matters literary – that the reader will be led to make the connection. Pliny's letter to Calvisius Rufus is unprompted; he simply wants to advertise how well he has been spending his time of late. Both writing and publishing such a letter have a particular self-fashioning intent. Here, indirectly, Pliny manages to be seen outdoing Cicero at his own game.[109]

In *epist.* 8.24, Pliny writes to a Valerius Maximus who is setting out to govern the province of Achaea. Although Pliny himself has not yet been a provincial governor, he does not shrink from sending Maximus a lengthy letter of advice. This epistle is without a doubt modeled on Cicero's letter to Quintus as he entered into the third year of his proconsulship of Asia (*ad Q. fr.* 1.1), as has been recognized since the commentary of Catanaeus in 1506 and elucidated in detail by Friedrich Zucker.[110] Cicero had not yet governed a province at the time he wrote his letter either, and so he provided Pliny with a valuable precedent.

Beyond the obvious situational parallels, there are several clear verbal reminiscences of Cicero in Pliny's letter. Pliny begins (*epist.* 8.24.1):

> amor in te meus cogit, non ut praecipiam (neque enim praeceptore eges), admoneam tamen, ut quae scis teneas et obserues, aut nescire melius.

---

[109] In *epist.* 6.34 Pliny may also look to Cicero in the context of the Roman games, consoling one Maximus about how his *Africanae* (panthers? see Keller [1909–1913] 1.64) did not manage to show up on time; cf. the correspondence of Cicero and Caelius (*fam.* 2.11.2, 8.8.10, 8.9.3). While Sherwin-White (1966) ad *epist.* 6.34.3 p. 401 rightly notes that "the reference is too circumstantial to be an absolute invention," Pliny can nevertheless capitalize on the coincidence (perhaps especially by placing the letter last in the book).

[110] Zucker (1929); see his p. 221 for Catanaeus.

> My love for you compels me, not to instruct you – for you don't need an
> instructor – but nevertheless to remind you to hold fast and use what you
> know; or else it's better to be ignorant.

As Sherwin-White notes, this passage is a tissue of Ciceronianisms. Writing
to Curio, Cicero had said *breue est quod me tibi praecipere meus incredibilis*
in te amor cogit ("there's one little thing that my extraordinary love for you
compels me to instruct you in," *fam.* 2.1.2).[111] Pliny has toned down his
own approach considerably; his *amor* still compels him, but he says that it
compels him "not to" do exactly what Cicero's had compelled him to do
(even if he goes on to do it anyway). Moreover, Pliny's *neque enim*
praeceptore eges ("for you don't need an instructor") looks directly to
Cicero's own parenthetical *neque enim prudentia tua cuiusquam praecepta*
desiderat ("for your prudence doesn't need anyone's instruction," *ad Q. fr.*
1.1.36).[112] Thus he begins his letter with a clear evocation of Cicero.
   Pliny continues (*epist.* 8.24.2):

> cogita te missum in prouinciam Achaiam, illam ueram et meram Graeciam,
> in qua primum humanitas litterae, etiam fruges inuentae esse creduntur;
> missum ad ordinandum statum liberarum ciuitatum, id est ad homines
> maxime homines, ad liberos maxime liberos.

> Remember that you have been sent to the province of Achaea, to that true-
> blue Greece, where civilization, literature, and even agriculture are believed
> to have been invented. You have been sent to set in order the affairs of free
> cities, that is, to those who are well and truly free men.

Here again Pliny plainly looks to multiple passages of Cicero. There is,
in the first instance, no doubt that he is thinking again of Cicero's letter
to Quintus, where Cicero describes the people of Asia as *ei generi . . . non*
modo in quo ipsa sit, sed etiam a quo ad alios peruenisse putetur humanitas
("that people . . . not just among whom *humanitas* itself is to be found,
but from whom *humanitas* is thought to have passed to others," *ad Q. fr.*
1.1.27). Elsewhere too Cicero remarks that the province of Asia is
composed *ex eo genere sociorum, quod est ex hominum omni genere*
humanissimum ("of that group of people which is the most humane of
the whole human race," *ad Q. fr.* 1.1.6).[113] But Pliny also seems to have

---

[111] Marchesi (2008) 223 n. 53 objects that "the nexus *amor cogit* is a commonplace," but not paired with
praecipere and the phrase *meus . . . in te.*

[112] Cf. too *ad Q. fr.* 1.1.18 *quid enim ei praecipiam quem ego in hoc praesertim genere intellegam prudentia*
non esse inferiorem quam me, usu uero etiam superiorem?

[113] For reasons that are not clear to me, Marchesi (2008) 224 n. 54 seems to doubt that Pliny alludes to
these Ciceronian phrases. She observes that *humanissimos homines* is found elsewhere in Cicero (e.g.
Arch. 19), but surely the fact that there is an overlap in both words and sentiment between Pliny and

incorporated the words and sentiment of a passage from Cicero's *Pro Flacco* (61–62):

> aspiciant hunc florem legatorum laudatorumque Flacci ex <u>uera atque integra Graecia</u> ... adsunt Athenienses, <u>unde humanitas, doctrina, religio, fruges, iura, leges ortae atque in omnis terras distributae putantur.</u>

> Let them look at the most distinguished deputations from the <u>true and authentic Greece</u> who have come as character witnesses for Flaccus ... men from Athens are present, <u>whence civilization, learning, religion, agriculture, justice, and laws are thought to have arisen and to spread across the entire world.</u>

We have both the motif of the *uera atque integra Graecia* (cf. Pliny's *ueram et meram Graeciam*, perhaps topping Cicero with sound-play), and also the notion that *humanitas, fruges,* and many other good things "are thought" (*putantur* here, *creduntur* in Pliny) to have arisen (*ortae, inuentae*) in Greece and flowed thence to the rest of the world. The correspondences are too detailed to be mere coincidence, and so it is clear that Pliny has deliberately conflated these passages. It is striking that Pliny evokes a passage from the middle of the *Pro Flacco*, because once again this speech is not one of Cicero's schoolroom texts, and so it reveals Pliny's detailed study of the Ciceronian corpus.[114] This was in a sense the "right" text to allude to: Flaccus was the governor of Asia in 62 BC. (There could even lurk a note of warning: Flaccus was prosecuted for *res repetundae* upon his return, after all.) In combining two Ciceronian passages on governors of Asia, Pliny has shown himself a fully engaged member of the tradition.

Pliny's letter is long by his standards (two pages of Oxford text), but it is miniature by comparison with Cicero's Brobdingnagian epistle (eighteen pages of Oxford text!). As he gets underway, Pliny's advice parallels Cicero's only in general terms, not in specific verbal allusions: one should treat the provincials with kindness and care; one should be conscious of one's own elevated station as a provincial administrator; one should tend to one's own good reputation. As Pliny begins to close his letter, however, he again alludes to Cicero: *accedit quod tibi certamen est tecum* ("furthermore, your competition is with yourself," *epist.* 8.24.8); that is to say, his addressee Maximus is his own greatest rival, since he already has such a good reputation as provincial administrator from his term as quaestor in

---

Cicero here, in a Plinian letter that elsewhere must be looking to this Ciceronian exemplar, is enough to convince even the radical skeptic that Cicero was on Pliny's mind.

[114] Note that Quintilian alludes to this passage at *inst.* 11.1.89.

Bithynia. Quintus, of course, had already been proconsul in Asia for two years at the time of Cicero's letter, and so it was entirely in place for Cicero to remind him of the same thing: "if you work toward being well spoken of by all, <u>not to contend with others but with yourself</u> . . . a single added year of labor will bring us many years of happiness" (*si te ipse uehementius ad omnis partis bene audiendi excitaris, <u>non ut cum aliis sed ut tecum iam ipse certes</u> . . . unus annus additus labori tuo multorum annorum laetitiam nobis . . . adferet, ad Q. fr.* 1.1.3). Pliny can thus blend a compliment to his addressee with a Ciceronian reminiscence. From beginning to end Pliny's letter is dyed in the color of Cicero's words and feelings.

Marchesi observes that Pliny's letter closes his eighth book, and Cicero's opens his correspondence with Quintus. Even someone skeptical of numerology can acknowledge that the first and last items of a book have a particular significance, and this placement has if nothing else the effect of drawing further attention to itself.[115] Marchesi thinks that Pliny's letter may be designed particularly to contrast his own careful process of revision and publication with Cicero's unrevised and unrefined correspondence.[116] Perhaps, although I am skeptical, and even more so of her further meta-literary claims.[117] A simpler approach is to assume that Pliny is writing a genuine letter to a genuine imperial legate setting out for his province.[118] At the same time he is engaged in a complex process of self-fashioning at every moment, and on at least two levels, first for the benefit of Maximus, his immediate addressee, and second for that of the reading public who are the ultimate audience of his published collection. We must examine the effect of Pliny's allusions in this light.

---

[115] It is interesting to observe that the last letters of books 3, 7, and 8 all deal with the relationship between Pliny and Cicero (the end of book 6 may also allude to Cicero; see n. 109 above), and book 1 in some sense opens with Cicero (1.2). Furthermore, within letters that have Ciceronian affinities, those affinities are often made clear both at the beginnings and the endings of the letters, and even within a letter Cicero is placed first in a list (see p. 312 above).

[116] Marchesi (2008) 225, in particular connection with both *epist.* 8.24/*ad Q. fr.* 1.1 and *epist.* 7.33/*fam.* 5.12 – both of which, however, received a remarkable amount of editorial care! See p. 332 below.

[117] In discussing the phrase *tibi certamen est tecum*, she writes: "*Q. Fr.* 1.1 is the actual alter-ego of Pliny's text. The competition in which his letter engages is a shadow combat with Cicero's text, ultimately a contest with itself" (Marchesi [2008] 224).

[118] I take this as a given. His contemporary audience would have known the addressee, and it would not have been a very convincing fiction if he had not in fact been sent to Greece. Whether the addressee can be identified with the quaestor mentioned in the *Panegyricus* (70.1) and/or with Sextus Quinctilius Valerius Maximus (see *ILS* 1018 = *CIL* III.384), however, is less certain. Birley (2000b) 84 is confident of the identification; Sherwin-White (1966) ad *epist.* 8.24.8 pp. 479–480 is skeptical but offers a detailed prosopographical note with his own suggestions and further bibliographical references (cf. Jones [1968] 122–123).

In writing to Maximus, Pliny is composing a propempticon.[119] He offers advice, to be certain, but it is of the vaguest sort: be nice, work hard, do a good job. Such a letter is rather different from Cicero's to Quintus, where Quintus had already been in the province two years, and Cicero dares to proffer some very detailed instructions tailored to Quintus' own character (he admonishes his brother not to let his notorious temper get the better of him, for example). Pliny here is really, I imagine, doing the polite thing by writing to his friend before he sets off for the provinces. He wants to fulfill his own obligations, and he is happy to have the opportunity to compliment his friend. None of this is to deny the sincerity of the sentiment: just as a thank-you note today may be full well meant, even though it is part of a thoroughly conventional genre and sent by the well-mannered whether they mean it or not, so too can Pliny really mean what he says. He is delighted to have the opportunity to weave in elegant compliments, which are naturally the sort of thing that one wants to say to a departing friend. Zucker calls this letter a "Denkmal antiker Humanität," "monument of ancient *humanitas*," believing that the profound admiration for Greece that Pliny expresses is deeply felt and sincerely meant.[120] Pliny is a man of culture and learning, and I would not be surprised if he does praise the virtues of Greece with genuine feeling, but his praise also gives him the opportunity to glorify his addressee implicitly – he must be a great man if he is to govern such a great province – and to offer rather innocuous advice.

For the broader reading public, Pliny's overriding aim is to be *seen* doing all these things. He wants to be seen giving sage advice, seen as a lover of Greek culture, seen as a friend of the Roman governing elite – and indeed himself superior to them, since he is in a position to dispense advice. More cynically, he will want to be seen as the kind of man who should himself be chosen for a provincial post, which, perhaps to his chagrin, he has not yet held.[121] Furthermore, for his learned readership in particular, Pliny will want to seem learned himself, both excelling in the propempticon genre and cleverly allusive. And so he alludes to Cicero, and does so in some detail. His readers would have known of Cicero's famous letter to Quintus, and Pliny, writing a letter to a new governor, could scarcely not refer to it. He does so clearly and programmatically right from the beginning, and he returns to it at the end. But his allusions are not completely straightforward, for he looks also to Cicero's *Pro Flacco* and blends his sources

---

[119] Cf. e.g. Stat. *silu.* 3.2, 5.2, with the introduction of Gibson (2006) to the latter containing helpful discussions of the propempticon in general.
[120] Zucker (1929) 209 and *passim*.   [121] Cf. too *epist.* 6.22 and Syme (1958) 80.

together. While the middle of the letter is "his own," so to speak, it is fundamentally predicated on the allusion to the *Pro Flacco* – all of Pliny's advice follows from the fact that "Athens" and "Greece" are names to conjure with, as Cicero had affirmed.

As Sherwin-White remarks, Pliny is here an authority – despite his lack of experience – writing to a younger man. So too Cicero, although he had never governed a province, writes to Quintus as the older and wiser big brother. Pliny thus assimilates himself not just to Cicero, but to Cicero's superior role. This is another key element in Pliny's self-fashioning: he is here a cultured and learned man, a philhellene, and a comfortably superior second Cicero. This is perhaps as confident as Pliny ever seems in setting himself up as Cicero, for he appears to voice no anxiety whatsoever in this letter, and he places it in a position of great prominence to close the book. But by comparison with the actual letter to Quintus, Pliny is a *Cicero dimidiatus*, at best: his letter is short, vague, and unspecific. He implicitly acknowledges that he cannot genuinely challenge Cicero in this field. He alludes to him, thus winning points for his learning and wit and assimilating himself to the great man's image, but ultimately we feel again that Pliny's world is not that of Cicero. It is in what Pliny does not or cannot do that we can detect an undercurrent of unease in tension with the self-confident exterior.

In *epist.* 5.8 and 7.33 Pliny discusses the writing of history, each time with implicit and explicit allusions to Cicero's thoughts on historiography. In 5.8 he writes to Titinius Capito, who had evidently suggested that Pliny compose historical works himself.[122] Pliny demurs with an elaborate *recusatio* that looks to the opening of Cicero's *De legibus*.[123] Once again the first sentence of Pliny's letter sets the stage for its allusiveness: *suades ut historiam scribam, et suades non solus: multi hoc me saepe monuerunt* ("you encourage me to write history, and you're not the only one: many people have given me this advice," *epist.* 5.8.1). So too the character of Atticus implores Cicero at the beginning of the discussion in the *De legibus*: *postulatur a te iam diu uel flagitatur potius historia* ("for a long time now there's been a desire – or rather a demand – for a history from you," *leg.* 1.5). Perhaps even more pertinently, Cicero writing to the real Atticus in 44 BC claimed that *hortaris me ut historias scribam* ("you urge me to write history,"

---

[122] On this letter, see the detailed and perceptive analysis of Woodman (2012). Further bibliography in Gibson and Whitton (2016) 30 n. 139.

[123] Pointed out by Leeman (1963) 1.333–336.

Att. 14.14.5).[124] Pliny thus has Ciceronian precedent for the self-praise implicit in reporting to the world the demands of his admiring public. Moreover, he at least has the plausible notion that Capito had genuinely urged him to write history – in the *De legibus* Cicero has to make his own character of Atticus do the urging.[125]

A cornerstone of Cicero's discussion is the difference between history and poetry (Quintus speaking: *intellego te, frater, alias in historia leges obseruandas putare, alias in poemate, leg.* 1.5). Cicero is clear on the over-riding distinction between the two (*leg.* 1.5):

> quippe cum in illa <omnia> ad ueritatem, Quinte, referantur, in hoc ad delectationem pleraque; quamquam et apud Herodotum patrem historiae et apud Theopompum sunt innumerabiles fabulae.

> Namely, Quintus, in history everything must be written with an eye to truth, whereas in poetry most things are written for the pleasure of the audience; although even in Herodotus, the father of history, and Theopompus there are stories without number.

Pliny chooses to contrast not history and poetry, but rather history and oratory, inasmuch as his excuse for not turning his hand to history is that he is too busy revising his speeches for publication (*epist.* 5.8.6). Oratory and poetry, he says, must be written with the highest standard of eloquence if they are to give pleasure, whereas history can be content with a presentation of the facts (*epist.* 5.8.4). History and oratory do indeed have much in common, he confesses, but there are great differences too (*epist.* 5.8.9–11):

> narrat illa narrat haec, sed aliter: huic pleraque humilia et sordida et ex medio petita, illi omnia recondita splendida excelsa conueniunt; hanc saepius ossa musculi nerui, illam tori quidam et quasi iubae decent; haec uel maxime ui amaritudine instantia, illa tractu et suauitate atque etiam dulcedine placet; postremo alia uerba alius sonus alia constructio. nam plurimum refert, ut Thucydides ait, κτῆμα sit an ἀγώνισμα; quorum alterum oratio, alterum historia est.

> They both tell stories, but rather differently: the one is concerned with trivial and everyday and common things, the other with the sublime and noble; a sinewy and bare-bones narrative characterizes the one, plumed

[124] Woodman (2012) 227–228 remarks on this connection and contends that Pliny has used a different verb – twice! – "because he is testing his knowledgeable readers." He does use *hortaris* in 5.8.14. Cf. Woodman (2012) 240 n. 35 on another possible "challenging" allusion.

[125] And Cicero's Atticus lays on his compliments with a trowel: *sic enim putant, te illam* [sc. *historiam*] *tractante effici posse, ut in hoc etiam genere Graeciae nihil cedamus* (*leg.* 1.5).

fullness the other; the one is especially pleasant by its force and bitterness and attack, the other by its sweet and pleasing treatment of the material; finally each employs different vocabulary, different rhythms, different structures. For it makes a great difference, as Thucydides said, whether you are writing a κτῆμα or an ἀγώνισμα: history is the former, a speech the latter.

This passage is beset by a difficulty that, although it appears simple, proves surprisingly challenging to resolve: does *haec = oratio* and *illa = historia*, or vice-versa?[126] I would tentatively adopt the minority position, namely that *haec* is *historia*, and so it is of lower stylistic register, concerned with quotidian events,[127] and pleasing however it is written (cf. *historia quoquo modo scripta delectat, epist.* 5.8.4). Oratory, by contrast, cannot be pleasing unless endowed with the highest measure of eloquence (*nisi eloquentia est summa, epist.* 5.8.4). There is no doubt, however, that history is a κτῆμα – this is after all what Thucydides claims – while a speech is an ἀγώνισμα. Pliny has probably either misunderstood or, more charitably, deliberately recast Thucydides' ἀγώνισμα as "forensic contest" instead of "display piece."[128] Thus, in both Pliny's and Cicero's *recusatio* of historical composition, each compares the demands of history with some other genre.

There is then the question of what kind of history one should write, and in particular what its chronological scope should be (*a quibus temporibus scribendi capiatur exordium,* Cic. *leg.* 1.8). Quintus suggests that his brother should begin from the very beginning, whereas Marcus apparently prefers to write about contemporary events, and Atticus agrees (*sunt enim maxumae res in hac memoria atque aetate nostra; tum autem hominis amicissimi Cn. Pompeii laudes inlustrabit, incurret etiam in <praeclarum> illum et memorabilem annum suum: quae ab isto malo praedicari quam, ut aiunt, de Remo et Romulo, leg.* 1.8). Pliny too is vexed by this question, but finds no suitable answer (*epist.* 5.8.12):

---

[126] See Marchesi (2008) 165–168 for discussion with extensive bibliography, and briefly Woodman (2012) 234.

[127] In the Aristotelian sense that history deals with particulars, poetry with general truths. This answers the objection of Leeman (1963) 1.336 that such a description is unsuitable for historians like Sallust and Tacitus.

[128] Cf. Leeman (1963) 1.336 for this interpretation, which may find some support in Quintilian's description of historiography: *totumque opus non actum rei pugnamque praesentem, sed ad memoriam posteritatis et ingenii famam* (*inst.* 10.1.31). Leeman glosses the first half of this definition as Thucydides' ἀγώνισμα ἐς τὸ παραχρῆμα and the second half as κτῆμά τ' ἐς ἀεί; if Pliny's teacher interpreted Thucydides thus, it is hardly surprising that Pliny did as well. Woodman (2012) 238 well notes that, whatever Pliny's interpretation, he has clearly "omitted the temporal dimensions with which Thucydides had filled out the comparison with historiography"; i.e., in Thucydides history was forever, but a speech only for the moment. Pliny, however, is trying to ensure the immortality of his speeches too.

> tu tamen iam nunc cogita quae potissimum tempora adgrediar. uetera et
> scripta aliis? parata inquisitio, sed onerosa collatio. intacta et noua? graues
> offensae leuis gratia.

> But you should now give some thought to what period I might best treat.
> Ancient history that has already been discussed by others? Materials are at
> hand for a ready investigation, but sifting through them is onerous. Recent
> events and virgin territory? The risk of causing offense is grave and the
> rewards are slight.

Although he feels that both *noua* and *uetera* bring with them various
disadvantages, Pliny nevertheless resolves that he will at some point pursue
whichever Capito suggests (*epist.* 5.8.14). He cannot, however, do so at
present, because he is too busy revising his speeches. So too does Cicero
plead that he would gladly undertake a historical project, if only he had the
time, for such a large and important project would require his full and
undistracted attention (*quem non recusarem, si mihi ullum tribueretur
uacuum tempus et liberum; neque enim occupata opera neque impedito
animo res tanta suscipi potest; utrumque opus est, et cura uacare et negotio,*
leg. 1.8; cf. *leg.* 1.9). Each thus refuses history in order to pursue another
kind of literary activity: oratory for Pliny, a legal treatise for Cicero (*leg.* 1.
13–14).

It seems, then, that Pliny's *recusatio* is loosely patterned on Cicero's.
Pliny's letter is no doubt a real refusal; the opening *suades ut historiam
scribam* begins a reply to a real letter of Capito's. The question is then why
Pliny has chosen to cast his response in a Ciceronian mold. There are
relatively few direct echoes of Cicero's words, but the pattern of Pliny's
argument is precisely that of Cicero: (1) people demand that he write
history, (2) history is compared with another genre (poetry/oratory),
(3) the question of whether he should write of *noua* or *uetera* is broached,
(4) ultimately he must refuse because he lacks sufficient time; he chooses
another literary pursuit instead.

There are nevertheless significant differences.[129] Cicero apparently has
no anxieties about his potential as a historian; he has never attempted such
a work, but like Lady Catherine de Bourgh's contrafactual musical abilities,
if he had he should have been a great proficient. His Atticus boldly asserts
that if only Cicero wrote history, then the Romans would rival the Greeks
in this sphere as well (*leg.* 1.5), and Quintus agrees with him (*leg.* 1.8).

---

[129] An obvious difference in Pliny's letter is the mention of his uncle, the Elder Pliny, who, Pliny says,
historias et quidem religiosissime scripsit (*epist.* 5.8.5). This is a genuine circumstance unique to Pliny,
and should again remind us that he is not exclusively playing literary games with Cicero.

Cicero's own character does not doubt his success, should he enter the lists, but simply claims to lack the time to do so. Pliny, by contrast, is immediately diffident: he likes the idea, not, he claims, because he is sure of success – he is but an amateur, after all – but because he could perhaps prevent worthy men from falling into oblivion (*ego uolo, non quia commode facturum esse confidam (id enim temere credas nisi expertus), sed quia mihi pulchrum in primis uidetur non pati occidere, quibus aeternitas debeatur, epist.* 5.8.1). He continues (*epist.* 5.8.3):

> itaque diebus ac noctibus cogito, si "qua me quoque possim tollere humo"; id enim uoto meo sufficit, illud supra uotum "uictorque uirum uolitare per ora"; "quamquam o – ": ...

> Therefore day and night I wonder whether "somehow I too might rise from the earth"; for that would suffice in answer to my prayer. "And to flit as victor on the lips of men" – that would be over and above what I have hoped. "Yet o if I could" – ...

This is as far as possible from Cicero's straightforward confidence about his abilities. Pliny's doubts are expressed in a series of Vergilian quotations (*georg.* 3.8–9 and *Aen.* 5.195), which might superficially make them seem more bantering and witty. And yet they are sincere for all that: Pliny lacks Cicero's confidence. And indeed he is so diffident that even when he expresses his lack of confidence, he distances himself and invokes a famous authority's words to say what he cannot.

What is the effect of these similarities and differences? Capito has issued a real request, and Pliny wants to decline. This in itself calls for some delicacy and finesse, and perhaps a refusal phrased in allusively literary terms comes across as more polite. Both Capito and the broader reading public can recognize Pliny's playfully learned reference; they will thus appreciate his learning and plume themselves on their own. More importantly, Pliny also gets to associate himself with Cicero for all to see – without ever having to come out and make an explicit statement to that effect. And yet here he becomes, as he often does, a more cautious version of Cicero, self-conscious about self-praise. He wants to be Ciceronian, but he does not dare go as far as Cicero himself had gone in his own refusal. Indeed, Cicero ends up by declining *tout court* to write history – he will write a legal treatise for the nonce, and he will never have sufficient leisure to devote himself to the labors of Clio. Pliny, by contrast, ends by promising that when his other obligations have been discharged, he will indeed take up whatever kind of history Capito suggests (*epist.* 5.8.14).

Pliny's *epist.* 7.33 frames itself even more obviously as a Ciceronian letter. He writes to Tacitus with the passionate desire to be included in his *Historiae* (*epist.* 7.33.1–2):

> auguror nec me fallit augurium, historias tuas immortales futuras; quo magis illis (ingenue fatebor) inseri cupio. nam si esse nobis curae solet ut facies nostra ab optimo quoque artifice exprimatur, nonne debemus optare, ut operibus nostris similis tui scriptor praedicatorque contingat?

> I predict – and I'm sure of it – that your *Historiae* will be immortal, and so I'm all the more eager to find a place in them (I admit it openly). For if it is customarily of concern to us that our portrait be painted by the best artist, should we not also want to find a writer such as yourself to sing the praises of what we have accomplished?

This opening recalls Cicero's famous letter to Lucceius (*fam.* 5.12, *ca.* 12 April 55).[130] Cicero had written of his ardent desire to be included and celebrated in Lucceius' writings (*ardeo cupiditate incredibili neque, ut ego arbitror, reprehendenda nomen ut nostrum scriptis illustretur et celebretur tuis, fam.* 5.12.1). Pliny's bold request to find a place in Tacitus' *Historiae* thus has an equally bold precedent in Cicero. And Cicero wished to be included precisely because he desires the *commemoratio posteritatis* and has *spes quaedam immortalitatis*, just as Pliny was eager for a place in Tacitus' "immortal" works. Even the complimentary analogy between the best painters and the best writers finds its origin in Cicero's letter: Alexander the Great did not want to be painted by Apelles and sculpted by Lysippus to curry favor, but because he thought that their art would bring glory both to them and to himself (*neque enim Alexander ille gratiae causa ab Apelle potissimum pingi et a Lysippo fingi uolebat, sed quod illorum artem cum ipsis tum etiam sibi gloriae fore putabat, fam.* 5.12.7); see too Cicero's flattering comparison of Lucceius with Timaeus, Herodotus, and Homer.

The content of the two letters is rather different. Both Cicero and Pliny have a story that they would like their encomiast to tell, but Cicero expresses his wish in general terms, saying only that the period from the Catilinarian conspiracy until his recall from exile would be ideal for separate treatment in a historical monograph (*fam.* 5.12.4–5). Pliny, on the other hand, has a very specific incident in the Senate that he would like recounted: in representing the province of Baetica he had cut down Baebius Massa with a choice *sententia* (*epist.* 7.33.8). Again, on the one

---

[130] On this letter, see the sensitive explication of Rudd (1992) 18–26, who, although he goes on to discuss Pliny, does not discuss *epist.* 7.33.

hand this only means that Pliny is doing more than playing a literary game; he is making a genuine request based on a genuine incident in his own life. Nevertheless, the contrast between the roiling seas of Cicero's struggles and the placid calm in which Pliny selects a single vaguely witty remark for memorialization is striking. Under the imperial dispensation he is yet again seen to be confined within narrow bounds.

In his last sentence, Pliny returns to his Ciceronian model with a twist (*epist.* 7.33.10):

> haec, utcumque se habent, notiora clariora maiora tu facies; quamquam non exigo ut excedas actae rei modum. nam nec historia debet egredi ueritatem, et honeste factis ueritas sufficit.

> These events, such as they are, you will make more known and famous and important; nevertheless I don't ask you to exceed the bounds of the facts. For history should confine itself to the truth, and the truth is enough for things done honorably.

No one with knowledge of Cicero's letter could read this sentence and not think immediately of Cicero's own, rather less modest, take on historical truth (*fam.* 5.12.3):

> itaque te plane etiam atque etiam rogo ut et ornes ea uehementius etiam quam fortasse sentis et in eo leges historiae neglegas gratiamque illam de qua suauissime quodam in prohoemio scripsisti, a qua te flecti non magis potuisse demonstras quam Herculem Xenophontium illum a Voluptate, eam, si me tibi uehementius commendabit, ne aspernere amorique nostro plusculum etiam quam concedet ueritas largiare.

> Therefore I ask you again, in plain words, to embellish this theme with greater enthusiasm than you perhaps feel. Waive the laws of history for this once. Do not scorn personal bias, if it urges you strongly in my favor – that sentiment of which you wrote very charmingly in one of your prefaces, declaring that you could no more be swayed thereby than Xenophon's Hercules by Pleasure. Concede to the affection between us just a little more even than the truth will license. (After Shackleton Bailey, Loeb)

Cicero knows full well how bold his request is – indeed, the first part of the letter is filled with discussion about just that.[131] Pliny obviously evokes Cicero's phrase, but he seems to correct the sentiment: Tacitus is not to exceed the laws of history or the bounds of truth. Pliny has thus positioned

---

[131] E.g. *fam.* 5.12.1 or, especially, *fam.* 5.12.3 *neque tamen ignoro <u>quam impudenter faciam</u> qui primum tibi tantum oneris imponam (potest enim mihi denegare occupatio tua), deinde etiam ut ornes me postulem. quid si illa tibi non tanto opere uidentur ornanda? <u>sed tamen, qui semel uerecundiae finis transierit, eum bene et nauiter oportet esse impudentem.</u>*

himself as following Cicero's precedent in asking a famous historian to sing his praises, and yet he has outdone him by claiming that Tacitus should stick only to the facts, because the facts are enough. Pliny's deeds need no amplification.

Epist. 7.33, like *epist.* 8.24 with advice for the new imperial legate, is placed at the end of its book. Marchesi's observation of this placement is perceptive, but her interpretation that "Pliny draws attention to two epistles [sc. *ad Q. fr.* 1.1 and *fam.* 5.12] in a corpus that did not receive as much editorial care from its author" seems flawed.[132] We know for a fact that *fam.* 5.12 received Cicero's most tender and exceptional care; he asks Atticus to obtain a copy of it from Lucceius and comments with satisfaction that the letter is quite pretty (*ualde bella est, Att.* 4.6.4). Moreover, the length and style of *ad Q. fr.* 1.1 make it all but certain that it was designed for a broader public.[133] Still, the placement is significant. In two consecutive books Pliny closes with a deeply Ciceronian letter. He is plainly inviting readers to compare him with Cicero – without, of course, ever making the comparison himself.

There are, to be certain, other letters where such a comparison is implicit. In the correspondence treating Pliny's activity as a trial lawyer, particularly in cases of *repetundae*, he may be inviting a comparison with Cicero's courtroom exploits and their descriptions in letters to Atticus and others.[134] The thorough-going researches of Heribert Pflips, however, turn up surprisingly few secure verbal echoes in this series of letters.[135] Their Ciceronianism feels forever fleeting and always seems to be slipping just out of our grasp. Consider only *epist.* 2.11 and 2.12, on the trial of Marius Priscus, which Whitton calls "a climax, not just for book 2 but for the whole *Epistles*, of P[liny]'s self-presentation as latter-day orator, statesman, and *littérateur* in

---

[132] Marchesi (2008) 225.

[133] See Shackleton Bailey (1980) 147: "Though not wholly lacking in personal touches ... it is rather a tract, *commentariolum de provincia administranda*, doubtless intended for wider circulation. In contrast with the rest of the Quintus correspondence, the style is literary, with observance of clausular rhythm."

[134] Letters on *repetundae*: *epist.* 2.11, 2.12, 3.9, 4.9, 5.20, 6.13, 7.6. Schenk (1999) 123–133 = (2016) 342–353 is a somewhat speculative attempt to tease Ciceronian echoes out of another legal letter, *epist.* 1.18, describing one of Pliny's early trials.

[135] Pflips (1973) is very strong on lexical notes and points of detail, but is less concerned with thematic resonances and larger issues (on p. 26 he seems to imply that the details will paint the broader picture). For his best evidence, about which I often remain skeptical, see pp. 359–378. For example, he believes (pp. 119, 365) that the height of Pliny's Ciceronianism is to be found in *epist.* 2.11.15 *gracilitas* ~ Cic. *Brut.* 313 *gracilitas*, but (1) *gracilitas* is used reasonably frequently to describe bodies (*TLL* vi.2.2132.66–79 [Burckhardt]) and (2) it is hard to see why the mature Pliny should allude to a description of Cicero's youthful weakness. Whitton (2013a) ad loc. p. 175 is more sympathetic to the possible intertext.

the Ciceronian mould."[136] Perhaps they are. On the one hand the addressee is Maturus Arrianus, recipient of two other letters mentioning Cicero (*epist.* 1.2, 4.8). On the other hand, this same Arrianus receives seven letters from Pliny and is mentioned in an eighth, and the rest of them do not seem particularly Ciceronian.[137] Again, on the one hand *epist.* 2.11 might be thought to come squarely in the center of book 2. On the other hand, maybe it does not,[138] and even if it does, how do we know whether that is significant or what it would mean? Whitton's detailed commentary likewise traces many "Ciceronian phrases," but as with Pflips's observations, some of these may just be Latin, where Cicero happens to bulk large through the accident of survival (e.g. *epist.* 2.11.1 *per hos dies*). In other cases – although much of this will depend on individual reader response – the parallels are not necessarily convincing.[139] Most problematically, even phrases that seem distinctly redolent of Cicero, like *uoci laterique* ("voice and lungs," *epist.* 2.11.15), are hard to pinpoint as specifically Ciceronian when they are also found in heavy rotation in Quintilian, Pliny's own teacher (e.g. *inst.* 1 pr. 27 *uox, latus patiens laboris*; 10.7.2, 11.3.29, 12.5.5). Such phraseology may thus be common in discussions of oratory – and we have lost the overwhelming majority of such texts between Cicero and Quintilian.[140] But of course it could be specifically Ciceronian; in another letter describing Pliny's actions on behalf of provincials, he certainly does seem to allude to one of Cicero's uses of that phrase, substituting polysyndeton for asyndeton: *epist.* 3.9.9 *uerebamur ne nos dies, ne uox, ne latera deficerent* ("we were afraid that time and my voice and my lungs would give out") – Cic. *Verr.* ii 2.52 *me dies uox latera deficiant* ("time, my voice, my lungs would give out" [*sc.* if I wished to describe one of Verres' many scandals]). Similar problems are presented by the letter's close: is it "exquisitely Ciceronian"?[141] Whitton believes it is "in tone, if not in specifics."[142] But that is a fair summary of the texture of a good portion of Pliny's correspondence. It is not, in general, Pliny's style to lard his prose with Ciceronian tags; he works at a more subtly evocative level.

---

[136] Whitton (2013a) 157–158.   [137] Cf. n. 54 above.   [138] Cf. n. 44 above.

[139] E.g. Whitton (2013a) ad *epist.* 2.11.11 p. 171 *quae solitudo . . . qui metus* – Cic. *Cluent.* 50–51; cf. Pflips (1973) 104, 363. At least one instance, however, is admittedly quite secure: *epist.* 2.11.11 *me tamen ut noua omnia nouo metu permouebant* – Cic. *Mil.* 1 *haec noui iudici noua forma terret oculos*.

[140] See *TLL* vii.2.1026.82–1027.24 for the preserved evidence.

[141] Cugusi (1983) 224 "squisitamente ciceroniana la chiusa di *epist.* 2, 11, § 25 *habes res urbanas*."

[142] Whitton (2013a) ad *epist.* 2.11.25 p. 185. He contrasts the close of the following letter, *epist.* 2.12.5, where he sees three echoes of Cicero's *De re publica*. Are these commonplace ideas or deliberate references? If they are deliberate, what is their effect? Cf. too his remarks ad *epist.* 2.12.6 p. 192, where he considers the mention of a *tabellarius* a "reality reference" that indicates the "specifically Ciceronian mode." Perhaps, but then again, references to couriers must have been common in letters more generally; they were after all the delivery mechanism.

It is a challenge to evaluate how much Pliny tries to fit into a Ciceronian mold.[143] He took part in real trials,[144] and he genuinely wanted to publicize his leading and successful role in them, first by reporting on them to friends, then by recording them for posterity. Doubtless at some level he was thinking of Cicero, and Whitton may be right that *epist.* 2.10–11 are of central importance for Pliny's self-presentation as a Ciceronian orator and man of letters. But if they are, Pliny has played an exceptionally subtle game with very few clear signals. We should not forget that winning fame and sometimes fortune through successful oratory was a favorite activity of the upper-class Roman male. Cicero is just one piece of a bigger picture.

Conclusion

"Cicero is just one piece of a bigger picture" – true enough, but he is a very important piece of that picture. While Pliny was not thinking of Cicero at every single moment when writing his *Epistulae*, he nevertheless found in him a dominating and domineering model whose influence was inescapable. Cicero is a crucial element in Pliny's larger project of constructing an ideal image of himself in his published correspondence, both for his contemporaries and for posterity. His Cicero is very much the Cicero of Quintilian's classroom, the classroom in which he was educated. He is a model for style and eloquence, a precedent for publishing and for poetry, and a great man; by and large, however, he is apparently not a political figure. This might seem rather different from Tacitus' Cicero, whose elegant oratory is intimately bound up with the politics of the late Republic. But Pliny is in fact fully aware of the Cicero of Tacitus, as we see when he lets his guard down and mentions Cicero's different political circumstances or the poverty of oratory in the contemporary centumviral courts. He simply would prefer not to dwell on these points, because they reveal underlying anxieties that conflict with the confident self-portrait he is trying to paint: by his own acknowledgement, he cannot hold a candle to Cicero's greatness in the political realm.

Cicero's greatness had been hammered into Pliny's head for years in Quintilian's classroom. He knew that Cicero should serve as his model, not only for polished Latinity but also for published letters. And yet Pliny, in trying to bring that Cicero out of the classroom and into the real world, finds himself caught in a web of contradictions. He is supposed to vie with Cicero

---

[143] The challenge is well noted by Marchesi (2008) 216–218, Gibson and Morello (2012) 75.

[144] And there had been many extortion trials since Cicero's time, for the details of which see Brunt (1990) 54–95 (90–94 a list of attested cases from Augustus to Trajan), 487–506.

in oratory and epistolography, but he realizes that neither his native *ingenium* nor the changed political circumstances of Trajan's empire will allow him to do so successfully. In his *Epistulae* we see this tension time and again, as Pliny, torn between following Quintilian's prescription to become a Cicero *rediuiuus* and the persistent anxiety that he will fall short, struggles not to put a foot wrong in presenting his carefully crafted image to the public eye.

Epilogue: The Early Empire and Beyond

As I hope I have shown throughout this book, the image of Cicero fashioned by declamation and the rhetorical classroom exerted a powerful influence on the version of Cicero found in literature and the educated imagination in the early Roman Empire. Not every ancient writer is limited to this schoolroom construction of Cicero, of course, but for everyone it is foundational. Some are able to rise above it and can react against it in sophisticated ways, like Seneca the Younger or Tacitus in his *Dialogus* or Pliny in his *Epistulae*, but even in these cases we cannot fully understand the authors' literary projects unless we understand what they are reacting against. The Cicero of the early Roman Empire was neither the Cicero of the late Republic nor, for that matter, the Cicero of today. In the first 150 years after his death, Romans engaged with a particular image of the man, stripped of the complex contradictions of his own lifetime and polarized into a literary and political symbol.

The reception of Cicero in the early Roman Empire is thus molded in the rhetorical schoolroom. By understanding how this process works, we gain further insight into ancient education and how it created and transmitted Roman identity and ideology. Cicero's reception also serves as a case study of how memories of the late Republic were constructed in the early Empire, and we see in particular how important the schoolroom can be in mediating those memories. Furthermore, in coming to grips with the way in which early imperial writers understood Cicero, we find ourselves better able to understand their writing too, because the whole history of Latin prose literature after Cicero is predicated on his dominating and domineering influence as mediated by the rhetorical schoolroom. These reflections also help us better understand the filters through which we view Cicero today.

For centuries Cicero was understood first and foremost as a "rhetorical figure," but that image did not remain eternally static, and a brief glance forward at those changes will help demarcate the early imperial reception.

With the rise of Christianity, Cicero began to be seen in new ways. One striking absence from his early reception, as we have seen in discussing Seneca the Younger, is consideration of his philosophical writings. Romans of the first and second centuries AD seem to have paid little or no attention to Cicero the philosopher.[1] There could, of course, be many reasons for this; perhaps it is just the notorious Roman distrust of philosophy, or perhaps those who do explicitly write philosophy, like Seneca the Younger, feel compelled to strike out on their own. Furthermore, philosophically inclined Romans had no need to read their Greek philosophy filtered through Cicero's Latin translations. Cicero insists very self-consciously that all his *philosophica* do is clothe Greek thoughts in Latin garb (e.g. *fin.* 1.1), and he feels compelled to defend at some length the very idea of doing philosophy in Latin (e.g. *fin.* 1.1–10). He was not just tilting at windmills here; it really does seem that contemporary Romans preferred to betake themselves to Greek sources when their minds turned to philosophy.

Seneca the Younger scarcely adduces Cicero at all as a philosophical precedent. Or take Quintilian: while he dutifully nods to Roman philosophy in his reading list (*inst.* 10.1.123–124), it is almost an afterthought, tacked on as the last thing he mentions before a special closing paragraph on Seneca the Younger. He confesses that Roman literature has brought forth very few eloquent authors of philosophy (*quo in genere paucissimos adhuc eloquentes litterae Romanae tulerunt, inst.* 10.1.123), among whom Cicero, "as in everything else," stands out. When Quintilian talks about Greek philosophers, by contrast, he is effusive. Consider just what he says about Xenophon: "I don't need to mention Xenophon's charm: effortless, but such as no effort could achieve. The Graces themselves seem to have shaped his style, and we may justly transfer to him what a writer of Old Comedy wrote of Pericles, that some goddess of persuasion sat upon his lips" (*quid ego commemorem Xenophontis illam iucunditatem inadfectatam, sed quam nulla consequi adfectatio possit? – ut ipsae sermonem finxisse Gratiae uideantur, et quod de Pericle ueteris comoediae testimonium est in hunc transferri iustissime possit, in labris eius sedisse quandam persuadendi deam, inst.* 10.1.82). Moreover, although Quintilian quotes Cicero more than 700

---

[1] Apparently Suetonius wrote something on Cicero's *De re publica* in response to an earlier treatise by Didymus Chalcenterus (*Suda* τ 895; cf. Amm. Marc. 22.16.16). Note too Cicero's unexpectedly marginal presence in the early imperial jurists, on which see Wibier (2016), who writes that "Cicero's role as a [legal] philosopher is passed over in complete silence" (121). This is not to say that Cicero's *philosophica* were completely unknown, only that they paled in significance compared to his other works.

times in the *Institutio oratoria*, I count only 10 citations from the philosophical works.[2] This is lip service at best: Quintilian's Cicero is no philosopher.

But times change. Cicero's philosophical writings evidently garnered enough attention to have survived into late antiquity, if only because they were attached to the great name of Cicero. At that point his stock as a philosopher began to rise in direct proportion to the decline of Greek in the Latin West, which was itself closely correlated with the ascendance of Christianity. Christian writers in the West, a group collectively obsessed with discussions of morality and philosophy, often had limited or no access to Greek originals, and for them Cicero proved a supremely useful and usable mediator of Greek philosophical thought. His *philosophica* were also easy to repurpose for Christian ends. As Sabine MacCormack put it, "Christian apologists found in Cicero's [*sc.* philosophical] dialogues a voice that they used so as to explain their religion while at the same time claiming to support the established order of things by way of offering a better way of maintaining it."[3] Moreover, the Latin language itself was changing, as were political conditions in the Roman world. The issues that had once been so sensitive for the imperial regime had long since died out, and scope for public speaking continued to shrink. Cicero was no longer primarily useful as a model for budding orators, and the social and political context of his orations was fast becoming incomprehensible.[4] The late antique and Christian philosophical turn in the reception of Cicero helps mark off the earlier imperial reception as a distinct and discrete period.[5]

Many Christian authors could be adduced as examples of these trends.[6] Ambrose, for example, alluded to Cicero's philosophical works in his sermons and wrote a three-book *De officiis ministrorum* which both

---

[2] See ch. 6 n. 19 for the statistics.

[3] MacCormack (2013) 261, with special reference to Tertullian, Minucius Felix, Arnobius, and Lactantius. To give just one example, Lactantius cites Cic. *rep.* 3.33 on the *uera lex* (natural law) and claims that Cicero here spoke as a proto-Christian (Lact. *inst.* 6.8.6). Already Zielinski (1929) had observed the particular importance of the philosophical Cicero for early Christian authors.

[4] It is uncharitable to pick out examples of medieval confusion, but consider the following gloss in a manuscript of Priscian, cited by Herren (2013) 41: *Helena: Vxor Menelai quam postea rapuit Marcus Cicero!* For knowledge and ignorance of Cicero in the Middle Ages, see Herren (2013) and Ward (2015). Cicero's rhetorical works, especially the *De inuentione* and the *Ad Herennium*, which was believed to be Ciceronian, did continue to be influential and popular; the former attracted commentaries by Marius Victorinus and Grillius. These rhetorical treatises were also reapplied to new ends, like preaching sermons.

[5] Bishop (2015), although not explicitly framing her discussion in these terms, implicitly points to an early reception of Cicero as "Roman Demosthenes" and a late antique and medieval reception as "Roman Plato."

[6] Cf. Bishop (2015) 294–303 on the Cicero of Macrobius, probably a Christian.

imitates Cicero's own *De officiis* and refashions it for the new world of the Christian ministry. Perhaps the best case to look at, however, is that of Augustine, himself a *rhetor* and so a suitable book-end for a study of Cicero in the classroom.[7] Although he had suffered through childhood instruction in the rudiments of Greek, Augustine never gained much facility with the language, and Greek literature remained a closed book for him.[8] In a remarkable passage in a letter to one Dioscorus, he actually has the effrontery to criticize his correspondent – a native speaker of Greek who nevertheless had a Latin education – for his ignorance of Greek philosophy in the original, and he does so in scathing terms (*epist.* 118.2.10):

> nonne magis caues, ne multo facilius existant, qui te ... de ipsis philoso-
> phorum libris aliqua interrogent, quae Cicero in suis litteris non posuit?
> quod si acciderit, quid responsurus es? potius te ista in Latinorum auctorum
> libris quam in Graecorum nosse uoluisse? qua responsione primo Graeciae
> facies iniuriam et nosti, quam illi homines hoc non ferant; deinde iam
> exulcerati et irati quam cito te, quod nimis non uis, et hebetem iudicabunt,
> qui Graecorum philosophorum dogmata uel potius dogmatum particulas
> quasdam discerptas atque dispersas in Latinis dialogis quam in ipsorum
> auctorum libris Graecis tota atque contexta discere maluisti, et indoctum.

> Aren't you much more worried that it would be quite a bit easier for men
> to ... ask you about some things in the original works of their philoso-
> phers which Cicero may not have put into his writings? If this happens,
> what are you going to say? That you preferred to learn these things in
> books written by Latin authors rather than by Greek? With that sort of
> answer you will first of all insult Greece; and you know how those Greeks
> can't stand that. Furthermore, now that they're irritated and angry, how
> quickly will they judge you (that which you are only too anxious to avoid!)
> both stupid, because you preferred to learn the tenets of the Greek
> philosophers – or rather, some snippets of their philosophy yanked out
> of context and scattered about – in Latin dialogues, rather than to study
> the complete and connected system of their opinions in the Greek origi-
> nals, and ignorant.

Augustine might as well have added a marginal annotation, "This is me." These must have been his own fears and anxieties, and he must have had a constant sense of inferiority in the field of Greek learning: his Greek philosophy was cribbed from the pages of Cicero. Thus, as Peter Brown

---

[7] It is admittedly also the most complex, and I will present only a few aspects of the picture. For more details, see Hagendahl (1958), Testard (1958), and Hagendahl (1967); briefly Shanzer (2012) 165–168. Müller (2015) discusses Augustine's educational career, pp. 363–365 on his activities as a *rhetor*; for a synopsis, see Kaster (1988) 246–247.

[8] See e.g. *conf.* 1.12.19 and 1.14.23, as well as Brown (2000) 24, 268–270.

writes, Augustine "will become the only Latin philosopher in antiquity to be virtually ignorant of Greek."[9]

Nevertheless, become a Latin philospher he did. When Augustine read through Cicero's *Hortensius* at the age of nineteen, he claims that it changed his whole life, and he resolved to devote himself to philosophy and, eventually, Christianity (*conf.* 3.4.7–8). He continued a close engagement with Cicero's philosophical works throughout his life; in the early stages of his Christianity, for example, he was keen to refute Cicero's Academic skepticism in his own dialogue *Contra academicos*.[10] Later on, he seems to have girded himself to write the *De ciuitate Dei* by undertaking a systematic rereading of classical literature, including especially Cicero.[11] Book 5 of that work, for example, is concerned to refute Cicero's *De fato*. Cicero's *De re publica*, *De natura deorum*, *De finibus*, *Tusculanae disputationes*, and *Timaeus* are all likewise especially prominent in various parts of the *De ciuitate Dei*.[12] In sum, Augustine and other Christian authors in late antiquity engage with Cicero's philosophical writings in a way that no one seems to have done in the early imperial period. Both the rise of Christianity and the fall of Greek in the West gave a new impetus to the study of Cicero the philosopher.

Cicero the Christianized philosopher continued to be influential through the Middle Ages and beyond,[13] but with the rediscovery of "lost" Ciceronian texts and the rise of Ciceronianism in the Renaissance, old Tully began to be read again as a model for classical eloquence as well.[14] Around the same time, technological innovations like the printing press dramatically changed the accessibility of Cicero's writings, as did the commentaries and lexical aids and translations that followed. But to trace this story further would require a whole series of books, for Cicero's rich, varied, and complex influence from late antiquity to the present defies any easy summary.[15] The influence of the schoolroom on Cicero's reception, however, is ever present, and those interested in these later "schoolroom Ciceros" will find that their history stretches back in an unbroken tradition to the rhetorical schools of antiquity.

---

[9] Brown (2000) 24.   [10] MacCormack (2013) 274, with reference to Jolivet (1948).
[11] O'Donnell (1980) 151–157.   [12] See O'Donnell (1980) 157 for a summary.
[13] See e.g. MacCormack (2013) and Ward (2015), along with several of the essays in van Deusen (2013).
[14] On Renaissance Ciceronianism, see recently Tunberg (2012) 47–68, as well as the foundational Sabbadini (1885) and the texts conveniently assembled and translated in Delleneva and Duvick (2007); cf. Springer (2018) on the "Reformation" Cicero of Luther and subsequent Lutherans.
[15] For a start, see some of the essays assembled in Steel (2013), Altman (2015a), and Manuwald (2016), as well as the classic Zielinski (1929) and Weil (1962).

Nevertheless, after antiquity education underwent great changes, and the Cicero of the schoolroom changes as well. The classroom of the Middle Ages was a fundamentally different place from the ancient *rhetor*'s school, and the classroom of the early modern period only more so. For centuries, to be certain, Europeans and European colonists sought "models, standards, and projects in antiquity,"[16] and Cicero was ideally placed to fill those roles. But however much it wanted to model itself on the ancient world, such a cultural program, aimed at inculcating a kind of virtuous Christian humanism, was entirely different from the education of the early Roman Empire. An English-speaking colonist studying Cicero at the Boston Latin School in the seventeenth century is worlds away from his first-century counterpart in Rome. Over the *longue durée*, changes in language, religion, culture, political structure, and so forth fostered different and complex forms of engagement with the "schoolroom Cicero."

Students were still reading many of the same texts, however, and so continuities and discontinuities existed side by side. As long as Latin remained a major language of written communication, for example, Cicero's prose provided a model that would be beaten into schoolboys from the moment they entered the grammar school – even if their native language was English and climbing the rungs of the Roman *cursus honorum* or publishing Latin oratory was the furthest thing from their minds. Cicero's philosophical and political thought was also an important part of this cultural project, and through the eighteenth century philosophers and statesmen took Cicero seriously as a politician and man of letters; that is to say, they read him even after their toil in the grammar grind was finished.[17] The decline of Latin as *lingua franca* and the diminishing influence of humanism as a cultural force changed all that, and I do not think that even the most optimistic classicist among us could claim such a readership for Cicero anymore.

In the twentieth and twenty-first centuries yet another classroom is again the dominant influence on Cicero's reception. Although Cicero's texts are more widely disseminated than ever, his readers probably are not. Such readers might be divided into two categories, those who read Cicero in Latin and those who read him in translation. Those who read him in the original are almost exclusively students and their teachers; there are very few Thomas Babington Macaulays nowadays who spend their time spared

---

[16] Shelford (2007) 2.
[17] In Enlightenment Europe and Revolutionary War–era America, for example. On the former, see briefly Fox (2013); on the latter Reinhold (1984), e.g. 94–100, Bederman (2008), and Richard (2015).

from governing the Raj in rereading the entirety of classical literature.[18] Of those who read him in translation, I would suspect again that the vast majority are college and university students who are dutifully completing course assignments. Moreover, by comparison to a Julius Caesar, say, Cicero gets very few mentions in modern popular literature and film.[19] What contemporary educated people know about Cicero, they probably learned in high school or college. And so the schoolroom, however much it has changed over two millennia, remains even today the foundation of Cicero's reception.

---

[18] Even the redoubtable Macaulay confesses to not having quite finished Cicero complete in his leisure moments in India. His reading list for 1835 (Pinney [1974–1981] II.159–160): "During the last thirteen months I have read Aeschylus twice; Sophocles twice; Euripides once; Pindar twice; Callimachus; Apollonius Rhodius; Quintus Calaber [!]; Theocritus twice; Herodotus; Thucydides; almost all Xenophon's works; almost all Plato; Aristotle's *Politics*, and a good deal of his *Organon*, besides dipping elsewhere in him; the whole of Plutarch's *Lives*; about half of Lucian; two or three books of Athenaeus; Plautus twice; Terence twice; Lucretius twice; Catullus; Tibullus; Propertius; Lucan; Statius; Silius Italicus; Livy; Velleius Paterculus; Sallust; Caesar; and, lastly, Cicero. I have, indeed, still a little of Cicero left; but I shall finish him in a few days. I am now deep in Aristophanes and Lucian." On Macaulay's attitude toward Cicero, see Wiseman (2009) 99–106.

[19] On the rare appearances of Cicero in popular novels and films, see Fotheringham (2013a). In the influential HBO television series *Rome*, for example, he is a bit player at best. The only real exception to this generalization is Robert Harris' trilogy of novels about Cicero, told from Tiro's perspective, *Imperium* (2006), *Lustrum* (2009), and *Dictator* (2015).

Works Cited

Abbreviations

ALL	*Archiv für lateinische Lexikographie* (Munich 1884–1908).
ANRW	*Aufstieg und Niedergang der römischen Welt* (Berlin 1972–).
CIL	*Corpus inscriptionum Latinarum* (Berlin 1863–).
CLA	*Codices Latini antiquiores* (Oxford 1934–1971).
FRHist	T. Cornell (ed.) *Fragments of the Roman Historians*, 3 vols. (Oxford 2013).
GL	H. Keil (ed.) *Grammatici Latini*, 8 vols. (Leipzig 1855–1880).
ILS	H. Dessau (ed.) *Inscriptiones Latinae selectae* (Berlin 1892–1916).
LSJ	H. G. Liddell, R. Scott, and H. S. Jones (eds.) *A Greek–English Lexicon*, 9th edn. with revised supplement (Oxford 1996).
M–P³	Mertens–Pack³ (http://web.philo.ulg.ac.be/cedopal/base-de-donnees-mp3/).
OCD	S. Hornblower, A. Spawforth, and E. Eidinow (eds.) *Oxford Classical Dictionary*, 4th edn. (Oxford 2012).
OLD	P. G. W. Glare (ed.) *Oxford Latin Dictionary* (Oxford 1982).
ORF	H. Malcovati (ed.) *Oratorum Romanorum fragmenta*, 4th edn., 2 vols. (Turin 1976).
PHI	Packard Humanities Institute Latin texts (http://latin.packhum.org).
RE	A. Pauly, G. Wissowa, and W. Kroll (eds.) *Real-Encyclopädie der classischen Altertumswissenschaft* (Stuttgart 1893–1980).
RLM	K. Halm (ed.) *Rhetores Latini minores* (Leipzig 1863).
Schanz–Hosius	M. Schanz and C. Hosius (rev.) *Geschichte der römischen Literatur bis zum Gesetzgebungswerk des Kaisers Justinian*, 4th edn., 4 vols. (Munich 1935).
TLL	*Thesaurus linguae Latinae* (Leipzig 1900–).

Achard, G. (1981) *Pratique rhétorique et idéologie politique dans les discours "optimates" de Cicéron*. Leiden.

Adams, J. N. (1978) "Conventions of naming in Cicero," *CQ* n.s. 28: 145–166.

(2013) *Social Variation and the Latin Language*. Cambridge.

Ahl, F. (1976) *Lucan: An Introduction*. Ithaca.

Alewell, K. (1913) "Über das rhetorische Paradeigma: Theorie, Beispielsammlungen, Verwendung in der römischen Literatur der Kaiserzeit." Ph.D. diss., Christian-Albrechts-Universität, Kiel.

Alfonsi, L. (1965) "Dall''Hortensius' al 'Dialogus de oratoribus,'" *Latomus* 24: 40–44.

Allen, W. A. (1954) "Cicero's conceit," *TAPhA* 85: 121–144.

Altman, W. H. F. (ed.) (2015a) *Brill's Companion to the Reception of Cicero*. Leiden.

(2015b) "Cicero and the fourth triumvirate: Gruen, Syme, and Strasburger," in Altman (2015a): 215–246.

Anderson, G. (1993) *The Second Sophistic: A Cultural Phenomenon in the Roman Empire*. London.

Arena, V. (2012) *Libertas and the Practice of Politics in the Late Roman Republic*. Cambridge.

Badian, E. (1973) "Marius' villas: the testimony of the slave and the knave," *JRS* 63: 121–132.

Barchiesi, A. (1993) "Future reflexive: two modes of allusion and Ovid's *Heroides*," *HSPh* 95: 333–365.

Bardon, H. (1953) "Tacite et le 'Dialogue des orateurs,'" *Latomus* 12: 166–187.

Barnes, T. D. (1986) "The significance of Tacitus' *Dialogus de oratoribus*," *HSPh* 90: 225–244.

Bartsch, S. (1994) *Actors in the Audience: Theatricality and Doublespeak from Nero to Hadrian*. Cambridge, MA.

Bartsch, S., and A. Schiesaro (eds.) (2015) *The Cambridge Companion to Seneca*. Cambridge.

Barwick, K. (1929) "Zur Erklärung und Komposition des Rednerdialogs des Tacitus," in *Festschrift Walter Judeich zum 70. Geburtstag*. Weimar: 81–108.

(1954) *Der Dialogus de oratoribus des Tacitus: Motive und Zeit seiner Entstehung*. Berlin.

Beagon, M. (2005) *The Elder Pliny on the Human Animal: Natural History, Book 7*. Oxford.

Beard, M. (1993) "Looking (harder) for Roman myth: Dumézil, declamation and the problems of definition," in *Mythos in mythenloser Gesellschaft: Das Paradigma Roms*, ed. F. Graf. Stuttgart: 44–64.

(2002) "Ciceronian correspondences: making a book out of letters," in *Classics in Progress*, ed. T. P. Wiseman. Oxford: 103–144.

Beaujeu, J. (1991) *Cicéron: Correspondance*, vol. x. Paris.

Becher, F. (1882) "Ueber die Sprache der Briefe ad Brutum," *RhM* 37: 576–597.

(1885) "Die sprachliche Eigenart der Briefe ad Brutum," *Philologus* 44: 471–501.

Beck, J.-W. (1998) *"Germania"-"Agricola": zwei Kapitel zu Tacitus' zwei kleinen Schriften. Untersuchungen zu ihrer Intention und Datierung sowie zur Entwicklung ihres Verfassers.* Hildesheim.

Beck, M. (2001) "Das dramatische Datum des *Dialogus de oratoribus*: Überlegungen zu einer in Vergessenheit geratenen Streitfrage," *RhM* 144: 159–172.

Bederman, D. J. (2008) *The Classical Foundations of the American Constitution: Prevailing Wisdom.* Cambridge.

Bellen, H. (1985) "Cicero und der Aufstieg Octavians," *Gymnasium* 92: 161–189.

Berry, D. H. (1996) *Pro P. Sulla oratio.* Cambridge.

   (2000) *Cicero: Defence Speeches.* Oxford.

Berti, E. (2007) *Scholasticorum studia: Seneca il Vecchio e la cultura retorica e letteraria della prima età imperiale.* Pisa.

Bill, C. P. (1941) "Lecythizing," *CPh* 36: 46–51.

Bingham, W. J. (1978) "A Study of the Livian 'Periochae' and their relation to Livy's 'Ab Urbe Condita.'" Ph.D. diss., University of Illinois at Urbana-Champaign.

Birley, A. R. (2000a) "The life and death of Cornelius Tacitus," *Historia* 49: 230–247.

   (2000b) *Onomasticon to Pliny the Younger.* Munich.

   (2016) = 2000b, in Gibson and Whitton (2016): 51–66.

Bishop, C. (2015) "Roman Plato or Roman Demosthenes," in Altman (2015a): 283–306.

   (2016) "How to make a Roman Demosthenes: self-fashioning in Cicero's *Brutus* and *Orator*," *CJ* 111: 167–192.

Bloomer, W. M. (1992) *Valerius Maximus and the Rhetoric of the New Nobility.* Chapel Hill.

   (1997a) "Schooling in persona: imagination and subordination in Roman education," *ClAnt* 16: 57–78.

   (1997b) *Latinity and Literary Society at Rome.* Philadelphia.

   (2011) *The School of Rome: Latin Studies and the Origins of Liberal Education.* Berkeley.

   (ed.) (2015a) *A Companion to Ancient Education.* Malden, MA.

   (2015b) "Corporal punishment in the ancient school," in Bloomer (2015a): 184–198.

Bo, D. (1993) *Le principali problematiche del Dialogus de oratoribus: panoramica storico-critica dal 1426 al 1990.* Hildesheim.

Bodel, J. (2015) "The publication of Pliny's letters," in Marchesi (2015): 13–108.

Bonner, S. F. (1949) *Roman Declamation in the Late Republic and Early Empire.* Berkeley.

   (1977) *Education in Ancient Rome: From the Elder Cato to the Younger Pliny.* Berkeley.

Borda, M. (1961) "Iconografia Ciceroniana," in *Marco Tullio Cicerone: scritti nel bimillenario della morte*, ed. L. Alfonsi. Florence: 257–265.

Borgies, L. (2016) *Le conflit propagandiste entre Octavien et Marc Antoine: de l'usage politique de la uituperatio entre 44 et 30 a. C. n.* Brussels.

Bornecque, H. (1902) *Les déclamations et les déclamateurs d'après Sénèque le père.* Lille.

Bowersock, G. (1965) Review of Millar (1964), *Gnomon* 37: 469–474.

Boyle, A. J. (2014) *Seneca: Medea.* Oxford.

Bringmann, K. (1970) "Aufbau und Absicht des taciteischen Dialogus de oratoribus," *MH* 27: 164–178.

Brink, C. O. (1963–1982) *Horace on Poetry,* 3 vols. Cambridge.

(1989) "Quintilian's *De causis corruptae eloquentiae* and Tacitus' *Dialogus de oratoribus,*" *CQ* n.s. 39: 472–503.

(1994) "Can Tacitus' *Dialogus* be dated? Evidence and historical conclusions," *HSPh* 96: 251–280.

Briscoe, J. (1998) *Factorum et dictorum memorabilium libri* ix, 2 vols. Stuttgart.

Brodersen, K. (2015) "Epitaphios: Appianos and his treasured Eutychia θησαυρίζειν τὴν εὐτυχίαν," in Welch (2015a): 341–350.

Brown, P. (2000) *Augustine of Hippo,* 2nd edn. Berkeley.

Brunt, P. A. (1990) *Roman Imperial Themes.* Oxford.

Bütler, H.-P. (1970) *Die geistige Welt des jüngeren Plinius: Studien zur Thematik seiner Briefe.* Heidelberg.

Burckhardt, L. A. (1990) "Political elite of the Roman Republic: comments on recent discussion of the concepts *nobilitas* and *homo novus,*" *Historia* 39: 77–99.

Burden-Strevens, C. (2015) "Cassius Dio's Speeches and the Collapse of the Roman Republic." Ph.D. diss., University of Glasgow.

Burkard, T. (2016) "Zu den Begriffen divisio und color bei Seneca maior," in Poignault and Schneider (2016): 83–134.

Butler, S. (2015) *The Ancient Phonograph.* New York.

Caplan, H. (1970) *Of Eloquence: Studies in Ancient and Modern Rhetoric.* Ithaca.

Carlon, J. (2009) *Pliny's Women: Constructing Virtues and Creating Identity in the Roman World.* Cambridge.

Castagna, L., and E. Lefèvre (eds.) (2003) *Plinius der Jüngere und seine Zeit.* Munich.

Cavenaile, R. (1958) *Corpus papyrorum Latinarum.* Wiesbaden.

Citroni Marchetti, S. (2016) "Cicero as role-model in the self-definition of Pliny the Elder," in *Papers of the Langford Latin Seminar,* vol. xvi, ed. F. Cairns and R. Gibson. Oxford: 315–337.

Clark, A. C. (1895) *Cicero: Pro Milone.* Oxford.

(1907) *Q. Asconii Pediani Orationum Ciceronis quinque enarratio.* Oxford.

Clark, M. L. (1953) *Rhetoric at Rome: A Historical Survey.* London.

Clausen, W. V. (1994) *A Commentary on Virgil: Eclogues.* Oxford.

Coleman, K. M. (1988) *Statius: Silvae* iv. Oxford.

(2012) "Bureaucratic language in the correspondence between Pliny and Trajan," *TAPhA* 142: 189–238.

Coleman, R. (1977) *Vergil: Eclogues.* Cambridge.

Connolly, J. (2007) *The State of Speech: Rhetoric and Political Thought in Ancient Rome.* Princeton.

Consbruch, M. (1906) *Hephaestionis Enchiridion.* Leipzig.

Costa, C. D. N. (1969) "The 'Dialogus,'" in *Tacitus,* ed. T. A. Dorey. London: 19–34.

   (1973) *Seneca: Medea.* Oxford.

Courtney, E. (1980) *A Commentary on the Satires of Juvenal.* London.

   (2003) *The Fragmentary Latin Poets.* Oxford. (Repr. of 1993 with addenda.)

Cousin, J. (1967) *Etudes sur Quintilien,* 2 vols. Amsterdam. (Repr. of Paris, 1935–1936.)

Cowan, E. (ed.) (2011) *Velleius Paterculus: Making History.* Swansea.

Craig, C. (2002) "A survey of selected recent work on Cicero's rhetorica and speeches," in May (2002): 503–531.

Cribiore, R. (2001) *Gymnastics of the Mind: Greek Education in Hellenistic and Roman Egypt.* Princeton.

   (2015) "School structures, apparatus, and materials," in Bloomer (2015a): 149–159.

Crook, J. A. (1995) *Legal Advocacy in the Roman World.* Ithaca.

Cugusi, P. (1983) *Evoluzione e forme dell'epistolografia latina.* Rome.

   (1985) "Spunti di polemica politica in alcuni graffiti di Pompei e di Terracina," *ZPE* 61: 23–29.

   (2003) "Qualche riflessione sulle idee retoriche di Plinio il giovane," in Castagna and Lefèvre (2003): 95–122.

Dahlmann, H. (1975) *Cornelius Severus.* Mainz.

Delleneva, J. (ed.), and B. Duvick (trans.) (2007) *Ciceronian Controversies.* Cambridge, MA.

De Marco, M. (1967) *Marco Tullio Cicerone: La consolazione, le orazioni spurie.* Milan.

   (1991) *[M. Tulli Ciceronis]: Orationes spuriae.* Milan.

Dench, E. (2013) "Cicero and Roman identity," in Steel (2013): 122–140.

Desideri, P. (1992) "I documenti di Plutarco," *ANRW* II.33.6: 4536–4567.

Deufert, M. (2013) "Vergilische Prosa?," *Hermes* 141: 331–350.

Devillers, O. (ed.) (2015) *Autour de Pline le Jeune: mélanges à Nicole Méthy.* Bordeaux.

Dickey, E. (2012–2015) *The Colloquia of the Hermeneumata Pseudodositheana,* 2 vols. Cambridge.

Dienel, R. (1915) "Quintilian und der Rednersdialog des Tacitus," *WS* 37: 239–271.

Diliberto, O. (1981) *Ricerche sull'auctoramentum e sulla condizione degli auctorati.* Milan.

D'Ippolito, G. (2000) "Il concetto di intertestualità nel pensiero degli antichi," in *Intertextualidad en las literaturas griega y latina,* ed. V. Bécares, F. Pordomingo, R. Cortés Tovar, and J. C. Fernández Corte. Madrid: 13–32.

Döpp, S. (1986) "Die Nachwirkung von Ciceros rhetorischen Schriften bei Quintilian und in Tacitus' Dialogus: eine typologische Skizze," in *Reflexionen antiker Kulturen,* ed. P. Neukam. Munich: 7–26.

Dominik, W. (2007) "Tacitus and Pliny on oratory," in *A Companion to Roman Rhetoric*, ed. W. Dominik and J. Hall. Malden, MA: 323–338.

Douglas, A. E. (1966) *M. Tulli Ciceronis Brutus*. Oxford.

Dronke, E. (1828) *C. Corn. Taciti Dialogus de oratoribus*. Koblenz.

Dugan, J. (2005) *Making a New Man: Ciceronian Self-Fashioning in the Rhetorical Works*. Oxford.

Durry, M. (1938) *Panégyrique de Trajan*. Paris.

Dyck, A. (2002) "The 'other' *Pro Milone* reconsidered," *Philologus* 146: 182–185.
    (2008) *Cicero: Catilinarians*. Cambridge.

Edwards, C. (2015) "Absent presence in Seneca's *Epistles*: philosophy and friendship," in Bartsch and Schiesaro (2015): 41–53.

Edwards, R. (2008) "Hunting for boars with Pliny and Tacitus," *ClAnt* 27: 35–58.

Edwards, W. A. (1928) *The Suasoriae of Seneca the Elder*. Cambridge.

Elefante, M. (1997) *Ad M. Vinicium consulem libri duo*. Hildesheim.

Ernout, A. (1962) *Pseudo-Sallust: Lettres à César, Invectives*. Paris.

Evenepoel, W. (2007) "Cicero's *Laelius* and Seneca's letters on friendship," *AC* 76: 177–183.

Ewbank, W. W. (1933) *The Poems of Cicero*. London.

Fairweather, J. (1981) *Seneca the Elder*. Cambridge.

Fantham, E. (1978) "Imitation and decline: rhetorical theory and practice in the first century after Christ," *CPh* 73: 102–116.
    (2004) *The Roman World of Cicero's De oratore*. Oxford.

Fechner, D. (1986) *Untersuchungen zu Cassius Dios Sicht der römischen Republik*. Hildesheim.

Feddern, S. (2013) *Die Suasorien des älteren Seneca: Einleitung, Text und Kommentar*. Berlin.

Fedeli, P. (2004) "Cicerone e Seneca," *Ciceroniana* 12: 217–237.

Feeney, D. (2014) *Ovid's Ciceronian Literary History: End-Career Chronology and Autobiography* (UCL Housman Lecture). London.

Feldherr, A. (2013) "Free spirits: Sallust and the citation of Catiline," *AJPh* 134: 49–66.

Fischer, J. G. (1870) "De fontibus et auctoritate Cassii Dionis in enarrandis a Cicerone post Caesaris mortem a.d. XVI Kal. Apr. de pace et Kal. Jan. anni a. Chr. n. 43 habitis orationibus." Ph.D. diss., Leipzig.

Fisher, E. (1982) "Greek translation of Latin literature in the fourth century AD," *YClS* 27: 173–216.

Flower, H. I. (2006) *The Art of Forgetting: Disgrace and Oblivion in Roman Political Culture*. Chapel Hill.

Fotheringham, L. S. (2007) "Having your cake and eating it too: how Cicero combines arguments," in Powell (2007): 69–90.
    (2013a) "Twentieth/twenty-first-century Cicero(s)," in Steel (2013): 350–373.
    (2013b) *Persuasive Language in Cicero's Pro Milone: A Close Reading and Commentary*. London.

Fox, M. (2007) *Cicero's Philosophy of History*. Oxford.
    (2013) "Cicero during the Enlightenment," in Steel (2013): 318–336.

Friedrich, A. (2002) *Das Symposium der* XII *Sapientes: Kommentar und Verfasserfrage*. Berlin.

Fromentin, V., and E. Bertrand (2014) *Dion Cassius: Histoire romaine. Livre 47*. Paris.

Gabba, E. (1955) *Appiano e la storia delle guerre civili*. Florence.

(1957) "Note sulla polemica anticiceroniana di Asinio Pollione," *RSI* 69: 317–339.

Galinsky. K. (1996) *Augustan Culture: An Interpretive Introduction*. Princeton.

Gallia, A. (2012) *Remembering the Roman Republic: Culture, Politics, and History under the Principate*. Cambridge.

Gamberale, L. (1997) "Dal falso al vero Cicerone: note critiche all'orazione *Pridie quam in exilium iret* e alla *Pro Rabirio perduellionis reo*, 31," in *MOYΣA: Scritti in onore di Giuseppe Morelli*. Bologna: 331–343.

(1998) "Dalla retorica al centone nell'*Oratio pridie quam in exilium iret*: aspetti della fortuna di Cicerone fra III e IV secolo," in *Cultura latina pagana fra terzo e quinto secolo dopo Cristo: Atti del Convegno Mantova, 9–11 ottobre 1995*. Florence: 53–76.

Gamberini, F. (1983) *Stylistic Theory and Practice in Pliny the Younger*. Hildesheim.

Gambet, D. G. (1963) "Cicero's Reputation from 43 BC to AD 79." Ph.D. diss., University of Pennsylvania.

(1970) "Cicero in the works of Seneca *philosophus*," *TAPhA* 101: 171–183.

Gates, H. L. (2009) *Lincoln on Race and Slavery*. Princeton.

Gee, E. R. (2013) "Cicero's poetry," in Steel (2013): 88–106.

Gerber, A., and A. Greef (1877–1902) *Lexicon Taciteum*. Leipzig.

Gibson, B. (2006) *Statius: Silvae 5*. Oxford.

Gibson, R. K., and R. Morello (2012) *Reading the Letters of Pliny the Younger: An Introduction*. Cambridge.

Gibson, R. K., and C. Steel (2010) "The indistinct literary careers of Cicero and Pliny the Younger," in *Classical Literary Careers and their Reception*, ed. P. Hardie and H. Moore. Cambridge: 118–137.

Gibson, R. K., and C. Whitton (eds.) (2016) *Oxford Readings in Classical Studies: The Epistles of Pliny*. Oxford.

Gigante, M. (1979) *Civiltà delle forme letterarie nell'antica Pompei*. Naples.

Ginsberg, L. D. (2016) "Jocasta's Catilinarian oration (Sen. *Phoen.* 632–43)," *CJ* 111: 483–494.

Glei, R. F. (2002) "Catilinas Rede gegen Cicero: literarische Fälschung, rhetorische Übung, oder politisches Pamphlet?," *NLJ* 4: 155–196.

Goldberg, S. M. (1999) "Appreciating Aper: the defence of modernity in Tacitus' *Dialogus de oratoribus*," *CQ* n.s. 49: 224–237.

(2009) "The faces of eloquence: the *Dialogus de oratoribus*," in *The Cambridge Companion to Tacitus*, ed. A. J. Woodman. Cambridge: 73–84.

Goold, G. P. (1977) *Manilius: Astronomica*. Cambridge, MA.

Goukowsky, P., and P. Torrens (2010), *Appien: Histoire romaine. Tome X, livre XV: Guerres civiles, livre III*. Paris.

Gowing, A. (1992) *The Triumviral Narratives of Appian and Cassius Dio*. Ann Arbor.

(1998) "Greek advice for a Roman senator: Cassius Dio and the dialogue between Philiscus and Cicero (38.18–29)," in *Proceedings of the Leeds Latin Seminar*, vol. x, ed. F. Cairns and M. Heath. Leeds: 373–390.

(2005) *Empire and Memory: The Representation of the Roman Republic in Imperial Culture*. Cambridge.

(2010) "'Caesar grabs my pen': writing civil war under Tiberius," in *Citizens of Discord: Rome and its Civil Wars*, ed. B. W. Breed, C. Damon, and A. Rossi. Oxford: 249–260.

(2013) "Tully's boat: responses to Cicero in the Imperial period," in Steel (2013): 233–250.

Grattarola, P. (1988) *Un libello antiaugusteo: la lettera dello pseudo-Cicerone a Ottaviano*. Genoa.

Griffin, M. T. (1976) *Seneca: A Philosopher in Politics*. Oxford.

(1987) "Philosophy for statesmen: Cicero and Seneca," in *Antikes Denken – Moderne Schule*, ed. H. W. Schmidt and P. Wülfing. Heidelberg: 133–150.

Grilli, A. (1962) *Hortensius*. Milan.

(2002) "Seneca e l'*Hortensius*," in *Hommages à Carl Deroux*, vol. II: *Prose et linguistique, médecine*, ed. P. Defosse. Brussels: 196–205.

Grimal, P. (1984) "Sénèque juge de Cicéron," *Mélanges de l'Ecole française de Rome – Antiquité* 96: 655–670.

Gudeman, A. (1902) *The Sources of Plutarch's Life of Cicero*. Philadelphia.

(1914) *P. Corneli Taciti Dialogus de oratoribus*. Leipzig.

Guillemin, A.-M. (1929) *Pline et la vie littéraire de son temps*. Paris.

Gunderson, E. (2003) *Declamation, Paternity, and Roman Identity: Authority and the Rhetorical Self*. Cambridge.

Güngerich, R. (1951) "Der *Dialogus* des Tacitus und Quintilians *Institutio Oratoria*," *CPh* 46: 159–164.

(1980) *Kommentar zum Dialogus des Tacitus*. Göttingen.

Gurd, S. (2012) *Work in Progress: Literary Revision as Social Performance in Ancient Rome*. Oxford.

Häger, H.-J. (2015) "Das Briefcorpus des jüngeren Plinius: neuere Tendenzen in Altertumswissenschaft und Didaktik," *Gymnasium* 122: 559–596.

Häussler, R. (1986) "Aktuelle Probleme der Dialogus-Rezeption: Echtheitserweise und Lückenumfang," *Philologus* 130: 69–95.

Hagendahl, H. (1958) *Latin Fathers and the Classics: A Study of the Apologists, Jerome, and Other Christian Writers*. Gothenburg.

(1967) *Augustine and the Latin Fathers*, 2 vols. Stockholm.

Hahn, I. (1968) "Geschichtsphilosophische Motive in den Reden der Emphylia," in *Studien zur Geschichte und Philosophie des Altertums*, ed. J. Harmatta. Amsterdam: 197–203.

Håkanson, L. (1989a) *L. Annaeus Seneca Maior: Oratorum et rhetorum sententiae diuisiones colores*. Leipzig.

(1989b) "Zu den Historikerfragmenten in Seneca d. A. Suas. 6," in *Studies in Latin Literature in Honour of C. O. Brink*, ed. J. Diggle, J. B. Hall, and H. D. Jocelyn. Cambridge: 14–19.

(2014) "Zu den literarischen Vorbildern der *Declamationes maiores*: Cicero, Seneca, *Declamationes minores*," in *Unveröffentlichte Schriften*, vol. 1: *Studien zu den pseudoquintilianischen Declamationes maiores*, ed. B. Santorelli. Berlin: 15–38.

Hall, J. (2009) *Politeness and Politics in Cicero's Letters*. Oxford.

Harvey, P. B. (1991) "Cicero *Epistulae ad Quintum fratrem et ad Brutum*: content and comment," *Athenaeum* 69: 17–29.

Haß-von Reitzenstein, U. (1970) "Beiträge zur gattungsgeschichtlichen Interpretation des Dialogus 'De Oratoribus.'" Ph.D. diss., Cologne.

Heath, M. (1999) "Longinus, On Sublimity," *PCPhS* 45: 43–74.

Heldmann, K. (1982) *Antike Theorien über Entwicklung und Verfall der Redekunst*. Munich.

Helm, R. (1908) "Zwei Probleme des taciteischen Dialogs," *Neue Jahrbücher für das klassische Altertum, Geschichte, und deutsche Literatur und für Pädagogik* 21: 474–497.

Henderson, J. (2001) "On Pliny on Martial on anon . . . (*Epistles* 3.21/*Epigrams* 10.19)," *Ramus* 30: 56–87.

(2002) *Pliny's Statue: The Letters, Self-Portraiture, and Classical Art*. Exeter.

(2011) Review of Lefèvre (2009), *Gnomon* 83: 313–317.

Hercher, R. (1873) *Epistolographi Graeci*. Paris.

Herren, M. W. (2013) "Cicero redivivus apud scurras: some early medieval treatments of the great orator," in van Deusen (2013): 39–46.

Higham, T. F. (1949) *Some Oxford Compositions*. Oxford.

Hildebrandt, P. (1894) *De scholiis Ciceronis Bobiensibus*. Berlin.

Hirzel, R. (1895) *Der Dialogus: Ein literarhistorischer Versuch*, 2 vols. Leipzig.

Hoffer, S. E. (1999) *The Anxieties of Pliny the Younger*. Atlanta.

Hollis, A. (2007) *Fragments of Roman Poetry*. Oxford.

Homeyer, H. (1977) "Die Quellen zu Ciceros Tod," *Helikon* 17: 56–96.

Horsfall, N. (1989) *Cornelius Nepos: A Selection*. Oxford.

(2003). *Virgil: Aeneid 11. A Commentary*. Leiden.

Internullo, D. (2016) "P.Vindob. L 17 identificato: Cicero, *In Catilinam* 1, 14–15 + 27," *ZPE* 199: 36–40.

Inwood, B. (1995) "Seneca in his philosophical milieu," *HSPh* 97: 63–76.

(2007) "The importance of form in Seneca's philosophical letters," in *Ancient Letters: Classical and Late Antique Epistolography*, ed. R. Morello and A. D. Morrison. Oxford: 133–148.

Jolivet, R. (ed.) (1948) *Augustine, Dialogues philosophiques: problèmes fondamentaux*. Paris.

Jones, B. (2016) "Cassius Dio – *pepaideumenos* and politician on kingship," in *Cassius Dio: Greek Intellectual and Roman Politician*, ed. C. Lange and J. Madsen. Leiden: 297–315.

Jones, C. P. (1968) "A new commentary on the Letters of Pliny," *Phoenix* 22: 111–142.

(2015) "The Greek letters ascribed to Brutus," *HSPh* 108: 195–244.

Jones, F. (1996) *Nominum ratio: Aspects of the Use of Personal Names in Greek and Latin*. Liverpool.

Kambylis, A. (1965) *Die Dichterweihe und ihre Symbolik: Untersuchungen zu Hesiodos, Kallimachos, Properz und Ennius*. Heidelberg.

Kaster, R. A. (1988) *Guardians of Language: The Grammarian and Society in Late Antiquity*. Berkeley.

(1998) "Becoming 'CICERO,'" in *Style and Tradition: Studies in Honor of Wendell Clausen*, ed. P. Knox and C. Foss. Stuttgart: 248–263.

(2006) *Cicero: Speech on Behalf of Publius Sestius*. Oxford.

Keane, C. (2015) *Juvenal and the Satiric Emotions*. Oxford.

Keeline, T. J. (2013) "The literary and stylistic qualities of a Plinian letter: a commentary on Plin. *Ep.* 7.9," *HSPh* 107: 229–264.

Keller, O. (1909–1913) *Die antike Tierwelt*, 2 vols. Leipzig.

Kemezis, A. (2014) *Greek Narratives of the Roman Empire under the Severans: Cassius Dio, Philostratus, and Herodian*. Cambridge.

Kennedy, D. F. (1992) "'Augustan' and 'anti-Augustan': reflections on terms of reference," in *Roman Poetry and Propaganda in the Age of Augustus*, ed. A. Powell. London: 26–58.

Kennedy, G. A. (1969) *Quintilian*. New York.

(1972) *The Art of Rhetoric in the Roman World*. Princeton.

(2002) "Cicero's oratorical and rhetorical legacy," in May (2002): 481–501.

(2003) *Progymnasmata: Greek Textbooks of Prose Composition and Rhetoric*. Leiden.

Ker, J. (2004) "Nocturnal writers in imperial Rome: the culture of *lucubratio*," *CPh* 99: 209–242.

Kinsey, T. E. (1971) *Pro P. Quinctio oratio*. Melbourne.

Klaiber, R. (1914–1916) *Die Beziehungen des Rednerdialogs von Tacitus zu Ciceros rhetorischen Schriften*, 2 vols. Bamberg.

Kleiber, L. (1883) "Quid Tacitus in dialogo prioribus scriptoribus debeat." Ph.D. diss., Halle.

Köstermann, E. (1930) "Der taciteische Dialogus und Ciceros Schrift De re publica," *Hermes* 65: 396–421.

Kohl, R. (1915) "De scholasticarum declamationum argumentis ex historia petitis." Ph.D. diss., Münster.

Koster, S. (1980) *Die Invektive in der griechischen und römischen Literatur*. Meisenheim am Glan.

Krebs, C. B. (2011) *A Most Dangerous Book: Tacitus's Germania from the Roman Empire to the Third Reich*. New York.

Kristofferson, H. (1928) "Declamatio in L. Sergium Catilinam: Text och Tradition." Ph.D. diss., Göteborg.

Kroll, W., and F. Skutsch. (1910) *W. S. Teuffels Geschichte der römischen Literatur*, vol. ii, 6th edn. Leipzig.

Kroll, W. (1959) *C. Valerius Catullus*, 3rd edn. Stuttgart.

Kurczyk, S. (2006) *Cicero und die Inszenierung der eigenen Vergangenheit: Autobiographisches Schreiben in der späten Römischen Republik*. Cologne.

Lachenaud, G., and M. Coudry (2011) *Dion Cassius: Histoire romaine. Livres 38, 39 & 40*. Paris.

Lamacchia, R. (1967) *Epistula ad Octavianum*. Milan.

(1968) *Epistola ad Octavianum*. Florence.

(1975) "Il giudizio di Tito Livio su Cicerone (Sen. 'Suas.' VI 22)," *Studi urbinati di storia, filosofia e letteratura* 49: 421–435.

Lamberton, R. (2001) *Plutarch*. New Haven.

Lange, A. G. (1832) *Vermischte Schriften und Reden*. Leipzig.

Lausberg, H. (trans. M. T. Bliss, A. Jansen, D. E. Orton; ed. D. E. Orton and R. D. Anderson) (1998) *Handbook of Literary Rhetoric: A Foundation for Literary Study*. Leiden.

Lavery, G. B. (1965) "Cicero's Reputation in the Latin Writers from Augustus to Hadrian." Ph.D. diss., Fordham University.

Leach, E. (1990) "The politics of self-presentation: Pliny's letters and Roman portrait sculpture," *ClAnt* 9: 14–39.

Leeman, A. D. (1963) *Orationis ratio*, 2 vols. Amsterdam.

Leeman, A. D., and H. Pinkster (1981) *M. Tullius Cicero: De oratore Libri* III. *Kommentar*, vol. I. Heidelberg.

Leeman, A. D., H. Pinkster, and J. Wisse (1996) *M. Tullius Cicero: De oratore Libri* III. *Kommentar*, vol IV. Heidelberg.

Lefèvre, E. (2009) *Vom Römertum zum Ästhetizismus: Studien zu den Briefen des jüngeren Plinius*. Berlin.

Lentano, M. (2016) "Parlare di Cicerone sotto il governo del suo assassino: la controversia vii,2 di Seneca e la politica augustea della memoria," in Poignault and Schneider (2016): 375–391.

Leo, F. (1960) *Ausgewählte kleine Schriften*, 2 vols., ed. E. Fraenkel. Rome.

Levene, D. S. (2004) "Tacitus' 'Dialogus' as literary history," *TAPhA* 134: 157–200.

(2010) *Livy on the Hannibalic War*. Oxford.

Levick, B. (2010) *Augustus: Image and Substance*. Harlow.

(2011) "Velleius Paterculus as senator: a dream with footnotes," in Cowan (2011): 1–16.

Lewis, R. G. (2006) *Asconius: Commentaries on Speeches of Cicero*. Oxford.

Lintott, A. W. (1974) "Cicero and Milo," *JRS* 64: 62–78.

(1997) "Cassius Dio and the history of the late Roman Republic," *ANRW* II.34.3: 2497–2523.

(2013) *Plutarch: Demosthenes and Cicero*. Oxford.

Lobur, J. A. (2008) *Consensus, Concordia, and the Formation of Roman Imperial Ideology*. New York.

Luce, T. J. (1993) "Reading and response in the *Dialogus*," in *Tacitus and the Tacitean Tradition*, ed. T. J. Luce and A. J. Woodman. Princeton: 11–38.

Ludolph, M. (1997) *Epistolographie und Selbstdarstellung: Untersuchungen zu den "Paradebriefen" Plinius des Jüngeren*. Tübingen.

MacCormack, S. (2013) "Cicero in late antiquity," in Steel (2013): 251–305.

McDermott, W. C. (1972) "M. Cicero and M. Tiro," *Historia* 21: 259–286.

McElduff, S. (2013) *Roman Theories of Translation: Surpassing the Source*. New York.

McGill, S. (2012) *Plagiarism in Latin Literature*. Cambridge.

Madvig, J. N. (1828) *De Q. Asconii Pediani et aliorum veterum interpretum in Ciceronis orationes commentariis disputatio*. Copenhagen.

Malcovati, H. (1945) *Imperatoris Caesaris Augusti operum fragmenta*, 3rd edn. Turin.

Mankin, D. (2011) *Cicero: De oratore Book* III. Cambridge.

Manuwald, G. (2007) *Cicero: Philippics 3–9*, 2 vols. Berlin.

(2011) "Ciceronian praise as a step to Pliny's *Panegyricus*," in *Pliny's Praise: The Panegyricus in the Roman World*, ed. P. Roche. Cambridge: 85–103.

(ed.) (2016) *The Afterlife of Cicero*. London.

Marchesi, I. (2008) *The Art of Pliny's Letters: A Poetics of Allusion in the Private Correspondence*. Cambridge.

(ed.) (2015) *Pliny the Book-Maker: Betting on Posterity in the Epistles*. Oxford.

Marincola, J. (2007) "Speeches in Greek and Roman historiography," in *A Companion to Greek and Roman Historiography*, ed. J. Marincola. Malden, MA: 118–132.

Marrou, H. I. (trans. G. Lamb) (1964) *A History of Education in Antiquity*, 3rd edn. New York.

Marshall, B. A. (1985) *A Historical Commentary on Asconius*. Columbia, MO.

Martin, R. H. (1972) Review of Haß-von Reitzenstein (1970), *CR* n.s. 22: 356–357.

Martin, R. H., and A. J. Woodman (1989) *Tacitus: Annals Book* IV. Cambridge.

Martín Sanchez, M. A. F. (1989) "Cicerón en Seneca: las citas del pensador cordobés sobre el orador romano," *Myrtia* 4: 117–125.

Maurach, G. (1970) *Der Bau von Senecas Epistulae Morales*. Heidelberg.

May, J. M. (1988) *Trials of Character: The Eloquence of Ciceronian Ethos*. Chapel Hill.

(ed.) (2002) *Brill's Companion to Cicero: Oratory and Rhetoric*. Leiden.

May, J. M., and J. Wisse (2001) *Cicero: On the Ideal Orator*. Oxford.

Mayer, R. (2001) *Dialogus de oratoribus*. Cambridge.

(2003) "Pliny and *gloria dicendi*," *Arethusa* 36: 227–234.

Mazzoli, G. (1964) "Il frammento enniano *laus alit artis* e il proemio al XVI libro degli *Annales*," *Athenaeum* 42: 307–315.

(1970) *Seneca e la poesia*. Milan.

Melchior, A. (2008) "Twinned fortunes and the publication of Cicero's *Pro Milone*," *CPh* 103: 282–297.

Merguet, H. (1877–1884) *Lexikon zu den Reden des Ciceros*, 4 vols. Jena.

Merklin, H. (1991) "'Dialogus'-Probleme in der neueren Forschung: Überlieferungsgeschichte, Echtheitsbeweis, und Umfang der Lücke," *ANRW* II.33.3: 2255–2283.

Merwald, G. (1964) "Die Buchkomposition des jüngeren Plinius (Epistulae I–IX)." Ph.D. diss., Erlangen.

Méthy, N. (2007) *Les lettres de Pline le Jeune: une représentation de l'homme*. Paris.

Meyer, P. (1881) *Untersuchung über die Frage der Echtheit des Briefwechsels Cicero ad Brutum*. Stuttgart.

Michel, A. (1962) *Le "Dialogue des orateurs" de Tacite et la philosophie de Cicéron*. Paris.

Migliario, E. (2007) *Retorica e storia: una lettura delle Suasorie di Seneca padre*. Bari.

(2008) "Cultura politica e scuole di retorica a Roma in età augustea," in *Retorica ed educazione delle élites nell'antica Roma: Atti della* vi *Giornata ghisleriana di filologia classica, Pavia, 4–5 aprile 2006*, ed. F. Gasti and E. Romano. Pavia: 77–93.

Millar, F. (1961) "Some speeches in Cassius Dio," *MH* 18: 11–22.

(1964) *Cassius Dio*. Oxford.

Millnor, K. (2014) *Graffiti and the Literary Landscape in Roman Pompeii*. Oxford.

Mindt, N. (2013) *Martials epigrammatischer Kanon*. Munich.

Moles, J. (1988) *Plutarch: Life of Cicero*. Warminster.

(1997) "Plutarch, Brutus and Brutus' Greek and Latin letters," in *Plutarch and his Intellectual World*, ed. J. Mossman. London: 141–168.

(1998) "Cry freedom: Tacitus *Annals* 4.32–35," *Histos* 2: 1–54.

Morello, R. (2003) "Pliny and the art of saying nothing," *Arethusa* 36: 187–209.

Moreno Soldevila, R. (2010) *Panegírico de Trajano*. Madrid.

Moreschini, C. (1977) "Cicerone filosofo fonte di Seneca," *RCCM* 19: 527–534.

Morgan, T. (1998) *Literate Education in the Hellenistic and Roman Worlds*. Cambridge.

Morstein-Marx, R. (2004) *Mass Oratory and Political Power in the Late Roman Republic*. Cambridge.

Müller, H. (2015) "Challenges to classical education in Late Antiquity: the case of Augustine of Hippo," in Bloomer (2015a): 358–371.

Murgia, C. E. (1979) "The length of the lacuna in Tacitus' 'Dialogus,'" *ClAnt* 12: 221–240.

(1980) "The date of Tacitus' *Dialogus*," *HSPh* 84: 99–125.

(1985) "Pliny's letters and the *Dialogus*," *HSPh* 89: 171–206.

Narducci, E. (ed.) (2003a) *Aspetti della fortuna di Cicerone nella cultura latina: Atti del* iii *Symposium Ciceronianum Arpinas*. Florence.

(2003b) "Cicerone nella 'Pharsalia' di Lucano," in Narducci (2003a): 78–91.

Neger, M. (2015) "Pliny's Martial and Martial's Pliny: the intertextual dialogue between the *Letters* and the *Epigrams*," in Devillers (2015): 131–144.

Nicholson, J. (1998) "The survival of Cicero's letters," in *Studies in Latin Literature and Roman History* ix, ed. C. Deroux. Brussels: 63–105.

Nisbet, R. G. M. (1961) *In L. Calpurnium Pisonem oratio*. Oxford.

Noè, E. (1984) *Storiografia imperiale pretacitiana: linee di svolgimento*. Florence.

Norden, E. (1958) *Die antike Kunstprosa vom* vi. *Jahrhundert v. Chr. bis in die Zeit der Renaissance*, 5th edn., 2 vols. Darmstadt.

Noreña, C. F. (2007) "The social economy of Pliny's correspondence with Trajan," *AJPh* 128: 239–277.

Novokhatko, A. A. (2009) *The Invectives of Sallust and Cicero: Critical Edition with Introduction, Translation, and Commentary.* Berlin.

Nutting, H. C. (1926) "Cicero and the Younger Pliny," *CJ* 21: 420–430.

O'Donnell, J. (1980) "Augustine's classical readings," *RecAug* 15: 144–175.

Ogilvie, R. M., and I. A. Richmond (1967) *De vita Agricolae.* Oxford.

Opelt, I. (1965) *Die lateinischen Schimpfwörter und verwandte sprachliche Erscheinungen: Eine Typologie.* Heidelberg.

O'Sullivan, N. (1992) *Alcidamas, Aristophanes and the Beginnings of Greek Stylistic Theory.* Stuttgart.

Otto, A. (1890) *Die Sprichwörter und sprichwörtlichen Redensarten der Römer.* Leipzig.

Paratore, E. (1951) *Tacito.* Milan.

Passelac, M. (1972) "Le bronze d'applique de Fendeille," *Revue archéologique de Narbonnaise* 5: 185–190.

Patillon, M. (1998) *Aelius Théon: Progymnasmata.* Paris.

Pausch, D. (ed.) (2010) *Stimmen der Geschichte: Funktionen von Reden in der antiken Historiographie.* Berlin.

Peirano, I. (2012) *The Rhetoric of the Roman Fake: Latin Pseudepigrapha in Context.* Cambridge.

Pelliccia, H. (2010–2011). "Unlocking *Aeneid* 6.460: Plautus' *Amphitryon*, Euripides' *Protesilaus* and the referents of Callimachus' *Coma*," *CJ* 106: 149–219.

Pelling, C. (1988) *Plutarch: Life of Antony.* Cambridge.

(2002) *Plutarch and History: Eighteen Studies.* Swansea.

(2011a) *Plutarch: Caesar.* Oxford.

(2011b) "Velleius and biography: the case of Julius Caesar," in Cowan (2011) 157–176.

Peter, H. (1901) *Der Brief in der römischen Litteratur.* Leipzig.

Petzold, P. (1911) "De Ciceronis obtrectatoribus et laudatoribus Romanis." Ph.D. diss., Leipzig.

Pflips, H. (1973) "Ciceronachahmung und Ciceroferne des jüngeren Plinius: ein Kommentar zu den Briefen des Plinius über Repetundenprozesse." Ph.D. diss., Münster.

Pieper, C. (2014) "*Memoria saeptus*: Cicero and the mastery of memory in his (post-)consular speeches," *SO* 88: 42–69.

Pierini, R. Degl'Innocenti (2003) "Cicerone nella prima età imperiale: luci ed ombre su un martire della repubblica," in Narducci (2003a): 3–54.

Pinney, T. (1974–1981) *The Letters of Thomas Babington Macaulay*, 6 vols. Cambridge.

Plasberg, O. (1892) "De M. Tullii Ciceronis Hortensio dialogo." Ph.D. diss., Leipzig.

Poignault, R., and C. Schneider (eds.) (2016) *Fabrique de la déclamation antique (controverses et suasoires).* Lyons.

Pomeroy, A. J. (1991) *The Appropriate Comment: Death Notices in the Ancient Historians.* Frankfurt am Main.

Potts, A. W. (1886) *Hints towards Latin Prose Composition.* London.

Powell, J. (ed.) (2007) *Logos: Rational Argument in Classical Rhetoric.* London.

Radice, B. (1969) *Letters and Panegyricus of Pliny,* 2 vols. Cambridge, MA.

Rawson, E. (1985) *Intellectual Life in the Late Roman Republic.* London.

Rees, W. (2011) "Cassius Dio, Human Nature, and the Late Roman Republic." Ph.D. diss., University of Oxford.

Reinhardt, T., and M. Winterbottom (2006) *Quintilian: Institutio oratoria Book 2.* Oxford.

Reinhold, M. (1984) *Classica Americana: The Greek and Roman Heritage in the United States.* Detroit.

Reuters, A. (1887) "De Quintiliani libro qui fuit De causis corruptae eloquentiae." Ph.D. diss., Breslau.

Reynolds, L. D. (ed.) (1983) *Texts and Transmission: A Survey of the Latin Classics.* Oxford.

Rich, J. (2011) "Velleius' History: genre and purpose," in Cowan (2011): 73–92.
　(2015) "Appian, Polybius, and the Romans' war with Antiochus the Great: a study in Appian's sources and methods," in Welch (2015a): 65–124.

Richard, C. (2015) "Cicero and the American founders," in Altman (2015a): 124–143.

Richter, W. (1968) "Das Cicerobild der römischen Kaiserzeit," in *Cicero: Ein Mensch seiner Zeit,* ed. G. Radke. Berlin: 161–197.

Riggsby, A. M. (1995) "Pliny on Cicero and oratory: self-fashioning in the public eye," *AJPh* 116: 123–135.

Robb, M. A. (2010) *Beyond Populares and Optimates: Political Language in the Late Republic.* Stuttgart.

Roca-Puig, R. (1977) *Ciceró: Catilinàries (I et II in Cat.).* Barcelona.

Rochette, B. (1997) *Le latin dans le monde grec: recherches sur la diffusion de la langue et des lettres latines dans les provinces hellénophones de l'Empire romain.* Brussels.

Rolim de Moura, A. (2010) "Lucan 7: speeches at war," in *Lucan's Bellum civile: Between Epic Tradition and Aesthetic Innovation,* ed. N. Hömke and C. Reitz. Berlin.

Roller, M. (1997) "*Color*-blindness: Cicero's death, declamation, and the production of history," *CPh* 92: 109–130.
　(2015) "The dialogue in Seneca's *Dialogues* (and other moral essays)," in Bartsch and Schiesaro (2015): 54–67.

Romano, D. (1965) "Il significato della pseudo-ciceroniana 'Epistula ad Octavianum,'" in *Studi in memoria di Carmelo Sgroi.* Turin: 593–604.

Roos, P. (1984) *Sentenza e proverbio nell'antichità e i 'Distichi di Catone': il testo latino e i volgarizzamenti italiani.* Brescia.

Rudd, N. (1992) "Strategems of vanity: Cicero, *Ad familiares* 5.12 and Pliny's letters," in *Author and Audience in Latin Literature,* ed. A. J. Woodman and J. Powell. Cambridge: 18–32.

Ruebel, J. S. (1979) "The trial of Milo in 52 BC: a chronological study," *TAPhA* 109: 231–249.

Russell, D. A. (1970) *Longinus: On the Sublime*. Oxford.

(1979) "De imitatione," in *Creative Imitation and Latin Literature*, ed. D. West and A. J. Woodman. Cambridge: 1–16.

(2001) *Quintilian: Institutio oratoria*, 5 vols. Cambridge, MA.

Sabbadini, R. (1885) *Storia del Ciceronianismo*. Turin.

Sailor, D. (2008) *Writing and Empire in Tacitus*. Cambridge.

Sánchez-Ostiz, Á. (2013) "Cicero Graecus: notes on Ciceronian papyri from Egypt," *ZPE* 187: 144–153.

Sandys, J. E. (1885) *Ad Marcum Brutum orator*. Cambridge.

Santangelo, F. (2012) "Authoritative forgeries: late Republican history re-told in pseudo-Sallust," *Histos* 6: 27–51.

Schafer, J. (2011) "Seneca's *Epistulae morales* as dramatized education," *CPh* 106: 32–52.

Scheidegger Lämmle, C. (2017) "Last words: Cicero's late works and the poetics of a literary legacy," in *Self-Presentation and Identity in the Roman World*, ed. A. Gavrielatos. Newcastle upon Tyne: 17–36.

Schenk, P. (1999) "Formen von Intertextualität im Briefkorpus des jüngeren Plinius," *Philologus* 143: 114–134.

(2016) "Forms of intertextuality in the Epistles of Pliny the Younger," in Gibson and Whitton (2016): 332–354. (Trans. of Schenk [1999].)

Schilling, R. (1977) *Pline l'Ancien: Histoire naturelle. Livre* VII. Paris.

Schmeling, G. (2011) *A Commentary on the Satyrica of Petronius*. Oxford.

Schmidt, O. E. (1884) "Zur Kritik und Erklärung der Briefe Ciceros an M. Brutus," *Neue Jahrbücher für classische Philologie* 129: 617–644.

Schmitzer, U. (2000) *Velleius Paterculus und das Interesse an der Geschichte im Zeitalter des Tiberius*. Heidelberg.

Schurgacz, K. (2004) *Die Declamatio in L. Sergium Catilinam: Einleitung, Übersetzung, Kommentar*. Trier.

Scott, K. (1933) "The political propaganda of 44–30 BC," *Memoirs of the American Academy in Rome* 11: 7–49.

Seager, R. (1972) "Cicero and the word *popularis*," *CQ* n.s. 22: 328–338.

Sedley, D. (1997) "The ethics of Brutus and Cassius," *JRS* 87: 41–53.

Setaioli, A. (1965) "Esegesi virgiliana in Seneca," *SIFC* 37: 133–156.

(1976) "On the date of publication of Cicero's Letters to Atticus," *SO* 51: 105–120.

(2000) *Facundus Seneca: aspetti della lingua e dell'ideologia senecana*. Bologna.

(2003) "Seneca e Cicerone," in Narducci (2003a): 55–77.

(2014) "*Epistulae morales*," in *Brill's Companion to Seneca: Philosopher and Dramatist*, ed. G. Damschen and A. Heil. Leiden: 191–200.

Shackleton Bailey, D. R. (1965–1970) *Cicero: Epistulae ad Atticum*, 7 vols. Cambridge.

(1971) *Cicero*. New York.

(1977) *Cicero: Epistulae ad familiares*, 2 vols. Cambridge.

(1980) *Cicero: Epistulae ad Quintum fratrem et M. Brutum*. Cambridge.

(1982) "Notes on Tacitus' opuscula," *CJ* 77: 255–258.

(2002) *Cicero: Letters to Quintus and Brutus, Letter Fragments, Letter to Octavian, Invectives, Handbook of Electioneering.* Cambridge, MA.

Shanzer, D. (2012) "Augustine and the Latin classics," in *A Companion to Augustine*, ed. M. Vessey. Malden, MA: 161–174.

Shelford, A. (2007) *Transforming the Republic of Letters: Pierre-Daniel Huet and European Intellectual Life, 1650–1720.* Rochester.

Sherwin-White, A. N. (1966) *The Letters of Pliny: A Historical and Social Commentary.* Oxford.

Sillett, A. (2015) "'A Learned Man and a Patriot': The Reception of Cicero in the Early Imperial Period." Ph.D. diss., University of Oxford.

(2016) "Quintus Cicero's *Commentariolum*: a philosophical approach to Roman elections," in *Splendide mendax: Rethinking Fakes and Forgeries in Classical, Late Antique, and Early Christian Culture*, ed. E. P. Cueva and J. Martínez. Groningen: 177–191.

Sion-Jenkis, K. (2000) *Von der Republik zum Prinzipat: Ursachen für den Verfassungswechsel in Rom im historischen Denken der Antike.* Stuttgart.

Skidmore, C. (1996) *Practical Ethics for Roman Gentlemen: The Work of Valerius Maximus.* Exeter.

Smith, M. S. (1975) *Petronii Arbitri Cena Trimalchionis.* Oxford.

Soubiran, J. (2002) *Cicéron: Aratea. Fragments poétiques.* Paris.

Springer, C. (2018) *Cicero in Heaven: The Roman Rhetor and Luther's Reformation.* Leiden.

Stadter, P. A. (2006) "Pliny and the ideology of Empire," *Prometheus* 32: 61–76.

Stangl, T. (1886) "Die bibliothek Ashburnham," *Philologus* 45: 201–236.

(1964) *Ciceronis orationum scholiastae.* Hildesheim. (Repr. of Vienna 1912.)

Steel, C. (2005) *Reading Cicero: Genre and Performance in Late Republican Rome.* London.

(ed.) (2013) *The Cambridge Companion to Cicero.* Cambridge.

Stekelenburg, A. V. van (1971) "De Redevoeringen bij Cassius Dio." Ph.D. diss., Leiden.

Stone, A. M. (1980) "*Pro Milone*: Cicero's second thoughts," *Antichthon* 14: 88–111.

Stramaglia, A. (2016) "Il maestro nascosto: elementi 'metaretorici' nelle Declamazioni Maggiori pseudo-quintilianee," in Poignault and Scheider (2016): 21–47.

Stroh, W. (1975) *Taxis und Taktik: Die advokatische Dispositionskunst in Ciceros Gerichtsreden.* Stuttgart.

Summers, W. C. (1910) *Select Letters of Seneca.* London.

Sussman, L. (1978) *The Elder Seneca.* Leiden.

Suster, G. (1890) "De Plinio Ciceronis imitatore," *RFIC* 18: 74–86.

Syme, R. (1939) *The Roman Revolution.* Oxford.

(1958) *Tacitus.* Oxford.

(1964) *Sallust.* Berkeley.

(1968) "People in Pliny," *JRS* 58: 135–151. Reprinted in *Roman Papers*, vol. II, ed. E. Badian, Oxford: 694–723.

(1991) "Pliny's early career," in *Roman Papers*, vol. VII, ed. A. R. Birley. Oxford: 551–567.

Taldone, A. (1993) "Su *insania* e *furor* in Cicerone," *BStudLat* 23: 3–19.

Testard, M. (1958) *Saint Augustin et Cicéron*, 2 vols. Paris.

Thomas, B. P. (2009) *Abraham Lincoln: A Biography*. Carbondale, IL.

Too, Y. L. (2001) "Introduction," in *Pedagogy and Power: Rhetorics of Classical Learning*, ed. Y. L. Too and N. Livingstone. Cambridge: 1–16.

Torraca, L. (1959) *Marco Giunio Bruto: Epistole greche*. Naples.

Tunberg, T. (2012) *De rationibus quibus homines docti artem Latine colloquendi et ex tempore dicendi saeculis XVI et XVII coluerunt*. Leuven.

Tzounakas, S. (2013) "Martial's Pliny as quoted by Pliny (*Epist.* 3.21)," *C&M* 64: 247–268.

(2015) "Pliny the Younger as the Roman Demosthenes," in Devillers (2015): 207–218.

Uden, J. (2015) *The Invisible Satirist: Juvenal and Second-Century Rome*. Oxford.

Usener, H. (1873) "Vergessenes," *RhM* 28: 391–435.

van den Berg, C. (2006) "The Social Aesthetics of Tacitus' *Dialogus de oratoribus*." Ph.D. diss., Yale University.

(2014) *The World of Tacitus' Dialogus de oratoribus: Aesthetics and Empire in Ancient Rome*. Cambridge.

van den Berg, C., and Y. Baraz (eds.) (2013) *Intertextuality and its Discontents (AJPh* 134). Baltimore.

van den Hout, M. J. P. (1999) *A Commentary on the Letters of M. Cornelius Fronto*. Leiden.

van der Blom, H. (2010) *Cicero's Role Models: The Political Strategy of a Newcomer*. Oxford.

(2016a) *Oratory and Political Career in the Late Roman Republic*. Cambridge.

(2016b) "Creating a great orator: the self-portrait and reception of Cicero the orator," in *Autorretratos: la creación de la imagen personal en la Antigüedad*, ed. A. D. Fernández. Barcelona: 87–99.

van der Poel, M. (2009) "The use of *exempla* in Roman declamation," *Rhetorica* 27: 332–353.

van Deusen, N. (ed.) (2013) *Cicero Refused to Die: Ciceronian Influence through the Centuries*. Leiden.

van Mal-Maeder, D. (2007) *La fiction des déclamations*. Leiden.

Vasaly, A. (1993) *Representations: Images of the World in Ciceronian Oratory*. Berkeley.

Vogt-Spira, G. (2003) "Die Selbstinszenierung des jüngeren Plinius," in Castagna and Lefèvre (2003): 51–68.

Volk, K. (2013) "The genre of Cicero's *De consulatu suo*," in *Generic Interfaces in Latin Literature: Encounters, Interactions and Transformations*, ed. T. D. Papanghelis, S. J. Harrison, and S. Frangoulidis. Berlin: 93–112.

Volk, K., and J. E. G. Zetzel (2015) "Laurel, tongue and glory (Cicero, *De consulatu suo* fr. 6 Soubiran)," *CQ* n.s. 65: 204–223.

Vretska, K. (1961) *Sallust: Invektive und Episteln*, 2 vols. Heidelberg.

(1976) *De Catilinae coniuratione*, 2 vols. Heidelberg.

Wallace-Hadrill, A. F. (1984) *Suetonius: The Scholar and his Caesars*. New Haven.

Ward, J. O. (2015) "What the Middle Ages missed of Cicero, and why," in Altman (2015a): 307–328.

Weil, B. (1962) *2000 Jahre Cicero*. Zürich.

Weische, A. (1989) "Plinius d. J. und Cicero: Untersuchungen zur römischen Epistolographie in Republik und Kaiserzeit," *ANRW* 11.33.1: 375–386.

Welch, K. (ed.) (2015a) *Appian's Roman History: Empire and Civil War*. Swansea.

(2015b) "Programme and narrative in *Civil Wars* 2.118–4.138," in Welch (2015a): 277–304.

Westall, R. (2015) "The sources for the *Civil Wars* of Appian of Alexandria," in Welch (2015a): 125–168.

White, H. (1912) *Appian's Roman History*, 4 vols. Cambridge, MA.

Whitton, C. (2013a) *Pliny the Younger: Epistles Book* 11. Cambridge.

(2013b) "Trapdoors: false closure in Pliny," in *The Door Ajar: False Closure in Greek and Roman Literature and Art*, ed. F. Grewing, B. Acosta-Hughes, and A. Kirichenko. Heidelberg: 43–61.

(2015a) "Grand designs: unrolling *Epistles* 2," in Marchesi (2015): 109–143.

(2015b) "Pliny on the precipice (*Ep.* 9.26)," in Devillers (2015): 217–236.

(2015c) "Pliny's progress: on a troublesome Domitianic career," *Chiron* 45: 1–22.

(2018) "Quintilian, Pliny, Tacitus," in *Literary Interactions under Nerva, Trajan, and Hadrian*, ed. A. R. König and C. Whitton. Cambridge: 37–62.

Wibier, M. (2016) "Cicero's reception in the juristic tradition of the early Empire," in *Cicero's Law*, ed. P. J. du Plessis. Edinburgh: 100–122.

Wilkins, A. S. (1888) *M. Tulli Ciceronis De oratore libri tres*. Oxford.

Williams, Gareth (2003) *Seneca: De otio; De brevitate vitae*. Cambridge.

(2015) "Style and form in Seneca's writing," in Bartsch and Schiesaro (2015): 135–149.

Williams, Gordon (1978) *Change and Decline: Roman Literature in the Early Empire*. Berkeley.

Wilson, M. (1987) "Seneca's Epistles to Lucilius: a revaluation," *Ramus* 16: 102–121.

(2001) "Seneca's *Epistles* reclassified," in *Texts, Ideas, and the Classics: Scholarship, Theory, and Classical Literature*, ed. S. J. Harrison. Oxford: 164–187.

(2008) "Your writings or your life: Cicero's *Philippics* and declamation," in *Cicero's Philippics: History, Rhetoric and Ideology*, ed. T. Stevenson and M. Wilson. Auckland: 305–334.

Winkler, J. (1988) "Juvenal's attitude toward Ciceronian poetry and rhetoric," *RhM* 131: 84–97.

Winterbottom, M. (1964) "Quintilian and the *vir bonus*," *JRS* 54: 90–97.

(1974) *Seneca the Elder: Declamations*, 2 vols. Cambridge, MA.

(1982) "Cicero and the Silver Age," in *Eloquence et rhétorique chez Cicéron*, ed. W. Ludwig. Geneva: 237–274.

(1984) *The Minor Declamations Ascribed to Quintilian*. Berlin.

Wirszubski, C. (1950) *Libertas as a Political Idea at Rome during the Late Republic and Early Principate*. Cambridge.

Wiseman, T. P. (1971) *New Men in the Roman Senate 139* BC–AD *14*. Oxford.

(2009) *Remembering the Roman People*. Oxford.

Wisse, J. (2002) "*De oratore*: rhetoric, philosophy, and the making of the ideal orator," in May (2002): 375–400.

(2007) "The riddle of the *Pro Milone*: the rhetoric of rational argument," in Powell (2007): 35–68.

Wölfflin, E. (1933) "Zur Alliteration," in *Eduard Wölfflin: Ausgewählte Schriften*, ed. G. Meyer. Leipzig: 225–284.

Woerther, F. (2015) *Caecilius de Calè-Actè: fragments et témoignages*. Paris.

Wolff, E. (2004) "Pline et Cicéron: quelques remarques," in *Epistulae Antiquae* III: *Actes du* IIIe *colloque international "L'épistolaire antique et ses prolongements européens,"* ed. L. Nadjo and E. Gavoille. Leuven: 441–447.

Wolverton, R. (1964) "The encomium of Cicero in Pliny the Elder," in *Classical, Mediaeval, and Renaissance Studies in Honor of Berthold Louis Ullman*, ed. C. Henderson Jr. Rome: 159–164.

Woodman, A. J. (1983) *Velleius Paterculus: The Caesarian and Augustan Narrative (2.41–93)*. Cambridge.

(1988) *Rhetoric in Classical Historiography: Four Studies*. London.

(2012) "Pliny on writing history: *Epistles* 5.8," in *From Poetry to History: Selected Papers*, ed. A. J. Woodman. Oxford: 223–242.

(2014) *Tacitus: Agricola*. Cambridge.

Woolf, G. (2006) "Pliny's province," in *Rome and the Black Sea Region: Domination, Romanisation, Resistance*, ed. T. Bekker-Nielsen. Aarhus: 93–108.

(2015) "Pliny/Trajan and the poetics of Empire," *CPh* 110: 132–151.

Wooten, C. (1977) "Cicero's reactions to Demosthenes: a clarification," *CJ* 73: 37–43.

(1997) "Cicero and Quintilian on the style of Demosthenes," *Rhetorica* 15: 177–192.

Wright, A. I. (1997) "Cicero Reflected: The Image of a Statesman in the Century after his Death, and its Ideological Significance." Ph.D. diss., University of Sydney.

(2001) "The death of Cicero. Forming a tradition: the contamination of history," *Historia* 50: 436–452.

Yavetz, Z. (1990) "The personality of Augustus: reflections on Syme's *Roman Revolution*," in *Between Republic and Empire: Interpretations of Augustus and his Principate*, ed. K. Raaflaub and M. Toher. Berkeley: 21–41.

Zanker, P. (trans. A. Shapiro) (1988) *The Power of Images in the Age of Augustus*. Ann Arbor.

Zetzel, J. E. G. (1974) "Statilius Maximus and Ciceronian studies in the Antonine Age," *BICS* 21: 107–123.

(1995) *Cicero: De re publica.* Cambridge.

(2013) "Political philosophy," in Steel (2013): 181–195.

Zielinski, T. (1929) *Cicero im Wandel der Jahrhunderte,* 4th edn. Leipzig.

Zucker, F. (1929) "Plin. epist. VIII 24 – ein Denkmal antiker Humanität," *Philologus* 84: 209–232.

General Index

Index Locorum